2016-2017

EVANGELICAL SUNDAY SCHOOL LESSON COMMENTARY

SIXTY-FIFTH ANNUAL VOLUME

Based on the
Pentecostal-Charismatic Bible Lesson Series

Editorial Staff

Lance Colkmire—Editor
Tammy Hatfield—Editorial Assistant
Terry Hart—General Director of Publications

Lesson Exposition Writers

Lance Colkmire
Jerald Daffe
Lee Roy Martin

Homer G. Rhea
Joshua F. Rice
Sabord Woods

Published by

PATHWAY PRESS   Cleveland, Tennessee

*To place an order, call 1-800-553-8506.
*To contact the editor, call 423-478-7597 or
email at *Lance_Colkmire@pathwaypress.org*.

Lesson treatments in the *Evangelical Sunday School Lesson Commentary* for 2016-2017 are based on the outlines of the Pentecostal-Charismatic Bible Lesson Series prepared by the Pentecostal-Charismatic Curriculum Commission.

Copyright 2016

PATHWAY PRESS, Cleveland, Tennessee

ISBN: 978-1-59684-884-9 Hardbound
ISBN: 978-1-59684-885-6 Large Print

ISSN: 1555-5801

Printed in the United States of America

TABLE OF CONTENTS

INTRODUCTION TO THE 2016-2017 COMMENTARY

The *Evangelical Sunday School Lesson Commentary* contains in a single volume a full study of the Sunday school lessons for the months beginning with September 2016 and running through August 2017. The twelve months of lessons draw from both the Old Testament and the New Testament in an effort to provide balance and establish relationship between these distinct but inspired writings. The lessons in this 2016-2017 volume are drawn from the fourth year of a seven-year series, which will be completed in August 2020. (The series is printed in full on page 15 of this volume.)

The lessons for the *Evangelical Commentary* are based on the Pentecostal-Charismatic Bible Lesson Series Outlines, prepared by the Pentecostal-Charismatic Curriculum Commission. (The Pentecostal-Charismatic Curriculum Commission is a member of the National Association of Evangelicals.) The lessons in this volume, taken together with the other annual volumes of lessons in the cycle, provide a valuable commentary on a wide range of Biblical subjects. Each quarter is divided into two or more units of study.

The 2016-2017 commentary is the work of a team of Christian scholars and writers who have developed the volume under the supervision of Pathway Press. All the major writers represent a team of ministers committed to a strictly evangelical interpretation of the Scriptures. The guiding theological principles of this commentary are expressed in the following statement of faith:

1. WE BELIEVE the Bible to be the inspired, the only infallible, authoritative Word of God.

2. WE BELIEVE that there is one God, eternally existing in three persons: Father, Son, and Holy Spirit.

3. WE BELIEVE in the deity of our Lord Jesus Christ, in His virgin birth, in His sinless life, in His miracles, in His vicarious and atoning death through His shed blood, in His bodily resurrection, in His ascension to the right hand of the Father, and in His personal return in power and glory.

4. WE BELIEVE that for the salvation of lost and sinful men, personal reception of the Lord Jesus Christ and regeneration by the Holy Spirit are absolutely essential.

5. WE BELIEVE in the present ministry of the Holy Spirit by whose cleansing and indwelling the Christian is enabled to live a godly life.

6. WE BELIEVE in the personal return of the Lord Jesus Christ.

7. WE BELIEVE in the resurrection of both the saved and the lost—they that are saved, unto the resurrection of life; and they that are lost, unto the resurrection of damnation.

8. WE BELIEVE in the spiritual unity of believers in our Lord Jesus Christ.

USING THE 2016-2017 COMMENTARY

The *Evangelical Sunday School Lesson Commentary* for 2016-2017 is presented to the reader with the hope that it will become his or her weekly companion through the months ahead.

Quarterly unit themes for the 2016-2017 volume are as follows:
- Fall Quarter—Unit One: "More Great Stories of the Bible";
  Unit Two: "First and Second Peter and Jude"
- Winter Quarter—Unit One: "The Minor Prophets (Part 1)";
  Unit Two: "Letter to the Romans"
- Spring Quarter—Unit One: "The Era of the Judges";
  Unit Two: "Paul's Journey (Acts, Part 2)"
- Summer Quarter—Unit One: "Good Lessons From Bad Examples";
  Unit Two: "Good Lessons From Good Examples"

The lesson sequence used in this volume is prepared by the Pentecostal-Charismatic Curriculum Commission. The specific material used in developing each lesson is written and edited under the guidance of the editorial staff of Pathway Press.

INTRODUCTION: The opening of each week's lesson features a one-page introduction. It provides background information that sets the stage for the lesson.

CONTEXT: A time and place is given for most lessons. Where there is a wide range of ideas regarding the exact time or place, we favor the majority opinion of conservative scholars.

PRINTED TEXT: The printed text is the body of Scripture designated each week for verse-by-verse study in the classroom. Drawing on the study text the teacher delves into this printed text, exploring its content with the students.

CENTRAL TRUTH and FOCUS: The central truth states the single unifying principle that the expositors attempted to clarify in each lesson. The focus describes the overall lesson goal.

EXPOSITION and LESSON OUTLINE: The heart of this commentary—and probably the heart of the teacher's instruction each week—is the exposition of the printed text. This exposition material is organized in outline form, which indicates how the material is to be divided for study.

QUOTATIONS and ILLUSTRATIONS: Each section of every lesson contains illustrations and sayings the teacher can use in connecting the lesson to daily living.

QUESTIONS are printed throughout the lesson to help students explore the Scripture text and how it speaks to believers today.

CONCLUSION: Each lesson ends with a brief conclusion that makes a summarizing statement.

The GOLDEN TEXT CHALLENGE for each week is a brief reflection on that single verse. The word *challenge* is used because its purpose is to help students apply this key verse to their life.

DAILY DEVOTIONS: Daily Bible readings are included for the teacher to use in his or her own devotions throughout the week, as well as to share with members of their class.

SCRIPTURE TEXTS USED IN LESSON EXPOSITION

Genesis

3:15	December 25
6:5-14, 17-18, 22	September 4
7:1, 5-7	September 4
8:13-16, 20-22	September 4
12:1-5	September 11
13:10-13	June 11
14:11-12, 16	June 11
15:1-6	September 11
17:1-5, 15, 21	September 11
19:13-16, 26, 29	June 11

Exodus

4:14-17, 29-31	September 18
6:28-30	September 18
7:1-7	September 18
28:1-4	September 18
29:4-7	September 18

Numbers

13:1-2, 25, 27-28, 30-31	July 16
14:5-9, 20-24, 30	July 16
25:3, 7-8, 11	July 23

Deuteronomy

23:23	June 18

Joshua

2:1-4, 9, 11-15, 22-23	July 30
6:24-25	July 30
14:7-14	July 16
22:10, 13-14, 16, 23-24, 29, 31	July 23

Judges

2:3, 7-8, 10-12, 14, 16-23	March 5
3:7, 9-12, 15, 28-30	March 12
4:1-2, 4, 9, 14, 23-24	March 12
5:1-2	March 12
6:11-16, 27, 33-35	March 19
7:2-3, 6-7, 9, 13-14, 16, 20-21	March 19
9:1-2, 5-6, 19-25, 46-57	March 26
11:7-8, 11, 29-36, 39-40	June 18
13:1-5	April 2
16:4-6, 16-17, 20, 23, 25, 28, 30	April 2

Judges (cont.)

19:12, 15-16, 20, 22-23, 25, 30	April 9
20:12-14, 21, 25, 48	April 9

1 Samuel

2:12, 17, 24, 34	June 25

2 Kings

21:16	July 2

2 Chronicles

20:1, 3-6, 12, 15-18, 20-23, 25-26	August 6
29:1-5, 31, 36	September 25
30:1, 4-5, 13, 22, 26-27	September 25
32:21-23	September 25
33:1, 6, 9, 11-13, 15-16	July 2

Psalms

10:4	July 9

Proverbs

16:5, 19	July 9

Ecclesiastes

5:2, 4-7	June 18

Isaiah

9:6-7	December 25

Ezekiel

18:21-23	July 2

Daniel

1:5, 8-9, 12, 14-15	August 13
4:24-27, 30-31, 34, 36-37	July 9
6:3-5, 8-11, 16, 20-24, 26	August 13

Hosea

1:1-3	December 4
2:1-2, 5, 14, 19-20, 23	December 4
3:1-3	December 4
11:1-2, 7, 9	December 4

Joel

1:1-4, 8-10, 13-14	December 11
2:1-2, 13-15, 18, 25, 28-29, 32	December 11
3:12, 14, 16	December 11

Amos

7:1, 4, 7-9, 12-13, 17	December 18
8:2, 4-6, 11-13	December 18
9:1, 8, 11-12, 14-15	December 18

Jonah

1:1-4, 9, 11-12, 15-17	January 1
2:7-10	January 1
3:1-5, 9-10	January 1
4:1, 5-6, 10-11	January 1

Micah

1:1-2	January 8
6:2-3, 7-9, 13, 16	January 8
7:1, 4-7, 9, 11, 18-20	January 8

Matthew

1:5	July 30
27:57-60	April 16
28:1-10, 18-20	April 16
28:18-20	October 16

Luke

1:32-33	December 25
2:1-7	December 25
17:28-33	June 11

John

1:38-49	August 20
2:15-17	July 23
3:1-21	October 2
14:15-18, 26	June 4
15:26-27	June 4
16:7-14	June 4

Acts

2:1-4	June 4
4:32, 36-37	August 27
5:1-6, 8-9	June 25
6:8-12, 15	October 9
7:44, 47, 49-60	October 9
8:9, 18-20	June 25
8:29-31, 35-39	August 20
9:26-27	August 27
11:19-22	April 23
11:22-25	August 27
11:25-26, 29-30	April 23
13:1-2	April 23
13:2	August 27
13:3-8, 12	April 23

Acts (cont.)

13:14-17, 38, 44-45, 49-52	April 30
14:1	August 27
14:2	April 30
14:3	August 27
14:5-7, 19-22	April 30
14:21-22	August 27
14:23	April 30
15:1-7, 10-14, 19-21, 28-32	May 7
15:37	August 27
16:4-5	May 7
16:9-10, 13-18, 25-28, 31-33	May 14
17:1, 4-5, 10-11	May 14
18:1, 4	May 21
18:1-4	October 16
18:6, 8-11	May 21
18:18-19, 24-28	October 16
19:1-2, 5-12, 15, 17-20	May 21
23:11	May 28
25:10-12	May 28
27:21-25	May 28
28:16-17, 23-24, 27-31	May 28

Romans

1:1, 5-6, 14-17	January 15
2:4, 11	July 2
3:1-5, 9-12, 19-26	January 15
4:3-5, 11-13, 18-22	January 22
5:1-2, 5-6, 10-11	January 22
5:12-19	February 1
6:1-3, 8-14, 22-23	February 1
7:1, 4-9, 18-24	February 8
8:1-6, 11	February 8
8:12-15, 18-27	February 15
8:26-27	June 4
8:28, 31-32, 35-39	February 15
12:1-5, 9-11	February 22
12:11	July 23
12:12-13	February 22
12:13	October 16
12:14-15	February 22
13:1-7	February 22
13:8-10, 12	March 1
14:1-4, 7-8, 11-19	March 1
16:3-5	October 16

Galatians
4:4-9   December 25

Ephesians
4:11-12   October 16

Hebrews
1:1-3, 26-28   December 25
3:12-13   July 23
11:31   July 30

James
2:14, 17, 25   July 30
4:4   June 11

1 Peter
1:1-14, 17-22, 25   October 23
2:1-3   October 23
2:4-5, 9-12, 17-25   October 30
3:8-17   November 16
4:1-2, 7-19   November 6

1 Peter (cont.)
5:1-5   October 30
5:5   July 9
5:6-9   October 30

2 Peter
1:1-11, 15-21   November 13
2:1   November 13
2:7, 9   June 11
2:19-21   November 13
3:1-18   November 20

1 John
2:15-17   June 11

3 John
8   October 16

Jude
1-5, 8, 10, 12-13,   November 27
16, 20-25

SCRIPTURE TEXTS USED IN GOLDEN TEXT HOMILIES

Genesis
15:6 — September 11

Exodus
7:1 — September 18

Judges
2:10 — March 5
3:9 — March 12
6:12 — March 19
16:20 — April 2

2 Chronicles
20:15 — August 6
31:21 — September 25

Psalms
139:23-24 — June 25

Proverbs
5:22 — March 26

Ecclesiastes
5:2 — June 18

Jeremiah
29:13 — July 16

Ezekiel
18:21 — July 2

Hosea
2:19 — December 4

Joel
2:13 — December 11

Amos
5:14 — December 18

Jonah
3:10 — January 1

Micah
7:18 — January 8

Matthew
28:6 — April 16

John
1:41-42 — August 20
3:16 — October 2
15:26 — June 4

Acts
7:55 — October 9

Acts (cont.)
13:2 — April 23
14:27 — April 30
19:11, 20 — May 21

Romans
1:17 — January 15
1:28 — April 9
5:1 — January 22
5:15 — February 1
8:1 — February 8
8:14 — February 15
12:2 — February 22
12:11 — July 23
13:8 — March 1
14:19 — August 27

Galatians
3:8 — May 7
4:4-5 — December 25

Ephesians
4:1 — October 16

Philippians
1:12 — May 28

1 Thessalonians
1:5 — May 14

Hebrews
11:7 — September 4

James
2:17 — July 30

1 Peter
1:3 — October 23
1:7 — August 13
2:9 — October 30
2:21 — November 6
5:5 — July 9

2 Peter
1:10 — November 13
3:13 — November 20

1 John
2:15 — June 11

Jude
3 — November 27

ACKNOWLEDGMENTS

Many books and Web sites have been used in the research that has gone into the 2016-2017 *Evangelical Commentary*. The major books that have been used are listed below.

Bibles

Contemporary English Version (CEV), American Bible Society, New York

King James Version, Oxford University Press, Oxford, England

New American Standard Bible (NASB), The Lockman Foundation, La Habra, California

New English Translation, bible.org

New International Version (NIV), Zondervan Publishing House, Grand Rapids

New King James Version (NKJV), Thomas Nelson Publishers, Nashville

New Living Translation (NLT), Tyndale House Publishers, Carol Stream, Illinois

Ryrie Study Bible, The Moody Bible Institute, Chicago

The Nelson Study Bible, Thomas Nelson Publishers, Nashville

Commentaries

Acts of the Apostles, Pathway Press, Cleveland, Tennessee

Adam Clarke's Commentary, Abingdon-Cokesbury, Nashville

Barnes' Notes, BibleSoft.com

Commentaries on the Old Testament (Keil & Delitzsch), Eerdmans Publishing Co., Grand Rapids

Ellicott's Bible Commentary, Zondervan Publishing House, Grand Rapids

Jamieson, Fausset and Brown Commentary, BibleSoft.com

Matthew Henry's Commentary, BibleSoft.com

Social-Science Commentary on the Synoptic Gospels, Augsburg Fortress, Minneapolis

The Expositor's Bible Commentary, Zondervan, Grand Rapids

The Greatest Letter Ever Written, Pathway Press, Cleveland, Tennessee

The Wycliffe Bible Commentary, Moody Press, Chicago

Zondervan NIV Bible Commentary, Zondervan Publishing House, Grand Rapids

Illustrations

Quotable Quotations, Scripture Press, Colorado Springs

The Encyclopedia of Religious Quotations, Fleming H. Revell Co., Old Tappan, New Jersey

The Face of God, The Hands of God, and *The Heart of God,* Woodrow Kroll, Elm Hill Books, Nashville

Who Said That?, George Sweeting, Moody Press, Chicago www.ochristian.com

Reference Books

Nelson's Bible Dictionary, Thomas Nelson, Nashville

The Complete Word Study Old Testament, AMG Publishers, Chattanooga, Tennessee

Vincent's Word Studies in the New Testament, W. E. Vincent, Hendrickson Publishers, Peabody, Massachusetts

Vine's Complete Expository Dictionary of Old and New Testament Words, W. E. Vine, Thomas Nelson, Nashville

Wuest's Word Studies From the Greek New Testament, Kenneth Wuest, Eerdman's Publishing Co., Grand Rapids

Pentecostal-Charismatic Bible Lesson Series (2013-2020)

Fall Quarter September, October, November	Winter Quarter December, January, February	Spring Quarter March, April, May	Summer Quarter June, July, August
Fall 2013 1 • Great Events in Genesis 2 • Discourses in Matthew	**Winter 2013-14** 1 • Songs and Hymns in the New Testament 2 • Wisdom From Ecclesiastes & Proverbs	**Spring 2014** 1 • Hope in the Book of Isaiah 2 • Principles for Christian Living (1, 2, 3 John)	**Summer 2014** 1 • The Exodus 2 • The Doctrine of Salvation
Fall 2014 1 • Great Stories of the Bible 2 • Parables of Jesus (Stories Jesus Told)	**Winter 2014-15** 1 • Law and Grace in the New Testament 2 • Universal Moral Law (Genesis–Deuteronomy)	**Spring 2015** 1 • Life of Samuel 2 • The Early Church (Acts, Part 1)	**Summer 2015** 1 • Different Types of Psalms 2 • Practical Christianity (James)
Fall 2015 1 • The Book of Joshua 2 • Mark (Jesus in Action)	**Winter 2015-16** 1 • Messianic Prophecies 2 • Normal Christian Living (Ephesians)	**Spring 2016** 1 • Jeremiah and Lamentations 2 • Lessons From 1 Corinthians	**Summer 2016** 1 • David & Solomon 2 • Life's Transitions (Adult Life Stages)
Fall 2016 1 • More Great Stories of the Bible 2 • 1 & 2 Peter, Jude	**Winter 2016-17** 1 • Minor Prophets (Part 1) 2 • Letter to the Romans	**Spring 2017** 1 • The Era of the Judges 2 • Pauls Journeys (Acts, Part 2)	**Summer 2017** 1 • Good Lessons From Bad Examples 2 • Good Lessons From Good Examples
Fall 2017 1 • Luke (The Compassion of Jesus) 2 • The Holy Trinity	**Winter 2017-18** 1 • Kings of Judah 2 • The Christian Family	**Spring 2018** 1 • Ezekiel 2 • 2 Corinthians	**Summer 2018** 1 • Ezra & Nehemiah 2 • Philippians & Colossians (Philemon)
Fall 2018 1 • Abraham, Isaac, & Jacob 2 • Pastoral Letters	**Winter 2018-19** 1 • Minor Prophets (Part 2) 2 • Miracles of Jesus	**Spring 2019** 1 • Women of Faith 2 • Fruits & Gifts of the Spirit	**Summer 2019** 1 • Best-Known Psalms 2 • Hebrews
Fall 2019 1 • Job: A Life of Integrity 2 • John (The Son of God)	**Winter 2019-20** 1 • Major Christian Beliefs 2 • 1 & 2 Thessalonians	**Spring 2020** 1 • Daniel 2 • Galatians	**Summer 2020** 1 • The Bible's Influence in Society 2 • Revelation

Introduction to Fall Quarter

"More Great Stories of the Bible" (lessons 1-7) includes accounts of Noah, Abraham, Aaron, Hezekiah, Nicodemus, Stephen, and Aquila and Priscilla.

Dr. Sabord Woods, longtime professor of English at Lee University, who now lives in Jesup, Georgia, wrote the expositions. He holds B.A. and M.A. degrees from Georgia Southern College; M.A., Church of God Theological Seminary; Ph.D., University of Tennessee.

The second unit, "First and Second Peter and Jude" (lessons 8-13), provides faith-building lessons on the themes of hope, holiness, discipleship, the Day of the Lord, and faithfulness.

The lessons were compiled by Lance Colkmire (B.A., M.A.), editor of the *Evangelical Commentary* and the *Church of God Evangel* for Pathway Press. He also serves the South Cleveland (TN) Church of God as missions pastor.

Noah and the Ark

Genesis 6:5—8:22

Unit Theme:

More Great Stories of the Bible

Central Truth:

God keeps those who trust and obey Him.

Focus:

Consider Noah's obedience to God and trust Him to fulfill His word.

Context:

Traditional chronology dates the Flood around 2400 BC.

Golden Text:

"By faith Noah, being warned of God of things not seen as yet, moved with fear, prepared an ark to the saving of his house; by the which he condemned the world, and became heir of the righteousness which is by faith" (Heb. 11:7).

Study Outline:

  I. **Noah Obeys God** (Gen. 6:5-22)

  II. **God Preserves Noah** (Gen. 7:1-24)

  III. **God Delivers; Noah Worships** (Gen. 8:13-22)

INTRODUCTION

The disobedience of Adam and Eve brought sin, misery, suffering, and death into the world. However, while we are not told so directly, Scripture strongly implies that Adam and Eve repented and taught their sons to give honor and reverence to God. As evidence, both Cain and Abel presented sacrifices to the Lord; He considered Abel's as acceptable and Cain's as not acceptable. Nonetheless, overall, in succeeding generations, humankind followed the way of Cain in rebellion, godlessness, and lawlessness.

After the death of Abel, Eve bore to Adam a third son, Seth, whose name means "appointed." Adam believed God had appointed Seth to replace the seed of Abel (Gen. 4:25), his righteous son murdered by Cain. After the birth of Seth's son Enos, people "began to call on the name of the Lord [Yahweh]" (v. 26 NKJV). This might indicate that a system of worship had been established.

From Seth came a godly line consisting of eight successive generations that climaxed in the righteous Noah. Despite this positive fact, the descendants of both Cain and Seth, in the main, were ungodly. Only one line, stretching from Seth to Noah, was righteous. Scripture says of Enoch, the seventh from Adam in this line of descendants from Seth, that he "walked with God: and he was not, for God took him" (5:24). Hebrews 11:5 states, "By faith Enoch was taken away so that he did not see death, 'and was not found, because God had taken him'; for . . . he had this testimony, that he pleased God" (NKJV).

The tragic fact is that, in only a few generations, humankind—despite its material and technological gains—on the whole had descended to horrible depths of depravity. Some think there was no organized government in the pre-Flood world. If this was the case, such a condition of godless anarchy would have contributed to the state of rebellion and violence existent by the time of Noah.

Jesus speaks of Noah's generation in Luke 17:26-27: "As it was in the days of Noah, so it will be also in the days of the Son of Man. They ate, they drank, they married wives, they were given in marriage, until the day that Noah entered the ark, and the flood came and destroyed them all" (NKJV). Their lives were totally consumed with the material and the sensual, with no consciousness of God and His will for human life. Jesus states that, just prior to His second coming, a similar situation will exist. This is a good reason for us to study the texts of Scripture surrounding Noah and the Flood for their application to our own times.

I. NOAH OBEYS GOD (Gen. 6:5-22)

Study of the genealogical and narrative records in Genesis 4 and 5 reveal that the descendants of Cain followed his lead in lawlessness and rebellion against the Lord without any notable exception. On the other hand, Seth's descendants, while in the main equally self-devoted and spiritually insensitive, contained one line that maintained a high degree of moral and spiritual integrity.

A. God's Response to Human Depravity (vv. 5-7, 11-12)

⁵And God saw that the wickedness of man was great in the earth, and that every imagination of the thoughts of his heart was only evil continually. ⁶And it repented the Lord that he had made man on the earth, and it grieved him at his heart. ⁷And the Lord said, I will destroy man whom I have created from the face of the earth; both man, and beast, and the creeping thing, and the fowls of the air; for it repenteth me that I have made them.

¹¹The earth also was corrupt before God, and the earth was filled with violence. ¹²And God looked upon the earth, and, behold, it was corrupt; for all flesh had corrupted his way upon the earth.

By the tenth generation from Adam to Seth (see ch. 5), that of Noah, moral wickedness had reached an extremely high level. In fact, sexual depravity had resulted in the birth of giants who seemed to be physical and moral freaks (6:1-2, 4). The term *wickedness* (v. 5) refers generally to evil, moral wretchedness, mischief, and ethical malignancy. The very bent of human thought was toward ethical and moral evil.

There appears to have been a total insensitivity to spiritual values. Lawlessness and violence were so characteristic of human, social, and personal behavior that God saw no hope of recovery (vv. 11-12). There is the strong suggestion of a hopeless morass of individual and social evil, similar in degree, if not in kind, to the later sexual depravity of Sodom and Gomorrah (19:1-11). If (as He indeed had) the Lord had determined that total destruction was necessary, then there was evidently in this generation no sense of sin, no spiritual sensitivity, and no inclination toward repentance.

God himself does not "repent" in the human sense—a change of mind, heart, and direction; but He does repent in the sense of regret (see 6:6). In other words, despite human failure in the Garden of Eden, God had given humankind wonderful opportunities for growth and development materially, morally, and spiritually. God's omniscience and omnipresence assured Him full observation and comprehension of the personal human condition and of the social fabric across the inhabited earth. It was fully evident to Him that no upward movement had occurred or ever would occur. Therefore, God—probably with a broken heart—determined that annihilation of the existing population was necessary, with subsequent renewal of the human race to follow this necessary act of divine judgment.

---

1. What did God see (v. 5)?
2. How did God respond to what He saw, and why (v. 6)?
3. Compare what the Lord saw in Noah's day (vv. 11-12) with what He sees on earth today.

"We desperately need to understand something of the magnitude of sin, of evil, and of gross wickedness in this world if we are to appreciate our redemption. God's love, grace, and mercy shine all the brighter against the awful reality of evil. Indeed, the very existence of evil is a powerful proof of God's existence and holiness."—Dave Hunt

---

B. Noah's Grace From God (vv. 8-10)

8But Noah found grace in the eyes of the Lord. 9These are the generations of Noah: Noah was a just man and perfect in his generations, and Noah walked with God. 10And Noah begat three sons, Shem, Ham, and Japheth.

Noah, son of Lamech in the righteous line descending from Seth, was so named because the Hebrew word *Noah* means "comfort." This son, Lamech hoped, would be a capable partner in his farming enterprise, thereby providing comfort to the family and particularly to Lamech himself as he grew older (5:28-29). But God, behind the scenes, was assigning this name for His own larger purpose, *comfort* to Noah's own family, the surviving land animals, and the human race at large after the worldwide Flood—and maybe even comfort for the Lord himself. "Noah was a righteous man, blameless in his time" (6:9 NASB) whom God could use in a time of extreme crisis as an instrument of salvation and renewal.

The writer of the letter to the Hebrews sums up Noah's righteous life by stating, "By faith Noah, being divinely warned of things not yet seen, moved with godly fear, prepared an ark for the saving of his household, by which he condemned the world and became heir of the righteousness which is according to faith" (11:7 NKJV). Noah was counted righteous by God because he trusted in Him and walked with Him by faith. Noah listened to the voice of God and became an instrument of God for the salvation of his own family and selected land animals.

Faith means trusting in the wisdom and leadership of God and leaning on Him for direction. Noah was able to act in faith because he had found "grace," or favor, in the sight of God (Gen. 6:8). But Noah, however spiritually sensitive, did not reach upward toward God; instead, as is always the case with God's grace, He reached down to Noah. The Lord chose to work through a human instrument that He, in His infinite wisdom, saw as pliable and usable for a divinely ordained purpose.

Noah, like his great-grandfather Enoch, walked out his faith in daily relationship with his Maker. Noah's Creator was his Companion, much like the walk of Adam and Eve in the Garden of Eden before the Fall. However, Noah's was a walk of faith; whereas Adam and Eve had forfeited an actual physical experience of the presence of Deity right there in the garden—no faith (in the sense of "evidence of things not seen," Heb. 11:1) necessary.

---

1. Why is the word "but" so significant in verse 8?
2. From verses 9 and 10, list four facts about Noah.

> "Either we are adrift in chaos or we are individuals, created, loved, upheld and placed purposefully, exactly where we are. Can you believe that? Can you trust God for that?"—Elisabeth Elliot

---

C. God's Instructions to Noah (vv. 13-21)
(Genesis 6:15-16, 19-21 is not included in the printed text.)

¹³And God said unto Noah, The end of all flesh is come before me; for the earth is filled with violence through them; and, behold, I will destroy them with the earth. ¹⁴Make thee an ark of gopher wood; rooms shalt thou make in the ark, and shalt pitch it within and without with pitch.

¹⁷And, behold, I, even I, do bring a flood of waters upon the earth, to destroy all flesh, wherein is the breath of life, from under heaven; and every thing that is in the earth shall die. ¹⁸But with thee will I establish my covenant; and thou shalt come into the ark, thou, and thy sons, and thy wife, and thy sons' wives with thee.

Noah was the sole righteous man among his contemporaries. When one contemplates the pull toward conformity within the typical human mind, it becomes evident that the counter pull within Noah can be attributed to only two possible factors—a strong tradition of faith within his family and the attraction toward God through the divine grace operating within him. Noah learned how to listen to God's voice and had the discernment to follow that divine leading.

God had a startling message for Noah: *I have observed your contemporaries and now realize that there is no inclination within them toward spiritual change. The lawlessness and violence evident among them will only get worse; therefore, I have resolved to annihilate completely all human life. The means chosen is a worldwide flood.*

Noah and the Ark

Some Old Testament scholars hold that the flood planned by God was merely local. However, if that were true, Noah and his family could have simply left the area. Also, it would have been unnecessary to put animals in the ark because a local flood would not destroy all animal life. In fact, however, descriptive language in the Genesis account points to a worldwide flood that would destroy all human and land-animal life on the planet.

God dictated to Noah His directions for construction of the ark as the place of refuge to ride out the onrush of water that would spread across the surface of the planet. The building material, "gopher wood" (v. 14), is from an unidentifiable tree, but some scholars believe *cypress* wood is the writer's intention. The "pitch" used to cover the wood and make it watertight (v. 14) is different from the "pitch" sealing the "ark of bulrushes" that held the infant Moses (Ex. 2:3), according to the Hebrew language, so we cannot be certain of its exact nature. But we can assume it was totally appropriate for God's purpose.

The dimensions of the ark are given in cubits. If one assumes that a *cubit* is equivalent to 18 inches (the smallest measurement for the cubit typically suggested), then the ark was to be 450 feet long, 75 feet wide, and 45 feet high. This structure would be appropriate for riding floodwaters, but would not be much of a sailing vessel. However, God did not intend the occupants of the ark to sail; rather, they were to be tossed to and fro without capsizing. This structure contained rooms on three levels and, just beneath its roof, an 18-inch-high window that apparently reached all the way around the vessel and served as a means of air and light. There was also a single door and possibly another window on the side of the ark (see Gen. 8:6). God must have left to Noah and his sons many details of the construction or else directed them as they proceeded with the project.

Noah had at least one hundred years to complete the ark. We can imagine the jeers and jests of his contemporaries as they, over the decades, observed the slow but sure movement toward completion. With absolutely no belief in the God of revelation, these neighbors of Noah would quite likely see him as a quaint old man who was trustworthy, despite his odd convictions and actions.

God informed Noah in detail concerning His act of judgment: only specified individuals and selected animals would survive the Flood. A male and female of each "kind" would be spared (v. 20). I believe the reference here is specifically to the kinds of animals created in Genesis 1:24-25. The countless sub-species existent today, if they even existed then, would not necessarily survive. Moses (the writer of Genesis) also comments that seven of each kind of clean animals were to come into the ark (7:2-3; for identification, see Deut. 14:9-20). Noah also was to store sufficient food to last throughout the time of enclosure (6:21).

God informed Noah before the Flood began that He would establish His "covenant" with him (v. 18). This in itself was an assurance that he would survive the Flood. While Noah (by faith) constructed the ark, he most certainly, being human, was beset by doubts and questions, both as the construction phase stretched over the decades and after entering the ark and waiting for the rain to begin. Only if Noah had already learned to trust God implicitly would this period of waiting have been anything less than nerve-wracking. When

God promised to establish the covenant, He was assuring Noah that he, his family, and the animals would survive the onslaught of watery terror soon to come; hence, the covenant was an aid to faith. It was promised by God before the Flood, with its detail to be given afterward.

---

1. How destructive would the flood be (vv. 13, 17)?
2. Describe the ark's layout (vv. 14-16).
3. How was the ark part of God's covenant with Noah (v. 18)?

No Other Solution

If we read Genesis 6 carefully and thoughtfully, we must conclude that the sinfulness of humanity was enormous and gross because of what we learn elsewhere in Scripture about the great mercy of God. If any other solution than a worldwide flood had existed, then the merciful, loving Creator and Sustainer of the universe would surely have resorted to it rather than exacting wholesale destruction.

D. Noah's Total Obedience (v. 22)

22Thus did Noah; according to all that God commanded him, so did he.

Noah obeyed God completely, although he likely found bewildering the tasks He was asking him to perform. God, having observed Noah's character during his five hundred years of living among hostile contemporaries, knew this righteous servant would comply with His directions without deviation. God loves unconditionally, but He rewards obedience. Noah must have absorbed this spiritual principle from his forebears' oral transmission of long, reassuring experience with the God of heaven. In fact, obedience without comprehension of God's purpose, but with full awareness that He is in control, is the highest level of faith.

"I find that doing of the will of God leaves me no time for disputing about His plans."—George MacDonald

---

II. GOD PRESERVES NOAH (Gen. 7:1-24)

A. Divine Invitation to Noah (vv. 1-5)

(Genesis 7:2-4 is not included in the printed text.)

1And the Lord said unto Noah, Come thou and all thy house into the ark; for thee have I seen righteous before me in this generation.

5And Noah did according unto all that the Lord commanded him.

By Noah's six hundredth year, the construction of the ark was complete. Now God graciously said to Noah, "Come . . . into the ark" (v. 1). He was inviting

---

Noah, his wife, his sons, and his sons' wives to enter the ark of safety. It was God's unique vessel of protection from the imminent advent of destruction of the world by water. Noah and his household were to be spared because, among his contemporaries, he alone had proved to be just before God.

Noah was to take with him into the ark one pair of each unclean animal and seven (three pairs plus one) clean animals so all kinds of animals would remain alive on the earth after the Flood (vv. 2-3). The seventh clean animal was likely for sacrifice. God announced to Noah that, after seven more days, the rain would begin and all living things on the land surface of the planet would be destroyed (v. 4).

We are informed in verse 5 that Noah did precisely what the Lord ordered him to do, making him fully usable in the kingdom of God.

---

1. What does God reiterate in verse 1?
2. How does God show His concern for animal life (vv. 2-3)?
3. Why do you suppose God gave Noah such a specific forecast (v. 4)?
4. How does Genesis 7:5 echo 6:22?

> "See in the meantime that your faith brings forth obedience, and God in due time will cause it to bring forth peace."—John Owen

---

B. A Divine Provision of Safety (vv. 6-15)

(Genesis 7:8-15 is not included in the printed text.)

⁶And Noah was six hundred years old when the flood of water was upon the earth. ⁷And Noah went in, and his sons, and his wife, and his sons' wives with him, into the ark, because of the waters of the flood.

God commanded Noah to enter the ark—with the animals—seven days before the rain began to fall. God must have caused the animals to come to the ark. For Noah to have tracked them down and coax them inside would have been a humanly impossible task.

There would be two main sources of water. The first source would be from under the earth's surface—"the fountains of the great deep" (v. 11). A great supply of water exists beneath the surface of the earth, and even more must have existed back then. If that huge amount of water suddenly spewed out onto earth's surface, it alone would cause cataclysms and an enormous contribution to coverage of the planet with water.

The second source would be that canopy of moisture existing above earth since the Creation (see 1:7). According to 2:5-6, rain did not occur before the time of the Flood; instead, "a mist went up from the earth and watered the whole face of the ground" (NKJV). When the enormous amount of water from both above and below the earth accumulated quickly on its surface, the inevitable result must be thousands of feet of water covering the entire planet. This engulfment of the entire earth surface by such a weight of water would destroy all humans, animals, birds, and insects—all dependent on oxygen and now covered completely by water—and create a vast upheaval of the crust of the planet. Such punishment by being swallowed up by water sounds extremely cruel, but must be seen to occur only because no other viable alternative presented itself to the omniscient mind of the Creator.

---

1. When the flood came, how old was Noah (v. 6)? How could this be?
2. What happened during the first week on the ark (vv. 7-9)? How do you suppose this happened?
3. What factors caused the worldwide flood (vv. 10-12)?
4. How did the ark fare (v. 15)?

> "There are three kinds of faith in Christ: (1) struggling faith, like a man in deep water desperately swimming; (2) clinging faith, like a man hanging to the side of a boat; (3) resting faith, like a man safely within the boat."—D. L. Moody

---

C. Divine Judgment Through Water (vv. 16-24)

(Genesis 7:16-24 is not included in the printed text.)

Once all eight humans and all selected animals were inside the ark, God himself shut the door (see v. 16). Perhaps God was showing His deep personal respect for His righteous servant Noah and His special personal concern for the well-being of His carefully selected survivors amidst the devastating flood. The rain from the "windows of heaven" would continue for forty days and nights, and the "fountains . . . of the deep" would spew forth water at the same time (8:2). This result would be a greatly altered topography across the entire planet. Noah and his family would eventually disembark, only to find an earth surface habitable but greatly changed, with the results of death and decay still evident everywhere.

---

1. What took place outside the ark (vv. 20-22)?
2. Today, where can we find safety from the worldwide flood of sin and its consequences?

> "Yet, in the maddening maze of things/And tossed by storm and flood/To one fixed trust my spirit clings;/I know that God is good!"—John Greenleaf Whittier

---

III. GOD DELIVERS; NOAH WORSHIPS (Gen. 8:13-22)

For 150 days, Noah and his family rode the waves in the ark God had designed for their safety and survival, while the water during the first forty days increased steadily, then for 110 days held its high level 22 feet above the highest mountain. Then God caused a *wind* (Hebrew, *ruach*) "to pass over the earth, and the waters subsided" (v. 1 NKJV). A number of scholars believe that, since *ruach* means both *wind* and *spirit*, the *wind* might plausibly be the

Holy Spirit, the third person of the divine Trinity. He could have acted on these waters in a similar fashion as He did during the first day of Creation—"the Spirit of God was hovering over the face of the waters" (1:2 NKJV).

On the seventeenth day of the seventh month (six months after Noah and his family entered the ark), the ark rested "upon the mountains of Ararat" (8:4). Then, on the first day of the tenth month (almost nine months after Noah and his family entered the ark), the tops of the mountains were visible (v. 5).

A. The Departure From the Ark (vv. 13-19)

(Genesis 8:17-19 is not included in the printed text.)

13And it came to pass in the six hundredth and first year, in the first month, the first day of the month, the waters were dried up from off the earth: and Noah removed the covering of the ark, and looked, and, behold, the face of the ground was dry. 14And in the second month, on the seven and twentieth day of the month, was the earth dried. 15And God spake unto Noah, saying, 16Go forth of the ark, thou, and thy wife, and thy sons, and thy sons' wives with thee.

One year after God had shut Noah inside the ark, by the beginning of the first month of the 601st year, all waters on the earth's surface had dried up, as Noah saw for himself when he removed the "covering" (v. 13) off the top and observed conditions outside. One month later, God spoke to Noah, giving him the signal to leave the ark with all his family and all animals that had gone into the ark (v. 16). The divine intention was that these surviving humans and animals thrive and multiply throughout the earth (v. 17).

God had directed Noah step-by-crucial-step throughout the entire ordeal (for it was an ordeal for Noah and his family). God's reason for such hands-on direction was so Noah might not, at any point, misstep and suffer any kind of loss through ignorance. The stakes were too high for such a risk.

---

1. When did Noah leave the ark (vv. 13-16)?
2. How had God proven His faithfulness to Noah (vv. 18-19)?

> "It is foolish to move into the future on our own when God is waiting to guide us. His plan is the best. If we yield to Him, He can save us from Satan's snares."—Zac Poonen

---

B. The Divine Covenant With Creation (vv. 20-22)

20And Noah builded an altar unto the Lord; and took of every clean beast, and of every clean fowl, and offered burnt offerings on the altar. 21And the Lord smelled a sweet savour; and the Lord said in his heart, I will not again curse the ground any more for man's sake; for the imagination of man's heart is evil from his youth; neither will I again smite any more every thing living, as I have done. 22While the earth remaineth, seedtime and harvest, and cold and heat, and summer and winter, and day and night shall not cease.

Noah immediately worshiped God, using the prescribed ritual—a burnt offering; in this case, an elaborate sacrifice from every kind of clean beast and bird. Noah's priorities were right: attending first to his spiritual duties, an expression of his relationship with the Lord. God accepted Noah's sincere worship and responded positively toward all the survivors of the Flood. Noah, as head of household, led his entire family in this act of worship.

God resolved to "never again curse the ground on account of man," recognizing the inevitable dominance of the sin nature in fallen, unrepentant men and women (v. 21 NASB). Yet, God invited fellowship of humanity with Himself, while also making individuals answerable to Him for their moral and spiritual state. God also made an unbreakable promise to "never again destroy every living thing" by water (v. 21 NASB).

In six cryptic lines of Hebrew verse, God also enunciated the following vow:

> While the earth remains,
> Seedtime and harvest,
> Cold and heat,
> Winter and summer,
> And day and night
> Shall not cease (v. 22 NKJV).

Genesis 9 states in detail the post-Flood conditions covering Noah and all creation. Noah and his sons should "be fruitful, and multiply, and replenish the earth" (v. 1). Their relationship with animals would change: from this point on, animals would fear man (v. 2). Humans now could include meat from animals in their diet, but should avoid eating blood (v. 4; Lev. 3:17). Because man is made in the image of God, any person who sheds human blood must pay with his own life (Gen. 9:6).

In God's covenant with Noah and all creation, He promised that never again would all humans and animals be destroyed by a worldwide flood. As a sign of this covenant, He placed a rainbow in the sky. Since there had been no rain before the Flood, whenever there was rain and a rainbow appeared once the sun began to shine again, people should then remember God's gracious promise. Moreover, God himself would "look on [this rainbow] to remember the everlasting covenant between God and every living creature of all flesh that is on the earth" (v. 16 NKJV).

---

1. How did Noah respond to God's faithfulness (v. 20)?
2. How are you responding to God's faithfulness?
3. What did God promise would never happen again (v. 21)?
4. What did God say would "not cease" (v. 22)?

"The unceasing activity of the Creator, whereby in overflowing bounty and goodwill, He upholds His creatures in ordered existence, guides and governs all events, circumstances, and free acts of angels and men, and directs everything to its appointed goal, for His own glory."—J. I. Packer

---

CONCLUSION

God saw that Noah—a righteous man of faith who lived in daily relationship with Him—could rebuild human civilization on a better foundation. So an ark of safety was prepared according to God's instructions, and Noah, his household, and selected animals of every kind were preserved from the Flood. God has a righteous remnant in our own generation, to be preserved from the Great Tribulation and brought back to Planet Earth to join the righteous Jewish remnant in ruling and reigning with Christ. The challenge to you and me is to be a part of God's blood-bought, raptured Church at the end of this age.

GOLDEN TEXT CHALLENGE

"BY FAITH NOAH, BEING WARNED OF GOD OF THINGS NOT SEEN AS YET, MOVED WITH FEAR, PREPARED AN ARK TO THE SAVING OF HIS HOUSE; BY THE WHICH HE CONDEMNED THE WORLD, AND BECAME HEIR OF THE RIGHTEOUSNESS WHICH IS BY FAITH" (Heb. 11:7).

Noah's faith was the foundation for his fearful obedience and his deliverance. Without faith, he too would have experienced God's judgment. Faith in God is absolutely essential to live for Him.

When Noah responded obediently to the command of the Lord to prepare for the Flood, it was an act of faith. When he obediently entered the ark, it was an act of faith. And when he accepted the covenant after the Flood, signified with the token of the rainbow, it was an act of faith.

The importance of faith in the Lord cannot be overstated. The entire chapter of Hebrews 11 recognizes individuals who were delivered, endured great hardship, and were mightily used of God.

Through faith in God and obedience to Him, we too can carry out exploits with God in service to His kingdom.

Daily Devotions:

M. God Blesses Noah • Genesis 9:1-3
T. God's Covenant With Noah • Genesis 9:8-17
W. All Are Descendants of Noah • Genesis 10:1-7
T. Similarities With Noah's Day • Matthew 24:36-44
F. A Hero of Faith • Hebrews 11:1-2, 6-7
S. The Righteousness of Jesus Christ • 1 Peter 3:18-22

Abraham and the Covenant

Genesis 12:1-8; 15:1-16; 17:1-22

Unit Theme:
More Great Stories of the Bible

Central Truth:
Christians trust God to faithfully keep His covenant promises.

Focus:
Recognize and emulate Abraham's great faith in God's promises.

Context:
Over a twenty-five-year period, God establishes and reaffirms His covenant with Abraham (around 2091—2067 BC).

Golden Text:
"And he [Abraham] believed in the Lord; and he counted it to him for righteousness" (Gen. 15:6).

Study Outline:
   I. **Obeying God's Call** (Gen. 12:1-8)
  II. **Believing God's Promise** (Gen. 15:1-16)
 III. **Entering God's Covenant** (Gen. 17:1-10, 15-21)

INTRODUCTION

After Noah and his family left the ark, received God's promises, and started their new lives, Noah's three sons—Japheth, Ham, and Shem—and their immediate descendants were forced by the confusion of languages at Babel to migrate to different parts of the world. They produced lines of descendants who began what ultimately became the many nations of the earth. Genesis 10 offers genealogies of Noah's three sons. In general, descendants of Japheth migrated north, east, and west; descendants of Ham went south and east; and descendants of Shem either stayed put or moved generally southwest. Shem's descendants, however, ultimately remained in a more contained area than did those of his brothers (in what we now call the Middle East).

Arphaxad, one of Shem's sons, began a line of descendants that eventually produced Abraham, father of two major ethnic groups and major contributor to three major world religions—Judaism, Islam, and Christianity. Abraham was likely a moon-god worshiper back in Ur, near the Euphrates River, when he heard a "strange" new God address him with a mighty challenge and several astounding promises. This initial encounter with Deity led Abraham to an obedient response and an eventual trek into and throughout the land of Canaan. During a twenty-four-year period in their mature years, Abraham and his wife, Sarah, experienced the beginning of a gradual unfolding of God's plan for their family, succeeding ethnic groups, and eventually the entire human race.

According to scholars, in Bible times, God made approximately seven covenants with all or part of humankind: (1) Adamic, (2) Noahic, (3) Abrahamic, (4) Sinaitic, (5) Palestinian, (6) Davidic, and (7) new covenant. The list varies a little according to definitions of *covenant* and ideas of what must appear in one. It is generally accepted that a *covenant*, unlike a *contract*, does not have two equal parties, and requires relationship between its parties.

God originated every covenant in the seven listed above. Since He is omnipotent and omniscient, He (by right) initiated each covenant and gave the conditions, rewards, and penalties. In some cases, He also gave a "sign" (Gen. 17:11) and/or "seal" (Rom. 4:11) of the covenant. In at least one crucial case (Gen. 15), God "cut a covenant"; that is, He arranged an awesome ceremony in which sacrificial animals were cut in two pieces, between which He walked, signifying that He would unconditionally keep the promises He was making. The Hebrew word for *covenant* (*berith*) likely means "space between" (*Hastings' Dictionary of the Bible*), with reference to the space between the two halves of animals in which the parties to the covenant walked as they pledged to keep covenant (see also Jer. 34:18).

Abraham experienced successive stages in what is called the "Abrahamic covenant." In the first stage (Gen. 12:1-3), God appeared to Abram (Abraham's original name) in Ur of the Chaldees and invited him to travel to a destination He would reveal precisely later. God then gave him unconditional promises. In the second stage (ch. 15), God literally cut His covenant with Abram, and the narrator first specified the word *covenant* in verse 18. In the third stage (ch. 17), God gave promises, conditions, and a sign of the covenant and specified that Abraham's heir would come from his wife, Sarah.

I. OBEYING GOD'S CALL (Gen. 12:1-8)

A. A Sovereign Lord (v. 1)

¹Now the Lord had said unto Abram, Get thee out of thy country, and from thy kindred, and from thy father's house, unto a land that I will shew thee.

Abram probably had no idea who this God was when He spoke to him while he was still back in Ur, a pagan city in what is now southern Iraq. Moon worship dominated the culture of this idolatrous city. It is possible that knowledge of the true God had gradually been either totally lost or else very greatly diminished in the generations after some of Shem's descendants settled here. But Abram felt compelled to obey the bodiless Voice and induced his family to begin a fateful journey. At that time, Abram's obedience was likely a partial one at first—a response which led his family to the city of Haran, where Abram remained until his father, Terah, died.

It is remarkable that descendants of Noah so quickly moved in a direction similar to that of descendants of both Cain and Seth before the worldwide Flood, though certainly not as totally evil. Moreover, there was still a sovereign Lord dwelling in heaven whose presence yet filled the earth He had created. He was now initiating a long series of encounters in what we presently call "salvation history"—encounters that would repeatedly call perennially wandering humans back to Himself and His revealed purposes.

Note that God's name was specified so there could be no mistake about who was calling Abram. His name was (and is) *Yahweh*. In ancient history, this name consisted of four Hebrew language consonants transliterated into modern English as *YHWH*. Two probable vowels were added sometime later in the written language to form the word *Yahweh*. R. Kent Hughes wrote that *Yahweh* is "the personal covenant name of God who relates to and redeems His people" (*Genesis*). It is therefore fitting that God should introduce Himself to Abram by this name, though at the time a name only faintly understood by him.

• Has God ever told you to "get out" of somewhere, as he told Abram? If so, how did you respond?

> "Our lifestyle, language, attitudes, and manner of dress reflect on His name. He leads us in paths of righteousness for His name's sake. Unless you are honestly convinced that the thing in question will bring glory to God, then don't do it."—Curtis Hutson

---

B. An Amazing Call (v. 2)

2And I will make of thee a great nation, and I will bless thee, and make thy name great; and thou shalt be a blessing.

God gave Abram one condition—to leave his country and go to a land God would show him. What was so amazing about this call, especially to Abram, was that he should have received it at all. Isn't this typically true of our calls by the Lord? Poor, uneducated, limited in measurable abilities, satisfied where we are, or overwhelmed by any thoughts of great change—we are accosted by Divinity and jerked up and out by a call from God. That call may come in one or more ways, whether an impression, a dream, a long-term gnawing at our innards, or a suggestion from someone else that we cannot shake. Rarely does a person hear a voice outside his head, as did Abram.

Abram's call must have been so obvious and strong that he could not push it aside. So after a while, he took a step, halting at first, but to be followed by a second much greater step that would set him and the entourage (which he had, by then, accumulated in Haran) on their way south to Canaan. Abram, by then, had at least some indication that he was to go south, and that would mean toward and into Canaan. His accompanying family group would include his wife, his nephew Lot, and a considerable number of servants—in addition to sheep, goats, donkeys, camels, and necessary supplies.

• Describe the "greatness" God had in mind for Abram.

> "Many do not recognize the call of God simply because they have never taken the time to really talk with Him long enough to know what He is like."—Winkie Pratney

C. Unconditional Promises (vv. 3-8)

(Genesis 12:6-8 is not included in the printed text.)

³And I will bless them that bless thee, and curse him that curseth thee: and in thee shall all families of the earth be blessed. ⁴So Abram departed, as the Lord had spoken unto him; and Lot went with him: and Abram was seventy and five years old when he departed out of Haran. ⁵And Abram took Sarai his wife, and Lot his brother's son, and all their substance that they had gathered, and the souls that they had gotten in Haran; and they went forth to go into the land of Canaan; and into the land of Canaan they came.

In His first call to Abram, God gave him seven great commitments by Himself that imposed no conditions on Abram other than taking God's commanded trip—His one imperative. These remarkable promises (vv. 2-3) are rooted in God's nature and in His long-term intentions for all humankind. Abram would obediently start a great chain of commitments with remarkable results for time and eternity.

The seven promises by God to Abram are as follows: (1) "I will make of you a great nation." (2) "I will bless you." (3) "I will make your name great." (4) "I will make you a blessing." (5) "I will bless those who bless you." (6) "I will curse those who curse you." (7) "In you shall all the families of the earth be blessed."

First, God would make out of Abram a *great nation*—the nation of Israel. This nation would come from Abram's seed. There could be no compromise, no substitute; there must be a biological heir. Second, there would flow a *general blessing* ("I will bless you"); an obedient Abram would receive divine blessing—*favor* received not by chance, but by the direct action of the Lord.

Third, Abram's *name would become great* as he moved in obedience to God throughout his lifetime. Fourth, Abram *would be a blessing* during his lifetime and long afterward. Abram would be a blessing to all who surrounded him and to all who came into contact with him. God's blessings on Abram would overflow onto those nearby. Fifth, those who blessed Abram, thereby cooperating with God's purposes centering on Abram's life in his generation, would be *blessed by God*. Sixth, those who cursed him would hinder God's purposes being wrought in and through Abram, and they *would be cursed by God*. To be cursed by God could bring many negative results—for instance, defeat by enemies, disease, or even death.

The seventh great promise reached forward in time to the coming of the Messiah. The seed of Abraham would pass through Isaac and Jacob; into Jacob's son Judah; through generations proceeding directly from Judah down to Ruth and Boaz and their beloved son, Obed; his descendant Jesse; and Jesse's youngest son, David. David would become king of Israel, and from David's seed would come Jesus, the Messiah, through the long line of the kings of Judah and, during the intertestamental period, through obscure descendants of the Judean kings. The Messiah—Jesus Christ the Lord—is God's eternal Son, who will return to reign on earth. Through Him, *all the families of the earth are blessed.*

Abram and his family trekked slowly down through Canaan, stopping at certain sites and building altars there, then tarrying until circumstances moved them further (thereby continuing God's unfolding purpose). These stops on Abram's physical and spiritual journey consisted of Shechem, a spot near Bethel; a detour from God's plan down into Egypt; and separation from Abram's nephew Lot, leading to Lot's subsequent rescue by Abram (Gen. 12:5—13:13; 14:1-16). They take us to a second great encounter of Abram with God.

---

1. How would one man influence the whole world (v. 3)?
2. Who traveled with Abram (v. 5)?
3. What did God promise (v. 7)?
4. What did Abram do in two locations, and why (vv. 7-8)?

> "To obey God in some things, and not in others, shows an unsound heart. Childlike obedience moves toward every command of God, as the needle points where the loadstone draws."
> —Thomas Watson

II. BELIEVING GOD'S PROMISE (Gen. 15:1-16)

A. Hearing God's Voice (v. 1)

¹After these things the word of the Lord came unto Abram in a vision, saying, Fear not, Abram: I am thy shield, and thy exceeding great reward.

Abram had rescued his nephew after Lot had been captured by powerful kings who had defeated Sodom and other nearby cities. Some believe Abram was beset by anxieties and misgivings after his victorious battle and chase of the powerful kings that had captured Lot and his possessions. Perhaps he was worried about possible reprisal. Whatever the case, the Lord appeared to him in a remarkable vision. Yahweh gave Abram a cryptic two-part revelation of Himself that would crucially affect his present and long-term future.

Shield is a military term that pertains to defensive warfare. When the spears and arrows came against Abram, whether physical or spiritual, they would be stopped or deflected by Yahweh himself. When we are pursuing God's objectives, we cannot ultimately be defeated. When the battle is over, we will remain standing on the side of victory, for God will have prevented opposing forces—Syrian or Canaanite, physical or spiritual, human or demonic—from achieving any aim that opposes divine plans for a particular time and place on Planet Earth.

Yahweh was also Abram's "exceeding great reward." This superlative is as extreme as could possibly be stated. And the *reward* was Yahweh himself—and whatever an obedient relationship with the God of heaven and earth would bring to Abram as the years and generations passed.

• Describe God's relationship with Abram.

B. Looking to the Heavens (vv. 2-5)

²And Abram said, Lord God, what wilt thou give me, seeing I go childless, and the steward of my house is this Eliezer of Damascus? ³And Abram said, Behold, to me thou hast given no seed: and, lo, one born in my house is mine heir. ⁴And, behold, the word of the Lord came unto him, saying, This shall not be thine heir; but he that shall come forth out of thine own bowels shall be thine heir. ⁵And he brought him forth abroad, and said, Look now toward heaven, and tell the stars, if thou be able to number them: and he said unto him, So shall thy seed be.

Abram could not see how such a great future could be possible when he had no heir and, according to social custom, all his accumulation of possessions would go to Eliezer, his Syrian chief servant (v. 2). Eliezer was a long-term servant with a multigenerational connection to Abram, but he was not his biological son. Abram complained to the Lord, "You have given no offspring to me" (v. 3 NASB); in Abram's time and culture, having an heir produced from his body and by his wife was imperative.

Yahweh assured Abram that he would have an heir from his "own bowels" (v. 4)—a son produced from a sexual relationship between the mother and Abram. However, God at this point did not specify that Sarai would be the mother, leaving room for Abram to choose to continue trusting in the Lord or to shift to attempted achievement through his own devices.

Yahweh now took Abram outside his tent so he could view the countless stars in a cloudless heaven. He said to Abram, "Look up at the heavens and count the stars—if indeed you can count them" (v. 5 NIV). This is a suggestion of the vast number of Abram's future descendants. God had a plan for the birth of nations from Abram's seed (through a single biological son and heir). Since God had decreed it, it would happen.

---

1. Explain Abram's concern (vv. 2-3).
2. Describe God's incredible promise (v. 5).

C. Trusting God's Commitment (v. 6)

⁶And he believed in the Lord; and he counted it to him for righteousness.

By now Abram had experienced a number of years of listening, trusting, walking, and obeying. Abram also had failures—times when he seized the initiative and went ahead of God. He was gradually learning to trust this invisible Deity with a consistent voice and a perfect record of deliverance and protection. Abram was ethical and moral but, nonetheless, prone to mistakes and failures, as are we all.

God made a calculation (*counted* means "making a legal reckoning")—not lining up the good deeds and the bad deeds, but seeing Abram's trust and reliability portrayed in his overall daily walk. According to the *New Spirit-Filled Life Bible*, "God added up everything that Abraham's belief meant to Him, and computing it all together, determined that it was equal to righteousness." Yahweh took Abram's faith (his trust) and *counted* him just. This verse became the apostle Paul's chief piece of Scriptural historical evidence for his contention that faith, not works, brings salvation (see Rom. 4:1-5). According to Derek Kidner (*Genesis: An Introduction & Commentary*), "This story and the argument of Romans 4 present faith not as a crowning merit but as readiness to accept what God promises."

• How are faith and righteousness related?

> "God never alters the robe of righteousness to fit the man. Rather, He alters the man to fit the robe."—John Hagee

---

D. Cutting an Unconditional Covenant (vv. 7-16)

(Genesis 15:7-16 is not included in the printed text.)

Abram asked God a crucial question, not out of unbelief, but from a heart that needed to see how he could possibly get from being landless and negotiating water and grazing rights to the position of owner and master of the whole of Canaan with eventual boundaries from the Nile to the Euphrates: "How can I know that I will gain possession of it?" (v. 8 NIV). God's awesome promise strained ordinary credulity, but thereby gave Abram's incipient faith a great opportunity for growth and development. At this point, Yahweh chose to speak to Abram in a way that would be understandable in terms of his cultural background.

As Abram's vision continued, the Lord had him bring Him "a three-year-old heifer, a three-year-old female goat, a three-year-old ram, a turtledove, and a young pigeon" (v. 9 NKJV). Abram was instructed to cut in half each of the large animals. The pieces of the larger animals were placed opposite to each other and apparently the two birds opposite to each other.

When darkness fell, Abram fell into a deep sleep with "horror and great darkness" (v. 12 NKJV). In this unusual state of awe and receptivity, Abram received from the Lord remarkably precise information about the future of his descendants (vv. 13-14). They would go as strangers to another land and serve and suffer affliction there four hundred years. Then God would judge the oppressive nation and bring Abram's descendants out with great wealth. This accurately foretold the fate of the Hebrew nation in Egypt and their divine deliverance.

A "smoking oven and a burning torch" (v. 17 NKJV)—in "a theophany, a visual manifestation of God" (Kent Hughes, *Genesis*)—passed between the pieces of the sacrificed animals. Since only representations of Deity and not Abram (the other party to the covenant) passed between the animals, this was a sign of God's unalterable determination to keep, without conditions, His covenant with Abram. The Lord also covenanted to give Abram land with specific boundaries—"from the river of Egypt to . . . the River Euphrates" (v. 18 NKJV)—and specified the nations that would be ejected from this land promised to Abram's descendants (vv. 19-21).

---

1. List specifics God gave to Abram about the nation that would come from him (vv. 13-14, 16).
2. What personal assurance did God give to Abram (v. 15)?

> "A consciousness of our powerlessness should cast us upon Him who has all power. Here then is where a vision and view of God's sovereignty helps, for it reveals His sufficiency and shows us our insufficiency."—A. W. Pink

---

III. ENTERING GOD'S COVENANT (Gen. 17:1-10, 15-21)

As years passed and no biological heir seemed possible, Sarai urged Abram to take her Egyptian handmaid Hagar as a concubine and have her produce an heir. Custom of the times allowed the practice. However, this failure to trust God completely, instead of relying on human machination, not only created domestic strife but, over several millennia, has produced great ethnic enmity and violence. The account is recorded in Genesis 16:1-12.

A. Challenged to Holiness (v. 1)

¹And when Abram was ninety years old and nine, the Lord appeared to Abram, and said unto him, I am the Almighty God; walk before me, and be thou perfect.

Abram and Sarai had entered Canaan when he was seventy-five and she was sixty-five. They had lived through two-and-a-half decades of the vicissitudes of their lives, developing spiritually as they enjoyed and endured adventures of living in a new and strange land whose customs they did not always understand or appreciate. Scripture does not record any communication between Yahweh and Abraham during the years between chapters 15 and 17, though we cannot know whether unrecorded encounters occurred.

As Christians, we have the completed canon of Scripture to guide us, whereas Abram had to depend only on visions, the divine voice, and applications of truth from Yahweh. He did not have the guidance of inspired writers' records of the lifetime experiences of scores of faithful adherents to God's covenants.

Now, when Abram was ninety-nine, he experienced once more an appearance of Yahweh. The mode of the Lord's appearance—visionary or literal—is not specified. The narrator gave the name *Yahweh*, while reporting that He revealed Himself as *El Shaddai*, which means "the Almighty, the Powerful One, or the Mighty One" (*The Complete Word Study Old Testament*).

This time, God gave Abram a challenge to holiness of character: "Walk before me, and be thou perfect" (17:1). The word *perfect* represents "the divine standard which man must attain" (*The Complete Word Study Old Testament*). Abram had walked in fellowship with Yahweh for a quarter century now. God had revealed to him His character; now Abram must measure himself morally against that standard and strive for excellence. God knew Abram would never succeed fully, but he must lead an exemplary life and faithfully represent the God of revelation who had called him.

• How is God's instruction to Abram relevant to all believers?

> "To place ourselves in range of God's choicest gifts, we have to walk with God, work with God, lean on God, cling to God, come to have the sense and feel of God, refer all things to God."
> —Cornelius Plantinga

B. Presented With a Covenant (vv. 2-8)

(Genesis 17:6-8 is not included in the printed text.)

2And I will make my covenant between me and thee, and will multiply thee exceedingly. 3And Abram fell on his face: and God talked with him saying, 4As for me, behold, my covenant is with thee, and thou shalt be a father of many nations. 5Neither shall thy name any more be called Abram, but thy name shall be Abraham; for a father of many nations have I made thee.

Promise by promise, Yahweh was beginning the fulfillment of the seven divine commitments of 12:1-3—the blessings of Abram's twenty-four-year walk, the promises of chapter 15, and now (in this renewal of covenant) the spelling out of some of the implications of promises one, six, and seven. The full implications of Yahweh's covenant with Abram and Sarai would be much more fully specified. "Abram fell on his face" before God and listened to Him speak (17:3). God's general commitment in this renewed covenant was to "multiply [Abram] exceedingly" (v. 2). We will see some of its detail.

Abram means "exalted father." He had lived up to that name, as he was already a highly respected patriarch of a growing clan with impressive wealth. He was now promised that he would father "many nations" (v. 4); that is, from Ishmael would come twelve nations (vv. 18-20), and from Abram's principal heir, Isaac, would come Jacob and Esau. From Esau would come Edom, and from Jacob's twelve sons would come the twelve tribes of Israel, eventually dividing into two kingdoms. These are examples of the many peoples arising eventually from Abram's seed. Because of this extended divine commitment,

God changed Abram's name to *Abraham*, which means "father of a multitude" (*New Spirit-Filled Life Bible*). God also pledged to Abraham that both he and his descendants throughout the coming generations would be in an everlasting covenant with Himself and that Canaan would be an everlasting possession of Abraham's descendants (vv. 7-8).

---

1. How did Abram respond to God's promise, and why (vv. 2-3)?
2. Why did God change Abram's name (vv. 4-6)?
3. Describe the duration of the covenant God established (vv. 7-9).
4. What would symbolize the covenant (v. 10)?

> "When you plant your seed in the Kingdom of God, the Lord will multiply it far better than Wall Street."—John Hagee

---

C. Required to Carry Out the Sign (vv. 9-10)

(Genesis 17:9-10 is not included in the printed text.)

As the sign of God's covenant with Abraham and his descendants, every male in Abraham's household and all of his male descendants throughout the generations must be circumcised on the eighth day following their birth. Male circumcision might have been common among the cultures of Abraham's era, but now it was to be an unbreakable sign of an unbreakable covenant. In fact, any uncircumcised male must be permanently ejected from covenant life.

---

1. Why would Sarai's name be changed (vv. 15-16)?
2. Why did Abraham laugh (v. 17)?
3. How would Ishamel and Isaac's blessings differ (vv. 18-20)?
4. Do you still believe God gives time-specific promises to His people, as He did in verse 21? Have you ever received such a promise?

The New Covenant

In the Bible, divine covenants contained certain characteristics: (1) institution solely by God; (2) a mediator of the covenant; (3) provisions setting forth expectations; (4) rewards for abiding by the covenant and penalties for failing to keep covenant; (5) a sign of the covenant; (6) a seal of the covenant.

Jeremiah 31:31 prophesies the coming of a new covenant; Jesus, in Luke 22:20, celebrates with the disciples the new covenant in His blood; and Hebrews 12:24 identifies Jesus as the Mediator of the new covenant. The new covenant is divinely instituted, is mediated by Christ himself, offers eternal life to those within it and eternal death to those outside it, has baptism for its sign, and has the Holy Spirit for its seal.

D. Flabbergasted by the Details (vv. 15-21)

(Genesis 17:16-20 is not included in the printed text.)

¹⁵And God said unto Abraham, As for Sarai thy wife, thou shalt not call her name Sarai, but Sarah shall her name be.

²¹But my covenant will I establish with Isaac, which Sarah shall bear unto thee at this set time in the next year.

Abraham's wife, Sarai, would now be called *Sarah* (v. 15)—a change in name to indicate her changed status as a "mother of nations," since Abraham's heir would come from her womb (v. 16).

Abraham was so surprised and amazed by the details of this covenant—particularly by the possibility of Sarah's bearing his son at ninety years of age—that he fell on his face and laughed in consternation. Abraham did not doubt God's power; rather, he saw the natural impossibility of the fulfillment of this promise. He also felt grief for Ishmael, the son he had fathered by Hagar and now loved deeply.

"Abraham said to God, 'If only Ishmael might live under your blessing!'" (v. 18 NIV). God would honor Ishmael for Abraham's sake (v. 20). However, He would give a son and heir to Abraham and Sarah in the following year, to be named *Isaac*, meaning "laughter" invoking continual memory throughout time of Abraham's faith and Sarah's doubt (18:12) and the joyous laughter during the celebration of Isaac's birth (17:19), which would occur "next year" (v. 21).

CONCLUSION

The Abrahamic covenant contains provisions (Gen. 12:1-3) that offer blessings to every Christian both now and in time to come. How? First, according to the apostle Paul, in Romans 11:24, Gentiles redeemed by the blood of Christ are grafted into the olive tree, which is the nation of Israel, so that we enjoy privileges in Christ as spiritual Israel. Second, the seventh provision in Genesis 12:3 assured Abram that through his seed "all nations of the earth shall be blessed." One source of such blessing is the coming of Messiah, who has brought spiritual redemption and will bring worldwide restoration when He comes to reign as King over all the earth during the Millennium. We, as believers, are the spiritual seed of Abraham and enjoy today and forever blessings granted us through provisions of the Abrahamic covenant.

GOLDEN TEXT CHALLENGE

"AND HE [ABRAHAM] BELIEVED IN THE LORD; AND HE COUNTED IT TO HIM FOR RIGHTEOUSNESS" (Gen. 15:6).

The Lord saw that Abraham now understood that all His promises were received by faith and all blessings that came to people were by God's unmerited favor; they were not deserved or earned—they came purely because God wanted to bless humanity. Abraham felt his own unworthiness and inability to keep the covenant in his own strength. God counted Abraham's faith as righteousness.

The greatest blessing of all is God's gift of His Son, Jesus Christ, for the salvation of everyone who believes on Him. Just as Abraham seemed physically incapable of keeping the covenant by having children, we are spiritually incapable of pleasing God by ourselves. We can be saved only by believing that Jesus saves us.

Daily Devotions:

M. Canaan Promised to Abraham • Genesis 15:17-21
T. Abraham Promised a Son • Genesis 18:1-10
W. The Birth of Isaac • Genesis 21:1-7
T. Jesus Speaks of Abraham • John 8:54-59
F. Abraham Justified by Faith • Romans 4:1-8
S. The Faith of Abraham • Hebrews 11:8-19

Aaron, Spokesman and High Priest

Exodus 4:10-17, 27-31; 6:28—7:7; 28:1—29:9

Unit Theme:
More Great Stories of the Bible

Central Truth:
God empowers all who submit to His will.

Focus:
Examine how God used Aaron and submit to God's will for our lives.

Context:
In the fifteenth century before Christ, Aaron serves as Moses' spokesman and Israel's first high priest.

Golden Text:
"The Lord said unto Moses, See, I have made thee a god to Pharaoh: and Aaron thy brother shall be thy prophet" (Ex. 7:1).

Study Outline:
 I. **Respond to God's Direction** (Ex. 4:10-17, 27-31)
 II. **Be Faithful and Fearless** (Ex. 6:28—7:7)
 III. **Consecrated for Service** (Ex. 28:1-4, 29-38; 29:4-9)

INTRODUCTION

Aaron was a younger brother of Miriam and the older brother of Moses. Moses was the reluctant spokesman for God to the Pharaoh of Egypt. God chose Aaron to speak for Moses and, at Moses' command, perform miraculous signs designed to convince the Pharaoh of God's omnipotence and fully determined and unchangeable intention to deliver Israel from Egypt. Aaron continued to share leadership with Moses during the Exodus and during Israel's wanderings in the wilderness. God chose Aaron as high priest and his sons as priests subordinate to him once the Tabernacle was constructed and in service as the center of Israel's worship.

When the prophesied time for Israel's departure from Egypt was nearing, God began to select and groom their deliverer. His servant, the infant Moses, was preserved from sure death by placement in an ark made of bulrushes, which was then left in the reeds along the bank of the Nile River. Moses, the third child of Amram and Jochebed from the tribe of Levi, was rescued by the daughter of the Pharaoh of Egypt and reared in the royal palace. There he "was educated in all the wisdom of the Egyptians" (Acts 7:22 NIV).

God had placed Moses where, as he matured to adulthood, he would gradually acquire the right qualifications for confrontation with the Pharaoh when the time arrived. Moses was the only person of Hebrew descent in existence properly qualified for that task.

God revealed Himself to Moses when he was eighty years of age through a supernatural phenomenon—a burning bush not consumed—in the vicinity of Mount Sinai. God spoke out of the bush, identifying Himself as Yahweh, the God of the Hebrew patriarchs. God challenged Moses to accept his mission to lead His people out of Egypt and showed to him supernatural signs designed to convince both the Hebrews and the Pharaoh of His and Moses' authenticity. Moses, however, greatly intimidated by this divine assignment, protested that he lacked eloquence. He finally said to Yahweh, "O Lord, please send someone else to do it" (Ex. 4:13 NIV). But God had the exactly right person already; He just must make him willing.

God had already prepared the heart of Moses' older brother, Aaron, to assist Moses in this task. In fact, God already had Aaron en route to the region of Sinai to meet with his younger brother when the above conversation between the Lord and Moses was occurring. Moses had the understanding of Egyptian culture and protocol, and Aaron was ready to serve humbly as Moses' spokesman—as if Moses were God and Aaron were his prophet (see v. 16; 7:1).

I. RESPOND TO GOD'S DIRECTION (Ex. 4:10-17, 27-31)

A. Moses' Initial Rejection of God's Call (vv. 10-13)

(Exodus 4:10-13 is not included in the printed text.)

Moses had no desire to take on this enormous burden of leadership. In fact, he initially refused, provoking God to anger. Moses felt inadequate for such a leadership role. After all, he had spent the past four decades as a simple shepherd. Possibly, however, he had been shaped spiritually at the hand of his priestly father-in-law, Jethro. As becomes apparent to the careful reader of the entire Book of Exodus, Moses had a reservoir of spiritual strength and emotional maturity not even readily apparent to himself early on.

Although possessed of an emotional temperament and subject to depression during times of great pressure, Moses would demonstrate an obedient spirit, necessary to one leading under divine appointment, with only one recorded public failure. Of what person in leadership today could this be said? Despite Moses' reluctance, he was now prepared to be malleable—ready to be continually shaped by God for service. And Aaron would be not only Moses' voice, but also a steadying companion who stood strongly by his side through every test—except for one major failure.

The reluctant Moses finally became an exemplary servant of Yahweh—to the extent that he could be called "very meek, above all the men which were upon the face of the earth" (Num. 12:3). He became willing to do the Lord's bidding when He spoke, even when the task was overwhelming and his people uncooperative.

---

1. Why did the Lord respond to Moses' complaint with questions (vv. 10-11)?
2. What did the Lord promise, and how did Moses respond (vv. 12-13)?

B. Aaron Chosen as Moses' Assistant (vv. 14-17)

14And the anger of the Lord was kindled against Moses, and he said, Is not Aaron the Levite thy brother? I know that he can speak well. And also, behold, he cometh forth to meet thee; and when he seeth thee, he will be glad in his heart. 15And thou shalt speak unto him, and put words in his mouth: and I will be with thy mouth, and with his mouth, and will teach you what ye shall do. 16And he shall be thy spokesman unto the people: and he shall be, even he shall be to thee instead of a mouth, and thou shalt be to him instead of God. 17And thou shalt take this rod in thine hand, wherewith thou shalt do signs.

While Moses continued to protest, God had already spoken to Aaron, who (as far as we can tell from Scripture) went to meet Moses in the desert near Sinai without any protest. This man seemed ready to "play second fiddle" to his younger brother, an out-of-the-ordinary role reversal. Moses likely would appear to the royal audience to be a mysterious silent figure as he, step-by-step, heard from God, then privately instructed his brother in what to say and how and when to use the shepherd's staff as an entrance into the miraculous. Scripture presents this fraternal duo as being in unity as God's men called out to confront a colossal pagan ruler. Their human resources—God-given intelligence, appropriate experience, and matched temperaments—were limited in the face of the horrendous obstacles, but they also had the voice of God directly to Moses and the unbreakable promise of God.

• Describe the roles Aaron and Moses would play in confronting Pharaoh.

C. Meeting With the Elders (vv. 27-31)

(Exodus 4:27-28 is not included in the printed text.)

29And Moses and Aaron went and gathered together all the elders of the children of Israel: 30And Aaron spake all the words which the Lord had spoken unto Moses, and did the signs in the sight of the people. 31And the people believed: and when they heard that the Lord had visited the children of Israel, and that he had looked upon their affliction, then they bowed their heads and worshipped.

Moses first told Aaron everything the Lord had told him and communicated to Aaron the three supernatural signs given to convince their own people, then the Pharaoh. Afterward, Aaron, as the mouthpiece of Moses, relayed to the assembled Hebrews God's promise of deliverance and performed three miraculous signs in front of this willing-to-believe audience. The signs were (1) Moses' staff becoming a serpent and then turning back again; (2) Moses' hand becoming leprous and then being healed; (3) water turning into blood (see vv. 6-9).

It was welcome news to these long-demoralized people that God had seen their suffering. Their response is noteworthy—they worshiped. They acknowledged the goodness and the greatness of the God of revelation and bowed humbly in His presence.

- How did the Israelites respond in their hearts to this word from the Lord? How did they respond outwardly, and why (v. 31)?

> "It is in the process of being worshipped that God communicates His presence to men."—C. S. Lewis

---

II. BE FAITHFUL AND FEARLESS (Ex. 6:28—7:7)

A. Aaron as Moses' Spokesman (6:28—7:1)

6:28 And it came to pass on the day when the Lord spake unto Moses in the land of Egypt, ²⁹That the Lord spake unto Moses, saying, I am the Lord: speak thou unto Pharaoh king of Egypt all that I say unto thee. ³⁰And Moses said before the Lord, Behold, I am of uncircumcised lips, and how shall Pharaoh hearken unto me?

7:1 And the Lord said unto Moses, See, I have made thee a god to Pharaoh: and Aaron thy brother shall be thy prophet.

Moses' excuse of having "uncircumcised lips" (6:30) can be translated as being "unskilled in speech" (NASB) or having "faltering lips" (NIV). Moses, who had been a shepherd for the past forty years, was overwhelmed by the idea of confronting the most powerful ruler of his day—the Pharaoh of Egypt.

The Lord responded by saying something that could be seen as blasphemy or idolatry if spoken by any human mouth. He said He had made Moses not *like* a god, but a *god* to Pharaoh (7:1). Pharaoh himself was considered a god by the Egyptian populace; now he was seeing another man in the role of a god. The true God knew this was a necessary step in the process of humiliation of this hard-hearted despot. Moses himself said not a word in the Pharaoh's presence; he did not wave the rod that initiated a miraculous sign. Aaron served as prophet, as spokesman to Pharaoh. The Lord had a great role for the nation of Israel to play in future years. The humiliation of pagan Egypt was a necessary step toward realization of His divine plan. Moses and Aaron learned immediately a crucial lesson: to do precisely what God said to do.

1. How did God identify Himself to Moses, and why (6:29-29)?
2. How did Moses feel about God's plan (v. 30)? Why does God challenge us to do difficult tasks?
3. How would Moses be like "a god to Pharaoh" (7:1)?

"There is great force hidden in a gentle command."—George Herbert

B. Aaron's Role in the Supernatural Signs (7:2-7)

²Thou shalt speak all that I command thee: and Aaron thy brother shall speak unto Pharaoh, that he send the children of Israel out of his land. ³And I will harden Pharaoh's heart, and multiply my signs and my wonders in the land of Egypt. ⁴But Pharaoh shall not hearken unto you, that I may lay my hand upon Egypt, and bring forth mine armies, and my people the children of Israel, out of the land of Egypt by great judgments. ⁵And the Egyptians shall know that I am the Lord, when I stretch forth mine hand upon Egypt, and bring out the children of Israel from among them. ⁶And Moses and Aaron did as the Lord commanded them, so did they. ⁷And Moses was fourscore years old, and Aaron fourscore and three years old, when they spake unto Pharaoh.

In verses 2-4, the Lord spoke to Moses concerning the three signs to be demonstrated to Pharaoh at the outset. The Hebrew word *oth* means "miracle, miraculous sign, proof," and the Hebrew word *mopheth* signifies "wonderful deed, wonder, miraculous sign, miracle, prodigy, portent, omen" (*The Complete Word Study Old Testament*). "Signs and wonders" (v. 3), then, an oft-occurring Biblical phrase, contains two approximate synonyms that emphasize by repetition.

The genuinely supernatural signs from God were brushed aside when skilled, but cynical, manipulators impressed the Pharaoh by apparent duplication (vv. 10-12). Pharaoh had an enormous unpaid workforce at his command, and this hard, stubborn man was not about to risk losing them or slowing down the latest building project.

After Pharaoh's initial rejection of Moses and Aaron, God would send ten supernatural judgments on Egypt, progressively more and more devastating. Some scholars hold that these judgments related directly to Egyptian deities, including the Pharaoh himself (considered a god), and showed the true God's power over all these possibly demonic so-called deities. Aaron was Moses' mouthpiece, but he also wielded the shepherd's staff that signaled each forthcoming divine act. In some cases we are told specifically that Aaron spoke for Moses and waved the rod (7:9, 19; 8:6, 17); in other cases (e.g., 8:20; 9:23), we are told that Moses himself spoke or acted. However, Aaron was always present, and he might have been the actual spokesman and actor, even when not specifically named as such (cf. 4:30; 7:1-2). We are told, moreover, "Moses and Aaron did all these wonders before Pharaoh; and the Lord hardened Pharaoh's heart, and he did not let the children of Israel go out of his land" (11:10 NKJV).

That Aaron's role did not diminish or disappear becomes apparent to the reader of the Book of Exodus once the exodus from Egypt and the trek through the wilderness ensued. "The Lord spake unto Moses and Aaron" regarding institution of Passover (12:1). After the crossing of the Red Sea, a supernatural phenomenon in which Aaron is not specifically mentioned; in 16:2, "the children of Israel complained against Moses and Aaron in the wilderness" (NKJV); and in verse 6, Moses and Aaron together presented God's plan to send manna to feed the people. While Aaron is not mentioned in every case, evidently he is beside Moses throughout and may be the actual spokesman when unnamed.

---

1. What would "multiply," and how would Pharaoh respond (vv. 3-4)?
2. What would God accomplish in Egypt (v. 5)?
3. How did Moses and Aaron cooperate (v. 6)?

> "It is impossible on reasonable grounds to disbelieve miracles."
> —Blaise Pascal

III. CONSECRATED FOR SERVICE (Ex. 28:1-4, 29-38; 29:4-9)

The tribe of Levi was set apart for sacred service on behalf of the entire nation of Israel. Aaron, his sons, and their descendants were to be priests serving in the Tabernacle in the offering of required animal sacrifices, whereas other adult males from the tribe of Levi cared for the Tabernacle itself—particularly taking it down and setting it up when the camp of the Israelites moved. Aaron, as high priest, was responsible at the highest level for the entire sacrificial system and everything associated with the Tabernacle and its function.

Chapters 25-27 and 30 describe the Tabernacle and its components, chapters 36-39 describe its construction, and chapter 40 presents its erection. Many Christian scholars believe that every aspect of the Tabernacle served to typify elements associated with Jesus Christ, His sacrifice for our sins, and His present role in heaven.

At the point of Jesus' death on the cross when His sacrifice for our sins was complete, the thick curtain separating off the Holy of Holies was split in two (Mark 15:37-38), signifying the tearing down of this means of separation and limitation by Christ's all-sufficient sacrifice. This made it possible for every believer to approach God directly for forgiveness and restoration in the name of Jesus, our great High Priest now at the right hand of His Father (see Heb. 4:15-16).

A. Separation to the Priesthood (28:1)

¹And take thou unto thee Aaron thy brother, and his sons with him, from among the children of Israel, that he may minister unto me in the priest's office, even Aaron, Nadab and Abihu, Eleazar and Ithamar, Aaron's sons.

The institution of the Mosaic covenant necessitated the consecration of a class of men to attend to the duties that arose from God's direct commands regarding the Tabernacle itself and the animal sacrifices offered there. Aaron,

Moses' brother, was already second in leadership and therefore well known to the Hebrew people. It was entirely natural and understandable from a purely human viewpoint that this man and his family perform these God-ordained duties. But God spoke expressly to Moses, instructing him to take Aaron and his sons "from among the children of Israel" to minister as priests.

Under the new covenant, each believer in Christ is a part of a "royal priesthood" of believers (1 Peter 2:9), offering "the sacrifice of praise to God" (Heb. 13:15).

"How different the world would look, how different the state of our nation would be, if there were more sanctified priestly souls! These are souls who have the power to bless, for they intercede with sanctified hearts. They never begin their daily time of intercessory prayer without having first brought to the cross all that is unholy in their lives, so that their old self can be crucified there with Jesus, the sacrificial Lamb."—Basilea Schlink

---

B. Priestly Garments (28:2-4)

²And thou shalt make holy garments for Aaron thy brother for glory and for beauty. ³And thou shalt speak unto all that are wise hearted, whom I have filled with the spirit of wisdom, that they may make Aaron's garments to consecrate him, that he may minister unto me in the priest's office. ⁴And these are the garments which they shall make; a breastplate, and an ephod, and a robe, and a broidered coat, a mitre, and a girdle: and they shall make holy garments for Aaron thy brother, and his sons, that he may minister unto me in the priest's office.

The garments of the high priest were elaborate, gorgeous, and precisely ordered by God. The *ephod* "probably was a high priestly waistcoat woven of blue, purple, scarlet, and white linen thread—all entwined with gold thread" (*The Expositor's Bible Commentary*). Highly decorated with precious stones, and sleeveless, it was hung from the shoulders by straps. Etched on onyx stones mounted on golden clasps on either shoulder were the names of the twelve tribes of Israel (vv. 9-12).

On a breastplate made similarly to the ephod but folded to form a pouch were twelve precious stones, again with the names of the twelve tribes of Israel (vv. 15-21). Inside the pouch were the Urim and the Thummim, mysterious stones used by the high priest to determine God's will (v. 30). A. Paul Davis and E. L. Gilmore suggest that "the stones remind us of the value God sets on each individual made in His image and particularly on the sons of Israel" (*The Expositor's Bible Commentary*).

Next to his body, the high priest wore a blue sleeveless robe that reached just below his knees (v. 31). It had slits for the arms and, at the top, a hole for the head to go through (v. 32). Along the bottom hem were alternating purple pomegranates and golden bells (v. 34). The tinkling of the bells assured listeners that the high priest was still alive when he was ministering inside the

Holy Place (v. 35). The high priest wore a linen turban on which was a golden plate engraved with the words "Holy to the Lord" (v. 36 NASB). The high priest also wore a tunic under his robe and just over his linen undergarments (vv. 39, 42). Aaron's sons also wore the undergarments plus a white linen tunic with a sash and also a hat—all "for glory and for beauty" (v. 40).

---

1. What was the purpose of Aaron's "holy garments" (v. 2)?
2. Describe two distinct callings of God described in verse 3.

> "It does not take great men to do great things; it only takes consecrated men."—Phillips Brooks

---

C. Consecration of Aaron and His Sons (29:4-9)

(Exodus 29:8-9 is not included in the printed text.)

⁴And Aaron and his sons thou shalt bring unto the door of the tabernacle of the congregation, and shalt wash them with water. ⁵And thou shalt take the garments, and put upon Aaron the coat, and the robe of the ephod, and the ephod, and the breastplate, and gird him with the curious girdle of the ephod: ⁶And thou shalt put the mitre upon his head, and put the holy crown upon the mitre. ⁷Then shalt thou take the anointing oil, and pour it upon his head, and anoint him.

Leviticus 8 presents in even greater detail than the Book of Exodus the service of consecration for Aaron and his sons. First, both Aaron and his sons were washed with water. Then Aaron was invested with his high-priestly garments in the sight of all the people, gathered in front of the Tabernacle. All objects in the Tabernacle were anointed with the special anointing oil and, afterward, Aaron and his sons. Appropriate animal sacrifices were offered, with Aaron and his sons and all objects in the Tabernacle sprinkled with the blood of sacrificed animals.

This impressive service of consecration would serve to remind Aaron, his sons, and all the people of Israel of the high importance of the post of high priest and of the entire sacrificial system. This was the divinely ordained system of bringing God's people into contact with Him for forgiveness and fellowship under the old covenant. Aaron's role was paramount, and that of his sons was also crucial; they must carry out their duties with exactitude and recognition of the spiritual nature of their tasks. Aaron served as high priest until shortly before Israel crossed over the Jordan River into Canaan. Then, at the direct command of the Lord, Aaron's position as high priest ended, his son Eleazar was consecrated in his place, and Aaron "was gathered unto his people" (Num. 20:22-29).

---

1. Explain the significance of the water (v. 4) and the oil (v. 7) for the priests.
2. What roles do water and anointing play in the spiritual lives of Christians today?

The Temple Restored

In the second century BC, Antiochus IV Epiphanes of Syria persecuted the people of Israel to the extent of offering a pig on the brazen altar in front of the Holy Place in the Temple. God, at this time, raised up a leader named Judas Maccabeus—one of the sons of the high priest, Mattathias. *Maccabeus* means "the Hammer." Judas led an army of faithful Jewish adherents in several battles that resulted in the recapture of the area surrounding the Temple in Jerusalem. The Temple was cleansed and re-dedicated, and the golden candelabra in the Holy Place re-lit. This time of celebration became Hanukah, a joyous Jewish festival celebrated each December today (*Jewish Encyclopedia*).

CONCLUSION

Emphasized throughout the account of the deliverance of the children of Israel from Egypt and their wanderings in the wilderness is unwavering obedience to the commands of the Lord. Since they faced obstacles that were humanly impossible, they must follow divine directions without fail to be assured of victory. Moses' one public failure was punished severely by God, and Aaron, always at Moses' side, shared that punishment. They both forfeited their right to enter the land of Canaan (Num. 20:8, 23-24).

The Lord's covenant loving-kindness (Hebrew, *chesed*) caused Him to be always gracious and forgiving (Ex. 34:5-7), but did not cancel out retribution for sin. If we as believers in Christ today are to be usable in His kingdom work, we too must walk in careful obedience before God (see 1 Sam. 15:22; John 15:5).

GOLDEN TEXT CHALLENGE

"THE LORD SAID UNTO MOSES, SEE, I HAVE MADE THEE A GOD TO PHARAOH: AND AARON THY BROTHER SHALL BE THY PROPHET" (Ex. 7:1).

Moses was authorized to speak and act in God's name and stead, and, under the divine direction, was endued with a divine power to do that which is above the ordinary power of nature, and invested with a divine authority to demand obedience from a sovereign prince and punish disobedience. Moses was a "god," but he was only a made god, not essentially one by nature; he was no good but by commission. He was a god, but he was a god only to Pharaoh; the living and true God is a God to all the world.—*Matthew Henry's Commentary*

Daily Devotions:

M. Aaron Stands Before Pharaoh • Exodus 7:10-13

T. The Exodus Begins • Exodus 12:31-36

W. Consecrated for the Priesthood • Exodus 40:12-16

T. The Death of Aaron • Numbers 20:22-29

F. Jesus Christ Our High Priest • Hebrews 8:1-7

S. A Royal Priesthood • 1 Peter 2:4-10

Hezekiah the Reformer

2 Chronicles 29:1—30:27; 32:1-23

Unit Theme:
More Great Stories of the Bible

Central Truth:
Christians are to serve God wholeheartedly.

Focus:
Observe and imitate Hezekiah's zeal for the Lord.

Context:
Hezekiah serves as king of Judah (726-697 BC).

Golden Text:
"In every work that he [Hezekiah] began in the service of the house of God, and in the law, and in the commandments, to seek his God, he did it with all his heart, and prospered" (2 Chron. 31:21).

Study Outline:
 I. **Restore Worship** (2 Chron. 29:1-11, 27-36)
 II. **Return to God's Word** (2 Chron. 30:1-13, 22-27)
 III. **Witness God's Glorious Power** (2 Chron. 32:1:23)

INTRODUCTION

King Hezekiah proved to be one of Judah's greatest kings, in terms of external accomplishment and quality of character. He stood strong against Assyrian invasion and led his people back to faithfulness to the God of revelation in both worship and daily living.

After the division of Israel into two rival kingdoms in approximately 931 BC, following King Rehoboam's unwise and provocative actions, the northern kingdom (led by King Jeroboam, 931-910 BC) abandoned acceptable worship of the true God and gradually fell into idolatry, never to return to the Lord. The southern kingdom—consisting of the tribes of Judah, Simeon, and Benjamin—was governed by descendants of King David, some of whom were godly rulers, but others of whom took Judah in a direction similar to that taken by the northern kingdom.

Judah experienced periods of reform when a godly king would lead the nation back toward moral living and worship according to the Mosaic Law. Unfortunately, these royal efforts toward reform would typically be halting and incomplete. Shrines to heathen gods would remain in the high places, since they were deeply entrenched and required more diligent effort to dislodge than would be put forth by lukewarm people and rather weak kings. King Asa (911-870 BC), for instance, led the nation in destruction of idols and restoration of worship, but rejected the genuine word of the Lord from the prophet

Hanani and had him imprisoned, purely because of the king's arrogant spirit. Asa's son, Jehoshaphat (870-845 BC), in contrast, proved to be consistently strong both militarily and spiritually because "his heart took delight in the ways of the Lord" (2 Chron.17:6 NKJV).

Intermarriage of Judean royalty with the family of King Ahab of the northern kingdom led to the introduction (into Judah) of heinous idolatry, particularly widespread Baal worship. Return to morality and authentic worship occurred briefly when reform under King Joash (842-802 BC) led to the repair of the Temple and restoration of worship there. But this king soon fell under bad influence and allowed idolatry to return. Joash was succeeded by three kings who were inclined, but lukewarm, toward true religion and morality—Amaziah, Uzziah, and Jotham. But Jotham's son Ahaz (742-726 BC) was an avid worshiper of false gods, particularly Baal, and even offered sacrifices to the gods of Syria, a country which (in cooperation with the northern kingdom of Israel) had defeated Judah in battle.

Ahaz's son Hezekiah (726-697 BC) rose to the throne as a bright light of hope because of his strong fidelity to truth in lifestyle and worship. Apparently, Hezekiah benefitted from maternal influence toward allegiance to the true God, inasmuch as his father, by no means, influenced him toward righteousness. After initial co-regency with his father had ended, Hezekiah introduced reform in worship, led in cleansing of the Temple, and offered strong leadership of Judah when threats from Assyria arose. Hezekiah "did that which was right in the sight of the Lord, according to all that David his father had done" (2 Chron. 29:2).

I. RESTORE WORSHIP (2 Chron. 29:1-11, 27-36)

A. King Hezekiah's Accession to the Throne (vv. 1-2)

¹Hezekiah began to reign when he was five and twenty years old, and he reigned nine and twenty years in Jerusalem. And his mother's name was Abijah, the daughter of Zechariah. ²And he did that which was right in the sight of the Lord, according to all that David his father had done.

Hezekiah ascended to the throne at a time when Judah was under strong military pressure from Assyria. The neighboring state of Samaria (the northern kingdom of Israel) was conquered by Assyria during Hezekiah's reign, and most of its Jewish inhabitants resettled in provinces within Assyria, to be replaced in Israel by settlers from other lands. Assyria, at this juncture, was concerned primarily with elimination of threats from Egypt. Both Samaria and Judah were small pawns to be removed at will, in Sennacherib's view, as that Assyrian ruler looked toward elimination of its major threat in the area, Egypt. King Ahaz, fearful that Judah would suffer a fate similar to that occurring in Samaria, attempted to placate Assyria. Ahaz unsuccessfully solicited Assyria's aid against Edomites and Philistines, and paid periodic tribute to Assyria. However, when Hezekiah came into sole royal power after his father's death, he refused to continue paying tribute. Second Kings 18:7 states that "he rebelled against the king of Assyria and did not serve him" (NKJV). Instead, he "trusted in the Lord God of Israel; so that after him was none like him among all the kings of Judah, nor any that were before him" (v. 5).

At the beginning of his reign, then, Hezekiah signaled his return to strong obedience to the Lord God and to dependence on Him. According to verse 4, "He removed the high places and broke the sacred pillars, cut down the wooden image and broke in pieces the bronze serpent that Moses had made; for until those days the children of Israel burned incense to it, and called it Nehushtan ['thing of brass']" (NKJV).

The chronicler stressed Hezekiah's strong spiritual leadership by stating that "he did what was right in the sight of the Lord, according to all that his father David had done" (2 Chron. 29:2 NKJV). This reference to King David indicated the thoroughness of Hezekiah's efforts toward reform as well as making clear to the reader that David's reign had long since become the standard of measurement "of the godly walk" for later kings of Judah (*The Expositor's Bible Commentary*). Hezekiah's reign was viewed as a return to the "gold standard," as it were.

• Describe Hezekiah.

John Wesley's Influence

During the eighteenth century, John Wesley ministered across the British Isles, usually riding horseback. Wesley preached to large crowds several times each day, typically in open-air locations. The results were, on the part of numerous people, a return to holiness of lifestyle, the organization of support groups (a method of teaching and fellowship used often ever since), translation of theology into practical Christianity, and a decades-long impact on the entire culture in the United Kingdom. This great revival eventually spread to the United States.

B. Hezekiah's Directive to Priests and Levites (vv. 3-11)

(2 Chronicles 29:6-11 is not included in the printed text.)

³He in the first year of his reign, in the first month, opened the doors of the house of the Lord, and repaired them. ⁴And he brought in the priests and the Levites, and gathered them together into the east street. ⁵And said unto them, Hear me, ye Levites, sanctify now yourselves, and sanctify the house of the Lord God of your fathers, and carry forth the filthiness out of the holy place.

Immediately upon his accession to the throne, Hezekiah made clear his intention to serve the true God when he turned his attention to the magnificently constructed and appointed, but (under his father King Ahaz) the sadly neglected and misused Temple. This sacred edifice in Jerusalem, dedicated by King Solomon solely to sacrifice to and worship of the Lord God (2 Chron. 6), had fallen into extreme disrepair under the rule of Ahaz. (One notes particularly here the strong significance of the influence of one's father, whether positive or negative and whether absorbed or rejected by offspring.)

Ahaz had closed the doors leading into the Holy Place and the Holy of Holies, discarded or destroyed important implements of sacrifice, and carelessly cast aside (or piled into corners) the exquisite symbolic furniture of the Holy Place, including the table of shewbread, the altar of incense, and the lampstand along with their articles of service. Ahaz also had the priest Urijah construct an altar in the Temple court patterned after an altar in Syria dedicated to idol worship (see 2 Kings 16:10-16). King Ahaz moved the great brass altar constructed according to Moses' original instructions (Ex. 27:1-8) away from its central position in front of the door leading into the Holy Place and placed the new altar there, while relocating the original altar to the north side (away from its former central location). Ahaz, then, had led his constituents away from the true God into idolatry and inexcusable disrespect for the central representation in the capital of Israel of the holiness and redemptive power of God.

In contrast, his son Hezekiah opened the doors to the Holy Place and repaired them. He then called a meeting of the priests and Levites "in the East Square" (2 Chron. 29:4 NKJV) near the Temple and gave them brief, pointed instructions. First, they were to *sanctify* themselves—that is, undergo ritual purification and spiritual dedication required by the Mosaic Law. Then they were to cleanse thoroughly the interior space of the Temple and remove the debris accumulated there during the reign of the previous king. This process of cleansing, removal, and restoration would constitute an essential first step to precede the return to sacrifice initiated by Moses (under God) and the accompanying worship through music added by King David.

Hezekiah stressed continuity with past glory in worship when he required the sanctifying of the "house of the Lord God of your fathers" (v. 5). King Solomon had experienced supernatural signs of divine favor when he dedicated that awe-inspiring Temple (7:1-3) and initiated a strong tradition of faithfulness to the commands regarding worship of God given through Moses (vv. 4-11). Now the spiritually wise Hezekiah was recalling his people to holiness of heart and life and to strict adherence to that authentic worship required by the living God, rather than continued imitation of false worship patterns and indulgent lifestyles practiced by neighboring idolatrous countries.

King Hezekiah believed Judah had suffered defeat at the hand of its enemies because of neglect of God's house, evil living, and overall abandonment of faithfulness to its covenant with the true God (29:6-9). This rebellion against truth and right had ignited God's wrath and caused Him to punish Judah by allowing military and civilian casualties during battles with nearby enemies. The young king intended to turn things around by making a covenant with God on behalf of His people (v. 10). He instructed the spiritual leaders of his nation—priests and Levites—to resume their posts of duty, inasmuch as the Lord had "chosen" them to "stand before Him, to serve Him, and . . . [to] minister to Him and burn incense" (29:11 NKJV). In other words, they were to lead the way in resumption of proper worship of God.

Those placed at the helm of religious leadership hold positions of trust before God, provided they are heading organizations devoted to the service of true religion. If they fail to be faithful to Scripture, they participate in the resulting sin and shame in the sight of God when their constituents fall away to worldliness and apostasy.

It took the Levites and priests two weeks to cleanse the Temple (v. 17). "Then they went in to King Hezekiah and reported: 'We have purified the entire temple of the Lord, the altar of burnt offering with all its utensils, and the table for setting out the consecrated bread, with all its articles" (v. 18 NIV).

---

1. What was top priority for Hezekiah when he became king (vv. 3-5)?
2. How had God's people failed Him (vv. 6-7)?
3. How had the people suffered (vv. 8-9)?
4. What was in the king's heart, and why (v. 10)?

> "The foundation of true holiness and true Christian worship is the doctrine of the Gospel, what we are to believe. So when Christian doctrine is neglected, forsaken, or corrupted, true holiness and worship will also be neglected, forsaken, and corrupted."
> —John Owen

C. Humble and Joyful Worship (vv. 27-30)

(2 Chronicles 29:27-30 is not included in the printed text.)

King Hezekiah now assembled the rulers of the city of Jerusalem and went with them to the newly cleansed Temple (v. 20). They brought with them seven bulls, seven rams, seven lambs, and seven male goats to serve as a sin offering. The king held a dedicatory service at the Temple, leading the way in an occasion of repentance, confession, and remission according to the sacrificial system authorized under the old covenant. The king commanded the priests to perform their ritual duties (v. 21). (Had the priests been properly doing their duties at their posts, it should not have been necessary for the king to command their performance of ordinary tasks.)

Instrumental musicians among the Levites were stationed in the Temple court with cymbals, stringed instruments, and harps, while priests stood ready with trumpets (vv. 25-26). The instrumental musicians accompanied the offering of sacrifices with appropriate music. Also, vocalists performed and trumpeters sounded until the offering of sacrifices had ended (vv. 27-28). "When the offerings were finished, the king and everyone present with him knelt down and worshiped" (v. 29 NIV). Hezekiah then commanded the Levites to sing psalms of praise (v. 30).

Thus, we learn that this rededication of the Temple was a grand worship experience in which sin was atoned for through blood sacrifice made at the great brass altar, now back in its proper place. The king led the congregation in humbly worshiping God.

- List three words that describe this occasion of worship.

D. Appropriate Voluntary Sacrifices (vv. 31-36)

(2 Chronicles 29:32-35 is not included in the printed text.)

³¹Then Hezekiah answered and said, Now ye have consecrated yourselves unto the Lord, come near and bring sacrifices and thank offerings into the house of the Lord. And the congregation brought in sacrifices and thank offerings; and as many as were of a free heart burnt offerings.

³⁶And Hezekiah rejoiced, and all the people, that God had prepared the people: for the thing was done suddenly.

At the close of the service of dedication, the congregation was invited to bring voluntary "sacrifices and thank offerings" (v. 31). Early chapters in the Book of Leviticus explain in detail how the priest accepted and processed these offerings brought as means of worship. The five kinds of offerings explained include the *burnt offering,* the *grain offering*, the *peace offering*, the *sin offering,* and the *trespass offering*, each type of sacrifice having its own ritual protocol.

King Hezekiah was encouraging God's people to return to prescribed procedures in the Mosaic Law in order to obtain forgiveness, to worship, and to present gifts of thanksgiving. The response was overwhelming—worshipers brought "seventy bulls, a hundred rams and two hundred male lambs—all of them for burnt offerings to the Lord. The animals consecrated as sacrifices amounted to six hundred bulls and three thousand sheep and goats" (vv. 32-33 NIV). The Temple activity now would return to normalcy as the entire nation resumed faithfulness to God in their overall living. Everyone "rejoiced" because the turnaround had happened so quickly (v. 36).

1. What was "established again" (v. 35 NASB)?
2. Who "rejoiced," and why (v. 36)?

II. RETURN TO GOD'S WORD (2 Chron. 30:1-13, 22-27)

A. Planning Celebration of Passover (vv. 1-4)

(2 Chronicles 30:2-3 is not included in the printed text.)

¹And Hezekiah sent to all Israel and Judah, and wrote letters also to Ephraim and Manasseh, that they should come to the house of the Lord at Jerusalem, to keep the passover unto the Lord God of Israel.

⁴And the thing pleased the king and all the congregation.

Perhaps as a means of immediate spiritual reinforcement after the rededication of the Temple, King Hezekiah decided to celebrate Passover. Apparently, celebration of this important feast had ceased, some time before, to occur on a culture-wide basis. Because the cleansing of the Temple had not been completed until the sixteenth day of Nisan, an insufficient number of priests had consecrated themselves, and there was not enough time to send notices to those outside the Jerusalem area, the Passover could not be celebrated at its regular time during the first month. So the king and his advisers decided to celebrate the feast beginning on the fourteenth day of the second month instead. There was precedent in Numbers 9:10-11 for such a delay.

---

1. Describe the invitation sent by Hezekiah (v. 1).
2. Why was the celebration delayed, and what might we learn from this (vv. 2-3)?

B. Informing the People (vv. 5-13)

(2 Chronicles 30:6-12 is not included in the printed text.)

⁵So they established a decree to make proclamation throughout all Israel, from Beersheba even to Dan, that they should come to keep the Passover unto the Lord God of Israel at Jerusalem: for they had not done it of a long time in such sort as it was written.

¹³And there assembled at Jerusalem much people to keep the feast of unleavened bread in the second month, a very great congregation.

King Hezekiah and his advisers decided to extend an invitation to all Israel—from the southern border to the northern border—to attend this feast. The Passover had not been celebrated as a feast for all Jewish people in many years. The king and his advisers sent runners with an invitation which was conciliatory, yet negative, in tone. Note verse 8: "Do not be stiff-necked, as your fathers were, but yield yourselves to the Lord; and enter His sanctuary, which He has sanctified forever" (NKJV).

The response from the northern kingdom was mixed: some laughed and mocked (v. 10), but others—particularly people from Manasseh, Asher, and Zebulun—"humbled themselves, and came to Jerusalem" (v. 11). "The hand of God" intervened, creating "singleness of heart" among the people of Judah to obey the call to observe the Passover in agreement with "the word of the Lord" (v. 12 NKJV).

---

1. What did Hezekiah urge the people not to "be" (vv. 7-8)?
2. Describe the conditional promise in verse 9.
3. How do the different responses to Hezekiah's letter (vv. 10-11) mirror people's responses to the Gospel today?
4. What did God do for the people of Judah (v. 12)?

> "When a train goes through a tunnel and it gets dark, you don't throw away the ticket and jump off. You sit still and trust the engineer."—Corrie Ten Boom

---

C. Celebrating Passover (vv. 22-27)

(2 Chronicles 30:23-25 is not included in the printed text.)

²²And Hezekiah spake comfortably unto all the Levites that taught the good knowledge of the Lord: and they did eat throughout the feast seven days, offering peace offerings, and making confession to the Lord God of their fathers.

²⁶So there was great joy in Jerusalem: for since the time of Solomon the son of David king of Israel there was not the like in Jerusalem. ²⁷Then the priests and the Levites arose and blessed the people: and their voice was heard, and their prayer came up to his holy dwelling place, even unto heaven.

On the fourteenth day of the second month, the celebration began with the bringing of the Passover lambs to the Temple to be slaughtered in the approved manner. The roasted lamb was eaten with unleavened bread and bitter herbs. Throughout the week, only bread made without yeast was eaten.

Many people had not prepared themselves by ritual cleansing to celebrate the feast. But King Hezekiah prayed for forgiveness for them, "and the Lord hearkened to Hezekiah, and healed the people" (v. 20). Such great joy and gladness prevailed that the king and his leadership decided to extend the celebration for another seven days (v. 23). The king and the princes supplied thousands of additional bulls, sheep, and goats so this could happen (v. 24). The king and his advisers had signaled to the entire nation their settled intention to return to faithfulness to the Law of Moses in worship and lifestyle.

The glories of Solomon's kingdom were long gone. The nation had split into two kingdoms. But, because of the dedication of one king named Hezekiah, the two peoples (remnant that they were) were again in harmony for these two weeks of celebration. Most importantly, God honored the prayers of blessing offered by the religious leaders—"their prayer came to His holy dwelling place, to heaven" (v. 27 NASB).

III. WITNESS GOD'S GLORIOUS POWER (2 Chron. 32:1-23)

A. The Threat to Judah From Assyria (v. 1)

(2 Chronicles 32:1 is not included in the printed text.)

In Hezekiah's fourteenth year as king, Sennacherib invaded and conquered all the walled cities of Judah. Only Jerusalem, among major cities of Judah, was still unoccupied by Assyrian troops. Rather than surrendering to Sennacherib, Hezekiah strengthened the defenses of Jerusalem. However, when Assyrian forces began to move toward Jerusalem, Hezekiah resumed the lapsed payment of tribute to Assyria, a mistaken and useless conciliatory act (2 Kings 18:14-16). This action by Judah's king, showing weakness rather

---

than strength, did not cause the Assyrian army to desist from its movement toward the Holy City.

• Describe the crisis Hezekiah faced.

> "That which is bitter to endure is sweet to remember."—Thomas Fuller

---

B. Hezekiah's Strong Righteous Leadership (vv. 2-8)
(2 Chronicles 32:2-8 is not included in the printed text.)

Despite Hezekiah's temporary show of weakness, he consulted with his officials to defend the city. First, they "stopped all the springs and the brook that ran through the land" (v. 4 NKJV). Next, "he strengthened himself, built up all the wall that was broken, raised it up to the towers, and built another wall outside; also he repaired the Millo by the City of David, and made weapons and shields in abundance" (v. 5 NKJV). The *Millo* was a fortified area in Jerusalem formerly occupied by the Jebusites, who had been hard to dislodge from this highly protective area of the city, an indication of its importance as a place of safety.

The king organized the entire populace under military captains. He then gave an encouraging message to the assembled occupants of the city: "Be strong and courageous; do not be afraid nor dismayed before the king of Assyria, nor before all the multitude that is with him; for there are more with us than with him" (v. 7 NKJV). The king might have been referring here to the hosts of angels under the command of God Almighty, who was on Israel's side when they were obedient to the terms of their covenant with Him. This strong message from the king "strengthened" the people.

---

1. Explain Hezekiah's first defensive action (vv. 2-4).
2. Describe the construction project (v. 5).
3. Describe Hezekiah's faith and its impact (vv. 6-8).

> "When God speaks, oftentimes His voice will call for an act of courage on our part."—Charles Stanley

---

C. King Sennacherib's Attempt to Intimidate Judah (vv. 9-19)
(2 Chronicles 32:9-19 is not included in the printed text.)

King Sennacherib of Assyria with his mighty military force was, at this point, besieging Lachish, less than forty miles southwest of Jerusalem (v. 9). This aggressive enemy sent an intimidating message to the populace of Jerusalem through what was probably Sennacherib's chief of staff or governor. This oral and written message mocked Judah's supposed reliance on Egypt (not a fact) and their trust in the Lord for safety (indeed the fact). The missive attempted to destroy the confidence of the populace of Jerusalem in their God and their king (vv. 10-17).

Sennacherib's messengers "called out with a loud voice in Hebrew to the people of Jerusalem who were on the wall, to frighten them and trouble them, that they might take the city" (v. 18 NKJV).

King Hezekiah, upon receipt of this message, tore his garment and donned sackcloth and ashes, a traditional sign of mourning and distress. He then went to the Temple, spread the taunting message from Sennacherib before the Lord, and cried out to Him for help (Isa. 37:1). He also sent a delegation to Isaiah the prophet, who gave the king the following reassuring message from God: "Thus says the Lord: 'Do not be afraid of the words which you have heard, with which the servants of the king of Assyria have blasphemed Me. Surely I will send a spirit upon him, and he shall hear a rumor and return to his own land; and I will cause him to fall by the sword in his own land'" (vv. 6-7 NKJV).

---

1. List two false accusations Sennacherib brought against Hezekiah (vv. 11-12).
2. Describe Sennacherib's boasts (vv. 13-15).
3. How did Sennacherib's agents attempt to intimidate the people of Jerusalem (vv. 17-18)?
4. What foolish mistake were the Assyrians making (v. 19)?

> "The principal act of courage is to endure and withstand dangers doggedly rather than to attack them."—Thomas Aquinas

---

D. The Defeat of Assyria (vv. 20-23)

(2 Chronicles 32:20 is not included in the printed text.)

²¹And the Lord sent an angel, which cut off all the mighty men of valour, and the leaders and captains in the camp of the king of Assyria. So he returned with shame of face to his own land. And when he was come into the house of his god, they that came forth of his own bowels slew him there with the sword. ²²Thus the Lord saved Hezekiah and the inhabitants of Jerusalem from the hand of Sennacherib the king of Assyria, and from the hand of all other, and guided them on every side. ²³And many brought gifts unto the Lord to Jerusalem, and presents to Hezekiah king of Judah: so that he was magnified in the sight of all nations from thenceforth.

The method used by the destroying angel is not altogether clear. It might have been a highly contagious disease, or it might have been a direct action by the destroying angel. Angels are messengers from God who convey verbal messages from God and protect God's people from enemies. Through this divine intervention—in response to the desperate prayers of King Hezekiah and the prophet Isaiah (v. 20)—Sennacherib lost 185,000 fighting men in a single night.

After this devastating military blow from Judah's (and the only) God, Sennacherib crept ashamedly home, where some years later he was assassinated by two of his own sons (v. 21). Contrarily, Hezekiah was honored. Presents were brought to him in recognition of the divine deliverance of Judah in the face of impossible odds (vv. 22-23).

God can be trusted to care for His own. The means, however, will vary according to the need and according to what will give God the most glory and further His kingdom work.

———————————

1. How did the people of Jerusalem respond to Assyria's threats (v. 20)?
2. Contrast Sennacherib's loss with Hezekiah's gain (vv. 21-23).

> "God does not guide those who want to run their own life. He only guides those who admit their need of His direction and rely on His wisdom."—Winkie Pratney

———————————

CONCLUSION

Hezekiah's reign was a glorious period of return to covenant with God and reliance upon Him for strength and preservation. This king, while not perfect, was consistently faithful to God. Hezekiah, quite understandably, became fearful when the Assyrian army was bearing down on Jerusalem and resorted to useless compromise. Moreover, after victory over Assyria through divine help, Hezekiah became rather proud of his nation's prosperity and unwisely showed Judah's God-given wealth to Babylonian emissaries (2 Kings 20:12-13). The prophet Isaiah warned that this failure would cause Judah trouble in a later generation (vv. 16-18). However, two remarkable miracles also marked Hezekiah's rule: the divine rout of the Assyrians and the personal healing granted to Hezekiah himself when he otherwise would have died an early death (vv. 1-7).

Overall, King Hezekiah was a model of faithfulness to Israel's covenant with the Lord. We should rely on Hezekiah's example, extracting principles that apply universally in the spiritual realm—particularly faith in God and consistent faithfulness to God.

GOLDEN TEXT CHALLENGE

"IN EVERY WORK THAT HE [HEZEKIAH] BEGAN IN THE SERVICE OF THE HOUSE OF GOD, AND IN THE LAW, AND IN THE COMMANDMENTS, TO SEEK HIS GOD, HE DID IT WITH ALL HIS HEART, AND PROSPERED" (2 Chron. 31:21).

Because Hezekiah served the Lord "with all his heart . . . [he] prospered"— "he was very successful" (NLT).

The Temple was in shameful disrepair, and Hezekiah would not rest until it was thoroughly cleansed. Earlier kings had haphazardly followed God's commands (or intentionally ignored them), but Hezekiah followed "God's laws and commands . . . wholeheartedly" (NLT).

If you are currently in a difficult situation, "you will find [God] if you seek Him with all your heart and with all your soul. . . . He will not forsake you nor destroy you" (Deut. 4:29, 31 NKJV).

Wholehearted service and obedience to God is the path to genuine success.

Daily Devotions:

M. Hezekiah's Devotion to God • 2 Kings 18:1-8

T. Hezekiah's Healing • Isaiah 38:1-7

W. Hezekiah's Praise to God • Isaiah 38:15-20

T. Zeal for God's House • John 2:13-17

F. The Dynamic Ministry of Apollos • Acts 18:24-28

S. Stir Up the Gift of God • 2 Timothy 1:3-7

Nicodemus and Jesus

John 3:1-21

Unit Theme:
More Great Stories of the Bible

Central Truth:
Jesus is God's provision for our salvation.

Focus:
Study Nicodemus' encounter with Jesus and affirm that salvation comes only through Jesus Christ.

Context:
In AD 27, Nicodemus talks with Jesus.

Golden Text:
"For God so loved the world, that he gave his only begotten Son, that whosoever believeth in him should not perish, but have everlasting life" (John 3:16).

Study Outline:
  I. **Seeking Jesus** (John 3:1-6)
 II. **Confronted by Jesus** (John 3:7-13)
III. **The Way of Salvation Explained** (John 3:14-21)

INTRODUCTION

Nicodemus was a member of the Sanhedrin, that traditional body of seventy highly respected Jewish elders which was allowed to decide Jewish religious matters and some infractions of civil and criminal law under the tight fist of Roman rule. Nicodemus was also a respected "teacher of Israel," which indicates that he was learned both in the Old Testament texts and in interpretations of those revered texts. Moreover, he was a Pharisee—a member of the Jewish sect known for conservatism, piety, acceptance of the entire canon of the Old Testament, and strict adherence to the Law with rigorous interpretation and application of all its minutiae. Jesus criticized the Pharisees for attending to external piety while neglecting inner purity, calling them hypocrites (see Matt. 23).

Nicodemus evidently had witnessed some of Jesus' mighty signs and wonders wrought during the early days of His ministry while He was still in the vicinity of Jerusalem (John 2:23-25). Impressed by the evident supernatural character of what he had seen, Nicodemus came to Jesus privately to discuss with Him what he thought would be matters of mutual interest. Jesus, instead, pointed the Jewish leader to what mattered most—birth into spiritual life through the inner action of the Spirit.

The apostle John, close companion of Jesus throughout His earthly ministry, penned the Gospel in which Nicodemus' story occurs to induce faith in

Jesus as the Son of God (20:30-31). John likely was interested in reaching Jewish settlers in late-first-century Ephesus and regions beyond since John was resident there during these years. In his Gospel, John presented seven great signs as basic narrative structure. Around that structure, he wove both conversations with individuals impacted by Jesus and discourses to His disciples that grew out of the signs He performed.

Those mighty works—from turning water into wine to resurrecting Lazarus—pointed beyond themselves to deep spiritual truths basic to life in Christ. John, like the three writers of other Gospels, climaxed his book with a riveting narration of Jesus' passion, resurrection, and post-resurrection appearances. John thereby ended his book with the most conclusive reasons for faith in Jesus as Messiah and Lord. Early in Jesus' ministry, Nicodemus was pointed toward faith in Jesus' coming redemptive death as essential to birth into spiritual life.

Those private conversations with Jesus recorded in John's Gospel, in addition to that with Nicodemus, included those with Andrew and John himself; Nathanael; the woman at the well; the man born blind; and the powerful dialogue with Simon Peter that closes the book. These conversations reveal Jesus as the divine teacher, leading individuals, point-by-point, toward spiritual truth.

Though we see no direct portrayal of it, we have good reason to believe Nicodemus gradually moved toward comprehension and acceptance of the Gospel. This is suggested by his defense of Jesus (7:50-52) and his participation with Joseph of Arimathea in preparation of Jesus' body for burial (19:38-42).

I. SEEKING JESUS (John 3:1-6)

A. The Seeker (vv. 1-2)

¹There was a man of the Pharisees, named Nicodemus, a ruler of the Jews: ²The same came to Jesus by night, and said unto him, Rabbi, we know that thou art a teacher come from God: for no man can do these miracles that thou doest, except God be with him.

The Synoptic Gospels (Matthew, Mark, and Luke) share a basic core of material, while in each case also containing narratives and teachings not shared with the other two. The Gospel of John, however, offers the reader a large amount of narrative and teaching occurring only therein, while sharing a relatively small portion of material with the other Gospels. The encounter of Jesus with Nicodemus occurs only in the fourth Gospel, as do the references to Nicodemus in 7:50-52 and 19:38-42.

The Synoptic Gospels, on the whole, present the Pharisees as declared enemies of Jesus. Therefore, it might come as a surprise to the thoughtful reader that Nicodemus was, to say the least, open-minded where Jesus was concerned. Perhaps the explanation is that, in John 3, we are still in the early Judean stage of Jesus' ministry—before His bold declarations regarding the Sabbath and performing of miracles on the Sabbath had hardened the attitudes of the typical legalistic Pharisees, who appeared more interested in preserving minute distinctions than expressing compassion toward their less fortunate contemporaries. Jesus' compassion, however, never caused Him to violate Mosaic Law; rather, He fulfilled that Law by expressing and acting in accordance with the very heart of it.

Nicodemus, nonetheless, was an exception among his fellow Pharisees and Sanhedrin members. He likely was among those who, when Jesus "was in Jerusalem at the Passover, during the feast, . . . believed in His name when they saw the signs which He did" (2:23 NKJV). However, "Jesus did not commit Himself to them, because He knew all men, and had no need that anyone should testify of man, for He knew what was in man" (vv. 24-25 NKJV). Over time, Nicodemus' early superficial faith might develop into a strong, enduring faith after opportunities to hear more truth from the Master Teacher.

In this first encounter, Nicodemus appears to have approached Jesus privately to escape criticism from more vocal colleagues among the Pharisees and rulers. Nicodemus had examined the observable evidence concerning Jesus and arrived at a plausible conclusion. He called Jesus "Rabbi" (3:2)—"a title of honor and respect given by the Jews to teachers of the Law" (*Nelson's Bible Dictionary*). Then Nicodemus made an unexpected admission.

He had seen the miracles performed by Jesus during this early stage of His ministry, and he evidently had heard His teaching. He was now ready to confess (a dangerous admission should it get out to his colleagues) that Jesus had to be "a teacher come from God"—not the Prophet predicted by Moses and certainly not the Messiah but, beyond reasonable doubt, a teacher sent by God. Jesus was what Nicodemus declared Him to be, but He was so much more, as Jesus himself declared and proved in John's Gospel.

Jesus' miracles were acts of compassion—first and always. They were performed to save and/or improve the lot of human lives. And Jesus' teaching was typically rooted in Old Testament texts, reinterpreted and applied specifically to first-century problems. Jesus was not only a *teacher* but, as is evident from what He said and did, also a *prophet* who powerfully taught and proclaimed the kingdom of God with attesting miracles.

The apostle John, moreover, would demonstrate conclusively in his Gospel that Jesus was also the Messiah predicted in Old Testament prophecy and the unique, eternally existent Son of God—the second person in the Trinity. So, Nicodemus' confession was somewhat lukewarm and the least that could have been expected, given even a degree of honest soul-searching. It was the heartless opposition to Jesus soon to be evident among Nicodemus' peers that would be both heart-rending and worthy of divine judgment. Pharisees like Nicodemus were indeed exceptional.

---

1. Who was Nicodemus?
2. What truths about Jesus did Nicodemus realize?

> "Seek not to understand that thou mayest believe, but believe that thou mayest understand."—Augustine

B. An Unexpected Challenge (v. 3)

³Jesus answered and said unto him, Verily, verily, I say unto thee, Except a man be born again, he cannot see the kingdom of God.

Jesus did not enter into a comfortable discussion with Nicodemus. In fact, He did not even respond to Nicodemus' opening remarks. Instead, He pierced to the heart of the matter—where Nicodemus now was and what he must now do if he was to be serious about his spiritual life. Opening with a phrase that expressed strong emphasis ("verily, verily"), Jesus asserted that unless Nicodemus was "born again," or "born from above" (the Greek word allows either translation), he would not even "see" God's kingdom. Nicodemus would not even comprehend the Kingdom's nature (much less enter into it since it had its beginning in renewed human hearts), unless he experienced *regeneration*, or the *new birth*. "Born from above" is the more precise term for this experience.

John had earlier alluded to this topic in his Gospel. After sadly stating that Jesus, God's Son, had been rejected by His own people, John asserted that to all who received Him, Jesus gave the *right*, or *authority*, "to become children of God, to those who believe in His name: who were born, not of blood, nor of the will of the flesh, nor of the will of man, but of God" (1:11-13 NKJV).

In John 3:3, Jesus contrasted *natural birth*, originating in human impulse or passion, and the *second birth*, an act of the Holy Spirit occurring in conjunction with the person's faith, or trust, in His power and authority. Through this supernatural experience, a person becomes a child of God. After Adam and Eve's fall, human beings had lost that relationship with the divine. It would now be restored with resulting gradual growth in spiritual life.

---

1. What does God require for entrance into His kingdom, and why?
2. List other ways that people try to enter God's kingdom.

> "To be born again is, as it were, to enter upon a new existence; to have a new mind, a new heart, new views, new principles, new tastes, new affections, new likings, new dislikings, new fears, new joys, new sorrows, new love to things once hated, new hatred to things once loved; new thoughts of God, and ourselves, and the world, and the life to come, and salvation."—J. C. Ryle

---

C. Nicodemus' Puzzled Response (v. 4)

⁴Nicodemus saith unto him, How can a man be born when he is old? Can he enter the second time into his mother's womb, and be born?

Nicodemus might well have realized, to some extent, the importance of what Jesus was saying to him. If that was the case, his response might well have been an expression of hopelessness. He wondered how anyone who had passed through the developmental stages of life and become "old" (probably a personal reference) could do so again. The fact that he had come to Jesus reveals that Nicodemus recognized his spiritual shortcomings. Was it possible for him to start his life over again and live it the way he knew God would have him live it? Just *how* it could happen was his problem; the power and the process perplexed him.

• What questions do you have about the New Birth?

> "Even to earnest minds the difficulty of grasping the truth at all has always proved extreme. Philosophically, one scarcely sees either the necessity or the possibility of being born again. Why a virtuous man should not simply grow better and better until in his own right he enter the kingdom of God is what thousands honestly and seriously fail to understand."—Henry Drummond

---

D. Enlightening Interpretation (vv. 5-6)

⁵Jesus answered, Verily, verily, I say unto thee, Except a man be born of water and of the Spirit, he cannot enter into the kingdom of God. ⁶That which is born of the flesh is flesh; and that which is born of the Spirit is spirit.

As a religious leader, Nicodemus should have known such Old Testament Scripture as Ezekiel 36:25-27: "I will sprinkle clean water on you, and you shall be clean; I will cleanse you from all your filthiness and from all your idols. I will give you a new heart and put a new spirit within you; I will take the heart of stone out of your flesh and give you a heart of flesh. I will put My Spirit within you and cause you to walk in My statutes, and you will keep My judgments and do them" (NKJV). He might then have realized that the Spirit of God could enable spiritual birth through "water and . . . the Spirit" (John 3:5), which would transform him into the "new creation" Paul would later describe in 2 Corinthians 5:17: "If anyone is in Christ, he is a new creation; old things have passed away; behold, all things have become new" (NKJV).

When Jesus spoke of "water" in John 3:5, He was not contrasting *flesh* and *spirit*; He was symbolizing the renewal of life through the Spirit that He would later speak of in 7:38: "He who believes in Me, as the Scripture has said, out of his heart will flow rivers of living water" (NKJV).

In 3:6, Jesus makes a clear distinction between the natural and the spiritual. Man's natural life, though derived from the Creator, is not the life of God. The new birth is not a self-improvement project or a physical makeover. The flesh may be battered, but it is still the flesh. The sinful man or woman must be transformed by God's Spirit—this alone is new birth.

---

1. What does it mean to be "born of the water and of the Spirit" (v. 5)?
2. What birth do all people experience, and what birth do only some people experience (v. 6)?

A New Creation

Recently, a confused, hurting teenager, encouraged by a high school teacher, attended a youth conference titled "Forward." This young man had grown up in a broken home, where he received no Christian values or training. As a result, he had drifted into activities that violated both basic moral values and legal restrictions. As he heard dynamic presentations of Gospel truth, he was convinced of his need for a Savior and gave his life to Christ. Now he is an enthusiastic witness to Bible truth, even as he delves into deeper understanding of Christian living.

II. CONFRONTED BY JESUS (John 3:7-13)

A. Provocation (vv. 7-8)

⁷Marvel not that I said unto thee, Ye must be born again. ⁸The wind bloweth where it listeth, and thou hearest the sound thereof, but canst not tell whence it cometh, and whither it goeth: so is every one that is born of the Spirit.

Jesus was prodding Nicodemus' mind into consideration of a different way of viewing spiritual life—not merely as religious duty but as a Holy Spirit-directed birth into new life with a re-ordering of priorities and an infusion of inner power. This is more important than the external miracles, significant as they were, both as acts of compassion and as indicators of the truth concerning the divine identity of Jesus as both Son of Man and Son of God—Messiah and second person of the Trinity.

In first-century Judea, four languages were spoken: Aramaic, Hebrew, koine Greek, and Latin. The Old Testament documents had been composed primarily in Hebrew, but with a few writings in Babylonian Aramaic. First-century Jews spoke a version of Aramaic, brought home with them from their Babylonian captivity. The common Greek was the language of commerce and daily activity outside the Jewish communities, but known somewhat to the Jews. The Roman overlords, including the military occupiers of both Galilee and Judea and their political rulers, spoke and wrote Latin. In Hebrew, the word for both *wind* and *spirit* was *ruach*; in Greek, it was *pneuma*; in Latin, the word for a *breeze* or *breath*, as well as for *spirit*, was *spiritus*.

This coincidence of a single word for two different realities—one physical and the other spiritual—made it possible to convey, through a symbol from everyday reality, profound insight into the Holy Spirit's work in the human heart. Today, wind is charted by meteorologists, but in the first century it was a total mystery. However, even today, we do not know how and why a particular local breeze behaves exactly as it does, particularly if we aren't scientists.

The work of the Spirit in the human heart is also mysterious. We feel its effects, but cannot fully understand or explain its work in the individual heart. If we listen to the voice of the Spirit and follow His leadings, we too will not be fully understood by those who move primarily within a physical and social world ruled by pragmatic impulse and common logic.

- How is the wind similar to the Holy Spirit (v. 8)?

> "He is intangible and invisible. But His work is more powerful than the most ferocious wind. The Spirit brings order out of chaos and beauty out of ugliness."—R. C. Sproul

B. Consternation (vv. 9-10)

⁹Nicodemus answered and said unto him, How can these things be? ¹⁰Jesus answered and said unto him, Art thou a master of Israel, and knowest not these things?

Nicodemus was baffled by these words of Jesus. He did not move and live on such a highly spiritual plane. Instead, he likely was preoccupied with personal, religious, and political considerations. He could not understand how and why God would work in such a baffling spiritual way within human hearts. He likely thought in terms of an eventual return to home rule: Jews governing Jews and the hated Romans finally expelled. He did not see that such a supposed solution would fail to change the underlying issue. As "the teacher of Israel" (v. 10 NKJV), Nicodemus should have known from Israel's history that a change in human hearts was the only lasting solution. Spiritual transformation—rather than a social or political solution—was the need.

- Why do religious people sometimes find it difficult to grasp Biblical truths?

> "The spiritual man is no mere development of the natural man. He is a new creation born from above."—Henry Drummond

C. Authoritative Elaboration (vv. 11-13)

¹¹Verily, verily, I say unto thee, We speak that we do know, and testify that we have seen; and ye receive not our witness. ¹²If I have told you earthly things, and ye believe not, how shall ye believe, if I tell you of heavenly things? ¹³And no man hath ascended up to heaven, but he that came down from heaven, even the Son of man which is in heaven.

Jesus was attempting to move Nicodemus to a higher level of spiritual comprehension. He spoke now of a heavenly rather than earthly way of thinking. One might ask, "What is the reference of 'We'?" The answer lies in the connections of Jesus. As the Son of God incarnate fulfilling a heavenly mission on earth, He was associated primarily with His Father and the Holy Spirit. At this point, "we" probably did not refer to His disciples, men who were then probably slightly ahead of Nicodemus when it came to spiritual insight and particularly insight into the messianic nature of Jesus.

On the earthly plane, Jesus was not a priest nor a scribe but, as Matthew 7:29 states, "He taught them as one having authority, and not as the scribes." His references were to Scripture only, and His authority came first from His divine origin and additionally from the sheer inner force, inherent truth, and faultless logic of His words.

His source of authority lay in heaven itself, not in the quotation of numerous sayings from the rabbis that had been spoken and/or written during the intertestamental period (ca. 400-1 BC), as teachers among the Pharisees might prefer. His heavenly Father himself was the One who backed up Jesus' words, as attested by the voice from heaven at His baptism (Matt. 3:17) and at His transfiguration (17:5). In other words, Jesus was speaking about what He knew because of His attested heavenly origins. However, the religious establishment in Jerusalem would not accept that authentic witness to truth, even though it was from heaven.

In order to grow in understanding of God's truth, Nicodemus must begin with the elementary things (cf. Heb. 6:1), then move (under the direction of Jesus) into understanding of "heavenly things" (John 3:12)—a gradual growth in faith and true knowledge. Jesus had come down from heaven; therefore, He knew of those heavenly things and could direct Nicodemus in his gradual growth in understanding of them. Did Nicodemus gradually grow in understanding and experience genuine transformation through regeneration by the Holy Spirit as he exercised faith in Christ the Son? We have reason to believe he did, because of John 7:50-52 and 19:38-42.

---

1. What does Jesus say about Himself in verses 11 and 13?
2. Why are "earthly things" harder to believe than "heavenly things" (v. 12)?

> "This new birth in Christ, thus firmly believed and continually desired, will do everything that thou wantest to have done in thee, it will dry up all the springs of vice, stop all the workings of evil in thy nature, it will bring all that is good into thee, it will open all the gospel within thee, and thou wilt know what it is to be taught of God."—William Law

---

III. THE WAY OF SALVATION EXPLAINED (John 3:14-21)

A. The Serpent in the Wilderness (v. 14)

¹⁴And as Moses lifted up the serpent in the wilderness, even so must the Son of Man be lifted up.

Numbers 21:4-9 relates how the bronze snake upon a pole was a God-sent remedy for the terrible result of Israel's unbelief and murmuring. The people had to merely *look up* to live. When anyone was bitten by one of the venomous snakes sent to punish them, he or she would be healed by looking at the bronze snake.

Jesus resembled the bronze snake in His vicarious dying primarily because God the Father "made Him who knew no sin to be sin for us, that we might become the righteousness of God in Him" (2 Cor. 5:21 NKJV). The Israelites looked on a representation of the agent of punishment for their sin and were healed. Jesus took on Himself the guilt and the punishment for our sin; He became our sin offering. If we look to Him in faith, we are spiritually and morally healed. Jesus became an offering for sin for us. We should, in turn, make our lives an offering of obedience to Him (see Eph. 2:10).

- How was Jesus' being "lifted up" greater than the lifting up of the bronze snake?

> "Let your tears fall because of sin; but, at the same time, let the eye of faith steadily behold the Son of Man lifted up, as Moses lifted up the serpent in the wilderness, that those who are bitten by the old serpent may look unto Jesus and live."—Charles Spurgeon

---

B. Salvation by Faith in Christ (vv. 15-17)

15That whosoever believeth in him should not perish, but have eternal life. 16For God so loved the world that he gave his only begotten Son, that whosoever believeth in him should not perish, but have everlasting life. 17For God sent not his Son into the world to condemn the world; but that the world through him might be saved.

As looking upon the bronze serpent brought life to the Israelites, so those who look on the crucified, resurrected, and ascended Christ in genuine faith receive deliverance. They escape present life without meaning and eternal death through separation from God and they gain present and eternal life in Jesus Christ. In verse 16, perhaps the most widely known statement in all Scripture, Jesus captured the central theological and experiential reality in Christian faith.

God so loved—that is, the triune God who created us (but here primarily God the Father) loved us entirely unselfishly, with no hope of perfect return of that love. *He gave* the completely free gift of *His only begotten Son* (the greatest gift imaginable). He gave *that we should not perish* (something we fully deserved), *but have everlasting life* (an eternal gift of divine grace poured selflessly upon us). What more could we ask or want?

What is it to *believe*? It is to lean heavily on Christ, God's Son, trusting in Him to save us and to keep us safe and secure forever. That faith is not founded on emotions or logic, but on trust in God and His Word. It is an everyday companionship with the divine. Who would not want this relationship with the Lord?

The opposite of faith-based and faithful living is *condemnation*; that is, carrying the full load of guilt for one's sin. This is a burden that never stops gnawing at you, destroying your inner peace, and moving you toward eternal destruction.

---

1. What does it mean to "perish" (v. 15)?
2. Explain the term "only begotten Son" (v. 16).
3. What does it to "believe in" Jesus (v. 16)?
4. Explain the term "world," and God's plan for the world (v. 17).

> "Faith is not belief without proof, but trust without reservation."
> —Elton Trueblood

C. Condemnation Through Unbelief (vv. 18-21)

¹⁸He that believeth on him is not condemned: but he that believeth not is condemned already, because he hath not believed in the name of the only begotten Son of God. ¹⁹And this is the condemnation, that light is come into the world, and men loved darkness rather than light, because their deeds were evil. ²⁰For every one that doeth evil hateth the light, neither cometh to the light, lest his deeds should be reproved. ²¹But he that doeth truth cometh to the light, that his deeds may be made manifest, that they are wrought in God.

The faithful man, woman, or child does not live in condemnation because he or she accepts God's gift of salvation through faith. In verse 18, "the name" is the full authority of Jesus Christ to give spiritual life fully and permanently to any person who comes to Him without recrimination or reservation. He is *only begotten*—He stands forever in that unique relationship of divine Son to His heavenly Father. If people refuse to come, it is because they like their sinning. They hate the bondage, but they love aspects of the daily experience of lust, illegitimate power, and acquisition of material goods as if they were the only goods life had to offer.

What is involved in God's gift of "light" (v. 19)? First is the sheer ability to see reality through Christ. Next is the purity inside, achieved by allowing and trusting the light to burn away the sin that stains our mind, emotions, attitudes, and will with selfish desire, tainting even our apparent good. When we allow God's eternal light of reality to penetrate to the essence of our being, we begin to become more transparent (vv. 20-21). We don't mind people seeing us through and through, though we know a lot of flaws and "muck" remain.

Don't be surprised if former "allies," in the cause of self-centered living, turn against you once you come to the light. They will question your motives and find it difficult to believe and accept the changes in your lifestyle and character. Why? Because, in comparison, they will look as bad as they truly are. Besides, they like their sinning and don't wish to be reminded that it is *sinning*—against God and the forever-valid standards in His Word.

1. What is "condemnation," and what causes it (v. 18)?
2. Why do people love "darkness rather than light" (vv. 19-20)?
3. Compare verse 21 with Jesus' words in Matthew 5:14. Do you fit this description? Why or why not?

> "Most laws condemn the soul and pronounce sentence. The result of the law of my God is perfect. It condemns but forgives. It restores—more than abundantly—what it takes away."—Jim Elliot

---

CONCLUSION

Are you a Nicodemus, torn inside by conflicting motives, and seeing the need to be transformed? Have you already been changed by coming to the light of God's truth, personified in Christ himself? If you have, allow the Holy Spirit to continue His work in you. Avail yourself of daily sanctifying grace to live, walk, and witness through and to Jesus, who will give us life together forever.

GOLDEN TEXT CHALLENGE

"FOR GOD SO LOVED THE WORLD, THAT HE GAVE HIS ONLY BEGOTTEN SON, THAT WHOSOEVER BELIEVETH IN HIM SHOULD NOT PERISH, BUT HAVE EVERLASTING LIFE" (John 3:16).

God's love reaches back into eternity and culminates at Calvary. Such love in the heart of God moved Him to send His Son down from heaven to die on the cross. At an early time, man fell into sin and rebellion against God's plan. Being the kind of God He is, God has sought to win man back into His joyful fellowship. He has not remained serenely detached but has become passionately involved in our joys and heartaches—"the Word was made flesh, and dwelt among us" (John 1:14).

The purpose of Christ's coming has been to disclose the love of God and to redeem His people. The great outpouring of God's love has been through His Son—loving, searching, and even dying for godless sinners (Rom. 5:6-10).

The cross-death of Christ is the supreme demonstration of God's love. Such love proceeds from the loving heart of the heavenly Father and is poured out in our hearts by the Holy Spirit (v. 5). It has no limits; it is wide enough to embrace all humanity.

Daily Devotions:

M. The Blessing of Forgiveness • Psalm 32:1-7

T. The Gift of Salvation • Isaiah 55:1-7

W. Promise of the New Covenant • Jeremiah 31:31-34

T. The Great Invitation • Matthew 11:28-30

F. Jesus Is the Only Way • John 14:6-14

S. The Assurance of Salvation • Romans 10:5-13

The First Christian Martyr

Acts 6:8—7:60

Unit Theme:
More Great Stories of the Bible

Central Truth:
The Holy Spirit anoints Christians to proclaim the Gospel.

Focus:
Consider the anointed courage of Stephen and proclaim God's truth without fear.

Context:
In AD 35 in Jerusalem, Stephen is killed for the cause of Christ.

Golden Text:
"He [Stephen], being full of the Holy Ghost, looked up steadfastly into heaven, and saw the glory of God, and Jesus standing on the right hand of God" (Acts 7:55).

Study Outline:
  I. **Full of Faith and Power** (Acts 6:8-15)
 II. **Anointed to Speak Boldly** (Acts 7:1-8, 44-53)
III. **A Glorious Homegoing** (Acts 7:54-60)

INTRODUCTION

The word *martyr* is derived from a Greek noun meaning "witness." A martyr makes the strongest possible witness to Christian faith by giving his or her life for the Gospel. Stephen, a dynamic witness to Gospel truth, was the first martyr; he set the high standard for authentic Christian martyrdom. Then, during the time of the church fathers, some unquestionably sincere, highly dedicated believers mistakenly *sought* martyrdom as the highest possible way to honor their Lord. Christians, instead, should seek to honor our Lord by all-out dedication to lifetime witness, while leaving in God's hand the time and mode of the ending of our life journey.

In the earliest days of the Christian church, in Jerusalem, Stephen was selected by the congregation as one of seven men to assist the apostles by attending to practical matters affecting Greek-speaking widows of the church. Stephen was singled out among these men as being "full of faith and the Holy Spirit" (Acts 6:5 NKJV).

He soon branched out into powerful evangelistic ministry characterized by "wonders and miracles" (v. 8). Luke, the writer of the Book of Acts, does not specify the exact supernatural signs that occurred in Stephen's ministry. However, the Gospel of Luke records Jesus' healing the sick, casting out of demons, raising the dead, and affecting the physical environment (walking on water and multiplying bread). Stephen's supernatural actions, then, were probably types of miracles like those in that list, subtracting the last category.

"Wonders and miracles" like those accompanying Stephen's ministry also accompanied the ministry of Peter and John (Acts 3), Paul (14:8-10), and Philip the evangelist (8:6). Such supernatural phenomena did not persuade extreme proponents of traditional Judaism. They might even have attributed them to Satan rather than to God, as opponents of the Gospel did those of Jesus himself (Luke 11:14-26). The concern of enemies of Stephen was that powerful, persuasive followers of Jesus of Nazareth would pull more and more people away from adherence to the Law of Moses and from Temple worship. So they were willing to present false evidence regarding Stephen to the Sanhedrin to stop this fervent preacher of the gospel of Christ.

I. FULL OF FAITH AND POWER (Acts 6:8-15)

Stephen was one of seven laymen chosen to attend to the practical needs of Greek-speaking Jewish widows who had been neglected in the distribution of food, perhaps because of their language difference (Acts 6:1). These widows were entirely dependent on assistance from the church for their livelihood. The apostles specified three qualifications that the congregation should require of the seven men selected: (1) good character, (2) fullness of the Spirit, and (3) fullness of wisdom (v. 3).

It is interesting that being full of the Spirit was specifically attributed to Stephen (v. 5), since the seven men selected were required to have this characteristic. Stephen's spiritual manifestations must have been outstanding for him to elicit such special mention. French Arrington states that Stephen "was endowed with the gift of faith that works miracles" (*The Acts of the Apostles*). The apostles prayed over these men and laid their hands on them, thus consecrating them to their task.

A. Called to Evangelize (v. 8)

⁸**And Stephen, full of faith and power, did great wonders and miracles among the people.**

By insistent repetition, Luke hammered into his readers' consciousness the remarkable supernatural quality of Stephen's Gospel ministry. The attesting signs in verse 8 appear to have been of two different kinds—*wonders* and *miracles*. However, in their Greek origins, these two words have practically the same meaning, and the repetition is probably more for emphasis and emotional effect than for division into different kinds. Luke, guided by the Spirit, was stretching for the ultimate vocabulary choice to express remarkable supernatural phenomena.

God appeared to be drawing attention to a choice servant who was sold out to Him, thereby giving to doubting minds far more than sufficient evidence of Gospel truth. This truth would be capable of converting minds and hearts through the demonstration of supernatural power able to heal bodies and even to raise the dead. This is not mere speculation, since such miraculous events occur throughout the Book of Acts.

In our own age in places where the Christian "good news" is being presented for the first time, not only physical healings but also astounding resurrections from the dead have occurred. This conforms to the provision for healing in the Atonement through the sacrifice of Christ and the supernatural manifestations of "faith," "gifts of healing," and "the working of miracles" listed by the apostle Paul (1 Cor. 12:8-9). The Lord seems to be saying to naturally ignorant, rather than willfully ignorant, hearers of the Gospel, "Witness My miraculous work among you and trust in the redemptive power of My Son to set you free from sin and to set you on a victorious spiritual journey."

• How was Stephen able to do mighty ministry?

"Miracles are the swaddling clothes of infant churches."—Thomas Fuller

---

B. Challenged by Nonbelievers (vv. 9-11)

⁹Then there arose certain of the synagogue, which is called the synagogue of the Libertines, and Cyrenians, and Alexandrians, and of them of Cilicia and of Asia, disputing with Stephen. ¹⁰And they were not able to resist the wisdom and the spirit by which he spake. ¹¹Then they suborned men, which said, We have heard him speak blasphemous words against Moses, and against God.

We can tell from Stephen's address to the Sanhedrin in Acts 7 that he did not hesitate to declare the whole truth of God, however much it might sting and agitate opposing individuals. However, 6:8 contains no reference to Stephen's proclamation of the gospel, though we can assume he did it, but only the reference to supernatural signs attesting that he was "full of faith and power." We can therefore assume that the opposition to Stephen was a spiritual resistance to authentic evidence of divine favor—resistance that can be called satanic. When one determines to act contrary to divine truth, clearly shown to be such through miraculous attestation, he places himself at the disposal of the enemy of divine truth, Satan himself. There is a difference between sincere misunderstanding of truth and determined resistance to truth, regardless of the evidence.

The opponents of Stephen who "disputed," or "argued," with him therefore appeared to question the source of his miracle-working power. This was a dangerous course to pursue, since it might easily be tantamount to blasphemy against the Holy Spirit, who enabled Stephen's remarkable acts (see Matt. 12:32).

These Jewish opponents of Stephen had formed synagogues in Jerusalem. The first group was the synagogue of the "Libertines" (freed men), former slaves existing in sufficient numbers in the capital city to form their own unit of worship. A second group was from Cyrene in North Africa, another from Alexandria in Egypt, and others from the Roman provinces of Cilicia and Asia (areas of what is now Turkey). These indignant opponents of Gospel truth could not argue successfully against Stephen. (Once an acquaintance of mine argued, without success, day after day regarding the ultimate source of Christian authority. Frustrated each time, he would send me a book on

---

the subject. Soon I acquired a sizable library on the subject from his point of view. He was determined to continue to hold his point of view, but could not successfully defend it.)

These men, however, were completely out-sized by the anointed brilliance of Stephen. Nonetheless, they took an opposing course. They contended that, regardless of supernatural demonstration and unassailable presentation of truth, Stephen could not be right. So they would resort to whatever means they could concoct to silence him.

The Old Testament clearly and repeatedly speaks regarding the ethical principle violated by these men. Of chief importance, is the ninth of the Ten Commandments: "You shall not bear false witness against your neighbor" (Ex. 20:16 NKJV). A basic character deficiency must exist in individuals who are willing to resort to carefully planned lying to make their case, especially those likely steeped in Old Testament Scripture from childhood. The word *suborned* (Acts 6:11) means to "put someone up to something; perhaps pay (secretly) or bribe" ("Dictionary," *The Greek New Testament*). So they got unprincipled men to agree to lie about Stephen, and they might have bribed them by giving them money.

The lie told against Stephen was that he had spoken blasphemous words against Moses and against God. They obviously had no evidence that Stephen had spoken such words. Even if Stephen had expressed the conviction that the Law of Moses was fulfilled in Jesus Christ (as Jesus said in Matt. 12:1-13) and that Jesus was the Son of God, he would have been speaking truth and not blasphemy. But they could offer no specific evidence that Stephen had said this. Instead, they made up evidence and had their bribed men speak it.

---

1. What did "certain [men] of the synagogue" do, and how successful were they (vv. 9-10)?
2. Describe the second method they used to silence Stephen (v. 11).

"Men can see the greatest miracles and miss the glory of God."
—Tom Wells

C. Brought Before the Sanhedrin (vv. 12-15)
(Acts 6:13-14 is not included in the printed text.)
¹²And they stirred up the people, and the elders, and the scribes, and came upon him, and caught him, and brought him to the council.
¹⁵And all that sat in the council, looking stedfastly on him, saw his face as it had been the face of an angel.

These opponents of Stephen used their false evidence to stir up ordinary people who likely were more principled and, therefore, otherwise would never have participated in this evil action, particularly secretly suborning lying witnesses. The elders were leaders of the Jews, perhaps in the synagogues frequented by these persecutors, and the scribes were respected teachers of the Law.

With their testimony from false witnesses and their support from authority figures in the community in hand, these furious men caught Stephen and took him before the Sanhedrin. The Sanhedrin was the highest governing body of the Jews, consisting of seventy highly respected elders—Pharisees, Sadducees, important rabbis, and Temple authorities, including the high priest. This is the same body—probably, in the main, the same individuals—that had unjustly condemned Jesus. This body could pronounce guilt or innocence according to Jewish law, but could not legally, according to Roman law (which by effective state power prevailed), execute sentenced lawbreakers. They must have permission from the Roman government to carry out the death sentence.

The false charge against Stephen was as follows: "This man does not cease to speak blasphemous words against this holy place and the law; for we have heard him say that this Jesus of Nazareth will destroy this place and change the customs which Moses delivered to us" (vv. 13-14 NKJV). First, the accusers had not heard Stephen speak these words. Second, although Jesus had indeed prophesied in Matthew 24:2 that the Temple would be destroyed, He had not said He would destroy it Himself. Third, the Law of Moses would be superseded by the law of Christ; but if Stephen had said that, it would not have been blasphemy since Moses himself had predicted the coming of a Prophet like himself to whom the people should listen (Deut. 18:15).

Psalm 26:9-10 also speaks directly to this situation, referring to "bloodthirsty men, in whose hands is a sinister scheme, and whose right hand is full of bribes" (NKJV). As these spurious charges were made to the Sanhedrin against Stephen, all observers, "looking steadfastly at him, saw his face as the face of an angel" (Acts 6:15 NKJV). God was, thereby, giving His witness on behalf of His faithful servant Stephen.

---

1. Compare the accusations against Stephen with those used against Jesus (vv. 12-14; see Matt. 26:59-61).
2. Contrast Stephen's countenance (v. 15) with that of his accusers.

"Unbelief is not a misfortune to be pitied; it is a sin to be deplored."—John Stott

---

II. ANOINTED TO SPEAK BOLDLY (Acts 7:1-8, 44-53)

A. Defense Through History (vv. 1-8)

(Acts 7:1-8 is not included in the printed text.)

The high priest asked Stephen a direct question, "Are these things so?" (v. 1), and Stephen began his defense. Rather than attempting a point-by-point rebuttal of the false charges, he recounted events from the early history of Israel.

Stephen began his presentation with God's call to Abraham when he was still in Ur, a city in what is now southern Iraq. Stephen recounted Abraham's move to Haran and his journey into Canaan after the death of his father. The eloquent speaker emphasized Abraham's living as a stranger there who possessed no land, even though God had promised the entire land to him and his descendants. Abraham received from God the covenant of circumcision and the divine prediction that his descendants would be in bondage in "a foreign land" for four hundred years (v. 6 NKJV). Abraham became the father of Isaac, the father of Jacob, who fathered the "twelve patriarchs" (v. 8). Stephen thus began the unfolding of Israel's history according to God's plan.

• Why did Stephen begin his defense with the story of Abraham?

Persecuted Pioneers

In the early twentieth century, pioneers of the Pentecostal Movement in the United States underwent much opposition and persecution because of their departure from religious traditions in the communities where revivals eventually called "Pentecostal" occurred. The music tended to be loud, fast, and joyful. Spirit-filled participants danced before the Lord. Spirit-filled believers spoke in tongues, and there were frequent reports of physical healings through prayer. The worship infuriated staid community and church leadership. Also, rowdies who could not care less about doctrinal issues and worship traditions jumped at the chance to act out. As a result, opponents threw rocks, burned tents, and, in a few cases, inflicted serious injuries on sincere worshipers. However, the Pentecostal Movement persisted and prevailed.

B. From Moses to Solomon (vv. 44-48)

(Acts 7:45-46 is not included in the printed text.)

⁴⁴Our fathers had the tabernacle of witness in the wilderness, as he had appointed, speaking unto Moses, that he should make it according to the fashion that he had seen.

⁴⁷But Solomon built him an house. ⁴⁸Howbeit the most High dwelleth not in temples made with hands; as saith the prophet.

As Stephen continued to recount the history of the nation, he focused on God's faithfulness—first to Joseph and his brothers (vv. 9-16), then to the nation through Moses (vv. 17-43). Moses had an encounter with Yahweh at the burning bush in the desert near Mount Sinai. In that encounter, a reluctant Moses was commanded by God to lead His people out of Egyptian slavery. God performed "wonders and signs" before Pharaoh, at the Red Sea, and in the wilderness during Israel's forty years of wandering (v. 36).

Stephen emphasized particularly Moses' prophecy of God's intention to raise up a Prophet "like unto me" (v. 37). Only one human being could fulfill that prophecy—the Messiah, for only He could be the mediator of a new covenant, succeeding that of Moses. Stephen did not disparage either Moses or the Law given to him; rather, he gave Moses high honor while also recounting Israel's immediate fall into idolatry.

Next, Stephen began to emphasize Israel's perennial disobedience and idolatry: at Mount Sinai, and then during the forty years of wandering in the wilderness (vv. 38-41). Stephen quoted Amos 5:25-27, which indicted Judah for their worship of Molech and heavenly bodies (Acts 7:42-43).

As he now made a transition in his emphasis, Stephen mentioned David's desire to build a permanent house for God to replace the Tabernacle, and his son Solomon's fulfillment of that desire (vv. 44-47). Stephen here indirectly referred to the charge against him concerning the Temple. He stressed the high motives of King David in desiring to build God a house and of his son King Solomon, who constructed that magnificent Temple—likely at the location of the place where Stephen was speaking.

Stephen did not disparage Solomon's building of the Temple, and he did not deny that the localized presence of God was over the mercy seat in the Holy of Holies (although there was no ark of the covenant in Herod's temple in the first century AD). Stephen emphasized the impossibility of containing the omnipresent God of Israel and of the entire universe in a building made by human hands (v. 48). He referred to a statement in King Solomon's dedicatory prayer upon completion of that Temple: "But will God indeed dwell on the earth? Behold, heaven and the heaven of heavens cannot contain You. How much less this temple which I have built!" (1 Kings 8:27 NKJV).

---

1. What did Moses do for the Lord God (v. 44), and what did Solomon do (v. 47)?
2. In verse 48, how does Stephen describe God's superiority?

> "Those who don't know history are destined to repeat it."
> —Edmund Burke

C. Indictment of Contemporaries (vv. 49-53)

⁴⁹Heaven is my throne, and earth is my footstool; what house will ye build me? Saith the Lord: or what is the place of my rest? ⁵⁰Hath not my hand made all these things? ⁵¹Ye stiffnecked and uncircumcised in heart and ears, ye do always resist the Holy Ghost: as your fathers did, so do ye. ⁵²Which of the prophets have not your fathers persecuted? And they have slain them which shewed before of the coming of the Just One; of whom ye have been now the betrayers and murderers: ⁵³Who have received the law by the disposition of angels, and have not kept it.

Stephen was now quoting that magnificent poetic passage in Isaiah 66:1-2, in which the Lord himself spoke through the prophet. The Lord conveyed a marvelous sense of His omnipotence and omnipresence as the Creator of the universe, as He posed this question: "What is the place of my rest? Hath not My hand made all these things?" (Acts 7:49-50). Stephen was conveying clearly and eloquently, under the anointing of the Holy Spirit, the limitations of any human construction since the Lord has made all things and, therefore, could not be contained within any object of His direct or indirect creation.

Stephen was speaking the same insight that Jesus himself stressed in John 4:21, 23: "The hour is coming when you will neither on this mountain, nor in Jerusalem, worship the Father. . . . The hour is coming, and now is, when the true worshipers will worship the Father in spirit and truth" (NKJV).

Stephen, under the anointing of the Holy Spirit, now interrupted his discourse and moved immediately to an indictment of the self-righteous men sitting before him. He had recounted the rebellion, idolatry, and murder of God's prophets by leaders of Israel in the past. Now, he followed the indictment of the Jewish leadership made by Jesus himself in Matthew 23, as Stephen called the men before him "stiffnecked and uncircumcised in heart and ears" and asserted that they "always" resisted the Holy Spirit (Acts 7:51).

In the past, their fathers had persecuted the prophets who had predicted the coming of the Messiah, and these contemporary leaders had betrayed and murdered the Messiah (v. 52). Stephen called Him "the Just One," referring to the perfect inherent holiness of Jesus Christ, Son of Man and Son of God. God had given them the Law of Moses through angels, and they had not kept that law (v. 53).

Stephen covered every charge made against him, either through forthright assertions within his narration or by his references to the Temple at its close. The charges made against him were false, but Stephen did not hesitate to state clearly his positions regarding those charges. Note how closely Stephen's indictment, arrest, and execution followed that of the Lord himself and how Stephen showed a Christlike spirit. There was righteous indignation in each case, but also unhesitating, clear-cut statement of truth without rancor or bitterness.

---

1. How should we view the works we do for God (vv. 49-50)?
2. How were these religious leaders like their ancestors (v. 51)?
3. How did Stephen defend Jesus Christ (v. 52)?
4. What had these teachers of the Law done (v. 53)?

"An attitude can murder just as easily as an ax."—Woodrow Kroll

---

III. A GLORIOUS HOMEGOING (Acts 7:54-60)

A. Fury and Ecstasy (vv. 54-56)

⁵⁴When they heard these things, they were cut to the heart, and they gnashed on him with their teeth. ⁵⁵But he, being full of the Holy Ghost, looked up stedfastly into heaven, and saw the glory of God, and Jesus standing on the right hand of God, ⁵⁶And said, Behold, I see the heavens opened, and the Son of man standing on the right hand of God.

Here we see the irrational response of Stephen's hearers to his bold indictment of them because of their rejection of Jesus, God's Messiah: "They began gnashing their teeth at him" (v. 54 NASB). Stephen had seen beneath their veneer of piety and exposed their evil hearts. If they had been sincere men of God, they would have responded with repentance when convicted by the Spirit (contrast the response in 2:37). Instead, these men responded like voracious beasts in their hatred of a man who dared challenge them.

Once again, Luke emphasized Stephen's fullness of the Spirit (7:55)—in contrast with the spiritual leaders of the Jews, who, now showing their true colors, were full of Satan-inspired fury. As Stephen kept his eyes unremittingly on heaven, he saw the glory of God. He also saw Jesus, God's Son, whom he was defending, "standing" at the right hand of God (v. 56). Jesus was looking on as His faithful servant made his great personal defense and that of his Lord. Stephen spoke audibly of his vision of Jesus in heaven as his final testimony to his persecutors.

---

1. Describe the rage of Stephen's opponents (v. 54).
2. Describe the roles of the Holy Spirit, the Son, and the Father in this scene (vv. 55-56).

"Those early Christians were beaten, stoned to death, thrown to the lions, tortured, and crucified. Every conceivable method was used to stop them from talking."—Josh McDowell

---

B. Mob Violence and Christian Response (vv. 57-60)

⁵⁷Then they cried out with a loud voice, and stopped their ears, and ran upon him with one accord, ⁵⁸And cast him out of the city, and stoned him: and the witnesses laid down their clothes at a young man's feet, whose name was Saul, ⁵⁹And they stoned Stephen, calling upon God, and saying, Lord Jesus, receive my spirit. ⁶⁰And he kneeled down, and cried with a loud voice, Lord, lay not this sin to their charge. And when he had said this, he fell asleep.

As far as we can tell from the text, the Sanhedrin resorted to mob violence (v. 57). They took Stephen outside the city of Jerusalem by force—something Jesus' own hometown, early in His ministry, had done in an attempt to kill Him (see Luke 4:16-30). Outside the city, self-appointed witnesses to Stephen's stoning—"whose grisly duty it was to knock the offender down and throw the first stones" (*The Expositor's Bible Commentary*)—laid their outer garments at the feet of "a young man" named Saul, so that they could more freely perform their despicable act (Acts 7:58). There is, then, no evidence of a judiciously considered verdict, followed by the required delay of one day, during which time permission from the Roman government might have been secured.

Stephen's response during this terrible ordeal was exemplary. First, he prayed a simple prayer: "Lord Jesus, receive my spirit" (v. 59). As he experienced a vision in which his Lord was standing at the Father's right hand, he committed himself to divine care. Kneeling, he continued to pray, loudly beseeching, "Lord, lay not this sin to their charge" (v. 60). In this final moment, Stephen showed himself to have the attitude of the Lord himself, who had prayed, "Father, forgive them; for they know not what they do" (Luke 23:34).

---

1. How had the religious leaders "stopped their ears" (v. 57) throughout Stephen's trial?
2. Describe the role Saul played (v. 58).
3. Describe Stephen's death (vv. 59-60).

> "True Christianity is to manifest genuinely Christlike behavior by dependence on the working of the Spirit of God within, motivated by a love for the glory and honor of God."—Ray C. Stedman

CONCLUSION

Stephen's martyrdom led to great growth in conversions to Christian faith in the first century. In recent decades, similar responses to persecution have occurred in China and in several nations in Africa. Our response to a contemporary church under fire throughout the world should be to pray, to give our time and money, and to listen closely to the Spirit, lest we miss His urge to us personally to join the great missionary movement of our age. Stephen gave his all for God and His church. What would God have you and me do today?

GOLDEN TEXT CHALLENGE

"HE [STEPHEN], BEING FULL OF THE HOLY GHOST, LOOKED UP STEDFASTLY INTO HEAVEN, AND SAW THE GLORY OF GOD, AND JESUS STANDING ON THE RIGHT HAND OF GOD" (Acts 7:55).

In the midst of violent rage, God strengthened His servant with a vision of glory. Stephen was not overcome by fear, or even aware of those who raged about him; he seems to have been conscious only of the heavenly goal set before him. The inference is that he did not keep his eyes on his enemies, but "looked up stedfastly into heaven."

Stephen exclaimed of the glory and beauty of what he saw: Jesus was standing in the companionship of God the Father. And the first Christian martyr would soon join them.

Daily Devotions:

M. A Prophet Promised • Deuteronomy 18:15-18
T. Elijah's Obedience, God's Provision • 1 Kings 17:1-6
W. A Courageous Faith Displayed • Daniel 3:14-26
T. The Bold Ministry of John • Matthew 3:1-10
F. Emboldened by the Holy Spirit • Acts 4:5-13
S. Paul Encourages Timothy • 2 Timothy 1:8-14

A Dynamic Ministry Couple

**Matthew 28:18-20; Acts 18:1-4, 18-19, 24-28;
Romans 12:13; 16:3-5; Ephesians 4:11-12; 3 John 5-8**

Unit Theme:
More Great Stories of the Bible

Central Truth:
Christians are called to serve God by ministering to others.

Focus:
Survey Aquila and Priscilla's ministry and serve God wholeheartedly.

Context:
Principles of ministry exhibited by Aquila and Priscilla, and highlighted in practical teaching

Golden Text:
"I therefore, the prisoner of the Lord, beseech you that ye walk worthy of the vocation wherewith ye are called" (Eph. 4:1).

Study Outline:
   I. **Ministry of Hospitality** (Acts. 18:1-4; Rom. 12:13; 3 John 5-8)
  II. **Ministry of Discipleship** (Matt. 28:18-20; Acts 18:18-19, 24-28)
 III. **Pastoral Ministry** (Rom. 16:3-5; Eph. 4:11-12)

INTRODUCTION

Aquila and Priscilla were a married couple remarkably dedicated to Christian ministry. Luke presents them in Acts 18 as partners in ministry with Paul and as seasoned believers who instructed the brilliant Apollo in certain essential basics of the Christian faith. Paul mentioned this couple in three of his letters—Romans, 1 Corinthians, and 2 Timothy. He found them plying their trade of tent-making (Acts 18:3) in Corinth, his own trade. They were probably already Christian believers when Paul first arrived in Corinth on his second missionary journey. They had been forced to leave Rome because of Emperor Claudius' edict requiring all Jews to leave Rome, allegedly due to conflicts between traditional Jews and Christian Jews.

Aquila and Priscilla could easily set up their trade in various places. So they were able to move from place to place witnessing for Jesus Christ, teaching about Christian faith to new converts, modeling a godly lifestyle in conspicuous settings in urban environments, and opening their home to house churches. *Hospitality*, well exemplified by Aquila and Priscilla, is an important means of sharing the Gospel with "neighbors" (as defined by Jesus in Luke 10:29-37).

Several Old Testament contexts reveal the importance of hospitality. Consider Abraham's graciousness to divine travelers (Gen. 18:1-8), the horrific lack of hospitality displayed by the men of Sodom (19:4-11), and the contrasting hateful denial of hospitality seen in Nabal and the abundant graciousness shown by his wife, Abigail (1 Sam. 25). In the New Testament, Mary and Martha and their brother Lazarus opened their home to local friends and neighbors, as well as their special friends Jesus of Nazareth and His disciples (John 12:1-8; Luke 10:38-42).

Priscilla and Aquila's Christian hospitality developed into pastoral ministry when they welcomed newly established house churches into their home. This dynamic ministry couple illustrated total dedication to Christ that continually extended its scope and depth, leading to repeated commendation and recommendation by the apostle Paul (Rom. 16:3-5; 1 Cor. 16:19; 2 Tim. 4:19).

I. MINISTRY OF HOSPITALITY (Acts 18:1-4; Rom. 12:13; 3 John 5-8)

A. Hospitality Extended (Acts 18:1-4)

[1]After these things Paul departed from Athens, and came to Corinth; [2]And found a certain Jew named Aquila, born in Pontus, lately come from Italy, with his wife Priscilla; (because that Claudius had commanded all Jews to depart from Rome;) and came unto them. [3]And because he was of the same craft, he abode with them, and wrought: for by their occupation they were tentmakers. [4]And he reasoned in the synagogue every Sabbath, and persuaded the Jews and the Greeks.

On his second missionary journey, the apostle Paul retraced the steps he had taken on his first missionary journey by revisiting churches he had established earlier in Syria, Cilicia, Phrygia, and Galatia. He paused at Troas, after being forbidden by the Holy Spirit to preach in Bithynia and Asia. But, after experiencing a vision in which a man urged him to "come over into Macedonia, and help us" (Acts 16:9-10), he crossed the Aegean Sea into Europe, landing at the port city of Neapolis. He went about ten miles inland to Philippi (v. 12) and there birthed, with the Lord's help and the assistance of Silas and Timothy, the wonderful church that supported him consistently throughout the rest of his ministry (see Phil. 4).

After undergoing extreme persecution in Philippi, Paul went westward across Macedonia and, with his assistants, established two other strong churches in that province, Berea and Thessalonica. Constant opposition dogged Paul's steps, but he pressed on into the Roman province of Achaia, stopping in Athens, where he witnessed fearlessly and brilliantly to Greek intellectuals, but with few converts (Acts 17). He then went to Corinth, where he soon met a vibrant Christian couple named Aquila and Priscilla (ch. 18).

While Aquila and Priscilla had more recently come to Corinth from Rome, driven out with all other Jewish people by the edict of Claudius, Aquila was "a native of Pontus, a region in northern Asia Minor on the south shore of the Black Sea" (*The Expositor's Bible Commentary*). We are not told Priscilla's country of origin, but some speculate that she might have come from a prominent family in Rome. Paul had likely been looking for fellow "tentmakers" (v. 3). As a Rabbi, Paul was required to have a trade to support himself to conform to Jewish law, and he had chosen tent-making (or perhaps his parents had chosen it for him).

Paul found Aquila and Priscilla, likely already converts to Christianity, and began to live and work with them. We can assume they were well located for commerce and for witnessing in Corinth. What better way could there be to witness to their faith than in their shop as they served customers?

As was his custom, Paul visited the Jewish synagogue in Corinth on the Sabbath day and confronted the Jews meeting there with the claims of Jesus Christ as Messiah and Lord. Paul "reasoned" with them (v. 4). As a Jewish rabbi, Paul knew the Old Testament thoroughly. As a result, he was able to present evidence for the messiahship of Jesus of Nazareth in relation to prophecy throughout the Old Testament (with likely emphasis on the Psalms and the prophets Isaiah, Micah, and Zechariah). Priscilla and Aquila must have assisted him as they also pursued their own witness to Christ.

Paul also witnessed effectively to the original population of Corinth—the Greeks. And his tactics likely were quite different from those he used in dialoging in the Jewish synagogue. And Priscilla and Aquila certainly pursued relentlessly the Greek population surrounding them every day. Paul's letters indicate that this witness to Greeks was effective.

---

1. Describe the circumstances that joined Paul with Aquila and Priscilla (vv. 1-2).
2. Explain the relationship between Paul and this couple (v. 3).
3. How did Paul minister in Corinth (v. 4)?

> "Our love to God is measured by our everyday fellowship with others and the love it displays."—Andrew Murray

---

B. Hospitality Practiced (Rom. 12:13)

13Distributing to the necessity of saints; given to hospitality.

In Romans 12, the apostle Paul gives practical instructions for Christian living growing out of the opening injunction: "I beseech you therefore, brethren, by the mercies of God, that ye present your bodies a living sacrifice, holy, acceptable unto God, which is your reasonable service. And be not conformed to this world: but be ye transformed by the renewing of your mind, that ye may prove what is that good, and acceptable, and perfect, will of God" (vv. 1-2).

In verse 9, Paul says, "Love must be sincere" (NIV). The succeeding verses present a variety of instructions that, in essence, show what sincere love looks like when honestly and faithfully lived out. The directive at the end of verse 13 to "practice hospitality" (NIV) is one of those ways of living out genuine love.

Christians in the first century had great need to practice hospitality, and Priscilla and Aquila were fine examples. There were few places to stay when brothers and sisters in the Lord were traveling, and "the need among Christians was exacerbated by the many traveling missionaries and other Christian workers" (Douglas Moo, *The Epistle to the Romans*). A pragmatic need does not explain sufficiently a Biblical injunction, for we must obey God's Word whether it proves practical in a given situation or not. However, the pragmatic need can lead to more frequent exercise of a spiritual grace. New Testament writers frequently advise the regular practice of hospitality (see 1 Tim. 5:10; 1 Peter 4:9; 3 John 8).

A Dynamic Ministry Couple

- How can you and your church better follow this command?

Hospitable Home

My family was rather poor in the early 1950s, but also enthusiastic members of a Pentecostal congregation. My dad was a skilled laborer at a large sawmill in Doctortown, Georgia. We also grew several acres of vegetables for feeding our large family and corn for feeding both us and several farm animals. We always ate well and nutritiously, but not lavishly.

Nonetheless, practically every Sunday afternoon, young couples from the local church could be found eating at our table. My parents demonstrated the fact that Christian hospitality was not dependent on abundant means, but that it instead rested in a common faith, a genuine Scriptural hope, and an abundance of sincere Christian love.—Sabord Woods

---

C. Hospitality Denied (3 John 5-8)

(3 John 5-7 is not included in the printed text.)

⁸We therefore ought to receive such, that we might be fellowhelpers to the truth.

In the third letter of the apostle John, we read about a church leader's persistent refusal to practice Christian hospitality. As John wrote to Gaius, a brother in that church, he informed him of Diotrephes' denial of hospitality to traveling missionaries (vv. 9-10). Diotrephes apparently was a haughty "church boss" insistent on total control of whatever happened in the local church. Despite the respect accorded John by other believers because of his role as an apostle, Diotrephes rejected both the apostle and the traveling Christian teachers he had sent out.

The apostle provided for Gaius a contrasting example—Demetrius, a brother in that particular body of believers who was quite willing to receive traveling Christians (vv. 11-12). Already, Gaius was "faithful" in hosting Christian "brothers, even though they [were] strangers to [him]" (v. 5 NIV). Those traveling ministers had told others about Gaius' love. They deserved to be treated in a godly manner as they were traveling in God's name (vv. 6-7).

Verse 8 offers an important ministry principle, as explained by Albert Barnes: "All Christians cannot go forth to preach the Gospel, but all may contribute something to the support of those who do; and . . . have a joint participation in the work of spreading the truth."

Luke's characterization in Acts 18:1-4 of Aquila and Priscilla stands in great contrast to John's description of Diotrephes. Aquila and Priscilla (the order of their names varying, but Priscilla's name coming first in four of six occurrences in Scripture) demonstrated great dedication to Christ and His work in the world. This couple led house churches, but never seemed eager to establish their own precedence. Rather, they always deferred to the apostle Paul, hosting him, traveling with him, and praised by him.

---

1. How did John commend Gaius (v. 5), and how did others commend him (v. 6)?
2. How should local congregations treat godly evangelists, and why (vv. 7-8)?

> "The chief characteristic of Christian leaders, [Jesus] insisted, is humility, not authority, and gentleness, not power."—John Stott

---

II. MINISTRY OF DISCIPLESHIP (Matt. 28:18-20; Acts 18:18-19, 24-28)

A. Discipleship Commanded (Matt. 28:18-20)

¹⁸And Jesus came and spake unto them, saying, All power is given unto me in heaven and in earth. ¹⁹Go ye therefore, and teach all nations, baptizing them in the name of the Father, and of the Son, and of the Holy Ghost: ²⁰Teaching them to observe all things whatsoever I have commanded you: and, lo, I am with you always, even unto the end of the world. Amen.

Priscilla and Aquila were superb examples of first-century believers who were dedicated to living out and propagating the gospel of Christ as they traveled from one locale to another—whether because of spiritual opposition or evangelistic opportunity. Whether or not they knew the Great Commission as expressed at the conclusion of Matthew's Gospel, this couple lived and worked in the spirit of it.

Jesus had asserted His universal authority under His heavenly Father—"All authority in heaven and on earth has been given to me" (v. 18 NIV). Though two separate persons, the Father and the Son always acted in total unity. In verse 19, the Holy Spirit is also mentioned in reference to how converts should be baptized—"in the name of the Father and of the Son and of the Holy Spirit" (NIV).

In the Great Commission, the Trinity is cooperatively commanding the church of Jesus Christ to go throughout the world and "make disciples" (v. 19 NIV)—faithful followers and learners who seek to receive and emulate the principles of Christian faith and standards for daily living established in the four Gospels. Discipleship is a teaching-learning process. Believers learn to "obey everything" Christ commands (v. 20 NIV) as they absorb into their inner being the character and teaching of Jesus.

In studying the lives of Priscilla and Aquila, we see obedience to the Great Commission. They went, they worked, they modeled, they taught.

---

1. Describe the authority of Jesus (v. 18).
2. What did Jesus authorize His followers to do (vv. 19-20)?
3. What did Jesus promise His witnesses (v. 20)?

> "The greatest form of praise is the sound of consecrated feet seeking out the lost and helpless."—Billy Graham

---

B. Discipleship in Transit (Acts 18:18-19)

18And Paul after this tarried there yet a good while, and then took his leave of the brethren, and sailed thence into Syria, and with him Priscilla and Aquila; having shorn his head in Cenchrea: for he had a vow. 19And he came to Ephesus, and left them there: but he himself entered into the synagogue, and reasoned with the Jews.

Paul remained in Corinth about eighteen months, reasoning with opponents and prospects with the help of Silas, Timothy, Priscilla, and Aquila. But Paul had become eager to return to "home base" in Antioch of Syria. Earlier, Paul had taken what was likely a Nazarite vow, which involved not cutting his hair for a period of time, and which he concluded by shaving his head at the port city of Cenchrea. Accompanied by Priscilla and Aquila, he then sailed to Ephesus.

Priscilla and Aquila would remain in Ephesus for a long while, having transferred their tent-making trade to that city. The ministry duo continued the evangelistic work started by Paul at Ephesus, while he made his way on to Syria to conclude his second missionary journey by reporting to the church in Antioch. Priscilla and Aquila would seek out prospects for conversion to Christian faith in Ephesus and begin to create, under the guidance of the Spirit, another fledgling church in their house.

• Describe Paul's continuing relationship with Priscilla and Aquila.

> "I care not where I go, or how I live, or what I endure so that I may save souls. When I sleep I dream of them; when I awake they are first in my thoughts."—David Brainerd

---

C. Discipleship Exemplified (vv. 24-28)

24And a certain Jew named Apollos, born at Alexandria, an eloquent man, and mighty in the scriptures, came to Ephesus. 25This man was instructed in the way of the Lord; and being fervent in the spirit, he spake and taught diligently the things of the Lord, knowing only the baptism of John. 26And he began to speak boldly in the synagogue: whom when Aquila and Priscilla had heard, they took him unto them, and expounded unto him the way of God more perfectly. 27And when he was disposed to pass into Achaia, the brethren wrote, exhorting the disciples to receive him: who, when he was come, helped them much which had believed through grace: 28For he mightily convinced the Jews, and that publicly, shewing by the scriptures that Jesus was Christ.

After telling of the continuation of Paul's journey (vv. 20-23), Luke returned to Priscilla and Aquila's life in Ephesus. This dedicated couple soon came into contact with the learned and eloquent Apollos, an Alexandrian Jew privileged to be brought up in the city where the greatest library of ancient times existed and where the Septuagint translation of the Old Testament, the primary Scripture of first-century Christians, had been created. They heard this master of rhetoric speak convincingly of the gospel of Jesus Christ according to his understanding gained from followers of John the Baptist, and possibly also from disciples of the Lord Jesus.

But when Priscilla and Aquila heard Apollos, however much they admired his eloquence and spiritual fervor, they detected doctrinal errors. Since they were tactful and loving servants of Jesus, they took Apollos aside to discuss the limitations and flaws in his message. They desired to help him come to a greater fullness of understanding.

Various interpreters arrive at different conclusions as to the nature of Apollos' limitations in understanding the Gospel. The consensus is that Apollos had been immersed according to John the Baptist's baptism for repentance and had learned much about the gospel of Jesus Christ, but lacked full understanding of Jesus' blood atonement. Old Testament prophecies of the coming Messiah mention both a suffering Messiah and a reigning Messiah. Perhaps Apollos did not understand fully the redemptive suffering of the Messiah that would result in the spiritual salvation of all repentant men, women, and children.

Apollos' water baptism must have been found acceptable since there is no record of a re-baptism; while in Acts 19, disciples baptized according to John's baptism would be required to be baptized again. It is significant that Apollos accepted Priscilla and Aquila's corrective teaching. He obviously had great confidence in this missionary couple, and they must have been solid in their convictions, and plausible and convincing in their arguments, for this brilliant man to accept their ministry to him and humbly correct his misunderstanding.

---

1. Describe how Apollos was "mighty" and "fervent" (vv. 24-25).
2. How did Aquila and Priscilla minister to Apollos (v. 26)?
3. Describe Apollos' ministry in Achaia (vv. 27-28).

> "My principal method for defeating error and heresy is by establishing the truth. One purposes to fill a bushel with tares; but if I can fill it first with wheat, I may defy his attempts."—John Newton

---

III. PASTORAL MINISTRY (Rom. 16:3-5; Eph. 4:11-12)

A. Partners in Pastoral Ministry (Rom. 16:3-5)

³Greet Priscilla and Aquila my helpers in Christ Jesus: ⁴Who have for my life laid down their own necks: unto whom not only I give thanks, but also all the churches of the Gentiles. ⁵Likewise greet the church that is in their house. Salute my wellbeloved Epaenetus, who is the firstfruits of Achaia unto Christ.

In the conclusion of his epistle to the church in Rome, Paul included greetings to a number of friends and former associates, apparently residing in Rome at the occasion of Paul's writing. Near the beginning of that list stood Priscilla and Aquila, who by now had left Ephesus and returned to Rome (only later to return to Ephesus). Paul called them his "fellow workers in Christ Jesus" (v. 3 NKJV). We have seen already why Paul so designated them since we have viewed their association with him in both Corinth and Ephesus. They had allowed Paul to live in their house and work with them at their mutual trade, providing him a trade and a place of daily witness.

We don't know exactly on what occasion these friends of Paul hazarded their own lives to protect Paul's (v. 4); it might have been in Corinth when Jews in the synagogue "became abusive," causing Paul to shake "out his clothes in protest" and to say, "Your blood be on your own heads! I am clear of my responsibility" (Acts 18:6 NIV). Aquila and Priscilla were certainly there to assist him despite personal risk to their own valuable and much-loved "necks" (Rom. 16:4).

---

* What did Priscilla and Aquila do for Paul?

> "If the ultimate, the hardest, cannot be asked of me; if my fellows hesitate to ask it and turn to someone else, then I know nothing of Calvary love."—Amy Carmichael

---

B. Ministry Offices (Eph. 4:11-12)

[11]And he gave some, apostles; and some, prophets; and some, evangelists; and some, pastors and teachers; [12]For the perfecting of the saints, for the work of the ministry, for the edifying of the body of Christ.

Paul designates, under the inspiration of the Spirit, four orders of Christian ministry—apostles, prophets, evangelists, and pastor-teachers. Clearly, this classification of set-forth believers is seen as a gift given by the crucified Christ to His church. Priscilla and Aquila qualified as gifts to God's church—perhaps as evangelists and teachers, but surely as pastors who nurtured believers, modeled them, and interceded on their behalf. They were a pastoral team, with her role being as significant as his.

Paul named three crucial purposes for the existence and service of the orders of ministry: "the perfecting of the saints . . . the work of the ministry . . . the edifying of the body of Christ" (v. 12). Aquila and Priscilla were deeply engaged in the fulfillment of each of these purposes. The first has to do with the growth in maturity of the "saints"—believers who are set apart by Jesus Christ through His sanctifying blood. God views us as fully sanctified in Christ, but in practice in this present age, we must participate with God in a perfecting process of equipping and training. If we are pleasing God in our daily walk, we are in constant forward and upward motion.

Second, "the work of the ministry" is service to the saints—assisting them according to their individual need, whether financial, spiritual, emotional, or nutritional. Priscilla and Aquila helped to fulfill this divinely mandated aspect of Christian ministry as a team every day in whatever place they were needed.

Third, to *edify* is to "build up." We build up by blessing. We bless by both word and action. A positive Scriptural word is a Biblical blessing. We thereby fill a person's emotional tank, as well as his or her spiritual container, to capacity. If leaders perform Christ's ministry purpose of building up the saints, His local and universal body will be enabled to function as Jesus Christ intended it to function—planting, watering, cultivating until maturity in Christ is attained.

In Paul's last known written document, the apostle took special notice of Aquila and Priscilla. He told Timothy, "Salute Prisca [Priscilla] and Aquila" (2 Tim. 4:19). He wanted Timothy to serve as his proxy in giving them a "holy kiss," an acceptable Christian greeting in this early formative stage of God's church because it was customary in that time and place. Since Timothy most likely was ministering as a bishop and an evangelist in Ephesus then, Paul wanted him to greet this remarkable couple who could bring sustenance, ministry assistance, and intimate spiritual fellowship wherever God and circumstance led them.

---

1. How are apostles and prophets different?
2. What is an evangelist?
3. Can someone be a pastor without being a teacher? Why or why not?
4. What is the responsibility of God-called leaders (v. 12)?

"Teaching may be less dramatic than evangelism, less emotional than prophecy, but it is no less important."—Charles W. Conn

---

CONCLUSION

When twentieth-century Pentecostalism was bursting into significant growth in the mid-century South, many "saints" in local congregations resembled Priscilla and Aquila in their fervent spiritual dedication. Witnessing of their salvation and the indwelling, empowering presence of the Holy Spirit was the norm, not the exception. Their homes were typically open to both fellow believers and to needy unsaved members of the surrounding community. Have we lost something of our earlier zeal? Perhaps methods of outreach have changed, but our consecration and personal witness must not change. We must, like Priscilla and Aquila, view our trades or professions as spiritual vocation—as means to witness through our Christian lifestyle and spoken testimony.

GOLDEN TEXT CHALLENGE

"I THEREFORE, THE PRISONER OF THE LORD, BESEECH YOU THAT YE WALK WORTHY OF THE VOCATION WHEREWITH YE ARE CALLED" (Eph. 4:1).

The term *walk* implies daily living or a lifestyle. Our society today advocates living for the moment, much like a sprinter running the 100-yard dash. Our life in Christ must be continuous without ceasing, not as the sprinter running for a short time and then taking a break.

The dictionary defines *worthy* as "useful, valuable, respectable, or admirable." *Vocation* is defined as a "profession," especially one to which an individual is particularly suited. These traits should be exemplified on the job, and, as Christians, we must remember that our conduct in every setting will have great impact on all those who observe us. But God's Word is speaking to a different kind of *vocation*, a higher calling: "But all these worketh that one and the selfsame Spirit, dividing to every man severally as he will. For as the body is one, and hath many members, and all the members of that one body, being many, are one body: so also is Christ" (1 Cor. 12:11-12).

As members of the body of Christ, we all have important jobs—vocations that require us to live daily at a standard much higher than this world would have us live. We must live every day as respectable, valuable members of the body of Christ.

Daily Devotions:

M. Help the Poor • Leviticus 25:35-38
T. Do Good • Micah 6:6-8
W. Serve God in Righteousness • Malachi 3:16-18
T. Salt and Light • Matthew 5:13-16
F. Barnabas Befriends Paul • Acts 9:23-31
S. Serve God and One Another • 1 Peter 4:7-11

A Living Hope

1 Peter 1:1—2:3

Unit Theme:
First and Second Peter and Jude

Central Truth:
God, through Christ, gives us a hope that orders our lives.

Focus:
Acknowledge and live consistent with our hope in Jesus Christ.

Context:
Simon Peter's first epistle was probably written in Rome around AD 64.

Golden Text:
"Blessed be the God and Father of our Lord Jesus Christ, which according to his abundant mercy hath begotten us again unto a lively hope by the resurrection of Jesus Christ from the dead" (1 Peter 1:3).

Study Outline:
  I. **Born Again to Hope** (1 Peter 1:1-5)
 II. **The Basis of Our Hope** (1 Peter 1:6-12)
III. **Living by Hope** (1 Peter 1:13—2:3)

INTRODUCTION

Simon Peter was a native of Bethsaida, a village on the northeastern tip of the Sea of Galilee (John 1:44). He made his living as a fisherman along with his father, Jonas, and his brother Andrew (vv. 40, 42). After his marriage, Simon and his wife apparently moved to a nearby town, Capernaum (see Matt. 8:5, 14). The record does not show whether they had any children.

Andrew became convinced that Jesus was the Messiah. He then introduced Simon personally to Jesus (John 1:41-42). On this occasion, Simon was given the additional name of *Cephas* (Aramaic), or *Peter* (Greek), both meaning "a rock." Shortly after this event, Christ called Peter to become a full-time follower or disciple (Matt. 4:18-20). Peter was the first to be chosen by Jesus to be one of the Twelve from among His followers. He became the leading member of this select group during the remaining years of Christ's earthly ministry. He also became the leading apostle during the early days of the Church.

Peter wrote his letter to "the strangers scattered throughout Pontus, Galatia, Cappadocia, Asia, and Bithynia" (1 Peter 1:1). The letter has several purposes: to explain the relationship of trials to God's purpose in salvation (vv. 2-12); to provoke the readers to lives of holiness, love, growth, and testimony (1:13—2:12); to call for submission of believers to civil authorities (vv. 13-17), of servants to masters (vv. 18-25), and of wives to husbands (3:1-8); to discuss the proper attitude of believers to suffering (3:9—4:19); to give guidelines to the elders for the proper performance of their ministry (5:1-4); to call them to humility (vv. 5-7); to warn them against the tactics of Satan (vv. 8-11); and to send greetings (vv. 12-14).

I. BORN AGAIN TO HOPE (1 Peter 1:1-5)

A. Chosen (vv. 1-2)

¹Peter, an apostle of Jesus Christ, to the strangers scattered throughout Pontus, Galatia, Cappadocia, Asia, and Bithynia, ²Elect according to the foreknowledge of God the Father, through sanctification of the Spirit, unto obedience and sprinkling of the blood of Jesus Christ: Grace unto you, and peace, be multiplied.

Peter wrote this letter not as a fisherman from Galilee, but as an apostle of Jesus Christ, as a man sent from God. He identified his readers as "strangers" in the world. His reference was to Jewish Christians who were scattered over various areas.

The readers were identified as individuals whom God knew and chose. They became the chosen ("elect") when they accepted God's call to salvation. God decreed a plan of redemption in which Christ would die for all. Anyone who calls upon Him will be saved. Thus, Paul could write that those whom God "foreknew, He also predestined to be conformed to the image of His Son" (Rom. 8:29 NKJV).

Peter attributed the work of sanctification to the ministry of the Holy Spirit. God the Father calls and elects, but the Holy Spirit brings us to the place of conviction, conversion, and cleansing. Through the sanctifying work of the Holy Spirit, believers are taught to obey Jesus Christ. The disciples demonstrated this inner work when they determined they would obey God, even if it meant suffering and death.

The apostle prayed that the blessing and peace of God would be with his readers in an ever-increasing measure. Believers are always in need of God's grace. Only through His grace can we find a satisfying, fulfilling lifestyle.

• How does the Trinity work together in our salvation?

> "There are two great truths which from this platform I have proclaimed for many years. The first is that salvation is free to every man who will have it; the second is that God gives salvation to a people whom He has chosen; and these truths are not in conflict with each other in the least degree."—Charles Spurgeon

---

B. A Living Hope (vv. 3-5)

³Blessed be the God and Father of our Lord Jesus Christ, which according to his abundant mercy hath begotten us again unto a lively hope by the resurrection of Jesus Christ from the dead, ⁴To an inheritance

incorruptible, and undefiled, and that fadeth not away, reserved in heaven for you, ⁵Who are kept by the power of God through faith unto salvation ready to be revealed in the last time.

The people to whom Peter wrote were entering a period of severe trial. The apostle wanted to send them encouragement and support. So, in this letter he burst forth with praise. The reason for such gratitude is the believer's hope. Paul was preeminently the apostle of faith, John the apostle of love, and Peter the apostle of hope.

What is there about this "lively hope" that caused Peter to rejoice and bless God? God has made us His children by regeneration and heirs to an incorruptible inheritance in heaven. This means something follows our earthly life. Life does not vanish into nothingness at death, leaving no trace of its glory. "I am the resurrection, and the life," Jesus said; "he that believeth in me, though he were dead, yet shall he live." Then He asked, "Believest thou this?" (John 11:25-26).

Beyond the kingdom of this world is a kingdom forever with the Father. This inheritance is permanent: "incorruptible, and undefiled, and that fadeth not away" (v. 4). These three descriptions all imply permanence, but they treat it in different ways. "Incorruptible" refers to spiritual, not material, inheritance. The blessedness of that state will not depend on anything that can decay. "Undefiled" means untainted, unblemished by earthly defects and human infirmities. "That fadeth not away" means this spiritual inheritance is everlasting.

Peter also said this inheritance is certain—"reserved in heaven for you, who are kept by the power of God" (vv. 4-5). No earthly heritage is sure, but this one is. "Reserved in heaven" means it is safe. That we are "kept by the power of God" means we are safe in God's love.

Our inheritance is made sure to us by the resurrection of Jesus Christ from the dead. Jesus Christ—our brother (see Heb. 2:11-12, 17), representative, and Lord—identified Himself with us in life and death, and made us one with Himself in resurrection, which is God's seal (the amen) to all Jesus said and did.

---

1. Explain the phrase "lively hope" (v. 3).
2. Describe the inheritance of Christians (v. 4).
3. How can a believer be faithful until the end (v. 5)?

> "God's faithfulness has never depended on the faithfulness of His children."—Max Lucado

---

II. THE BASIS OF OUR HOPE (1 Peter 1:6-12)

A. A Glorious Faith (vv. 6-8)

⁶Wherein ye greatly rejoice, though now for a season, if need be, ye are in heaviness through manifold temptations: ⁷That the trial of your faith, being much more precious than of gold that perisheth, though

it be tried with fire, might be found unto praise and honour and glory at the appearing of Jesus Christ: ⁸Whom having not seen, ye love; in whom, though now ye see him not, yet believing, ye rejoice with joy unspeakable and full of glory.

First Peter reflects for us, as in a mirror, the dark shadows that were gathering over the scattered saints—partakers of Christ's suffering. They were rebuffed for doing well, reviled and punished, exposed to terror, tried in fiery trials, and reproached for the name of Christ. They experienced the same afflictions as brethren throughout the world. To suffer as Christians sometimes meant the loss of business, reputation, and home; desertion by parents, children, and friends; misrepresentation, hatred, and even death.

For us, trials generally come from three sources: those brought on us by others; those caused by our own sins, mistakes, and indiscretions; and those permitted as tests from God, our Father. No wonder that, at times, the heart is bowed down beneath such pressures.

According to the apostle, our joy can grow out of "manifold" trials—joy experienced even during times of sorrow (v. 6). We ought to always rejoice. The idea that a believer ought to rejoice *only* is as foolish as it is false; but it is possible *always* to rejoice, "as sorrowful, yet always rejoicing" (2 Cor. 6:10 NKJV). In Peter's words, we have grounds for joy; they are *faith*, *hope*, and *love*.

The heaviness—grief, suffering—that we have to endure through the trials of life is for the purpose of proving and purifying our faith. "Trial" (1 Peter 1:7) is equivalent to *trying, testing, proving.* Is it not in darkness that our faith is tested? "Heaviness" (v. 6) is the time when we discover who we are. Just as gold is tested by fire and the impurities removed so all that remains is pure gold, when we are tried by fire, our pure faith will prove its genuineness—with the result of bringing praise, honor, and glory to God.

The heaviness of our trials contributes to the enlargement of our hope. In every aspect of life, we are cheered on through difficulties by the hope of eternal life. Hope points us to the blessed end and whispers, "Do not give up." We shall not only survive the storms of life, but we shall also be stronger became of them.

---

1. Why is the phrase "for a little while" significant (v. 6 NASB)?
2. When do our trials bring glory to Christ (v. 7)?
3. How does verse 8 describe the relationship Christ wants to have with you?

"Trials should not surprise us, or cause us to doubt God's faithfulness. Rather, we should actually be glad for them. God sends trials to strengthen our trust in Him so that our faith will not fail. Our trials keep us trusting; they burn away our self-confidence and drive us to our Savior."—Edmund Clowney

B. An Everlasting Future (vv. 9-12)

⁹Receiving the end of your faith, even the salvation of your souls. ¹⁰Of which salvation the prophets have enquired and searched diligently, who prophesied of the grace that should come unto you: ¹¹Searching what, or what manner of time the Spirit of Christ which was in them did signify, when it testified beforehand the sufferings of Christ, and the glory that should follow. ¹²Unto whom it was revealed, that not unto themselves, but unto us they did minister the things, which are now reported unto you by them that have preached the gospel unto you with the Holy Ghost sent down from heaven; which things the angels desire to look into.

Our present existence becomes unbearable if this life is all there is. But Peter said salvation awaits believers. The end result of our faith is our eternal salvation, brought to us by God's grace (vv. 9-10).

The Old Testament prophets "spoke of the grace that was to come . . . [through] the sufferings of Christ and the glories that would follow" (vv. 10-11 NIV). Now we who believe on Christ are living in that grace. If the gifted prophets and holy angels found sacred joy in pondering the provisions of God's love and mercy, how urgent it becomes for us to heed the Gospel which offers gracious pardon, a spiritual cleansing, and a dauntless life!

---

1. Describe "the end" for Christians (v. 9).
2. What advantage do we have over the ancient prophets (vv. 10-12)?

"In Christ, troubles are turned into triumph, so in Him we look at what is coming as the times of the greatest triumphs the world has ever known! The conclusion of all things is that we win! The cross will prevail. This is the foundational truth that all of our understanding of these times must be based on."—Rick Joyner

---

III. LIVING BY HOPE (1 Peter 1:13—2:3)

A. Called to Be Different (vv. 13-14)

¹³Wherefore gird up the loins of your mind, be sober, and hope to the end for the grace that is to be brought unto you at the revelation of Jesus Christ; ¹⁴As obedient children, not fashioning yourselves according to the former lusts in your ignorance.

When Peter said "gird up [your] loins," he was referring to the type of clothing worn in the East. The hot climate dictated the wearing of long, loose, flowing robes. That was fine as long as the movement of the body was deliberate. But if there had to be movement in a hurry, the clothing could be hampering. Therefore, they must tuck in their clothing so as not to impede their progress.

When the Israelites were expecting the summons to leave Egypt, they stood around the tables on which the paschal lamb was smoking. They were ready for the journey with their clothes tucked in. Elijah, the prophet of fire,

---

girded himself for the swift run before Ahab's chariot from Carmel to Jezreel (1 Kings 18:46).

Peter urged his readers to guard their tastes, appetites, affections, and inclinations. "Gird up the loins of your mind" is an appropriate imagery, because sin begins in the thought life. The idea is entertained before the behavior emerges. We must not let our thoughts stream as they will; to do so puts us at great peril.

One ancient preacher said, "We must 'gird up' the habits of our souls, and trim ourselves, so as to pass as quickly and easily as possible through the thorny jungle of the world." Elders, deacons, women, aged men, young men, and young women are all urged in the New Testament to be "sober" (1 Peter 1:13), meaning "self-controlled."

Peter urged believers to "hope to the end." *Hope* motivates us, strengthening us through the discomforts of the journey. It provides inward joy that looks forward.

The object of the believer's hope is *grace*, which comes from God—His favor. Someone aptly said that *grace* is glory begun and *glory* is grace completed. So it is for the one who surrenders to Jesus Christ.

In verse 14, those who are fashioned "according to the former lusts" have allowed their natural inclinations to run wild, overthrowing wholesome restraints and asserting their own arrogant will. They live in darkness, allowing their lusts to dominate their lives. They become molded (or fashioned) by their fleshly desires, as a potter molds clay. Being ignorant of how abominable sin is, unbelievers yield to it, creating a tyrant that eventually ruins their lives.

---

1. How should Christians live (v. 13)?
2. How must we not live (v. 14)?

> "The image of Christ that is forming within us—that is life's one charge. Let every project stand aside for that."—Henry Drummond

---

B. Be Holy (vv. 15-16)
(1 Peter 1:15-16 is not included in the printed text.)

The essence of religion consists in imitating the One we worship. However, Christians cannot perfectly imitate God's holiness, because holiness is inherent in God; in believers it is acquired. In God, holiness is infinite and unchangeable; it allows no increase and no loss. Holiness in believers admits degrees and can only be maintained through walking with God. Only God can make us and keep us holy.

• Describe genuine holiness.

> "Nowhere can we get to know the holiness of God, and come under His influence and power, except in the inner chamber. It

---

> has been well said: 'No man can expect to make progress in holiness who is not often and long alone with God.'"—Andrew Murray

---

C. Called to Unity (vv. 17-21)

17And if ye call on the Father, who without respect of persons judgeth according to every man's work, pass the time of your sojourning here in fear: 18Forasmuch as ye know that ye were not redeemed with corruptible things, as silver and gold, from your vain conversation received by tradition from your fathers; 19But with the precious blood of Christ, as of a lamb without blemish and without spot: 20Who verily was foreordained before the foundation of the world, but was manifest in these last times for you, 21Who by him do believe in God, that raised him up from the dead, and gave him glory; that your faith and hope might be in God.

Holy fear, which is befitting for all Christians, is made gracious and purifying by our knowledge that the Father's eye is upon us and the Father's heart never ceases to cherish us. Verses 17-21 contain one long reason why we who have salvation through Christ should live in reverence.

Our salvation is certain. We are "elect"; we have an inheritance reserved for us, and we are kept for it. Loving Christ, we now have the salvation of our souls. The revelation of this salvation, being given through the Holy Spirit, is infallible. After all that, He bids us pass the time of our sojourning here in "fear"—an emphatic contradiction of the idea that the doctrine of grace fosters a spirit of carelessness. A reverent concern about our souls is the natural result of God's free salvation.

---

1. How should Christians conduct themselves, and why (v. 17)?
2. Describe your worth in God's eyes (vv. 18-19).
3. Why can you put your "faith and hope" in God (vv. 20-21)?

> "You will not stroll into Christlikeness with your hands in your pockets, shoving the door open with a careless shoulder. . . . It takes all one's strength, and all one's heart, and all one's mind, and all one's soul, given freely and recklessly and without restraint."
> —A. J. Gossip

D. Called to Love (vv. 22-25)

(1 Peter 1:23-24 is not included in the printed text.)

22Seeing ye have purified your souls in obeying the truth through the Spirit unto unfeigned love of the brethren, see that ye love one another with a pure heart fervently:

25But the word of the Lord endureth for ever. And this is the word which by the gospel is preached unto you.

"Love one another" is the theme of these verses. Verse 22 says that only after we have become pure through our acceptance of and obedience to the Gospel truth are we able in the highest sense to love, or to live a life of love. This is love from the heart. It is intense, sincere, genuine, and fervent. Jesus told His disciples, "By this shall all men know that ye are my disciples, if ye have love one to another" (John 13:35).

We can love as Christ commands only if we have been "born again . . . by the word of God" (1 Peter 2:23). The Gospel is "imperishable . . . living and enduring . . . [and] stands forever" (vv. 23, 25 NIV). The natural world, including all humanity, will perish (v. 24), but the born-again people of God will be raised to eternal life.

• Why is the preaching and teaching of God's Word so important?

"What does love look like? It has the hands to help others. It has the feet to hasten to the poor and needy. It has eyes to see misery and want. It has the ears to hear the sighs and sorrows of men. That is what love looks like."—Augustine

---

E. Called to Progress (2:1-3)

¹Wherefore laying aside all malice, and all guile, and hypocrisies, and envies, and all evil speakings, ²As newborn babes, desire the sincere milk of the word, that ye may grow thereby: ³If so be ye have tasted that the Lord is gracious.

Peter identified a representative selection of the evils that are harmful to the spiritual life. These are probably mentioned here rather than others because, judging from Peter's frequent exhortations to love and to be subject to one another, they represent a class of sins to which the Christians to whom he wrote were especially prone. These were the sins which most "easily beset" them (Heb. 12:1).

The term "newborn babes" (1 Peter 2:2) emphasizes there is Christian character not yet perfected in all Christians, and especially in newborn believers. As we cannot see what a baby can become, neither can we see in the newborn child of God the perfected saint bowing in the eternal glory before His throne. Spiritual maturity comes through growth. The nourishment of God's Word provides for the balanced growth of all our spiritual faculties, so we become more and more like Christ.

The graciousness of Christ is a delight to our spiritual appetite (v. 3). We who have tasted His love have developed a desire to be fed by His Word and to grow in His grace. We must come repeatedly to the Word to satisfy our appetite which, though always being fed, is ever-increasing.

---

1. Which of these five sins is most tempting to you, and how can you rid yourself of it (vv. 1-2)?

---

2. How can we know "the Lord is good" (v. 3 NIV)?

> "Gradual growth in grace, growth in knowledge, growth in faith, growth in love, growth in holiness, growth in humility, growth in spiritual-mindedness—all this I see clearly taught and urged in Scripture, and clearly exemplified in the lives of many of God's saints."—J. C. Ryle

CONCLUSION

The Christians to whom Peter wrote had never personally seen the Lord; yet, they had steadfast faith in Him. To have this faith in One whom they had never seen brought to them a joy beyond description (1 Peter 1:8). If Peter was blessed by having seen Jesus, then those who believed without having seen Him were doubly blessed. As Jesus said, "Blessed are they that have not seen, and yet have believed" (John 20:29).

This is an assurance to all of us who have lived in subsequent generations. Christ in us is our "hope of glory" (Col. 1:27).

GOLDEN TEXT CHALLENGE

"BLESSED BE THE GOD AND FATHER OF OUR LORD JESUS CHRIST, WHICH ACCORDING TO HIS ABUNDANT MERCY HATH BEGOTTEN US AGAIN UNTO A LIVELY HOPE BY THE RESURRECTION OF JESUS CHRIST FROM THE DEAD" (1 Peter 1:3).

The Christian hope is not static or passive, for its basis is on a living Lord. The hope is not in the words of Christ or even the death of Christ, but, in fact, that He arose from the dead and extends His life to all who receive Him. Believers have been "begotten," or born again, through the abundant mercy He has provided.

Daily Devotions:

M. Hope in God's Sovereignty • Exodus 6:1-8
T. Hope in God's Calling • Deuteronomy 26:16-19
W. Hope in God's Mercy • Psalm 33:18-22
T. Hope Is an Anchor • Hebrews 6:10-20
F. Hope Satisfies • Romans 5:1-5
S. The Blessed Hope • Titus 2:11-15

A Holy Nation

1 Peter 2:4-25; 5:1-11

Unit Theme:
First and Second Peter and Jude

Central Truth:
Christians are citizens of God's kingdom and live by the law of Christ.

Focus:
Understand and live worthy of our heavenly citizenship.

Context:
Simon Peter's first epistle was probably written in Rome around AD 64.

Golden Text:
"Ye are a chosen generation, a royal priesthood, an holy nation, a peculiar people; that ye should shew forth the praises of him who hath called you out of darkness into his marvellous light" (1 Peter 2:9).

Study Outline:
  I. **Chosen in Mercy** (1 Peter 2:4-10)
 II. **Imitate Christ** (1 Peter 2:11-25)
III. **Shepherding, Serving, and Standing** (1 Peter 5:1-11)

INTRODUCTION

Christians are pilgrims; but we should never forget that while our true citizenship is in heaven, we also retain citizenship on earth (see 1 Peter 2:11; Phil. 3:20). As citizens of two kingdoms, we are called to live by the principles of God's kingdom while existing physically for a time in the kingdom of Caesar (see John 14:15).

Some laws of life are common to both kingdoms. Problems arise, however, when people either (1) deny the existence of God's laws or (2) when they acknowledge them but refuse to abide by them. Even we, as Christians, can hinder God's plan when we fail to obey His law.

How are we, as Christians, different from non-Christians? We are different because we have experienced a second (or new) birth (1 Peter 1:23) and have been redeemed by the blood of Christ. We are not yet perfect, and we will not be glorified until the end of the age. Christians lead a new life between justification and glorification.

Christians are different from non-Christians because we experience a new and different estrangement. Prior to becoming Christians, we were the enemy of God; we loved the world and the world loved us. But once we became children of God, we became estranged from the world. Formerly, the world loved us, whereas now it hates us (John 15:18-19). So people, whether saved or lost, experience alienation in this life—either from God or from the world.

I. CHOSEN IN MERCY (1 Peter 2:4-10)

A. Living Stones (vv. 4-8)

(1 Peter 2:6-8 is not included in the printed text.)

⁴To whom coming, as unto a living stone, disallowed indeed of men, but chosen of God, and precious, ⁵Ye also, as lively stones, are built up a spiritual house, an holy priesthood, to offer up spiritual sacrifices, acceptable to God by Jesus Christ.

Peter referred to Christians as "living stones" (v. 5 NKJV). Perhaps the apostle was remembering that Jesus had given him a new identity as a rock (Matt. 16:17-18). Jesus also said that if men did not praise Him, the rocks would cry out in praise (Luke 19:40). Jesus, the rejected "living stone" (1 Peter 2:4), had proclaimed the truth that a dead body could be raised from the grave into everlasting life.

The Christian grows by coming to that "living stone," which had been "disallowed" by the Jews. Here was the Son of God, "chosen of God, and precious," but He did not meet the approval of men. These men discarded Him, killing Him as a worthless pretender. But He was truly *the* Living Stone.

Because we are in Him, we also are living stones. As "stones," we are being built up into a "spiritual house" (v. 5). This "building" is His body, the Church, fashioned by the Holy Spirit to be His own dwelling on earth. Peter had in mind a contrast with the Temple in Jerusalem. Those who served in that building, meant to house the Spirit of God, were no longer a "holy priesthood," because they had rejected Jesus. The Church is the temple of the Holy Spirit where sanctified men and women offer up "spiritual sacrifices, acceptable to God." Thus, the emphasis falls on the holiness of this priesthood in knowing what pleases God and is approved by Him.

Unbelievers are offended by Christ's claims and, therefore, stumble over Him (vv. 7-8), while those who believe "in Him will not be disappointed" (v. 6 NASB).

---

1. How does verse 4 contrast God's view of Jesus Christ with the world's view of Him?
2. What "spiritual sacrifices" does God command us to "offer up" (v. 5)?
3. Contrast the results of rejecting Christ with accepting Him (vv. 6-8).

"The Church is in Christ as Eve was in Adam."—Richard Hooker

B. Royal and Holy (vv. 9-10)

⁹But ye are a chosen generation, a royal priesthood, an holy nation, a peculiar people; that ye should shew forth the praises of him who hath called you out of darkness into his marvellous light; ¹⁰Which in time past were not a people, but are now the people of God: which had not obtained mercy, but now have obtained mercy.

Verse 9 continues to show what we are called to be. We are a "chosen generation." We are chosen by God's grace, not by our merit.

We are a "royal priesthood." As a "holy priesthood" (v. 5), we know how to offer the sacrifices that please the Lord. We also know how to enter His presence in deference to His holiness. As a "royal priesthood," we belong to His kingdom. We are not primarily citizens of this world; we relate to this world as citizens of His coming Kingdom. This is not a priesthood of fear but of love, knowing we are accepted in Christ.

We are a "holy nation." A *nation* is identified by certain essential characteristics: territory, sovereignty, people. As God's holy nation—the church of our Lord Jesus—our essential characteristics are similar but, in a spiritual sense, will be more fully manifested when Jesus returns.

Finally, we are a "peculiar people." This Old English phrase has led some believers to unbiblical extremes regarding holy living. However, it does not mean we are an "odd people." The Greek word for *peculiar* means "an acquisition, possession." It is also used in Ephesians 1:14, where it refers to God's people as "the purchased possession." In Old English, the word *peculiar* was popularly understood in relation to its Latin root, *peculium*, which referred to a slave held as private property. The slave was the exclusive possession of the owner. Thus, we are people who belong to one Lord and Master, the Lord Jesus Christ.

How is this possible? Verse 10 says it is because of God's mercy. Prior to Calvary, people everywhere were a dispossessed non-people. But in Christ Jesus, people of faith become "the people of God."

---

1. What has God chosen His people to *be* and to *do*, and why (v. 9)?
2. Explain what God's mercy accomplishes (v. 10).

> "The Christian is called out from the world. His life is not to be as the lives of those about him."—Harry Ironside

---

II. IMITATE CHRIST (1 Peter 2:11-25)

A. Principles for Living (vv. 11-12)

¹¹Dearly beloved, I beseech you as strangers and pilgrims, abstain from fleshly lusts, which war against the soul; ¹²Having your conversation honest among the Gentiles: that, whereas they speak against you as evildoers, they may by your good works, which they shall behold, glorify God in the day of visitation.

Peter called the believers of Asia Minor "strangers and pilgrims." A *stranger* was one who lived in a foreign country but had no citizenship rights in that country (see Acts 7:6; Heb. 11:9). The word *pilgrim* refers to a person visiting in a foreign country with no intentions of permanently remaining (Heb. 11:13). Peter reminded them that heaven is their true home and origin of citizenship. While we can and should use our national citizenship rights to good advantage to spread the Gospel, we must remember that the world is, by its sinful nature, against believers.

Because we are "strangers and pilgrims," we should abstain from fleshly lusts (1 Peter 2:11). These desires are characteristic of the citizens of this world. They "war against the soul." If they are victorious, they destroy our service for Christ. The word *war* means to have a strategy against something or someone. Thus, Satan uses fleshly lusts as a planned strategy to defeat us.

Verse 12 indicates we are to live with proper conduct ("conversation") among the Gentiles. Such a life will ultimately have its effect on worldly people and bring glory to God on the day of Christ's return.

---

1. Name some "fleshly lusts," and describe how they "war against the soul" (v. 11).
2. How can a life of Christian integrity impact unbelievers (v. 12)?

> "Be like Christ at all times. . . . We are watched; our words are caught; our lives are examined—taken to pieces."—Charles Spurgeon

---

B. Relating to Government (vv. 13-17)

(1 Peter 2:13-16 is not included in the printed text.)

¹⁷Honour all men. Love the brotherhood. Fear God. Honour the king.

The "ordinances" are governments God has instituted as the organizational framework for human community. God has not committed Himself to any particular form of government. He is concerned that leadership and laws be righteous and just. Whenever government has a certain level of righteousness, that government comes under the blessings of God. However, government can transgress those limits and demand for itself the loyalties belonging to God alone. When that occurs, government steps outside of God's blessings and falls victim to the manifestations that ultimately lead to its downfall.

In verses 13 and 14, Peter applied the principle of Christian respect for government to both the king (emperor) and to local governors, and he noted the two primary functions of government. First, it preserves law and order through "the punishment of evildoers." Government provides stability and order so offenders are removed as a threat. Second, government praises "them that do well." This means government should provide structures for goodness to be advanced and to affirm the dignity and well-being of citizens.

In verse 15, Peter showed that obedience to such government is an expression of doing God's will. This enables government to recognize the validity of Christianity and its claim that Jesus is King of kings and Lord of lords. Such a claim is not a threat to proper government. In fact, leaders in a godly government recognize that they lead under divine sovereignty and, thus, govern righteously. The nation that lives in this fashion surely is blessed!

Peter admonished Christians to live like free people, but not to use their freedom as a guise for independence from obedience to the laws of government (v. 16). Such "freedom" is nothing more than moral slavery. The way to be truly free is to live as servants of God. This servanthood is accomplished through loving the brotherhood, fearing God, and honoring the leaders in government (v. 17).

---

1. Which "ordinance of man" is hardest to abide by, yet why must we do so (v. 13)?
2. What is the purpose of good government (v. 14)?
3. How should Christians use their freedom in Christ (vv. 15-16)?
4. How do the four commands in verse 17 interrelate?

> "The obligation of human beings to support and obey human governments, while they legislate upon the principles of the moral law, is as unalterable as the moral law itself."—Charles Finney

---

C. A Purpose for Suffering (vv. 18-20)

18Servants, be subject to your masters with all fear; not only to the good and gentle, but also to the froward. 19For this is thankworthy, if a man for conscience toward God endure grief, suffering wrongfully. 20For what glory is it, if, when ye be buffeted for your faults, ye shall take it patiently? but if, when ye do well, and suffer for it, ye take it patiently, this is acceptable with God.

Peter's remarks in verses 13-17 had been oriented toward free people in the empire. Yet, he knew many Christians were household servants and slaves (v. 18). The church was the one place in ancient society where freed men, slave owners, and slaves met on equal footing with equal voice. The elder in the church could be a slave who would preach the Gospel to his master.

Peter advised servants to submit to their masters in a spirit of "fear," or respect (v. 18). Even if the master is "froward" (crooked, overbearing, harsh, dishonest), the Christian servant should maintain a godly attitude. If we suffer wrongly and patiently endure it, God regards us favorably (v. 19).

There is no merit, however, in suffering at the hands of authority because of our own misdeeds (v. 20). This suffering is just and does not count as suffering for the cause of Christ.

These principles should be applied to the contemporary workplace. Employees should serve their employers, whether harsh or understanding, with a Christian attitude.

---

1. How should you respond to an "unreasonable" boss (v. 18 NASB)?
2. What is "commendable" (v. 19 NKJV)?

> "If you and I have taken the place of owning Christ as Lord, we shall be sure to have a little bit of suffering. . . . I must give up this thing and not do the other, cost what it may, if He is Master."—G. V. Wigram

---

D. Our Sinless Example (vv. 21-23)

²¹For even hereunto were ye called: because Christ also suffered for us, leaving us an example, that ye should follow his steps: ²²Who did no sin, neither was guile found in his mouth: ²³Who, when he was reviled, reviled not again; when he suffered, he threatened not; but committed himself to him that judgeth righteously.

Peter understood that the cross of Jesus provides the clearest picture of how we are to respond to suffering unjustly: by submission to God's will and the manifestation of sacrificial love in our actions.

Peter knew firsthand what it meant to suffer for Christ. Earlier in Jerusalem, he had faced what he thought was his last night of life only to be delivered (Acts 12). That experience did not cause him to reject following Christ as too dangerous or unreasonable. Rather, he accepted that "hereunto were ye called" (1 Peter 2:21).

Christ suffered for us, leaving us an example to follow. The word *example* refers specifically to the copy a child was given to use as an example. Suffering for Christ is not reserved for a select group of holy martyrs; it is foundational for every believer. Jesus, our perfect example, was without sin (v. 22). No "guile" was found in His mouth; that is, He did not stoop to the deceit so often practiced by servants to shield themselves from punishment. When He was reviled, He did not retaliate but committed Himself to God, the righteous Judge (v. 23). We too are called to follow in His steps.

---

1. What are Christians "called" to do (v. 21)?
2. Why was Jesus able to remain silent before His accusers (vv. 22-23)?

"His great act of condescension in becoming man and His willingness to be completely humiliated in the death on the cross is set before us here as the supreme example of what our attitude should be."—John F. Walvoord

---

E. A Place of Healing (vv. 24-25)

²⁴Who his own self bare our sins in his own body on the tree, that we, being dead to sins, should live unto righteousness: by whose stripes ye were healed. ²⁵For ye were as sheep going astray; but are now returned unto the Shepherd and Bishop of your souls.

We think of suffering as a terrible experience. We do all we can to avoid pain. We want to follow Jesus, but we do not want to give up our comforts. We want the benefits of salvation, but not the responsibilities of following the Lord. Somehow we got the notion that suffering is a sign of failure, a sign of a lack of blessings.

Although we are instructed to follow Jesus' example, there is an aspect of His suffering we cannot imitate—His sinless death on the cross in atonement for our sins. Verses 24 and 25, then, must be understood as intended to elicit our gratitude rather than an attempt to follow His example in this action.

The suffering of Jesus led to our healing. This is more than healing of physical sickness; it is the healing of a sin-sick world. It brings reconciliation and peace, bears godly fruit, and leads the lost to God.

---

1. What did Christ's suffering accomplish for humanity (v. 24)?
2. Explain Christ's titles in verse 25.

> "Yes, give thanks for 'all things,' for, as it has been well said, 'our disappointments are but His appointments.'"—A. W. Pink

---

III. SHEPHERDING, SERVING, AND STANDING (1 Peter 5:1-11)

A. The Responsibility of Elders (vv. 1-4)

¹The elders which are among you I exhort, who am also an elder, and a witness of the sufferings of Christ, and also a partaker of the glory that shall be revealed: ²Feed the flock of God which is among you, taking the oversight thereof, not by constraint, but willingly; not for filthy lucre, but of a ready mind; ³Neither as being lords over God's heritage, but being examples to the flock. ⁴And when the chief Shepherd shall appear, ye shall receive a crown of glory that fadeth not away.

Since "elders" as mature overseers of the church were responsible members and most in danger of judgment, Peter's exhortation is very important. Peter, however, does not give apostolic orders here but takes his place as a fellow-elder; and with sympathetic concern, as one called to a similar responsibility, he encourages and urges them in devotion to duty.

Peter claimed to be a "witness" of Christ's sufferings and of the glory to be revealed. A proper witness is one who testifies truthfully and fearlessly of that which he has seen and heard.

Peter gave testimony of Christ's sufferings from personal observation and declared His resurrection as a guarantee of future glory. As a "partaker" of this glory (v. 1), Peter may have been referring to his presence at Christ's transfiguration (2 Peter 1:16-18). This event, then, was a preview of Christ's glory as revealed at His second coming.

In 1 Peter 5:2, the apostle gives to the elders the same command that the risen Lord had given him (John 21:16). To "feed the flock of God" involves all the duties of a shepherd to his sheep. Believers are like sheep that need food, guidance, and protection.

This is God's flock, and the elders are but under-shepherds of the Chief Shepherd. They were not to serve from a sense of compulsion but with willingness and with first concern for the will of God. Nor were they to be moved by a desire for material advantage, but rather by a desire to serve the Lord with eagerness. A pastor is not to commercialize his ministry, nor ought a Christian to join the church to promote his or her business.

In verse 3 of the text, the apostle exhorts pastors not to exercise high-handed, autocratic rule over the flock but, rather, to lead the flock by example. "Examples" connotes a pattern or model. According to Wuest, "Under-shepherds should be living patterns or models of the chief Shepherd, the Lord Jesus."

Having instructed the elders concerning their responsibilities to God's flock and the spirit in which such responsibilities should be discharged, the apostle announces the incentive for faithfulness in such a ministry (v. 4). The reward assured is a "crown of glory," and the time of reward is at the appearing of the "chief Shepherd." The expression "fadeth not away" shows the Christian servant's reward has eternal duration and value.

---

1. How does Peter describe himself (v. 1)?
2. List three traits of godly church leaders (vv. 2-3).
3. What is promised to godly leaders (v. 4)?

> "The welfare of sheep depends solely upon the care they get from their shepherd. Therefore, the better the shepherd, the healthier the sheep."—Kay Arthur

---

B. Humility and Trust (vv. 5-7)

⁵Likewise, ye younger, submit yourselves unto the elder. Yea, all of you be subject one to another, and be clothed with humility: for God resisteth the proud, and giveth grace to the humble. ⁶Humble yourselves therefore under the mighty hand of God, that he may exalt you in due time: ⁷Casting all your care upon him; for he careth for you.

The response of all members of the Christian community, both to each other and to circumstances, should reflect godly attitudes. The younger members who might be tempted to unhealthy self-assertion are exhorted to act in ready submission to their elders as church overseers and senior citizens. They were to put on humility as an apron and to express their humility in serving others, taking orders, and fitting into the life of the church. The exhortation is enforced by a quotation from Proverbs 3:34, which emphasizes that God watches the people's attitudes and actions and treats them accordingly. He is against the haughty and the proud, but to the lowly He grants favor.

In verse 6 of the text, Christians are called on to submit to the humbling process of God by yielding to such circumstances as He would allow to effect such humbling. We are to recognize "the mighty hand of God" in our circumstances and trust Him as the supreme Governor who providentially controls what happens. In this awareness and confidence, we can rightly refuse to be oppressed by anxiety or alarm, but rather throw all our cares upon the Lord who has promised to sustain us. Not only does the Lord care for His own, but He has promised to exalt us at the proper time.

Verse 7 partly quotes and partly interprets Psalm 55:22: "Cast thy burden upon the Lord, and he shall sustain thee." When troubles beset us, we cannot just shake them off as though they were unreal, but we can unload our anxieties upon our heavenly Father, who lovingly cares and desires our good.

---

1. Describe the proper relationship between younger and older Christians (v. 5).
2. Who will be exalted by God, and when (v. 6)?
3. Which cares should you *not* "cast" on God (v. 7)?

> "Do not desire to be the principal man in the church. Be lowly. Be humble. The best man in the church is the man who is willing to be a doormat for all to wipe their boots on, the brother who does not mind what happens to him at all, so long as God is glorified."—Charles Spurgeon

---

C. Steadfast in God (vv. 8-11)
   (1 Peter 5:10-11 is not included in the printed text.)

⁸Be sober, be vigilant; because your adversary the devil, as a roaring lion, walketh about, seeking whom he may devour: ⁹Whom resist stedfast in the faith, knowing that the same afflictions are accomplished in your brethren that are in the world.

Behind the forces antagonistic to the church, Peter saw another great force—the master foe, "your adversary the devil." We are given three ways by which we may resist the devil. First, we are to be *sober. Sobriety* is the opposite of *intoxication*. Anything that intoxicates strengthens the baser forces in our nature, deadening the conscience and reason. We can become intoxicated not only on drugs or alcohol but also on money, power, work, worldly status, applause, and many other things in life.

Second, we are to *be vigilant*, or watchful. Victory is sure in no other way. Sometimes Satan so takes us by surprise that we hardly know we are doing wrong until we have sinned. Take heed that he does not catch you off guard.

Third, Peter urged his readers to *be steadfast in the faith*. Faith in God is the fort from which the adversary would dislodge us, so we must keep trusting in Him even when "sufferings" come (v. 9 NKJV), realizing they are not unique to us.

"After you have suffered for a little while, the God of all grace . . . will Himself perfect, confirm, strengthen and establish you" (v. 10 NASB).

---

1. Why is the lion an appropriate symbol for Satan (v. 8)?
2. What should encourage us in our resistance of evil (v. 9)?
3. For the Christian, what follows suffering (v. 10)?

> "The great and important duty which is incumbent on Christians is to guard against all appearance of evil; to watch against the first risings in the heart to evil; and to have a guard upon our

actions, that they may not be sinful, or so much as seem to be so."
—George Whitefield

CONCLUSION

In the midst of the dark and habitual chaos of earth, a light penetrates the darkness. It cannot be extinguished; it is the light of the kingdom of God. His kingdom *has* come, in His people today, and it is yet to come as well, in the great consummation of human history.—Charles Colson (*Kingdoms in Conflict*)

GOLDEN TEXT CHALLENGE

"YE ARE A CHOSEN GENERATION, A ROYAL PRIESTHOOD, AN HOLY NATION, A PECULIAR PEOPLE; THAT YE SHOULD SHEW FORTH THE PRAISES OF HIM WHO HATH CALLED YOU OUT OF DARKNESS INTO HIS MARVELLOUS LIGHT" (1 Peter 2:9).

Christians are a chosen people. The Christian is called out of insignificance into significance. A Christian is chosen for three things: (1) *Obedience*: The Christian is not chosen to do as he or she likes but to do as God likes. (2) *Privilege*: This means a new and intimate relationship and fellowship with God through Christ will exist. (3) *Service*: A Christian's honor is being a servant of God, used for the purpose of God.

Christians are a royal priesthood. Every Christian has the right of access and approach to God, and each one must offer their work, their worship, and themselves to God. As a priest, he or she speaks to God in behalf of fellow believers and the unrighteous.

Christians are a holy nation. The basic meaning of the word *holy* in Greek is "different." When God chose us, He chose us to be different from other people. That difference lies in the fact that the Christian is dedicated to God's will and service. Other people may follow the standards of this world, but for the Christian the only law is the standard of God and the will of God.

Christians are God's special possession. In any museum, you will find ordinary things which are of value only because they were once possessed and used by some great person. The ownership gives them worth. This is true of the Christian. You may have been a very ordinary person; but when Christ came into your life, you acquired a new value, dignity, and greatness because you belong to God.

Daily Devotions:

M. God's Treasured People • Deuteronomy 7:6-9
T. The Lord Establishes His People • Psalm 118:15-24
W. Praise God for His Calling • Psalm 135:1-7
T. Called to Belong to Christ • Romans 1:1-6
F. Our Heavenly Citizenship • Philippians 3:17-21
S. Our Capital City • Revelation 21:1-7

A Holy Nation

Follow in Christ's Footsteps

1 Peter 3:8—4:19

Unit Theme:
First and Second Peter and Jude

Central Truth:
Christ has shown us how to live and die pleasing to God.

Focus:
Examine the pattern of Christ's life and follow Him in all circumstances.

Context:
Simon Peter's first epistle was probably written in Rome around AD 64.

Golden Text:
"For even hereunto were ye called: because Christ also suffered for us, leaving us an example, that ye should follow his steps" (1 Peter 2:21).

Study Outline:
  I. **Live Blamelessly** (1 Peter 3:8-17)
 II. **Live Uprightly** (1 Peter 4:1-11)
III. **Endure Suffering** (1 Peter 4:12-19)

INTRODUCTION

Simon Peter knew firsthand what it meant to live through trials, loss, and suffering. Consider some of his personal experiences recorded in the Gospels and Acts.

Peter lost it all. When Jesus called him, Peter and his brother Andrew "at once . . . left their nets and followed him" (Matt. 4:20 NIV). He left everything familiar to him—his career, his home, his security—to follow Christ.

Peter had a near-death experience. In the midst of a storm-tossed lake, Peter became frightened and began to sink. He cried out, "Lord, save me" (14:30).

Peter suffered rebuke. When Peter declared Jesus would never be killed by the religious leaders, Jesus said to him, "Get thee behind me, Satan: thou art an offence unto me" (16:23).

Peter miserably failed Christ. As Jesus was being tried, three times Peter denied knowing Him. "And he went out, and wept bitterly" (26:75).

Peter suffered physically. Peter was arrested, beaten, and threatened for preaching in the name of Jesus (Acts 5:40-41).

Peter experienced criticism. Fellow Christians accused Peter of doing wrong by winning Gentiles to Christ (11:1-3).

Peter faced certain death. When he was again arrested for preaching the Gospel, Peter was chained, locked up, and a date was set for trial (12:4-6).

In looking back at Peter's life, we can see the purposes served in his difficulties:

- By losing it all, he gained everything.
- In his near drowning, he witnessed Christ's power over nature.
- In Christ's rebuke, he heard how even Christ's followers can hinder the purposes of God.
- After denying Christ three times, the Lord restored Peter with a three-part calling (John 21:15-17).
- Through the persecution of Peter and the other apostles, the Gospel was spread and the church grew.
- In his willingness to face criticism, Peter helped open the door of the Gospel to the Gentile nations.
- Through Peter's miraculous deliverance from prison, the early church's confidence in prayer was multiplied.

I. LIVE BLAMELESSLY (1 Peter 3:8-17)

A. The Blessed Life (vv. 8-12)

⁸Finally, be ye all of one mind, having compassion one of another, love as brethren, be pitiful, be courteous: ⁹Not rendering evil for evil, or railing for railing: but contrariwise blessing; knowing that ye are thereunto called, that ye should inherit a blessing. ¹⁰For he that will love life, and see good days, let him refrain his tongue from evil, and his lips that they speak no guile: ¹¹Let him eschew evil, and do good; let him seek peace, and ensue it. ¹²For the eyes of the Lord are over the righteous, and his ears are open unto their prayers: but the face of the Lord is against them that do evil.

Believers are expected to be of "one mind" (v. 8). This term is in keeping with the expression "with one accord," found so frequently in the Book of Acts. In Philippians 2:2, Paul said, "Be likeminded, having the same love, being of one accord, of one mind."

Peter gives a list of attitudes Christians must hold in their relationships with one another. Love and respect are graces that must be prominent in all Christian living. We must love one another, have compassion for one another, and be tenderhearted and courteous to one another.

Earlier in his epistle, Peter had repeated much of Christ's teaching regarding Christian submission (2:12-20). In 3:9, he comes back to the same subject: "Do not repay evil with evil or insult with insult, but with blessing" (NIV). In Matthew 5:39, Jesus forbade His followers from seeking revenge when they are persecuted or reviled.

In verses 10-12 of our text, Peter quoted Psalm 34:12-16 to show the way of blessing and life is to do good toward others. Those who are spiteful, vindictive, and self-serving can never enjoy life. Fullness of life and the blessing of the Lord come to those who are righteous in word and deed. Anyone who is always critical or contentious merely reflects the unhappiness and the emptiness of his or her own life.

Peace does not usually come automatically. It must be sought and followed with persistence. Peace with others is dependent upon peace with God and oneself.

Verse 12 of the text should bring comfort to those who do good and condemnation to those who do evil. The eyes of the Lord are over us to protect and guide us, and His ears are sensitive to the prayers of those who live righteously. As surely as He benefits the righteous, however, just as surely will He judge those who do evil.

---

1. List five ways Christians should act toward each other (v. 8).
2. How can Christians "inherit a blessing" (v. 9)?
3. Describe the Christian's speech (v. 10).
4. What does verse 12 say about the Lord's eyes, ears, and face?

> "If God be one, let all that profess Him be of one mind, and one heart, and thus fulfill Christ's prayer, 'that they [all] may be one' (John 17:11)."—Thomas Watson

---

B. Conduct in Suffering (vv. 13-17)

13And who is he that will harm you, if ye be followers of that which is good? 14But and if ye suffer for righteousness' sake, happy are ye: and be not afraid of their terror, neither be troubled; 15But sanctify the Lord God in your hearts: and be ready always to give an answer to every man that asketh you a reason of the hope that is in you with meekness and fear: 16Having a good conscience; that, whereas they speak evil of you, as of evildoers, they may be ashamed that falsely accuse your good conversation in Christ. 17For it is better, if the will of God be so, that ye suffer for well doing, than for evil doing.

The principle that people are not punished for doing good is universal, though at times inconsistent. If the wrath of unbelievers sometimes perverts this principle, we can be sure their wrath will have a short life. Ultimately, we will be blessed for the good we do.

There is a special blessing for those who endure persecution, as Christ stated in Matthew 5:11-12. The apostles rejoiced that they were counted worthy to suffer for Christ (Acts 5:41). Peter now writes to those who might face persecution in its fiercest form. They would be ordered to denounce the Christian faith or lose their lives. Yet, Peter called upon them to have courage in the face of such danger.

A complete dedication to the Lord is the only possible way we can stand in the face of persecution. In 1 Peter 3:15, the apostle quoted from Isaiah 8:13, "Sanctify the Lord of hosts himself; and let him be your fear, and let him be your dread." Only our awe of God is able to overcome our dread of man. With a healthy fear of God, we will be able to meet the expectations of courage laid upon us (Matt. 10:28).

Because the disciples lived in a time of persecution and injustice, they were given much instruction about how they should reply to the accusations brought against them. In Mark 13:11, Jesus taught, "When they shall lead you, and deliver you up, take no thought beforehand what ye shall speak, neither do ye premeditate: but whatsoever shall be given you in that hour, that speak ye: for it is not ye that speak, but the Holy Ghost."

Once again the apostle calls his readers to a life of "good conscience" (1 Peter 3:16). If they were to suffer, then it should be as servants of the Lord and not as evildoers. Accusations will come against Christians, but our lives should be so exemplary that all accusations against us will be proven false.

Some people who are subjected to false accusations take the attitude that they would not mind suffering if they deserved it. Peter contradicts this common opinion. When suffering comes as a result of good, then it is a temporary and peripheral experience. If it is caused by our wrongdoing, then the penalties we suffer outwardly are less than our inner suffering of sin and guilt. Furthermore, suffering for righteousness' sake brings spiritual blessings to us both now and in eternity.

---

1. What is the implied answer to the question in verse 13?
2. Does verse 14 surprise you? Why or why not?
3. What does it mean to "sanctify the Lord God in your hearts" (v. 15)?
4. How must Christians prepare for and respond to opposition (vv. 15-16)?
5. What is "better," and why (v. 17)?

"Those times when you feel like quitting can be times of great opportunity, for God uses your troubles to help you grow."
—Warren Wiersbe

II. LIVE UPRIGHTLY (1 Peter 4:1-11)

A. Arm Yourselves (vv. 1-6)

(1 Peter 4:3-6 is not included in the printed text.)

¹Forasmuch then as Christ hath suffered for us in the flesh, arm yourselves likewise with the same mind: for he that hath suffered in the flesh hath ceased from sin; ²That he no longer should live the rest of his time in the flesh to the lusts of men, but to the will of God.

"Arm yourselves" (v. 1) was Peter's exhortation to those who were already suffering. The thrice-repeated "in the flesh" (vv. 1-2) was to reinforce the Christians' confidence that they could obtain victory over their persecutors just as Christ has won the victory over His.

Peter was telling his readers that those who had armed themselves with the mind of Christ had been set free from their earlier life of sin. The memory of their sinful past was to serve as a warning against any tendency to relapse into the old lifestyle.

The rest of their lifetime must be occupied with doing the will of God, which starts by knowing what His will is. As Christians, they were no longer to live "to the lusts of men, but to the will of God." The "lusts of men" refers to a life controlled by the varied sinful desires that characterize fallen human beings. The plural *lusts* indicates the many cravings of fallen human nature, while the singular *will* indicates the unitary will of God for His people.

In their pre-Christian days, the recipients of Peter's letter "wrought the will of the Gentiles" (v. 3). The six evils enumerated form a dark picture of life in the pagan world. The list is not intended to be complete. The terms are in the plural to indicate the variety and frequency of those vices. They are sins of impurity and drunkenness generally associated with open idolatry.

The evils Peter listed here were characteristic of many social parties in the towns of Asia Minor in the first century. The heathens saw a profound difference between themselves and the Christians. These godless people thought it strange that their friends who had become Christians would "no longer plunge into the flood of wild and destructive things they do" (v. 4 NLT).

The reluctance of the Christians to participate in the routine of contemporary life, civic ceremonies, and functions involving contact with idolatry caused them to be despised, and they themselves were then suspected of illicit practices. This estrangement produced irritation against, misunderstanding of, and opposition to the Christians. The verb "speaking evil of" means "to injure the reputation of" or "to defame." The persecutors of Christians will face "God the Judge of all" (Heb. 12:23) who is "ready to judge" (1 Peter 4:5). It is God's essential character to exercise judgment. Both "the quick and the dead"—people of all generations—will be called into judgment.

---

1. Describe the example Christ set (vv. 1-2).
2. What surprises ungodly people, and why (vv. 3-4)?

> "However dark and profitless, however painful and weary, existence may have become, life is not done, and our Christian character is not won, so long as God has anything left for us to suffer, or anything left for us to do."—Frederick W. Robertson

---

B. Be Good Stewards (vv. 7-11)

7But the end of all things is at hand: be ye therefore sober, and watch unto prayer. 8And above all things have fervent charity among yourselves: for charity shall cover the multitude of sins. 9Use hospitality one to another without grudging. 10As every man hath received the gift, even so minister the same one to another, as good stewards of the manifold grace of God. 11If any man speak, let him speak as the oracles of God; if any man minister, let him do it as of the ability which God giveth: that God in all things may be glorified through Jesus Christ, to whom be praise and dominion for ever and ever. Amen.

The readers of Peter's letter had suffered grievously and were told to accept it in the light of Christ's coming. This fact provided them with a further reason for abandoning a lifestyle of self-indulgence and for practicing self-discipline, prayer, and loving service.

In chapter 1, Peter had referred to "the last time" (v. 5), the appearance of Christ (v. 7), and "the revelation of Jesus Christ" (v. 13). Now, he referred to that time with the words "the end of all things is at hand" (4:7), which summarizes the Christian's anticipation concerning the future.

"Be clear minded and self-controlled" (v. 7 NIV) conveys that Christians should not become so excited by the proximity of the end that they allow it to upset the routine of their lives or to fall into excesses of any kind. If believers are to be sane and sober in the face of trials, they must develop consistent prayer habits. Being clear-minded and self-controlled are essential for unhindered prayer.

In verse 8, Peter prefaced his exhortation to love one another with the words "above all." Such love should be fervent. Peter contended for the power of love—the kind of love that covers all kinds of sins. Love's action was necessary because the believers were still weak and failing.

He enforced his advice by loosely quoting Proverbs 10:12. "Sins" denotes all that misses the mark of God's standards, including sins of weakness and moral shortcomings as well as overt acts of sin. Whenever offenses occur, love will deal with them according to the principles Jesus set forth in Matthew 18:15-17. The "multitude of sins" calls for a love that is fervent and willing to forgive "until seventy times seven" (v. 22).

Another way Christian love may find active, practical expression is showing hospitality (v. 9). The practice of hospitality was highly valued in the early church. Without its practice, the early missionary work of the church would have been greatly hindered.

There was a great deal of coming and going in the early church. The public inns were often the scene of drunkenness and impurity. The Christian faith had cut the believer off from the pagan practices that prevailed there. It was only natural, then, that Christian visitors should be invited to stay with fellow Christians.

For the first two hundred years there were no church buildings; each local congregation would meet in the home of one of the members. That practice would put hospitality to the test. "Without grudging" is a frank recognition that the practice of hospitality could easily become costly, burdensome, and irritating.

The thought passes from mutual love to mutual service (vv. 10-11). Peter implied that every Christian had received some gift from God, to be exercised in the ministry for the good of others. The Biblical principle is that all can and should minister in one way or another. Each Christian has his own distinctive function. The ultimate purpose is to glorify God through ministry.

---

1. What does verse 7 teach about prayer?
2. What can "fervent love" accomplish (v. 8 NKJV)?

3. When is "hospitality" not genuine (v. 9)?

4. How are Christians to be "good stewards" (vv. 10-11)?

> "Self-control is the exercise of inner strength under the direction of sound judgment that enables us to do, think, and say the things that are pleasing to God."—Jerry Bridges

---

III. ENDURE SUFFERING (1 Peter 4:12-19)

A. The Certainty of Persecution (vv. 12-13)

¹²Beloved, think it not strange concerning the fiery trial which is to try you, as though some strange thing happened unto you: ¹³But rejoice, inasmuch as ye are partakers of Christ's sufferings; that, when his glory shall be revealed, ye may be glad also with exceeding joy.

Peter addresses these words to his "beloved," which could be translated "divinely loved ones." The true believer has never been loved or appreciated by the world. Persecution is inevitable. That is because the Christian's ways are so different that only scorn and resentment are elicited from an unappreciative and misunderstanding world. Paul also had spoken of the tribulations and trials that would beset the true child of God (2 Pim. 3:12; Acts 14:22).

The inevitable persecution of the Christian is really a test, or "fiery trial" (1 Peter 4:12). The word literally means "a burning," but is used here to refer to a smelting furnace and the process in which gold or silver ore is purified. The believer should not "think it . . . strange" if we are tested; we should rather wonder why we are *not* tested. God is refining us; and, as He accomplishes this, there must be some sacrifice and suffering on our part. The devotion of anyone to a principle can best be measured by our willingness to suffer for that principle. We will never wear the crown if we never bear the cross.

What a joy it is to know that if we suffer with Him we will be glorified with Him (see Rom. 8:17). By suffering with Him, we not only walk as He walked, but we also share in the cross He carried. It must bring joy to the heart of the Savior to know that His followers love Him enough to suffer for Him.

• When should Christians "keep on rejoicing," and why (NASB)?

> "We were promised sufferings. They were part of the program. We were even told, 'Blessed are they that mourn.'"—C. S. Lewis

---

B. The Blessedness of Persecution (vv. 14-16)

¹⁴If ye be reproached for the name of Christ, happy are ye; for the spirit of glory and of God resteth upon you: on their part he is evil spoken of, but on your part he is glorified. ¹⁵But let none of you suffer as a murderer, or as a thief, or as an evildoer, or as a busybody in other

---

men's matters. ¹⁶Yet if any man suffer as a Christian, let him not be ashamed; but let him glorify God on this behalf.

Peter now assures the persecuted believer of a great and present blessing. The Christian who is able to bear the reproach and abuse of a sinful world is not only being tested, but he is also showing forth the presence of God's glory.

The persecutors who looked on Stephen "saw his face as it had been the face of an angel" (Acts 6:15). All the fire of the persecutors cannot keep the glory of God from shining forth from the faces of His beloved.

The phrase "resteth upon you" (1 Peter 4:14) is the translation of a Greek word used as a technical term in agriculture. "The writer speaks of a farmer resting his land by sowing light crops upon it. He relieved the land of the necessity of producing heavy crops, and thus gave it an opportunity to recuperate its strength" (Wuest). The Spirit of God, therefore, rests the tormented and persecuted believer with His refreshing power. In spite of the venom and hatred of an evil world, we can live a life that pleases God and gives glory to Him as well.

In verse 15, it is easy to understand Peter's meaning regarding murder, theft, and evildoing. The word translated "busybody" literally means "looking upon, or into, that which belongs to another." It could, first of all, mean "covetous of someone's property." Then, too, it could refer to those who pry into other people's affairs. Finally, it could mean that the Christian should not engage in any act or business that does not become a Christian. There are some things a true believer should not do.

To be a Christian in Peter's day meant that you were opposed to the Caesar cult. Christianity was a rival claimant to world worship and dominion. The followers of our Lord looked for Him to return and overthrow the Roman kingdom. For this hope the believers underwent ten bloody persecutions during the early days of the church. Peter warned his friends not to be ashamed because of this tribulation (v. 16). We should be glad to be numbered among His followers, regardless of the suffering it might entail.

---

1. What is a sign of God's blessing (v. 14)?
2. Contrast two types of suffering (vv. 15-16).

"God will not permit any troubles to come upon us, unless He has a specific plan by which great blessing can come out of the difficulty."—Peter Marshall

---

C. The Certainty of Our Safety (vv. 17-19)

¹⁷For the time is come that judgment must begin at the house of God: and if it first begin at us, what shall the end be of them that obey not the gospel of God? ¹⁸And if the righteous scarcely be saved, where shall the ungodly and the sinner appear? ¹⁹Wherefore let them that suffer according to the will of God commit the keeping of their souls to him in well doing, as unto a faithful Creator.

God always judges most sternly where privilege has been greatest. Judgment should "begin at my sanctuary" (Ezek. 9:6). God expects His children to walk uprightly; and, if He expects honor from them, how much more will be the terror of those who have not cared so much for Him as to even attempt to serve Him.

Today we live in a world that has lost the fear of God. Sin is rampant even in churches, and evil is not only tolerated, but loved. However, God, in His goodness, has chosen to redeem humanity. We merited only banishment forever; but God, who is Love, made a way of escape. He paid dearly for our salvation. He gave His best to redeem us from the power, presence, and penalty of sin.

What can the ungodly person who laughs in the face of God and mocks at His offer of salvation expect? Love that is spurned can render an awful penalty. He who goes to hell has no one to blame but himself. It was a difficult task to save us from sin, and woe be to the person who makes a mockery of Calvary!

In verse 19, Peter uses a financial term to portray what he wants to say. When someone went on a trip, he might leave left his money in the safekeeping of a friend. This friend was honor-bound to keep the funds and to return them when they were called for. So it is with our Lord. He and He alone can be trusted with the care of our souls. Did He not create the universe? Why then should we wince when it comes to committing our souls to Him?

---

1. Where must "judgment . . . begin," and why there (v. 17)?
2. Answer the question in verse 18.
3. What is God called in verse 19, and why?

> "God is not a security *from* storms. He is a security *in* storms."
> —Kathy Troccoli

CONCLUSION

"If we suffer unjustly, it is not by chance, but according to the divine will. God wills nothing or appoints nothing but for the best reason," said John Calvin. "They are led by Him to the contest . . . under His protection to give proof of their faith."

Jesus was "the Holy One and the Just" (Acts 3:14), yet He was treated unjustly. Why? That He might die, "the just for the unjust, [and] bring us to God" (1 Peter 3:18).

GOLDEN TEXT CHALLENGE

"FOR EVEN HEREUNTO WERE YE CALLED: BECAUSE CHRIST ALSO SUFFERED FOR US, LEAVING US AN EXAMPLE, THAT YE SHOULD FOLLOW HIS STEPS" (1 Peter 2:21).

The early church, for the most part, was comprised of people whose economic levels were very low. Among the church population were people who were made slaves by the Roman government. It was estimated the slave population in New Testament times reached into the millions. Each time Rome conquered, people were taken into slavery to serve the government and people of the Roman Empire. These slaves included both professional and nonprofessional people. Some of them formed a part of the early church.

In his letter, Peter instructed the Christians, whatever their life's conditions were, to live a life that would exemplify and exalt Jesus Christ, remembering that Christ himself had been reduced to the status of a criminal and executed before the eyes of many people. In a world where the persecution of Christians is rampant, suffering believers can know they are following in the steps of Christ.

Daily Devotions:

M. Rest in the Lord • Psalm 37:1-11
T. The Lord Repays • Psalm 37:12-24
W. The Lord Preserves His People • Psalm 37:25-33
T. Wait for the Lord's Justice • Psalm 37:34-40
F. Follow the Good Shepherd • John 10:11-18
S. Persist in Doing Good • Galatians 6:1-10

Make Your Salvation Certain

2 Peter 1:1—2:3, 18-22

Unit Theme:
First and Second Peter and Jude

Central Truth:
God has provided everything necessary for salvation and obedience.

Focus:
Comprehend the certainty of our salvation and praise God for it.

Context:
Peter wrote his second epistle around AD 66.

Golden Text:
"Wherefore the rather, brethren, give diligence to make your calling and election sure: for if ye do these things, ye shall never fall" (2 Peter 1:10).

Study Outline:
  I. **Sufficient for Life and Godliness** (2 Peter 1:1-11)
 II. **Remember Your Calling** (2 Peter 1:12-21)
III. **Guard Your Salvation** (2 Peter 2:1-3, 18-22)

INTRODUCTION

Peter knew it was his responsibility to remind his readers of proper Christian doctrine and ethics (1:12-13). However, he also knew he was soon to die (v. 14). In order for his readers to have a permanent written record of his teaching after his death, he purposed to write (v. 15; 3:1).

In this epistle, therefore, he wanted to encourage his readers to grow into Christian maturity (1:3-11), to explain the imminence of his death (vv. 12-15), to show how the transfiguration of Christ guaranteed His second advent (vv. 16-18), and to inform them that the truth of the Second Coming was not a concept originated by humans (vv. 19-21). He also wanted to describe the moral and doctrinal characteristics of the false teachers (2:1-22), to explain the delay in Christ's return (3:1-9), to describe the destruction of the universe in the Day of the Lord (vv. 12-13), and to motivate his readers to vigilance and growth.

I. SUFFICIENT FOR LIFE AND GODLINESS (2 Peter 1:1-11)

A. Provisions (vv. 1-4)

¹Simon Peter, a servant and an apostle of Jesus Christ, to them that have obtained like precious faith with us through the righteousness of God and our Saviour Jesus Christ: ²Grace and peace be multiplied unto you through the knowledge of God, and of Jesus our Lord, ³According as his divine power hath given unto us all things that pertain unto

life and godliness, through the knowledge of him that hath called us to glory and virtue: ⁴Whereby are given unto us exceeding great and precious promises: that by these ye might be partakers of the divine nature, having escaped the corruption that is in the world through lust.

Peter described himself in his first letter as "an apostle of Jesus Christ" (1:1). In this letter he again claimed that lofty title, but added the lowlier title of "servant" (2 Peter 1:1). Christ's servants must learn of their Master and remember they are the bondservants of Jesus Christ.

Who were the readers of Peter's epistle? They were believers. They had listened to the preaching of the Gospel. They had "obtained like precious faith" with those who had preached the faith to them. Now faith was also their possession and their inheritance.

The apostle invoked a blessing on his readers in verse 2. It is the same form of salutation he used in his first letter—the prayer that grace and peace be multiplied to them. He could express no holier wishes for them. What more could they need than God's all-sufficient grace and peace that surpasses understanding?

God's blessings of grace and peace are above what we can ask or think. We shrink from asking for blessings so far above what we deserve. But God has called us. The invitation comes from Him; freely of His own sovereign bounty He bids us come to Him. He attracts us by His own glory and virtue, manifesting His love and power in the ceaseless activity of His providence and grace. Thus He kindles in us the strong desire for the knowledge of God and satisfies that desire by the revelation of Himself. Through that full and holy knowledge, He gives us "everything we need" (v. 3 NIV). These are within our grasp, weak and helpless as we are, because God has given them.

In keeping with the worthiness of the Giver, His gifts are "great and precious" (v. 4). Two of those gifts are an escape from corruption and the privilege of partaking of the divine nature.

The sinful corruption of the world is all around us. We see the results of its workings every day, so it is hard to escape from it. As God's angels once laid hold of the hand of Lot, brought him out of the doomed city, and said to him, "Escape for thy life . . . escape to the mountain, lest thou be consumed" (Gen. 19:17), so now the Holy Spirit alone can give us strength to escape the many sins which would so easily ensnare us.

To be kept safe from sin, we need the abiding presence of the Holy Spirit. We need to be made "partakers of the divine nature" (2 Peter 1:4). This lofty state seems to be above our reach. The promise of the Spirit is a precious and exceedingly great promise. Will God indeed dwell with us? Can these poor bodies of ours become the temples of the Holy Spirit? Yes. We have His promise, and we know God is true to His word. By the gift of the Holy Spirit we can partake of the divine nature.

---

1. Explain the titles Peter ascribes to himself (v. 1).
2. What two things does Peter call "precious," and why (vv. 1, 4)?
3. How can we lead godly lives (vv. 3-4)?

B. Diligence (vv. 5-7)

⁵And beside this, giving all diligence, add to your faith virtue; and to virtue knowledge; ⁶And to knowledge temperance; and to temperance patience; and to patience godliness; ⁷And to godliness brotherly kindness; and to brotherly kindness charity.

Verse 5 is an exhortation to earnest effort. It is a call to duty. We are enjoined to be diligent in our living for Christ. God's divine power is with us, thus we should be all the more diligent. This gift of power is the ground on which the apostle based his exhortation to persevering, self-denying labor.

God's power is fighting for us. It may seem strange to be told to put our weak, trembling endeavors beside the strength of God, but the infinite and finite work together. The work is God's work. He began it and He "will perform it until the day of Jesus Christ" (Phil. 1:6). It is on this ground that we must also work—in trusting faith, love, and gratitude.

Faith is the first of God's gifts for Christian living (2 Peter 1:5). This is the precious faith of which Peter spoke so warmly throughout his first letter. Faith cannot remain alone, however. As it works, virtue issues out of its active energies.

Virtue is the holy courage which enables Christians to act with boldness in the service of Christ. In the midst of temptations, we need a resolute determination to do what is right in the sight of God, a steadfast strength of will to always choose what is good. This is the virtue of the Christian, and this is the result of faith.

With virtue comes *knowledge*. Courage and firmness may do harm unless they are directed by knowledge. Christian virtue leads to knowledge. Double-minded and undecided people waver between right and wrong. They do not develop that deep perception of good and evil that evolves with Christlike virtue. Holy discretion grows from Christian virtue.

The next grace on Peter's list is *temperance* (v. 6). The union of virtue and knowledge will produce self-control, which enables the Christian to govern his or her appetites and keep them under the rule of a Christian conscience. Without self-control there is no unity of purpose. Christians must strive to devote their energies to the service of Christ.

Side-by-side with self-control comes *patient endurance*. One who controls his or her appetites will learn to endure hardness. Some of God's people have to wait in patient endurance; others labor in active service. Both may serve with equal faithfulness. It is not work itself, but inner faithfulness of spirit, that wins praise from God.

Godliness is next on the list; it is the spirit of reverence, the holy fear of God. The godly person sets God always before him; the thought of God controls his whole life. His effort is to do all things in the name of the Lord Jesus, to live for the Lord, to seek His glory only. This holy reverence for God can only be maintained through faith and self-control. It cannot flourish in an atmosphere of worldly living.

Brotherly kindness (v. 7) naturally follows godliness. John tells us, "If a man say, I love God, and hateth his brother, he is a liar: for he that loveth not his brother whom he hath seen, how can he love God whom he hath not seen?" (1 John 4:20). God's people are knit together in one family and fellowship. As we all love the same Father in heaven, we must, for love's sake, love all who by the new birth are made the children of God.

The last grace in Peter's list is *charity*—Christian love, which must not be confined within the limits of the church. It is especially due to those who are of the household of faith, but it cannot stop there. Love comes from God, who is love and whose love is without limits. Godly love continually increases in depth and extent.

---

1. What is the foundational element of Christian living, and why (v. 5)?
2. What type of "knowledge" is vital to Christians?
3. What is the relationship between "self-control" and "perseverance" (v. 6 NASB)?
4. How is "godliness" seen in our treatment of others (v. 7)?

> "It is doubtful we are Christian in anything if we are not Christian in everything."—A. W. Tozer

---

C. Victory (vv. 8-11)

8For if these things be in you, and abound, they make you that ye shall neither be barren nor unfruitful in the knowledge of our Lord Jesus Christ. 9But he that lacketh these things is blind, and cannot see afar off, and hath forgotten that he was purged from his old sins. 10Wherefore the rather, brethren, give diligence to make your calling and election sure: for if ye do these things, ye shall never fall: 11For so an entrance shall be ministered unto you abundantly into the everlasting kingdom of our Lord and Saviour Jesus Christ.

When we possess all these qualities (vv. 5-7), we will be effective and productive "in the knowledge of our Lord Jesus Christ" (v. 8). When (by the help of divine power working in and with us) the precious graces of Christ are made our own, they will not let us be unfruitful. *Love*, the crown of all graces of Christian character, is not mere sentiment; it is active spiritual energy. It will not allow us to be idle; it must work and, in its working, it will bring us nearer to the full knowledge of Christ.

People are spiritually blind without these graces of Christian character (v. 9). They cannot discern the cross of the Lord Jesus Christ, see the blessed realities of the eternal world, or discern the spiritual powers that are working in the Church. Through spiritual blindness they forget they were cleansed from their "past sins" (NIV).

In verse 10, Peter again urged his readers to be diligent. He used the language of entreaty, saying "brethren," in tones of affectionate appeal. He knew how hard it is to persevere and how much we all need encouragement.

Working with that divine power which alone is the source of our salvation, we can "make [our] calling and election sure." While we are diligent in working out our own salvation, we feel God working in us. Doubts arise if we relax our efforts. If we put ourselves into perilous situations to which He has not called us, our doubts increase and our souls are vexed. On the other hand, earnest work for God deepens our assurance of God's love and our election to eternal life.

---

1. Who is called "nearsighted and blind" (v. 9 NIV), and why?
2. What does it mean to "make your calling and election sure" (v. 10)?
3. How must Christians be "diligent" (v. 10 NKJV), and why?

> "Spiritual blindness sets in when we cease to lift our eyes to Him."
> —*Quotable Quotations*

II. REMEMBER YOUR CALLING (2 Peter 1:12-21)

A. Concern (vv. 12-15)

(2 Peter 1:12-14 is not included in the printed text.)

[15]Moreover I will endeavour that ye may be able after my decease to have these things always in remembrance.

Peter was aware that most of his life was behind him. He knew there was a need for a continuing witness for Christ after his death. This weighed heavily on his heart. Because of this burden, he not only determined to continue a personal ministry while living, but also to write an account of his experiences so his readers and those who would come after them would have an account and a defense of the faith.

Those to whom Peter wrote had knowledge of the Gospel. They had heard it from Paul and his companions. Peter gladly acknowledged this, but he also had a duty to perform. He felt, like Paul, that he was a debtor both to Jews and Gentiles. He felt he must do his utmost to preach the gospel of Christ and to keep alive the holy flame of love in those who knew the truth. Therefore, he took advantage of every opportunity to stir his readers. He refused to relax his efforts so long as he lived.

Peter looked forward to his death with holy and peaceful calmness (v. 14). He felt it was near at hand, for he was now an old man and the hour of which the Lord had spoken could not be delayed long (see John 21:18-19). He called *death* the "putting off of his tabernacle." His earthly body was regarded as a tent. The tent was old, worn out; it could not last long. He knew, like Paul, that he had "a building of God, an house not made with hands, eternal in the heavens" (2 Cor. 5:1). Knowing this, he calmly awaited the dissolution of his earthly tabernacle. The approach of death, however, was also a reason for more earnest work while there was time.

The thought of our approaching death should be kept before us. It will help us to calmly and thoughtfully reflect upon it. Such meditation throws a clear light on the meaning of our earthly life and impresses on us the importance of finishing the work God has given us to do. Often, testimony seems to be deeper and more convincing from individuals at the point of departure, whose immediate future is in the world beyond the grave.

• What had the Lord revealed to Peter, and how did this motivate him?

> "Many Christians have enough religion to make them decent, but not enough to make them dynamic."—Kenneth Grider

---

B. Corroboration (vv. 16-18)

16 For we have not followed cunningly devised fables, when we made known unto you the power and coming of our Lord Jesus Christ, but were eyewitnesses of his majesty. 17 For he received from God the Father honour and glory, when there came such a voice to him from the excellent glory, This is my beloved Son, in whom I am well pleased. 18 And this voice which came from heaven we heard, when we were with him in the holy mount.

Peter proclaimed the certainty of the truths of the Gospel. He stated first that these truths are not "fables" (v. 16). There were many legends and religious myths circulating among the people at that time in history. However, the gospel of Christ stands apart from them all in its unimpeachable truthfulness. The story of Jesus contains wonderful works of power and wonders of grace, but all of these are related with a simplicity that bears the stamp of truth.

The Gospel truths Peter presented were verified by eyewitnesses, including Peter himself. Likewise, John wrote concerning the Christ, the Son of God, "We beheld his glory" (John 1:14). There were also many other eyewitnesses of the Lord's life and works. More than five hundred brethren at one time saw Him after He had risen from the dead (1 Cor. 15:6). But there were three who had been eyewitnesses of His majesty when He was transfigured on the mountain and declared by God to be the Son of God (Matt. 17:1-5). Peter was one of those three who had seen Jesus in His majesty on the Mount of Transfiguration (2 Peter 1:17).

Compelling evidence of the Savior's divine majesty was granted to the eyes and ears of Peter, James, and John on the day of His transfiguration. That radiant glory came from God the Father. The highly favored three had a preview of the glorious Christ whom the redeemed will behold in heaven. That blessed vision was to prepare them for and sustain them through the terrible events of crucifixion that would soon follow.

From time to time, God gives to His saints glimpses of the blessings of heaven. The Savior manifests Himself to His chosen in a different way than the world. Sometimes, those who are most highly favored with the vision of His love are called in a special manner to be partakers of His sufferings, to bear in their body the marks of the dying Lord Jesus (see Gal. 6:17).

The Lord Jesus was "despised and rejected of men" (Isa. 53:3), but He belonged to the Lord God omnipotent—He was the most holy Son of God. Surely, as God was well pleased with His Son, who "humbled himself, and became obedient unto death" (Phil. 2:8), so He is well pleased now with those to whom the only begotten Son has given power to "become children of God" (John 1:12 NKJV).

Peter, James, and John heard God speak from heaven (2 Peter 1:18). They heard it with their own ears, and there was no way to mistake it. The three chosen witnesses heard it as they were with Christ on "the holy mount." We have their testimony, the testimony of eyewitnesses.

---

1. Name some "cunningly devised fables" (v. 16) about God that people have created.
2. Of what event does Peter give a firsthand account, and why (vv. 16-18)?

> "There in front of the disciples, Jesus was completely changed. His face was shining like the sun, and his clothes became white as light."—Matthew 17:2 (CEV)

C. Assurance (vv. 19-21)

¹⁹We have also a more sure word of prophecy; whereunto ye do well that ye take heed, as unto a light that shineth in a dark place, until the day dawn, and the day star arise in your hearts: ²⁰Knowing this first, that no prophecy of the scripture is of any private interpretation. ²¹For the prophecy came not in old time by the will of man: but holy men of God spake as they were moved by the Holy Ghost.

Many to whom the apostle wrote had experienced the knowledge of the "day star" in their hearts. But what about those of whom this was not true? What could they do? For them there was the "sure word of prophecy"—the Holy Scriptures—to confirm the Gospel proclaimed by the apostles (v. 19). Let them take heed to that, and it would bring them to the dawn. Many of the predictions about the Messiah in the Old Testament had seemed vague and mysterious; but now that they had been fulfilled in Jesus of Nazareth, their meaning and truth were apparent. They could be read and pondered with a confidence not possible before.

No testimony could be more explicit to the inspiration of the Scriptures than verses 20 and 21. Christians have no difficulty accepting the New Testament. We understand that the Savior spoke the words of God by a direct and self-evident inspiration. We understand, on the strength of Christ's promise, that the apostles were inspired by a direct gift of the Holy Spirit. For the inspiration of the Old Testament we look to the New. The treatment of the Old Testament by our Lord, His frequent appeals to it in controversy, His many references to it as fulfilled in Himself, and the express assertion of its inspiration by Paul and Peter are the grounds on which we believe the Old Testament is the inspired Word of God.

---

1. What does Peter describe as "a lamp shining in a dark place" (v. 19 NASB)?
2. What do verses 20 and 21 teach about the Holy Scriptures?

> "By this process of inbreathing or inspiration, the divine mind was impressed upon the human mind so that what was written by man was written of God."—Charles W. Conn

---

III. GUARD YOUR SALVATION (2 Peter 2:1-3, 18-22)

A. False Prophets (vv. 1-3)

(2 Peter 2:2-3 is not included in the printed text.)

¹But there were false prophets also among the people, even as there shall be false teachers among you, who privily shall bring in damnable heresies, even denying the Lord that bought them, and bring upon themselves swift destruction.

Counterfeits are as old as Satan. He is the great deceiver and has in his domain everything from false Christians to false christs. Peter suggested that as Israel was constantly being led astray by false prophets, so the church would be beset with false teachers (v. 1).

These false teachers are characterized by false messages, methods, and words. Their behavior is deliberate. They know the truth but reject it. In fact, they deny the Lord who bought them. This will make their judgment even more severe.

"Pernicious ways" (v. 2) is another way of referring to "sensuality" (NASB). These false teachers deny the Christian faith because they would rather satisfy their own lusts and make it appear they are very religious.

Since many people would rather believe a lie than believe the truth, these false teachers are successful. Their followers condemn themselves and bring a disgrace to the cause of Christ.

Greed is the name of the game for the false teachers (v. 3). They use words that can mean whatever anyone wants them to mean. Anything goes if the price is right.

---

1. What is the ultimate heresy (v. 1)?
2. Describe the damage caused by false teachers (v. 2).
3. What motivates false teachers (v. 3)?
4. How can Christians distinguish between godless and godly ministers?

B. False Freedom (vv. 18-22)

(2 Peter 2:18, 22 is not included in the printed text.)

¹⁹While they promise them liberty, they themselves are the servants of corruption: for of whom a man is overcome, of the same is he brought in bondage. ²⁰For if after they have escaped the pollutions of the world through the knowledge of the Lord and Saviour Jesus Christ, they are again entangled therein, and overcome, the latter end is worse with them than the beginning. ²¹For it had been better for them not to have known the way of righteousness, than, after they have known it, to turn from the holy commandment delivered unto them.

The false teachers promise everything, yet deliver nothing (v. 18). Still they are able to allure followers. Warren Wiersbe writes of these false teachers:

> They know how to impress people with their vocabulary, inflated words that say nothing. . . . Do not be impressed with religious oratory. Apollos was a fervent and eloquent religious speaker, but he did not know the right message to preach (Acts 18:24-28). Paul was careful not to build his converts' faith on either his words or his wisdom (1 Cor. 2:1-5). Paul was a brilliant man, but his ministry was simple and practical. He preached to express and not to impress. He knew the difference between communication and manipulation (*Be Alert*).

The Preacher's Homiletic Library, Volume 5, has an interesting treatment of verse 20:

> Peter is giving a grave warning against the enslavement and entanglement of error. The Christian who thinks he needs no warnings is a fool. He may make a profession of faith and rest in a carnal security from which he has a disastrous fall. The practical aim is to encourage adherence to the full truth of Christ. This is "the way of truth" (v. 2), "the right way" (v. 15), and "the way of righteousness" (v. 21).

In verse 22, Peter quoted from Proverbs 26:11: "As a dog returneth to his vomit, so a fool returneth to his folly." People in Bible times were also aware that hogs delight in bathing in filthy mudholes. The false teachers to whom Peter referred—cleaned up on the outside, experiencing an outward moral reformation but not an inward regeneration—like the pig, went back to their wallowing in the gross forms of sin from which they had been outwardly delivered by the cleansing action of an intellectual knowledge of the Word of God (*In These Last Days*, Kenneth Wuest).

---

1. Whom do false teachers try to deceive, and how (vv. 18-19)?
2. Who is "worse off at the end than they were at the beginning" (NIV), and how (vv. 20-21)?

> "Just because a person waves a Bible and acts spiritual does not mean that his ministry is God-anointed. Religious deception is the worst of all demonic control."—Ron Phillips

---

CONCLUSION

We who are Christians can confidently declare that we are saved, having already passed from death to life. But as God continues His work in us and we work out our salvation, we await the time when we will be finally and completely saved from all sin and evil, changed into the Lord's likeness with transformed bodies.—French L. Arrington

GOLDEN TEXT CHALLENGE

"WHEREFORE THE RATHER, BRETHREN, GIVE DILIGENCE TO MAKE YOUR CALLING AND ELECTION SURE: FOR IF YE DO THESE THINGS, YE SHALL NEVER FALL" (2 Peter 1:10).

Can you know without a doubt that your name is written in the Lamb's Book of Life? Can you know without a shadow of a doubt that you are on your way to heaven? Emphatically, yes!

The apostle Peter offers tremendous reassurance to all believers. We can know without reservation that we are in a right relationship with our heavenly Father and that He is eagerly awaiting us. This assurance comes by our adopting a lifestyle of attitudes and actions that are consistent with the divine nature and Christ's teaching. This lifestyle is totally different from a "works" salvation, which consists of doing certain deeds and then receiving merit points.

Knowing the tremendous gift of life eternal, which is being offered, should be a stimulus for us to attain the assurance God wants us to have. Isn't it wonderful to know we don't have to fail? We don't have to live in uncertainty, wondering if we are ready to meet the Lord.

That's how the apostle Paul could make such a final testimony: "I have fought a good fight, I have finished my course, I have kept the faith" (2 Tim. 4:7).

Daily Devotions:

M. Taste and See God's Goodness • Psalm 34:1-8
T. Forget Not His Benefits • Psalm 103:1-10
W. New Mercies Daily • Lamentations 3:22-24
T. Stand Fast by Faith • Galatians 5:1-6
F. Persuaded to Trust Christ • 2 Pimothy 1:8-14
S. Contend for the Faith • Jude 1-4

The Day of the Lord

2 Peter 3:1-18

Unit Theme:
First and Second Peter and Jude

Central Truth:
The coming Day of the Lord should reorder the lives of Christians.

Focus:
Live in anticipation of the Day of the Lord.

Context:
Peter wrote his second epistle around AD 67.

Golden Text:
"Nevertheless we, according to his promise, look for new heavens and a new earth, wherein dwelleth righteousness" (2 Peter 3:13).

Study Outline:
I. **The Day Will Come** (2 Peter 3:1-9)
II. **All Things Will Be New** (2 Peter 3:10-13)
III. **Live for That Day** (2 Peter 3:14-18)

INTRODUCTION

Scoffers speak with derision of the second advent of Christ. They say nothing has changed for centuries; everything goes on the same as it always has. Where, then, they ask, is the fulfillment of the promise of His coming? (2 Peter 3:4). But they have failed to take into consideration that "with the Lord one day is as a thousand years, and a thousand years as one day" (v. 8 NKJV).

The apostle Peter had no such doubts that Christ would keep His promise to return. He had been a witness of Christ's transfiguration on the holy mount and thus had experienced a foretaste of the future glory.

The purpose of this epistle is twofold: (1) that believers should not be seduced by the teachers of false doctrine, especially their disbelief in the Second Coming; (2) that believers might grow in grace and in the knowledge of their Lord and Savior, and thereby be found blameless in the day of the Lord's return.

I. THE DAY WILL COME (2 Peter 3:1-9)

A. Reflection (vv. 1-2)

¹This second epistle, beloved, I now write unto you; in both which I stir up your pure minds by way of remembrance: ²That ye may be mindful of the words which were spoken before by the holy prophets, and of the commandment of us the apostles of the Lord and Saviour.

The apostle took a personal interest in the spiritual welfare of the Christians of Asia Minor. He felt a great affection for them. He called them "beloved" four times in this chapter. We do not know whether he had seen them face-to-face. In his first letter, he comforted them in the presence of persecution. In the second, he warned them about the seductions of false teachers.

Peter wrote to "stir up [their] pure minds" (v. 1). Their minds were pure. They were single-minded Christians. Their commitment to Christ was genuine. Nevertheless, it was appropriate to stir them up. The Holy Spirit used Peter as His agent to stir up the minds of the Christians in Asia Minor.

Peter wanted the Christians in Asia Minor to be mindful of, or remember, the words of the prophets and apostles (v. 2). The writings of the prophets and apostles both have a message for us. It is important that we recognize that message. To neglect it shows a lack of reverence and gratitude to Him from whom the message comes. The commandments delivered to us by the apostles are truly the commandments of our Lord.

• What must Christians remember, and why?

The Master's Book

Amidst the flood of dangerous reading, I plead for my Master's book; I call upon you not to forget the book of the soul. Do not let newspapers, novels, and romances be read, while the prophets and apostles be despised. Do not let the exciting and the sensual swallow up your attention, while the edifying and the sanctifying can find no place in your mind.—J. C. Ryle

---

B. Reaction (vv. 3-4)

³Knowing this first, that there shall come in the last days scoffers, walking after their own lusts, ⁴And saying, Where is the promise of his coming? for since the fathers fell asleep, all things continue as they were from the beginning of the creation.

The apostle warned that scoffers would come (v. 3). It has always been so. There have always been people who mocked those who trusted in God. It was so with Lot in Sodom; with Isaac, the heir of promise; with the psalmist David; with the Lord Jesus himself. Those mockers of whom Peter spoke were men of sensual habits, walking after their own lusts. There is such a thing as "honest doubt," such as that of Thomas. As it has been in all ages, however, many of those who profess skepticism are using the claim to cover up an ungodly life—individuals who reject the faith because they are unwilling to believe. The pure morality of the Gospel offends their self-judgment; it is a reproach to them. The teaching of Scripture concerning judgment is repulsive to them; therefore, they try to keep such thoughts from their minds. Besides this, sin hardens their hearts. A sensual life blinds the eye of the soul and makes men and women incapable of appreciating spiritual truth.

The Day of the Lord

The scoffers will say, "Where is the promise of his coming?" (v. 4). The Fathers have fallen asleep; generation after generation has passed. Christians have lived in expectation of the Lord's coming, but still He has not come. Are we to spend our lives waiting for an Advent which seems to be continually delayed? Yes, we are to wait for and expect the Lord to come. The scoffers are wrong. The Lord will come again as He promised.

- How would you reply if a doubter asked you, "What happened to the Second Coming?"

"After the prophets, the false prophets; after the apostles, the false apostles; after Christ, Antichrist."—John Chrysostom

---

C. Recounting (vv. 5-7)

5For this they willingly are ignorant of, that by the word of God the heavens were of old, and the earth standing out of the water and in the water: 6Whereby the world that then was, being overflowed with water, perished: 7But the heavens and the earth, which are now, by the same word are kept in store, reserved unto fire against the day of judgment and perdition of ungodly men.

Peter began to answer the scoffers in verse 5. He says all things have not always continued as they were. Creation itself was the introduction of a vast change, a mighty interposition of divine power. "In the beginning God created the heaven and the earth" (Gen. 1:1). "Through faith we understand that the worlds were framed by the word of God, so that things which are seen were not made of things which do appear" (Heb. 11:3).

Scoffers willfully ignore this. They shut their eyes to this unalterable truth and forget that He who made the world can also destroy it. They disregard the fact that the Creator has the power to make other great changes in the future.

Verse 6 of the text is a reference to the Flood. The earth, which God had pronounced to be "very good" (Gen. 1:31), became corrupt and was filled with violence. Then God brought the Flood upon the world of the ungodly. By His word "were all the foundations of the great deep broken up, and the windows of heaven were opened. . . . And all flesh died that moved upon the earth" (7:11, 21). That awful judgment was a warning of coming judgments. All things did not go on in the same unvarying course as the scoffers said. When the earth was corrupted by sin, God interposed His justice; and the earth, by a baptism of water, was restored and purified, prepared for a new beginning.

The time Peter referred to in verse 7 will be a day of destruction to the ungodly. It will sweep them into eternal death. A state of separation from the life of God—separation from light and joy and love—will be felt in all its blank and utter misery. Then all things will not continue as they are. He who made the world in the beginning, He who swept away the wicked with the waters of the Flood, will visit the earth "in flaming fire taking vengeance on them that know not God, and that obey not the gospel of our Lord Jesus Christ" (2 Thess. 1:8).

---

1. According to verses 5 and 6, what do skeptics "deliberately ignore" (RSV)?
2. What awaits the earth, and why (v. 7)?

> "Faith has in it the recognition of the certainty and the justice of a judgment that is coming down crashing on every human head."
> —Alexander MacLaren

D. Realization (vv. 8-9)

⁸But, beloved, be not ignorant of this one thing, that one day is with the Lord as a thousand years, and a thousand years as one day. ⁹The Lord is not slack concerning his promise, as some men count slackness; but is longsuffering to us-ward, not willing that any should perish, but that all should come to repentance.

Peter borrowed a concept from Psalm 90:4, a prayer of Moses, to impress upon his readers the reason for God's patient dealings with humanity in their sin and unbelief: "A thousand years in thy sight are but as yesterday when it is past." The apostle not only adopted the concept, but he also adapted the words for his own purpose.

George Cramer says: "This cannot be construed as a standard by which God works in time, nor can it be used as a key for interpreting all temporal references in prophecy. Because Peter equates a thousand years as one day and one day as a thousand years . . . he is clearly saying that God recognizes no temporal measure for the working out of His purposes.

"The apostles shared this hope [of Christ's second coming] with the early church. [God's] longsuffering with man in his sinful ways has spanned more than 1,900 years, although the door of grace could have been closed at any time" (*First and Second Peter*).

The apparent delay in Christ's coming does not mean indifference (2 Peter 3:9a). It does not mean the Lord is unaware of the conduct of godless people. They say, "God has forgotten; He hides His face; He will never see" (Ps. 10:11 NKJV). It is not so. The delay of judgment comes from a far different reason. The Lord is "not willing that any should perish, but that all should come to repentance" (2 Peter 3:9b).

The power to choose good or evil has been given to us by God. Without that power there could be no moral action, responsibility, obedience, holiness, or love. Life without power of choice would be the working of a machine, not the energy of a creature made after the likeness of God. We have often abused our freedom and turned that which should have led to holiness into an occasion to sin. But God has no pleasure in the death of the wicked. His desire is that all would be saved.

Pulpit Commentary states: "Therefore He gives us time. The delay comes from the longsuffering of God. How sad that men should scoff at that which should be the basis of deep gratitude."

---

1. Explain the message of verse 8.
2. How is God different from people, and why is this good news (v. 9)?

> "Time is the brush of God, as He paints His masterpiece on the heart of humanity."—Ravi Zacharias

---

II. ALL THINGS WILL BE NEW (2 Peter 3:10-13)

A. Warning (v. 10)

¹⁰But the day of the Lord will come as a thief in the night; in the which the heavens shall pass away with a great noise, and the elements shall melt with fervent heat, the earth also and the works that are therein shall be burned up.

The apostle sounded a warning when he said, "The day of the Lord will come." It must be so, for it is so decreed in the counsels of God. The scoffers may mock and ask in bitter sarcasm, "Where is the promise of His coming?" The Christian knows the answer; it is hidden in the secret purposes of God.

The Day of the Lord *will* come, though we do not know the time. Its coming is certain, as sure as the Word of God. It will come suddenly, as a thief comes unexpectedly. People will be carrying on with the daily round of activities—"eating and drinking, marrying and giving in marriage" (Matt. 24:38)—without a thought of God and the future, when He returns. As Christians, the coming of Christ and the Day of the Lord should not take us unawares. We must live daily in anticipation of the Lord's coming.

The Day of the Lord will be terrible for the ungodly. Peter's words bring vividly before our minds the awful scenes: the crash of falling mountains, the roar of destroying flames, the dissolution of the elements into chaos, the fire that will burn up the earth. All the works of the earth will be swept away in one tremendous ruin. This is the apostle's answer and warning to scoffers.

• Describe "the day of the Lord."

> "We ought to be living as if Jesus died yesterday, rose this morning, and is coming back this afternoon."—Adrian Rogers

---

B. Provision (vv. 11-13)

¹¹Seeing then that all these things shall be dissolved, what manner of persons ought ye to be in all holy conversation and godliness,

¹²Looking for and hasting unto the coming of the day of God, wherein the heavens being on fire shall be dissolved, and the elements shall melt with fervent heat? ¹³Nevertheless we, according to his promise, look for new heavens and a new earth, wherein dwelleth righteousness.

The catastrophe of judgment that is to follow the second coming of Christ is here spoken of with such certainty it is almost as though it was already accomplished. In view of this, we are to lead holy and godly lives.

The picture so vividly presented is given as a reason for being concerned about our behavior. Holy living is the lifestyle of those who are set apart to the service of a holy God. Godliness points to this living as based on our relationship to God. Godly living includes a dependence on God and reverence toward Him; a desire for the blessings of God and a trust in Him for those blessings; ardent love for God because of who He is and gratitude toward Him for His mercies; a knowledge of God's will and a resolve to do His will. All of these are part of a holy and godly life.

Peter referred to the believer's attitude toward the second coming of Christ in these words: "Look forward to the day of God and speed its coming" (v. 12 NIV). This reference to the end of the age as "the day of God" has the same meaning as the more usual wording, "day of the Lord." Both refer, of course, to Christ's second coming. Our attitude toward that day is to be one of expectancy. We are to look for His coming. The first Christians longingly looked for it to come in their day; we should desire it no less eagerly.

The idea of hastening the coming of the Lord is expressed elsewhere by Peter. He preached, "Repent therefore and be converted . . . so that times of refreshing may come from the presence of the Lord, and that He may send Jesus Christ" (Acts 3:19-20 NKJV). It is thus Scriptural to think of the coming of Christ as an event which may be hastened on by repentance and prayers and the spread of the Gospel.

The apostle continued his description of the end of the age: "The heavens being on fire shall be dissolved, and the elements shall melt with fervent heat" (2 Peter 3:12). Even the heavens have been defiled by those who live under them. When Christ comes to the earth in judgment, the material universe will melt from the glory of His presence. Revelation 20:11 says earth and heaven will flee from the face of Him who sits on the throne.

Second Peter 3:13 identifies the Christian's hope for the future. Peter's writing agrees with John's in Revelation 21:1: "And I saw a new heaven and a new earth: for the first heaven and the first earth were passed away." The promise cited by Peter is recorded in Isaiah 65:17: "For, behold, I create new heavens and a new earth: and the former shall not be remembered, nor come into mind."

Some scholars believe the present heaven and earth will be destroyed into nonexistence by the judgment of God. Then God will create a new heaven and earth. Other scholars believe the fiery judgment will merely cleanse the heaven and earth of evil, and the new heaven and earth will be the same which now exists, only renovated or regenerated by God so as to be a new creation. (Compare the new creation of the believer in Christ as recorded in 2 Corinthians 5:17.)

1. How does God expect His people to live (v. 11)?
2. What is the proper Christian attitude regarding Christ's coming, and why (vv. 12-13)?

> "This, and this alone, is Christianity, a universal holiness in every part of life, a heavenly wisdom in all our actions, not conforming to the spirit and temper of the world but turning all worldly enjoyments into means of piety and devotion to God."
> —William Law

III. LIVE FOR THAT DAY (2 Peter 3:14-18)

A. Attitude (vv. 14-16)

¹⁴Wherefore, beloved, seeing that ye look for such things, be diligent that ye may be found of him in peace, without spot, and blameless. ¹⁵And account that the longsuffering of our Lord is salvation; even as our beloved brother Paul also according to the wisdom given unto him hath written unto you; ¹⁶As also in all his epistles, speaking in them of these things; in which are some things hard to be understood, which they that are unlearned and unstable wrest, as they do also the other scriptures, unto their own destruction.

The apocalyptic language of fire and destruction is not meant to scare people, but to motivate us to see things correctly—that is, from God's perspective. It also enables us to see the provision of God for believers, including the new heavens and earth, and even in the midst of judgment. Consequently, we must make every effort with haste ("be diligent") to manifest four characteristics in particular when Jesus returns (vv. 14-15): (1) be free from anxiety ("in peace"); (2) remain pure and uncorrupted ("without spot"); (3) be morally "blameless" and without reproach; and (4) manifest patient steadfastness in the midst of difficulty ("longsuffering"), which is a virtue of Christ. These things help assure final salvation and deliverance.

In a parenthetical section, Peter mentions "our beloved brother Paul" and his writings, which confirm what Peter is saying (vv. 15-16). Subtly, it reminds the readers that people and situations can change. In Galatians 2:11-14, Paul confronted Peter concerning his actions, but now Peter calls Paul "beloved." God can turn even the most contentious of situations around.

Even at this early stage of the church, the writings of the apostles were recognized as the inspired Word of God. Yet, even Peter had trouble understanding some of Paul's writings (v. 16). Like us, Peter needed the Holy Spirit to be his Teacher.

1. How can you "be found by Him in peace" (v. 14 NASB)?
2. Explain the statement "Our Lord's patience means salvation" (v. 15 NIV).
3. What is deadly, and why (v. 16)?

> "God will work when He pleases, how He pleases, and by what means He pleases. He is not bound to keep our time, but He will perform His word, honor our faith, and reward them that diligently seek Him."—Matthew Henry

---

B. Declaration (vv. 17-18)

¹⁷Ye therefore, beloved, seeing ye know these things before, beware lest ye also, being led away with the error of the wicked, fall from your own stedfastness. ¹⁸But grow in grace, and in the knowledge of our Lord and Saviour Jesus Christ. To him be glory both now and for ever. Amen.

Peter closes out his epistle reminding his readers they have been warned and now they need to manifest the essence of his teaching and the provision and knowledge of "our Lord and Saviour Jesus Christ." He closes with a doxology, or declaration of praise, unto the One who saves and keeps us—and who shall return again! "To him be glory [and honor] both now and for ever. Amen" (v. 18).

- Describe the potential "fall" (v. 17) with the necessary growth (v. 18).

> "Take care of giving up your first zeal; beware of cooling in the least degree. You were hot and earnest once; be hot and earnest still."—Charles Spurgeon

---

CONCLUSION

Peter has warned of both the danger and error of the false teachers' heresy. The doctrine of the Second Coming serves to motivate Christians to live in a way that is consistent with the example of Jesus, through knowledge of Him as revealed in the Old and New Testaments. As well, God's mercy should not be construed as aloofness or delay, for He is sending His Son again and preparing a place for those who serve Him—a place in which He reigns supremely!

GOLDEN TEXT CHALLENGE

"NEVERTHELESS WE, ACCORDING TO HIS PROMISE, LOOK FOR NEW HEAVENS AND A NEW EARTH, WHEREIN DWELLETH RIGHTEOUSNESS" (2 Peter 3:13).

Christians are forward-lookers. Rather than dwelling on past victories and failures, we are to deal with the challenges of today while always anticipating the return and reign of Christ. In fact, it is the hope of a new world where righteousness rules that motivates us to live holy today.

God's promises are certain: Jesus will return, He will establish a new heaven and a new earth, righteousness will prevail, and Christ's righteous people will reign with Him.

Daily Devotions:

M. The Days of Lot • Genesis 19:17-26
T. The Day Is Coming • Malachi 4:1-6
W. No One Knows the Day • Matthew 24:36-44
T. Watch for the Day • Mark 13:32-37
F. As in the Days of Lot • Luke 17:28-33
S. The Eternal Day • Revelation 22:1-5

Beware of False Teachers

Jude 1-25

Unit Theme:

First and Second Peter and Jude

Central Truth:

God will punish false teachers, but will preserve and reward faithful Christians.

Focus:

Beware of false teachers and hold faithfully to the truth.

Context:

Jude probably wrote his epistle around AD 66.

Golden Text:

"Beloved, when I gave all diligence to write unto you of the common salvation, it was needful for me to write unto you, and exhort you that ye should earnestly contend for the faith which was once delivered unto the saints" (Jude 3).

Study Outline:

  I. **Danger of False Teachers** (Jude 1-7)
 II. **Characteristics of False Teachers** (Jude 8-16)
III. **Response of Faithful Disciples** (Jude 17-25)

INTRODUCTION

The general Epistle of Jude is a polemic for the Christian faith and is most severe in its denunciation of apostasy. While displaying loving concern for true believers, at the same time it burns with fiery indignation and fierce pronouncements of judgment upon apostates and religious sensualists. As such, it stands in our English Bibles as a fitting introduction to the Book of Revelation.

After the author's identification of himself and a Christian greeting, he states the occasion and purpose for writing. He then proceeds to give historical examples of apostasy and consequent judgment, followed by vivid descriptions and severe denunciation of the apostates of his day, and warning of certain judgment at Christ's coming. Believers are exhorted to be aware of this apostasy, and to make sure they have a right spiritual attitude toward God and those who need instruction and guidance.

The similarity of the contents of Jude to the Second Epistle of Peter suggests that the author is aware of Peter's letter and is resolved to join the apostle in sending forth the warning of apostasy and judgment. The epistle, though brief, is rich in doctrine and practical lessons for Christians of all times.

I. DANGER OF FALSE TEACHERS (Jude 1-7)

A. Contending for the Faith (vv. 1-3)

¹Jude, the servant of Jesus Christ, and brother of James, to them that are sanctified by God the Father, and preserved in Jesus Christ, and called: ²Mercy unto you, and peace, and love, be multiplied. ³Beloved, when I gave all diligence to write unto you of the common salvation, it was needful for me to write unto you, and exhort you that ye should earnestly contend for the faith which was once delivered unto the saints.

The writer called himself "Jude, the servant of Jesus Christ, and brother of James" (v. 1). This self-identification of linking himself to his brother apparently indicates the brother was well-known. Since the New Testament mentions more than one James, it is not easy to know to which one Jude was referring. It is possible that Jude was a half-brother of our Lord Jesus Christ (see Mark 6:3).

Acts 1:14 informs us that Christ's "brethren" were a part of the praying group in Jerusalem that was waiting for the Holy Spirit. Perhaps Jude, with James, was among them. In verse 1 of the text, Jude made three significant statements about Christians: (1) They are "sanctified by God," (2) "preserved in Jesus Christ," and (3) "called."

"Sanctified by God the Father" means God has set them apart for His use. "Preserved in Jesus Christ" suggests they not only were once but continue to be objects of God's love and care. Jude was referring to the continuous preservation with which Jesus keeps those who trust Him. He keeps that which we commit to Him.

The word *called* stresses the basis for their preservation. They were called by God to be "a people for his name" (Acts 15:14)—a people who would be "holy and without blame" before Him (Eph. 1:4). The word *called* came to be used synonymously with the term *Christian*.

In verse 2, Jude gave another triad of qualities which he desired for his readers. He wanted them to have mercy, peace, and love multiplied to them. These three relate us properly to God, to our inner being, and to our brethren around us.

Mercy refers to God's tender compassion and pity. Although mercy is initially extended to the sinner in his or her misery, it is also a necessary resource for the Christian.

Peace is the serenity of soul which springs from the assurance of being kept safe; therefore, peace is the quietness of soul that belongs to one who is properly related to God.

Love originates with God himself and becomes a strengthening and motivating force in the Christian's life. The assurance of God's love and the love of other believers can sustain the church when apostasy is rampant.

In verse 3, the Christian experience is summarized by one word, *salvation*, and Christian belief as "the faith." So important is this faith that believers must "earnestly contend" for it. This means "to contend strenuously in defense of." The Greek word for this expression implies an intense, agonizing struggle.

"The faith" is a body of beliefs, as opposed to the more usual meaning of *faith* as "trust." What this body of beliefs is, Jude did not explain; however, he did designate it as "the faith which was once delivered unto the saints." In other words, Christianity is viewed as a system of revealed teachings that are unalterable and normative. This is the force of the phrase "once for all" (NKJV).

---

1. What is the relationship between *sanctification*, *preservation*, and *calling* (v. 1)?
2. Explain the term "common salvation" (v. 3).
3. What is the purpose of Jude's letter (v. 3)?

> "We must never cease to earnestly contend for the faith. . . . And how? By loving the faith. By learning the faith. By living the faith. And by loosing the faith."—O. S. Hawkins

---

B. Warning to the Faithful (vv. 4-7)

(Jude 6-7 is not included in the printed text.)

⁴For there are certain men crept in unawares, who were before of old ordained to this condemnation, ungodly men, turning the grace of our God into lasciviousness, and denying the only Lord God, and our Lord Jesus Christ. ⁵I will therefore put you in remembrance, though ye once knew this, how that the Lord, having saved the people out of the land of Egypt, afterward destroyed them that believed not.

Jude said believers must contend for the faith because "certain men crept in unawares" (v. 4)—they had slipped in secretly and without the congregation's knowledge. This is the peril that caused Jude to dash off this sudden, short letter. Those threatening the church had not challenged the faith openly; instead, by underhanded methods, they had gained influence in the church. The Old Testament, the teachings of Jesus, and that of the apostles all contain ample warnings against the advent of false teachers. So eager was the writer to warn his readers against these people that, even before mentioning the nature of their error, he indicated these apostates were long ago marked for condemnation. As such, they are to be shunned by the faithful but not to be feared because, dangerous as they may seem, they could not alter divine purpose.

Jude further described these false teachers as "ungodly men." They were guilty of two major errors. The first was that they turned the grace of God into *lasciviousness*, or license to immorality—their attitude was irreverent, their deeds were shameless, and their desires were illicit. Their second great error was their denial of the Lord Jesus Christ. Jude did not give any details of their denial. It may be simply that, by their unrestrained wickedness, these men were denying Christ and His Father.

Verses 5-7 give examples of the certain doom of such men. The first example is that of Israel who experienced the great display of God's grace in the Exodus, yet many of them rebelled. The second example is the fallen angels. The third example of judgment is that of the cities of the plain, Sodom and Gomorrah.

---

1. How had "certain men" twisted the doctrine of God's grace (v. 4)?
2. List the three solemn examples given in verses 5-7.

> "In these last days, demons are seducing and deceiving many through false teaching."—Ron Phillips

---

II. CHARACTERISTICS OF FALSE TEACHERS (Jude 8-16)

A. Polluted Dreamers (vv. 8-13)

(Jude 9, 11 is not included in the printed text.)

⁸Likewise also these filthy dreamers defile the flesh, despise dominion, and speak evil of dignities.

¹⁰But these speak evil of those things which they know not: but what they know naturally, as brute beasts, in those things they corrupt themselves.

¹²These are spots in your feasts of charity, when they feast with you, feeding themselves without fear: clouds they are without water, carried about of winds; trees whose fruit withereth, without fruit, twice dead, plucked up by the roots; ¹³Raging waves of the sea, foaming out their own shame; wandering stars, to whom is reserved the blackness of darkness for ever.

From the preceding examples in verses 5-7, Jude drew three clear points. The false teachers are arraigned (1) for lust, (2) for rebellion, and (3) for irreverence. These men are ungodly dreamers who defile the flesh. They also "despise dominion" (v. 8) and attack the constituted authorities of the church, by what Jude calls "speak[ing] evil of dignities." However, Michael the archangel exhibited the kind of restraint the Christian should practice when he said to Satan, "The Lord rebuke thee" (v. 9). These words spoken by Michael are identical to the words spoken by the Lord to Satan in Zechariah 3:2.

These ungodly men whom Jude described railed not only at those in authority over them but also at truths that were above their knowledge. They followed in the footsteps of Cain "and ran greedily after the error of Balaam for reward" (v. 11). Jude indicated they "perished in the rebellion of Korah" (NKJV).

Cain was the first murderer. He killed Abel, his brother (Gen. 4:8).

Balaam was bribed by Balak to curse Israel and attempt to lead her astray (Num. 22—24; 31:16). Later, Jews would consider Balaam the one who misled the youth. By the end of the first century AD, Christians were having to combat this heresy which was affecting some of the churches in Asia Minor (Rev. 2:12, 14).

Korah rebelled against Moses, who was in the God-ordained position of authority (Num. 16). Rebellion in the church was a major problem facing the church in the last part of the first century (1 Tim. 1:19-20; 2 Tim. 2:16-18, 23-25; Titus 1:9-11; 3 John 9-10).

A figurative and graphic description of the polluted dreamers follows in Jude 12-13. They are *spots*, literally "hidden rocks," thus sources of unsuspected peril, spoiling the fellowship of Christians, like weeds in the vegetation. They are like clouds that bring no refreshing showers, like trees that wither without bearing fruit, like waves of the sea that cannot rest, and like shooting stars of the sky that go out in darkness.

---

1. What do verses 8 and 9 teach about spiritual authority?
2. How were Cain, Balaam, and Korah alike (v. 11)?
3. How do verses 12 and 13 describe false teachers?

"The purpose of life is not to find your freedom, but your master."
—P. T. Forsyth

B. Coming Judgment (vv. 14-16)

(Jude 14-15 is not included in the printed text.)

¹⁶These are murmurers, complainers, walking after their own lusts; and their mouth speaketh great swelling words, having men's persons in admiration because of advantage.

The Lord will return to bring judgment against the ungodly (vv. 14-15). Note how Jude took the word *ungodly* and applied it to everything that was done by these false teachers. "Hard speeches" referred to the things these men said against the Lord. At the last day, all sinners will know the extent of their sin against the Lord. One of the characteristics of hell will be the sinner's knowledge that his or her sins could have been forgiven but were not because of their failure to repent.

The ungodliness that will be judged is spelled out in verse 16. "Murmurers" are grumblers. The Greek for this noun was used in Exodus 16:8; Numbers 11:1, 14-27, 29. Inherent in the word is the secrecy of murmured discontent. It is the style of those who refuse to speak up and get their views into the open, but who return to secret, small groups, and speak against God's plans.

"Complainers, walking after their own lusts" (Jude 16) are those who are so self-centered they are unable to see beyond themselves. They follow their passions of discontent. They have no desire to serve anyone. They are habitual complainers. Nothing can be done to please them.

Those who speak "great swelling words" are people who boast with loud mouths. The purpose of their boasting is to gain advantage over other people. These are manipulators of God's people.

---

1. How do verses 14 and 15 characterize false teachers, and what awaits them?
2. What do these "grumblers" love to find, what do they follow, and why do they flatter (v. 16 NASB)?

III. RESPONSE OF FAITHFUL DISCIPLES (Jude 17-25)

A. Remember the Apostles' Words (vv. 17-19)

(Jude 17-19 is not included in the printed text.)

Throughout his brief epistle, Jude intermingled accusations, illustrations, and condemnation, drawing heavily on Old Testament events and allusions. Now, his plea was that there would be dejection, since the apostles themselves had given a forecast of these alarming developments. Forgetfulness of the teaching and warnings of God in Scripture causes spiritual loss.

Perhaps the appeal to apostolic teaching would be more readily accepted from the pen of Jude, since he himself was not an apostle. Jude called attention to the words that were *spoken* by the apostles because, at that time, the New Testament was still being written.

Jude's point is that when the apostles proclaimed their message, they addressed it to all generations of Christians, including his own. It is clear the writer was not thinking of any specific statement by the apostles, or any single apostle, but of a characteristic element in the teaching of the apostolic church. The word *mocker,* or *scoffer,* literally means "one who plays with, trifles with, makes fun of, or mocks," as when the soldiers put a purple robe on Jesus, a crown of thorns on His head, and a reed in His hand, bowed and cried out, "Hail, King of the Jews."

Jude considered the end times as in the process of actualization. He found proof of this, as did others, in the shameless revelation of the blasphemers of God and scoffers who were following their own ungodly desires.

What else could he have said about the heretics? Verse 19 reveals a lot. He called them "they who separate themselves," that is, men who cause division. Thus, we may see here a separation caused partly by wealth, attaching themselves to the rich (v. 16); partly by social position, rebelling against the authority of the officials who were not always men of means (v. 8); and partly by assuming an intellectual superiority.

Not only do false teachers divide the church, but they also deceive the church because they are "sensual, having not the Spirit" (v. 19). Thus, we see that the *sensual* people are those who live in the world of sense and are ruled by human feeling and human reason. The word *sensual* means the opposite of *spiritual.*

In spite of their vaunted claims and teaching, the false teachers are devoid of the Holy Spirit. A Christian, however, is baptized by the Spirit into the body of Christ, sealed by the Spirit, indwelt by the Spirit, taught by the Spirit, and led by the Spirit.

---

1. What must Christians "remember," and why (v. 17-18)?

2. What do "sensual persons" cause, and why (v. 19 NKJV)?

> "The Internet has given atheists, agnostics, skeptics—the people who like to destroy everything you and I believe—almost equal access to your kids as your youth pastor and you have . . . whether you like it or not."—Josh McDowell

---

B. Help Yourselves and Others (vv. 20-23)

20 But ye, beloved, building up yourselves on your most holy faith, praying in the Holy Ghost, 21 Keep yourselves in the love of God, looking for the mercy of our Lord Jesus Christ unto eternal life. 22 And of some have compassion, making a difference: 23 And others save with fear, pulling them out of the fire; hating even the garment spotted by the flesh.

Jude again addresses his readers as "beloved," in contrast to the false teachers (v. 20). The expression "building up" in the New Testament is always used in the sense of believers forming a temple. The Greek word carries the notion of one stone being placed on another, so that upward progress is made.

In face of the threat of heretical teaching, the foundation that will sustain the building and keep it safe is declared. Appropriately enough, it is what Jude called "your most holy faith"—the Christian revelation handed down by the apostles.

The faith here is called "most holy" because it comes to us from God. *Holy* means "set apart" and, thus, different. This "holy faith" is entirely set apart from all others because it reveals God to humanity. It is unique in the message it teaches and in the moral transformation it produces. We bear the responsibility for self-development, for growth in Christian character, for the rearing of a structure that will glorify Christ in everything. This is a lifelong task.

Again, a contrast is deliberately drawn to those who do not possess the Spirit (v. 19) and so have no true prayer. Praying in the Holy Spirit is necessary because the battle against false teaching is not won by argument.

This building process in the Christian's life involves the Word of God, the Spirit of God, and prayer. To these things Jude added another factor, abiding in the love of God (v. 21).

Jesus said, "As the Father hath loved me, so have I loved you: continue ye in my love" (John 15:9). We bear the responsibility for keeping ourselves, or continuing, within the sphere where the love of God is able to bless us. It was His love that first drew the believers to Himself, but as evidenced in the false teachers, it is possible to turn one's back on the love of God.

Jude concluded his exhortation in verses 20 and 21 by encouraging Christians to look ahead. We are to "wait for the mercy of our Lord Jesus Christ to bring [us] to eternal life" (v. 21 NIV). In Titus 2:13, Christians are told to be "looking for that blessed hope."

It is because of God's mercy that we are not consumed, and it is because of His mercy that we are given eternal life. The mention of *mercy* reminds

Christians that salvation is never a matter of good works and that only in Christ is their hope of salvation.

According to Jude, *salvation* is not merely to be defined in terms he has already given—faith, prayer, love, and hope—but service is also involved. Without a hint of transition, he counseled how his readers should behave toward fellow members of the community who have fallen.

In verses 22 and 23, Jude sets forth three groups of people who need help: "Be merciful to those who doubt; snatch others from the fire and save them; to others show mercy, mixed with fear—hating even the clothing stained by corrupted flesh" (NIV).

The first group are those who need compassionate tenderness because sincere doubts trouble them. When individuals begin to waver is the time for well-taught Christians to act.

The second group are in a worse plight; they have been completely carried away by dangerous propaganda. These require urgent boldness if they are to be snatched from an eternal fiery judgment. They are on the wrong path and need to be informed and then rescued.

The third group is composed of those who must be dealt with in cautious compassion, lest the soulwinner himself be contaminated by their sins. The idea is that these were so corrupt their very clothes were defiled. This is, of course, a hyperbole, but with Scriptural support.

The principle Jude was laying down is that stronger believers must never think they are beyond satanic influence. The faithful are urged to show all possible tenderness for the fallen but, at the same time, to have a fear lest they themselves or others whom they influence should be led to think too lightly of the sin whose ravages they are endeavoring to repair. Christians are to retain their hatred of sin even as they love the sinner.

---

1. How can Christians strengthen themselves (v. 20)?
2. What does it mean to "keep yourselves in the love of God" (v. 21)?
3. What must Christians continually anticipate (v. 21)?
4. How should Christians minister to others (vv. 22-23)?

"If I should neglect prayer but a single day, I should lose a great deal of the fire of faith."—Martin Luther

---

C. Trusting Almighty God (vv. 24-25)

24Now unto him that is able to keep you from falling, and to present you faultless before the presence of his glory with exceeding joy, 25To the only wise God our Saviour, be glory and majesty, dominion and power, both now and ever. Amen.

As Jude concluded his letter, he drew his readers' attention away from the sordid spectacle of apostasy and turned it toward God, who cared for them. The writer was acutely conscious of the perils to which his readers were exposed. Thus, he deliberately framed his statement to emphasize that God, and God alone, is able to keep them safe and to present them faultless.

The word translated "to keep" means "to guard." In a world full of pitfalls, God keeps a watch over His own to prevent them from stumbling.

Jude indicated that the believer will be presented faultless in eternity. *Faultless* is a term used to describe Christ; however, since the Christian is in Christ, he or she too can be presented faultless and without blame.

To God alone be the glory (v. 25)! This is the final note of Jude's epistle. *Glory* is the brightness, the manifest excellence of God. It is a divine radiance which shines (Luke 2:9), blinds (Acts 22:11), and cannot be endured by the unglorified human race.

Majesty is a word used only of God in the Bible. It means "greatness and magnificence" and refers to the incomparable regal presence of the Ruler of the universe.

Dominion has to do with God's sovereignty and rule over all things. The Scripture declares that He upholds "all things by the word of his power" (Heb. 1:3). The Greek word translated "dominion" means "strength and might" and carries the idea of complete control over all things. *Dominion* denotes that absolute power of God which assures Him ultimate victory.

Power suggests the authority of the sovereign freedom of action God enjoys as Creator and expresses His ability to do anything He chooses.

Thus, Jude brings his letter to a close with a noble and beautiful doxology that not only sums up the message of this epistle but also makes a fitting conclusion to the whole group of the New Testament Epistles.

---

1. What can God accomplish in our lives (v. 24)?
2. How does verse 25 describe God?

> "God never alters the robe of righteousness to fit the man; He changes the man to fit the robe."—Unknown

---

CONCLUSION

Jude warns the Christian against the apostasy that will arise within the Christian church. We are not to be surprised when error arises and even seeks to prevail in the Christian church. Rather, we ought to comfort ourselves in the midst of confusion that Christ will maintain His church and make good His promise that "the gates of hell shall not prevail against it" (Matt. 16:18).

GOLDEN TEXT CHALLENGE

"BELOVED, WHEN I GAVE ALL DILIGENCE TO WRITE UNTO YOU OF THE COMMON SALVATION, IT WAS NEEDFUL FOR ME TO WRITE UNTO YOU, AND EXHORT YOU THAT YE SHOULD EARNESTLY CONTEND FOR THE FAITH WHICH WAS ONCE DELIVERED UNTO THE SAINTS" (Jude 3).

The language of this verse suggests it was the author's original intention to write about our "common salvation"—the common spiritual property of all believers. This is the salvation which had been granted to Jew and Gentile alike on condition of faith in the Savior—a doctrine and spiritual experience of real interest and concern to all true Christians. But the situation that has arisen in the church created the immediate necessity to exhort his readers relative to Christian doctrine. Because of this dangerous situation, they are exhorted to "earnestly contend for the faith which was once delivered unto the saints."

H. A. Ironside said:

> Evolution in theology there may be, for theology is simply the reasoning of man's mind as to the things of God. But evolution in regard to the truth, the faith once delivered, there is none. God has given His last word on the subject.

Daily Devotions:

M. Discerning False Prophets • Deuteronomy 18:18-22

T. Reject Ungodly Counsel • Psalm 1:1-6

W. Dangers of Falsehood • Psalm 5:1-12

T. Beware of False Prophets • Matthew 7:15-20

F. Do Not Be Deceived • Colossians 2:1-10

S. Test the Spirits • 1 John 4:1-6

Introduction to Winter Quarter

"The Minor Prophets (Part 1)" comprises the first unit (lessons 1-3, 5-6). Studies come from the books of Hosea, Joel, Amos, Jonah, and Micah.

This unit was written by Homer G. Rhea (L.H.D.), who has served the church in many capacities, including editor in chief of Church of God Publications, pastor, district overseer, and chairman of the Ministerial Internship Program (Mississippi). An ordained minister since 1966, Rhea is the author of three books, has contributed to other books, and has written numerous magazine articles.

The Christmas lesson (4) was written by Lance Colkmire (see biographical information on page 16).

The second unit (lessons 7-13) is "Letter to the Romans," lifting up vital Christian doctrines: righteousness, justification, grace, victory over sin, Spirit-filled living, and godly love.

The expositions were written by the Reverend Joshua F. Rice (B.A., M.A., Th.M.), who earned his Ph.D. in New Testament Studies from Lutheran School of Theology. He serves as teaching pastor of Mount Paran North Church of God in Marietta, Georgia, and is an adjunct professor at Lee University and Pentecostal Theological Seminary. Josh and his wife, Johanna, have two children.

God, Faithful Husband and Father

Hosea 1:1—3:5; 11:1-11

Unit Theme:
The Minor Prophets, Part 1

Central Truth:
God can be trusted completely.

Focus:
Acknowledge God's faithfulness, and trust and obey Him.

Context:
Hosea ministered between 780 and 722 BC.

Golden Text:
"I will betroth thee unto me for ever; yea, I will betroth thee unto me in righteousness, and in judgment, and in lovingkindness, and in mercies" (Hos. 2:19).

Study Outline:
I. **A Wife's Adultery** (Hos. 1:1—2:13)
II. **A Husband's Love** (Hos. 2:14—3:5)
III. **A Father's Love** (Hos. 11:1-11)

INTRODUCTION

The greatest story in the Bible—indeed, the greatest story ever told—is that of Jesus Christ and His redeeming work. That blessed story includes His virgin birth, holy life, atoning death, and victorious resurrection. Some have suggested that the second-greatest story in the Bible is the story of Hosea because it anticipates the story of Christ.

Nothing is known about Hosea's family history except that he was born to Beeri. His ministry was conducted over a period of several decades in the second half of the eighth century BC. It began near the end of Uzziah's reign in Judah, and Jeroboam II's reign in Israel. Four kings of Judah and one king of Israel are mentioned as serving in office during the time Hosea prophesied. It is uncertain why there are more Judean kings mentioned than Israelite kings, since the prophet's message is primarily addressed to Israel.

The name *Hosea* means "salvation." He lived at the same time as Isaiah and Amos. Isaiah's focus was on the southern kingdom of Judah, and Amos concentrated on the northern kingdom of Israel.

James Montgomery Boice puts Hosea's role in perspective:

It would seem that on one occasion, no doubt early in his life, God came to Hosea to ask him to do a very difficult thing. God said, "Hosea, I want you to marry a woman who is going to prove unfaithful to you but to whom you are nevertheless going to be faithful. You will love her, but she will disgrace your love. I am asking you to do this because we are to present a pageant to Israel by your marriage. It is going to be symbolic, an object lesson. You are going to play the part of God. The woman is going to play the part of My people. The reason she is going to run away and be unfaithful is that this is the way My people act in the spiritual marriage that I have established with them. You are going to be faithful, because I am faithful to Israel, even though she dishonors My name" (*The Minor Prophets,* Vol. 1).

The story of Hosea switches back and forth between *judgment* and *salvation.* It presents the trauma Hosea felt because of his wife's unfaithfulness and the happiness they found in their restored relationship.

I. A WIFE'S ADULTERY (Hos. 1:1—2:13)

A. A Wife and Children (1:1-9)

(Hosea 1:4-9 is not included in the printed text.)

¹The word of the Lord that came unto Hosea, the son of Beeri, in the days of Uzziah, Jotham, Ahaz, and Hezekiah, kings of Judah, and in the days of Jeroboam the son of Joash, king of Israel. ²The beginning of the word of the Lord by Hosea. And the Lord said to Hosea, Go, take unto thee a wife of whoredoms and children of whoredoms: for the land hath committed great whoredom, departing from the Lord. ³So he went and took Gomer the daughter of Diblaim; which conceived, and bare him a son.

In unquestioning obedience to the Lord, Hosea took Gomer, the daughter of Diblaim, to be his wife. Gomer seemed to have no interest in or care for the ministry to which Hosea had been called. She chose a wanton and wicked way of life as opposed to the earnest devotion he was giving to his ministry. Hosea was doing everything in his power to save his people from national disaster, but she was unconcerned about their destiny. There was trouble in the parsonage, and nothing can hinder a ministry more.

To this couple, three children were born: two sons and a daughter. Each of them was given a divinely chosen name, and each name was symbolic. The first son was named *Jezreel* (v. 4), which meant "the Lord will scatter." He was given this name as a reminder that God would punish the house of Jehu for the massacre in Jezreel. The Lord himself had ordered the elimination of Jezebel and the descendants of Ahab. However, Jehu acted with a treacherous mind, and with an eye to his own greatness when he destroyed the house of Ahab. The judgment of God upon the wicked house of Ahab was just, but Jehu carried out His instructions not as the will of God, but as his own will. This action by Jehu demonstrates that we can do a right thing in a wrong way and for the wrong reasons. The end result of God's punishment of Jehu was that God would destroy the military power of Israel in the Valley of Jezreel and cut off Jehu's dynasty forever. The demise of Jehu's dynasty also meant the downfall of the northern kingdom of Israel.

The second child Gomer gave birth to was a daughter named *Lo-Ruhamah* (v. 6), which meant "not loved." The Lord continues to express His displeasure with Israel. Throughout the years, He had shown marvelous patience and tender mercy toward Israel, saving her many times from her enemies. But the Israelites had reached a stage where God would no longer show mercy to them, no longer protect them from their enemies. Though it might come about slowly, the withdrawal of God's mercy meant the sure and ultimate destruction of the nation. In contrast to His attitude toward proud, flourishing, secure, and sinful Israel, He promised mercy and preservation to poor, oppressed, and impoverished Judah (v. 7).

The third child born to Gomer was named *Lo-Ammi* (vv. 8-9), which meant "not My people." His name represents the whole house of apostate Israel, who first cast off the house of David and the Temple, and finally rejected God; so God says He will no longer be their God.

---

1. What was Hosea commanded to do, and why (vv. 1-2)?
2. How were the names of Hosea's three children similar (vv. 3-9)?

"When adultery walks in, everything worth having walks out."
—Woodrow Kroll

B. Reversal of Israel's Fortunes (1:10—2:1)

(Hosea 1:10-11 is not included in the printed text.)

2:1 Say ye unto your brethren, Ammi; and to your sisters, Ruhamah.

The tone expressed toward Israel changes completely in this passage, and the Lord assures them that the effects of this judgment will pass and Israel will be restored to greatness. Though God cast off the ten tribes of the northern kingdom, in His time He will bring together great numbers of true Israelites (1:10). This restoration will come as the fulfillment of God's irrevocable covenant with Abraham recorded in Genesis 22:17-18: "I will certainly bless you. I will multiply your descendants beyond number, like the stars in the sky and the sand on the seashore. Your descendants will conquer the cities of their enemies. And through your descendants all the nations of the earth will be blessed—all because you have obeyed me" (NLT).

Hosea speaks of a time when Judah and Israel will be united again (v. 11). This could be a reference to the return from captivity in Babylon. It could also have a much more extensive view with reference to Christ himself. Through the Lord, the promise to David of an everlasting throne will be fulfilled. It may also be speaking of what is happening to Israel in our day. In 1948, Israel was declared a state again for the first time in almost two thousand years. Jews from all over the world returned to the land of Israel, settling in their homeland.

God dropped the negative connotation from the names of Gomer's children. He changed *Lo-Ruhamah* to *Ruhamah*, meaning instead of "she is not loved" to "she is loved" (2:1). He changed *Lo-Ammi* to *Ammi*, meaning instead of "not My people" to "My people." He changed the meaning of *Jezreel* from "scattered" to "planted" (see 1:11). Thus, the Lord announced His intention to gather His people and plant them again in their homeland.

Hosea foretells a time in the future when the covenant promises made to Abraham concerning the expanse of his descendants and to David concerning an everlasting kingship will be fulfilled in Christ.

---

1. How would God eventually bless Israel (1:10-11)?
2. What is the significance of the two changed names (2:1)?

> "God is not at a loss when He moves to bring us back to Himself. He can woo or whip. He can draw or drive. He can work rapidly or slowly, as He pleases. In other words, He is free to be God! And in His own way, at His own pace, He brings us back."—Tom Wells

---

C. Punishment (2:2-13)

(Hosea 2:3-4, 6-13 in not included in the printed text.)

²Plead with your mother, plead: for she is not my wife, neither am I her husband: let her therefore put away her whoredoms out of her sight, and her adulteries from between her breasts;

⁵For their mother hath played the harlot: she that conceived them hath done shamefully: for she said, I will go after my lovers, that give me my bread and my water, my wool and my flax, mine oil and my drink.

The Lord calls upon the children to plead earnestly with their mother—meaning Israel—to abandon her adulteress lifestyle and sexually immoral behavior (v. 2). He wants them to let her know that He is greatly displeased with her ways; to call to her attention her unfaithful, lewd, and sinful conduct; and to remind her that God will judge her for her wayward lifestyle.

In the little word "lest" hangs hope for Israel (v. 3). The Lord is offering His people a time to repent and be reconciled. If they fail to do that, they face a great threat at His hands. If adulterous Israel does not repent and turn to God, He will strip her to the skin, as it were, lead her into captivity, and leave her in a desolate and comfortless condition. She will be left as barren as the wilderness because all the joy will be taken out of her life. He threatens her with passing through a parched land where she will face the possibility of dying of thirst. In Moses' day, God led His people through the wilderness to a place of habitation; now He will lead them through the wilderness that they may perish in it.

Not only is God's displeasure shown to the Israelites, but He has also withdrawn His mercy from their children (v. 4). The reason is that the children are as idolatrous as they are. Notice that none of them belong to God by birth; they are called "her children," not God's children.

Because of Israel's shameless ways, God could have abandoned them altogether, but instead He chooses to discipline them. It is sad to see Israel giving credit to Baal for the blessings God has bestowed upon her (v. 8). The Lord will set bounds around the Israelites so they will find little satisfaction in their wanderings and little pleasure in the sinful course they are following (vv. 5-7). From this, they should learn they can never have peace unless they follow the divinely provided way. Their circumstances should teach us also that God knows how to "hedge up [our] way with thorns" (v. 6).

---

1. What charges did God bring against Israel (vv. 2, 5)?
2. What can you learn from verses 6-8 about praying for backslidden loved ones?
3. How would God allow His people to suffer (vv. 9-12), and why (v. 13)?

> "God has no pleasure in afflicting us, but He will not keep back even the most painful chastisement if He can but thereby guide His beloved child to come home and abide in the beloved Son." —Andrew Murray

---

II. A HUSBAND'S LOVE (Hos. 2:14—3:5)

A. Restoration (2:14-20)

(Hosea 2:15-18 is not included in the printed text.)

14Therefore, behold, I will allure her, and bring her into the wilderness, and speak comfortably unto her.

19And I will betroth thee unto me for ever; yea, I will betroth thee unto me in righteousness, and in judgment, and in lovingkindness, and in mercies. 20I will even betroth thee unto me in faithfulness: and thou shalt know the Lord.

God speaks of the ways He will use to win Israel back. Using holy enticements and persuasion, He will allure her to Himself (v. 14). He will show her joy beyond any earthly joy she might experience. He will thrill her with a taste of His love. Beyond that, He will lead her back into the wilderness away from where her past lovers can influence her and where she can be open to His advances. In that environment, He will speak tenderly to her. His gracious promises and wonderful mercy will be words of comfort to a wayward Israel.

When Israel leaves the wilderness and returns to the homeland, God will abundantly enrich her with blessings that include restoring her vineyards (v. 15). This does not mean everything will always be rosy for Israel, for even as she returns to the Promised Land she will pass through "the valley of Achor." *Achor* means "troubling." It was in Achor that Achan sinned and caused Israel's conquest of Ai to fail (Josh. 7:1-5, 24-26). But now the valley will be "a door of hope" opening to Israel where, once again, she will walk in favor with God (Hos. 2:15).

After returning to the Land of Promise, Israel will acknowledge in a loving, tender manner that God is her husband and she takes delight in Him (vv. 15-16). The names of Baal will no longer be on her lips; her talk will be of Him and Him only (v. 17).

The Lord will enter into a new covenant relationship with repentant Israel and she will find peace when she returns to the land. In this full and gracious promise, the creatures that would otherwise cause them harm will be a comfort to them (v. 18). Even bloodthirsty men will become tame and peaceful in their dispositions. The Lord will remove all weapons of warfare from the land so the people can live securely.

In verses 19 and 20, God makes an incredible promise to them showing that He will always be with them. He will walk in their midst in righteousness, justice, steadfast love, tender compassion, and faithfulness. He will be their God and they would be His people.

---

1. How would God demonstrate His love for unfaithful Israel (vv. 14-15)?
2. Describe the new relationship God would have with His people (vv. 16-18).
3. What vows would God make to His people (vv. 19-20)?

> "Repentance is the true turning of our life to God, a turning that arises from a pure and earnest fear of Him; and it consists in the mortification of the flesh and the renewing of the Spirit."
> —John Calvin

B. The Great First Cause (2:21-23)

(Hosea 2:21-22 is not included in the printed text.)

²³And I will sow her unto me in the earth; and I will have mercy upon her that had not obtained mercy; and I will say to them which were not my people, Thou art my people; and they shall say, Thou art my God.

In the poetry of verses 21 and 22, a conversation is going on between the heavens and the earth. We see a picture of the harmony between all parts of the universe in response to the needs of God's people. The sky will no longer be like iron or brass, withholding its dew and rain; the earth will no longer be parched, unable to nourish the plants; nor will the fruits be denied the support of the earth.

God is the great First Cause of all nature's phenomena. God had threatened to "take back the ripened grain and new wine I generously provided each harvest season" (v. 9 NLT). But here the One who ultimately controls the agricultural cycles says He will hearken to the clouds and fill them with rain, and the skies will listen to the plea of the earth and supply it with the rain it needs. In turn, the earth will answer the thirsty cries of the corn, wine, and oil, begging it to bring them forth and make them productive.

Not only will there be a great change resulting in agricultural prosperity, but Israel will also experience a different and better standing with the Lord. No longer will she be *Jezreel* in the sense of "God scattering" (see 1:4), but in the sense of "God planting" (see v. 11). The Lord promises to bless Israel with a wonderful increase so that she will multiply and become as the sand of the sea, which cannot be measured nor numbered.

Not only will the number of God's people increase, but He will show mercy to them. He will show love to those who were called "Not loved"; and to those who were called "Not my people," He will say, "Now you are my people." And their response will be, "You are our God!" (2:23 NLT).

Verse 23 is quoted by both Paul and Peter to show both Jews and Gentiles will be converted to Christ during the church age. Paul speaks of this in Romans 9:24-25, and Peter addresses the matter in his first epistle (2:10).

---

1. What do verses 21 and 22 reveal about God's relationship with nature?
2. What would God plant for Himself, and what would be the result (v. 23)?

> "To love God is the greatest of virtues; to be loved by God is the greatest of blessings."—Author unknown

---

C. God's Love for Israel (3:1-5)
(Hosea 3:4-5 is not included in the printed text.)
¹Then said the Lord unto me, Go yet, love a woman beloved of her friend, yet an adulteress, according to the love of the Lord toward the children of Israel, who look to other gods, and love flagons of wine. ²So I bought her to me for fifteen pieces of silver, and for an homer of barley, and an half homer of barley: ³And I said unto her, Thou shalt abide for me many days; thou shalt not play the harlot, and thou shalt not be for another man: so will I also be for thee.

Hosea is instructed to take back his wife whom he still loved, although she had been unfaithful to him. Although Gomer had left Hosea and was living with another man, he obeyed the Lord's instructions.

Hosea's actions are an illustration of God's love for Israel, even though the nation had been unfaithful to Him. Although He had been the source of all the good she had ever enjoyed or could ever hope for, she had forsaken Him. She chose to worship other gods and to offer, as several translations have it, "raisin cakes to idols" (v. 1 NET). Apparently these were delicacies offered in feasts associated with Baal worship. Yet God shows mercy to Israel. What a picture of the matchless mercy of God toward a sinful nation, a people laden with iniquity, whom He loved freely as though she had never offended Him! What is said of His attitude toward Israel can be said of His regard for the whole world: "For God so loved the world, that he gave his only begotten Son, that whosoever believeth in him should not perish, but have everlasting life" (John 3:16).

When Gomer was put up for sale, her clothes would have been removed, and the men bid for her as she stood nude before them. We don't know what amount was bid first, but we do know that Hosea, obeying God's instruction to buy his wife back, bid "fifteen pieces of silver and about ten bushels of grain" (Hos. 3:2 CEV). This was a substantial price—about the price of a slave.

Herein we have a picture of the price paid for us to buy us back out of sin. God's great love saw us in sin's bondage and bought us out through the blood of His Son, Jesus Christ. The world had put in its bid for us, offering us "the lust of the flesh, and the lust of the eyes, and the pride of life" (1 John 2:16). But Jesus said, "I have a better offer for hopeless, enslaved humanity. I bid the price of My blood." God accepted that bid, being satisfied with the price Christ paid for our sins. When we believed on Christ, God forgave our sins and clothed us in robes of righteousness.

In Hosea 3:5, the prophet declares the coming reign of the Messiah over all the earth. God's people "will come trembling to the Lord and to his blessings in the last days" (NIV).

---

1. Describe Gomer's status when Hosea is told to marry her again (v. 1).
2. How did Hosea respond to this command (v. 2)?
3. Describe the prophet's vow to Gomer (v. 3).

> "Nothing humbles and breaks the heart of a sinner like mercy and love. Souls that converse much with sin and wrath, may be much terrified; but souls that converse much with grace and mercy, will be much humbled."—Thomas Brooks

---

III. A FATHER'S LOVE (Hos. 11:1-11)

A. A Kind God and an Unthankful People (vv. 1-4)

(Hosea 11:3-4 is not included in the printed text.)

¹When Israel was a child, then I loved him, and called my son out of Egypt. ²As they called them, so they went from them: they sacrificed unto Baalim, and burned incense to graven images.

Early in His relationship with the Israelites, the Lord demonstrated His great love for them. He treated them with tender and paternal affection, increasing their numbers and wealth and honor. When they were in bondage in Egypt, He brought them out (v. 1). He led them through the wilderness and planted them in the Promised Land. They suffered many hardships at the hands of the Egyptians, but God never forsook them. Instead, in His wonderful love, He redeemed them out of bondage. However, it seemed the more He did for them, the further they moved away from Him (v. 2).

When the prophets called them back to God—advising and persuading, and urging them to walk in His ways—they moved further away from the truth. They participated in the worship of Baal, worshiped the golden calf, made graven images to other gods, burned incense to them, and performed other acts of idolatry.

With tender care, a mother or nurse helps the child to form its first steps. Likewise, the Lord dealt with Israel with patience and tenderness in its infancy

(v. 3). He led them by the hand, giving them strength to grow and mature. He treated them with compassion and kindness, removing the yoke from their neck so they could eat more easily the food He provided for them (v. 4). Did they appreciate what God did for them? Obviously not! They showed an unthankful attitude, even refusing to acknowledge it was God who had helped them through the years. Instead, they attributed their deliverance to a golden calf. "All the people took the gold rings from their ears and brought them to Aaron. Then Aaron took the gold, melted it down, and molded it into the shape of a calf. When the people saw it, they exclaimed, 'O Israel, these are the gods who brought you out of the land of Egypt!'" (Ex. 32:3-4 NLT).

• List ways God had been a loving mother to Israel (vv. 1-4).

> "Love is proportional to hurt. God is love, so He is enormously grieved by our sins."—Winkie Pratney

---

B. An Unrepentant Attitude (vv. 5-7)

(Hosea 11:5-6 is not included in the printed text.)

⁷And my people are bent to backsliding from me: though they called them to the most High, none at all would exalt him.

Although God dealt kindly with the Israelites, they stubbornly continued to worship idols. Even when His prophets called them to repentance, they refused to return to Him. This resulted in their being taken captive by the Assyrians, who were a proud and cruel people. Since the Israelites ran from God and refused to heed the warning of His prophets, the difficulties they faced at the hands of their conquerors was their own fault (v. 5).

Because of their unrepentant attitude, the sword of foreign people would be unleashed against them (v. 6). The attack would be more than an overnight incursion; it would be a war that would last for years. It is dreadful when the sword abides upon a people. The enemy would have the courage to seize the cities of the land and sack and burn their "branches" (the lesser towns and villages). All of this would be done because of the Israelites' "own counsels"—following their way instead of God's design.

The people were determined to walk in their backslid ways (v. 7). As one person, the godly prophets called the Israelites to return to God; but, as one person, the Israelites refused to turn from their waywardness. None would exalt Him.

How it must grieve God for His own people to turn away from Him and follow a course of action that displeases Him. What a message and warning to the Church not to abandon its allegiance to the Lord, but to give Him first place in all things!

• How would God's people suffer, and why?

C. God's Mercy (vv. 8-11)

(Hosea 11:8, 10-11 is not included in the printed text.)

⁹I will not execute the fierceness of mine anger, I will not return to destroy Ephraim: for I am God, and not man; the Holy One in the midst of thee: and I will not enter into the city.

The Israelites deserved the same treatment as the cities of the plains (including Admah and Zeboim) received, which was utter destruction (v. 8; Gen. 19:25). They had forgotten God and openly showed their devotion to false gods, but the Lord reveals how strong His feelings are for Israel. The thought of giving up on them and letting them go caused Him inner turmoil, stirring His compassion and tearing at His heart.

The Lord determined He would not unleash His fierce anger and completely destroy the people; rather, He would act in mercy and not execute justice (Hos. 11:9). He is compassionate and forgiving, a God who is holy, just, and faithful. He relates to Christians in the same way today. Justice is reconciled with mercy through the atoning death of Jesus Christ. In Him, God "is faithful and just to forgive us our sins, and to cleanse us from all unrighteousness" (1 John 1:9) when we confess our sins to Him.

The Lord saw a day when Israel would walk with Him again. They would respond to His call and come from all directions—the west, Egypt, and Assyria (Hos. 11:10–11). God's love reaches to the farthest distance, His power is without limits, and no enemy can keep His people when He calls them to Himself. One thinks of the words of Jesus about the end time: "I say unto you, That many shall come from the east and west, and shall sit down with Abraham, and Isaac, and Jacob, in the kingdom of heaven" (Matt. 8:11).

---

1. Describe God's feelings toward Israel (v. 8).
2. What did God promise not to do (v. 9)?
3. How would Israel eventually respond to the Lord's love (vv. 10-11)?

"When you stray from His presence, He longs for you to come back. He weeps that you are missing out on His love, protection,

---

and provision. He throws His arms open, runs toward you, gathers you up, and welcomes you home."—Charles Stanley

CONCLUSION

The Israelites, of all people, should have known that God can be trusted. Although they failed Him on numerous occasions, He was always faithful to them. He repeatedly received them back after they wandered away. His compassion and love was on display time and again. He is the same God today. We can trust Him completely. He will never fail us. Have you put your trust in Him?

GOLDEN TEXT CHALLENGE

"I WILL BETROTH THEE UNTO ME FOR EVER; YEA, I WILL BETROTH THEE UNTO ME IN RIGHTEOUSNESS, AND IN JUDGMENT, AND IN LOVINGKINDNESS, AND IN MERCIES" (Hos. 2:19).

All who are sincerely devoted to God are betrothed to Him. To them He gives the most sacred and inviolable promise that He will love, protect, and provide for them. In this betrothal He forgets the past, forgives sin, espouses anew, and that forever. Christ betroths both His church and individual Christians to Himself forever. They are not only pardoned, but joined to Him in service; not only reconciled to God through Him, but admitted into the inner circle of warm fellowship.

Daily Devotions:

M. Disobedience Has Consequences • Genesis 6:5-8
T. Teach Children to Obey God • Deuteronomy 6:1-7
W. Obeying God Can Be Costly • Daniel 3:13-20, 28
T. Jesus Was Obedient for Us • Romans 5:12-21
F. Jesus, the Model of Obedience • Hebrews 5:1-9
S. God Loves Us as Children • 1 John 3:1-3

God of Judgment and Mercy

Joel 1:1—3:21

Unit Theme:
The Minor Prophets, Part 1

Central Truth:
The penitent experience God's mercy.

Focus:
Recognize God's judgment against sinners and seek His mercy through repentance.

Context:
The occasion of the book was a devastating locust plague in Israel. The date is uncertain.

Golden Text:
"Rend your heart, and not your garments, and turn unto the Lord your God: for he is gracious and merciful, slow to anger, and of great kindness, and repenteth him of the evil" (Joel 2:13).

Study Outline:
I. **Call on God** (Joel 1:1-20)
II. **Repent and Turn to God** (Joel 2:1-2, 11-17)
III. **God's Mercy and Judgment** (Joel 2:18-20, 25-32; 3:12-16)

INTRODUCTION

Apart from identifying Joel as the son of Pethuel, nothing else is told us about him. It is probable that Joel was a contemporary of Elisha. Although the book consists only of three chapters, it is a literary gem. Of its style, the book has been described as "preeminently pure. It is characterized by smoothness and fluency . . . strength [and] tenderness" (*JFB Commentary*).

The prophet's writing is indeed impressive. Joel has a knack for drawing a most descriptive word picture. The reader can visualize the swarm of locusts descending upon the land, which has been called the grandest description in all literature of locust devastation.

The prophet pictures absolute devastation on one hand, and the golden age of plenty on the other. No one can deny the clear call to repentance Joel makes and its obvious results. Joel knew that genuine repentance is the basis for real revival.

The section of the book most often discussed concerns the outpouring of the Holy Spirit fulfilled on the Day of Pentecost. This would be a time characterized by prophecy, dreams, and visions. It offers a perfect description of the Pentecostal age in which we now live.

Joel has been called both a *foreteller* and a *forthteller*. As the latter, his message was intended for his own generation. As the foreteller, he was inspired to look into the future and speak to a coming generation.

Equally intriguing are his thoughts on the invasion of the locusts and the apocalyptic view of the coming Day of the Lord. He spoke of things which were evident to those to whom he addressed his words, and warned of an immediate judgment, but also looked into the distant future to the ultimate Day of the Lord. The remarkable prophecies Joel uttered extended in scope from his day to the end of time.

I. CALL ON GOD (Joel 1:1-20)

A. A Divine Visitation (vv. 1-4)

¹The word of the Lord that came to Joel the son of Pethuel. ²Hear this, ye old men, and give ear, all ye inhabitants of the land. Hath this been in your days, or even in the days of your fathers? ³Tell ye your children of it, and let your children tell their children, and their children another generation. ⁴That which the palmerworm hath left hath the locust eaten; and that which the locust hath left hath the cankerworm eaten; and that which the cankerworm hath left hath the caterpiller eaten.

The message Joel brings has come to him from the Lord (v. 1). It is not the product of his imagination, but a divine communication and must be taken seriously.

Joel addresses the results of a devastating locust attack on the crops of the land. Since man and beast depended on this produce for survival, the plague had far-reaching effects. He asks the oldest inhabitants of the land if they have ever seen anything like this or had they ever heard their forefathers speak of a circumstance this bad (v. 2). All the produce of the land, from the various sorts of corn to their choicest fruit trees, was gone. In addition to the destruction of their crops, the excessive heat and drought that accompanied this invasion would leave the herds and flocks without water and, therefore, about to perish.

Joel would have all the inhabitants of the land to understand this is a divine visitation. This is a warning to those who would choose to disregard the works of the Lord. Furthermore, they are to tell the great works of God to their children and to their children's children (v. 3). The psalmist said, "This shall be written for the generation to come" (102:18). He also said they are to "declare his righteousness unto a people that shall be born, that he hath done this" (22:31).

Joel describes four sets of locusts which came in successive waves and completely destroyed the land's vegetation, resulting in a grievous famine (v. 4). This calamity came upon a land God once protected and blessed. The guilt must be great that leads God to punish His own land. This is a lesson Christians must learn. Desolation awaits the believer or the church that succumbs to sin and fails to bear fruit to the glory of God.

• What needed to be passed on to the next generation, and why?

> "For those who have not yet turned to the Lord for His salvation, their condition of suffering often creates compelling opportunities for them to cry out to God for His help."—T. A. McMahon

---

B. A Time of Mourning (vv. 5-12)

(Joel 1:5-7, 11-12 is not included in the printed text.)

⁸Lament like a virgin girded with sackcloth for the husband of her youth. ⁹The meat offering and the drink offering is cut off from the house of the Lord; the priests, the Lord's ministers, mourn. ¹⁰The field is wasted, the land mourneth; for the corn is wasted: the new wine is dried up, the oil languisheth.

The prophet calls for drunkards to awaken from their stupor and to weep and wail because the source of their wine is gone; the grapes are ruined (v. 5). He describes a vast army of locusts too numerous to count who had invaded the land and stripped bare the grapevines and fig trees, leaving nothing but white and bare branches (vv. 6-7). Their ability to devour was like the power of a lion as they stripped the bark from the trees and left them in ruin.

The prophet turns his attention away from the godless among the Jews to address the godly among them, warning them to prepare for a time of mourning. He speaks of calamitous times to come that call for weeping. He describes deep mourning similar to that of a virgin whose husband to be is snatched away from her by an untimely death (v. 8).

Like the rest of the population, the priests have reason to mourn (v. 9). He reminds them the land is ruined, the grain is devoured, and the oil of the olive is lost; thus they could not offer proper sacrifices on the altar.

He then turns his attention to the farmers and tells them the pomegranate, palm, and apple trees are ruined; the ground is dried up and the harvest of the field is destroyed (vv. 10-12).

Joel has given a wake-up call to the Israelites and their leaders. The Scripture calls on believers to awake from their sleep and busy themselves in the work of the Lord. Paul cautioned, "Now it is high time to awake out of sleep: for now is our salvation nearer than when we believed" (Rom. 13:11). He also admonished, "Awake thou that sleepest, and arise from the dead, and Christ shall give thee light" (Eph. 5:14). He further wrote, "Therefore let us not sleep, as do others; but let us watch and be sober" (1 Thess. 5:6). Peter also addressed the issue, saying, "Be sober, be vigilant; because your adversary the devil, as a roaring lion, walketh about, seeking whom he may devour" (1 Peter 5:8).

---

1. Describe the loss pictured in verses 5-7.
2. How did the devastation affect religious life (vv. 8-10)?
3. How does verse 12 compare the people's emotional condition with the trees?

> "Many mourn for their sins that do not truly repent of them, weep bitterly for them, and yet continue in love and league with them."—Matthew Henry

---

C. A Solemn Assembly (vv. 13-20)

(Joel 1:15-20 is not included in the printed text.)

¹³Gird yourselves, and lament, ye priests: howl, ye ministers of the altar: come, lie all night in sackcloth, ye ministers of my God: for the meat offering and the drink offering is withholden from the house of your God. ¹⁴Sanctify ye a fast, call a solemn assembly, gather the elders and all the inhabitants of the land into the house of the Lord your God, and cry unto the Lord.

Joel calls on the priests to lead the nation in mourning. They were to weep bitterly like one would who mourned the death of a loved one. While others might mourn in the day, the priests were to mourn night and day lying wrapped in sackcloth as an outward expression of their sorrow (v. 13). Their duty was to offer up sacrifices for their own sins and the sins of others, but the ingredients of certain daily offerings were no longer available. Because of the terrible conditions upon the land, the grain and drink offerings were not being brought to the Temple, therefore the priests could not do their job.

Joel instructed the priests to call the people to a time of fasting, and to gather for a solemn, sacred assembly (v. 14). The leaders and the other inhabitants of the land were to gather at the house of God, laying everything else aside and cry unto the Lord. They were to go without food, confess their sins, repent of them, and return to God. They were to shed tears of repentance, seeking God with a broken heart, pleading His promises and waiting for His mercies.

What a picture Joel paints of the devastation that besets the land! All the joy of celebration is gone (vv. 15-16). The land is parched so that if one turns over a clod of dirt, he finds the seeds still lying there with no signs of germination (v. 17). There is no pasture left for the animals, so they wander about searching for something to eat. Specifically, he says the sheep and goats "groan" (v. 18). The barns and storehouses stand empty, since no harvest is available. "Fire has devoured the open pastures and flames have burned up all the trees of the field" (v. 19 NIV).

The wild animals suffer as much as the domesticated. The prophet pictures them crying out to God for help since the streams had dried up (v. 20).

---

1. How must the religious leaders respond to the crisis, and why (v. 13)?
2. Describe the "solemn assembly" Joel called for (v. 14).
3. What is "the day of the Lord" (v. 15)?
4. How were animals affected by Israel's condition (vv. 18, 20)?

> "Prayer is reaching out after the unseen; fasting is letting go of all that is seen and temporal. Fasting helps express, deepen, confirm the resolution that we are ready to sacrifice anything, even ourselves, to attain what we seek for the kingdom of God."
> —Andrew Murray

II. REPENT AND TURN TO GOD (Joel 2:1-2, 11-17)

A. The Day of the Lord (vv. 1-2)

¹Blow ye the trumpet in Zion, and sound an alarm in my holy mountain: let all the inhabitants of the land tremble: for the day of the Lord cometh, for it is nigh at hand; ²A day of darkness and of gloominess, a day of clouds and of thick darkness, as the morning spread upon the mountains: a great people and a strong; there hath not been ever the like, neither shall be any more after it, even to the years of many generations.

After describing the horrible results of the invasion of the locusts, we would think Joel might now have a word of encouragement for the people. Perhaps he would say something like times have been bad, but better times are coming. But that is not the case. In fact, his message is that things are going to get worse; what is coming is far more destructive than what has been.

This chapter looks in a different direction than the previous one. In chapter 1, Joel speaks of events that have already taken place; in chapter 2, he looks to the future. He sees the events of the first chapter as a warning of things to come. He now calls for the blowing of the trumpet and the sounding of an alarm throughout the land (v. 1). The trumpet was a ram's horn and the blowing thereof signaled a time of great danger. The sound of this alarm should bring fear and trembling to the people.

Joel reminds the people that "the day of the Lord" is coming, that it is even at hand. Several of the writers of this era address this dreadful day. It is described as a day such as had never been before and would never be after. That day is always described as a time of gloominess, destruction, and darkness (v. 2).

Isaiah described the day of the Lord this way:

> Wail, for the day of the Lord is at hand! It will come as destruction from the Almighty. . . . Behold, the day of the Lord comes, cruel, with both wrath and fierce anger, to lay the land desolate; and He will destroy its sinners from it. For the stars of heaven and their constellations will not give their light; the sun will be darkened in its going forth, and the moon will not cause its light to shine (Isa. 13:6, 9-10 NKJV).

Amos paints this gloomy scene, "Will not the day of the Lord be darkness, not light—pitch-dark, without a ray of brightness?" (Amos 5:20 NIV).

In Joel 2:3-10, he continues his description of the coming Day of the Lord. Whatever troublesome times the earth has seen—locusts, invasions, plagues, famines, wars, and natural catastrophes—are minor judgments compared to it. The reader needs to take heed because Joel is talking about wrath that is yet to come.

The invading army is compared to a roaring fire that wipes out everything in its path. Land as luscious as the Garden of Eden may lie before it; but once it passes through, there is nothing left but desolation. In contrast to the orderly advance of this army is the cosmic disorder of the entire world. The earth trembles and the heavens shake. The sun and the moon become dark and the stars stop shining. All of this is characteristic of the Day of the Lord.

---

1. How and why must the Church "blow the trumpet" today (v. 1)?
2. How does verse 2 describe the Day of the Lord?

> "It is not a true Gospel that gives us the impression that the Christian life is easy, and that there are no problems to be faced."—Martyn Lloyd-Jones

---

B. A Call to Repent (vv. 11-17)

(Joel 2:11-12, 16-17 is not included in the printed text.)

¹³And rend your heart, and not your garments, and turn unto the Lord your God: for he is gracious and merciful, slow to anger, and of great kindness, and repenteth him of the evil. ¹⁴Who knoweth if he will return and repent, and leave a blessing behind him; even a meat offering and a drink offering unto the Lord your God? ¹⁵Blow the trumpet in Zion, sanctify a fast, call a solemn assembly.

The Day of the Lord is a day of God's judgment. The disastrous happenings described in this chapter are minor compared to the outpouring of divine wrath that is to come. So severe are these future events that the prophet asks, "Who can possibly survive?" (v. 11 NLT). Make no mistake about it, the divine Commander is in charge of this invasion.

Confronted by such a massive invasion and its horrific outcome, the nation's only hope is to repent before the Lord. In a direct and moving appeal, the Lord calls on them to do just that. Since the time of this invasion was uncertain, there is an urgency about the call. They are to repent immediately (v. 12).

The Lord urges the people to call on Him with all their heart (v. 13). He is more interested in their being brokenhearted over sin than to participate in any mere outward show of concern. At an earlier time, God said to Samuel concerning one of Jesse's sons, "Look not on his countenance, or on the height of his stature; because I have refused him: for the Lord seeth not as man seeth; for man looketh on the outward appearance, but the Lord looketh on the heart" (1 Sam. 16:7). It is only when we rend our hearts that we gain again the favor of the Lord.

The Lord appeals to His character as an incentive to repent. After all, He is "merciful and compassionate, slow to get angry and filled with unfailing

---

love" (Joel 2:13 NLT). If the people truly repent, God might give a reprieve and extend to them a blessing instead of a curse.

The Lord makes an appeal to the leaders of Israel to be in the forefront by setting an example for all to see. They are to "*blow* the trumpet . . . *sanctify* a fast, *call* a solemn assembly: *gather* the people, *sanctify* the congregation, *assemble* the elders, *gather* the children" (vv. 15-16, italics added). The entire congregation of Israel was to be brought together. No one was to be left out: from the oldest to the youngest, all were to assemble. The priests were to lead in the worship, crying out to God for mercy and to spare them from the derision of other nations who might bring the accusation that God had abandoned His people (v. 17).

---

1. Respond to the question in verse 11.
2. What does wholehearted turning to God look like (v. 12)?
3. How does verse 13 describe God?
4. How urgent is the sacred assembly Joel calls for, and who is to participate (vv. 15-16)?
5. When and why should we fast?
6. How does Joel instruct the religious leaders to pray (v. 17)?

Plea for Forgiveness

By his investigation and meditations and calculations, the great Polish mathematician Copernicus revolutionized human thought about the universe. Yet, before God, Copernicus saw himself not as an astronomer or a scholar but as a sinner.

Today on his grave at Frauenburg you can read the epitaph which he chose for himself: "I do not seek a kindness equal to that given to Paul; nor do I ask the grace granted to Peter; but that forgiveness which Thou didst give to the robber—that I earnestly pray."—*Macartney's Illustrations*

III. GOD'S MERCY AND JUDGMENT (Joel 2:18-20, 25-32; 3:12-16)

A. The Promise of Blessing (2:18-20)

(Joel 2:19-20 is not included in the printed text.)

¹⁸Then will the Lord be jealous for his land, and pity his people.

When the people of God turn to Him in repentance, He shows compassion for them and restores lost blessings. In verse 19, His blessings on Israel include green pastures and fruitful trees, resulting in plentiful grain and new wine and oil.

God provides for the needs of His people. This does not mean believers will automatically become wealthy, though some may; but God will take care of us according to His promise. Jesus addressed this matter in the Sermon

---

on the Mount. He declared believers to be of more value than "the birds of the air" or "the lilies of the field" (Matt. 6:26-28 NKJV). He says life is "more than food and the body more than clothing" (v. 25 NKJV). He exhorts us not to worry about what we are going to eat, drink, or wear. These are the things, He says, that unbelievers concern themselves about. He assures us He knows we "need . . . all these things" (v. 32). Then Jesus declares, "Seek ye first the kingdom of God, and his righteousness; and all these things shall be added unto you" (v. 33).

Not only did the Lord promise material blessings to Israel, He also assured them of a secure environment (Joel 2:20). He promised to stop the invading armies, sending them into a parched and barren land. He would drive the armies on the front (leading the invasion) into the Dead Sea, and those bringing up the rear He would drive into the Mediterranean Sea. The stench from the dead bodies would permeate the air. Isaiah described a similar scene: "Their dead will be left unburied, and the stench of rotting bodies will fill the land" (34:3 NLT).

For a people who had come to fear the future, they were reminded that God had done great and mighty things (Joel 2:21). In His hands, they were secure. In these uncertain days in which we live, we need to remember the words of Jesus concerning the signs of the times: "When these things begin to come to pass, then look up, and lift up your heads; for your redemption draweth nigh" (Luke 21:28).

---

1. How did God feel toward His people (v. 18)?
2. Describe the change God would initiate (v. 19).
3. Why would God's people feel secure (v. 20)?

> "The Lamb has conquered, and the doom of the devil is sealed for all eternity. Righteousness will triumph. The Word of God, which is established forever, has declared it."—David M. Griffis

---

B. The Outpouring of the Holy Spirit (vv. 25-32)
   (Joel 2:26-27, 30-31 is not included in the printed text.)
25And I will restore to you the years that the locust hath eaten, the cankerworm, and the caterpiller, and the palmerworm, my great army which I sent among you.

28And it shall come to pass afterward, that I will pour out my spirit upon all flesh; and your sons and your daughters shall prophesy, your old men shall dream dreams, your young men shall see visions: 29And also upon the servants and upon the handmaids in those days will I pour out my spirit.

32And it shall come to pass, that whosoever shall call on the name of the Lord shall be delivered: for in mount Zion and in Jerusalem shall be

deliverance, as the Lord hath said, and in the remnant whom the Lord shall call.

The Lord promised His people that He would reverse the lost years (v. 25). Only He could do that and only because they returned to Him. This promise means they would have all the food they wanted (v. 26). This abundant provision would prompt them to praise the name of the Lord and recognize His miraculous working (v. 27).

Anyone whose life has been destroyed by the ravishes of sin—who has seen divine blessing stripped away and the soul made barren—can have life restored by returning to God. He alone can make the barren life fruitful again.

Joel wrote of a day when the Spirit of the Lord would be poured out "on all people" (v. 28 NIV). In Numbers 11:26-28, Joshua objected to a couple of the elders of Israel prophesying. Moses responded by saying, "I wish that all the Lord's people were prophets and that the Lord would put his Spirit upon them all!" (v. 29 NLT).

Well, Joel spoke of a day when that would happen . . . a day when sons and daughters would prophesy; when old men would dream dreams and young men would see visions; when the Holy Spirit would be poured out on men and women alike (vv. 28-29). This prophecy began to be fulfilled on the Day of Pentecost (Acts 2), and it is continuing. Since near the turn of the twentieth century, a fresh outpouring of the Spirit has swept across the world, and now millions of individuals have received this blessed Pentecostal experience!

Joel also spoke of that "great and dreadful day" (2:31 NIV) when the sun would become dark and the moon would turn blood-red. However, he ends this section with the promise that "whoever calls on the name of the Lord will be delivered" (v. 32 NASB).

---

1. Describe the restorative ability of God (v. 25).
2. What would God do for His people, and why (vv. 26-27)?
3. What does God promise to "pour out," and why (vv. 28-29)?
4. What will happen before the Day of the Lord comes (vv. 30-31)?
5. Who can receive salvation, and how (v. 32)?

"The Spirit-filled life is not a special, deluxe edition of Christianity. It is part and parcel of the total plan of God for His people."
—A. W. Tozer

C. The Valley of Decision (3:12-16)

(Joel 3:13, 15 is not included in the printed text.)

¹²Let the heathen be wakened, and come up to the valley of Jehoshaphat: for there will I sit to judge all the heathen round about.

¹⁴Multitudes, multitudes in the valley of decision: for the day of the Lord is near in the valley of decision.

God of Judgment and Mercy

¹⁶The Lord also shall roar out of Zion, and utter his voice from Jerusalem; and the heavens and the earth shall shake: but the Lord will be the hope of his people, and the strength of the children of Israel.

Chapter 3 opens with God's charge against the nations for mistreating His people and scattering them among the nations. They made slaves of His people, sold their boys as payment to obtain prostitutes, and sold girls to get enough wine to get drunk. They stole silver and gold and carried them off to pagan temples (vv. 1-6). The Lord assured the heathen nations He would bring His people back from wherever they have been scattered, and that He would pay the offending nations back for everything they had done (vv. 7-8).

Joel gives us more detail about the coming Day of the Lord than is found in other areas of Scripture. He addresses the judgment of the nations (vv. 11-13) in terms that agree with what the Lord says in Matthew 25:31-46. Joel's reference to "the valley of decision" (3:14) is not a call to decide to follow Christ. Rather, it speaks of the day when the great Judge will announce final decisions about humanity, dividing those who lived right from those who did not. The Lord will separate those who will share His kingdom from those who will enter into eternal punishment.

In verse 16, the Lord's voice roars and thunders, causing creation to tremble. However, His people need not fear, for the Lord will be their refuge and stronghold forever.

---

1. What awaits the nations (vv. 12-13)?
2. What will happen in "the valley of decision" (v. 14)?
3. How should Christians be comforted by verse 16?

"When the Author walks on the stage, the play is over. God is going to invade, all right—something so beautiful to some of us and so terrible to others. . . . It will be too late then to choose your side."—C. S. Lewis

---

CONCLUSION

A day of accounting is coming for all people. We can accept the work of redemption Christ accomplished for us and have our sins forgiven and be welcomed to a home in heaven, or we can stand before God in that great day of judgment and be sentenced to eternal separation from Him. Those who repent of their sins and believe on the Lord Jesus Christ will be saved from any future condemnation.

GOLDEN TEXT CHALLENGE

"REND YOUR HEART, AND NOT YOUR GARMENTS, AND TURN UNTO THE LORD YOUR GOD: FOR HE IS GRACIOUS AND MERCIFUL, SLOW

TO ANGER, AND OF GREAT KINDNESS, AND REPENTETH HIM OF THE EVIL" (Joel 2:13).

Here stands the Lord God. He is *gracious* (inclined to pardon) and *merciful* (overflowing with compassion). He is filled with *loving-kindness* (exuberant goodness), and is *slow* to anger, giving the backslider every chance to repent.

There stands the backslider, his back turned toward God by his own choice. God wants to pardon and receive him, but the conditions are clear: The backslider must have a broken, repentant heart, making a turn away from sin and toward God. Then God's forgiveness will flow.

Daily Devotions:

M. Return to the Lord • Deuteronomy 30:1-10
T. Repentance and Restoration • Job 42:1-10
W. God Offers Mercy to Backsliders • Jeremiah 3:6-13
T. Rejoice Over the Penitent • Luke 15:1-7
F. Godly Grief Produces Repentance • 2 Corinthians 7:8-13
S. God Desires All to Repent • 2 Peter 3:8-13

Salvation Through God's Judgment

Amos 1:1-2; 7:1—9:15

> **Unit Theme:**
> The Minor Prophets (Part 1)
>
> **Central Truth:**
> God disciplines erring Christians in order to restore fellowship with Him.
>
> **Focus:**
> Perceive how God uses judgment to reform His people and yield to His loving discipline.
>
> **Context:**
> The prophet Amos ministered in the northern kingdom of Israel during the eighth century BC.
>
> **Golden Text:**
> "Seek good, and not evil, that ye may live: and so the Lord, the God of hosts, shall be with you, as ye have spoken" (Amos 5:14).
>
> **Study Outline:**
> I. **Inescapable Judgment** (Amos 1:1-2; 7:1-17)
> II. **Terrible End** (Amos 8:1-14)
> III. **Restoration Assured** (Amos 9:1-15)

INTRODUCTION

The only thing we know about Amos is what we find in his book. Therein he tells who he is, where he came from, and when he prophesied. Amos is clear that he was called of God to be His messenger. His message was primarily one of judgment. He condemns the ethical mistreatment of the misfortunate of society. Such conduct violates the moral laws that hold a society together.

Amos rails against the misuse of privilege. Instead of acknowledging God's blessing as the source of their standing, the Israelites used the advantages they had in a sinful manner. Such action always results in the judgment of God. In this case, God used a neighboring country as a rod with which to smite Israel.

Amos conveyed five visions of judgment which the Lord had shown him. Each vision was presented in the form of a specific object: locusts, fire, a plumb line, summer fruit, and a smitten sanctuary. Each object represented a different phase of divine judgment which was to come.

Amos concludes the book on a positive note. He announces the restoration of the Davidic kingdom and the blessings of God poured out on those who are faithful to Him. For them a brighter day was coming.

Several characteristics mark the message from Amos. He sees God as the Creator of the world and its Sustainer. He pictures God as very active in the affairs of humanity and underscores His particular interest in Israel, acknowledging Him as the God of Israel.

The burden of Amos' heart was to call for righteousness in the name of the Lord. All the rituals, festivals, and offerings the people might participate in were meaningless unless their hearts were right with God. Their violations of the moral laws established by God were a provocation resulting in divine judgment. It is unfortunate that the message Amos brought went unheeded by many who heard it. Instead of receiving his words favorably, Amaziah the priest invited him to leave the country and take his message to Judah.

I. INESCAPABLE JUDGMENT (Amos 1:1-2; 7:1-17)

A. The Coming Wrath (1:1-2)

(Amos 1:1-2 is not included in the printed text.)

Amos, by interpretation, means "a burden." His words expressed the burden of the word of the Lord to Israel for her sin. Amos was a passionate prophet whose message included reproofs and threatenings so strong that many had difficulty bearing them. Obstinate sinners did not want to hear about God's displeasure, but Amos spoke the truth anyhow.

Of his own admission, Amos was not a prophet, not even the son of a prophet; he was a herdsman and a gatherer of sycamore fruit (7:14). Amos is an example of how God "has chosen the foolish things of the world to put to shame the wise, and God has chosen the weak things of the world to put to shame the things which are mighty" (1 Cor. 1:27 NKJV).

Amos was a shepherd and a farmer from Tekoa (1:1)—a town in the hill country of Judah about six miles from Bethlehem and ten miles south of Jeru-salem. He was given a vision concerning Israel, a revelation from the Lord. It was bad news for that nation whose ten tribes had rebelled against God and had been warned many times of the consequences of their errant ways. This vision came in the days when Uzziah reigned in Judah and Jeroboam was king in Israel. These were also the days of Hosea, Isaiah, and Micah.

Under the reign of these two kings, Judah and Israel enjoyed great pros-perity and lost all sense of their dependence on God. The psalmist described their situation: "They are not in trouble as other men; neither are they plagued like other men. Therefore pride compasseth them about as a chain; violence covereth them as a garment" (73:5-6). Amos was sent to warn them of the evil of their ways and urge them to turn back to God.

We are told this message came to Amos two years before what is called "the earthquake" (Amos 1:1). It must have been a notable earthquake that was still in the minds of the people. It was so terrible that Zechariah 14:5 says the people fled from it. Josephus says "half a great hill was removed by it out of its place, and carried four furlongs another way; so that the highway was obstructed, and the king's gardens utterly marred." By such extraordinary works, God shows His justice and displeasure against sin.

Amos shows the judgment of God is about to fall on Israel and other nations who had sinned against Him. Wherever the breath of God reached, the land would dry up, wither, and die (1:2). Those who heard the words coming from Amos would understand the wrath of God had moved against the land.

- How did God change the life of Amos?

> "God whispers to us in our pleasures; He speaks to us in our work; He shouts at us in our pain."—C. S. Lewis

---

B. God's Unrelenting Judgment (7:1-9)

(Amos 7:2-3, 5-6 is not included in the printed text.)

¹Thus hath the Lord God shewed unto me; and, behold, he formed grasshoppers in the beginning of the shooting up of the latter growth; and, lo, it was the latter growth after the king's mowings.

⁴Thus hath the Lord God shewed unto me: and, behold, the Lord God called to contend by fire, and it devoured the great deep, and did eat up a part.

⁷Thus he shewed me: and, behold, the Lord stood upon a wall made by a plumbline, with a plumbline in his hand. ⁸And the Lord said unto me, Amos, what seest thou? And I said, A plumbline. Then said the Lord, Behold, I will set a plumbline in the midst of my people Israel: I will not again pass by them any more: ⁹And the high places of Isaac shall be desolate, and the sanctuaries of Israel shall be laid waste; and I will rise against the house of Jeroboam with the sword.

In chapters 3-6, the prophet spells out the reasons for God's judgment against His people. Repeatedly, they had violated the covenants they had agreed to before the Lord. In chapters 7-9, the Lord describes the results of this coming judgment. Amos records five visions which detail the devastation that will come to the land, its buildings, and its people. What a warning these chapters give to those who would spurn God's will and grace!

The first vision shows God preparing to send a vast swarm of locusts over the land at the most vulnerable time of the year (7:1). The first cutting of the crop went to the king for the feeding of the military animals. So the best of the crop went for the king's use. The second phase of the crop—either that which grew after the first cutting or what was planted later—was for the people. If this harvest was lost, it could bring famine upon the land.

In this vision, Amos saw locusts completely consume the earth's vegetation. The prophet knew if this vision became a reality, the nation could not survive. So, he did the best thing any of us can do in a dire circumstance—he went to the Lord in prayer. He followed Elijah's example in the face of possible famine. James wrote: "The effective, fervent prayer of a righteous man avails much. Elijah . . . prayed earnestly . . . and the heaven gave rain, and the earth produced its fruit" (James 5:16-18 NKJV).

Amos knew sin was the cause of Israel's misery, so he interceded with the Lord to pardon them. He knew if God had cast them down, no one else could lift them up (Amos 7:2). He also knew they were too small, too weak, and too few to resist their enemies if God did not show them mercy. Amos' prayer prevailed; a famine caused by locusts did not come, for the Lord's judgment was diverted (v. 3).

In the second vision, Amos saw destruction come to the land by means of fire (v. 4). The fire spread in all directions, and any attempt to stop it was futile. Again Amos interceded with the Lord, and the Lord heard his prayers and declared this would not come to pass (vv. 5-6).

In the third vision, Amos sees the Lord holding a plumb line in His hand (v. 7). A *plumb line* was a cord used by builders to make sure the walls were constructed straight up and down. The nation had been built true to plumb, but now was out of line and needed to be torn down. Unlike the other visions, this time God would not relent; the matter was settled (v. 8). God said He would not overlook their sin. He would pull down all that was faulty—the pagan shrines and temples of Israel—and bring the dynasty of Jeroboam to an end (v. 9).

---

1. Describe the first vision, Amos' reaction, and God's answer (vv. 1-3).
2. Describe the second vision, Amos' reaction, and God's answer (vv. 4-6).
3. What was the third vision, and how would it be fulfilled (vv. 7-9)?

> "Our God is a consuming fire. He consumes pride, lust, materialism, and other sin."—Leonard Ravenhill

---

C. God's Instruction to Amos (vv. 10-17)

(Amos 7:10-11, 14-16 is not included in the printed text.)

¹²Also Amaziah said unto Amos, O thou seer, go, flee thee away into the land of Judah, and there eat bread, and prophesy there: ¹³But prophesy not again any more at Bethel: for it is the king's chapel, and it is the king's court.

¹⁷Therefore thus saith the Lord; Thy wife shall be an harlot in the city, and thy sons and thy daughters shall fall by the sword, and thy land shall be divided by line; and thou shalt die in a polluted land: and Israel shall surely go into captivity forth of his land.

When Amos began to prophesy about the ruin that would come to the house of Jeroboam because of their sin, Amaziah, the chief priest of Bethel, spoke out against him. Bethel was one of the state sanctuaries Jeroboam had established when he broke away from Jerusalem. It was designed to duplicate the religious system and bring stability to the northern kingdom.

Amaziah sent a message to King Jeroboam accusing Amos of high treason by openly and publicly encouraging rebellion against the king (v. 10). He declared that Amos' message was intolerable and, in the end, would bring well-ordered government to an end. Amos had prophesied against the house of Jeroboam, foretelling that Israel would be led away captive (v. 11).

Amaziah then ordered Amos to get out of Bethel, to return to the land of Judah and do his prophesying there (v. 12). He insinuated that Amos was in the prophesying business just to earn a living and that he could do that in

Judah. He reminded the prophet that Bethel is "the king's sanctuary and the national place of worship!" (v. 13 NLT). His preaching was not welcome here, and he would be wise to follow Amaziah's advice and leave the country.

Amos had a ready answer for the priest. He said he was not a professional prophet, rather he was a shepherd and a farmer (v. 14). More importantly, the Lord had commanded him to go to Israel and prophesy, instructing Israel by foretelling what was coming (v. 15). The Lord had not only told him what to say but where to say it. His message was to be given in Israel and not in Judah. The prophet was doing exactly what the Lord had directed him to do.

Amos then painted a bleak picture of what Amaziah could expect. Because he had so directly and strenuously opposed the Lord, his wife would be forced into prostitution, and all would take notice (v. 17). His sons and daughters would be killed. The land would be divided among foreigners. Amaziah himself would die in a foreign land and the people of Israel would be sent into exile.

---

1. Of what did Amaziah accuse Amos before the king (vv. 10-11)?
2. Why was Amos such a bold prophet (vv. 12-15)?
3. What did Amos prophesy concerning Amaziah (vv. 16-17)?

> "Courage is the indispensable requisite of any true ministry. . . . Do not keep on all your life preaching sermons which shall say not what God sent you to declare, but what they hire you to say."—Phillips Brooks

---

II. TERRIBLE END (Amos 8:1-14)

A. The Ruin of Israel (vv. 1-3)

(Amos 8:1, 3 is not included in the printed text.)

²And he said, Amos, what seest thou? And I said, A basket of summer fruit. Then said the Lord unto me, The end is come upon my people of Israel; I will not again pass by them any more.

In the fourth vision the Lord gives to Amos, the ruin of Israel is again foretold. Amos sees "a basket of summer fruit" (v. 1). By *summer fruit*, he means fruit at the end of the season, fully ripened, and with a short edible life.

When Amos acknowledges he sees a basket of summer fruit, the Lord explains what it means. The summer fruit represents "the end" for Israel (v. 2). The working of God's providences, mercies, chastenings, visitations, instructions, and warnings are completed.

Sinful works consist of three stages: a *beginning*, *progress*, and *completion*. Its progress leads to a ripening in wickedness which results in destruction by the hand of the Lord. Israel has reached the place where God will no longer overlook their sin. God's patience toward Israel has run out, and it means the end of their peace, growth, and glory. Until now they could boast they were God's people, and the nations around them recognized them as such. Until now God had spared Israel the punishment they often so richly deserved, but that day is over. They now face severe punishment without the possibility of pardon. They can forget about a stay of execution or a last-minute reprieve; God will no longer delay their punishment.

The singing in the Temple, which heretofore was set to the sweetest tunes and sung by the most skillful singers to the best musical instruments, will now turn into the howls and wailings of a despairing people (v. 3). Instead of bringing joy and delight, their singing will grate against the ears of the Lord. Their songs will be words of lamentation and disbelief as they observe what the hand of the Lord is doing in their midst.

Their grief is understandable when considering there will be dead bodies lying everywhere. This gruesome sight will be the bloody effects of enemies' swords, along with the wastes of famine and pestilence. These bodies will be taken out of the city in silence.

---

1. How was Israel like "summer fruit" (vv. 1-2)?
2. Describe the sounds that would be heard in Israel (v. 3).

> "Sin is first pleasing, then it grows easy, then delightful, then frequent, then habitual, then confirmed; then the man is impenitent, then he is obstinate, then he is resolved never to repent, and then he is ruined."—Robert Leighton

---

B. God's Judgment Against Dishonesty (vv. 4-10)

(Amos 8:7-10 is not included in the printed text.)

⁴Hear this, O ye that swallow up the needy, even to make the poor of the land to fail, ⁵Saying, When will the new moon be gone, that we may sell corn? and the sabbath, that we may set forth wheat, making the ephah small, and the shekel great, and falsifying the balances by deceit? ⁶That we may buy the poor for silver, and the needy for a pair of shoes; yea, and sell the refuse of the wheat?

The businessmen of that day couldn't wait for the New Moon festivals and the Sabbath worship to be over so they could continue their unlawful practices. Their dishonesty included overcharging customers by using dishonest scales, giving them less product than they paid for, and mixing chaff with the wheat they were selling (v. 5). The needy would be forced into slavery for a sum as small as the cost of a pair of sandals (v. 6). These evildoers needed to be aware that the Lord was observing all their activities.

God's judgment against those who acted out of greed and dishonest practices is given in considerable detail in the next few verses. He was fully aware of how the poor were being treated. The only recourse the poor had was to call upon the Lord. But that is all they needed to do because He is the poor man's King. He is the refuge to which they can turn.

In verse 7, the Lord begins to speak in the sternest terms. He whose words are immutably true and steadfast will punish His people for their sins. It is a warning they had heard many times before when God had plainly told them that unless they repented of their sins, He would punish them. This time He takes an oath to that effect. He cautions them that He will never forget their sins but instead will punish them for their evil deeds. It must be a comfort to those who have suffered injustices that not one of the cruelties perpetrated on them will go unnoticed. The wrath of God toward the evildoers would affect the land—it would rise and fall like the annual swelling and receding of the great Nile River (v. 8).

In the day of God's wrath, the sun would go down at noon, causing a day of darkness; their times of celebration would turn into times of mourning; their festivals would be turned into funerals and their songs into funeral dirges; and they would wear funeral clothes, shave their heads, and mourn as if their only son had died (vv. 9-10). What an awful, horrible day that would be!

---

1. Describe the merchants' greed (vv. 4-6).
2. How would the natural world be affected by God's judgment (vv. 7-9)?
3. Characterize the bitterness that would befall Israel (v. 10).

> "That which is won ill, will never wear well, for there is a curse attends it which will waste it. The same corrupt dispositions which incline men to sinful ways of getting, will incline them to the like sinful ways of spending."—Matthew Henry

---

C. A Famine of the Word (vv. 11-14)

(Amos 8:14 is not included in the printed text.)

¹¹Behold, the days come, saith the Lord God, that I will send a famine in the land, not a famine of bread, nor a thirst for water, but of hearing the words of the Lord: ¹²And they shall wander from sea to sea, and from the north even to the east, they shall run to and fro to seek the word of the Lord, and shall not find it. ¹³In that day shall the fair virgins and young men faint for thirst.

Because Israel had rejected the word of the Lord, God will now withdraw His words from them (v. 11). The result will be a famine of the soul. This will happen to the people to whom God had so openly communicated through the years. God had spoken "by the mouth of his holy prophets, which have been since the world began" (Luke 1:70). "He made known his ways unto Moses, his acts [and monuments] unto the children of Israel" (Ps. 103:7).

When the word of the Lord was abundantly available to them, they despised it. When the Lord sent prophets to warn them of the troubles they faced because of their sin, they hated them; they rejected the wise counsel the prophets offered. However, in that day when there will be a famine of the

Word, they will long for it but not have it. They will search for prophets to tell them when their troubles will end, but there will be none to offer them counsel (Amos 8:12). They will search all places from sea to sea, over mountainous terrain, running to and fro looking for a revelation from God at the mouth of a prophet, but will find none.

The young women and the strong men, those most capable of enduring in the search for the longest, will faint with despair because they cannot find a word from the Lord to comfort them (v. 13). Those who have turned to idolatry will fall, irrecoverably, into calamity, ruin, and destruction—by and for their sins—and never recover (v. 14).

---

1. How would the people become desperate, and what would result (vv. 11-12)?
2. What happens to those who trust in false gods (vv. 13-14)?

> "We must allow the Word of God to confront us, to disturb our security, to undermine our complacency, and to overthrow our patterns of thought and behavior."—John Stott

---

III. RESTORATION ASSURED (Amos 9:1-15)

A. No Hiding Place (vv. 1-10)

(Amos 9:2-7, 9-10 is not included in the printed text.)

¹I saw the Lord standing upon the altar: and he said, Smite the lintel of the door, that the posts may shake: and cut them in the head, all of them; and I will slay the last of them with the sword: he that fleeth of them shall not flee away, and he that escapeth of them shall not be delivered.

⁸Behold, the eyes of the Lord God are upon the sinful kingdom, and I will destroy it from off the face of the earth; saving that I will not utterly destroy the house of Jacob, saith the Lord.

In Amos' fifth vision, the Lord is standing beside the altar ready to bring judgment upon the disobedient among His people (v. 1). He was not standing at the altar to bless the people, but rather destroy the sinners among them. The Lord commanded that the tops of the pillars be struck with such force that the foundations tremble and the roof fall down on their heads. If any survived, He would pursue and kill them with the sword.

There would be no way to escape His wrath. If they dug down to the place of the dead, He would reach down and pull them up; or if they climbed into the sky, He would pull them down (v. 2). If they hid among the forests of Mount Carmel or in the caves, He would find them and bring them out. If they imagined they could hide from Him at the bottom of the sea, He would call upon "the serpent" to bite them (v. 3). Even if their enemies captured them and drove them like cattle into exile, the sword of the Lord would still be raised against them (v. 4). There was no escape for them; the Lord was absolutely determined to destroy them.

With the touch of His finger, the Lord can cause the earth to quake and the mountains to flatten, or the oceans to flood the earth, and all the people to go into mourning (vv. 5-6). Although the Lord's wrath is coming against Israel, He will not completely destroy its inhabitants (vv. 7-8). Those who have been faithful will be spared, while the rebellious will be sifted out and destroyed (vv. 9-10).

_____

1. Describe the inescapable nature of God's judgment (vv. 1-6).
2. What does God promise in verse 8?
3. How would God show justice (vv. 9-10)?

> "Man can certainly flee from God, but he cannot escape Him."
> —Karl Barth

_____

B. When God Speaks (vv. 11-12)

11In that day will I raise up the tabernacle of David that is fallen, and close up the breaches thereof; and I will raise up his ruins, and I will build it as in the days of old: 12That they may possess the remnant of Edom, and of all the heathen, which are called by my name, saith the Lord that doeth this.

This passage has a double meaning. It refers to the return of God's people out of captivity, but it also speaks to the establishment of the Messiah's kingdom. The phrase "in that day" (v. 11) appears often in Scripture and refers to a fixed time God has determined but unknown to us. An example is found in the words of Jesus, who said of the end times, "But of that day and hour knoweth no man, no, not the angels of heaven, but my Father only" (Matt. 24:36).

This phrase "in that day" sometimes refers to a time of devastation and gloom; but in this case (Amos 9:11), it speaks to us of a time of renewal and blessing. Looking ahead to the messianic aspect of this prophecy, the day is coming when the Lord will reign supreme. Both Jews and Gentiles will submit themselves to the name of the Lord and live under His rule. Thus will be fulfilled the Lord's promise to Abraham that through his descendants all people of the earth will be blessed. This promise is immutably confirmed by the Lord when He says, "The Lord has spoken, and he will do these things" (v. 12 NLT). When God speaks, He both says a thing and does it; He wills a thing and effects it; His command is almighty. His Word is true, His power is great, His grace is effective, and He will accomplish all that He has promised and foretold.

_____

1. What would God restore (v. 11)?
2. Whom besides Israel would God bless (v. 12)?

_____

C. A Day of Abundant Blessings (vv. 13-15)

(Amos 9:13 is not included in the printed text.)

¹⁴And I will bring again the captivity of my people of Israel, and they shall build the waste cities, and inhabit them; and they shall plant vineyards, and drink the wine thereof; they shall also make gardens, and eat the fruit of them. ¹⁵And I will plant them upon their land, and they shall no more be pulled up out of their land which I have given them, saith the Lord thy God.

Here is a sovereign declaration that the best days Israel has ever known are yet to be. It will be an era without any curses and with blessings abundant. Prosperity will prevail and peace will permeate the land. Israel will be able to relax and enjoy their country without fear of foes driving them out. The land will be so productive that "the grain and grapes will grow faster than they can be harvested" (v. 13 NLT). The vineyards will be so fruitful that the juice will drip from the vines and overflow the vats until trickling streams will run down from the mountains. What an elegant picture of the abundance of outward blessings promised to God's people!

The time is coming when Israel will be fully restored to her land and enjoy peace and prosperity in abundance (v. 14). They will build cities and live in them. They will plant vineyards and gardens that will be very fruitful, and the planters will live in their houses safely; they will eat and drink as they enjoy the labor of their hands.

God will plant Israel in their land and give assurance that they will never be uprooted again (v. 15). When God plants, man cannot uproot or destroy. That assurance comes from God who is faithful and never fails His people. He can bring it to pass because He is Jehovah; and He will do it, because He is their God.

- List the promises God makes in these verses.

CONCLUSION

Sin has its consequences. The unrepentant will face the judgment of God. His wrath is sometimes felt in this life; its full impact will be manifest in the next. But there is a remedy. Jesus' death on the cross and His subsequent resurrection provided redemption for all who will turn from their sin and put their faith in Him. Trusting Him leads to a life of abundant joy in this world, and a home in heaven in the next.

GOLDEN TEXT CHALLENGE

"SEEK GOOD, AND NOT EVIL, THAT YE MAY LIVE: AND SO THE LORD, THE GOD OF HOSTS, SHALL BE WITH YOU, AS YE HAVE SPOKEN" (Amos 5:14).

The message here is basic enough for a small child to understand. Here's how it reads in the *Contemporary English Version*: "If you really want to live, you must stop doing wrong and start doing right. I, the Lord God All-Powerful, will then be on your side, just as you claim I am."

Don't pretend to be on God's team if your living pleases the devil. You're only fooling yourself. Instead, show you are on God's team by doing right—from the inside out—and the Almighty will always be with you.

Daily Devotions:

M. The Lord Promises Discipline • 2 Samuel 7:12-16
T. God's Discipline Is a Blessing • Psalm 94:12-15
W. God Disciplines Justly • Jeremiah 30:4-11
T. Lovingly Discipline Your Children • Ephesians 6:1-4
F. God Disciplines His Children • Hebrews 12:4-13
S. God Disciplines Those He Loves • Revelation 3:14-22

Why Christ Came (Christmas)

Genesis 3:15; Isaiah 9:6-7; Luke 1:32-33; 2:1-7;
Galatians 4:4-7; Hebrews 1:1-3; 9:26-28

Unit Theme:

The Birth of Jesus

Central Truth:

Jesus came to redeem all people from sin.

Focus:

Examine why Christ came and appropriate the benefits of His coming.

Context:

Various Old and New Testament passages regarding the coming of Christ to redeem sinners

Golden Text:

"When the fulness of the time was come, God sent forth his Son, made of a woman, made under the law, to redeem them that were under the law, that we might receive the adoption of sons" (Gal. 4:4-5).

Study Outline:

I. **Timing of Christ's Coming** (Gal. 4:4; Heb. 1:1-3; Luke 2:1-7)

II. **Purpose of Christ's Coming** (Gal. 4:5; Isa. 9:6-7; Luke 1:32-33; Gen. 3:15)

III. **Benefits of Christ's Coming** (Gal. 4:6-7; Heb. 9:26-28)

INTRODUCTION

"No room in the inn." And it was doubtless a very ordinary inn at that. Bethlehem was not a large city. Its inns at best would be quite commonplace—but even these were not available. This is no reflection on the innkeeper. With his place filled (no advance notice from Joseph and Mary), he could hardly be blamed for offering only his second best. Rather, it is a penetrating comment on the divine plan for our redemption. God willed that His Son be born in a stable.

The world would have arranged for Jesus to be born in a royal palace, suitable surroundings for the King of kings. Human planners would have placed God's only-begotten Son in the lap of luxury. Surely nothing could be quite good enough for Him.

But such an arrangement would have missed the point entirely. It would have been an attempt to use pomp and circumstance to save a fallen race. In that case, an angel would have done better than a baby.

The Incarnation means infinite condescension. Not pomp but poverty is required; not heraldry but humiliation. Jesus, "being in the form of God . . .

took upon him the form of a servant" (Phil. 2:6-7) that He might bring "many sons unto glory" (Heb. 2:10). His birth made that stable glorious.

I. TIMING OF CHRIST'S COMING (Gal. 4:4; Heb. 1:1-3; Luke 2:1-7)

A. The Fullness of Time (Gal. 4:4)

⁴But when the fulness of the time was come, God sent forth his Son, made of a woman, made under the law.

Like a capstone to all the prophecies about Christ's coming, Paul said in Galatians 4:4, "But when the time had fully come, God sent his Son, born of a woman, born under law" (NIV). In his view of the fullness of time, Paul sees that all things were right and proper for His coming. The world had sunk to a desperate level of sin and godlessness, and yet it had been prepared for Him in various forms of readiness.

For example, the dispersion of the Jews had established synagogues in all parts of the known world; the conquering energies of Alexander the Great had made the Greek language an international form of communication; the military genius of the Romans had made worldwide travel possible by means of its sea traffic and network of roads. Jesus came at a propitious time. God's precision in prophecy and preparation brought the world to the point that it was prepared for the Messiah.

- What does this scripture reveal about God's timing?

B. In These Last Days (Heb. 1:1-3)

¹God, who at sundry times and in divers manners spake in time past unto the fathers by the prophets, ²Hath in these last days spoken unto us by his Son, whom he hath appointed heir of all things, by whom also he made the worlds; ³Who being the brightness of his glory, and the express image of his person, and upholding all things by the word of his power, when he had by himself purged our sins, sat down on the right hand of the Majesty on high.

The Book of Hebrews is basically a New Testament commentary on how Jesus has fulfilled Old Testament law and prophecy. It begins by affirming that the same God who spoke through Israel's prophets has now spoken through Israel's Messiah, His Son Jesus. Jesus has been "appointed heir of all things" (v. 2). The word *appointed* has the sense of "put in place" as an heir. Thus, Jesus has taken His rightful place as heir to all creation.

Jesus is "the brightness of his [God's] glory" (v. 3). This means that He shines forth with the glory of the Father. Revelation 1:16 describes Christ's countenance as the noonday sun, and 22:5 reveals that Christ, as the Lamb of God, is so bright in the heavenly city that there is no need of candle or sun. Thus, the reference to His brightness is a description of the purifying, revealing, and cleansing power of holy light that is the Father and is manifested in the Son.

Finally, Hebrews 1:3 tells that Jesus is "the express image of his [God's] person." The Greek word used for "express image" is *charakter*, from whence our English word for *character/characteristic* is derived. It denotes an engraving and a stamped impression by which the seal makes the identical impression on the item it presses against. Vine quotes Liddon on this passage: "The phrase expresses the fact that the Son 'is both personally distinct from, and yet literally equal to, Him of whose essence He is the adequate imprint.'" Vine continues, "The Son of God is not merely His image, He is the image, or impress, of His substance, or essence."

Why is this important? Our eternal redemption had to be purchased by God and not by animals or man. Only as God made provision of Himself and gave His own holy blood as He became flesh could our redemption be secured. If Jesus is not the eternal, only begotten Son of God, then we are not saved and His death was only that of a martyr.

---

1. Compare God's work in the world in "time past" with "these last days" (vv. 1-2).
2. How does verse 3 describe Christ's relationship with the Father?

> "Jesus was God spelling Himself out in language humanity could understand."—S. D. Gordon

---

C. In Those Days (Luke 2:1-7)

¹And it came to pass in those days, that there went out a decree from Caesar Augustus, that all the world should be taxed. ²(And this taxing was first made when Cyrenius was governor of Syria.) ³And all went to be taxed, every one into his own city. ⁴And Joseph also went up from Galilee, out of the city of Nazareth, into Judaea, unto the city of David, which is called Bethlehem; (because he was of the house and lineage of David:) ⁵To be taxed with Mary his espoused wife, being great with child. ⁶And so it was, that, while they were there, the days were accomplished that she should be delivered. ⁷And she brought forth her firstborn son, and wrapped him in swaddling clothes, and laid him in a manger; because there was no room for them in the inn.

Censuses were carried out in the Roman world for two reasons: to assess taxes and to discover who was eligible for military service. Since the Jews were exempt from military service, a census conducted in Palestine would be for taxation purposes.

Discoveries have been made which provide definite information about the censuses. The information has come from actual census documents written on papyrus and discovered in the dustheaps of Egyptian towns and villages, and in the sands of the desert. It is almost certain that what happened in Egypt happened in Syria, too, and Judea was part of the province of Syria.

At one time, critics questioned the thought of every man going to his own city to be enrolled, but now people possess documents proving this is what happened. We have here another instance of additional knowledge confirming the accuracy of the New Testament record.

Actors on the stage of the world don't always know how to evaluate their role. Caesar Augustus, the first Roman emperor, issues a decree and it is obeyed and he is in control. Joseph and Mary, peasants from Nazareth, answer his decree and make their way to Bethlehem. How insignificant they seem amid the many who are returning to their hometown. Yet this woman, marching under the orders of Caesar Augustus, is carrying in her womb the Son of God.

No longer is the little puppet in the city on seven hills, Caesar Augustus, the main character in this drama. Joseph and Mary become the most significant personalities on the stage. Caesar is only an instrument that God is using to prepare the way for the fulfillment of prophecy. The prophecy revolves around the man and the woman. Things are not always as they appear to be.

Prior to this time, Mary had been living at the wrong address for the birth of the Christ child. Caesar's decree had changed all of that. She arrived in Bethlehem in the nick of time. Soon upon her arrival, the time of her delivery came.

Jesus was born in a stable. It is probable that the stable was built out of a cave. Travelers put up in such places, that is, in the open areas, while the back parts were used as stables. When the Child was born, Mary wrapped Him in "swaddling clothes" (v. 7), which consisted of a square of cloth with a long bandagelike strip coming diagonally off from one corner. The infant was first wrapped in the square of cloth and then the long strip was wound round and round Him. Jesus was then laid in a *manger*, meaning "a place where animals feed."

The fact that there was no room for Jesus in the inn anticipated the reception He would receive from humanity. John recorded, "He came unto his own, and his own received him not. But as many as received him, to them gave he power to become the sons of God, even to them that believe on his name" (John 1:11-12). Some did come to Him reverently. God sent visitors of His own to pay homage to the newborn King. And in every generation, some have come and bowed before Him.

---

1. What does verse 4 reveal about Joseph?
2. How did Caesar's decree affect Jesus' birth?

> "Each of us is an innkeeper who decides if there is room for Jesus."
> —Neal A. Maxwell

II. PURPOSE OF CHRIST'S COMING (Gal. 4:5; Isa. 9:6-7; Luke 1:32-33; Gen. 3:15)

A. Redeem Lost People (Gal. 4:5)

⁵To redeem them that were under the law, that we might receive the adoption of sons.

God's purpose is the redemption of humanity under conditions conformable to His holy nature. Past ages clearly demonstrated that men and women were unable to measure up to God's moral standard of righteousness, much less achieve a righteousness of their own.

Living under law, we lived under a curse—under the law's judgment. But under grace, we receive from a gracious God the gift of sonship. Here, truly, is one of the marvels of redeeming grace: God actually adopts into His household those who formerly belonged to the family of the devil (see John 8:44), and He gives to them as a free gift the right to all the privileges and blessings of sons (1:12).

• Why did Christ come to earth?

B. Establish His Government (Isa. 9:6-7)

⁶For unto us a child is born, unto us a son is given: and the government shall be upon his shoulder: and his name shall be called Wonderful, Counsellor, The mighty God, The everlasting Father, The Prince of Peace. ⁷Of the increase of his government and peace there shall be no end, upon the throne of David, and upon his kingdom, to order it, and to establish it with judgment and with justice from henceforth even for ever. The zeal of the Lord of hosts will perform this.

This first proclamation of Christ's kingdom comes through the ministry of Isaiah during the latter half of the eighth century BC (Isaiah's ministry was from 740 to 700 BC). The setting is one of misery and despair. Because of the people's disobedience, in the present they can see only destruction and havoc wreaked by an invading army. However, the future provides a contrast when a remnant of this nation experiences both spiritual and material blessings.

The focus of this kingdom of peace is the King. It all hinges on His authority and power. The distinctiveness of this Child is seen in chapter 7 through His virgin birth (v. 14). Now the prophet proclaims Christ's authority over the coming kingdom. The special names given to this Ruler demonstrate His distinctiveness and dominion that is different from other human rulers.

In 9:6 there are four elements to the compound name. This really isn't too unusual as can be seen in the naming of Isaiah's son (8:3-4). However, the Child who becomes ruler over this kingdom is more than a human child. The elements of His name indicate this to be God himself through a member of the Trinity coming to earth to establish a continuous kingdom.

1. *Wonderful, Counsellor.* This element is better interpreted as a single term and embodies the wisdom of future authority.

2. *Mighty God.* This is the absolute declaration of His being deity, God himself through Christ coming to bring light into the darkness.

3. *Everlasting Father.* The term *father* provides the concept of love and protection. This future kingdom won't fade or dissolve because of the lack of authority or power. It will continue forever. Instead of temporary kingdoms, which may be fortunate to survive several centuries, this one will be without end.

Why Christ Came

4. *Prince of Peace*. The desire for the future is peace rather than war. It is important to understand that the point in time for complete peace isn't stated. We know He brings spiritual peace, but world peace would be in the distant future.

Verse 7 says this kingdom, unlike those of the world, will not cease. Also, it will be an extension of David's throne and kingdom (2 Sam. 7:13, 16). Finally, this kingdom upholds justice and righteousness, rather than personal pride and earthly greed.

------

1. Why does Isaiah twice use the phrase "unto us" (v. 6)?
2. How was Jesus Christ a ruler like none other (v. 6)?
3. How is Christ's kingdom like none other (v. 7)?

Dangerous Peace

There comes into the world One who is announced as the world's Savior and the Prince of Peace—and this leads immediately to the murder of children. It is almost as though the forces of evil, recognizing the extreme menace to their authority which the coming of Jesus portended, intensified to a new pitch of viciousness their determination to destroy the good.—Michael Stancliffe

------

C. Reign Forever (Luke 1:32-33)

³²He shall be great, and shall be called the Son of the Highest: and the Lord God shall give unto him the throne of his father David: ³³And he shall reign over the house of Jacob for ever; and of his kingdom there shall be no end.

Having announced Mary's imminent conception and the subsequent birth of Jesus, Gabriel proceeds to define the greatness of His character and the majesty of His destiny. As to His character, He would be acknowledged as "the Son of the Most High" (NIV). As a divine name, "the Most High God" belongs to the early patriarchal worship of one supreme Deity. Thus Melchizedek was the priest of "the most high God" (Gen. 14:18). So the angel declares that Mary's son is to be the unique Son of the one living and true God. It refers to Jesus' deity.

But His royalty is also clearly announced in that He is destined to inherit the dynasty of His father David, and to rule over Israel. This was a prophecy of a kingship and a perpetual kingdom which has not yet been literally fulfilled. The fact that the angelic announcement of the Savior's conception and birth was literally fulfilled in Nazareth and Bethlehem certifies a literal fulfillment of the related kingdom prophecy. This mediatorial kingdom on earth will be fully realized at Christ's second advent, and will be perpetuated and perfected in the eternal counsels of God (see Acts 1:6-7; 15:15-18; 1 Cor. 15:22-28).

• Explain the phrase "Son of the Highest" (v. 32).

D. Crush Satan (Gen. 3:15)

15And I will put enmity between thee and the woman, and between thy seed and her seed; it shall bruise thy head, and thou shalt bruise his heel.

The earliest prophecy concerning the coming of Christ was in the Garden of Eden when God spoke to the Serpent following the fall of Adam and Eve. The seed of the woman would be Jesus, who would inflict a mortal wound upon Satan. It was the plan of God that the Redeemer should be the seed of a woman, that is, becoming a man. His life on earth would be for the purpose of bruising the devil, defeating him and establishing the foundation whereby people might be restored to their rightful place with God. In the process of His bruising the head of the Serpent, His heel would also be bruised. This is a reference to the Passion and Crucifixion.

- Whose heel would be "bruised" (struck), and whose head would be "bruised" (crushed)?

III. BENEFITS OF CHRIST'S COMING (Gal. 4:6-7; Heb. 9:26-28)

A. A New Relationship (Gal. 4:6-7)

6And because ye are sons, God hath sent forth the Spirit of his Son into your hearts, crying, Abba, Father. 7Wherefore thou art no more a servant, but a son; and if a son, then an heir of God through Christ.

As proof of our new status as children of God, "God sent the Spirit of his Son into our hearts" (v. 6 NIV). "The Spirit of his Son" suggests the intimate relation of the Spirit and the Son, just as the "Spirit of God" suggests His intimate relation to the Father. The Trinity is forever one and inseparable in essence, yet triune in its personal manifestations.

The Spirit has come in answer to the intercession of Christ the Son (John 14:16); He bears witness to the work of Christ in the heart of the newborn believer (15:26; 16:14; Rom. 8:14-16). This witness is also represented here in Galatians 4:6 by the word *crying*, a verb that expresses deep, heart-moving emotion. "Abba, Father" is an Aramaic form of address which was carried over into early Christian prayer. This cry may be inarticulate, like the "groans that words cannot express" mentioned in Romans 8:26 (NIV), for it is the Spirit who cries within our hearts to give assurance of our adoptive position.

As grace delivers us from the power of darkness and translates us "into the kingdom of his dear Son" (Col. 1:13), so grace lifts us out of the context and bondage of legalistic servitude (bondslaves) into the position of sons. The logical consequence of this new status is that each believer becomes "an heir of God through Christ" (Gal. 4:7). Inasmuch as the entire redemptive purpose centers in Christ the Son, it must follow that the privileges and rights of sonship and heirship come to us through Christ (Rom. 8:17).

- Describe the believer's relationship with God, and how this is made possible.

> "Christ was content with a stable when He was born so that we could have a mansion when we die."—Anonymous

---

B. A New Covenant (Heb. 9:26-28)

26For then must he often have suffered since the foundation of the world: but now once in the end of the world hath he appeared to put away sin by the sacrifice of himself. 27And as it is appointed unto men once to die, but after this the judgment: 28So Christ was once offered to bear the sins of many; and unto them that look for him shall he appear the second time without sin unto salvation.

The old covenant between God and humanity was inferior. The mediator was not involved in the sacrifice itself except to offer it. In this sense the priest was removed from the sacrifice.

The new covenant was established by a new mediator (Christ) and in a new manner (in the very presence of God, v. 24). Christ gave 100 percent to the sacrifice by making Himself the sacrifice. The purity of His sacrifice was in its content and in the commitment of the One giving it. Christ was completely committed to the redemption of the lost.

The new magnitude of the covenant established by Christ is that the burden of sin's punishment is now removed for those who repent and serve the Lord. The severity of sin's penalty was certain death. Death came with the Fall and was part of the certainty of sin's guilt. However, just as certain was the all-sufficient sacrifice of Christ.

Christ's perfect sacrifice "was once offered to bear the sins of many" (v. 28). *Once* stresses the magnitude of Christ's sacrifice. So perfect, His sacrifice needed to be offered only once. *Bear* conveys the extent to which the sacrifice was efficient. All of the guilt of sin is borne by that one sacrifice.

The word *many* declares that the effect of the sacrifice reaches to everyone who believes. The sacrifice of Christ was not only perfect within itself, but it was perfect in the distance it covered—it reached thoroughly into every individual's heart who would believe.

The reconciling work of Christ's sacrifice is not only a spiritual reality within the hearts of believers, but it is also a work that will transform the very body of the Christian at the second coming of Christ. Thus transformed, the believer will be ushered into the heavenly presence of the Father. Those who "look for him" (v. 28) also "love his appearing" (2 Tim. 4:8). Loving the appearing of the Lord implies repenting of sins and renewing one's desires. There must be a heavenly desire for an eternal reunion in the heavenly presence of the Father.

---

1. What did Christ have to do only "once" (v. 26)?
2. What is the destiny of every human being (v. 27)?
3. What is the destiny of Jesus Christ (v. 28)?

> "Christ was content with a stable when He was born so that we could have a mansion when we die."—Anonymous

---

CONCLUSION

"Christmas—the Advent—is the first step of Calvary's journey. The coming of Christ to man was a journey no one had ever taken before—or since. But all can travel the road from man to God."—C. Neil Strait

GOLDEN TEXT CHALLENGE

"WHEN THE FULNESS OF THE TIME WAS COME, GOD SENT FORTH HIS SON, MADE OF A WOMAN, MADE UNDER THE LAW, TO REDEEM THEM THAT WERE UNDER THE LAW, THAT WE MIGHT RECEIVE THE ADOPTION OF SONS" (Gal. 4:4-5).

The ages prior to the First Advent were *periods of preparation* for a climactic event which had been planned in the eternal counsels of the Godhead. And when God saw that the world was ready for the advent of His Son—in "the fulness of the time"—He "sent forth his Son." Previous generations had been prepared through the disciplines of conscience and external laws for the gifts of grace which God's Son came to bestow upon fallen humanity. In one sense, "God sent forth his Son"; but the Son needed no external constraint other than the will of the Father. He was "sent" in the sense that He came from a state of preexistent glory. He came voluntarily to give Himself sacrificially.

First, He identified Himself fully with humanity: He was "made of a woman," that is to say, He entered humanity by the process of birth. He was subject to the laws of human growth and development, yet this process was initiated by the direct agency of the Holy Spirit (cf. Luke 1:34-35; Matt. 1:20).

Second, Jesus was "made under the law." The Jewish people were first of all subject to the law of God, a system of moral government that set them apart from their contemporaries. Jesus was thus born "under the law"—as a growing child He was subject to its ordinances, and as Man, He honored its claims upon Himself as an expression of the will of God for the life of man.

Living under law, people lived under a curse, under the law's judgment. But under grace, people receive from a gracious God the gift of sonship.

Daily Devotions:
M. God Lights the Darkness • Isaiah 9:2-7
T. God Promises the Savior • Micah 5:1-4
W. Christ Is Found by Seekers • Matthew 2:1-11
T. God Redeems His People • Luke 1:67-79
F. Christ Makes God Known • John 1:10-18
S. Christ: the Sacrificial Lamb • John 1:25-36

God of Grace and Compassion

Jonah 1:1—4:11

Unit Theme:

The Minor Prophets (Part 1)

Central Truth:

Because God is gracious, Christians must extend grace to others.

Focus:

Thank God for His compassionate grace and emulate His character.

Context:

Around 780 BC, God calls Jonah to preach in Nineveh, the capital of Assyria.

Golden Text:

"God saw their works, that they turned from their evil way; and God repented of the evil, that he had said that he would do unto them; and he did it not" (Jonah 3:10).

Study Outline:

I. **A Surprising Call** (Jonah 1:1-17)

II. **A Surprising Response** (Jonah 2:7—3:9)

III. **God's Amazing Compassion** (Jonah 3:10—4:11)

INTRODUCTION

God called Jonah to go to Nineveh to condemn the wickedness of that city and to call its inhabitants to repentance. For whatever reason, Jonah rebelled against that call and headed in the opposite direction. He boarded a ship to take him away from where the Lord was sending him. Before long, he found himself in the midst of a storm at sea. The storm was so strong that it sent fear through the others aboard. By the casting of lots, they determined Jonah was their problem. Eventually they cast Jonah overboard . . . something he suggested they do. A great fish then swallowed the prophet.

From the belly of the fish, Jonah prayed to the Lord. The fish deposited Jonah on the shore, after which he made his way to Nineveh to do what God had asked him to do initially. Jonah became angry when the people of Nineveh accepted his message, repented of their sin, and God withdrew His wrath from them. God's message to Jonah was that he needed to have compassion for all people.

The lesson Jonah could take from this experience is that God's mercy reaches beyond the nation of Israel and includes people from all walks of life and all nationalities. This story also draws a contrast between the openness of the Ninevites to the message from God and the slowness of the Jews, at times, to heed the Lord's words. There is also a contrast between the readiness of the people of Nineveh to believe the message and the lack of faith exhibited by those He claimed as His own people.

Jesus tied Jonah's story to His burial and resurrection by spending a similar period of time in the tomb. He stated: "For as Jonah was three days and three nights in the belly of the great fish, so will the Son of Man be three days and three nights in the heart of the earth" (Matt 12:40 NKJV). Furthermore, Jesus said, "This evil generation keeps asking me to show them a miraculous sign. But the only sign I will give them is the sign of Jonah. What happened to him was a sign to the people of Nineveh that God had sent him. What happens to the Son of Man will be a sign to these people that he was sent by God" (Luke 11:29-30 NLT).

I. A SURPRISING CALL (Jonah 1:1-17)

A. Jonah's Disobedience (vv. 1-3)

¹Now the word of the Lord came unto Jonah the son of Amittai, saying, ²Arise, go to Nineveh, that great city, and cry against it; for their wickedness is come up before me. ³But Jonah rose up to flee unto Tarshish from the presence of the Lord, and went down to Joppa; and he found a ship going to Tarshish: so he paid the fare thereof, and went down into it, to go with them unto Tarshish from the presence of the Lord.

We do not know a lot about Jonah, apart from what is recorded in this book. He is mentioned only one other time in the Old Testament. From 2 Kings 14:25, we learn he was from Gath Hepher, he was the son of Amittai, and he was a servant of the Lord who was called to be a prophet to Israel. Gath Hepher was a town in the tribe of Zebulun located north of Nazareth. Jonah lived during the time when Jeroboam II was king in the northern kingdom.

Although Jonah was a prophet to Israel, God called him to go to a heathen nation and deliver His message. God spoke to Jonah in his day, and He speaks to us in our day. He speaks through a number of avenues, including the written Word of God and the Holy Spirit.

God called Jonah to go to the city of Nineveh, the second-largest city in the region, second only to Babylon. Nineveh was situated on the east bank of the Tigris River, about 550 miles from Samaria, the capital of the northern kingdom. To travel to Nineveh would take Jonah about a month if he averaged 15 to 20 miles a day. Nineveh was located in modern-day Iraq, where the city of Mosul is today. The Lord referred to Nineveh as a "great city" (Jonah 1:2). The words *great* and *greatly* occur several times in this book. Some of the expressions are "great city," "great wind," "great storm," "greatly feared," "great fish," and "greatly displeased." It could be added that Nineveh was "great" in wickedness.

The message the Lord gave to Jonah to deliver to the Ninevites was clear. He was to cry out against their wickedness, letting them know God knew how wicked they were. How did Jonah react to these instructions from the Lord? Instead of heading to Nineveh, he struck out in the opposite direction toward Tarshish. His aim was to get as far away from where the Lord told him to go as he could. So he went down to Joppa, bought a ticket on a ship leaving for

Tarshish, and jumped aboard. Perhaps he thought God would forget about him in this strange country; he wrongly thought he could "flee from the Lord" (v. 3 NIV).

---

1. Describe Nineveh's condition (v. 2).
2. Have you ever tried to "flee from the Lord" (v. 3 NIV)? If so, what happened?

> "The greatness of a man's power is the measure of his surrender."
> —William Booth

B. Jonah's Lot (vv. 4-9)

(Jonah 1:5-8 is not included in the printed text.)

⁴But the Lord sent out a great wind into the sea, and there was a mighty tempest in the sea, so that the ship was like to be broken.

⁹And he said unto them, I am an Hebrew; and I fear the Lord, the God of heaven, which hath made the sea and the dry land.

Jonah had not journeyed far in his quest to reach Tarshish when God, from whom he was running, overtook him. The almighty and eternal God personally intervened, sending a powerful wind that caused a violent storm which threatened to rip the ship apart. The storm was so fierce that these well-seasoned sailors were afraid for their lives. This was not the first storm they had been through, but it was the worst one. They realized there was something supernatural about what was happening, so that each one began to cry aloud "unto his god" (v. 5).

They then did what experienced seamen were trained to do; they lightened the ship by throwing cargo overboard. When the apostle Paul was being transported to Rome, the ship taking him there encountered gale-force winds similar to what the ship to Tarshish faced. In Acts 27:18-19, we read that to save themselves and the ship, the crew started throwing cargo overboard, and even cast some of the ship's gear into the sea.

So what was Jonah doing during the violent storm? He had gone below the deck and was sound asleep. "So the captain went down after him. 'How can you sleep at a time like this?' he shouted. 'Get up and pray to your god! Maybe he will pay attention to us and spare our lives'" (Jonah 1:6 NLT). The others saw that prayers to their gods had availed nothing; perhaps Jonah's God would see their distress and deliver them. There is no indication that Jonah prayed at this point; for he was not yet ready to repent of his disobedience to God.

Finding themselves in extraordinary danger, the mariners decided to "cast lots" to see who was the cause of their plight (v. 7). The casting of lots was an appeal to heaven amid doubtful circumstances. The lot fell on Jonah. Immediately, they asked him what he had done that God was so angry with him. Jonah confessed to being a Hebrew who feared and worshiped the

---

almighty and eternal God. He acknowledged God made the sea that threatened him and all of them, because of his sin, and only God could calm its furious waves.

---

1. What does verse 4 say about the Lord?
2. Describe the religion of the mariners and their captain (vv. 5-6).
3. Why did the mariners ask Jonah so many questions (vv. 7-8)?
4. Did Jonah truly "fear the Lord" (v. 9)? Explain your answer.

> "Guilt is to danger, what fire is to gunpowder; a man need not fear to walk among many barrels of power, if he has no fire about him."—John Flavel

---

C. Jonah Overboard (vv. 10-17)
(Jonah 1:10, 13-14 is not included in the printed text.)
[11]Then said they unto him, What shall we do unto thee, that the sea may be calm unto us? for the sea wrought, and was tempestuous. [12]And he said unto them, Take me up, and cast me forth into the sea; so shall the sea be calm unto you: for I know that for my sake this great tempest is upon you.

[15]So they took up Jonah, and cast him forth into the sea: and the sea ceased from her raging. [16]Then the men feared the Lord exceedingly, and offered a sacrifice unto the Lord, and made vows. [17]Now the Lord had prepared a great fish to swallow up Jonah. And Jonah was in the belly of the fish three days and three nights.

As the tempest raged, fear among the mariners increased. It appears Jonah told them the whole story of how he was attempting to flee from the presence of the Lord. This information greatly concerned the men, who were "exceedingly afraid" and asked Jonah, "Why hast thou done this?" (v. 10). These mariners who worshiped false gods had a greater realization of the power of the true God than the prophet Jonah did!

Seeing that Jonah was the cause of the problem, they asked what they should do to him that the sea might be calm again (v. 11). When the storms of life are raging against us, the smartest thing we can do is determine the cause of the storm. By discovering the cause, we may also find the remedy.

Jonah realized the only way to save the other men on the ship was to have him thrown overboard (v. 12). Even though Jonah was ready to face the penalty for his sin, the mariners were reluctant to cast him into the sea (v. 13). They made one more effort to get the ship to land. But the harder they rowed, the stronger the winds blew and the more hopeless their situation became. They saw no solution, apart from what Jonah had suggested. If they did not cast him into the sea, they would drown with him. So they cried out for mercy, not to their gods, but to Jonah's God, Jehovah. They also prayed that they would not be held responsible for Jonah's death (v. 14). Having done everything they knew to do, as a last resort, they yielded to Jonah's advice. They picked him up and hurled him into the raging sea (v. 15). As Jonah had assured them, suddenly the sea was calm. The moment sin was judged, God intervened and the elements were silenced.

When the seamen saw the handiwork of God, they showed deep reverence for Him and His mercy. They offered a sacrifice to Him, the true God, and made vows to serve Him, the Creator of heaven and earth (v. 16).

If Jonah thought by being cast overboard with the prospect of drowning, he would escape the assignment he had been given, God had another plan. The Lord had arranged for a great fish to swallow Jonah. He would take up residence in the fish for "three days and three nights" (v. 17). Sent from God, this fish became Jonah's receiver and deliverer. God has the command of all His creatures, and can make any of them serve His designs of mercy to His people.

---

1. What "terrified" the seamen (v. 10 NIV)?
2. What was Jonah certain about (v. 12)?
3. Describe the seamen's prayer (v. 14).
4. How did the seamen show their newfound reverence for God (vv. 15-16)?
5. How did the Lord show His power to provide (v. 17)?

> "If a man finds the power of sin furiously at work within him, dragging his whole life downward to destruction, there is only one way to escape his fate—to take resolute hold of the upward power, and be borne by it to the opposite goal."—Henry Drummond

---

II. A SURPRISING RESPONSE (Jonah 2:7—3:9)

A. Jonah's Prayer (2:7-10)

⁷When my soul fainted within me I remembered the Lord: and my prayer came in unto thee, into thine holy temple. ⁸They that observe lying vanities forsake their own mercy. ⁹But I will sacrifice unto thee with the voice of thanksgiving; I will pay that that I have vowed. Salvation is of the Lord. ¹⁰And the Lord spake unto the fish, and it vomited out Jonah upon the dry land.

Out of the stomach of the great fish, Jonah offered a song of praise to God for sending the fish and saving him from drowning (vv. 1-9). Realizing he could have died in the sea, he lifted his voice in worship to God for His unfathomable mercy. He cried out to God with his whole heart when there was no one to hear him but God. Likewise, when we call out to the Lord from our secret place of prayer, God will hear our heart's cry and respond.

When Jonah reached the lowest possible point, God reached down and snatched him from the jaws of death. The rebellious prophet therefore avowed

---

that the Lord was his God. He promised to sacrifice to God alone, to sing praises to Him, and to keep the vows he had made (v. 9). He would do these things because "salvation comes from the Lord" (NIV). Safety and security come from a gracious God. In response to Jonah's prayer, God commanded the fish to deposit Jonah on dry land (v. 10).

• When was Jonah freed from the giant fish?

> "Your most profound and intimate experience of worship will likely be in your darkest days—when your heart is broken, when you feel abandoned, when you're out of options, when the pain is great—and you turn to God alone."—Rick Warren

---

B. Jonah's Message (3:1-4)

¹And the word of the Lord came unto Jonah the second time, saying, ²Arise, go unto Nineveh, that great city, and preach unto it the preaching that I bid thee. ³So Jonah arose, and went unto Nineveh, according to the word of the Lord. Now Nineveh was an exceeding great city of three days' journey. ⁴And Jonah began to enter into the city a day's journey, and he cried, and said, Yet forty days, and Nineveh shall be overthrown.

In *The Bible Knowledge Commentary*, we are told: "Seven miracles have taken place already in this short narrative: God caused a violent storm (1:4), had the lot fall on Jonah (v. 7), calmed the sea when Jonah was thrown overboard (v. 15), commanded the fish to swallow Jonah (v. 17), had the fish to transport him safely, had him throw Jonah up on dry land, and perhaps, greatest of all, melted the disobedient prophet's heart (evidenced by his thanksgiving prayer in ch. 2)."

Through whatever means He chose to use, God let the fish know it was time to throw Jonah up and return him to dry land. Even though fish cannot reason and understand as man can, this fish had ears to hear the voice of its Creator, and he responded immediately by obeying the Lord's command.

How do you suppose Jonah felt when he found himself standing on the shore? Immediately, God gave him a second chance to do the right thing. He reaffirmed that He was calling Jonah to go to Nineveh, and He gave him the message he was to deliver. Jonah was given another opportunity to be fruitful for God by representing Him before the Ninevites.

What would Jonah do? The first time God called him to go to Nineveh, he rebelled and went in the opposite direction. This time, however, he follows the right course. God's instructions to Jonah are clear. He is to go to Nineveh, a city large in size and large in sin. Once there, he is to preach publicly, plainly, and boldly denouncing their wickedness, calling them to repentance, and warning them of the judgment of God that will befall them in forty days. He was not to tell them what they wanted to hear, or even what he might like to have told them, but he was to give them the message God had given to him. As Jonah walked through the city, he proclaimed openly and plainly what God had commanded him to say: "Forty more days and Nineveh will be overturned" (3:4 NIV).

---

1. Why did God give Jonah a second chance?
2. How long did it take Jonah to walk around Nineveh, and what was his message?

> "Obedience to God must never be delayed."—Zac Poonen

C. Nineveh's Response (vv. 5-9)

(Jonah 3:6-8 is not included in the printed text.)

⁵So the people of Nineveh believed God, and proclaimed a fast, and put on sackcloth, from the greatest of them even to the least of them.

⁹Who can tell if God will turn and repent, and turn away from his fierce anger, that we perish not?

Jonah delivered his message with great passion, having seen firsthand what the wrath of God looked like. The Ninevites believed the message from God. Jonah had fully exposed their sin and what they deserved. They faced imminent judgment from God and only His mercy could save them. Realizing their plight, they declared a fast, knowing they must repent and seek the face of God. They clothed themselves in sackcloth, a symbol that they were in mourning. Everyone participated, "from the greatest to the least" (v. 5 NKJV).

When the king of Nineveh heard Jonah's message, he came down from his throne, took off his royal garments, covered himself with sackcloth, and sat on a heap of ashes, thereby expressing the deepest of sorrow for his sins and for the sins of his people (v. 6). With great haste, the king called for a fast throughout the city. He decreed the strictest fast possible, including man and beast: "No one, not even the animals from your herds and flocks, may eat or drink anything at all" (v. 7 NLT). Even the beasts were to be clothed with sackcloth (v. 8). The inhabitants of the city were called on to pray earnestly, and to turn from their wicked ways in the hope that God would relent and spare their city (v. 9).

God honors those who have a genuine change of heart. In 2 Chronicles 7:14, the Lord says, "If my people, which are called by my name, shall humble themselves, and pray, and seek my face, and turn from their wicked ways; then will I hear from heaven, and will forgive their sin, and will heal their land."

---

1. How did Nineveh's king and its residents outwardly demonstrate their sorrow over sin (vv. 5-6)?
2. What did the king command the people to do (vv. 7-8), and why (v. 9)?

> "I think there are many who would like to be saved but have been presented the faulty idea that repentance is turning from

---

III. GOD'S AMAZING COMPASSION (Jonah 3:10—4:11)

A. Jonah's Anger (3:10; 4:1-4)

(Jonah 4:2-4 is not included in the printed text.)

3:10 And God saw their works, that they turned from their evil way; and God repented of the evil, that he had said that he would do unto them; and he did it not.

4:1 But it displeased Jonah exceedingly, and he was very angry.

Jonah was not ready for what happened next. The people of Nineveh listened to his message, turned away from their sin, and turned to God for mercy. God responded to their change of heart by changing His intent toward them. A revival swept through the city, and God withheld His threatened destruction.

This brings up the question, "Does God repent?" There are certain circumstances when He does, but not when it comes to divine decrees. To every promise He has ever made, He says, "I am the Lord, I change not" (Mal. 3:6). However, when a lost soul believes on the Lord Jesus Christ and surrenders his or her life to Him, God's attitude changes immediately. When the people of Nineveh forsook their sins and surrendered their lives to God, the Lord changed their imminent peril to hope and blessing. The change was not in God but in the people. Everyone faces mercy or judgment. When one becomes a believer and accepts Christ as Savior, God changes His attitude from judgment to forgiveness.

Jonah did not like what he was seeing. This divine forbearance toward the city of Nineveh greatly upset him (4:1). The prophet said in effect, "Lord, I knew this is what You would do. That's why I fled to Tarshish. I knew You were merciful, compassionate, and slow to anger" (see v. 2). He felt God's pardon contradicted his preaching. He seemed to think it would be better to be dead and buried than to be branded a prophet whose word did not come to pass. God had spared Jonah; now He spared Nineveh, but Jonah didn't see the connection. The Lord asked him, "Is it right for you to be angry?" (v. 4 NKJV).

1. What does Jonah 3:10 reveal?
2. What had Jonah correctly assumed about God (4:2)?
3. Answer the Lord's question to Jonah (v. 4).

"Salvation is from our side a choice; from the divine side it is a seizing upon, an apprehending, a conquest by the Most High God."—A. W. Tozer

B. Jonah's Shelter (4:5-6)

⁵So Jonah went out of the city, and sat on the east side of the city, and there made him a booth, and sat under it in the shadow, till he might see what would become of the city. ⁶And the Lord God prepared a gourd, and made it to come up over Jonah, that it might be a shadow over his head, to deliver him from his grief. So Jonah was exceeding glad of the gourd.

There is a sadness in the words "Jonah went out of the city." This was no time for him to be leaving. God, in His great mercy, had saved the Ninevites because they had turned to Him. These new converts needed guidance and teaching. They were as sheep without a shepherd. However, at this point, Jonah was thinking only of himself.

How much time and effort do we devote to discipleship? We rejoice when individuals receive Christ, but what do we offer them after they become Christians? In what ways do we help them to mature in Christ?

Jonah built a crude shelter on the east side of the city on a higher elevation where he could sit under it for some shade. From this vantage point, he had a good view of the city. It appears he was still waiting to see if God would destroy Nineveh.

In spite of Jonah's pouting and depression, God showed him mercy. The Lord provided a vine to give Jonah a shade that his makeshift hut could not provide. It was a plant with long and large leaves to keep the scorching sun off him. The shade provided by the vine eased his discomfort and made him happy. Oh, that we could learn what it means to trust the Lord, depend on His Word, and follow His guidance. We could avoid the kind of predicament in which Jonah found himself.

• Explain Jonah's actions (v. 5).

> "His voice leads us not into timid discipleship but into bold witness."—Charles Stanley

---

C. Jonah's Misconception (vv. 7-11)

(Jonah 4:7-9 is not included in the printed text.)

¹⁰Then said the Lord, Thou hast had pity on the gourd, for the which thou hast not laboured, neither madest it grow; which came up in a night, and perished in a night: ¹¹And should not I spare Nineveh, that great city, wherein are more than sixscore thousand persons that cannot discern between their right hand and their left hand; and also much cattle?

By the same power which caused the vine to suddenly spring forth and spread its leaves, causing Jonah to be very pleased, God caused a worm to come along the next morning, chew the vine, and cause it to wither (v. 7). After the vine withered and the sun blazed, God sent a dry, scorching wind to blow on Jonah (v. 8). As the sun beat down on his head, he grew faint; his strength of body and courage of mind failed him. Jonah concluded that even death was better than this.

God confronted Jonah about his anger over the withering of the vine as opposed to God's concern for the people of Nineveh (vv. 9-11). Jonah did nothing to produce the vine; it did not belong to him. He did not plant it, nor did he take care of it. On the other hand, God created the Ninevites. They were souls facing eternity who were in need of His grace. They were a people walking in darkness who did not know right from wrong. Seeing that they had turned to God for forgiveness, why shouldn't He spare them?

Oh, the value of one soul, to say nothing of thousands of souls! Absolutely nothing is of greater value than the human soul. Jesus asked, "For what shall it profit a man, if he shall gain the whole world, and lose his own soul? Or what shall a man give in exchange for his soul?" (Mark 8:36-37).

• How does God contrast Himself with Jonah (vv. 10-11)?

The Eternal Soul

Over the doorway of the cathedral at Milan are three inscriptions spanning the arches. Upon one arch is carved a wreath of roses, and underneath this sentence: "All that which pleases is but for a season." Over the second is carved a cross with these words: "All that which troubles is but for a moment." But on the central arch is this statement: "That is only important which is eternal."
—Macartney's Illustration

CONCLUSION

Is it well with your soul? Many things in this life demand our attention. Our responsibility to care for the family weighs heavily upon us. Personal matters, such as taking care of our health, are a major concern. But nothing is more important than taking care of our soul. Our eternal destiny depends on how we address this matter and what we choose to do about Jesus.

GOLDEN TEXT CHALLENGE

"GOD SAW THEIR WORKS, THAT THEY TURNED FROM THEIR EVIL WAY; AND GOD REPENTED OF THE EVIL, THAT HE HAD SAID THAT HE WOULD DO UNTO THEM; AND HE DID IT NOT" (Jonah 3:10).

That God would change His mind ("God repented") is not new to the Old Testament. Jonah knew God had treated Israel in exactly the same manner on numerous occasions (see Ex. 32:14; 2 Sam. 24:16; Amos 7:3, 6). It did not mean God's nature had changed; rather, it meant He was responding to the change in the lives of the people of Nineveh.

This change on His part was consistent with His nature. It meant that if He called people to repentance, then He would respond to their repentance by shifting His judgment. Their dependence on His mercy made possible the atoning (by faith) of His rightful wrath. By faith in Him, they placed themselves under the covenant of His holiness and love.

God makes the same offer to sinners today. He calls them to repent of their sins. If they will repent, divine judgment will be avoided.

Daily Devotions:

M. God Declares Himself Gracious • Exodus 34:1-9

T. A Grace-Laden Blessing • Numbers 6:22-27

W. God, the Gracious Shepherd • Ezekiel 34:7-16

T. Grace for a Sinner • Luke 23:33-43

F. Grace-Fueled Effort • 1 Corinthians 15:9-11

S. Saved by Grace Through Faith • Ephesians 2:1-10

God Judges and Restores

Unit Theme:

The Minor Prophets (Part 1)

Central Truth:

God restores those who humble themselves before Him.

Focus:

Affirm that God restores the penitent and humbly submit to Him.

Context:

The Book of Micah was written in Judah between 735 and 698 BC.

Golden Text:

"Who is a God like unto thee, that pardoneth iniquity, and passeth by the transgression of the remnant of his heritage? he retaineth not his anger for ever, because he delighteth in mercy" (Mic. 7:18).

Study Outline:

I. **God Rebukes Sin** (Mic. 1:1-7; 6:1-13)

II. **Sin Has Consequences** (Mic. 6:14—7:6)

III. **God Restores the Humble** (Mic. 7:7-20)

INTRODUCTION

The thread running through the Book of Micah is that injustice was rampant in his day. Governmental and administrative corruption seemed to be everywhere. Micah denounced both Israel and Judah for their wicked ways, and was especially disappointed in the waywardness he saw in Jerusalem. Having a rural background, he was sensitive to how wealthy landowners took advantage of the poor.

The religious leaders of his day were also objects of his scorn. He condemned them for their failure to act justly toward the people. Of all the people, they should have been the keepers of God's law, yet time and again they betrayed that trust. That they could carry out their corrupt deeds in the name of religion was especially bothersome to Micah.

The prophet had a strong sense of the righteousness of God, and he expected the people who claimed to be followers of God to reflect that righteousness. The moral character of the individual and of communities should be evident for all to see. After all, they were in a covenant relationship with God. However, the religious leaders were routinely violating that covenant.

Micah used the strongest possible language in his reprimand of the leaders of Israel and the false prophets. He envisioned the total destruction of Jerusalem because the corruption they perpetrated on the people had reached the heart of national life. The prophet could see God uses heathen countries to punish His own people for their iniquity.

In spite of the destruction and devastation that Micah saw coming, he also saw a day of restoration. He saw the day when the Messiah would arise from among the common people and deliver them from oppression and injustice. The saving grace of God would be extended to all. Walking in humility, mercy, and justice would become a way of life. And that way of life would be well-pleasing to God.

I. GOD REBUKES SIN (Mic. 1:1-7; 6:1-13)

A. Coming Judgment (1:1-7)

(Micah 1:3-7 is not included in the printed text.)

¹The word of the Lord that came to Micah the Morasthite in the days of Jotham, Ahaz, and Hezekiah, kings of Judah, which he saw concerning Samaria and Jerusalem. ²Hear, all ye people; hearken, O earth, and all that therein is: and let the Lord God be witness against you, the Lord from his holy temple.

Micah made it clear the message he was about to deliver was not his own; it came to him from the Lord. He told his readers he came from a little town about twenty-five miles southwest of Jerusalem called *Moresheth*. He also wanted them to know he prophesied during the reigns of "Jotham, Ahaz, and Hezekiah, kings of Judah" (v. 1). The prophecies he proclaimed pertained to Samaria (the capital of the northern kingdom) and Jerusalem (the capital of the southern kingdom).

Micah called the whole world to listen to what God had to say about the failure of His people to honor the covenant relationship they had entered into with Him (v. 2). He knew once they heard the Lord's case they would agree that His dealing with His people was just. Micah said God would speak out of His "holy temple." The Temple was the place where He had chosen to make His presence known. The Lord's message still goes forth from the local church. Do you identify with a local congregation, and are you involved in sending His message forth?

What a fearsome picture Micah painted of the awesome God coming to judge His people. He envisioned Him stepping from mountain to mountain and, as He does, the mountains melt like wax before a fire and run like an unstoppable rush of water flowing down a slope (vv. 3-4).

In language anyone could understand, Micah made it clear why judgment was coming. Sin and transgression had swept across the whole landscape; the entire nation was guilty before God (v. 5). The capital cities of Samaria and Jerusalem had been the pacesetters of this rebellion. Once again, we are reminded that sin has its consequences. Any individual, any people, any nation that persists in wrongdoing will eventually face the wrath of God.

Though the Lord would work through others to execute His judgment, He is behind the ruin that would befall Israel and Judah (v. 6). The Assyrians would destroy Samaria, and the structure that housed the idols of false gods would be leveled and burned (v. 7). The people would also be judged for committing adultery with temple prostitutes.

_____

1. Where did Micah's message originate (vv. 1-2)?
2. Why was judgment coming (v. 5)?
3. Contrast the actions of the Lord with the fate of idols (vv. 3-4, 7).

> "If loving God with one's whole being is the greatest command-ment, then not to do so must be the greatest sin—indeed, the root of all sin."—Dave Hunt

_____

B. What the Lord Requires (6:1-8)

(Micah 6:1, 4-6 is not included in the printed text.)

²Hear ye, O mountains, the Lord's controversy, and ye strong founda-tions of the earth: for the Lord hath a controversy with his people, and he will plead with Israel. ³O my people, what have I done unto thee? and wherein have I wearied thee? testify against me.

⁷Will the Lord be pleased with thousands of rams, or with ten thou-sands of rivers of oil? shall I give my firstborn for my transgression, the fruit of my body for the sin of my soul? ⁸He hath shewed thee, O man, what is good; and what doth the Lord require of thee, but to do justly, and to love mercy, and to walk humbly with thy God?

Earlier, the Lord had called on the nations to listen to His case against His people. Now, He invites the people of Israel and Judah to tell their side of the story. Let people from everywhere, represented by the mountains and hills, judge the fairness of their case (v. 1). Then, the Lord repeated His complaint against them for all the nations to hear. Who had the stronger case: God or His people?

As though He was puzzled by their accusations, the Lord inquired as to what He had done to justify their attitude (v. 3). Then, He reminded them by listing several historical events in their storied past where He had demon-strated His love for them and had shown them His goodness (vv. 4-5). Had they forgotten about Egypt . . . how God delivered them from slavery? Did they remember Aaron, who had been a priest to them . . . Miriam, who comforted them with her song unto the Lord . . . Moses, who had been such a faithful leader to them? Were they still aware that God, in His goodness, had given them these great servants of the Lord to guide their journey? Have you ever been guilty of forgetting how good God has been to you and walked a way-ward path? Have you always appreciated the leaders He has sent to guide you in your Christian experience?

The Lord reminded the people that when Balak would have cursed them through Balaam, He caused Balaam to bless them instead (Num. 22:12; 23:7-12). Had they forgotten their last encampment in the wilderness and their first encampment after they miraculously crossed the Jordan River? All along the way, God had demonstrated goodness and mercy, yet somehow they failed to see it. We, too, should be careful to see God in the blessings of life. James wrote, "Every good gift and every perfect gift is from above, and cometh down from the Father of lights, with whom is no variableness, neither shadow of turning" (1:17).

What did God expect of His people? Was He looking for sacrifices of animals or fruits of the vine? Did He want them to offer up their children as a sacrifice to Him? No, He asked for only three things: "to do what is right, to love mercy, and to walk humbly with your God" (Mic. 6:8 NLT).

---

1. Explain God's appeal to nature (vv. 1-2).
2. List three ways God had been faithful to Israel (vv. 4-5).
3. Answer the four questions in verses 6 and 7.
4. What is the relationship between justice, mercy, and humility (v. 8)?

"A God forgotten is as good as no God to us."—Stephen Charnock

---

C. A Corrupt Society (vv. 9-13)

(Micah 6:10-12 is not included in the printed text.)

⁹The Lord's voice crieth unto the city, and the man of wisdom shall see thy name: hear ye the rod, and who hath appointed it.

¹³Therefore also will I make thee sick in smiting thee, in making thee desolate because of thy sins.

We are reminded God stands ready to judge Israel for their failure to obey Him. To get the attention of the people, Micah reminds them it is the Lord's voice calling for their obedience (v. 9). Whether the message comes through a prophet or by another means the Lord chooses to use, the Lord is behind the warning. The call is intended for every city in Israel and Judah, but especially for Jerusalem and Samaria. Wisdom dictates that they respond to the words from the Lord with reverence and fear. Proverbs 9:10 says, "The fear of the Lord is the beginning of wisdom." In Ecclesiastes 12:13, Solomon wrote, "Let us hear the conclusion of the whole matter: Fear God, and keep his commandments: for this is the whole duty of man." How careful are we to heed this sage advice?

If there was any question in the minds of the Jewish people why the Lord was judging them, He provided a whole list of their sins. One of His three requirements was practicing justice (v. 8), yet His charges against them show they were operating unjustly. The wealth they obtained was through oppressive means. The fathers had accumulated goods by fraudulent means, and the children were doing nothing to change the situation. One specific example was "measuring out grain with dishonest measures" (v. 10 NLT). Even though Proverbs 11:1 says, "A false balance is abomination to the Lord: but a just weight is his delight," the merchants were using "dishonest scales" and "false weights" (Mic. 6:11 NIV).

The Lord called out the rich among them and declared them to be the most guilty of acquiring dishonest gain (v. 12). They should have been the ones who were setting a positive example and operating in integrity. Unfortunately, the people were influenced by them and had adopted their unjust practices. People had become so accustomed to lying that none could be trusted in any negotiation or transaction. As believers, are we setting a better example? Can our word be trusted? The people of Micah's day were beginning to experience ruin (v. 13), as will finally happen to all who traffic in greed and dishonesty.

1. What does the wise person do (v. 9)?
2. List four specific charges brought against God's people (vv. 10-12).
3. What could the people expect (v. 13)?

"There is no enemy can hurt us but by our own hands. Satan could not hurt us, if our own corruption betrayed us not."
—Joseph Hall

II. SIN HAS CONSEQUENCES (Mic. 6:14—7:6)

A. Disobedience Brings Disaster (6:14-16)

(Micah 6:14-15 is not included in the printed text.)

¹⁶For the statutes of Omri are kept, and all the works of the house of Ahab, and ye walk in their counsels; that I should make thee a desolation, and the inhabitants thereof an hissing: therefore ye shall bear the reproach of my people.

Because of their sins, judgment was coming. In clear language, Micah told the people what they could expect. Micah said they would "eat, but not be satisfied" (v. 14). Their efforts to store up food would be futile. What little they could put away for a "rainy day" would be destroyed by the enemy. They would go to great pains to till the soil and sow the seeds, but not be able to harvest from what they had planted (v. 15). Their labor would be in vain, either because the crops did not produce or their enemies came in and destroyed the crops. Also, all their labor in harvesting olives and pressing or treading them into oil would be of no use to them. Apparently, the enemy would rob them of this produce and the great refreshment olive oil gave to the body. The same thing was true of the wine they would make from their harvested grapes—they would never drink of it. Because of their sin, God will turn their blessings into curses. He is still in the business of doing that when we disobey Him.

Instead of following the Lord, the people had adopted the idolatrous practices of Omri and Ahab (v. 16). Because they had steeped themselves in idolatry, God would bring them to utter ruin. Taken into captivity, they would be subject to the ridicule of the nations. Disobedience brings disaster.

1. Describe the miserable conditions that were coming (vv. 14-15).

2. Describe the "reproach" the people would bear (v. 16).

> "When we think of eternity, and of the future consequences of all human conduct, what is there in this life that should make any man contradict the dictates of his conscience, the principles of justice, the laws of religion, and of God?"—William Wilberforce

---

B. A Corrupt Society (7:1-4)

(Micah 7:2-3 is not included in the printed text.)

¹Woe is me! for I am as when they have gathered the summer fruits, as the grapegleanings of the vintage: there is no cluster to eat: my soul desired the firstripe fruit.

⁴The best of them is as a brier: the most upright is sharper than a thorn hedge: the day of thy watchmen and thy visitation cometh; now shall be their perplexity.

Micah expressed personal distress over living in an environment absent of godly or righteous people. Finding a God-fearing person in the land was like trying to glean from a vineyard after the fruit had been harvested, discovering that all the grapes and figs were gone. Micah is grieved that the fruit of righteousness could not be found in society. The increase of evil among the people was appalling. Are we facing a similar situation in our day? Are we as Christians bearing godly fruit in a barren world?

Micah was looking at a bankrupt society devoid of upright people. Godly people who showed love and kindness to those in need, who displayed decency and goodness, and who had a godly heart and lived to please God were absent from Israel and Judah (v. 2). Honest people who would have nothing to do with deceitful and crooked living could not be found. Those left in the land watched for opportunities to do mischief and shed blood. It would be bad enough if they laid in wait for strangers, but they had dropped so low morally that they schemed to destroy their own. They spread a net to trap them, meaning they were involved in premeditated cruelty.

Micah said the people did "evil with both hands earnestly" (v. 3), meaning they devoted all their energy to successfully carrying out their evil deeds. Corruption was running rampant. Government officials and judges were taking bribes. Men of prominence and influence were using their power and position to take advantage of the less fortunate. Sadly, too much of this kind of thing goes on today among those in whom we have vested public trust.

Micah warned that a day of judgment was coming, just as the true prophets had foretold (v. 4). It would be a day of sorrows, confusion, and perplexity. The peace and prosperity the false prophets had predicted would not materialize, and the nation would face overwhelming trouble and utter ruin.

---

1. Explain the imagery of "summer fruits" (v. 1).

2. How were the governmental leaders, the judges, and the average citizen all alike (vv. 2-3)?
3. How does Micah describe "the best of them" (v. 4)?

> "During the last times, men will be lovers of pleasure more than lovers of God. When you think of our sports-driven society, and our media-driven society, and our leisure-driven society, then you understand we are living in the last days."—Jerry Falwell

---

C. A Breakdown in Society (vv. 5-6)

⁵Trust ye not in a friend, put ye not confidence in a guide: keep the doors of thy mouth from her that lieth in thy bosom. ⁶For the son dishonoureth the father, the daughter riseth up against her mother, the daughter in law against her mother in law; a man's enemies are the men of his own house.

Micah saw a total breakdown in friend and family relationships. He lived in a day of such treachery that no one could be trusted, not even a neighbor or one's best friend. He even advised them to be careful what they told their spouse. It is hard to imagine that a wife would disclose her husband's secrets in a way that would ruin him, but Micah raises that possibility.

Micah spoke of a breakdown in society so severe that it brought havoc to home and family. Sons were found to treat their fathers with such disrespect as to belittle them. Daughters were guilty of rising up against their mothers, challenging and defying them. In both cases—sons and daughters—they were in violation of the fifth commandment: "Honour thy father and thy mother: that thy days may be long upon the land which the Lord thy God giveth thee" (Ex. 20:12). Daughters-in-law despised their mothers-in-law. Household servants proved untrustworthy. A man's greatest enemies were those of his own household (Mic. 7:6). It sounds like the "last days" Paul wrote about:

> In the last days perilous times shall come. For men shall be lovers of their own selves, covetous, boasters, proud, blasphemers, disobedient to parents, unthankful, unholy, without natural affection, trucebreakers, false accusers, incontinent, fierce, despisers of those that are good, traitors, heady, highminded, lovers of pleasures more than lovers of God; having a form of godliness, but denying the power thereof: from such turn away (2 Tim. 3:1-5).

In what ways do these words describe the day in which we are living? What are we doing about our decadent society? How earnestly are we praying?

---

1. Who could not be trusted (v. 5)?
2. Describe the breakdown in relationships (v. 6).

> "Our society is filled with runaways, dropouts, and quitters. . . . We have seen others faint or walk away and we have followed in

their weakness. We have fainted when we could have persevered by exchanging our strength for His!"—Kay Arthur

---

III. GOD RESTORES THE HUMBLE (Mic. 7:7-20)

A. Looking to the Lord for Help (vv. 7-10)

(Micah 7:8, 10 is not included in the printed text.)

⁷Therefore I will look unto the Lord; I will wait for the God of my salvation: my God will hear me.

⁹I will bear the indignation of the Lord, because I have sinned against him, until he plead my cause, and execute judgment for me: he will bring me forth to the light, and I shall behold his righteousness.

After the bleak picture Micah has painted, is there any hope? Where does one turn? Micah, speaking for himself and the godly remnant, said he was going to turn to the Lord. He knew Him to be a God of mercy who had power sufficient to protect him and meet his needs. Knowing that God could and would help him, he was willing to patiently wait on God for deliverance (v. 7). He had full confidence that God knew his situation and would come to his aid. Do you have that kind of trust in a loving God?

Micah, still speaking as a representative of God's people, advised their enemies not to take any pleasure in any calamity that might have overtaken them (v. 8). He wanted them to know that, no matter how low they fell or how deep the distress Israel felt, God would come to their rescue. When they sat in darkness and affliction or depression covered them like a cloud, the Lord would be their light to bring comfort and deliverance. *Light* frequently symbolizes well-being, and Micah turned to the Lord as the source of a blessed life.

Micah identified himself with the sins of God's people (v. 9). He said he would patiently submit himself to the indignation of the Lord. He confessed that the sins of idolatry, injustice, and unfaithfulness had brought God's wrath against them. But Micah also knew the day was coming when God would judge his enemies and bring him out of the darkness into the light.

When God's people were restored to righteousness, their enemies would see God was with them. Their enemies would then be ashamed for taunting them by asking, "Where is the Lord thy God?" (v. 10). The tables will then be turned, and the people of God will see the downfall of their enemies. They will be "trampled down like mud in the streets" (NKJV).

---

1. Describe Micah's confidence (vv. 7-8).
2. What was Micah willing to do, and why (vv. 9-10)?

"Thanks be to God, there is hope today; this very hour you can choose Him and serve Him."—D. L. Moody

---

B. Israel Revisited (vv. 11-13)

(Micah 7:12-13 is not included in the printed text.)

¹¹In the day that thy walls are to be built, in that day shall the decree be far removed.

Micah foretold a day when the Jews would be reestablished in their homeland, signified by the reference to "building your walls" (v. 11 NASB). The Hebrew word used here for "walls" usually refers to a wall around a vineyard. However, if it does refer to city walls, then it was partially fulfilled when Nehemiah rebuilt the walls around Jerusalem in 445 BC.

As it relates to the places where the Jews were held captive, Micah sees them returning to Jerusalem. They will come from Assyria, Egypt, the Euphrates, even "from sea to sea, and from mountain to mountain" (v. 12). They will come from any geographical region where they had been exiled. But undoubtedly, there is a second meaning here. Micah saw a day when the people would come from all over the world and settle in the Promised Land. Since 1948, when Israel was declared a nation, Jews have been returning to their homeland.

Notwithstanding the blessing of God upon the land, Micah saw that some will continue to rebel against Him and persist in their evil deeds (v. 13). These will find the land desolate, even though Jerusalem will be an oasis of prosperity. Here we see the truth of Genesis 12:3, "I will bless them that bless thee, and curse him that curseth thee."

• Describe the homecoming that would take place (vv. 11-12).

> "He [God] longs for you to come back. He weeps that you are missing out on His love, protection, and provision. He throws His arms open, runs toward you, gathers you up, and welcomes you home."—Charles Stanley

---

C. Israel's Restoration (vv. 14-17)

(Micah 7:14-17 is not included in the printed text.)

Micah called on the Lord to watch over His people like a shepherd cares for his sheep (v. 14). No shepherd ever tended his sheep so well as does the Good Shepherd. Psalm 23 paints a beautiful picture of all the provisions God has for His people. He treats them in a way that they can enjoy relaxation; He leads them along pleasant paths; He keeps them amid dangerous situations; He provides for all their physical needs by spreading a table before them; He is with them in dark times; and He assures them of an eternal dwelling place.

Micah assured the people that God will once again do mighty miracles in their midst—miracles like He performed when He brought them out of Egypt (v. 15). The nations will stand in awe of God's great power and be embarrassed at their inability to stand in His presence (v. 16). Their fear of the Lord will reach panic proportions, and they will tremble in the presence of His people.

1. How is God like a shepherd (v. 14)?
2. What would astonish the nations (vv. 15-16)?

D. God's Compassion (vv. 18-20)

18Who is a God like unto thee, that pardoneth iniquity, and passeth by the transgression of the remnant of his heritage? he retaineth not his anger for ever, because he delighteth in mercy. 19He will turn again, he will have compassion upon us; he will subdue our iniquities; and thou wilt cast all their sins into the depths of the sea. 20Thou wilt perform the truth to Jacob, and the mercy to Abraham, which thou hast sworn unto our fathers from the days of old.

The final three verses of Micah's prophecy spring from a play on Micah's name (*Who is like God?*). He alone is Sovereign of the whole earth, Creator of all that exists, and Saviour of the undeserving. Only He can take away guilt and sin. He alone can remove sin's presence and pass over the transgression of His people.

God does not ignore our sin and declare us innocent. "Passeth by" (v. 18) carries the idea of moving from one point to another. The Lord deals with our sin and restores us to proper relationship through the cleansing blood of Jesus Christ (Isa. 53:11). He moves us from where we are (bound by sin) to where we need to be (free in Him). His blood does not save us *in* our sin, but *from* our sin. Sin is dealt with in actuality, not through mere declaration. A true transformation takes place.

Through the redemptive provision of Jesus Christ, He has taken upon Himself the anger of God for our sin, so that the divine wrath is removed from us (v. 4). He freely offers us His steadfast love ("mercy," Mic. 7:18) to bring us in covenant relationship with Him. He comforts us as a mother comforts her child through His compassions (v. 19). He subdues our iniquities by treading them under His feet as a person would violently stamp out a fire. He victoriously deals with our sin and removes transgressions from us, casting them into the sea's fathomless depth. They are out of sight, out of mind, and out of reach. There is no one like our God—the true, merciful, covenant-keeping, and eternal One (v. 20).

---

1. What brings delight to God (v. 18)?
2. What happens to the sins of those who repent (v. 19)?

Oceans of Mercy

Long ago, a poor woman from the slums of London was invited to go with a group of people for a holiday at the ocean. She had never seen the ocean before, and when she saw it, she burst into tears. Those around her thought it was strange that she should cry when such a lovely holiday had been given her.

"Why in the world are you crying?" they asked. Pointing to the ocean she answered, "This is the only thing I have ever seen that

CONCLUSION

Like the people of Micah's day, we have walked in darkness, but God has brought us to His glorious light. We have been cursed by sin, but God has removed that curse through the redemptive work of Christ. We have experienced the life-giving power of our Lord, and confess there is no God like Him. We walk in deliverance, having been restored to divine favor through His grace.

GOLDEN TEXT CHALLENGE

"WHO IS A GOD LIKE UNTO THEE, THAT PARDONETH INIQUITY, AND PASSETH BY THE TRANSGRESSION OF THE REMNANT OF HIS HERITAGE? HE RETAINETH NOT HIS ANGER FOR EVER, BECAUSE HE DELIGHTETH IN MERCY" (Mic. 7:18).

Micah looked into the future as he came to the close in his prophecy. The people would have to endure God's punishment, but His mercy and compassion would eventually restore them. The wonder of God's grace is extolled in the rhetorical question "Who is a God like unto thee?" Only the one true God would grant such mercy to an undeserving people.

God still longs to restore people today. He invites us to come as we are and repent of the sins we have committed. He is, as always, the Lord of mercy, compassion, and justice. He wants us to enjoy an unbroken relationship with Him.

Daily Devotions:

M. Refusal to Humble Oneself • Exodus 10:1-7
T.   God Desires a Humble Spirit • 2 Chronicles 7:11-18
W. Humble Yourself Before God • 2 Chronicles 33:10-13
T.   Humility Exemplified • John 13:1-5
F.   God Humbles Those He Calls • Acts 9:1-9
S.   God Exalts the Humble • James 4:4-10

The Way to Righteousness

Unit Theme:
Letter to the Romans

Central Truth:
Righteousness comes through faith in Christ.

Focus:
Understand what true righteousness is and live in it.

Context:
The apostle Paul wrote the letter to the Romans in AD 58 while he was in Corinth.

Golden Text:
"Therein is the righteousness of God revealed from faith to faith: as it is written, The just shall live by faith" (Rom. 1:17).

Study Outline:
  I. **God's Righteousness Revealed** (Rom. 1:1-6, 14-17)
 II. **No One Is Righteous** (Rom. 3:1-12, 19-20)
III. **Made Righteous Through Christ** (Rom. 3:21-26)

INTRODUCTION

The significance of Paul's letter to the Romans can hardly be overstated. No single document has had a greater effect on Western thought and civilization than Romans. In that regard, Paul's letter to the Romans should be placed alongside the Gospel of John, the Magna Carta, and the United States Constitution when analyzing documents that shaped life and ideology in the West. This shaping took place because of Paul's Spirit-inspired letter and because, throughout Church history, key readers of Romans have made major contributions to society as a result of their interpretation.

Perhaps the most famous example of this letter's impact is found in the Protestant Reformation, led by Martin Luther, a Roman Catholic monk who was riddled with guilt and doubts about his eternal destiny. When he was sent to pursue academic studies in theology, Luther read the Bible for the first time. He was arrested by the message of Romans with its focus on justification by faith alone. Convinced that the established church had veered off course, the Lutheran Church was born, and all of Protestantism with it. The rallying cries of the Protestant Reformation were rooted in Martin Luther's reading of Romans: *sola fide* (faith alone) and *sola sriptura* (Scripture alone).

Several centuries later, another major Christian movement was birthed from a particular reading of Romans. A seminary-trained Anglican priest named John Wesley struggled with a sense of inadequacy. During a Moravian meeting, he listened to a reading of the introduction of Martin Luther's commentary on Romans. Wesley recorded the experience in his journal:

> About a quarter before nine, while he was describing the change which God works in the heart through faith in Christ, I felt my heart strangely warmed. I felt I did trust in Christ, Christ alone, for salvation; and an assurance was given me that He had taken away my sins, even mine, and saved me from the law of sin and death.

Wesley went on from this meeting on Aldersgate Street to travel the equivalent of ten times around the globe—on horseback—preaching the Gospel and establishing the Methodist church. His revivals not only birthed a denomination, but sparked an awakening of revival throughout the Americas.

Stories like this abound throughout Church history. The message of Romans changed the world forever. It is still changing lives and shaping the Church today.

I. GOD'S RIGHTEOUSNESS REVEALED (Rom. 1:1-6, 14-17)

Romans 1 includes some of the most powerful teaching in the New Testament. Unlike any other Pauline letter, the apostle dives into natural theology, the personal and intentional revelation of God as God, and even a theology of human sexuality. In the letter's opening, we see a skilled thinker, orator, rhetorician, and theologian performing his most famous work through the anointing of God's Spirit. Everything that comes later in Romans is built on the foundation of chapter 1.

A. The Letter's Historical Context (vv. 1-6)

(Romans 1:2-4 is not included in the printed text.)

¹Paul, a servant of Jesus Christ, called to be an apostle, separated unto the gospel of God,

⁵By whom we have received grace and apostleship, for obedience to the faith among all nations, for his name: ⁶Among whom are ye also the called of Jesus Christ.

We should never give in to the temptation to skip over the introductions to Paul's letters. This is especially easy to do in Romans, since the preliminary material so quickly gives way to Paul's theological argument. However, the opening prayer, greeting, and well-wishing hold clues about the important themes Paul will treat throughout this letter.

Romans follows the expected standards and structures of ancient letter-writing. Because Paul has never visited the churches of Rome, he must present himself as an effective communicator. He accomplishes this from the outset of the letter. Ancient letters typically included six parts in order: (1) the name of the writer; (2) the name of the recipient; (3) greeting; (4) wish, prayer, or thanksgiving; (5) body of the letter; and (6) farewell. We see the first four elements open the letter to the Romans. In verse 1, Paul identifies himself as the author. However, his greeting does not occur until verse 7. What stands between is an elaborate introduction of the Gospel, which would have caught the ears of Paul's ancient audience. The thanksgiving, then, occurs in verses 8-10, which includes a reference to Paul's prayer. The body of the letter may be said to begin in either verse 14 or 16.

Paul's opening verses are intensely personal. This is a bit strange at first glance, given that Paul admits to having never traveled to meet these brothers and sisters. Yet Paul speaks about his own calling and the situation of his recipients with great affection. We must pay special attention to the contents of his words. Paul is not offering pleasantries. Instead, he chooses his words carefully.

> Paul's introductions to his letters are intentional. Adhering to ancient epistolary conventions, they do more than simply introduce the speaker, audience, and thesis. Instead, they suggest subjects, dynamics, and terminology that will be fleshed out later in the letter (Joshua Rice, *Paul and Patronage: The Dynamics of Power in 1 Corinthians*).

Paying attention to those subjects and terminology will help us get a grip on what to expect in the future chapters of Romans. Three dynamics quickly emerge.

First, *the letter to the Romans will primarily be about the Gospel.* Paul introduces the history of the Gospel in the opening verses of the letter. He wants to make it clear that the Gospel is not some new faith system on the scene of history. Instead, the entirety of the Old Testament story has paved the way for the coming of the Son of God.

Second, *the letter to the Romans is written out of Paul's passion to call Gentiles to faith in Jesus Christ.* Using the plural "we" in verse 5, Paul corresponds the breadth of the Gospel with the calling of his apostolic team to preach faith and obedience to Gentiles. This calling has great application in Rome, Italy, which was the center of the Gentile world.

Third, *the letter to the Romans has the practical purpose of preparing for Paul's ministry in Rome.* Paul admits his plans to visit Rome have been sidetracked many times, but now it seems that God has opened the door (v. 13). Interestingly, the only evidence we have that Paul did minister in Rome took place during his imprisonment there. The Book of Acts ends with this preaching ministry under house arrest:

> For two whole years Paul stayed there in his own rented house and welcomed all who came to see him. Boldly and without hindrance he preached the kingdom of God and taught about the Lord Jesus Christ (Acts 28:30-31 NIV).

In the end, Paul made it to Rome to advance the Gospel. However, God had far different plans as to how Paul would arrive and accomplish this goal. Though he came to Rome as a prisoner, the Gospel still went forth.

---

1. Explain Paul's self-description of being "separated unto the gospel of God" (v. 1).
2. How does Paul summarize the Gospel in verses 3 and 4?
3. How does Paul describe the people to whom he was writing (vv. 5-6)?

"In our manner of speech, our plans of living, our dealings with others, our conduct and walk in the church and out of it—all should be done as becomes the Gospel."—Albert Barnes

B. Not Ashamed of the Gospel (vv. 14-17)

14I am debtor both to the Greeks, and to the Barbarians; both to the wise, and to the unwise. 15So, as much as in me is, I am ready to preach the gospel to you that are at Rome also. 16For I am not ashamed of the gospel of Christ: for it is the power of God unto salvation to every one that believeth; to the Jew first, and also to the Greek. 17For therein is the righteousness of God revealed from faith to faith: as it is written, The just shall live by faith.

After developing relational rapport with the Roman churches, explaining his desire to move to Rome for a period of evangelistic ministry among the Gentiles there, Paul launches into his personal commitment to the Gospel (vv. 14-15). His feeling of obligation transcends conventional boundaries. The strange feature of this address is that Rome is in Italy, not Greece. Presumably, the Gentiles in Rome would consider themselves Roman/Italian. Paul is clearly drawing a differentiation. Greeks would have been considered wise and educated by Paul's Roman audience. Barbarians were peoples that were uneducated, unwise, and poor. In Paul's mind, the Romans have failed to be reached. This is why he is ready to set up camp in Rome.

Finally, after introducing fifteen verses of personal context, Paul provides the reason for the letter (vv. 16-17). This thesis statement is packed with a weightiness that can be summarized in three points.

First, *Paul's commitment is not to a movement or an ideology, but to the message he calls "the gospel."* The term *gospel* would have been well known to Paul's Roman audience. It was the preferred term used by the caesars to describe the blessings they had provided for the world. An illustrative example of this word is found in a letter of Paulus Fabius Maximus, governor of Asia, in 9 BC. It describes the reshaping of the world's calendar so that its first day coincided with the birthday of Caesar Augustus. "The birthday of the god [Augustus] was the beginning for the world of good news." Such statements were inscribed on many monuments around the Roman Empire. In the city of Rome, this supposed "good news" of the rule of the caesars would have been represented everywhere: in buildings, signage, coinage, speeches, plays, and gladiatorial games. Paul, however, preaches a different gospel about the Son of God: the Lord Jesus Christ.

Second, *the message of the Gospel enables Jews and Gentiles to come together in Christ's church.* This is the heart of Paul's message. Paul was not primarily preaching about heaven, the afterlife, or how to find atonement for sin. These themes grew out of his greater message: that through Jesus Christ, the covenant people of God have now been expanded to include all the nations of the world. This truth is no less than the fulfillment of God's ancient promise to Abraham—to bless all the nations of the world through him (Gen. 12:1-3).

Third, *the content of the Gospel is that God has opened up a new way of righteousness.* We can define *righteousness* in many ways, and Paul will have much to say about the term in later chapters. Broadly speaking, *righteousness* referred to both a state of being and a lifestyle. God declares sinners righteous, then enables them to live in a righteous manner. Righteousness does not come through religious ritual. Instead, the good news is righteousness is by faith, as Paul quotes from Habakkuk 2:4.

---

1. What was Paul eager to do, and why (vv. 14-15)?
2. Describe the power of the Gospel (vv. 16-17).
3. How can we access God's righteousness (v. 17)?

> "Faith, as Paul saw it, was a living, flaming thing leading to surrender and obedience to the commandments of Christ."
> —A. W. Tozer

II. NO ONE IS RIGHTEOUS (Rom. 3:1-12, 19-20)

Much transpires between Paul's introduction of the theme of righteousness (1:17) to its fuller explanation in chapter 3. For two chapters, Paul builds his case for the need for righteousness. In 1:18-32, we find humanity has largely turned away from the goodness of God, preferring their own passions and lusts over His will. In chapter 2, we find that righteousness through religion has been derailed by ethnic identity and ethnic conflict. Religion is supposed to produce family, but instead it has produced division. In this chapter, Paul deals with the Lord's inability to break down these boundaries.

A. The Founder of Faith (vv. 1-8)

(Romans 3:6-8 is not included in the printed text.)

¹What advantage then hath the Jew? or what profit is there of circumcision? ²Much every way: chiefly, because that unto them were committed the oracles of God. ³For what if some did not believe? shall their unbelief make the faith of God without effect? ⁴God forbid: yea, let God be true, but every man a liar; as it is written, That thou mightest be justified in thy sayings, and mightest overcome when thou art judged. ⁵But if our unrighteousness commend the righteousness of God, what shall we say? Is God unrighteous who taketh vengeance? (I speak as a man).

Throughout Romans, Paul often sets up an imaginary conversation partner to help him work through various theological issues. Sometimes he even plays "devil's advocate" to his own point. This approach keeps the letter lively and moving, engaging his audience with seasoned skill.

In chapter 2, Paul has introduced key problems in the early church: the place of the Law and circumcision. We know from the Jerusalem Council in Acts 15 that these Old Testament signs of covenant were becoming impediments to reaching Gentiles with the Gospel. After all, most of these Gentiles had never even heard of the Old Testament, and certain Jewish Christian groups were demanding that they be circumcised and eat kosher. Paul will have none of this, arguing that righteousness is by faith alone, not by following cultural traditions. Paul's posture posed a problem for his Jewish heritage

---

and constituency (Rom. 3:1). Does Judaism not matter at all anymore? This is not the case, since the story of God begins with His revelation to Israel (v. 2).

The problem is that Jews are not turning to Jesus in large numbers in the first century of the Christian movement. Instead, Christianity quickly shifts to the Gentiles where it is widely accepted. Paul begins to explore this crisis in chapter 3, a theme to which he will return in chapters 9-11.

Paul argues that faith is primarily not a matter of human effort, but of divine initiative. Just because certain Israelites were unfaithful did not end their covenant with God (3:3). The covenant is eternal. Because of this, even human sin is not destructive enough to affect God's faithfulness (v. 4). However, rebellion against God will bring about God's judgment, even though it causes His righteousness to stand out (v. 5).

God may bring good out of evil, but that does not relieve from guilt the person who does evil (vv. 6-8). If it did, then that would encourage us to do evil, hoping that good would come from it. Such a false assumption would destroy the distinction between right and wrong (French L. Arrington, *The Greatest Letter Ever Written*).

---

1. How did God singly bless the Jewish people (vv. 1-2)?
2. How does Paul answer his own question (vv. 3-4)?
3. How does Paul again answer his own question (vv. 5-6)?
4. Whose "condemnation is deserved" (v. 8 NIV), and why?

> "Two things on which Paul preeminently insisted—that salvation was provided by God's grace and that faith was the means by which men appropriated it."—F. F. Bruce

---

B. The Need for God (vv. 9-12, 19-20)

⁹What then? are we better than they? No, in no wise: for we have before proved both Jews and Gentiles, that they are all under sin; ¹⁰As it is written, There is none righteous, no, not one: ¹¹There is none that understandeth, there is none that seeketh after God. ¹²They are all gone out of the way, they are together become unprofitable; there is none that doeth good, no, not one.

¹⁹Now we know that what things soever the law saith, it saith to them who are under the law: that every mouth may be stopped, and all the world may become guilty before God. ²⁰Therefore by the deeds of the law there shall no flesh be justified in his sight: for by the law is the knowledge of sin.

Paul describes the reality of sin in a long list of Old Testament quotations (vv. 10-18). Turning to the Old Testament is a way to heighten the importance of God's covenant with the Jews that has just been described. But Paul is doing more here than calling attention to the Torah covenant. He is describing humanity's failure at that same covenant, highlighting the need for God to act on His own accord. Paul strings together a hybrid collection of Biblical verses to create a single powerful point: the gift of the Torah did not fix the sin problem. Man was, and is, inherently faithless. The dire situation is summarized as hopeless (vv. 10-12).

In verses 19 and 20, the Law takes on a new meaning in Paul's description. It does not produce justification, but it leads to justification through the awareness of sin. The problem has been identified. Now it is time for Paul to explain the solution.

---

1. How are all people the same (vv. 9-12)?

2. What did the Law accomplish, and what could it not do (vv. 19-20)?

> "Through the death of Christ on the cross making atonement for sin, we get a perfect standing before God. That is justification, and it puts us, in God's sight, back in Eden before sin entered. God looks upon us and treats us as if we had never sinned."
> —A. C. Dixon

III. MADE RIGHTEOUS THROUGH CHRIST (Rom. 3:21-26)

Up to this point in Paul's letter to the Romans, the overall message has been quite dark. Human sin and the failure of human religion, even God-ordained religion, have been dramatically illustrated. No one is righteous, even those with the covenant of circumcision and the Law, so humanity is in a terrible dilemma. Yet, when it appears that all hope may have been lost, God has powerfully acted. The diamond of the Gospel message can shine so brightly because it is effectively placed against the diseased backdrop of human darkness.

A. Time Has Changed (vv. 21-24)

²¹But now the righteousness of God without the law is manifested, being witnessed by the law and the prophets; ²²Even the righteousness of God which is by faith of Jesus Christ unto all and upon all them that believe: for there is no difference: ²³For all have sinned, and come short of the glory of God; ²⁴Being justified freely by his grace through the redemption that is in Christ Jesus.

Paul's Jewish conception of world history is an important feature of his theology, with history being divided into two epochs (ages). The "present age" is associated with sickness, deprivation, death, and sin. But Paul looked forward to a future age, "the last days," in which the Messiah would inaugurate a new time, full of life, healing, health, and righteousness. In Romans 3, Paul dramatically announces that this moment has come. The time has changed through Jesus Christ!

A righteousness without the need for observance of the Law (Genesis-Deuteronomy) has been created by God. However, Paul shows there is a fundamental connection between this new righteousness and the witness of the Old Testament (note that here Paul widens the scope beyond the Law to include the prophetic books). In short, the message of the Old Testament was pointing toward and leading up to the realities of the New Testament. This new message levels the playing field, destroying ethnic and religious boundaries to create a new people of God. Jesus Christ is now the redemption of all things—past, present, and future.

---

1. What must we "believe" to receive God's promise (vv. 21-22)?
2. What exactly is "the glory of God" of which we fall short (v. 23)?
3. Explain the use of the word "freely" (v. 24).

> "The core and essence of the Gospel is its tremendous and glorious revelation of how deadly is God's hatred of sin, so that He cannot stand having it in the same universe as Himself, and will go any length, and will pay any price, and will make any sacrifice, to master and abolish it."—A. J. Gossip

---

B. Atonement Accomplished and Applied (vv. 25-26)

25Whom God hath set forth to be a propitiation through faith in his blood, to declare his righteousness for the remission of sins that are past, through the forbearance of God; 26To declare, I say, at this time his righteousness: that he might be just, and the justifier of him which believeth in Jesus.

In verses 21-24, Paul used the language of *righteousness* and *redemption* to describe God's victory over sin through Christ Jesus. In verse 25, he shifts to the subject of *atonement* ("propitiation").

As a faithful Jew, Paul would have been shaped by several controlling stories, or "metanarratives" that cohere the Old Testament together. One of these stories would have been the movement from slavery to freedom that is embodied in Exodus. Another huge Old Testament story would have been the movement from exile to return that is relayed by the Prophets. Still another was the story of sin and atonement that was used by the priests, especially in Leviticus. The important point to remember is that Paul uses all of these stories, in different ways, to explain God's action through Christ. All too often, *atonement* has been the only story used by Christians to explain the Gospel. It is a critically important story, and Paul introduces it in his description of God's new righteousness.

The truth of the Gospel is not only framed in terms of the goodness offered to believers. There is also the matter of divine justice which must be taken into account. In Paul's language this connection would have been more clear, in that the word translated "justice" (NIV) is the same word that is translated "righteousness." For an individual to be declared righteous requires that the cosmic scales of justice be balanced. God is a God of order, so we live in a morally ordered universe.

Paul's reference to Jesus as "a sacrifice for atonement" (v. 25 NIV) brings to mind Jesus being called "the Lamb slain from the foundation of the world" (Rev. 13:8). The story of Jesus' atonement for sin is ancient. He took all of history's sins upon Himself, so as to justify all who would believe in His name.

Paul ends this section with the logical consequences of such a divine act (Rom. 3:27-31). No one is permitted to boast, because God has done all the work on our behalf. This exclusion of boasting encompasses the Law and circumcision. The only proper response to God's mercy is a believing faith that acknowledges our need for God.

---

1. What did God do "publicly" (v. 25 NASB)?
2. Why is it important that God is both "just" and "justifier" (v. 26)?

Focus on Identity

We live in a world saturated by advertising. Untold billions of dollars are spent on marketing campaigns to sell products. Recently, advertisers have steered away from pitching the actual products they are selling. Rather than extol the benefits of the item's quality, marketers now are selling an identity to the purchaser: "If I buy this product, I am this kind of person."

This focus on identity is actually a Christian innovation, found in Romans. When a person is justified by faith, they do not join a new religion; they take on a renewed identity.

CONCLUSION

The opening three chapters of Romans begin with the problem of human sin and end with the answer of God through Christ Jesus. As Paul explains, humanity has created many methods in the attempt to improve the situation. The foremost method of improvement has been religion. Yet even Jewish religion, illuminated by God, did not ultimately fix the problem of sin. As a result, God revealed Himself definitively through Jesus Christ. It is in Christ that righteousness can be attained through faith.

GOLDEN TEXT CHALLENGE

"THEREIN IS THE RIGHTEOUSNESS OF GOD REVEALED FROM FAITH TO FAITH: AS IT IS WRITTEN, THE JUST SHALL LIVE BY FAITH" (Rom. 1:17).

The righteousness which salvation produces is by faith, from first to last. *Faith*, as Paul used the term, means total acceptance and absolute trust. It means being utterly sure that what Jesus said is true, and staking all time and eternity on that assurance. In full-fledged faith, a person hears the Christian message, agrees it is true, and then casts himself or herself upon it in a life of total yieldedness.

Paul then uses that beautiful phrase, "The just shall live by faith." When God justifies us, He treats us as if we had not been a sinner at all; God treats us as a child to be loved. *Justification* means God reckons us not as His enemies but as His friends; not as lawbreakers to be punished, but as men and women to be loved. That is the essence of the Gospel.

Daily Devotions:

M. Faith Credited as Righteousness • Genesis 15:1-6

T. Righteous Judgment • Leviticus 19:11-18

W. Righteous Commandments • Deuteronomy 6:20-25

T. Jesus Fulfills All Righteousness • Matthew 3:13-17

F. An Enemy of Righteousness Judged • Acts 13:6-12

S. The Righteous Conqueror • Revelation 19:11-16

Justified by Faith

Romans 4:1—5:11

Unit Theme:
Letter to the Romans

Central Truth:
Justification is received by trusting in Christ.

Focus:
Comprehend that justification is by faith and rejoice in our salvation.

Context:
The apostle Paul wrote the letter to the Romans in AD 58 while he was in Corinth.

Golden Text:
"Therefore being justified by faith, we have peace with God through our Lord Jesus Christ" (Rom. 5:1).

Study Outline:
  I. **Abraham Justified by Faith** (Rom. 4:1-12)
 II. **Promise for All Who Believe** (Rom. 4:13-25)
III. **Justified by Faith in Christ** (Rom. 5:1-11)

INTRODUCTION

The overarching theme of "justification by faith" is introduced in Romans 1:17. There, Paul picks from a fairly obscure Old Testament text in Habakkuk to mark the significance of this theme. The context of this reference is important, as the quotation of Old Testament verses in the New Testament typically call to mind the "textual world" that surrounds the reference. Paul is not plucking out a verse because it suits his purposes based on a phrase; what is happening in Habakkuk is important to the apostle's argument.

Habakkuk is a mysterious book of the Bible with few clues about its historical setting. We do not know the identity of the author, only his name. We do know Habakkuk prophesies against the Babylonians, even as he grapples with their role as instruments of the will of God (1:6). Although God will use the Babylonian Empire to judge Israel's sin and cause the period of exile, the Babylonian rulers will one day be judged. In the context of this judgment, Habakkuk draws a distinction between the faithless and the faithful. Speaking of the Babylonian ruler, Habakkuk says, "Behold, his soul is puffed up; it is not upright within him, but the righteous shall live by his faith" (2:4 ESV). The righteous will remain faithful unto God, living a life characterized by that commitment.

This story of Israel's past fits easily into the context of Paul's letter to the Romans. It is no accident, for example, that early Christians and Jews frequently referred to Rome as "Babylon" (1 Peter 5:13; Rev. 18). Rome was the capital of sin and oppression over the earth, and in Christian eschatology she awaited the judgment of God. The Roman Christians are surrounded by such paganism. Their only hope is the injunction of Habakkuk: *to live by faith alone.*

As the letter to the Romans unfolds, this command to live by faith is further fleshed out. We discover *faith* is less about human effort and more about God's initiative to make us faithful. This is wrapped up in the nature of justification by faith, which Paul carefully explains.

I. ABRAHAM JUSTIFIED BY FAITH (Rom. 4:1-12)

To read the words of Paul's letters is not just to read, but to listen to a skilled preacher. This is true not only because Paul's letters would be read aloud to a mostly illiterate audience, but because Paul was a preacher. In Romans 4, this communication ability is put on full display as Paul reaches into the Old Testament story of Abraham to explain God's plan to justify believers by faith. As a faithful student, preacher, and writer of God's Word, Paul is careful to ensure that the Roman Christians understand the Christian story is not suddenly new on the world's scene. In fact, the story stretches thousands of years backward into history.

A. Belief Versus Works (vv. 1-8)

(Romans 4:1-2, 6-8 is not included in the printed text.)

³For what saith the scripture? Abraham believed God, and it was counted unto him for righteousness. ⁴Now to him that worketh is the reward not reckoned of grace, but of debt. ⁵But to him that worketh not, but believeth on him that justifieth the ungodly, his faith is counted for righteousness.

In chapter 3, Paul spotlighted the faithfulness of God in creating a way of salvation that is not through ethnic markers of identity, but through faith alone. In order to make this argument, Paul must walk through the problem of circumcised Jewish Christians versus uncircumcised Gentile believers. The question of whether or not Judaism was necessary for salvation was a lightning-rod issue in the early church, and Paul's view was considered extreme by many.

In Galatians 6:15, Paul proclaims that "neither circumcision nor uncircumcision means anything" (NIV). This is a bold statement. Some scholars believe Romans was written in response to the firestorm of confusion caused by the letter to the Galatians. Paul does seem to temper his view. We must also recognize, however, that there is a strong constituency of Jewish believers in Paul's Roman audience, which does not seem to be the case among the Galatian churches. Paul, therefore, has to give more attentiveness to matters of Jewish concern. He must be methodical in walking these Jewish Christians through the Scriptural understanding given to him by God.

Paul begins Romans 4, which will mostly be about *circumcision*, with the wider subject at hand: the relationship between *faith* and *works*. In this way, the topic of *circumcision* bookends the present discussion, having been originally introduced in chapter 2. Paul considers *circumcision* to be a "work," along with keeping the rituals of the Law. He writes, "For if Abraham was justified by works, he has something to boast, but not before God" (4:2 NASB).

Paul argues that God's preference for faith over works was in existence decades before Christ came.

Just as he pulled a single line from Habakkuk to introduce the subject of *justification by faith* in 1:17, Paul now draws from a single sentence of the Old Testament story about Abraham in Romans 4:3, declaring, "Abraham believed God, and it was credited to him as righteousness" (NASB). We can imagine that Paul often preached from this verse to relay a powerful truth.

Paul does not immediately cite any of the surrounding context to his quotation of Genesis 15:6. This does not mean the context in Genesis does not matter to Paul's argument in Romans 4; Paul will bring it back around in verse 16. Abraham's sudden belief in God's word comes at the point in which God makes an eternal covenant with Abraham, promising to make a great nation from his lineage. Abraham's response is belief, an act which God named as *righteousness*. Paul's point is simple: Abraham had performed no great works for God! Instead, he had been a worshiper of false gods. Yet, in His "completely sovereign grace," God came to "this undeserving idolater," as John Piper describes him, and declared him righteous upon the basis of belief alone.

In Paul's explanation of Genesis 15:6, he digs into the nature of the credit God gives. It might be easy to construe God's bestowal of righteousness upon Abraham as God's obligation to His own divine plan. Not so, says Paul. Abraham's belief did not earn the credit of righteousness in any way (Rom. 4:4). God is not a mathematical equation, waiting on Abraham to believe enough so as to attain righteousness. Instead, God responds to faith by joyfully giving the gift of righteousness (v. 5). This is what primarily sets apart faith from works.

Paul contends not only that Abraham received this righteousness, but even King David understood the nature of grace (v. 6). By using these two headlining figures in Jewish history, Paul appeals primarily to Jewish Christians who would be moved (and perhaps surprised) by such an appeal. He wants to show the Old Testament is filled with the language of *grace*, the theology of *justification by faith*.

In verses 7-8, Paul quotes from David himself: "Blessed are those whose lawless deeds have been forgiven, and whose sins have been covered. Blessed is the man whose sin the Lord will not take into account" (NASB; see Ps. 32:1-2).

---

1. What does verse 2 say about boasting?
2. In verse 3, can you honestly replace the name *Abraham* with your name? Why or why not?
3. What does God offer the "ungodly" person (vv. 4-5)?
4. Explain the phrase "God imputes righteousness" (v. 6 NKJV).
5. Describe the "blessed" person (vv. 7-8).

> "The difference between *grace* and *works* is the difference between *worship* and *idolatry*. The man inebriated with the thought that all he has is Yahweh's gift finds himself repeatedly on his knees, adoring, thanking, praising. But if we do not grasp grace

B. The Place of Circumcision (vv. 9-12)

(Romans 4:9-10 is not included in the printed text.)

¹¹And he received the sign of circumcision, a seal of the righteousness of the faith which he had yet being uncircumcised: that he might be the father of all them that believe, though they be not circumcised; that righteousness might be imputed unto them also: ¹²And the father of circumcision to them who are not of the circumcision only, but who also walk in the steps of that faith of our father Abraham, which he had being yet uncircumcised.

After the hiatus from the subject of *circumcision* in verses 1-8, Paul doubles back. This wrangling over circumcision can seem strange to modern ears. We must remember, however, that Jews identified themselves as the people of God through circumcision. It was a covenant stretching back to Abraham. It was difficult for Jews, even Jewish Christians, to imagine that God would include uncircumcised families among the redeemed. There may also have been the temptation among Gentile Christians to be identified as Jews, so as to fall under the religions that the Roman government allowed. New Testament scholar Bruce W. Winter makes just this point:

> If Christian Gentiles underwent circumcision they would be Jewish proselytes. If they also observed the Jewish law, as did their Christian Jewish brethren in Jerusalem (Acts 21:20), then in the eyes of the outside world they belonged to a [legal religion]. The social identification of Jews by the Gentile world was their observation of the law (*Seek the Welfare of the City: Christians as Benefactors and Citizens*).

The practice of circumcision had grave implications, not only for Jewish identity but perhaps for Christian safety.

Paul, however, knows what is most at stake is the role of circumcision in God's salvation history. He wants his Roman audience to understand the sequence of events in the Abraham story. God declared Abraham to be righteous prior to the covenant of circumcision, on the basis of belief alone (v. 11). Abraham's moment of faith occurs in Genesis 15, while the covenant of circumcision does not appear until chapter 17. The original story proves righteousness can be ascribed apart from circumcision.

If circumcision is not necessary for righteousness, then the standard of belief must have nothing to do with ethnic boundary markers (Rom. 4:12). Those who believe have the same right to claim Abraham as their father as those who are circumcised. So Abraham truly stands as the father of faith, for both the circumcised and uncircumcised.

---

1. Answer the question in verse 9, and explain your answer.
2. Explain the before-and-after statement in verse 10.

---

3. Who can claim Abraham as a spiritual father (vv. 11-12)?

> "Many of us are tempted to find the key in doing, but the answer is actually found in being. It is vital that we are routinely humbled by the reminder that Christian life is grounded, not in what we can do, but what has been done for us and what we need done to us."—Alistair Begg

---

II. PROMISE FOR ALL WHO BELIEVE (Rom. 4:13-25)

In Romans 4, the focus of God's saving power moves outward from Abraham to incorporate larger concentric circles. Like a rock thrown into a pond, what started as one man's righteousness by God's grace expands to all those who believe. This promise certainly includes the circumcised and those who practice the Law, a point often missed by modern readers. These things are not precluded from faith, but they are subject to it. It is only in this movement of outward expansion that the ultimate promise to Abraham can be fulfilled: to bless all the nations of the earth through his faith.

A. Law Versus Grace (vv. 13-17)

(Romans 4:14-17 is not included in the printed text.)l

¹³For the promise, that he should be the heir of the world, was not to Abraham, or to his seed, through the law, but through the righteousness of faith.

Paul has been speaking about works (vv. 1-5) and about circumcision, which is a form of works (vv. 9-12). Now, however, he expands his study to the entire Law. Paul wants to make it clear that the age of the Law has been replaced by a righteousness that comes by faith.

The Law (the first five books of the Old Testament) was not given to Moses until centuries after the life of Abraham. For him to become the father of many nations means God chose a different means to pass down the promise. That means, according to Paul, righteousness by faith (v. 13).

Verse 14 teaches, "If the Jews only be heirs of the promise made to Abraham, and that on the ground of prior obedience to the Law, then 'faith is made void'—is entirely useless—and 'the promise,' which was made to faith, is 'made of none effect'" (*Adam Clarke's Commentary*). Thankfully, that is not the case.

In verse 16, Paul reintroduces God's grace into the conversation, setting up chapters 5 and 6, where *grace* will be the primary subject. *Grace* can be defined as "divine covenant favor which God alone can give." The Law and the covenant of circumcision were considered to be gifts of God's grace for the ancient Jews. Paul does not dispute that. Instead, he applies grace to uncircumcised believers, the "many nations" (v. 17) promised to Abraham in Genesis 17:5. Grace has been lavishly poured out on all who believe.

---

1. Why was the law of God necessary (v. 15)?
2. What could not be accomplished through the Law (v. 14)?

---

3. How does verse 17 describe God? How have you experienced this in your own life?

> "The Law tells me how crooked I am. Grace comes along and straightens me out."—D. L. Moody

---

B. Hope Against Hope (vv. 18-25)
(Romans 4:23-25 is not included in the printed text.)

18Who against hope believed in hope, that he might become the father of many nations, according to that which was spoken, So shall thy seed be. 19And being not weak in faith, he considered not his own body now dead, when he was about an hundred years old, neither yet the deadness of Sarah's womb: 20He staggered not at the promise of God through unbelief; but was strong in faith, giving glory to God; 21And being fully persuaded that, what he had promised, he was able also to perform. 22And therefore it was imputed to him for righteousness.

In the final verses of chapter 4, Paul brings his argument to a rousing close. He jumps back into the Abraham story, now including Sarah's part, to depict the grandeur of the patriarch's faith. Paul wants to make the point that the story is outlandish. Both Abraham and Sarah were too old to become parents (v. 19), yet Abraham did not cease to believe that he would "become the father of many nations" (v. 18). Abraham had faith in the voice of God over the cold reality of the impersonal facts (v. 20). He was "fully persuaded" that God was powerful enough to keep His word (v. 21). For that reason, God declared him righteous (v. 22).

> Abraham recognized God as God—that He was the Creator and Life-giver. Unwavering in his faith, he believed God's promise, even though his belief went against human experience and human hope. Considering Abraham's splendid example of faith, we are inspired to look beyond the hopelessness of human circumstances and to rejoice in God's power which is able to overcome the difficulties of life and give us victory (French L. Arrington, *The Greatest Letter Ever Written*).

Paul's message is that Genesis 15 was not written simply to describe the life of Abraham. It was written to depict the eternal pathway of faith for all followers of God (Rom. 4:23). Because God has raised Jesus from the dead, we are called to walk down Abraham's faithful pathway (v. 24). Because of God's work in Christ, we are conclusively justified by faith (v. 25).

---

1. What did Abraham do "against [all] hope," and what was the result (v. 18)?
2. How can we bring "glory to God" (vv. 20-21)?
3. What does God call us to believe (vv. 23-24)?
4. How does Christ transform lives (v. 25)?

> "Grace is the free, undeserved goodness and favor of God to mankind."—Matthew Henry

III. JUSTIFIED BY FAITH IN CHRIST (Rom. 5:1-11)

In Romans 5, Paul reaches further back into history than Abraham, contrasting the life of Jesus with the life of Adam. Before he gets there, however, verses 1-11 act as a bridge, giving Paul the space to draw important conclusions about the life that is justified by faith.

A. A Lifestyle of Faith (vv. 1-5)

(Romans 5:3-4 is not included in the printed text.)

¹Therefore being justified by faith, we have peace with God through our Lord Jesus Christ: ²By whom also we have access by faith into this grace wherein we stand, and rejoice in hope of the glory of God.

⁵And hope maketh not ashamed; because the love of God is shed abroad in our hearts by the Holy Ghost which is given unto us.

It is not an exaggeration to say that some Christian groups so overstate their doctrine of justification that matters of lifestyle are almost left out. In other traditions, Christians are expected to be practically perfect. While the proof of justification can be seen in a godly lifestyle, justification is the entry point to the life of faith, not the finish line.

The results of the experience of justification include peace and a good standing with God. Such a posture can only lead to a life of rejoicing. All confessed strife between humanity and God has been reconciled through the victory of Jesus Christ! So, the Christian can be said to live "into this grace" which is full of God's glory (vv. 1-2).

This grace-filled life also casts personal suffering in a new light. In Paul's day, Roman Christians were learning to suffer for their faith. It would not be long before Nero became the first emperor to systematically persecute Christians in Rome, blaming them for the great fire of AD 64. The physical conditions in the city of Rome were difficult for the average Christian/citizen. The Gospel, however, afforded believers a new lens through which to understand suffering: "Suffering produces perseverance; perseverance, character; and character, hope" (vv. 3-4 NIV). This is a dramatic sequence of statements. The final equation is that suffering produces hope, rather than despair.

It has been said that the Jews who lost their faith in the God of Israel during the Holocaust were not the Jews in the death camps, but the Jews far away in America. Those who suffer in God find hope in God. As Christians, "hope of the glory of God" (v. 2) does not disappoint us, for God has poured His love into us through the indwelling presence of the Holy Spirit (v. 5). His presence gives us hope, even when our circumstances look hopeless.

---

1. List two blessings of being "justified by faith" (vv. 1-2).
2. What will godly perseverance eventually produce (vv. 3-4)?
3. What will not disappoint us, and why not (v. 5)?

> "The truth is that, though we were justified by faith alone, the faith that justifies is never alone (it always produces fruit—good works . . . a transformed life)."—J. I. Packer

B. The Fullness of Time (vv. 6-11)

(Romans 5:7-9 is not included in the printed text.)

⁶For when we were yet without strength, in due time Christ died for the ungodly.

¹⁰For if, when we were enemies, we were reconciled to God by the death of his Son, much more, being reconciled, we shall be saved by his life. ¹¹And not only so, but we also joy in God through our Lord Jesus Christ, by whom we have now received the atonement.

Just as God carefully timed the pattern of His engagement with Abraham, so that justification by faith precluded the covenant of circumcision, so also did God wait for the right time to act in Christ Jesus. It had to be a time when humanity was utterly lost, waiting on an act of God. If humanity was not in desperation, there would be no need for such a plan from God. If the Law and circumcision were enough to fulfill God's promise to Abraham, to bless all the nations of the world through the Jewish people, the results would be evident. Instead, these realities were mile markers along the road to God's ultimate salvation in Jesus.

Paul describes humanity's status as *lost* in terms of our powerlessness and inability to help ourselves achieve goodness (v. 6). In writing about the Law versus grace to the Galatians, Paul said, "When the time had fully come, God sent his Son" (4:4 NIV). Obviously, the timing of Christ's coming was crucial.

This timing is more wondrous because God takes all the initiative in the plan of salvation. Paul paints a provocative picture. We know a few stories from history in which someone died on behalf of a good man. God, however, works in the opposite direction (vv. 6-7). Had He waited on humanity to attain to goodness, salvation would have never been purchased. God purchased salvation so helpless people could become redeemed. Christ gave His life on behalf of bad, greedy, sinful, miserable folk like us (v. 8). This is the heart of the Gospel.

As a result of receiving the Gospel, the wrath of God is nothing to fear (v. 9). Make no mistake, God's wrath is real. Paul declared in 1:18 that such wrath is being poured out on wickedness. Believers, however, have been redeemed from that wrath because they are no longer enemies of God (5:10).

Rather than living in fear, we can lead joyful lives if we have been reconciled to God through Christ (v. 11). Salvation is not a single, instant event; it has implications for the past, present, and future. As believers in Christ, we have been saved, we are being saved, and we will be saved.

---

1. How are people "helpless" (v. 6 NASB)?
2. How do verses 7 and 8 explain God's remedy for lost humanity?
3. Why did Christ shed His blood (vv. 9-10)?
4. Why should Christians be joyful (v. 11)?

Free and Clear

A common analogy for justification by faith is the setting of a courtroom. Imagine a criminal, confessing and proven guilty, about to receive the sentence for his crimes. Surprisingly, after pronouncing the stiff sentence, the judge takes the criminal's place, paying a penalty that was not his. Because the penalty has been paid, the criminal's record is free and clear. He is no longer a criminal! He is justified by the grace of the judge.

CONCLUSION

The theme of "justification by faith" is at the center of Paul's letter to the Romans. In order to make his theology of justification shine, Paul must carefully deconstruct other methods of justification. Yes, God created the Law and circumcision as a part of the Old Testament covenant. He does not throw these to the side as if they do not matter. Instead, Paul shows how these were a part of God's perfect plan to point the way to Jesus Christ. It is through the grace of Christ that humanity can receive redemption and reconciliation with God.

GOLDEN TEXT CHALLENGE

"THEREFORE BEING JUSTIFIED BY FAITH, WE HAVE PEACE WITH GOD THROUGH OUR LORD JESUS CHRIST" (Rom. 5:1).

The word *therefore* indicates the present passage is a continuance of Paul's discussion in the previous chapter. Chapter 4 gives us the illustration of Abraham, and how his faith was the basis for his receiving God's deliverance, guidance, and rewards.

Now Paul explains that we, too, may participate in these blessings "by faith." By faith in Christ as our Savior, we are *justified*. That is, we have faith, and God justifies us. Someone has explained *faith* with this acrostic: Forsaking All, I Take Him (Christ). Faith is not a mere agreement with the historical fact that Jesus died on the cross to save people from their sins. It involves a complete commitment to Him and identification with Him.

Sin separates us from God and prevents us from having *peace* in our heart. The basis for peace between us and God is the Peacemaker, Jesus Christ, who brings us and God together by means of a peace offering—His death on the cross. God has agreed to accept this offering; and, when we agree to accept it also, then peace is established.

Daily Devotions:
M. A Reason to Believe • Deuteronomy 7:6-9
T. God's Faithful Promises • 1 Kings 8:54-56
W. Great Is Thy Faithfulness • Lamentations 3:21-26
T. A Message of Justification • Acts 13:32-41
F. God Is Faithful • 1 Corinthians 1:3-9
S. Justification Is Only by Faith • Galatians 2:16-21

A Matter of Life and Death

Romans 5:12—6:23

Unit Theme:
Letter to the Romans

Central Truth:
Sin and death came by Adam; grace and life come through Christ.

Focus:
Contrast Adam with Jesus and sin with grace, and live by grace.

Context:
The apostle Paul wrote the letter to the Romans in AD 58 while he was in Corinth.

Golden Text:
"If through the offence of one many be dead, much more the grace of God, and the gift by grace, which is by one man, Jesus Christ, hath abounded unto many" (Rom. 5:15).

Study Outline:
  I. **Adam and Christ Contrasted** (Rom. 5:12-19)
 II. **Sin and Grace Contrasted** (Rom. 5:20—6:4)
III. **Death Versus Life** (Rom. 6:5-14, 20-23)

INTRODUCTION

The relationship between the Old Testament and the New Testament represents one of the most profound challenges across the centuries of Christian thought. We Christians believe the promises of God in the Old Testament reach their ultimate fulfillment within the message of the New Testament. We believe with 2 Timothy 3:16 that "all Scripture is God-breathed" (NIV), and with 2 Peter 1:21 That "men spoke from God as they were carried along by the Holy Spirit" (NIV). Pentecostal New Testament scholar John Christopher Thomas explains:

> Both of these texts make clear that the Scriptures are of divine origin and that God himself was active in their composition, breathing into them, carrying them along. These verses demonstrate that Scripture cannot be properly appreciated apart from divine inspiration (*Ministry and Theology: Studies for the Church and Its Leaders*).

We have two Testaments—two inspired witnesses to the work of God in history. One way the New Testament writers make sense of this relationship is by claiming to properly interpret some of the larger themes and characters of the Old Testament. Keep in mind that these writers did not necessarily realize they were writing what would later become the New Testament. The Bible of Jesus and the early Christians was the Old Testament alone. So, in the New Testament documents we see them working out what God revealed about Jesus Christ in the context of particular church communities. In order to do this, they used the language, constructs, and terminology of the Old Testament. For example, Hebrews 8:5 refers to the Old Testament tabernacle as a "copy and shadow" (NKJV) of the heavenly temple mediated by Jesus. The Old Testament, then, lays a foundation that is built upon by the achievements of Jesus Christ and His church.

A major means by which this interrelationship is displayed is in New Testament preaching about Old Testament characters. We have already seen that Paul makes Abraham a centerpiece of his theological approach in Romans 4. In chapter 5, Paul turns to the father of us all, Adam, in order to link the story of Christ to the story of the entire human predicament.

I. ADAM AND CHRIST CONTRASTED (Rom. 5:12-19)

Romans 5:12 and following extends an argument that began in 2:1. There, Paul began to explore the tensions between Jewish and Gentile Christians. These tensions were the hottest around the covenant of circumcision (the other significant issues of kosher diet and meat-eating will not surface until ch. 14).

A. Sin and the Law (vv. 12-14)

¹²Wherefore, as by one man sin entered into the world, and death by sin; and so death passed upon all men, for that all have sinned: ¹³(For until the law sin was in the world: but sin is not imputed when there is no law. ¹⁴Nevertheless death reigned from Adam to Moses, even over them that had not sinned after the similitude of Adam's transgression, who is the figure of him that was to come.

We have grown accustomed to Paul's focus on a sequential reading of the Old Testament to make his point. In Romans 4, Paul begins with Abraham's righteousness by faith in Genesis 15, then moves forward in time to prove that the covenant of circumcision and the giving of the Law occurred after this event. Therefore, righteousness by faith is built into God's original design for His relationship with humanity. In verses 12-14, Paul will perform a similar maneuver with different elements. He asks big questions, not about *faith* versus *works*, but about the *Law* versus *sin*.

Adam is not yet named in verse 12, but Paul can assume the reference is clear. Interestingly, Eve is not important to Paul's retelling of the Creation story. His focus is on Adam and on the repercussions of Adam's sin. "You will not surely die," the serpent had said in Genesis 3:4 (NKJV), contradicting the voice of God in 2:17. God's promise, however, came true, and physical death was introduced as the norm for the human race.

In verses 13-14, Paul introduces the historical reality of the beginning of sin in order to then relate sin to the Law. He notes first that sin ran rampant prior to the giving of the Law, referring to the Law which was given by God to Moses on Mount Sinai, as narrated in the Book of Exodus. His point is that sin was yet to be identified as *sin*. Yet, even without the Law specifically designating the precise definitions of *sin*, death still reigned over the world—even over those who did not break the commands of the Law before it had been given!

Paul is offering here a specific theology of sin. He is moving beyond sin as infraction to sin as force. Sometimes we conceptualize *sin* as "infraction," as singular events of rule-breaking. Paul would not disagree with this definition; he simply broadens it. Because all die, sin has power over everyone, even on those who live righteously. No one is allowed to cheat death.

Dietrich Bonhoeffer, the famous Nazi resister who was martyred for his faith, wrote: "The most experienced psychologist or observer of human nature knows infinitely less of the human heart than the simplest Christian who lives beneath the cross of Jesus. The greatest psychological insight, ability, and experience cannot grasp this one thing: what sin is" (Dietrich Bonhoeffer, *Life Together*). Sin mars human nature, cannot be restrained by the Law of God, and ends in death. However, there is yet hope in God's plan of redemption through Jesus Christ.

___

1. How are we like Adam (v. 12)?
2. Describe sin's reign before and after Moses received the Law (vv. 13-14).

> "One great power of sin is that it blinds men so that they do not recognize its true character."—Andrew Murray

___

B. The New Adam (vv. 15-19)

15But not as the offence, so also is the free gift. For if through the offence of one many be dead, much more the grace of God, and the gift by grace, which is by one man, Jesus Christ, hath abounded unto many. 16And not as it was by one that sinned, so is the gift: for the judgment was by one to condemnation, but the free gift is of many offences unto justification. 17For if by one man's offence death reigned by one; much more they which receive abundance of grace and of the gift of righteousness shall reign in life by one, Jesus Christ.) 18Therefore as by the offence of one judgment came upon all men to condemnation; even so by the righteousness of one the free gift came upon all men unto justification of life. 19For as by one man's disobedience many were made sinners, so by the obedience of one shall many be made righteous.

Paul nimbly shifts from the terminology of *sin* to the terminology of *trespass*. These terms should be considered mostly interchangeable, except that *trespass* is a sin that is individually committed. It only took one personal sin from Adam to introduce death and chaos into the creation. It will take only one great act of righteousness for the Son of God to reverse this trend.

Paul portrays God as perfectly in control of the breadth of Creation history. God is the One telling the story of humanity, redeeming it with His gift (v. 15). Paul's words that contrast Adam and Jesus are so majestic that some have gone so far as to identify Paul as a universalist. Origen, an important early Christian theologian who seemed orthodox on most important matters, fell into this way of thinking, believing every person (and even every demon) must one day involuntarily succumb to the redemption of Jesus Christ. Against this view of universal salvation, Paul refers to God's grace as a gift. A gift cannot be forced; it must be willingly accepted. This reality of human participation should not dull the majesty of this verse. In Christ, God has reversed the tide of human sin—He has provided an ultimate answer! Jesus is the anti-Adam, and the life He unleashes pours out more powerfully than the results of Adam's sin.

Paul's language is probably meant to address the Jewish belief that the Law was a gift from God. Paul also believes this, but he understands the gift of Jesus is far greater than the gift of Law.

Through trespass, the whole of humanity was condemned. Just as Adam's single trespass ruined the Creation project, each person is accountable for a single breakage of God's law. Jesus' death, however, did not count trespasses. Regardless of the number of trespasses committed, His atoning death justifies the sinner so he or she is made perfect in the sight of God. Also, the recipient of God's gift of righteousness begins to "reign in life" (v. 17). No longer do Christians remain in a position of weakness, dominated by sin. They are saved to a position of strength, placed back into their rightful role as stewards over all creation. For, prior to his sin, Adam was given this calling: "Rule over the fish of the sea and the birds of the air, over the livestock, over all the earth, and over all the creatures that move along the ground" (Gen. 1:26 NIV). The gift of God's grace in Jesus Christ restores humanity to this original mission. We reign again over our domain of life.

Paul now summarizes the trajectory of these massive theological undertakings. He connects all the dots by depicting the wide sweep of God's grace (Rom. 5:18-19). The grace of Jesus works like the sin of Adam in one manner: it infects all, like a virus gone out of control. New Testament scholar Lita Cosner comments on the literal nature of this offering of grace:

> Paul is using a typology in this passage which requires Adam and Christ to be equally historical; he is arguing that both individuals acted in ways that had real and lasting consequences in human history. It is impossible for either to be symbolic for Paul's argument to be coherent. Paul sees Adam and Christ as history's two most important figures: Adam causing humanity's downfall by his disobedience, and Christ triumphing over that downfall by His obedience ("Romans 5:12-21: Paul's View of a Literal Adam," *Journal of Creation* 22, No. 2).

The consequences of trusting in God's grace through Christ are more powerful than the consequences of sin. Christ reigns victorious over sin, and invites His followers to reign over their lives according to God's original intent.

---

1. How is the "free gift" different from the "offence" (vv. 15-16)?
2. Who can "reign in life," and what does that mean (v. 17)?
3. What did Christ's obedience accomplish (vv. 18-19)?

> "*Grace* means undeserved kindness. It is the gift of God to man the moment he sees he is unworthy of God's favor."—D. L. Moody

II. SIN AND GRACE CONTRASTED (Rom. 5:20—6:4)

The questions Paul presents in Romans are not imaginary, even though he has never visited the church in Rome. The questions he inserts within the text of Romans are literally being asked by actual people. Perhaps these people have called Paul's theology into question. After all, we know from the Books of Galatians, 1 Corinthians, and 2 Corinthians that Paul had plenty of detractors. Through answering the questions he creates in the letter, Paul answers these detractors and carves out the majestic theology of Romans.

A. The Eternal Life of Grace (5:20-21)

(Romans 5:20-21 is not included in the printed text.)

In verse 20, Paul returns to the original subject of the passage, the relationship between Law and sin. Paul envisions a close interrelationship. The emergence of the Old Testament law does not cause sin; it identifies sin. This was one of the foremost purposes of the Law, Paul says, to aid God's people in identifying God's value system. Thus, trespasses increased with the knowledge of the definition of such trespasses.

What is the point of having the knowledge of sin without the ability to curtail its habits? This is where God's grace enters the equation, multiplying life far beyond the way sin multiplied death. Paul even shows the way grace leads to "eternal life" (v. 21), which encompasses the afterlife in heaven, but it cannot be reduced to this alone. It is the present possession of the believer. *Eternal life* is the position of "reigning in life" that Paul introduced in verse 17. A traditional Jewish prayer recites, "Blessed be thou . . . who hast given us the Torah . . . and hast planted within us eternal life" (Abraham Heschel, *The Sabbath: Its Meaning for Modern Man*).

Eternal life was already connected with the Law in Jewish thought, but Paul reframes this connection to focus on the grace of God. Henri Nouwen wrote, "Eternal life is not some great surprise that comes unannounced at the end of our existence in time; it is, rather, the full revelation of what we have been and have lived all along" (*Life of the Beloved: Spiritual Living in a Secular World*). Eternal life is a present possession of believers with grand future implications.

• How is grace superior to the Law, sin, and death (vv. 20-21)?

> "In proportion to the size of the vessel of faith, brought by us to the Lord, is the measure we draw out of His overflowing grace."
> —Cyprian

B. Prohibition Against Libertine Living (6:1-4)

(Romans 6:4 is not included in the printed text.)

¹What shall we say then? Shall we continue in sin, that grace may abound? ²God forbid. How shall we, that are dead to sin, live any longer therein? ³Know ye not, that so many of us as were baptized into Jesus Christ were baptized into his death?

Having extolled the marvelous grace of God for all of chapter 5, Paul stops to address a different audience. This audience may have been libertine Gentiles who thought the grace of God gave them a license to live without traditional morals. More likely, this audience consisted of traditional Jews who struggled to buy into Paul's argument. Paul's answer to them packs a powerful punch.

We can almost hear the opinions of Paul's detractors in this riveting response: "If the Law that we love did little else than to expose sin and is now unimportant because of God's grace, what's to keep every Gentile Christian from sinning like mad? They don't have the morality that we have in the Law. We have all received God's grace in Jesus, but we still need the Law to curb sin."

Paul explains that such an opinion reduces the power of God's grace. To receive God's grace is to die a strong death to sin. This is the purpose of water baptism—an outward symbol that represents this interior reality of dramatic change. Verse 4 declares, "We have been buried with Him through baptism into death, so that as Christ was raised from the dead through the glory of the Father, so we too might walk in newness of life" (NASB).

---

1. Explain the wrong thinking expressed in 6:1.
2. How is someone "baptized into Jesus Christ" (v. 3)?
3. How are Christians to "walk" (v. 4)?

"We must desire to be separated unto the Lord from the world and its evil system. We must reckon ourselves dead to sin and alive to God. This is true positionally, but it can be made true in our spiritual life only as we yield to the Holy Spirit's control."
—Theodore Epp

III. DEATH VERSUS LIFE (Rom. 6:5-14, 20-23)

In Romans, Paul often communicates by setting up stark contrasts. Already in the letter, we have seen *sin* versus *gift*, *law* versus *grace*, and *Adam* versus *Jesus*. In chapter 6, the controlling contrast is *death* versus *life*. This is the natural outflow of Paul's exposition on Jesus as the second Adam in chapter 5. As the One who destroys death and gives life, Jesus is the answer to the cause of personal sins and the sinful nature.

A. The Antidote to Sin (vv. 5-11)

(Romans 6:5-7 is not included in the printed text.)

⁸Now if we be dead with Christ, we believe that we shall also live with him: ⁹Knowing that Christ being raised from the dead dieth no more; death hath no more dominion over him. ¹⁰For in that he died, he died unto sin once: but in that he liveth, he liveth unto God. ¹¹Likewise reckon ye also yourselves to be dead indeed unto sin, but alive unto God through Jesus Christ our Lord.

For Paul's Jewish Christian audience, accepting Jesus was not a step away from the Law; the Law continued to define their cultural worldview. Paul has no problem with this. However, they should not expect the Law to be effective in guiding the Gentiles toward the way of Jesus. For Paul, the ultimate antidote to sin is becoming united with Christ.

Paul uses *baptism* language in verses 5-7. In the early Christian movement, baptism was the passage through which one's identity fundamentally changed. Many Christians took on new names as a result of their baptism, including Paul, who was formerly named Saul. In baptism, Paul sees a definitive death to sin and a rising to new life in Christ.

In the same way that Christ died once and for all, so does every believer at the point of his or her union with Christ. Christians now live for the glory of God. This is the answer to the sin problem: the fundamental life change brought by the Holy Spirit in the moment of salvation.

---

1. How are Christians in union with Christ (v. 5)?
2. How is the "old self" in slavery (vv. 6-7 NIV)?
3. What happened "once for all," and why was that enough (vv. 8-10 NKJV)?
4. How must Christians view themselves (v. 11)?

> "Baptism [is] putting a line in the sand saying that old man is dead and he is no longer alive anymore, and I rise up to walk in the newness of life."—T. D. Jakes

---

B. Practical Holy Living (vv. 12-14, 20-23)

(Romans 6:20-21 is not included in the printed text.)

¹²Let not sin therefore reign in your mortal body, that ye should obey it in the lusts thereof. ¹³Neither yield ye your members as instruments of unrighteousness unto sin: but yield yourselves unto God, as those that are alive from the dead, and your members as instruments of righteousness unto God. ¹⁴For sin shall not have dominion over you: for ye are not under the law, but under grace.

²²But now being made free from sin, and become servants to God, ye have your fruit unto holiness, and the end everlasting life. ²³For the wages of sin is death; but the gift of God is eternal life through Jesus Christ our Lord.

With the theology and imagery of baptism carrying the weight of Paul's meaning in chapter 6, Paul now becomes practical. God has done all of the work on our behalf, but this does not leave us without our own work to do. Paul is not afraid to challenge the Roman churches, and us, with our serious responsibility back to God.

Paul has already described the Christians' new place of "reigning in life" through Christ in 5:17, 21. If we are to reign in Christ, there is no place for sin to reign (6:12). Paul describes this potential reigning of sin in bodily terms. He is not speaking in the abstract, but the practical. He wants the Roman Christians to make sure they are not sinning with their bodies (v. 13). This includes all manner of sins: speech, sexual immorality, stealing, hoarding, fighting. All of these are off limits, rendered null and void by baptism in Christ and the power of the Gospel.

The reason for practical holiness summarizes everything Paul has been writing about since 5:12. The absence of Law now stands concurrently with the absence of the dominion of sin. All that is needed is grace.

In 6:14, Paul uses the metaphor of *slavery* to address the issue, "Isn't it easier to sin without the Law, now that we are under grace?" This metaphor had to be particularly powerful among the Christians in Rome, since Rome was the capital of the worldwide slave trade. Hundreds of thousands of slaves ran the daily economy of Rome. They were bought, sold, brutalized, yet sometimes honored by the masters of the Roman elites. It is this honoring that Paul has in mind here. Some slaves would refuse to be set free—such was their place of esteem in the household of their master. This was especially true of Caesar's slaves. In God's household, to be considered "slaves of God" (v. 22 NKJV) would have been a high honor.

Baptism and *slavery* represent the same concept for Paul: the transference of one's identity and ownership from one entity to another. We are no longer slaves to sin, but to God through Jesus Christ, resulting in holiness and the gift of eternal life.

---

1. Describe the "offering" we should not give (see v. 13).
2. How can sin be overcome (v. 14)?
3. Answer the question in verse 21 in reference to your own life.
4. Describe the blessed life (v. 22).
5. What have we earned, and what are we offered instead (v. 23)?

Family Tree

There are companies that help people trace their lineage back into time. Our hope is typically that some notable person will be in our past: a general, a hero, a national leader. In Romans 5, Paul traces the family tree of humanity, revealing that we all derive from a failure named Adam. The good news of the Gospel is that believing in Jesus Christ can forever change our family tree. Upon that belief, God himself becomes our Father.

CONCLUSION

Sin and *salvation* are matters of life and death, literally. Death entered the world through the sin of Adam, and sin colors all of life. The law of God shows us how we should live, but it does not give us the power to do so. However,

God has unleashed His grace on those who put their trust in Jesus Christ. Through Christ we find victory over sin.

GOLDEN TEXT CHALLENGE

"IF THROUGH THE OFFENCE OF ONE MANY BE DEAD, MUCH MORE THE GRACE OF GOD, AND THE GIFT BY GRACE, WHICH IS BY ONE MAN, JESUS CHRIST, HATH ABOUNDED UNTO MANY" (Rom. 5:15).

A sharp contrast is drawn between Adam and Christ. The word *offense* involved Adam's fall; the word *trespass* involves an act of Adam's will. In contrast to the offense and the transgression, Paul sets "the gift by grace."

Adam's offense deserved only condemnation. As a God of love, He delights "much more" to extend mercy and pardon than to execute judgment upon the offender. The gift which is "by one man, Jesus Christ," far surpasses the transgression.

If we choose to accept God's gracious gift, we will pass from the death we deserve to the life only Christ can give.

Daily Devotions:

M. The Forbidden Fruit • Genesis 2:4-9, 15-17
T. The Fall • Genesis 3:1-7
W. The Curse • Genesis 3:8-19
T. The Birth of Christ • Matthew 1:18-25
F. The Death of Christ • Matthew 27:33-37, 50-55
S. The Resurrection of Christ • Matthew 28:1-10

A Matter of Life and Death

No More Condemnation

Romans 7:1—8:11

Unit Theme:

Letter to the Romans

Central Truth:

Christ sets believers free from the law of sin and death.

Focus:

Understand the antidote to sin and live according to the Spirit of God.

Context:

The apostle Paul wrote the letter to the Romans in AD 58 while he was in Corinth.

Golden Text:

"There is therefore now no condemnation to them which are in Christ Jesus, who walk not after the flesh, but after the Spirit" (Rom. 8:1).

Study Outline:

I. **Death to Bondage** (Rom. 7:1-6)

II. **The Struggle With Sin** (Rom. 7:7-25)

III. **Victory Through the Spirit** (Rom. 8:1-11)

INTRODUCTION

Unbelievers often wonder why Christians talk so much about forgiveness. In some parts of our culture, this focus is openly criticized. Why do Christians believe in the inherent need for God's forgiveness? The answer is simple: We believe every human being has a condemnation complex. Every human being, in one way or another, is attempting to escape guilt.

In a recent article, famous Presbyterian preacher Joanna Adams recalls serving on a doctrinal committee for her denomination. The team was charged with modernizing some of the language in their statement of faith. She describes the tension around one particular confession in the statement:

> By far, the most controversial part of that confession, which is now a part of our *Book of Confessions*, was the line that reads, "We deserve God's condemnation." One unhappy Presbyterian suggested that the line read, "We deserve to be evaluated by God." Another offered this: "Some people deserve God's condemnation." Ah, the challenge of admitting our need to clean up and shape up ("Clean Up Your Act," *Journal for Preachers*).

Condemnation and guilt are tough subjects. We all feel them . . . we ascribe them to God . . . we ascribe them to ourselves. What is the answer?

Thankfully, the Bible contains the definitive answer to personal guilt. In the Old Testament, guilt was covered over by the ritual of animal sacrifice. In the

New Testament, guilt has been destroyed once and for all by the sacrifice of Jesus Christ. Hebrews 10:11-12 states: "Day after day every priest stands and performs his religious duties; again and again he offers the same sacrifices, which can never take away sins. But when this priest had offered for all time one sacrifice for sins, he sat down at the right hand of God" (NIV). Because Jesus is seated in power at God's right hand, we can be assured that our sins are forgiven. His blood has removed our guilt. As believers in Christ, we no longer live under condemnation.

I. DEATH TO BONDAGE (Rom. 7:1-6)

We have seen Paul use different metaphors up to this point in the letter to the Romans. After talking about the spiritual life through the lenses of baptism and slavery, Paul chooses a new metaphor, *marriage*, in chapter 7. The legal ramifications of marriage create a springboard for Paul to discuss the place of the Law in the lives of Christians.

A. The Release of the Law (vv. 1-4)

(Romans 7:2-3 is not included in the printed text.)

¹Know ye not, brethren, (for I speak to them that know the law,) how that the law hath dominion over a man as long as he liveth?

⁴Wherefore, my brethren, ye also are become dead to the law by the body of Christ; that ye should be married to another, even to him who is raised from the dead, that we should bring forth fruit unto God.

Verse 1 indicates Paul's precise audience. He is not speaking to Gentiles who are far from God, but to "men who know the law" (NIV) of the Old Testament. While this group includes Jews, it need not be exclusively Jews. The synagogues of Rome also routinely included "God-fearers." These were Gentiles who worshiped the God of Israel without converting to Judaism (often because they did not wish to be circumcised or to endure social ostracism from fellow Gentiles). For example, Cornelius, the first Gentile convert under the apostle Peter's ministry, is called a "devout God-fearer" (see Acts 10:2). He was a faithful supporter of the local synagogue.

The ministry of Paul in the Book of Acts had particular appeal among God-fearing Gentiles. Paul's routine of ministry was typically to begin by preaching in the synagogue, which usually led toward an eventual split with the conservative Jews there. Others, especially God-fearers, would leave the synagogue with Paul to begin a local church.

Whether traditional Jews or God-fearers, Paul contends that his audience knows the Law. The Law has a great deal to say about marriage, which allows Paul to build conceptual common ground with them. Paul's point is simple and direct: the marriage covenant is, in modern language, "till death do us part." No one is obligated to their spouse beyond the point of death, except by personal choice (Rom. 7:2). If a person were to enter into a different relationship having already been married, conservative Jews, regardless of the circumstances, often considered this adulterous. Paul echoes Jesus' words from Mark 10:11, "Anyone who divorces his wife and marries another woman commits adultery against her" (NIV).

Paul's audience is in agreement with what Paul is saying. *Finally*, they may think, *Paul is acting like a proper apostle, expounding what the Torah explicitly commands regarding marriage.* Not so fast; Paul does not adhere to conventional expectations. The most natural theological point would be the death of Jesus. We expect Paul to say, "Because Christ died, the marriage to the Law has been annulled." Instead, Paul refers back to his baptism treatise in Romans 6—the contention that "we died with Christ" in baptism (v. 8 NKJV). Because we have undergone spiritual death through baptism, the Law is no longer our obligation. We have been "married" to another—so "we can produce a harvest of good deeds for God" (7:4 NLT).

---

1. What point is Paul making in verses 1-3?
2. To whom are Christians "married" (v. 4), and what is the result?

"Indeed, baptism is a vow, a sacred vow of the believer to follow Christ. Just as a wedding celebrates the fusion of two hearts, baptism celebrates the union of sinner with Savior."—Max Lucado

---

B. The Release of the Sinful Nature (vv. 5-6)

5For when we were in the flesh, the motions of sins, which were by the law, did work in our members to bring forth fruit unto death. 6But now we are delivered from the law, that being dead wherein we were held; that we should serve in newness of spirit, and not in the oldness of the letter.

Paul introduces a massive term in the letter to the Romans (v. 5). That term, in Paul's language, is *sarx*. In most English translations, this term is rendered "flesh" or "sinful nature." Paul uses the term throughout his letters to describe the human condition. The term is a catch-all for everything that is wrong with an individual. In Paul's letters, we see *sin* is cosmic while *flesh* is personal. He must describe how Jesus has come to redeem the *sarx*.

The term has been used several times in Romans, but not yet in this broad way. In 1:3, it refers to the human nature of Jesus. In 2:28, it refers to the physical act of circumcision. In 3:20, it refers to human beings in general. In 4:1, it refers to the lineage of Abraham. In 6:19 it is introduced in relationship to the Roman Christians themselves; they are weak in the flesh, in the sinful nature.

In 7:5, *death* is the primary experience of the sinful nature. The Law was meant to stem the tide of the sinful nature. However, it only stimulated the flesh, proving the sinfulness of man. "A harvest of sinful deeds" resulted (NLT).

The situation was dire and the Law was of limited use when God acted definitively to set believers free from the sinful nature, and thus free from the Law as well (v. 6). Death to the sinful nature implied a similar release from the Law so believers could serve God through the power of the Spirit. This is Paul's concurrent point in Galatians 5:16: "Live by the Spirit, and you will not gratify the desires of the sinful nature" (NIV). The Greek word for *live* also means "walk." Paul envisions a daily walk, filled with the Spirit's power, to enable the believer to fulfill the righteous demands of the Law. This is God's vision for all Christians.

1. How did the law of God impact "the flesh" (v. 5)?
2. How does verse 6 contrast a person's life before and after meeting Christ?

> "The best argument for Christianity is Christians: their joy, their certainty, their completeness. But the greatest argument against Christianity is also Christians—when they are somber and joyless, when they are self-righteous and smug."—Sheldon Vanauken

II. THE STRUGGLE WITH SIN (Rom. 7:7-25)

Paul's complex discussion about the role of the Law in God's plan of salvation and of history continues into the heart of Romans 7. The Jewish believers in Rome might have been aware of Paul's letter to the Galatians, in which he asserts that the Torah has no place among Gentile Christianity. Of course, that argument was in the particular context of the Galatian churches. Here, Paul qualifies his theology of the Law, proving its intent from verses within the Law itself.

A. The Goodness of the Torah (vv. 7-13)

(Romans 7:10-13 is not included in the printed text.)

7What shall we say then? Is the law sin? God forbid. Nay, I had not known sin, but by the law: for I had not known lust, except the law had said, Thou shalt not covet. 8But sin, taking occasion by the commandment, wrought in me all manner of concupiscence. For without the law sin was dead. 9For I was alive without the law once: but when the commandment came, sin revived, and I died.

Paul makes it clear that one of the Law's primary functions is to make humanity aware of the reality of sin. The Law is not sinful; it stands as a testimony of God's values (v. 7). Through the Law we have knowledge of sin.

The problem is not with the Law, but with the sinful nature of humanity (v. 8). Torah itself was a supreme gift from God, a gift of His beautiful grace. The rabbinic sayings in the Jewish Talmud confirm this elevation of the gift of the Torah: "Torah study is superior to the saving of life. . . . Torah study is superior to building the temple. . . . Torah study is superior to the honor of father and mother."

These rabbinic sayings confirm what Laura F. Winner, a former practicing Jew turned evangelical Christian, writes about the gift of the Law:

> Being born a human was not the first time God made Himself small so that we could have access to Him. First He shrunk Himself when He revealed the Torah at Mount Sinai. He shrunk Himself into tiny Hebrew words, man's finite language, so that we might get to Him that way. Then He shrunk Himself again, down to the size of a baby, down into manger finiteness (*Girl Meets God: On the Path to a Spiritual Life*).

Paul is saying something similar in Romans 7: The Law prepared the way for Jesus Christ by indicating and even producing sin with us. God's commandments made it plain that we are sinners in need of a Savior.

---

1. How did sin take advantage of the Law (vv. 7-8)?
2. How does verse 12 describe God's laws?
3. How was sin made "exceedingly [or utterly] sinful" (v. 13)? Why did this need to happen?

> "Throughout the Old Testament this was always the idea of a sin-offering—that of a perfect victim; without offense on its own account, taking the place of the offender; the transference of the offender's sin to that victim, and that expiation in the person of the victim for the sin done by another."—Charles Spurgeon

---

B. The Difficult "I" (vv. 14-25)

(Romans 7:14-17, 25 is not included in the printed text.)

[18]For I know that in me (that is, in my flesh,) dwelleth no good thing: for to will is present with me; but how to perform that which is good I find not. [19]For the good that I would I do not: but the evil which I would not, that I do. [20]Now if I do that I would not, it is no more I that do it, but sin that dwelleth in me. [21]I find then a law, that, when I would do good, evil is present with me. [22]For I delight in the law of God after the inward man: [23]But I see another law in my members, warring against the law of my mind, and bringing me into captivity to the law of sin which is in my members. [24]O wretched man that I am! who shall deliver me from the body of this death?

Paul personalizes the conversation about the relationship between the Law and sin. The problem is not the Law, but sin in the individual's heart. However, here is where we run into some complexities. Scholars are divided over the nature of the "I" in Romans 7:14-24. There is more than meets the eye in Paul's exposition. William M. Greathouse and George Lyons describe the quandary:

Does chapter 7 refer to one's preconversion or postconversion experience? The past tense of verses 7-13 clearly seems to refer to preconversion experience, but what of the present tense of verses 14-25? Does this describe Paul's personal experience at the time he was writing? Is this normal Christian experience? (*Romans 1—8: A Commentary in the Wesleyan Tradition*).

Other commentators have even suggested that the "I" of Romans 7 stands for Israel and the nation's experience under the Law. What do we make of these options?

If Paul wanted to speak exclusively about Israel or the Christian life in general, such language was available to him. Instead, Paul speaks personally. His audience knows of his past in Judaism and in persecution. Paul admits to being the "chief of sinners" (see 1 Tim. 1:15). Therefore, regardless of what

Paul may be doing theologically in Romans 7, he is also speaking from his personal life and Christian walk.

Paul's problem is that he is in a quandary that characterizes the entire Christian life, but particularly for those who seek to follow the Law (vv. 18-20). The relationship between Torah and sin reaches its culmination in this description of the fundamental difficulty. The apostle has already proven that the Torah makes one conscious of sin without giving the ability to do anything about it. This is Paul's problem. He looks to his flesh for answers and receives none. He looks to the Torah for answers and receives condemnation. This is the result of sin that dwells within him.

Paul summarizes the dire result of the failure of the Torah to medicate, much less heal, the sinful nature: "When I want to do good, evil is right there with me" (v. 21 NIV). It is not that all is lost. There is still an inner light within Paul, for he takes "delight in God's law" (v. 22 NIV). He delights in what God loves, but the law of sin is wreaking havoc within Paul's body. He cries out in desperation, for His inner delight is not in alignment with his outward behavior.

In referring to "the body of this death" (v. 24), Paul may have been alluding to a specific practice of execution among the Roman Empire's Eastern kings. In certain regions, there is evidence that the body of the deceased victim (the "body of death") would be tied to the back of his or her murderer. Over time, the disease, stench, and death of the dead body would eat its way into the body of the criminal.

This was Paul's dire situation, yet there was hope "through Jesus Christ our Lord" (v. 25). Paul concludes there was nothing good in him, but God had acted through Jesus to rescue him from his sinful nature.

---

1. Choose three adjectives to describe Paul's dilemma (vv. 14-16).
2. How does Paul describe his "flesh" (v. 18)?
3. What does Paul say about his "inward man" (v. 22)?
4. Why did Paul feel like a "prisoner" (v. 23 NIV)?
5. Describe the hope Paul found (vv. 24-25).

> "If Christ had not gone to the cross and suffered in our stead, the just for the unjust, there would not have been a spark of hope for us. There would have been a mighty gulf between ourselves and God, which no man ever could have passed."—J. C. Ryle

---

III. VICTORY THROUGH THE SPIRIT (Rom. 8:1-11)

Paul has been building a singular argument since 5:12, showing how the Torah is powerless to save us from our sinful condition. Now, Paul turns to the ultimate consequences of God's saving work in Jesus. The Spirit of God is the controlling factor of our life as Christians.

A. The Law's Requirements Fulfilled (vv. 1-4)

¹There is therefore now no condemnation to them which are in Christ Jesus, who walk not after the flesh, but after the Spirit. ²For the law of

the Spirit of life in Christ Jesus hath made me free from the law of sin and death. ³For what the law could not do, in that it was weak through the flesh, God sending his own Son in the likeness of sinful flesh, and for sin, condemned sin in the flesh: ⁴That the righteousness of the law might be fulfilled in us, who walk not after the flesh, but after the Spirit.

Condemnation has been destroyed because believers have been empowered to walk contrary to their sinful nature (v. 1). The image of God has been restored within us so we can live up to our true self and potential by walking according to the Spirit. A new law is at work—not the Old Testament commandments, but "the law of the Spirit of life in Christ Jesus" (v. 2). This sets us "free from the law of sin and death.

The Law has been replaced by the Spirit through the coming of Jesus Christ. Jesus has turned the trajectory of sin's condemnation on its head. No longer does sin condemn humanity. Now, Jesus condemns sin (v. 3). Therefore, the believer is delivered from the powers of sin.

The final result of the role of the Law is not that it is unimportant, but that its fulfillment and possibility are reached in the life of the Spirit (v. 4). The goal of the Law is perfectly reached in Christians who leave the sinful nature behind in order to follow the voice and the call of the Spirit.

---

1. Explain the phrase "no condemnation" (v. 1).
2. What "likeness" did God's Son take, and why (vv. 3-4)?

Guilt Is Gone

In the 2005 film *Constantine*, Angela enters a confessional in a Roman Catholic cathedral. As a police officer, she admits to killing a perpetrator as a part of her job to protect other citizens. Still, she feels guilty. The priest assures Angela that God has a purpose for her life and urges her to not allow condemnation to overcome her faith.

Guilt can come from many directions, sometimes being brought on by the complexities of life. The Scriptural mandate rings true: "There is now no condemnation for those who are in Christ Jesus" (Rom. 8:1 NIV).

B. The Desire of the Spirit (vv. 5-11)

(Romans 8:7-10 is not included in the printed text.)

⁵For they that are after the flesh do mind the things of the flesh; but they that are after the Spirit the things of the Spirit. ⁶For to be carnally minded is death; but to be spiritually minded is life and peace.

¹¹But if the Spirit of him that raised up Jesus from the dead dwell in you, he that raised up Christ from the dead shall also quicken your mortal bodies by his Spirit that dwelleth in you.

The voice and the call of the Spirit come with specific demands and desires. This lifestyle is not abstract or difficult to define; it is not simply "spiritual."

We can literally see whether or not a person is walking by the Spirit. Are their desires in line with the desires of the Spirit of God? Do their actions show their minds are focused on the things of the Spirit of God? Paul says the battle is in the mind. Without winning that battle, God cannot be pleased.

Paul proclaims that the Spirit of God lives within the Roman Christians. This is the delineating marker as to whether one is in Christ. Paul declares this Spirit is much more powerful than the Law; this is the Holy Spirit, who raised Jesus from the dead. Therefore, the ownership of the Christian's body transferred from death to life.

---

1. Describe the difference between the carnally minded person and the spiritually minded person (vv. 5-8).
2. How does the indwelling Spirit of God change the believer (vv. 9-10)?
3. Why should verse 11 be such an encouragement to Christians?

> "God knows what each one of us is dealing with. He knows our pressures. He knows our conflicts. And He has made a provision for each and every one of them. That provision is Himself in the person of the Holy Spirit, indwelling us and empowering us to respond rightly."—Kay Arthur

CONCLUSION

The life without condemnation is a life of freedom. As believers, we have been set free from all forms of religious law-keeping. We have been set free from the sinful nature. We have also been set free to a glorious life, led by the Spirit of God within us.

GOLDEN TEXT CHALLENGE

"THERE IS THEREFORE NOW NO CONDEMNATION TO THEM WHICH ARE IN CHRIST JESUS, WHO WALK NOT AFTER THE FLESH, BUT AFTER THE SPIRIT" (Rom. 8:1).

Christians are free because God sees them in Christ. The power of the Law to condemn them has been decisively broken. Sin has been dealt with at Calvary, and through the indwelling presence of the Holy Spirit, the Christian can live victoriously.

Jesus declared, "If the Son makes you free, you shall be free indeed" (John 8:36 NKJV).

Daily Devotions:
M. Precursor to Redemption • Leviticus 25:47-53
T. God Offers Mercy and Grace • Psalm 103:8-14
W. Unable to Save Ourselves • Proverbs 5:21-23
T. Restore the Fallen • Galatians 6:1-5
F. Abounding in Grace • Ephesians 1:3-10
S. Overcome the World • 1 John 2:15-17

The Spirit-Filled Life

Romans 8:12-39

Unit Theme:
Letter to the Romans

Central Truth:
The Holy Spirit enables Christians to live as God's children.

Focus:
Review the benefits and responsibilities of the Spirit-filled life, and trust God in all circumstances.

Context:
The apostle Paul wrote the letter to the Romans in AD 58 while he was in Corinth.

Golden Text:
"As many as are led by the Spirit of God, they are the sons of God" (Rom. 8:14).

Study Outline:

  I. **Be Led by the Spirit** (Rom. 8:12-17a)
 II. **Anticipate and Trust** (Rom. 8:17b-30)
III. **Firmly Held in God's Hands** (Rom. 8:31-39)

INTRODUCTION

Sometimes the Bible describes God in personified form, as a King with a strong right hand that extends to humanity, especially in the Psalms. Obviously this is metaphor. Jesus said, "God is Spirit" (John 4:24 NKJV). He does not have a physical body. This is language we use to talk about God. In other places in the Bible, God is described more as a universal presence than a person. Again, He is all of these things and, in a sense, none of these things. No language can capture who He really is. Saint Augustine said in a fourth-century sermon, "We are talking about God. What wonder is it that you do not understand? If you do understand, it is not God."

The Holy Spirit is not somehow separate from God. The doctrine of the Trinity reminds us that the Holy Spirit is God's essence, as the three persons of God commune with one another.

In the Book of Acts, the Holy Spirit is the driver of the global Christian movement. In essence, He "takes over" the mission after the ascension of Jesus. In 1 Corinthians, the Holy Spirit is the driver of the local congregation and particularly its worship service. In John's Gospel, the Holy Spirit is our advocate who guides the Christian community into all truth, even as He convicts the world with regard to sin.

In Romans 8, the subject of the Holy Spirit is approached from another angle. Here, the Holy Spirit is a part of God's cosmic plan to rescue the whole of creation. He is at work in the lives of individual Christians, but He is also at work in the restoration of the cosmos.

I. BE LED BY THE SPIRIT (Rom. 8:12-17a)

In Romans 8, Paul introduces the centrality of the Holy Spirit within the Christian life. Chapters 6 and 7 explore the inability of the Law to correct the problem of the sin of humanity. The ultimate solution to this problem is the indwelling presence of the Holy Spirit. In 8:12-17, Paul teaches practically on how the reality of the Holy Spirit changes the status of the believer. As people who are captured by God's Spirit, we are incorporated into His family. This status comes with special privileges and serious obligations.

A. The Obligation of Holiness (vv. 12-13)

In verses 1-11, we see the Holy Spirit empowers the believer to fulfill the righteous requirements of God that were previously demanded by the Law: "For the law of the Spirit of life in Christ has made me free from the law of sin and death" (v. 2 NKJV). This theological reality leads to a strict obligation for each believer.

¹²Therefore, brethren, we are debtors, not to the flesh, to live after the flesh. ¹³For if ye live after the flesh, ye shall die: but if ye through the Spirit do mortify the deeds of the body, ye shall live.

Although the Holy Spirit is a gift of God's grace, this does not mean Christians are free to live according to the desires of the flesh. Paul has already negated this possibility in 6:1, 15. Instead, the grace of Christ ushers His followers into a reciprocal relationship with God.

In the ancient Greco-Roman world, *reciprocity* was the primary value that guided customs, the economy, and relationships. The principle of reciprocity required that when a gift was given, some form of return was expected.

The debt Paul says Christians owe to God should be seen through the lens of mutual reciprocity. God has given us a gift, so He expects an obligation in return. That obligation, however, is not a material gift, but a spiritual lifestyle that causes our lives to completely flourish in Him.

Our proper obligation to God in the light of His free grace is an obligation to a lifestyle of faith. Paul does not want the Roman Christians to believe the coming of the Spirit changes the fabric of the moral universe. In essence, in verse 13 he reminds them of the first words of God to Adam in Genesis 2:17: "You must not eat from the tree of the knowledge of good and evil, for when you eat of it you will surely die" (NIV).

God set up a stark contrast from the beginning of Creation: obeying Him leads to life while disobedience leads to death. The temptation of man was always to rule over the categories of good and evil for himself. God makes it clear that He alone sets those categories. Through the process and reality of being led by the Spirit, true human life is made possible.

- Why must Christians overcome "the flesh," and how is this done (vv. 12-13)?

B. Our Adoption as Children (vv. 14-17a)

(Romans 8:16-17a is not included in the printed text.)

14For as many as are led by the Spirit of God, they are the sons of God. 15For ye have not received the spirit of bondage again to fear; but ye have received the Spirit of adoption, whereby we cry, Abba, Father.

The obligations that the Christian has toward God are not cold, mechanistic, or religious. Our obligations are not like homework—a set of boxes or assignments that God checks off. Instead, through fulfilling our obligations we realize our rightful place in God's household. He has made us a part of His family through the death and resurrection of Jesus Christ. To be led by the Spirit is to be adopted into this heavenly family. Through a relationship with the Holy Spirit, we come to realize the truth about our status. We are all sons and daughters of God (v. 14).

In the next verses, Paul works interestingly with the image of the ancient Roman household. The Roman household contained differing roles that were associated with various social stations and statuses. The father was the ultimate authority over all manners of household business and relationships. Upper-status households with an esteemed father always included slaves. We must not mistake the slavery of the Roman world with the slavery of the early Americas. In fact, ancient slaves were often able to achieve great status and stature within their households and communities. Paul's point here is strong. Though we would be doubly blessed to be considered slaves in God's household, He has gone so far as to make us His children! We can call out to Him affectionately, as Jesus did, "Abba, Father" (v. 15). We are not just casual children; even though we are adopted, we are given the full rights of a household heir (v. 17a). What an amazing promise for the people of God both then and now!

---

1. List three blessings of being a child of God (vv. 14-16).
2. What does it mean to be "co-heirs with Christ" (v. 17 NIV)?

II. ANTICIPATE AND TRUST (Rom. 8:17b-30)

A. Anticipate Suffering (vv. 17b-18)

(Romans 8:17b is not included in the printed text.)

¹⁸For I reckon that the sufferings of this present time are not worthy to be compared with the glory which shall be revealed in us.

Paul introduces the idea of Christian suffering in verse 17, as a part of our necessary obligation to God. Paul knows that unleashing this subject requires explanation. He dives into an age-old question: Why is there such terrible evil in the world if the divine ruler of the world is purely and ultimately good? Theologians call this question the problem of *theodicy*. Though Paul does not answer all of our questions, he does treat the problem of theodicy in terms of God's plan for the cosmos.

In verse 17, Paul says Christians who share in the sufferings of Christ can expect to share in the glory of Christ. This connection is vital throughout Scripture, especially in John's Gospel, where glory and suffering as two Christian realities go hand-in-hand. Jesus said, "Now my heart is troubled, and what shall I say? 'Father, save me from this hour'? No, it was for this very reason I came to this hour. Father, glorify your name!" (12:27 NIV). Jesus understood His dreadful suffering was an expression of the glory of God. This is a great irony of the Gospel story and message.

In Romans 8:18, Paul encourages the Roman Christians to endure present suffering based on God's hopeful future for them. This known future recasts their perspective on everyday problems, no matter how dire. Glory will be revealed if God's people can learn to suffer.

• How should verse 18 encourage the suffering Christian?

> "Suffering, although it is a burden, is a useful burden, like the splints used in orthopedic treatment."—Soren Kierkegaard

---

B. Wait Patiently in Hope (vv. 19-25)

¹⁹For the earnest expectation of the creature waiteth for the manifestation of the sons of God. ²⁰For the creature was made subject to vanity, not willingly, but by reason of him who hath subjected the same in hope, ²¹Because the creature itself also shall be delivered from the bondage of corruption into the glorious liberty of the children of God. ²²For we know that the whole creation groaneth and travaileth in pain together until now. ²³And not only they, but ourselves also, which have the firstfruits of the Spirit, even we ourselves groan within ourselves, waiting for the adoption, to wit, the redemption of our body. ²⁴For we are saved by hope: but hope that is seen is not hope: for what a man seeth, why doth he yet hope for? ²⁵But if we hope for that we see not, then do we with patience wait for it.

In this passage, Paul describes his cosmic theology of sin and salvation. His purpose is to set the Romans' suffering in the context of God's greater story. Such majestic words must be treated in line with the whole of Scripture, for Paul is essentially retelling the entire Biblical narrative in these few verses.

The Bible is not simply a loose collection of sixty-six books with their own voices. Like a gospel choir, these unique voices contribute to a greater whole—the "metanarrative" or grand story of the Bible. This story is a massive movement from Creation to new creation that passes through the stages of the fall of man, the Law and the people of God, the victory of Christ, the establishment of the Church, and eventually the second coming of Christ. The end of the story is the renewal of all creation to its original intent. Revelation 21:5 describes this triumphant ending: "He who was seated on the throne said, 'I am making everything new!'" (NIV).

In Romans 8:19-25, Paul is peering into this grand story, retelling it in his own way. God's Spirit revealed to Paul that suffering is inevitable because sin has not infected just humanity, but the whole of creation (v. 20). God has yet to eradicate sin in the whole of creation, so creation waits for the consummation of God's plan (v. 19). What we see now is a state of decay: natural disasters, famines, dangerous conditions. One day, all will be made new and the creation will, once again, be glorious (v. 21). This will include all of nature and the cosmos.

Today, we can feel creation "groaning" in the suffering all around (v. 22 NIV). This groaning is shared by each Christian heart—a longing for the ultimate plan of God to be accomplished (v. 23). Clark H. Pinnock describes this connection between the creation and Christian existence:

> The universe is not divine but is filled with God's presence. The destruction of nature is hurtful to the God who formed it and loves it. The Spirit suffers along with nature and struggles against powers that despoil. God delights in creation and grieves over its despoliation (*Flame of Love: A Theology of the Holy Spirit*).

God longs for the restoration of His entire creation, just as we long for the redemption of our bodies. This is the essence of the Christian hope (v. 24). If it is not true, we are all foolish and should quit the life of faith! Because it is true, we are able to be patient in affliction, no matter what comes our way (v. 25).

---

1. What is all creation desperately longing for (vv. 19-22)?
2. What are "the firstfruits of the Spirit" (v. 23)?
3. Why is patience a necessary virtue (vv. 24-25)?

> "Some people feel guilty about their anxieties and regard them as a defect of faith but they are afflictions, not sins. Like all afflictions, they are, if we can so take them, our share in the passion of Christ."—C. S. Lewis

---

C. The Help of the Spirit (vv. 26-30)

(Romans 8:29-30 is not included in the printed text.)

26Likewise the Spirit also helpeth our infirmities: for we know not what we should pray for as we ought: but the Spirit itself maketh intercession for us with groanings which cannot be uttered. 27And he that

searcheth the hearts knoweth what is the mind of the Spirit, because he maketh intercession for the saints according to the will of God. **²⁸And we know that all things work together for good to them that love God, to them who are the called according to his purpose.**

Just as the Holy Spirit is at work in the cosmos, bringing God's grand story to a conclusion, He also works in the individual lives of believers. In verse 26, the Spirit is described as coming to the aid of the Christian during times of weakness. This is reminiscent of John's understanding of the Holy Spirit as Advocate, or Comforter (John 14:26). This particular work of the Spirit even incorporates the prayer life of the believer. During times of weakness and suffering, prayer can be a trial, but the Spirit knows how to pray on our behalf, interceding for us as Jesus also does, according to Hebrews 7:25.

The Spirit intercedes for us and searches deep within us. Romans 8:27 finds a helpful parallel in 1 Corinthians 2:10-11, where Paul expresses the same truth in a different context. Here, the Spirit is all-powerful and all-knowing, writing the stories of both Creation and the interior lives of believers. The Spirit brings God's will to bear on the world and on our lives.

Because of this majestic work of the Holy Spirit, we know we have a part to play in God's bigger plan (Rom. 8:28). The idea is not that "things just tend to work out" for people who love God or even that "all things happen for a reason." Certainly bad things happen to good people every day. Instead, this verse boldly proclaims God is the One who will tell a larger, good story, even with the sufferings of the world and of our lives. Like a quilt, He will patch together the dark experiences of life so they have a meaning and purpose within His greater plan. Verse 29 reminds us this has been His plan all along. We should be careful not to get bogged down in abstract theories depicting God as preselecting some individuals for salvation. This is not the point of predestination at all. Instead, Paul's teaching here is about a people. God's plan always included a redeemed people that are called, justified, and one day will be glorified (v. 30). This is the nature of God's predestination.

---

1. Why do we sometimes not know "how to pray as we should" (v. 26 NASB)?
2. Describe the Holy Spirit's ministry of intercession (vv. 26-27).
3. What does God promise about "all things" in a believer's life (v. 28)?
4. Describe four actions God does on behalf of His children (v. 30).

"Prayers prayed in the Spirit never die until they accomplish God's intended purpose. His answer may not be what we expected, or when we expected it, but God often provides much more abundantly than we could think or ask."—Wesley L. Duewel

---

III. FIRMLY HELD IN GOD'S HANDS (Rom. 8:31-39)

Paul has now summarized the enormity of the Gospel. His words are breathtaking in scope. God is bringing the entire creation project back to its original state of glory. This process begins with believers who are conformed to the image of God's Son. It will end with the complete restoration and renewal of creation. Until then, and because of this truth, believers are firmly held in the hands of a gracious, loving, and sovereign God.

A. God Is on Our Side! (vv. 31-34)

(Romans 8:33-34 is not included in the printed text.)

31What shall we then say to these things? If God be for us, who can be against us? 32He that spared not his own Son, but delivered him up for us all, how shall he not with him also freely give us all things?

At its heart, the Gospel is a message about God. Paul uses the term *God* over five hundred times in his letters. His message is about what God has accomplished through Jesus Christ. Jesus is a part of God and God's story. Another aspect of God's story is His wrath. It is an important feature in Scripture because God must judge sin and injustice. This does not mean God is anti-world—He is forcibly pro-world and pro-people. He is "for us" (v. 31). Because God is for us, He gave up His Son for us so instead of experiencing God's wrath, we can be part of God's chosen people, whom He justifies (vv. 32-33).

We can know we are held firmly in God's hand because of the gift of His Son. Christ is how we know God is lavishly good. God's condemnation was poured out, not on humanity, but on Himself. Now Jesus, the risen Savior, intercedes on our behalf before the Father, having achieved our salvation (v. 34).

---

1. What are the "all things" referred to in verse 32, and what makes them free to believers?
2. How is Jesus ministering to believers right now (v. 34)?

> "Often, we endure trials seeking God's deliverance from them. Suffering is painful for us to endure or to see those we love endure. While our instinct is to flee trials, remember that even in the midst of suffering, God's will is being done."—Paul Chappell

B. More Than Conquerors (vv. 35-39)

35Who shall separate us from the love of Christ? shall tribulation, or distress, or persecution, or famine, or nakedness, or peril, or sword? 36As it is written, For thy sake we are killed all the day long; we are accounted as sheep for the slaughter. 37Nay, in all these things we are more than conquerors through him that loved us. 38For I am persuaded, that neither death, nor life, nor angels, nor principalities, nor powers, nor things present, nor things to come, 39Nor height, nor depth, nor any other creature, shall be able to separate us from the love of God, which is in Christ Jesus our Lord.

Paul continues with the theme of *suffering*. This must indicate that the Roman Christians were beginning to face various trials. We do not see evidence that such suffering was at the hands of the Roman government in this letter, as we do in later New Testament documents, such as Revelation. But we can imagine that social pressures were beginning to heat up as the Roman government began to wonder about this strange new Christian faith.

In the midst of such social ostracism, Paul reminds the Romans that they have nothing to fear because God is with them (vv. 35-36). The quotation from Psalm 44:22—facing "death all day long" (Rom. 8:36 NIV)—graphically portrays the suffering the Romans could expect. Just as Jesus was persecuted, so they would be. This must not be taken to be a sign of God's disfavor, for they would never be separated from Him, no matter the opposition they faced.

Even under persecution and weakness, Paul encouraged the Romans not to succumb to pessimism. They instead must keep their eyes on the larger story of God. Some might look at the fledgling Christians and see weakness, but Paul saw conquering strength (v. 37). The Christians must remember that nothing holds a shred of power against God, whether in the realm of the spiritual or the natural (v. 38). The love of God has made itself eternally manifest in Christ Jesus (v. 39).

---

1. If we are in "the love of Christ," why might we face the things listed (vv. 35-36)?
2. How are Christians "more than conquerors" (v. 37)?
3. Describe the warfare believers often experience (vv. 38-39).

CONCLUSION

The Holy Spirit is vital to the life of the believer because He is vital to the life and constitution of God. We cannot properly speak of God without recognizing the necessity and reality of the Holy Spirit. In Romans 8, the apostle Paul describes the Spirit-filled life. It is life of being led by God's Spirit through God's story for creation and for the Church. When we believe that beautiful story, we are given the confidence that all things are God's, and He holds us firmly in His hands.

GOLDEN TEXT CHALLENGE

"AS MANY AS ARE LED BY THE SPIRIT OF GOD, THEY ARE THE SONS OF GOD" (Rom. 8:14).

As the children of God, we are led, not driven, by the Spirit. We are led as the student by our teacher, the traveler by our guide, the soldier by our captain. We are not treated as mere machines, but as reasonable creatures. We are open to and receptive of divine influence.

The Spirit leads us out of the darkness and blindness of self-love into the light and clear vision of Christ-love. He will lead us from the shifting scenes of earth, through the dark valley of death, to the paradise of God. Thus have the redeemed through all ages been led, and thus will we continue to be led to the close of this age.

Daily Devotions:

M. The Spirit Creates • Genesis 1:1-3
T. The Spirit Empowers for Service • Numbers 11:16-17, 24-29
W. The Spirit Promised • Joel 2:26-29
T. The Spirit Moves on Jesus • Matthew 3:13—4:1
F. The Spirit Poured Out • Acts 2:1-4
S. The Spirit Gives Life • 2 Corinthians 3:1-6

Expectations for Everyday Living

Romans 12:1—13:7

Unit Theme:

Letter to the Romans

Central Truth:

Living for God demands dying to self.

Focus:

Examine Biblical expectations for Christian living and apply them to our daily lives.

Context:

The apostle Paul wrote the letter to the Romans in AD 58 while he was in Corinth.

Golden Text:

"Be not conformed to this world: but be ye transformed by the renewing of your mind, that ye may prove what is that good, and acceptable, and perfect, will of God" (Rom. 12:2).

Study Outline:

I. **Become a Living Sacrifice** (Rom. 12:1-8)

II. **Hate Evil, Cling to Good** (Rom. 12:9-21)

III. **Find Freedom in Submission** (Rom. 13:1-7)

INTRODUCTION

The New Testament does not draw any distinction between Christian doctrine and practice, between belief and ethics. This is an easy connection for us to miss, because of the emphasis on "right belief" in modern Christianity. It is easy to mistake true faith with simply assenting to abstract doctrines. Christian author Dallas Willard writes:

> The theology of Christian trinkets says there is something about the Christian that works like the bar code. Some ritual, some belief, or some association with a group affects God the way the bar code affects the scanner. Perhaps there has occurred a moment of mental assent to a creed, or an association entered into with a church. God "scans" it, and forgiveness floods forth. An appropriate amount of righteousness is shifted from Christ's account to our account in the bank of heaven, and all our debts are paid. We are, accordingly, "saved." Our guilt is erased. How could we not be Christians? (*The Divine Conspiracy: Rediscovering Our Hidden Life in God*).

The practice of infant baptism especially accelerated this view among some Christian groups, with the belief that the ritual of the sacrament assures heaven, regardless of lifestyle. How is all of this different from New Testament thought? The answer is simple, most seen in the writing of Paul. For him, *right belief* and *holy living* are two sides to the same coin.

Paul's typical practice is to begin his letters with theology, then work toward ethics. We see this most clearly in Ephesians and Colossians. In Ephesians, chapters 1-3 deal with theology and chapters 4-6 with ethics. Colossians breaks down similarly. Yet, even this structural approach can be misleading, in that Paul writes interchangeably about *belief* and *practice*. In the Bible, a belief that is not lived out is not a belief. Belief is far more than simply mental assent, agreeing that certain truths are true. As James 2:19 says, "Even the demons believe . . . and shudder" (NIV). Instead, true belief requires and inspires life change. This is the same transformed life Paul is describing in Romans 12 and 13.

I. BECOME A LIVING SACRIFICE (Rom. 12:1-8)

Romans 9—11 represent one of the biggest digressions in the letters of Paul. A *digression* was a popular ancient rhetorical device that a writer might use to address a sensitive subject. In this section, that subject is the place of Israel in the plan of God. The first eight chapters are essentially devoted to explaining why the Jewish Law is no longer the definitive, delineating marker for the people of God. But this reality does not make the story of Israel irrelevant. Instead, Paul explains that God's gifts and call over His Old Testament people still have value and relevance. After this digression is completed in the doxology at the end of chapter 11, Paul moves on to address the Roman church as a whole. Because Jews and Gentiles have been brought together within a single new people of God, they must learn to live in God's ways each day.

A. Discerning the Will of God (vv. 1-2)

¹I beseech you therefore, brethren, by the mercies of God, that ye present your bodies a living sacrifice, holy, acceptable unto God, which is your reasonable service. ²And be not conformed to this world: but be ye transformed by the renewing of your mind, that ye may prove what is that good, and acceptable, and perfect, will of God.

The catalyst for the commandments of Romans 12 is what God has accomplished in creating a new, diverse people to be His own. In this sense, the whole of the letter has been building to this chapter, for this is where the ethical instruction begins. We have seen that Romans is the closest thing to "pure theology" in all of Paul's letters. Typically, Paul is addressing specific congregational concerns. However, because he has never visited Rome, Paul is simply interested in expounding the Gospel to them. He is a controversial figure, according to Acts 15, so perhaps he does this to quell some of the rumors about him in preparation for his visit. In Romans 12, the pure theology ends, as Paul begins to speak practically about daily Christian living.

Paul begins his ethical instruction from the perspective of God's merciful character—"in view of God's mercy" (v. 1 NIV)—which he describes in 11:28-32. In response to His incomparable mercy, Christians should offer themselves as "a living sacrifice" (12:1).

The city of Rome knew well the blood of sacrifices. We tend to take this language more abstractly or metaphorically than it seemed to Paul's original audience. Hundreds of temples to various gods and goddesses—Apollo, Isis,

Osiris, Zeus, and Aphrodite, to name only a few—filled Rome. In each of these temples, animal sacrifice was the norm.

Meat for sale in the markets of Rome would have been sacrificed and devoted to some deity or another as a normative part of its processing. Meat sacrifices were a rare delicacy for most of the city. Only in special city festivals or games was meat available for the poor. So sacrifice was sought after.

One of the predominant features of early Christianity was that the celebration of the Lord's Supper took the place of celebrating animal sacrifices. Of course, synagogues in Rome were not houses of animal sacrifice, but Roman Jews could send money to the Jerusalem Temple so a sacrifice might be made on their behalf. Christians were highly suspect to their surrounding culture because they did not participate in these sacrificial rituals. They believed, instead, that Jesus was sacrificed once and for all, thus ending the need for the practice (see Heb. 10:10).

Paul calls this life of daily sacrifice a "spiritual act of worship" (Rom. 12:1 NIV). However, this is no pie-in-the-sky spirituality. Instead, the spiritual act of worship is intensely practical, in that we are to offer our bodies unto the daily service of God. Albert Hogeterp explains this connection:

> The fact that Paul refers to the bodies of the Roman believers as a living sacrifice may be explained in the context of dangers of persecution. The body as a living sacrifice could then represent the idea of endurance of hardships for the sake of the faith in Christ (*Paul and God's Temple*).

So, not only does Paul bring in the theme of sacrifice to the obligatory commitments of the Roman Christians; he also offers overtones of enduring hardships. The hardships the Romans must endure were not just bodily; they were also related to the mind (v. 2). The believers were to decompress themselves out of the world's mold and learn different patterns of thought. They were to be resocialized and retrained. Their way of thinking before coming to Christ was invalid. If they could not receive God's renewal for their mind, they would miss His will. But because He would empower them, they could grasp and walk in His will. As Paul says in 1 Corinthians 2:16, "We have the mind of Christ."

---

1. Why do some people consider the command in verse 1 "unreasonable"?
2. How can you discover the will of God (v. 2)?

O'Connor's Passion

One of the finest writers in the history of American literature is Flannery O'Connor. Though she died young, she left behind novels of the Deep Southern United States that stirred the hearts of her readers. She was also a committed Christian. As a college student, O'Connor journaled in her diary of her desire to live for God. "If I have to sweat for it, dear God, let it be as in Your service. I would like to be intelligently holy" (*A Prayer Journal*). Her success as a skilled writer was certainly related to this desire to live for God in her daily life.

B. One Body of Christ (vv. 3-8)

(Romans 12:6-8 is not included in the printed text.)

³For I say, through the grace given unto me, to every man that is among you, not to think of himself more highly than he ought to think; but to think soberly, according as God hath dealt to every man the measure of faith. ⁴For as we have many members in one body, and all members have not the same office: ⁵So we, being many, are one body in Christ, and every one members one of another.

Now that Paul has challenged the Romans both as individuals and as a community to offer themselves as living sacrifices and to be renewed in their minds, he turns to relationships within the congregations. This is critical when we realize there was a tendency for the various house congregations of Rome to see themselves as distinct. This was precisely the problem of 1 Corinthians—the house churches had divided into schisms (1:10). Paul has a greater hope of unity for the Romans.

Paul's communal strategy for the Roman church begins with humility. It starts with individuals taking a hard look at their own limitations and embracing them (v. 3). Paul considers this instruction to be a "grace" of God—a part of God's gift that we do not deserve. This gracious message is, "Do not think of yourself more highly than you ought" (NIV). Instead, we should examine ourselves with sober judgment. Only then will our faith remain pure.

In verses 4 and 5, Paul describes the Church as the body of Christ. This image is expanded in 1 Corinthians 12, but it is needed in the Roman church, where Jews and Gentiles are attempting to do life together. This image of a body of people would have been familiar to the Romans. For example, Philostratus, a Greek philosopher during the Roman period, compares a healthy city to a group of people operating a ship:

> Now look at that ship's crew, how some of them being rowers have embarked in the tugboats, while others are winding up and making fast the anchors, and others again are spreading the sails to the wind, and others are keeping an outlook at bow and stern. Now if a single member of this community abandoned any one of his particular tasks or went about his naval duties in an inexperienced manner, they would have a bad voyage and would themselves impersonate the storm; but if they vie with one another and are rivals only with the object of one showing himself as good a man as the other, then their ship will make the best of all havens, and all their voyage be one of fair weather and fair sailing, and as the precaution they exercise about themselves will prove to be as valuable as if Poseidon our lord of safety were watching over them (*Lives of the Sophists;* Cambridge: Harvard, 1921).

This example shows the motivation to work together was not new in the ancient world. Paul utilizes this convention for God's purposes (Rom. 12:4-8). His point is that each Christian has a role to play in the life and witness of the Church. Paul speaks of these roles in terms of spiritual gifts.

Though 1 Corinthians 12 and 14 more comprehensively explain spiritual gifts, Paul does make an important distinction in Romans 12: Some of the gifts are used in the worship service (prophecy, teaching), others are used in daily Christian living (encouraging, mercy), and others are used in the administration of church life (generosity, leadership). All are included and all have an equal place in building the kingdom of God.

---

1. How should you view yourself (v. 3)?
2. How should Christians view each other (vv. 4-5)?
3. How are some of the gifts in verses 6-8 actively in your congregation?

> "The Church is everywhere represented as one. It is one body, one family, one fold, one kingdom. It is one because it is pervaded by one Spirit. We are all baptized into one Spirit so as to become, says the apostle, one body."—Charles Hodge

---

II. HATE EVIL, CLING TO GOOD (Rom. 12:9-21)

Now that the Corinthians have been encouraged to live as a faithful community, witnessing and working as one body for the glory of God, Paul moves onto the particulars of community life. This section is built on short, pithy commandments, a common genre in the letters of Paul (usually toward the end of his letters). But simply because these commandments are short does not mean they are not practical and powerful. Paul expects them to be obeyed. For it is in the relationships between the Roman Christians that the Gospel movement will grow in Rome. As Jesus said in John 13:35, "By this all men will know that you are my disciples, if you love one another" (NIV).

A. Positive Affirmations (vv. 9-13)

⁹Let love be without dissimulation. Abhor that which is evil; cleave to that which is good. ¹⁰Be kindly affectioned one to another with brotherly love; in honour preferring one another; ¹¹Not slothful in business; fervent in spirit; serving the Lord; ¹²Rejoicing in hope; patient in tribulation; continuing instant in prayer; ¹³Distributing to the necessity of saints; given to hospitality.

At its heart, the Gospel is a communal message. Not only is it a message about the foundation and formation of a new Christian community, where all are welcome and included, but it also speaks to communally minded people in its original context. We now live in a profoundly individualistic world, especially among Western cultures, in which we discover our identity by standing apart from the group. We talk of "finding" ourselves and expressing ourselves. In ancient Rome, however, people first understood themselves as a part of a group. New Testament scholars Bruce J. Malina and Richard L. Rohrbaugh explain:

> In the ancient Mediterranean world, such a view of the individual did not exist. There every person was understood to be embedded in others and had his or

---

her identity only in relation to these others who formed this fundamental group. For most people, this was the family, and it meant that individuals neither acted nor thought of themselves as persons independent of the family group (*Social-Science Commentary on the Synoptic Gospels*).

Because the Church is the new family of God, Paul must reorient the Romans to understand the people of God as their new primary family.

Paul's commandment begins with *sincerity*—purity of heart, mind, and motives (v. 9). Without sincerity there will be no space created for right relationships. Paul also speaks highly of the Christian responsibility to honor one another (v. 10). *Honor* was a primary social value of the Roman world. People fought to gain honor for themselves. Paul encourages the Romans to radically give honor away. In the center of these commandments is a reminder to remain spiritually centered (v. 11). God alone ultimately sustains Christian relationships. Living in this truth will allow the Romans to share with one another and to practice hospitality (v. 13). They will be "joyful in hope, patient in affliction, faithful in prayer" (v. 12 NIV).

---

1. What must "love be without," and why (v. 9)?
2. When might verse 10 be difficult to obey?
3. Explain the fervency Christians must have (v. 11).
4. How do the three qualities in verse 12 relate to each other?

"Christianity offers a worldview that leads to the generation of moral values and ideals that are able to give moral meaning and dignity to our existence."—Alister McGrath

---

B. Responding to Negativity (vv. 14-21)

(Romans 12:16-21 is not included in the printed text.)

14Bless them which persecute you: bless, and curse not. 15Rejoice with them that do rejoice, and weep with them that weep.

The life of a genuinely Christian community cannot be lived inside a bubble. Paul knows the Romans also have a network of friends and family members outside the Church. They will also face opposition. It is one thing to be loving toward fellow Christians; it is another thing to love one's persecutors. Still, Paul commands this posture as normative for all Christians (v. 14).

Inside the body of Christ, believers must not be envious over each other's successes, nor be uncaring regarding each other's woes. Instead, Christians must "rejoice" and "weep" together (v. 15). Rather than being "proud" and "conceited" (v. 16 NIV), Christians must live together in harmony regardless of differences in social status.

The love that fills the inside of the Church must spill over to the outside. People will not experience Christian witness unless they are loved. When believers are tempted to "repay . . . evil for evil," they must instead "do what is right in the eyes of everybody" (v. 17 NIV).

Revenge will always be alluring (vv. 19-20), but Paul quotes Deuteronomy 32:35 and Proverbs 25:21-22 to warn against it. Revenge is nothing but a temporary fix, a narcotic.

Goodness and love will win if they remain the Christian's mode of operation (v. 21). These are long-term strategies for dealing with evil.

---

1. Restate verse 14 so an eight-year-old could understand it.
2. What do you need someone to "rejoice" or "weep" with you about today (v. 15)? Why is that important?
3. Explain the message of verse 16.
4. When have you been tempted to trade "evil for evil" (v. 17), and how did you respond?
5. How far should Christians go to make peace (v. 18)?
6. How can you overcome evil (vv. 19-21)?

> "Two types of voices command your attention today. Negative ones fill your mind with doubt, bitterness, and fear. Positive ones purvey hope and strength. Which one will you choose to heed?"
> —Max Lucado

III. FIND FREEDOM IN SUBMISSION (Rom. 13:1-7)

Paul begins Romans 13 by addressing one of the most difficult issues for the early church: how to understand their relationship and response to the civic government. We see Paul himself navigating this tricky line in the Book of Acts, as he is frequently called before government officials, both local and regional. The subject was all the more important in the city of Rome, where the first systematic persecution of Christians was soon to begin at the hands of Caesar Nero. On the whole, Paul demands that the Christian community get along with the secular government. However, there is more happening in these verses than first meets the eye.

A. The Institution of Government (vv. 1-3)

¹Let every soul be subject unto the higher powers. For there is no power but of God: the powers that be are ordained of God. ²Whosoever therefore resisteth the power, resisteth the ordinance of God: and they that resist shall receive to themselves damnation. ³For rulers are not a terror to good works, but to the evil. Wilt thou then not be afraid of the power? do that which is good, and thou shalt have praise of the same.

Rome was the center of the known world at the time Paul wrote this letter. It was the seat of Caesar, the sole ruler over this world. At the time Paul wrote Romans, the Caesars were at the height of their power. The Empire controlled over forty-four nations, over four thousand cities, and large pieces of three continents. Nothing seemed out of the reach of the emperor's power.

Because the Caesars so quickly clamped down on the emerging Christian movement, we might expect the New Testament to ridicule their rule. The

Christians were not afraid to oppose Rome in the name of the right, and we see this in many New Testament references, especially the Book of Revelation. Paul begins his treatise by reminding the Romans that government itself is a gift of God (v. 1).

Paul's focus is on the authority of the government at large, not on individual rulers. If Paul wanted to explicitly name Caesar, he could have done so. He could have said, "Everything Caesar says should be obeyed." He did not do this, but he did recognize the role government plays in the good of society.

Some new Christians perhaps had been accustomed to stealing or breaking the law in other ways to get by. Paul says this is not allowed in the Christian community. He calls Christians to do right in the eyes of the civil law.

---

* What does this passage reveal about local, state, and national governments?

> "No man can possibly be benevolent or religious, to the full extent of his obligations, without concerning himself, to a greater or less extent, with the affairs of human government."—Charles Finney

---

B. Caesar Is Accountable to God (vv. 4-7)

4For he is the minister of God to thee for good. But if thou do that which is evil, be afraid; for he beareth not the sword in vain: for he is the minister of God, a revenger to execute wrath upon him that doeth evil. 5Wherefore ye must needs be subject, not only for wrath, but also for conscience sake. 6For for this cause pay ye tribute also: for they are God's ministers, attending continually upon this very thing. 7Render therefore to all their dues: tribute to whom tribute is due; custom to whom custom; fear to whom fear; honour to whom honour.

In verse 4, Paul begins to speak specifically about the individual who wields supreme governmental authority. Rome had an army, but no official police force. When it came to governmental power, Caesar was the only show in town.

It is easy for Paul's context to be lost to us. In order to interpret this text properly, we must be aware that Caesar was considered to be a god. "The Divine Caesar" was printed on Rome's statues, buildings, roads, and coins. Against this context, Paul makes it clear Caesar was not god; he was God's slave ("minister," v. 4). Like Nebuchadnezzar in the Old Testament, Caesar was subject fully to God. In this sense, Paul subverted the power of Caesar. The Christians must submit to his laws, but not to his idolatry; for they were serving the one true God.

Paul goes on to draw a greater distinction between Caesar and the necessity of human government (vv. 5-7). To answer the question of taxation (one also famously posed to Jesus), Paul connects taxes to the institution of government under God, not Caesar. Christians are to pay what they owe, to fulfill their civic duty, and to leave the outcome to God.

---

1. Why should Christians be good citizens (vv. 4-5)?
2. What is the Christian response to taxation?

> "As Caesar demands of us the stamp of his likeness, so does God also. And as we render money to the one, so we give our souls to the other, our souls enlightened and sealed with the light of His countenance."—Venerable Bede

CONCLUSION

The Christian life is equally earthly and spiritual. We should not draw a sharp line of demarcation between the two. Our spiritual act of worship is to live according to God's expectations on a daily basis. This is the focus of Romans 12 and 13. Paul lays out God's expectations for individuals who live within a Christian community. They are to walk in His purposes toward their Christian brothers and sisters, toward suspicious outsiders, and toward their government.

GOLDEN TEXT CHALLENGE

"BE NOT CONFORMED TO THIS WORLD: BUT BE YE TRANSFORMED BY THE RENEWING OF YOUR MIND, THAT YE MAY PROVE WHAT IS THAT GOOD, AND ACCEPTABLE, AND PERFECT, WILL OF GOD" (Rom. 12:2).

The world system contrasts with the kingdom of Christ in the reality of its present and in the promise of its future. As subjects of Christ's kingdom, however, we inhabit two worlds. We live and work in a temporal world that contains elements at odds with the standards of that Kingdom which commands our allegiance. The only means of survival as a Christian, given such spiritual and moral tension, lies in being "living sacrifices," perpetually on the altar as our Christian stance in the world. That process involves transformation.

Instead of being *con*formed, we must be *trans*formed. In a sense, every Christian has the world system inside his or her head. We are constantly bombarded by its images, words, and values, so that often they echo in our minds. But the Christian's allegiance to the Kingdom is not merely a surface emotional commitment, leaving untouched the deepest springs of thought and behavior. The *mind* has been renewed; therefore, our habitual thought patterns and resulting behavior patterns reflect the contrasting values of Christ's kingdom and cause us to embark on a continuous quest—to discover the will of God in each successive life challenge, that "good, pleasing and perfect will" (NIV).

Daily Devotions:

M. Love God • Exodus 20:1-11
T. Love Others • Exodus 20:12-21
W. The Blessed Life • Psalm 1:1-6
T. Jesus Overcomes the Devil's Temptations • Luke 4:1-13
F. Responsibilities of Freedom • Galatians 5:13-16
S. Advice for Everyday Living • Philippians 4:4-9

A Life Governed by Love

Romans 13:8—14:23

Unit Theme:

Letter to the Romans

Central Truth:

Christians should live by the law of love.

Focus:

Appreciate what it means to live in the love of God and love others as we should.

Context:

The apostle Paul wrote the letter to the Romans in AD 58 while he was in Corinth.

Golden Text:

"Owe no man any thing, but to love one another: for he that loveth another hath fulfilled the law" (Rom. 13:8).

Study Outline:

I. **The Debt of Love** (Rom. 13:8-14)

II. **Me, You, and Jesus** (Rom. 14:1-12)

III. **Seek Peace, Not Conflict** (Rom. 14:13-23)

INTRODUCTION

Love—no other word is spoken so often with so little meaning. Love is typically boiled down to an emotion, a feeling, a chemical released by a synapse in the brain. Songs are sung and movies are made about "falling in love." Such a definition bears little resemblance to love in the Bible.

The New Testament conception of love is rooted in the Old Testament. The Hebrew word typically translated "love" is *hesed*. *Hesed* refers not to an emotion, but to a direct character trait of God, specifically His "covenant faithfulness" toward His people. This love stems from God's shared story with those whom He freed from Egyptian bondage. This love was forged in the contractual obligations of a solemn covenant. This love is stoked by worship, by ritual, by adherence to God's Word. In short, the Biblical concept of *love* cannot exist apart from God.

This Hebrew tradition in the Old Testament continues in the life of the New Testament church. The shift between the two happens at the Cross. Because the Cross is where God's love is ultimately expressed, the Church is birthed out of love. She is the bride of Christ. Love, therefore, is the mode of life for God's people.

This love begins toward God. A Christian is someone who has been swept up in God's love. The point of salvation is the acceptance of this divine love.

We begin to rightfully claim our place as God's beloved. We learn to be in love with God before we can even obey Him.

The fruit of this love of God is love of neighbor. These branches are inextricably tied together and can never be separated. Paul's letters start with the branch of God's love for us, move to our obligation to love God, and end with our need to express love to the family of God. Dietrich Bonhoeffer describes this three-pronged relationship: "Without Christ we should not know God. . . . But without Christ we also would not know our brother, nor could we come to him. The way is blocked by our own ego" (*Life Together*). The call of Romans 13 and 14 is to drop our egos so love might reign supreme in our heart.

I. THE DEBT OF LOVE (Rom. 13:8-14)

Paul has been slowly building the theme of *love* since his introduction of spiritual gifts in 12:4. For the Church to truly become the interdependent body of Christ, the "glue" of love is required and preeminent. Paul's instruction about obedience toward governmental institutions in 13:1-7 fits into this theme. Because Christians have been formed to be a people of love, they can be expected to act as productive members of civil society in addition to fulfilling their responsibilities within the Church. Paul continues this exposition on Christian responsibility beginning in verse 8. He claims that love is not only a grace of God; it is also our most reasonable obligation.

A. The Fulfillment of the Law (vv. 8-10)

8Owe no man any thing, but to love one another: for he that loveth another hath fulfilled the law. 9For this, Thou shalt not commit adultery, Thou shalt not kill, Thou shalt not steal, Thou shalt not bear false witness, Thou shalt not covet; and if there be any other commandment, it is briefly comprehended in this saying, namely, Thou shalt love thy neighbour as thyself. 10Love worketh no ill to his neighbour: therefore love is the fulfilling of the law.

Financial metaphors are not infrequent in Scripture. Paul has already built much of the argument of Romans on Genesis 15:6, where God "credited" Abraham with righteousness (NIV). *Credit* is obviously a financial term. Here in Romans 13, Paul uses the language of debt to describe the Christian obligation to love within the redeemed community (v. 8).

The concept of debt was no doubt a powerful motivator for the Roman Christians. Bruce J. Malina and Richard L. Rohrbaugh describe the common ancient problem of debt:

> The processes by which peasants fell into debt were many. Population growth affected some: more mouths to feed reduced a farmer's margin of livelihood and made borrowing more likely in lean years. Unreliable rainfall contributed as well. Two significant famines occurred in the period of Christian origins, one in 25 BC during the reign of Herod the Great, and the other in AD 46 under Claudius (Acts 11:28). The chief reason for indebtedness, however, was the excessive demand placed on peasant resources. (Evidence suggests that 35-40 percent of the total agricultural production was usually extracted in various taxes.) Peasants unable to repay loans of

seed or capital frequently became tenant sharecroppers on their own land (*Social-Science Commentary on the Synoptic Gospels*).

This situation of debt would have been especially acute in the city of Rome, which was loaded with masses of poor people. The indebted would naturally be seeking a way out of their problem.

In the ancient world, *debt* was a shady and dirty business. Since credit cards and other modern instruments of everyday debt were not available to ancient peoples, lenders typically charged exorbitant interest, and debtors' prisons were real entities. We see the impact of debt throughout the parables of Jesus, which reflect the life of common Israelis in the first century. In Rome, predatory moneylenders were everywhere. It is likely that some members of the Roman church had been exploited at the hand of a moneylender. Paul's command then, is powerful in its context. We Christians have a debt to pay! That debt is more powerful than finances. The debt is to *love one another.*

Paul has spent significant time in Romans working through the place of the Law. Writing to both conservative Jews and more liberal Gentiles, he can take nothing for granted. He has already made His point that the new Law of the Spirit has supplanted the old Law of the letter (8:2-3). In 13:9-10, he describes again the manner in which Christians fulfill the Law.

It is not that the Law has been set aside; it is that it is now being properly obeyed. This passage reflects on the teachings of Jesus, who said, "All the Law and the Prophets hang" on the commandments to love God and neighbor (Matt. 22:40 NIV). One of the most famous Jewish rabbis of the day, Hillel, said, "What is hateful to yourself, do not do to your fellow man. That is the whole Torah; the rest is just commentary." So we see the centrality of love among the people of God is not a new concept. However, the Church is charged first and foremost to live this commandment out in everyday life.

---

1. What "debt" can we never fully pay, and why not (v. 8)?
2. Which of the five laws listed in verse 9 is the greatest, and why?

> "Do not waste time bothering whether you 'love' your neighbor; act as if you did."—C. S. Lewis

---

B. The Coming Judgment (vv. 11-14)

(Romans 13:11, 13-14 is not included in the printed text.)

¹²The night is far spent, the day is at hand: let us therefore cast off the works of darkness, and let us put on the armour of light.

The commandment to *love* is not some abstract principle, disconnected from God's plan of history. It is not merely a good, utilitarian ideal that helps societies to function. The consequences of love stretch beyond this life to the next. Loving (or not loving) has eternal consequences.

Paul advised his readers to wake up (v. 11) and clean up (v. 12) in preparation for the Lord's return. As believers wait for the coming of the Lord Jesus

---

Christ, we must refrain from doing those things which He would not approve. We ought to spurn the deeds of darkness.

Dean Bosworth states the "armor of light" (v. 12) could mean *weapons* (John 18:3), in which case the figure is that of a soldier rising in the darkness of the early morning to put on his armor. Or, Bosworth says, it could mean *tools*, in which case the figure is that of a workman going out to the day's work (*Bible for Home and School*).

The word *rioting* (v. 13), or reveling, meant "a nocturnal and riotous procession of half-drunken and frolicsome fellows who, after supper, parade through the streets with torches and music in honor of Bacchus, or some other deity, and sing and play before the houses of their male and female friends; it was used generally of feasts and drunken parties that lasted all night and included all kinds of revelry" (J. C. Thayer).

Some scholars translate the word *chambering* as "debauchery" and indicate it refers primarily to sexual sins. *Wantonness* means "licentiousnes, lawless insolence, and riotous excess." The apostle also warned against *strife*, or contention, in the Christian life. He also urged his readers to avoid *envying*, or jealousy.

The Christian life is not so much empty of the things of the world as it is filled with the things of Christ. We will not walk in darkness if we "put on the Lord Jesus Christ" (v. 14). As H. C. G. Moule says, "The decisive, the satisfying, the thorough moral victory and deliverance comes to the Christian man, not by trampling about with his own resolves, but by committing himself to his Saviour and Keeper" (*The Expositor's Bible*).

---

1. Explain Paul's statement about time (v. 11).
2. How can believers overcome the "works of darkness" (vv. 12-14)?

> "We should be holy people eager to greet our Lord when He returns, ready at any moment for the trumpet's call, people of optimism, busy in evangelism, hands to the plow, eyes on the prize."
> —David Jeremiah

II. ME, YOU, AND JESUS (Rom. 14:1-12)

In chapter 14 we receive practical information that helps us understand the necessity of love within the Roman congregation. Disputes had arisen over dietary customs. These customs divided the Roman Christians into two schisms: the "weak" and the "strong." Remarkably, Paul identified himself as a member of the "strong" group, yet led the way in deferring to the "weak." This is love in action.

A. The Weak and the Strong (vv. 1-4)

¹Him that is weak in the faith receive ye, but not to doubtful disputations. ²For one believeth that he may eat all things: another, who is weak, eateth herbs. ³Let not him that eateth despise him that eateth not; and let not him which eateth not judge him that eateth: for God hath

received him. **⁴Who art thou that judgest another man's servant? to his own master he standeth or falleth. Yea, he shall be holden up: for God is able to make him stand.**

In our language, "weak" and "strong" are stark categories. Strength is always preferred over weaknesses. It is likely that the "strong" Romans were using this language to deride the "weak." Paul uses their language in order to not just treat their symptoms, but the root of their sickness. They must set aside personal differences that are not significant to their Gospel calling. They must love beyond the cultural limitations that were holding them back from one another.

The principal disagreement is over those who eat "all things" versus those who eat only vegetables (v. 2). The same problem occurs in the Corinthian church, which can help shed light on the controversy. It was a widespread point of conflict throughout the early churches that were located in pagan cities.

In 1 Corinthians 8:4, Paul addresses the issue of meat that has been sacrificed to idols. In Corinth and Rome, all meat, whether sold in the marketplace or offered at a dinner party, would have been sacrificed to an idol as a normal part of its processing. Pagan temples were the most common settings for dinner parties. In this verse, Paul indicates the mentality of the meat-eaters: "We know that an idol is nothing at all in the world and that there is no God but one" (NIV). Paul is in agreement, to some extent, with the meat-eaters. Their mentality is that the idols are not real, so eating meat is perfectly safe. True, but there is more at stake. What is most important is not what is philosophically true, but what is helpful for the edification of the community of faith.

The point is not who has the better argument. Regardless of personal opinion, no one in the Christian community is to look down on anyone else when it comes to matters that are not immediately moral (Rom. 14:3-4).

This teaching shows us the space that early Christianity created for profound individual conscience. Paul expects there to be differences of opinion within the church. He desires that such individuality is cherished and maintained. All too often, unfortunately, mob rule can take the place of mutuality. Paul is guarding against this tendency.

---

1. What are some "disputable matters" (v. 1 NIV) today over which Christians should not wrangle?
2. Explain the principle in verse 4.

> "I shall pass through this world but once. Any good thing therefore that I can do, or any kindness that I can show to any human being, let me do it now. Let me not defer it or neglect it, for I shall not pass this way again."—Henry Drummond

---

B. The Place of Cultural Traditions (vv. 5-8)
   (Romans 14:5-6 is not included in the printed text.)

7For none of us liveth to himself, and no man dieth to himself. 8For whether we live, we live unto the Lord; and whether we die, we die unto the Lord: whether we live therefore, or die, we are the Lord's.

Paul's encouragement of individuality and diversity within the Roman congregation takes on theological overtones in verses 5-8. Paul begins by describing calendar concerns. Because this is a mixed congregation, full of Jews and Gentiles, the two groups are living according to different calendars. The Gentile Christians would have no need or desire to celebrate the Passover, the Day of Atonement, or other Jewish holidays. The Gentiles may have even disagreed with the Jews over the weekly Sabbath observance. Paul simply allows for such diversity of practice, encouraging each group to be fully convinced that their way is holy and pleasing to God.

Diversity is possible because of the mutual obligations between members of the Church (v. 7). Christians are dependent on one another. This interdependence was even more pronounced in the first century, when Christianity was still a tiny sect within the larger pagan world. Therefore, Paul relegates matters of personal opinion, subjugating them to the need for relationships, all the while protecting the rights of believers to maintain such diverse opinions, even passionately. Because Christians are oriented toward the Lord, in life and death, every opinion is set in the context of belonging to God (v. 8).

- What do verses 7 and 8 teach about a Christian's responsibility and accountability?

> "A man of a right spirit is not a man of narrow and private views, but is greatly interested and concerned for the good of the community to which he belongs, and particularly of the city or village in which he resides, and for the true welfare of the society of which he is a member."—Jonathan Edwards

---

C. Do Not Judge (vv. 9-12)

(Romans 14:9-10 is not included in the printed text.)

11For it is written, As I live, saith the Lord, every knee shall bow to me, and every tongue shall confess to God. 12So then every one of us shall give account of himself to God.

Paul summarizes the Gospel story as a whole in verse 9: Jesus is Lord of all, having died and resurrected. Paul reveals the silliness of petty disputes to the Roman church by elevating the magnificence of Jesus. Because He is the ultimate Judge, Christians should allow Jesus to do His job.

The judgment that matters most is not between Christians, especially when they concern things that are not of eternal consequence (v. 10). The judgment that matters is the one we all will face before God himself (vv. 11-12). Because of this, there is no need to judge other brothers and sisters. We can leave judgment where it belongs—in the hands of God.

A Life Governed by Love

1. Contrast the two judgments in verse 10.
2. If we believe verses 11 and 12, how will we live?

> "I will not judge a person to be spiritually dead whom I have judged formerly to have had spiritual life, though I see him at present in a swoon (faint) as to all evidences of the spiritual life. And the reason why I will not judge him so is this—because if you judge a person dead, you neglect him, you leave him; but if you judge him in a swoon (faint) . . . you use all means for the retrieving of his life."—John Owen

---

III. SEEK PEACE, NOT CONFLICT (Rom. 14:13-23)

In the final section of chapter 14, the subject of food once again comes to the forefront. Because Paul goes into greater detail here about the dispute, a survey of the historical context of the Roman congregation might be helpful. It is likely that the situation of the Roman church is unlike any other in the New Testament period. Its membership includes Jews and Gentiles. Many of these Jews are staunchly conservative, with a high view of the Torah. This is why Paul writes so much about matters pertaining to the Law in Romans. There are other mixed churches in the New Testament, so this is nothing new. What has probably thrown the Roman church into tumult is called the *edict of Claudius*.

In Acts 18:2, Luke tells us "Claudius had ordered all the Jews to leave Rome" (NIV). This fact is corroborated by a pagan author, Suetonius, who records a similar statement: "Since the Jews constantly made disturbances at the instigation of Chrestus, he [the emperor Claudius] expelled them from Rome" (Louis Feldman, *Jewish Life and Thought Among Greeks and Romans*). Suetonius' statement is especially curious since no other historical record exists for this mysterious "Chrestus." A popular theory among Christian and non-Christian scholars is that the growing Christian community endured a violent clash with the large Jewish community in Rome. The disagreement was over groups of Jews accepting Christ, but Suetonius does not know this term. He mishears it, mistaking it for the name "Chrestus." We also know that Claudius quickly relents from his edict, allowing Jews to return to Rome. The return of Jewish Christians to the church at Rome may have created tension. Against this backdrop, Paul's admonitions for unity and mutuality are urgent.

A. Defer to the Weak (vv. 13-15)

¹³Let us not therefore judge one another any more: but judge this rather, that no man put a stumblingblock or an occasion to fall in his brother's way. ¹⁴I know, and am persuaded by the Lord Jesus, that there is nothing unclean of itself: but to him that esteemeth any thing to be unclean, to him it is unclean. ¹⁵But if thy brother be grieved with thy meat, now walkest thou not charitably. Destroy not him with thy meat, for whom Christ died.

Paul says believers must "stop passing judgment on one another" (v. 13 NIV), and to avoid setting up obstacles in others' way. Such "stumbling blocks" could take many forms. Believers might be tempted to threaten, backbite, or rally a schism to stand with them for a certain cause. Paul was not interested in causes, but instead yearned for believers to stand as Christ's church.

Paul was a part of the debate over meat-eating. Therefore, he offered the Roman Christians his personal strategy (v. 14). Paul was firmly in the camp of "the strong." Even though he was a Jew, he did not feel the need to fight for a kosher diet. According to Paul, this was a matter of personal choice because Jesus had nullified the importance of such matters.

What is important in the Church is not what people *think* but what they *do*. Paul was not interested in debating a philosophy of food, but in helping the Romans live out the Gospel (v. 15). What counts is love, and certain Romans were destroying this mandate. Paul did not command them to cease eating meat, but to abstain from eating meat in the presence of those brothers and sisters who might take offense because they had a differing view.

---

1. What are "stumbling blocks" (v. 13), and what did Jesus say about them (Mark 9:42)?
2. If we are "walking in love," what will we not do (v. 15 NKJV)?

> "We need not all agree, but if we disagree, let us not be disagreeable in our disagreements."—M. R. DeHaan

---

B. Mutuality and Individuality (vv. 16-23)

(Romans 14:20-23 is not included in the printed text.)

16Let not then your good be evil spoken of: 17For the kingdom of God is not meat and drink; but righteousness, and peace, and joy in the Holy Ghost. 18For he that in these things serveth Christ is acceptable to God, and approved of men. 19Let us therefore follow after the things which make for peace, and things wherewith one may edify another.

Paul encouraged the strong to defer to the weak; he did not want to nullify the importance of personal opinion. Some considered eating meat a gift from God, and the "weak" must respect that. The commandment not to judge flowed between the strong and the weak groups. None should speak evil of the other (v. 16). Instead, they should focus on the bigger picture.

This discussion was not really about food. It was about the values that hold Christian communities together: *righteousness*, *peace*, and *joy* (v. 17). These are the practices and habits of the heart that please God (v. 18). Therefore, they should be the primary domain of Christians.

In verses 19-23, Paul again makes a plea for unity and cooperation. This unity may require silence if the Romans cannot lower the temperature of the debate (v. 22). No one should condemn himself (v. 23) nor harm another (vv. 20-21) by his actions. Instead, *edification* is the goal of shared Christian life (v. 19).

A Life Governed by Love

1. Explain the phrase, "Do not let your good be spoken of as evil" (v. 16 NKJV).
2. How does verse 17 describe genuine Christianity?
3. What should Christians pursue (v. 19), and how (vv. 20-21)?
4. Explain the statement, "Everything that does not come from faith is sin" (v. 23 NIV).

Transformed by the Gospel

The Waroani tribe in the Amazon jungle of Ecuador was once considered the most dangerous people group on earth. Roughly half of the men could expect to be murdered by another tribesman. Thankfully, the story of this tribe has dramatically changed. They are now a people of peace. What happened? Missionaries arrived in 1958, bringing the message of God's love.

CONCLUSION

The Christian life is governed by love of God and neighbor. This love is put on public display most notably in relationships between Christians. We are indebted to one another as brothers and sisters in Christ, but this indebtedness does not equal forced conformity. Instead, Scripture not only allows but encourages diverse forms of culture and practice in living out the Christian faith. When our diversity is embraced within an attitude of unity, God is glorified.

GOLDEN TEXT CHALLENGE

"OWE NO MAN ANY THING, BUT TO LOVE ONE ANOTHER: FOR HE THAT LOVETH ANOTHER HATH FULFILLED THE LAW" (Rom. 13:8).

There is one debt the Christian will continue to owe—the debt "to love one another." One can satisfy earthly or civil claims, but love's claims can never be fulfilled. The more one pays this debt of love, the deeper one seems to be in debt. The practice of love makes the principle of love deeper and more active.

The word *another* has reference to one's neighbor. The whole Law can be summed up in loving God and loving one's neighbor. If one honestly seeks to discharge this debt of love, he or she will automatically keep all of the commandments.

Daily Devotions:

M. Brotherly Love • 1 Samuel 20:11-17
T. God's Tender Love • Psalm 23:1-6
W. God So Loved the World • John 3:16-21
T. Abide in Love • John 15:9-17
F. Do All for God's Glory • 1 Corinthians 10:23-33
S. Love One Another • 1 John 3:11-18

Introduction to Spring Quarter

"The Era of the Judges" (lessons 1-6) was a harrowing time in Israel's history. Important principles are drawn from the lives of Deborah, Othniel, Ehud, Gideon, Abimelech, Samson, and other deliverers.

This unit was written by Dr. Lee Roy Martin (D.Th., University of South Africa), professor of Old Testament and Biblical Languages at the Pentecostal Theological Seminary (Cleveland, TN). He has written several books and is the editor of the *Journal of Pentecostal Theology*.

The Easter lesson (7) was compiled by Lance Colkmire (see biographical information on page 16).

The second unit, "Paul's Journeys (Acts, Part 2)," begins with Acts 11 and concludes with Acts 28, examining how the Gospel spread through the first evangelists and missionaries.

Lessons 8-13 were compiled by Lance Colkmire (see biographical information on page 16).

A Generation That Forgot God

Judges 2:1—3:4

Unit Theme:

The Era of the Judges

Central Truth:

Christians are responsible for passing their faith to the next generation.

Focus:

Cherish and pass on our heritage of faith in God.

Context:

Events beginning around 1390 BC

Golden Text:

"There arose another generation after them, which knew not the Lord, nor yet the works which he had done for Israel" (Judg. 2:10).

Study Outline:

  I. **Declining Faith in God** (Judg. 2:1-10)

 II. **A Deadly Cycle** (Judg. 2:11-19)

III. **God Tests Israel** (Judg. 2:20—3:4)

INTRODUCTION

In a recent article on *Charisma* magazine's website, Joseph Mattera describes "Ten Signs Your Church Has Been Secularized." Essentially, Mattera attempts to point the church back to its God-given purpose and role in the world. He observes that, rather than being salt and light to the world, the church has often conformed to the ways of the world. Moreover, in conforming to the world, the church has lost its saving influence and prophetic impact. Mattera's article illustrates many of the reasons some people are accusing the church of being irrelevant.

If the church is to have a positive effect on society and reach the lost for Christ, it must gain a firm grasp on its calling to be the people of God. The church must answer the following vital questions: What is the message of the church in this world? How does the church maintain integrity? What are the church's priorities? What does God require of His people? Are obedience and holiness necessary today?

The answers to many questions like these can be found in the Book of Judges, which serves as the Biblical text for our next six lessons. The message of the Book of Judges is that God desires to walk in covenant relationship with His people. Our study of Judges will help us to understand how God's people should live out that covenant relationship faithfully.

Judges is the seventh book in the Bible, and it follows the Book of Joshua. Joshua recounts Israel's great victories over Jericho and the other cities of

Canaan. Throughout Joshua, the people of Israel were obedient and faithful, and God rewarded their faithfulness with His blessings. After Joshua died, however, the Israelites began to drift away from the Lord and forget their covenant obligations. Thus, the Book of Judges narrates Israel's downward spiral from victory to defeat, from unity to fragmentation, and from faithfulness to idolatry. Judges concludes on a tragic note: "In those days there was no king in Israel; everyone did what was right in his own eyes" (21:25 NASB). Judges, therefore, serves as a profound warning to Christians that we cannot rest upon the victories of the past—we must continue to be faithful in the present.

In this first lesson, we learn the important role that discipleship plays in the life of the church. More specifically, we see the value of transmitting our faith to the next generation. The Pentecostal-Charismatic Movement is now more than one hundred years old; and, in that time, God has worked wonders in our midst. We must be diligent to share these wonders with our children, grandchildren, and new converts so they too may experience the glory and majesty of God's mighty presence.

I. DECLINING FAITH IN GOD (Judg. 2:1-10)

A. Declining Faith Coincides With Disobedience (vv. 1-2)

(Judges 2:1-2 is not included in the printed text.)

The Book of Judges tells the struggles of the Israelites as they face new challenges in the Promised Land. Joshua had led them into the land of Canaan, but now that Joshua has died (Judg. 1:1), Israel must claim the remaining portions of the Promised Land (see Josh. 23:4-10). The work of Joshua's generation is finished. A new work remains, however, for the new generation. The work of the new generation is to live courageously and victoriously like Joshua's generation, and to go forward with new victories until every promise of God has been claimed and every enemy has been vanquished.

The Lord had directed Israel to drive out all of the Canaanites from the land, but we learn in Judges 1 that Israel disobeyed the Lord. Instead of driving out all of the Canaanites, Israel allowed many of them to remain. Israel even made covenants with some of the Canaanites—covenants that were in clear violation of God's orders (2:2).

Because of their refusal to drive out the Canaanites, the Lord sends His angel to rebuke the Israelites and to call them to repentance. The Lord's messenger, called "the angel of the Lord" (v. 1), is the special manifestation of God's presence, a *theophany*. The angel of Yahweh is mentioned seventeen times in Genesis through Numbers. Here, the angel travels from Gilgal to Bochim. Gilgal was Joshua's headquarters during the conquest, and it was a place of Israel's renewal and blessing. Therefore, the movement of the angel of Yahweh from Gilgal to Bochim recalls the victories of Joshua as they stand in sharp contrast to the defeats just recounted in Judges 1.

Also, the mention of Gilgal recalls the angel who is described as the "captain of the Lord's army" who appeared to Joshua there (see Josh. 5:13-15), where he stands with his sword drawn as in Numbers 22. In Joshua 6:1-2, he speaks as the voice of the Lord as he does in Genesis 16:13; Exodus 3:4-7; Judges 6:14. The angel who came to aid the Israelites at the beginning of the conquest now comes to rebuke them because they have not finished the work.

The angel begins his message with a reference to the Exodus, declaring, "I brought you out of Egypt into this land that I swore to give to your ancestors" (2:1 NLT). The reference to the Exodus reminds Israel that their future prospects in Canaan are based not on their commitment to the Lord but on His commitment to them. The mention of the ancestors affirms God's continuing faithfulness in His relationship with the people of Israel. This is not a new God who speaks; He is the God of Abraham, the God of Isaac, and the God of Jacob. He is the God who can be trusted, the God of covenant faithfulness. Furthermore, He promises to be faithful forever.

The Israelites' failure to obey the voice of the Lord is their fundamental and underlying error. Israel had vowed eagerly to obey the Lord (Josh. 24:24), but now their vows are broken. While the Lord has been faithful to His covenant with the Israelites, they have been unfaithful to Him.

- Contrast the covenant God made (v. 1) with the covenant made by Israel (v. 2).

"Though men are false, God is faithful."—Matthew Henry

B. Declining Faith Brings Discipline From God (vv. 3-5)

(Judges 2:4-5 is not included in the printed text.)

³Wherefore I also said, I will not drive them out from before you; but they shall be as thorns in your sides, and their gods shall be a snare unto you.

The Lord promises He will never break His covenant (v. 1)—a covenant that includes His giving of the land to Israel. However, because of Israel's disobedience, He will discipline them by allowing some of the Canaanites to remain as thorns and snares (v. 3). As thorns, they will be a constant source of pain to disobedient Israel. As snares, they will entice the Israelites to forsake the Lord and to serve the gods of Canaan.

After they hear the angel's message of judgment, the Israelites show signs of repentance by weeping and offering sacrifices (vv. 4-5). The name of the place is *Bochim*, which, in Hebrew, means "weepers." Israel had entered the Promised Land with shouts of victory, but their disobedience had brought them to a place of sorrow and regret. Biblical scholars believe *Bochim* (the place of weeping) was originally *Bethel* ("the house of God"), where Jacob had encountered the transforming presence of God. From this, we learn that disobedience will take us away from the presence of God and lead us into a place of sorrow.

1. Describe the effects of Israel's covenant with other nations (v. 3).
2. What happened at Bochim (vv. 4-5)?

C. Declining Faith Results From Carelessness (vv. 6-10)
(Judges 2:6, 9 is not included in the printed text.)

⁷And the people served the Lord all the days of Joshua, and all the days of the elders that outlived Joshua, who had seen all the great works of the Lord, that he did for Israel. ⁸And Joshua the son of Nun, the servant of the Lord, died, being an hundred and ten years old.

¹⁰And also all that generation were gathered unto their fathers: and there arose another generation after them, which knew not the Lord, nor yet the works which he had done for Israel.

Just as the Book of Joshua concludes with two versions of Joshua's final speech—one version focused on Israel's battles (ch. 23) and the other on Israel's worship (ch. 24)—the Book of Judges begins with two versions of what happened after Joshua died. Judges 1 tells about the battles that ensued after Joshua's death and the failure of Israel to drive out all of the Canaanites. Chapter 2 covers the same time period, but from a different perspective. While chapter 1 focuses on Israel's battles, chapter 2 focuses on Israel's worship. At the same time Israel began to disobey the Lord in battle, they also began to drift away from the Lord in their worship.

Before we learn the details of Israel's departure from the Lord in worship, we are reminded that the people of Joshua's generation "served the Lord" (2:7). One reason they were able to maintain their faith in God was that they had personally witnessed "all the great works" God had done. They remembered crossing over the Jordan River. They remembered how the walls of Jericho had fallen down. Their personal experiences of God's grace and power gave them the confidence to endure faithfully in their service to God.

The generation that followed after Joshua, however, had not witnessed the mighty acts of God. They did not know the "the works which he [God] had done for Israel" (v. 10), nor did they know the Lord. This troubling verse suggests the Israelites had failed in their discipleship of the younger generation. Could it be that the older generation had not testified about God's powerful acts? Had they failed to keep the sacred days and festivals? Had they shirked their responsibility to share their faith with their children and grandchildren? Apparently, the older generation had disregarded the Lord's instruction, which says, "And these words, which I command thee this day, shall be in thine heart: And thou shalt teach them diligently unto thy children" (Deut. 6:6-7).

1. Why is verse 6 significant?
2. Describe Joshua's generation with the next generation (vv. 7, 10).

Concrete Lesson

If we travel to archaeological sites from the ancient Roman Empire, we will find monuments, buildings, and other structures made of concrete. However, if we examine structures built between AD 500 and 1300, we will find no concrete. That is because the Romans failed to share their knowledge of how to make it. Thankfully, the method for making concrete was rediscovered in modern times. The lessons of life are sometimes learned through much struggle and through trial and error. However, those lessons must be shared with the next generation.

II. A DEADLY CYCLE (Judg. 2:11-19)

A. Ingratitude Leads to Rebellion (vv. 11-12)

¹¹And the children of Israel did evil in the sight of the Lord, and served Baalim: ¹²And they forsook the Lord God of their fathers, which brought them out of the land of Egypt, and followed other gods, of the gods of the people that were round about them, and bowed themselves unto them, and provoked the Lord to anger.

Israel's failure to drive out the inhabitants of the land meant Israel would be continually tempted to worship the gods of their neighbors. Just as the Lord had predicted (v. 3), the Canaanites enticed Israel to forsake the Lord and to worship the gods of Canaan. Their worship of false gods was "evil in the sight of the Lord" (v. 11). The most prominent gods of the Canaanites were Baal and Ashtaroth. Baal was the storm god, believed to control the rain and, therefore, instrumental in assuring successful crops. He also was a war god whose wife, Ashtaroth, was a fertility deity. The worship of Baal and Ashtaroth was intended to ensure the fertility of the earth.

Israel's forsaking of the Lord is even more troubling in light of His delivering them from the bondage of Egypt (v. 12). Because they did not know the Lord nor the works He had done for them, their commitment to God waned. When they discarded the Lord and adopted the gods of Canaan, the Israelites were demonstrating gross ingratitude. They were trampling under foot the grace of God. Their worship of Baal was a clear violation of Exodus 20:3, "Thou shalt have no other gods before me," which was based on God's identity as their Savior who had brought them up "out of the land of Egypt, out of the house of bondage" (v. 2).

Israel's worship of other gods "provoked the Lord to anger" (Judg. 2:12). The Lord had every right to be angry. He had saved them from bondage and claimed them as His people. Therefore, Israel was God's covenant people, His bride, His "treasured possession" (Ex. 19:5-6 NIV). However, they had forsaken Him and had pursued other gods. What's more, their idolatry was intentional—"followed other gods" (Judg. 2:12) indicates a willful and deliberate action. Thus, their worship of other gods was spiritual adultery.

• Describe Israel's new relationship with false gods.

B. Rebellion Calls for God's Judgment (vv. 13-15)

(Judges 2:13, 15 is not included in the printed text.)

¹⁴And the anger of the Lord was hot against Israel, and he delivered them into the hands of spoilers that spoiled them, and he sold them into the hands of their enemies round about, so that they could not any longer stand before their enemies.

The disobedience and idolatry of the Israelites called for strong disciplinary measures from the Lord. He delivered them over into the power of their enemies (v. 14), and they were oppressed on every side. Whenever they went out to battle, the Lord "was against them" (v. 15). Israel had been oppressed in Egypt, but the Lord had saved them. Now, however, their sins caused them to be oppressed once more.

• How did God respond to Israel's idolatry?

C. Judgment Leads to Mercy (vv. 16, 18)

¹⁶Nevertheless the Lord raised up judges, which delivered them out of the hand of those that spoiled them.

¹⁸And when the Lord raised them up judges, then the Lord was with the judge, and delivered them out of the hand of their enemies all the days of the judge: for it repented the Lord because of their groanings by reason of them that oppressed them and vexed them.

Israel's distress touched the heart of God. His discipline was meant to save them, mold them, and change them; it was not meant to destroy them. Therefore, when they had suffered enough, God would raise up a judge who would save them from the power of their oppressor. The Biblical term "to judge" also means "to rule." The office of judge was created by Moses, and the judges would mediate disputes and answer questions concerning the law of Moses. In the Book of Judges, however, the role of the judges went beyond their normal duties. In times when Israel was suffering oppression from the enemy, God would raise up judges who would lead Israel to victory, deliverance, and liberty (v. 16). Unlike the later office of king, the office of judge was not hereditary. The judges were charismatic leaders who were chosen by God and empowered by the Holy Spirit.

Verse 18 reveals the Lord's motivation for saving Israel, and it explains how the judges were able to bring victory against Israel's enemies. First, the judges were successful because the Lord "raised them up." They were chosen by the Lord for a particular time and a specific assignment. Second, they were successful because "the Lord was with" them. It was not their own abilities and wisdom that brought victory. Victory came because the Lord gave them special gifts, strategies, and supernatural power. Furthermore, everything the Lord did to bring victory was motivated by His compassion, love, and grace. The Lord was moved by their suffering; He heard their "groanings" just as He had heard their cries when they were in Egypt. Because the Lord loves His people, He cannot bear to see them suffer endlessly, even when that suffering is a result of God's own disciplinary actions. God is compassionate and merciful.

• How did the Lord respond to the people's groaning (vv. 16, 18)?

"Physicians say the memory is the first thing that decays; it is true in spirituals."—Thomas Watson

---

D. God's Mercy Taken for Granted (vv. 17, 19)

17And yet they would not hearken unto their judges, but they went a whoring after other gods, and bowed themselves unto them: they turned quickly out of the way which their fathers walked in, obeying the commandments of the Lord; but they did not so.

19And it came to pass, when the judge was dead, that they returned, and corrupted themselves more than their fathers, in following other gods to serve them, and to bow down unto them; they ceased not from their own doings, nor from their stubborn way.

Unfortunately, the Israelites were stubborn in their pursuit of other gods. Each time they were delivered from their enemies, they "turned quickly" away from the path of obedience their forefathers had laid down for them (v. 17). Once again we see a contrast between the new generation, who did not serve God, and Joshua's generation ("their fathers") who had obeyed God. Moreover, Israel's backsliding grew progressively worse—each generation "behaved more corruptly than their fathers" (v. 19 NKJV). Repeatedly the Lord saved them, and repeatedly they turned their backs on the Lord.

Apparently, the Israelites were dissatisfied with their covenant relationship with God, and they desired freedom from all restrictions. They would not cease "from their own doings," and they would not turn loose of their own "stubborn way." Herein lies the heart of Israel's problem. They refused to fulfill their obligation to keep the Lord's commandments and to be loyal to Him as their divine King. They must have assumed incorrectly that freedom from Egypt meant freedom to do as they pleased, but that is not the case. The Lord saved His people *from* Egypt, and He saved them *for* Himself. Israel was freed from bondage so they could live in the liberty of God's kingdom. However, their desire to abandon the Lord would lead them back into bondage.

The passage in 2:11-19 forecasts the downward spiral of the Book of Judges. The repeated cycle is made up of the following sequence of events: (1) The Israelites worship other gods. (2) God turns Israel over to an enemy who oppresses them. (3) Israel cries out for help. (4) The Lord raises up a judge who saves Israel. (5) The land enjoys a time of peace. (6) The Israelites backslide again, and the cycle repeats itself.

1. What would the Israelites "quickly" do (v. 17)?
2. Describe Israel's downhill slide (v. 19).

III. GOD TESTS ISRAEL (Judg. 2:20—3:4)

A. The Broken Relationship (v. 20)

[20]And the anger of the Lord was hot against Israel; and he said, Because that this people hath transgressed my covenant which I commanded their fathers, and have not hearkened unto my voice.

For the third time, we read that the Lord was angry with Israel. He was angry because Israel had broken the covenant relationship. Joshua 24 describes a covenant renewal ceremony, in which Israel promised to be faithful and to serve the Lord, but now they have disregarded their promise by worshiping other gods. Although the Lord called out to them, they did not listen. Instead, they listened to the voices of their neighbors in Canaan. God had brought Israel into the Promised Land, but they had allowed the Canaanites to influence them and draw them away from their Savior.

God does not force us to be obedient. He invites us to join with Him in covenant, and He gives us His Word. However, He allows us the freedom to rebel against Him. The choice is ours: we can heed the voice of God, or we can listen to the voice of the crowds and compromise with the world around us.

• Do you think the Lord would make this statement to our nation today? Why or why not?

"God, having placed good and evil in our power, has given us full freedom of choice; He does not keep back the unwilling, but embraces the willing."—John Chrysostom

B. The Opportunity for Restoration (2:21—3:4)

(Judges 3:1-4 is not included in the printed text.)

[21]I also will not henceforth drive out any from before them of the nations which Joshua left when he died: [22]That through them I may prove Israel, whether they will keep the way of the Lord to walk therein, as their fathers did keep it, or not. [23]Therefore the Lord left those nations,

without driving them out hastily; neither delivered he them into the hand of Joshua.

Although the Lord is very angry with Israel because of their disobedience and unfaithfulness, His steadfast devotion to His people causes Him to provide opportunities for restoration. The Lord disciplines those whom He loves, and in the case of Israel, their discipline involves the nations that surround them.

When God gave the Promised Land to Israel, He commanded that they drive out the Canaanites, Perizzites, Hittites, Amorites, Jebusites, and every other nation that inhabited Canaan. Under the leadership of Joshua, Israel had driven out most of them. Israel's disobedience, however, caused God to leave remnants of those nations which would serve as a test for Israel in the future. First, Israel would be tested in their determination to continue conquering the people that remained in Canaan. The new generations must learn how to fight against the enemy (3:2). Second, Israel would be tested in their devotion to the Lord as the only true God. Essentially, the presence of the Canaanites would test Israel's obedience to all of God's commands (v. 4).

We are like Israel. When God saved us, He did not take us out of the world. We are in the world, but we are not of the world (John 17:15-16). While we are in the world, we are continually tested and tried. However, God does not test us in order to harm us; rather, the tests are meant to produce in us faith and endurance (James 1:3; 1 Peter 1:7). Like the Israelites, we must put on the armor of God (Eph. 6:10-18) and fight against the Enemy. Even the Son of God "learned . . . obedience by the things which he suffered" (Heb. 5:8).

• What would the Lord no longer do, and why not?

> "Obedience is the only reality. It is faith visible, faith acting, and faith manifest. It is the test of real discipleship among the Lord's people."—R. C. Ryle

---

CONCLUSION

Just as Israel's salvation from Egypt was not the end of their battles, so our salvation from sin is not the end of our struggles. When we fall down before the Cross and confess our sins, we are reconciled to God, and we enter into the new covenant. That moment is our new birth, our new beginning of life in covenant with God.

However, we will always be tempted to settle down and accommodate ourselves to the world. We will always be tempted to rest in the victories of the past, forgetting that a new generation of Christians needs our witness, our teaching, and our example. The power of the blood of Jesus and the glory of Pentecost must be passed on to new believers in order for the world to be saved. We must never let it be said that a new generation arose who did not know the Lord nor the works that He has done for us.

Discipleship is vital, and the faith of the next generation is in our hands.

GOLDEN TEXT CHALLENGE

"THERE AROSE ANOTHER GENERATION AFTER THEM, WHICH KNEW NOT THE LORD, NOR YET THE WORKS WHICH HE HAD DONE FOR ISRAEL" (Judg. 2:10).

Tragically, after Joshua's generation passed on, their walk with God and their teachings about God were buried with them. Matthew Henry wrote: "There arose another generation of Israelites who had so little sense of religion, and were in so little care about it . . . one might truly say that they knew not the Lord, knew Him not aright, knew Him not as He had revealed Himself, else they would not have forsaken Him.

"They were so entirely devoted to the world, so intent upon the business of it or so indulgent of the flesh in ease and luxury, that they never minded the true God and His holy religion, and so were easily drawn aside to false gods and their abominable superstitions."

In many Christian families and churches, the same tragedy is taking place today—the young generation is rejecting God to embrace false gods. We as Christian leaders, parents, and grandparents must intentionally, deliberately, and prayerfully do all we can, through the anointing God gives us, to help the next generation embrace Christ and Christianity.

Daily Devotions:

M. A Father's Failure • 1 Samuel 3:10-18
T. A Father's Intercession • Job 1:1-5
W. The Generation to Come • Psalm 78:1-7
T. A New Example • Acts 16:27-34
F. A Godly Home • Ephesians 6:1-4
S. Duty to the Family • 1 Timothy 3:1-5

The First Judges (Othniel, Ehud, Deborah)

Judges 3:5—5:7

Unit Theme:
The Era of the Judges

Central Truth:
The Lord responds to His people's cry for deliverance.

Focus:
Acknowledge that God can raise up deliverers and ask Him to do so today.

Context:
Over a period of 200 years, God raises up Othniel, Ehud, and Deborah as deliverers.

Golden Text:
"When the children of Israel cried unto the Lord, the Lord raised up a deliverer to the children of Israel, who delivered them" (Judg. 3:9).

Study Outline:
I. **Othniel, Spirit-Empowered Warrior** (Judg. 3:5-11)
II. **Ehud, a Left-Handed Champion** (Judg. 3:12-30)
III. **Deborah, a Fearless Leader** (Judg. 4:1-14, 21-24; 5:1-7)

INTRODUCTION

The Church is facing unprecedented spiritual conflict, wrestling against "the spiritual forces of evil in the heavenly realms" (Eph. 6:12 NIV). Jesus, however, is our captain, and He has declared the Church will not be defeated (Matt. 16:18). The Church will triumph because "the weapons we fight with . . . have divine power" (2 Cor. 10:4 NIV) and the One who is in us is "greater than the one who is in the world" (1 John 4:4 NIV). God is calling His people to rise up in the power of the Spirit and proclaim the victory of the Kingdom, setting the captives free, opening the eyes of the blind, and giving liberty to those who are oppressed by Satan (Luke 4:18).

Our challenges today are similar to those encountered by Israelites when they first came into the Promised Land. When Joshua led the Israelites into Canaan, they won the battle of Jericho and defeated the major forces of the Canaanites. After Joshua's death, however, the Israelites began to assimilate to the culture that surrounded them. They lived among the Canaanites, intermarried with them, and served the gods of the Canaanites (Judg. 3:5-6). Although they had been saved from the bondage of Egypt, they continued to be surrounded by enemies who distracted them from their worship of Jehovah God.

However, the Book of Judges offers good news. Whenever God's people came under the attack of the enemy, God raised up Spirit-empowered leaders to bring deliverance. In this lesson, we will examine the ministries of Othniel, Ehud, and Deborah to discover how their stories might speak to our situations of spiritual conflict.

We will learn that God can use all kinds of people from various and diverse backgrounds. Othniel was an experienced soldier and leader, Ehud was a farmer, and Deborah was a prophetess. Despite their individual differences and qualifications, God uses each of them to bring salvation to Israel. Unlike us, God does not have a preconceived notion of the perfect leader, because He knows every person has flaws. God is able to form and shape imperfect people into effective leaders.

I. OTHNIEL, SPIRIT-EMPOWERED WARRIOR (Judg. 3:5-11)

A. Forgetting the Lord (vv. 5-7)

(Judges 3:5-6 is not included in the printed text.)

⁷And the children of Israel did evil in the sight of the Lord, and forgat the Lord their God, and served Baalim and the groves.

Othniel is the first of twelve judges mentioned in the Book of Judges. His story begins after the Israelites find themselves in bondage to the Canaanites. Their bondage was a direct result of their spiritual decline that took them out of God's favor.

Israel's spiritual decline happened in three stages.

1. *Careless Accommodation.* The loss of spiritual commitment began with the acceptance of evil in their midst. "The sons of Israel lived among the Canaanites, the Hittites, the Amorites, the Perizzites, the Hivites, and the Jebusites" (v. 5 NASB). Israel had been told to drive out the inhabitants and tear down their idolatrous altars, but they did not obey the Lord. Instead of driving out the inhabitants, Israel accepted them as neighbors and friends.

2. *Irresponsible Alliances.* Their loss of spiritual commitment to God became more severe when they intermarried with the enemy. "They took their daughters for themselves as wives, and gave their own daughters to their sons" (v. 6 NASB).

3. *Reckless Embrace of Idolatry.* Israel's loss of spiritual commitment culminated when they worshiped with the Canaanites and "served their gods" (v. 6). God had called Israel to be His holy people who were devoted only to Him, but they allowed the culture and society around them to destroy their relationship with God.

Israel's idolatry was centered on the Canaanite gods *Baal* and *Ashtaroth* (v. 7). As we learned in the previous lesson, Baal was a storm and warrior god, and Ashtaroth was his wife. Ashtaroth is referred to in the King James Version as "the groves" because she was worshiped in the form of carved tree trunks or poles that were placed around an altar.

---

1. Describe the Israelites' connection with the peoples around them (vv. 5-6).

2. Describe Israel's relationship with the Lord (v. 7).

> "To have a faith, therefore, or a trust in anything, where God hath not promised, is plain idolatry, and a worshipping of thine own imagination instead of God."—William Tyndale

---

B. Calling to God for Help (vv. 8-9)

(Judges 3:8 is not included in the printed text.)

⁹And when the children of Israel cried unto the Lord, the Lord raised up a deliverer to the children of Israel, who delivered them, even Othniel the son of Kenaz, Caleb's younger brother.

The idolatry of Israel provoked God's anger and caused Him to punish them by turning them over to the king of Mesopotamia, *Cushan-rishathaim* (*KU-shan-rish-a-THAY-im*), whose name means "twice-wicked Cushan." Israel suffered oppression at his hand for eight years. The fact that Israel is said to have "served" Cushan-rishathaim (v. 8) teaches us that unfaithfulness to God leads to bondage.

The word translated as *served* is the same Hebrew word that represents Israel's bondage in Egypt (Ex. 1:13-14). Also, the word *cried* expresses their prayers in both situations (Judg. 3:9; Ex. 2:23). In Judges, just as in Exodus, the Israelites cry out in the midst of their suffering and the Lord hears their cries. He responds with compassion and raises up a savior who delivers them.

The pattern of deliverance in Judges teaches us we should not underestimate the power of prayer. When the Israelites call out to God, He comes to their rescue. Similarly, if we will cry out to God, He will hear us and meet our needs (Matt. 7:7; Luke 18:7; Rom. 8:15; Phil. 4:6). Encouraging us to pray, the apostle James advises that we "have not" because we "ask not" (4:2).

Sometimes, God chooses to use people who already have extensive experience. Othniel, for example, is a trained soldier who has already won victories against the Canaanites (Judg. 1:12-13). He is the nephew of Caleb, and he had defeated the town of Kiriath-sepher and achieved notoriety as a local leader. Once the Lord determines to save Israel from the Canaanites, He chooses Othniel as the first of the judges. Othniel's anointing propels him beyond the level of local leader to the status of national deliverer. The first judge, therefore, is a person who is recognized as a local leader but is subsequently authorized and empowered by the Spirit of the Lord to enter a larger arena of influence.

• How did God punish Israel, and how did He help them?

> "The great thing in prayer is to feel that we are putting our supplications into the bosom of omnipotent love."—Andrew Murray

C. Experiencing Liberty (vv. 10-11)

¹⁰And the Spirit of the Lord came upon him, and he judged Israel, and went out to war: and the Lord delivered Chushanrishathaim king of Mesopotamia into his hand; and his hand prevailed against Chushanrishathaim. ¹¹And the land had rest forty years. And Othniel the son of Kenaz died.

These judges, raised up by the Lord, are not members of a hereditary line of leaders; their authority derives from the charismatic endowment of the Spirit. Also, Othniel does not seek the position of judge nor does he, in any way, control the working of the Spirit. It is the Lord who takes the initiative to "raise up" Othniel (v. 9), and it is the Spirit of the Lord who moves upon him (v. 10). Only after the Lord chooses Othniel and the Spirit of the Lord comes upon him does Othniel take action to judge Israel and go to war.

The anointing of the Holy Spirit is the necessary prerequisite for a position of leadership over God's people. For example, the Spirit anointed Joseph (Gen. 41:38; 50:20). The Spirit was upon Moses and was given to seventy elders who prophesied and then served as assistants to Moses (Num. 11:17-29). Joshua was chosen to be Moses' successor because the Spirit was "in" him (27:18), and when Moses laid his hands upon Joshua he was "filled" with the Spirit (Deut. 34:9). The coming of the Spirit upon Othniel places him in the company of these previous mighty leaders who were endowed with the Spirit. Like the earlier leaders, Othniel does not receive the Spirit for the sake of his own enjoyment or fulfillment, but for the sake of the people of God. The Spirit is given as the anointing for leadership, marking Othniel as God's chosen vessel.

• Describe and explain Othniel's success.

"It is the signature of the Holy Ghost upon our work and witness that makes all the difference."—Duncan Campbell

---

II. EHUD, A LEFT-HANDED CHAMPION (Judg. 3:12-30)

A. An Ongoing Need for Deliverance (vv. 12-14)

(Judges 3:13-14 is not included in the printed text.)

¹²And the children of Israel did evil again in the sight of the Lord: and the Lord strengthened Eglon the king of Moab against Israel, because they had done evil in the sight of the Lord.

The cycle of rebellion begins again. The Israelites disregard the Lord's commandments and do "evil" in His sight. The evil activity referred to here and throughout the Book of Judges is *idolatry*, "the worship of pagan gods." God demands that His people worship Him only.

Because of Israel's sin, the Lord once again turns them over to their enemy for punishment. This time the enemy is Eglon, king of Moab. The Moabites were descended from Lot (Gen. 19:37) and were a long-time enemy of Israel (see Num. 21—23), whose territory bordered Israel on the eastern side of the Dead Sea in what is now Jordan.

In Judges 3:13, Eglon formed a coalition with the Ammonites and the Amalekites, and they attacked Israel and conquered the "City of Palms" (another name for Jericho). Therefore, the sin of Israel caused them to lose control of territory they had conquered earlier. Instead of moving forward in fulfilling the promises of God, the Israelites were moving backward. Eglon's oppression of Israel lasted eighteen years (ten years longer than in the previous cycle).

- Describe the significance of the verbs *strengthened* (v. 12), *gathered* (v. 13), and *served* (v. 14).

> "Those that disobey the commandments of God do so foolishly for themselves. Sin is folly, and sinners are the greatest fools."
> —Matthew Henry

B. An Unlikely Deliverer (vv. 15-27)

(Judges 3:16-27 is not included in the printed text.)

¹⁵But when the children of Israel cried unto the Lord, the Lord raised them up a deliverer, Ehud the son of Gera, a Benjamite, a man lefthanded: and by him the children of Israel sent a present unto Eglon the king of Moab.

The Israelites could not break free from the tyrannical grip of Eglon, so they again "cried unto the Lord" (v. 15). The compassion of God moved Him to raise up a deliverer who would lead Israel out of bondage. The first of the judges, Othniel, had possessed all of the qualities we might expect in a leader. Ehud, however, was a farmer with no military experience and no weapons. Furthermore, he was "lefthanded." The original Hebrew text says he was "impaired in his right hand," a statement that may imply disability, or at the least it makes him abnormal. As a little boy, Ehud would have been considered an oddball. Even in modern times, lefthanded people have been mistreated and forced to use their right hands. Ehud's abnormality, along with his inexperience in warfare, made him an unlikely candidate to lead Israel against Moab.

However, when Ehud saw his family and his community suffering at the hands of an evil tyrant, he decided to do something about it. He may not have had training, and he may not have had weapons, but he had ingenuity. With that ingenuity, he came up with a cunning plan. Ehud made himself a dagger about eighteen inches long, and he hid the dagger under his robe on his right thigh (v. 16). He also made arrangements to deliver to Eglon the tribute money that was due from Israel (v. 17).

When Ehud was admitted into King Eglon's presence, he said he had a secret message for the king (v. 19). Therefore, Ehud asked to be left alone with the king. As he approached King Eglon, Ehud reached for his dagger with his left hand. The king did not suspect an attack, because Ehud's right hand was empty, and the right hand would be the normal means of grasping a weapon. Suddenly, Ehud stabbed and killed the evil king (v. 21). Ehud then escaped unseen, returned to his people, and blew the trumpet of war (v. 27).

Ehud risked his own life when he dared to attack King Eglon. He was willing to surrender himself to God, even when striving against overwhelming opposition. Ehud responded in obedience to God's call; and with God's promise as his only assurance, he placed himself at risk to deliver Israel. Therefore, Ehud's story compels us to participate enthusiastically and sacrificially in God's work of salvation.

---

1. How did Ehud arrange a private meeting with Moab's king (vv. 15-20)?
2. How did Ehud rally Israel's troops (v. 27)?

Unlikely Heroes

When the Jews came under attack in Nazi Germany, they expected the policy of discrimination would be overturned by government officials, religious authorities, and business leaders. However, no help came from those quarters. Instead, the Jews were aided by people like Corrie ten Boom and her family. Corrie's family were Christians who, at the risk of their own lives, helped many Jews escape the Holocaust.

C. Victory Through Unified Effort (vv. 28-30)

28 And he said unto them, Follow after me: for the Lord hath delivered your enemies the Moabites into your hand. And they went down after him, and took the fords of Jordan toward Moab, and suffered not a man to pass over. 29 And they slew of Moab at that time about ten thousand men, all lusty, and all men of valour; and there escaped not a man. 30 So Moab was subdued that day under the hand of Israel. And the land had rest fourscore years.

Ehud's personal victory over King Eglon proved to Israel that God was at work to deliver them, but it was only the beginning of the deliverance. Ehud called on the people to follow him into battle against Moab's army, and Israel defeated all of Moab's best soldiers, who were "stout men of valor" (v. 29 NKJV). Ehud's victory brought eighty years of peace to Israel.

The mission of the judges is not far from that of Jesus the Messiah, who declared, "The Spirit of the Lord is upon Me, because He has anointed Me to preach the gospel to the poor; He has sent Me to heal the brokenhearted, to proclaim liberty to the captives and recovery of sight to the blind, to set at liberty those who are oppressed" (Luke 4:18 NKJV).

It is not that we have lost our will to fight but that, in too many cases, we fight among ourselves rather than fighting the Enemy. We fight over church politics, budgets, recognition, church programs, denominational pride, music styles, and so on. If our energy is expended by internal strife, we will have no strength to fight for those in bondage. We should be fighting to save the alcoholic, the drug addict, the prostitute, and the pornographer. We should be fighting in prayer for the laid-off worker, the abandoned child, the widow, and the single mother struggling to survive.

- Describe Ehud's confidence in the Lord (v. 28), and the result (vv. 29-30).

> "The first step on the way to victory is to recognize the enemy."
> —Corrie ten Boom

III. DEBORAH, A FEARLESS LEADER (Judg. 4:1-14, 21-24; 5:1-7)

A. The Woman Judge (4:1-5)

(Judges 4:3, 5 is not included in the printed text.)

¹And the children of Israel again did evil in the sight of the Lord, when Ehud was dead. ²And the Lord sold them into the hand of Jabin king of Canaan, that reigned in Hazor; the captain of whose host was Sisera, which dwelt in Harosheth of the Gentiles.

⁴And Deborah, a prophetess, the wife of Lapidoth, she judged Israel at that time.

Israel's backsliding produced a repeat of the previous cycle of rebellion and punishment. This time, Israel was oppressed for twenty years by Canaanite king Jabin of Hazor, a northern city Joshua had conquered many years earlier (Josh.11:10-11). The people of Hazor were able to rebuild their city and regain their strength because Israel had failed to drive them out completely (see Judg. 1:33, 35). The captain of Jabin's army was Sisera, who lived in Harosheth of the Gentiles, another northern city. The Israelites were oppressed terribly and lived in fear of Sisera's army because he had nine hundred chariots of iron.

Out of the midst of their suffering, the Israelites cried out to God (4:3); and in His compassion, God raised up another deliverer. This time, God chose a woman. Deborah (whose name means "bee") is introduced as a prophetess who was already "judging Israel" in Ephraim (vv. 4-5 NKJV). As a judge, the people came to her for justice, and as a prophetess, she spoke for Yahweh. It is significant that a woman was filling these roles that were traditionally assigned to men. Ironically, after Moses' words in Deuteronomy 18:15, "The Lord your God will raise up for you a prophet like me from among your own brothers" (NIV), the first person who is called a prophet is not a "brother" but a "sister."

---

1. When did Israel backslide again, and why (v. 1)?
2. What finally motivated Israel to cry out to God (vv. 2-3)?

3. Describe Deborah (vv. 4-5).

> "All places where women are excluded tend downward to barbarism; but the moment she is introduced, there come in with her courtesy, cleanliness, sobriety, and order."—Harriet Beecher Stowe

---

B. The Wavering General (vv. 6-10)

(Judges 4:6-8, 10 is not included in the printed text.)

⁹And she said, I will surely go with thee: notwithstanding the journey that thou takest shall not be for thine honour; for the Lord shall sell Sisera into the hand of a woman. And Deborah arose, and went with Barak to Kedesh.

Deborah's first authoritative act is to summon Barak, and by the word of the Lord she commissions him to lead the Israelite army and to attack King Jabin (vv. 6-7). She specifies the location where Barak is to encamp, the number of soldiers that he is to recruit, the names of the tribes who will be involved, the name of the enemy general, and the exact location of the battle. Speaking as the messenger of Lord, she assures Barak of victory, declaring, "I [God] will deliver him into your hand" (v. 7 NKJV).

There is no indication that Barak questions Deborah's credentials or that he is disturbed by her gender; nevertheless, his response is less than enthusiastic. He requires that Deborah accompany him to the battle (v. 8), and because of his demand that she be physically present, he is deprived of the glory (v. 9). Consequently, Deborah proclaims the glory of victory will go to a woman. Verse 10 records that Barak "went up with ten thousand men under his command, and Deborah went up with him" (NKJV).

---

1. Describe Deborah's prophetic word to Barak (vv. 6-7).
2. Describe Barak's reluctance (v. 8).
3. How did Deborah say this situation would turn out (v. 9)?

> "God is looking for imperfect men and women who have learned to walk in moment-by-moment dependence on the Holy Spirit. Christians who have come to terms with their inadequacies, fears, and failures. Believers who have become discontent with 'surviving' and have taken the time to investigate everything God has to offer in this life."—Charles Stanley

---

C. The Winning Combination (vv. 11-14, 21-24)

(Judges 4:11-13, 21-22 is not included in the printed text.)

¹⁴And Deborah said unto Barak, Up; for this is the day in which the Lord hath delivered Sisera into thine hand: is not the Lord gone out

before thee? So Barak went down from mount Tabor, and ten thousand men after him.

23 So God subdued on that day Jabin the king of Canaan before the children of Israel. 24 And the hand of the children of Israel prospered, and prevailed against Jabin the king of Canaan, until they had destroyed Jabin king of Canaan.

As soon as the Israelites encamp near Kedesh, they are betrayed by Heber the Kenite, who is a descendant of Moses' father-in-law. Therefore, Sisera assembles his army and prepares to engage in battle against Barak's forces. Deborah responds by commanding Barak, "Arise! For this is the day in which the Lord has given Sisera into your hands; behold, the Lord has gone out before you" (v. 14 NASB). In addition to Deborah's first prophetic word that served as the initial command to Barak, this second word specifies the exact timing for Barak's attack on the enemy. Deborah's words sound much like those of Moses, who had promised the Israelites, "The Lord himself goes before you and will be with you" (Deut. 31:8 NIV). Like Moses, she speaks with no hint of uncertainty, providing Barak with the assurance he needs to initiate the battle.

Why Deborah does not lead the army is left unstated, but perhaps it has something to do with her role as prophetess. Deborah's activity seems to parallel that of Moses when the Amalekites attacked Israel in the wilderness (Ex. 17:8-13). Just as Deborah directed Barak to engage in battle, Moses directed Joshua, who served as commander of the army in the wilderness. Similarly to Deborah, Moses issued the initial command, and he accompanied Joshua to the battle zone, but he did not participate in the battle nor issue orders regarding the conduct of battle.

The prophecies of Deborah are fulfilled when the Israelites win the battle, and the glory of killing Sisera goes to Jael, a woman who drives a tent peg through the head of the unsuspecting general (Judg. 4:21-22). Verse 24 indicates this "great victory was the beginning of a successful resistance to Jabin, by which the Israelites recovered their independence, and finally broke the Canaanite power. Accordingly, we hear no more of Canaanite domination in the Book of Judges" (*Barnes' Notes on the Whole Bible*).

---

1. Explain Deborah's confident order (v. 14).
2. Explain the use of the phrase "heavier and heavier" (v. 24 NASB).

> "No doubt [women of faith in the past] were reproached for His name's sake, and accounted mad women; but they had a faith which enabled them at that time to overcome the world, and by which they climbed up to heaven."—George Whitefield

---

D. The Worshiping Congregation (5:1-7)
   (Judges 5:3-7 is not included in the printed text.)

---

¹Then sang Deborah and Barak the son of Abinoam on that day, saying, ²Praise ye the Lord for the avenging of Israel, when the people willingly offered themselves.

Just as Israel's deliverance from Egypt was followed by a song of thanksgiving (Ex. 15), this battle is followed by a victory song. In light of the connections between prophecy and song (1 Sam. 10:5; 18:10; 1 Chron. 25), we might classify Deborah's song as prophetic praise. It is appropriate and important that God's people take the time to rejoice in their victories and to recognize the work of God in their midst. Whenever God intervenes to bring an answer to prayer, the meaning and significance of the event is not complete until we have offered our praises to God for His mighty works.

The Song of Deborah (Judg. 5) focuses on several important elements of the battle. First, it glorifies the Lord and gives Him full credit for the victory. Second, it acknowledges the willingness of the Israelites to risk their lives as they enter into the battle. Third, it celebrates the key roles played by Deborah, Barak, and Jael. Fourth, the song criticizes the Israelite tribes who refused to fight. Fifth, it ridicules Sisera, his army, and his people. Finally, the Song of Deborah concludes with words of hope and promise: "Thus let all Your enemies perish, O Lord! But let those who love Him be like the sun when it comes out in full strength" (v. 31 NKJV).

---

1. What does God expect from leaders (Judg. 5:2, 7)?
2. What does God expect from all of His followers (comp. v. 2 with Rom. 12:1).
3. What does Judges 5:3-5 declare about God?

"God is pleased with no music below so much as with the thanksgiving songs of relieved widows and supported orphans; of rejoicing, comforted, and thankful persons."—Jeremy Taylor

---

CONCLUSION

The Lord brought Israel out of Egypt and gave them liberty, but their liberty was forfeited when they rebelled against the Lord. The church is in a similar situation. We have liberty, but we could lose it; we are redeemed but still at risk; we have been brought out of bondage, but we continue to battle temptation. We may be Christians, but still our enemy pursues after us "like a roaring lion, seeking whom he may devour" (1 Peter 5:8 NKJV). He seeks to "steal, and to kill, and to destroy" (John 10:10) by enticing us to return to a deadly lifestyle of sin. The power of sin is not always obvious. We may be overcome by secret sinful thoughts and pursuits, such as Internet pornography, which has become a serious problem in today's church.

It is important that we acknowledge our weakness—we cannot save ourselves. Nevertheless, if we will call out to God, He will come to our rescue and deliver us from the power of sin and Satan.

Furthermore, many of us have friends and loved ones who are in bondage—children on drugs, parents who are alcoholics, sisters who are abused, brothers who are bound by sin. However, the gospel of Jesus Christ is the "power of God that brings salvation" (Rom. 1:16 NIV). Just as God saved Israel from the bondage of her enemies, so also God can save our friends and loved ones from the bondage of sin.

GOLDEN TEXT CHALLENGE

"WHEN THE CHILDREN OF ISRAEL CRIED UNTO THE LORD, THE LORD RAISED UP A DELIVERER TO THE CHILDREN OF ISRAEL, WHO DELIVERED THEM" (Judg. 3:9).

"The children of Israel cried unto the Lord" is a recurring expression throughout Judges (3:9, 15; 4:3; 6:7; 10:10, 12). To *cry out* here means to call on the Lord in repentance. The Lord is great in His mercy to hear us when we call on His name and repent of our sins. God is our Father in heaven and we are His children. He loves us and wants to take care of us. James tells us, "Every good and perfect gift comes from above, . . . from the Father of lights" (see. 1:17). Prayer begins by understanding that God is our loving Father and we are His children.

Daily Devotions:

M. The Ultimate Deliverer • 2 Samuel 22:1-7
T. Prayer for Deliverance • 1 Kings 8:46-53
W. Deliverance Through Hezekiah • 2 Chronicles 32:14-23
T. Delivered for a Purpose • Acts 26:15-23
F. Certain of Deliverance • Philippians 1:19-26
S. Deliverance for the Tested • 2 Peter 2:4-9

Gideon, an Unlikely Hero

Judges 6:11—7:25

Unit Theme:

The Era of the Judges

Central Truth:

God often calls the unlikely to do the unexpected.

Focus:

Study how God used Gideon and yield to God's call.

Context:

Gideon delivers Israel from Midianite oppression around 1160 B.C.

Golden Text:

"The angel of the Lord . . . said unto him, The Lord is with thee, thou mighty man of valour" (Judg. 6:12).

Study Outline:

  I. **God Calls Gideon** (Judg. 6:11-16, 25-27)

 II. **Gideon's Three Hundred Men** (Judg. 6:33-35; 7:1-9)

III. **Gideon's Triumph** (Judg. 7:12-15, 19-25)

INTRODUCTION

Researchers say 20 percent of church members do 80 percent of the work, which means most members never get involved in meaningful service to the Lord. We should ask ourselves why so many Christians simply sit on the pew. Why is it so hard to recruit workers? Why can't churches find teachers for Sunday school and other classes? Why do ministries of outreach, evangelism, and community involvement continue to suffer from lack of volunteers? While multiple answers to these questions might be offered, one crucial cause is Christians feeling they are neither qualified nor able to do effective ministry. When presented with the opportunity to get involved, they respond, "Who, me? I'm not a minister. . . . I'm not gifted in that area. . . . I don't have enough education. . . . I can't do it." Most people do not get involved because they feel inadequate for the task.

In this lesson we will learn that God often calls the unlikely to do the unexpected. God calls those who feel inadequate, and empowers them with His Holy Spirit. God calls and then He equips. Our willingness to serve is much more important to God than our qualifications. We are reminded of what the people of Jerusalem said about Jesus' apostles: "When they saw the courage of Peter and John and realized that they were unschooled, ordinary men, they were astonished and they took note that these men had been with Jesus" (Acts 4:13 NIV).

The apostles were "ordinary men," and so was Gideon. Like the disciples of Jesus, Gideon had no experience in leadership or ministry. He was just a farmer who tried to take care of his family, but God called him to lead Israel and to bring about deliverance from the oppression of the enemy. However, Gideon lacked confidence. He was discouraged and afraid, unsure of himself and his calling, and unsure of God's plan. Despite Gideon's weakness and insecurities, he was transformed by God into a mighty warrior. The church needs people like Gideon—ordinary people who will surrender to God, put on the whole armor of God, and withstand the attack of Satan (Eph. 6:10-18).

I. GOD CALLS GIDEON (Judg. 6:11-16, 25-27)

Once again, the Israelites commit idolatry and forsake the Lord (v. 1). The Lord then gives them into the hand of the Midianites and Amalekites, who, for seven years, rob the Israelites of their crops and livestock, leaving the land impoverished and the people helpless. The Midianites were descendants of Abraham, who lived as nomads in the desert regions southeast of Israel. The father-in-law of Moses was a Midianite priest (Ex. 2:16—3:1; 18:1-12). The Amalekites were descendants of Esau, who had been enemies of Israel from the time Israel came out of Egypt (17:8-10).

Israel's suffering under the Midianites is more severe than in earlier cycles, indicating things are growing worse. In fact, times are so hard that the Israelites resort to hiding in the hills and caves as protection from the invading enemy (Judg. 6:2). Furthermore, the Midianites destroy all of Israel's crops and livestock (vv. 3-4) and encamp on Israelite land in massive numbers: "like locusts for number, both they and their camels were innumerable, and they came into the land to devastate it" (v. 5 NASB). The Midianites are not content to rule or rob the Israelites. They are intent on rendering the land uninhabitable for the Israelites, thus displacing them entirely. The intense suffering of the Israelites causes them to cry out to God for help (vv. 6-7).

A. Providing for His People (v. 11)

11And there came an angel of the Lord, and sat under an oak which was in Ophrah, that pertained unto Joash the Abiezrite: and his son Gideon threshed wheat by the winepress, to hide it from the Midianites.

The cries of Israel reach God's ears, and He sends His angel to recruit a new leader who will save Israel from oppression. This new leader is Gideon. In the earlier stories in Judges, we did not learn exactly how God called them; we read only that "the Lord raised up judges" (2:16, 18). Here, however, we are told that God sent His angel to notify Gideon of his calling. The "angel of the Lord" is what theologians call a *theophany*—a personal appearance of God (see also 2:1; 13:3). The angel comes and sits under an oak tree on the property of Joash, the father of Gideon. His appearance in such a casual manner is perhaps a precaution intended to prevent Gideon from being afraid. After all, the Midianites have so terrified Gideon that he fearfully threshes his grain in his winepress so he will not be discovered and robbed.

However, we should not be too quick to criticize Gideon for his fear. Even though he is afraid, he risks his life to provide for his family. While other people are running away and hiding in caves, Gideon is working to put food on the table.

- What does this scripture reveal about Gideon?

> "Social responsibility becomes an aspect not of Christian mission only, but also of Christian conversion. It is impossible to be truly converted to God without being thereby converted to our neighbor."
> —John Stott

B. Unaware of God's Concern (vv. 12-13)

¹²And the angel of the Lord appeared unto him, and said unto him, The Lord is with thee, thou mighty man of valour. ¹³And Gideon said unto him, Oh my Lord, if the Lord be with us, why then is all this befallen us? and where be all his miracles which our fathers told us of, saying, Did not the Lord bring us up from Egypt? but now the Lord hath forsaken us, and delivered us into the hands of the Midianites.

There at the winepress, the angel of the Lord confronts Gideon with a surprising declaration: "The Lord is with you, mighty warrior" (v. 12 NIV). The angel's words are surprising for two reasons. First, Gideon has no previous experience as a warrior or as a leader; he is only a farmer, and not a valiant one. Second, Gideon doubts the Lord is "with" Israel at this point in time. Therefore, he asks, "If the Lord is with us, why has all this happened to us?" (v. 13 NIV). He reminds the angel that, although the Lord delivered Israel from Egypt, He has now "forsaken" them and turned them over to the Midianites. In the midst of oppression and widespread suffering, Gideon asks, "Where are all His miracles which our fathers told us about?" (v. 13 NASB).

However, God is already at work, even though Gideon does not know it. The Lord appears to Gideon precisely because He has heard Israel's cries and He has called Gideon to save them from the Midianites.

Gideon's response to the angel reveals that he unjustly blames God for his people's distressing circumstances, when it is Israel who had forsaken God (v. 1). Moreover, we learn later (v. 25) that Gideon's father owns an altar dedicated to the worship of Baal.

- Describe Gideon's complaint.

> "If you don't do your part, don't blame God."—Billy Sunday

C. Questioning His Potential (vv. 14-15)

¹⁴And the Lord looked upon him, and said, Go in this thy might, and thou shalt save Israel from the hand of the Midianites: have not I sent thee? ¹⁵And he said unto him, Oh my Lord, wherewith shall I save Israel? behold, my family is poor in Manasseh, and I am the least in my father's house.

The Lord turns to face Gideon and says, "Go in the strength you have and save Israel out of Midian's hand. Am I not sending you?" (v. 14 NIV). The Lord's command to Gideon suggests three important facts about serving God. First, instead of complaining about what we lack, we must take courage and utilize whatever strength God has given us. Second, the Lord declares Gideon will "save Israel," which means the call of God is always larger than ourselves. Gideon's encounter with God is not for him alone, but for the benefit of the entire community. Third, the success of our endeavors rests on God sending us. We might be weak, and we might have flaws; but if God has sent us, He will prepare us to do the work.

Gideon, however, is not yet convinced. He asks, "How can I save Israel?" (v. 15 NIV). Gideon sees nothing about himself, his family, or his tribe of Manasseh that would qualify him to be a deliverer. Nevertheless, God has chosen Gideon and He promises to be with him.

---

1. What was God's solution?
2. Describe Gideon's excuses.

Ronnie and Justin

I went to school with Ronnie and Justin. Ronnie was full of potential. He made a near perfect score on his SAT and received a scholarship to a prestigious university. Unfortunately, he spent his first semester partying, so he flunked out of college. Justin seemed to have no potential. He smoked, drank, rebelled against authority, and was expelled from high school on several occasions. However, one night, Justin attended a Church of God revival service and gave his heart to the Lord. He was transformed by Christ, and today he is a medical doctor. In our weakness, Jesus can show His strength.

D. Terrified by God's Presence (v. 16)

¹⁶And the Lord said unto him, Surely I will be with thee, and thou shalt smite the Midianites as one man.

The Lord's promise to be "with" Gideon should not be taken lightly. With these same words, God called Moses to deliver Israel from the bondage of Egypt (Ex. 3:12). The presence of the Lord is a powerful assurance that the mission can be accomplished. Yet the Lord adds another word of encouragement. He says to Gideon, "You shall defeat Midian as one man" (Judg. 6:16 NASB). This promise indicates Gideon should not think of the Midianites in terms of an army—he should not dwell on their great numbers (v. 5). Instead, he should expect the entire army to fall like a single individual.

• Rephrase God's promise in simple words.

E. Fearful of His Family and Neighbors (vv. 25-27)

(Judges 6:25-26 is not included in the printed text.)

27 Then Gideon took ten men of his servants, and did as the Lord had said unto him: and so it was, because he feared his father's household, and the men of the city, that he could not do it by day, that he did it by night.

After God's reassuring Gideon of divine favor through a supernatural sign (vv. 17-23), "Gideon built an altar to the Lord there and called it The Lord is Peace" (v. 24 NIV). That night, the Lord commanded him to tear down his father's altar that was used in Baal worship and cut down the grove beside the altar. The word "grove" (v. 25) refers to an idolatrous pole dedicated to the worship of Asherah (also called Ashtaroth), wife of Baal. Gideon was also instructed to "build a proper kind of altar to the Lord" (v. 26 NIV) and offer a sacrifice to the Lord, using the wood from the Asherah pole as fuel for the fire.

Gideon does all the Lord commands him. However, despite all of the encouraging words from the Lord, Gideon is not confident enough to fulfill this assignment in the daytime. Instead, he goes out at night because he fears his father's household and the men of the city (v. 27).

Gideon's destruction of the altar of Baal is significant for various reasons. In the big picture, his act is an important step toward obeying the Lord's earlier commands to tear down all the idolatrous altars of the Canaanites (Ex. 34:13; Deut. 7:5; 12:3; Judg. 2:2). Sadly, by building altars to Baal, the elders of Israel had failed to live exemplary lives in front of the younger generation. Still today, children pay closer attention to our actions than to our words.

On a personal level, Gideon's obedience in performing this task is the first step of his transformation into a leader. His faithfulness in this relatively small matter indicates he can be entrusted with larger assignments in the future. Jesus said, "Whoever can be trusted with very little can also be trusted with much" (Luke 16:10 NIV).

Furthermore, Gideon's deed thrusts him into prominence. Whereas he was once an unimportant and unrecognized son of Joash, he now becomes a well-known figure in the community. His new stature ensures he will be taken seriously when he assumes his calling as the Lord's chosen deliverer.

1. How would Gideon make good use of an idol (vv. 25-26)?
2. How did fear influence Gideon's actions (v. 27)?

II. GIDEON'S THREE HUNDRED MEN (Judg. 6:33-35; 7:1-9)

A. The Spirit's Empowerment (6:33-35)

³³Then all the Midianites and the Amalekites and the children of the east were gathered together, and went over, and pitched in the valley of Jezreel. ³⁴But the Spirit of the Lord came upon Gideon, and he blew a trumpet; and Abiezer was gathered after him. ³⁵And he sent messengers throughout all Manasseh; who also was gathered after him: and he sent messengers unto Asher, and unto Zebulun, and unto Naphtali; and they came up to meet them.

Gideon and his community have little time to reflect on the events of the previous night because the enemy is close at hand. The Midianites assemble their army, cross the Jordan River, and camp in the Valley of Jezreel. Then, the Spirit of the Lord comes upon Gideon and he sounds the trumpet (v. 34). The English translation "came upon" does not fully capture the meaning of the original Hebrew text, which says the Spirit "clothed" Gideon. The imagery of clothing is significant. The basic functions of clothing are to conceal (Gen. 3:21), protect (Hag. 1:6), adorn (2 Sam. 1:24), and categorize the wearer within a social situation (Gen. 38:19). The Spirit of the Lord, as the clothing of Gideon, protects him, empowers him, and identifies him as the Lord's chosen judge who will lead the Israelites to deliverance.

The effect of the Spirit's clothing is obvious and immediate. Before the Spirit clothes him, Gideon works only under the cover of darkness (Judg. 6:27), but after the Spirit comes upon him, he becomes a public leader who emerges into the light of day. Before the Spirit strengthens Gideon, he stands by in silence while his father defends his actions (vv. 28-32); but after the Spirit comes upon him, Gideon speaks for himself. The Spirit empowers Gideon to sound the trumpet (shofar). In Biblical times, the trumpet was an alarm that signaled an eminent threat, which called for the assembling of an army. In Gideon's case, the army is gathered from his own family (Abiezer), his own tribe (Manasseh), and from the neighboring tribes of Asher, Zebulun, and Naphtali.

• What is the most important phrase in these three verses, and why?

"Many Christians estimate difficulty in the light of their own resources, and thus they attempt very little and they always fail. All giants have been weak men who did great things for God because they reckoned on His power and presence to be with them." —Hudson Taylor

---

B. Separation of Soldiers (7:1-9)

(Judges 7:1, 4-5, 8 is not included in the printed text.)

²And the Lord said unto Gideon, The people that are with thee are too many for me to give the Midianites into their hands, lest Israel vaunt

themselves against me, saying, Mine own hand hath saved me. ³Now therefore go to, proclaim in the ears of the people, saying, Whosoever is fearful and afraid, let him return and depart early from mount Gilead. And there returned of the people twenty and two thousand; and there remained ten thousand.

⁶And the number of them that lapped, putting their hand to their mouth, were three hundred men: but all the rest of the people bowed down upon their knees to drink water. ⁷And the Lord said unto Gideon, By the three hundred men that lapped will I save you, and deliver the Midianites into thine hand: and let all the other people go every man unto his place.

⁹And it came to pass the same night, that the Lord said unto him, Arise, get thee down unto the host; for I have delivered it into thine hand.

In verse 1, Gideon is called *Jerubbaal*, which means "the enemy of Baal." This had become his honorary name after he tore down the altar of Baal at Ophrah (6:32). Gideon and his army of thirty-two thousand men camped beside the "spring of Harod" (7:1 NIV), which in Hebrew means "fearful spring," another reference to the theme of fear that permeates the Gideon story. Gideon had been quite successful in his effort to build an army, and the Lord knew the Israelites would claim victory through their own strength. Therefore, in order for the Lord to receive credit for the victory, He decided to reduce Gideon's army of thirty-two thousand to a small force. There at the "Fearful Spring," the Lord gives instruction for any who are "afraid and trembling" (v. 3 NASB) to return home.

It is also at the "Fearful Spring" that the Lord tests Gideon's army the second time and chooses only the three hundred who lap water like a dog (vv. 3-7). The second test includes a play on words that recalls the memory of one of Israel's bravest warriors. The Hebrew word for *dog* is the same as the name *Caleb*; therefore, when the Lord says He will use those who lap water "as a dog" (v. 5), He might be understood to say "like Caleb."

Why might the Lord allude to Caleb? Because out of all their generation, only Caleb and Joshua had the courage to enter the Promised Land. Caleb was a man with "another spirit" (Num. 14:24) and "wholly followed the Lord" (Deut. 1:36). He scoffed at the giants of Canaan and said, "Give me this mountain" (Josh. 14:12). Caleb's nephew Othniel was a mighty warrior and was the first of the judges (Judg. 3:9). Finally, Jael, who killed the Canaanite general Sisera, was a relative of Caleb (4:21). Israel needs more men of faith like Caleb. Thus, the Lord promises to save Israel through three hundred men who are "like Caleb."

---

1. What did the Lord say about Gideon's troops, and why (v. 2)?
2. How does fear again play a role in Gideon's story (v. 3)?
3. What happened to 21,700 soldiers (vv. 7-8)?

"We have ample evidence that the Lord is able to guide. The promises cover every imaginable situation. All we need to do is to take the hand He stretches out."—Elisabeth Elliot

III. GIDEON'S TRIUMPH (Judg. 7:12-15, 19-25)

A. Victory Foretold in a Dream (vv.12-15)

(Judges 7:12, 15 is not included in the printed text.)

¹³And when Gideon was come, behold, there was a man that told a dream unto his fellow, and said, Behold, I dreamed a dream, and, lo, a cake of barley bread tumbled into the host of Midian, and came unto a tent, and smote it that it fell, and overturned it, that the tent lay along. ¹⁴And his fellow answered and said, This is nothing else save the sword of Gideon the son of Joash, a man of Israel: for into his hand hath God delivered Midian, and all the host.

Gideon and his three hundred men camp for the night, and the Lord instructs Gideon to go down to the camp of the Midianites where a surprise had been prepared for him. The Lord says, "Listen to what they are saying. Afterward, you will be encouraged to attack the camp" (v. 11 NIV). Therefore, Gideon sneaks into the enemy camp and overhears a Midianite soldier recounting a dream that symbolizes the Midianites' defeat at the hand of Gideon (vv. 13-14). When Gideon hears the account of the dream and its interpretation, he bows in worship. He then returns to the camp of Israel and says to his men, "Arise, for the Lord has given the camp of Midian into your hands" (v. 15 NASB). Gideon's worshipful response and confident declaration to his troops indicate he is finally convinced of the Lord's promise.

Because it is the Lord who directs Gideon to slip into the camp of Midian suggests the Lord is the source of the prophetic dream. Ironically, although Gideon did not believe the declarations of the angel of Yahweh (6:12-15), questioned the voice of God himself (v. 36), and asked for multiple signs of confirmation (vv. 17-18, 37-40), he finally believes the voice of the Lord speaking through an enemy soldier.

_____

1. How does verse 12 describe Israel's opponent?
2. Describe the Midianite soldier's dream (v. 13).
3. Describe Gideon's two responses to the dream's interpretation (v. 15).

"With the power of God within us, we need never fear the powers around us."—Woodrow Kroll

_____

B. Victory Achieved by a Miracle (vv.16-25)

(Judges 7:17-19, 22-25 is not included in the printed text.)

¹⁶And he divided the three hundred men into three companies, and he put a trumpet in every man's hand, with empty pitchers, and lamps within the pitchers.

²⁰And the three companies blew the trumpets, and brake the pitchers, and held the lamps in their left hands, and the trumpets in their right hands to blow withal: and they cried, The sword of the Lord, and of

Gideon. ²¹**And they stood every man in his place round about the camp: and all the host ran, and cried, and fled.**

Immediately, Gideon rallies his army and prepares for battle, and God gives Gideon a very unusual strategy. Gideon's forces, assembled outside the camp of the Midianites, are divided into three companies of one hundred each. Gideon "put trumpets and empty pitchers into the hands of all of them, with torches inside the pitchers" (v. 16 NASB). In unison, the three hundred men sound their trumpets and break the pitchers, which reveals the hidden torches. Along with the sound of the trumpets, they shout, "The sword of the Lord, and of Gideon" (v. 20).

The Midianites are suddenly awakened from their deep sleep by the sound of the trumpets and the shouting. When they look out into the darkness, they see hundreds of torches surrounding the camp. The Lord causes them to be so confused that they begin to kill each other. Gideon then calls for reinforcements, and he and his army pursue the Midianites and drive them back across the Jordan River (vv. 23-25).

---

1. Describe the unusual weapons of Gideon's army (vv. 16-17).
2. Explain the timing of Israel's attack (vv. 18-19).
3. How effective was Gideon's battle plan, and why (vv. 20-22)?

> "To me, it has been a source of great comfort and strength in the day of battle, just to remember that the secret of steadfastness, and indeed, of victory, is the recognition that 'the Lord is at hand.'"
> —Duncan Campbell

CONCLUSION

God called Gideon to save Israel from the Midianites, but Gideon did not feel qualified for the assignment. Gideon's calling brings to mind the admonition of the apostle Paul to the Corinthian church: "For you see your calling, brethren, that not many wise according to the flesh, not many mighty, not many noble, are called. But God has chosen the foolish things of the world to put to shame the wise, and God has chosen the weak things of the world to put to shame the things which are mighty; and the base things of the world and the things which are despised God has chosen, and the things which are not, to bring to nothing the things that are, that no flesh should glory in His presence" (1 Cor. 1:26-29 NKJV).

GOLDEN TEXT CHALLENGE

"THE ANGEL OF THE LORD . . . SAID UNTO HIM, THE LORD IS WITH THEE, THOU MIGHTY MAN OF VALOUR" (Judg. 6:12).

When the Lord called Gideon a "valiant warrior" (NASB), this was not based on anything this farmer had already done, but on what God planned to do through him. As He revealed to Abraham centuries earlier, God "gives life to the dead and calls those things which do not exist as though they did" (Rom. 4:17 NKJV).

God has the power and authority to shape and reshape us into whatever He wants us to become. Our responsibility is to respond to His voice in faith and obedience.

Daily Devotions:

M. Rahab's Courageous Act • Joshua 6:17-25
T. A Shepherd Boy's Anointing • 1 Samuel 16:6-13
W. A Slave's Witness • 2 Kings 5:1-5, 14-15
T. A Sudden Evangelist • Mark 5:15-20
F. A Boy's Obedience • John 6:5-13
S. "Profitable" Onesimus • Philemon 10-17

Abimelech's Rise and Fall

Unit Theme:

The Era of the Judges

Central Truth:

Because sin has dreadful consequences, we should always reject it.

Focus:

Consider the consequences of wickedness and turn away from sin.

Context:

The murderous son of Gideon reigned three years in Shechem.

Golden Text:

"His own iniquities shall take the wicked himself, and he shall be holden with the cords of his sins" (Prov. 5:22).

Study Outline:

I. **Abimelech Seizes Power** (Judg. 9:1-21)

II. **Rebellion Against Abimelech** (Judg. 9:22-25, 42-49)

III. **Abimelech Judged by God** (Judg. 9:50-57)

INTRODUCTION

The church is in a difficult position today regarding morality and ethics. Outside the church, the world resents the church's "imposing" of morals on everyone else. Even within the church, some people insist on setting their own standards of right and wrong. Consider two factors contributing to this troubling situation.

First, we are living in a time of moral relativism in which there are no absolute standards for morals and ethics. The authority of the Bible is not respected; therefore, people are willing to dispense with the Bible and choose instead to live according to their own ideas. As the writer of Judges puts it, "Everyone did what was right in his own eyes" (21:25 NASB).

Second, the sovereignty of God is disregarded, which leads to the belief that humans will not be held accountable for their actions. The Bible's declaration that "the wages of sin is death" (Rom. 6:23) is not popular these days. Many people are unwilling to face the fact that their actions, whether good or bad, are noticed by God and He is judging their actions in the present and, eventually, will repay them at the Final Judgment. The world forgets or disbelieves that sin has dreadful consequences. Sometimes even Christians forget this truth.

In this lesson, we will take a close look at Abimelech—a man who disregarded the commandments of God, disrespected his own family, and was destroyed in the end. Abimelech, who was a son of Gideon, murdered his seventy brothers (except for Jotham) and proclaimed himself king. He reigned for three years, and then the Lord caused division between Abimelech and the men of Shechem in order that both Abimelech and the men of Shechem might be judged for their evil deeds. A battle ensued and Abimelech was killed by a woman who dropped a millstone on his head as he and his army were attacking the tower of Thebez. The narrator adds a summary statement to the end of the story: "Thus God repaid the wickedness of Abimelech" (Judg. 9:56 NKJV). Through the story of Abimelech we learn God is capable of inflicting swift punishment on evildoers.

I. ABIMELECH SEIZES POWER (Judg. 9:1-21)

A. Abimelech's Desire for Power (vv.1-2)

¹And Abimelech the son of Jerubbaal went to Shechem unto his mother's brethren, and communed with them, and with all the family of the house of his mother's father, saying, ²Speak, I pray you, in the ears of all the men of Shechem, Whether is better for you, either that all the sons of Jerubbaal, which are threescore and ten persons, reign over you, or that one reign over you? remember also that I am your bone and your flesh.

In last week's lesson, we learned about Gideon's victory over the Midianites (6:33—8:28). After the Midianites were defeated, Israel had peace for forty years, during which time Gideon served as judge. His prosperity is indicated by the fact that he married many wives, who bore him seventy sons (8:30). Gideon also had a secondary wife (concubine) who bore a son named Abimelech. As the son of Gideon's secondary wife (who probably resided with her parents) in Shechem, Abimelech would have been shunned by his brothers.

Shechem was a well-established and important city, located on a main road about thirty miles north of Jerusalem and about six miles northeast of Gideon's home in Ophrah. Episodes in the lives of Abraham, Jacob, and Joshua took place in Shechem (Gen. 12:6-7; 33:18-19; Josh. 24).

When Gideon died, Abimelech expected his brothers to promote themselves as leaders in the place of their father. Therefore, in order to foil their plans, Abimelech took the initiative to establish himself as king of Shechem. It should be remembered that the people had tried to persuade Gideon to be king, but he refused, saying, "I will not rule over you, nor shall my son rule over you; the Lord shall rule over you" (Judg. 8:23 NKJV). Ironically, Abimelech's name means "My father is king."

Abimelech's plan was to gain the support of the people of Shechem. He began by talking to his mother's family, then he expanded his efforts to "all the men of Shechem" (9:2). His argument was twofold. First, he argued that one ruler is much more advantageous than seventy rulers; therefore, Abimelech would make a better king than his seventy brothers. Second, he argued that out of all Gideon's sons, only he was a true Shechemite. He pleaded with them, saying, "Remember also that I am your bone and your flesh" (v. 2).

1. Describe Abimelech's strategy for seizing power.
2. Where and when might a Christian be tempted to use similar tactics?

_____

B. Abimelech's Destructive Methods (vv. 3-6)

(Judges 9:3-4 is not included in the printed text.)

⁵**And he went unto his father's house at Ophrah, and slew his brethren the sons of Jerubbaal, being threescore and ten persons, upon one stone: notwithstanding yet Jotham the youngest son of Jerubbaal was left; for he hid himself. ⁶And all the men of Shechem gathered together, and all the house of Millo, and went, and made Abimelech king, by the plain of the pillar that was in Shechem.**

Abimelech's relatives assisted him in his campaign to be king, and his uncles reached out to the men of Shechem on Abimelech's behalf (v. 3). The men of Shechem responded positively, and gave Abimelech seventy pieces of silver so he could hire a crew of thugs (v. 4). The money came from the temple of _Baal-Berith_, whose name means "Lord of the Covenant." Baal-Berith was probably the local Canaanite god of the city of Shechem, a manifestation of the idolatry that once again plagued the Israelites.

Abimelech and his troop of hired gangsters went to Ophrah and murdered sixty-nine of his half-brothers (v. 5). He killed them without mercy on a single altar stone in the manner of human sacrifice. His youngest brother, Jotham, was able to escape and hide.

With Gideon's sons out of the way, Abimelech proceeded to seize power. The men of Shechem and the "house of Millo" came together and installed Abimelech as king of Shechem (v. 6). The "house of Millo" refers to the upper class who lived in a part of the city that was called _Beth Millo_, meaning "house of the fortress."

_____

1. What convinced the men of Shechem to follow Abimelech?
2. Who did Abimelech's dirty work, and why (vv. 3-4)?
3. In verse 5, how is God's sovereignty seen?

_____

C. Abimelech's Demise Foretold (vv. 7-21)

(Judges 9:7-18 is not included in the printed text.)

¹⁹**If ye then have dealt truly and sincerely with Jerubbaal and with his house this day, then rejoice ye in Abimelech, and let him also rejoice in you:** ²⁰**But if not, let fire come out from Abimelech, and devour the men of Shechem, and the house of Millo; and let fire come out from the men of Shechem, and from the house of Millo, and devour Abimelech.** ²¹**And Jotham ran away, and fled, and went to Beer, and dwelt there, for fear of Abimelech his brother.**

Jotham, whose name means "Jehovah is perfect," heard about the coronation of his brother Abimelech, and he interrupted the ceremonies with a prophetic fable. From a safe distance on Mount Gerizim, Jotham addressed the men of Shechem and told a story in which the trees decided to anoint a king over them (v. 7). The trees approached the olive tree and asked it to reign over them. The olive tree, however, was unwilling to rule because he was too busy in the useful occupation of producing olive oil. Next, they went to the fig tree and asked it to reign, but the fig tree replied that it was unwilling to forsake its role as maker of sweet fruit. After the fig tree, they came to the grapevine and begged it to be their king. Like the others, however, the vine knew its proper role and its place in the divine scheme of things. The vine would not give up its job of providing fruit, juice, and wine, all of which brought great joy to all of humanity. Finally, the trees sought out the thornbush and asked it to serve as their king. The thornbush questioned the motives of the trees and said, "If you really want to anoint me king over you, come and take refuge in my shade; but if not, then let fire come out of the thornbush and consume the cedars of Lebanon!" (v. 15 NIV).

After telling the story, Jotham explains its meaning. He asks the men of Shechem, "Have you acted honorably and in good faith by making Abimelek king? Have you been fair to Jerub-Baal and his family? Have you treated him as he deserves?" (v. 16 NIV). Jotham confronts their act of murdering the seventy sons of Gideon (v. 18). Finally, he utters a prophetic word, declaring that if they have been honorable, may they and Abimelech live in peace (v. 19). However, if they have not acted honorably, may fire come out and destroy both Abimelech and the men of Shechem (v. 20). Once he had spoken his peace, Jotham escaped and fled to the city of Beer, where he could live in safety, beyond the reach of Abimelech (v. 21).

---

1. Explain Jotham's two uses of the word "listen" (v. 7 NKJV).
2. Who is represented by the olive tree, fig tree, and grapevine (vv. 8-13)?
3. How is Abimelech characterized (vv. 14-15)?
4. Of what did Jotham accuse the people of Shechem (vv. 17-18)?
5. Describe Jotham's prophetic word (v. 20).

"It is a shame for a man to desire honor only because of his noble progenitors, and not to deserve it by his own virtue."—John Chrysostom

II. REBELLION AGAINST ABIMELECH (Judg. 9:22-25, 42-49)

A. Conditions for Rebellion Arranged by God (vv. 22-25)

²²When Abimelech had reigned three years over Israel, ²³Then God sent an evil spirit between Abimelech and the men of Shechem; and the men of Shechem dealt treacherously with Abimelech: ²⁴That the cruelty done to the threescore and ten sons of Jerubbaal might come, and their blood be laid upon Abimelech their brother, which slew them; and upon the men of Shechem, which aided him in the killing of his brethren. ²⁵And the men of Shechem set liers in wait for him in the top of the mountains, and they robbed all that came along that way by them: and it was told Abimelech.

Abimelech reigned for three years without incident (v. 22). However, God would not allow him to continue indefinitely. Therefore, God created dissension between Abimelech and the men of Shechem by sending "an evil spirit" (v. 23). The words *evil spirit* are open to at least two interpretations.

The first possibility is that the evil spirit was a satanic messenger that God used to fulfill His divine purpose. The Old Testament affirms that even Satan is under God's control (Job 1:6-12; Zech. 3:1-2). Satan, as the father of lies and the creator of confusion, would have been more than happy to come between Abimelech and the Shechemites so they would end up spilling more blood.

The second interpretation is based on the fact that the word *evil* can mean "bad" and the word *spirit* can refer to human attitudes rather than to supernatural beings. This train of thought produces the translation, "God stirred up animosity between Abimelek and the citizens of Shechem" (Judg. 9:23 NIV). Other similar translations state that God sent "a spirit of ill will" (NKJV) or a "spirit of discord" (LJB).

Although translations may differ in their exact wording, one thing is clear—God was at work to create hostility between these two wicked parties so that in destroying each other they might be repaid for their evil actions. Abimelech and the Shechemites were complicit in the murders of Gideon's seventy sons, and both of them must be punished for their heinous sin.

The immediate effect of the "evil spirit" was that the men of Shechem "dealt treacherously with Abimelech" (v. 23). "Dealt treacherously" refers to actions that violate commitments which are part of a relationship. *Treachery* is a betrayal, an unfaithful and deceitful action. In making Abimelech their king, the men of Shechem had formed an allegiance to him, but now they were breaking that allegiance.

The treachery of the Shechemites took the form of unsanctioned robbery. They set men on the hilltops to ambush and rob travelers and traders that passed through the region (v. 25). As king of Shechem, Abimelech would be responsible to guarantee the safe passage of anyone who came through his territory. In exchange for his protection, these travelers would pay him tribute money and tolls. By robbing the travelers, the men of Shechem undermined Abimelech's authority and deprived him of the income that would issue from everyone who passed through Shechem.

1. What changed after three years of Abimelech's reign (vv. 22-23)?
2. How did God view Abimelech and the men of Shechem (v. 24)?
3. How did the men seek to undermine the king (v. 25)?

> "Evil by its very nature opposes the purposes of God, but God, in His sovereignty, can make even this evil serve His purposes."
> —David F. Wells

B. Response to Rebellion Organized by Abimelech (vv. 42-49)

(Judges 9:42-45 is not included in the printed text.)

⁴⁶And when all the men of the tower of Shechem heard that, they entered into an hold of the house of the god Berith. ⁴⁷And it was told Abimelech, that all the men of the tower of Shechem were gathered together. ⁴⁸And Abimelech gat him up to mount Zalmon, he and all the people that were with him; and Abimelech took an axe in his hand, and cut down a bough from the trees, and took it, and laid it on his shoulder, and said unto the people that were with him, What ye have seen me do, make haste, and do as I have done. ⁴⁹And all the people likewise cut down every man his bough, and followed Abimelech, and put them to the hold, and set the hold on fire upon them; so that all the men of the tower of Shechem died also, about a thousand men and women.

When a man named Gaal moves into Shechem with his extended family, the people of Shechem begin to put their confidence in him (v. 26). He claims to be descended from Hamor, the founder of Shechem (v. 28). Gaal makes light of Abimelech and questions why he had been made king. Gaal claims that if he had the opportunity, he would remove Abimelech from power. Finally, he issues a threat to Abimelech, saying, "Increase thine army, and come out" (v. 29).

On two consecutive days, Abimelech attacked the city of Shechem (vv. 40-42). On the second day, "he captured the city and killed the people who were in it; then he razed the city and sowed it with salt" (v. 45 NASB). Sowing the city with salt made it unfit for growing crops. Additionally, sowing with salt was a ritual that invoked a curse on the city.

Although the city had been defeated and destroyed, about a thousand men and women remained in "the stronghold of the temple of the god Berith" (v. 46 NKJV). "Temples and places of worship were commonly built on mountains or high places, either in the form of forts or with towers attached to them" (*JFB Commentary*). Because of the structure's fortification, Abimelech was unable to attack its inhabitants directly. Therefore, he and his soldiers collected tree branches and piled them up against the temple (vv. 48-49). When he lit the branches, they burned with sufficient heat so the tower was engulfed in flames and smoke, killing all of the people who had hidden inside. The burning of the structure was a direct fulfillment of the earlier words of Jotham, who had predicted that fire would go out from Abimelech and consume the people of Shechem.

- Based on this passage, list four or five adjectives that describe Abimelech.

> "Personal vanity still lies root of most dissensions in every local church today."—John Stott

III. ABIMELECH JUDGED BY GOD (Judg. 9:50-57)

A. Abimelech's Humiliating Judgment (vv. 50-55)

⁵⁰Then went Abimelech to Thebez, and encamped against Thebez, and took it. ⁵¹But there was a strong tower within the city, and thither fled all the men and women, and all they of the city, and shut it to them, and gat them up to the top of the tower. ⁵²And Abimelech came unto the tower, and fought against it, and went hard unto the door of the tower to burn it with fire. ⁵³And a certain woman cast a piece of a millstone upon Abimelech's head, and all to brake his skull. ⁵⁴Then he called hastily unto the young man his armourbearer, and said unto him, Draw thy sword, and slay me, that men say not of me, A woman slew him. And his young man thrust him through, and he died. ⁵⁵And when the men of Israel saw that Abimelech was dead, they departed every man unto his place.

His complete victory over Shechem gave Abimelech the confidence to expand his reach to the surrounding area. Therefore, he led his army to the nearby city of Thebez, and camped around it. The defenses of Thebez were weak, and Abimelech conquered it with little effort. However, Thebez had a tower fortress into which a number of citizens fled for refuge.

The people locked the doors of the tower and ascended to the top, where they felt safe. Remembering his recent strategy at Shechem, Abimelech tried to burn the doors of the tower. This time, however, his strategy backfired. A woman on top of the tower saw Abimelech standing near the door, and she threw an upper millstone on his head and fractured his skull.

Critics have argued this story is fictional, offering two reasons for their position. First, they have questioned what a millstone was doing on the top of a tower. Second, they have said a woman could not have lifted a millstone. However, recent archaeological discoveries show individual households used small millstones. These rounded millstones would be used on top of a separate flat stone. The woman would hold the upper stone and push it back and forth over the grain, grinding it into flour. Household millstones such as these would weigh from eight to ten pounds. Any average woman could lift a millstone of that weight. As to why the millstone was on top of the tower, the answer is simple. When the people ran into the tower, they carried with them any items necessary for sustaining life over a period of time. The woman with the millstone must have brought it along with a sack of grain so she might be able to make bread. However, she found a more beneficial use for the millstone. Recognizing an opportunity to slay the enemy, she cast the stone down from the tower and struck Abimelech.

Abimelech realized he was dying, but he did not want to suffer the shame of being killed by a woman. Therefore, he pleaded with his armor-bearer to finish him off with his sword. The young man obeyed orders and killed Abimelech. Nevertheless, Abimelech was not spared the shame he wished to avoid, for we know he was not brought down by a male warrior, but by a resourceful woman. Deprived of their leader, Abimelech's army retreated from Thebez and returned to their own villages and homes.

---

1. Describe Abimelech's campaign against Thebez (vv. 50-52).
2. Why was Abimelech's death particularly shameful (vv. 53-54)?
3. How did Abimelech's death affect his followers (v. 55)?

Action and Reaction

Newton's third law of physics states that for every action, there is an equal and opposite reaction. Thus, every action has consequences. The corresponding spiritual law states, "God cannot be mocked. A man reaps what he sows. Whoever sows to please their flesh, from the flesh will reap destruction; whoever sows to please the Spirit, from the Spirit will reap eternal life" (Gal. 6:7-8 NIV). Every action we take moves us in a direction either toward good or toward evil. If we continue onward in the same direction, we will arrive at either a happy or a disastrous end.

B. Abimelech's Just Judgment (vv. 56-57)

56 Thus God rendered the wickedness of Abimelech, which he did unto his father, in slaying his seventy brethren: 57 And all the evil of the men of Shechem did God render upon their heads: and upon them came the curse of Jotham the son of Jerubbaal.

Although a woman struck down Abimelech, God is credited for directing her actions (v. 56). The death of Abimelech was repayment for his cold-blooded murder of his innocent brothers. Because the men of Shechem had assisted Abimelech in his evil deeds, they also received repayment for their guilty role. The death of Abimelech and the men of Shechem was a fulfillment of the curse of Jotham, the only remaining son of Gideon.

The sins of Abimelech probably bear little resemblance to our sins. It is doubtful that any of us have killed all of our brothers and declared ourselves the ruler of a city. However, the sins of Abimelech originated in his heart—the sins of pride, arrogance, selfishness, hatred, envy, and strife. Even if we do not commit murder, we may harbor the same attitudes within our hearts. These "works of the flesh," if not confessed and forsaken, will keep us from entering the kingdom of God (Gal. 5:19-21).

• What does this passage reveal about the Lord?

> "Sin has the devil for its father, shame for its companion, and death for its wages."—Thomas Watson

CONCLUSION

The story of Abimelech is a severe warning to anyone who thinks they can escape the consequences of wickedness. Those who live unrighteous lives will eventually be judged. The psalmist Asaph was discouraged when he saw the "prosperity of the wicked" (Ps. 73:3). He observed their pride, vanity, violence, and riches. But then he "went into the sanctuary of God," and he "understood . . . their end" (v. 17). There in the house of God, Asaph recognized the future desolation and destruction of the wicked.

Jesus declared we would face God's judgment for our every action and every word (Matt. 12:36-37). The future judgment is certain. Moreover, it is not only in the afterlife that God dispenses justice. The apostle Paul declares, "The wrath of God is being revealed from heaven against all the godlessness and wickedness of people, who suppress the truth by their wickedness" (Rom. 1:18 NIV). This manifestation of the wrath of God is in the present tense! Just as Abimelech was repaid by means of a violent death, so also we may be subject to painful repercussions of our sinful acts and ungodly lifestyles.

God's present judgment extends into the body of Christ. Paul admonished the Corinthian church for their divisions and disregard of the sacredness of the Lord's Supper. Because of their carnality, some of the Corinthian believers had become sick and weak, and some had even died (1 Cor. 11:30).

Adam and Eve probably had no idea of the vast consequences that would result from their brief and singular act of disobedience. Similarly, it is doubtful David gave any thought to the devastation that would result from his selfish misuse of power. Do we consider the consequences when we disobey God? The story of Abimelech should remind us every sin will yield its consequences because God will ensure that justice prevails.

GOLDEN TEXT CHALLENGE

"HIS OWN INIQUITIES SHALL TAKE THE WICKED HIMSELF, AND HE SHALL BE HOLDEN WITH THE CORDS OF HIS SINS" (Prov. 5:22).

"Most people who follow unlawful pleasures think they can give them up whenever they please; but sin repeated becomes customary; custom soon engenders habit; and habit, in the end, assumes the form of necessity; the man becomes bound with his own cords, and so is led captive by the devil at his will" (*Adam Clarke's Commentary*).

Daily Devotions:
M. Sin at the Door • Genesis 4:1-8
T. Escape From Sin • Genesis 39:1-12
W. High Cost of Sin • Jeremiah 16:10-18
T. Plucking Out Sin • Mark 9:43-50
F. Run From Sexual Sins • 1 Corinthians 6:15-20
S. The Vileness of Sin • 2 Peter 2:10-22

Samson, the Unstable Strongman

Judges 13:1-14; 16:1-31

Unit Theme:
The Era of the Judges

Central Truth:
God judges those who follow their own ways apart from Him.

Focus:
Learn from Samson's example and trust in God's power rather than our own.

Context:
In the twelfth century BC, Samson is destined to oppose the Philistines.

Golden Text:
"He awoke out of his sleep, and said, I will go out as at other times before, and shake myself. And he wist not that the Lord was departed from him" (Judg. 16:20).

Study Outline:
I. **Samson's Miraculous Birth** (Judg. 13:1-14, 24-25)
II. **Samson's Weakness** (Judg. 16:4-20)
III. **Samson's Final Act** (Judg. 16:21-31)

INTRODUCTION

The modern Pentecostal Movement was born among the poor and the powerless more than a century ago. From the hills and farms of Appalachia came the Church of God, and from an abandoned building in Los Angeles came the Azusa Street revival. Today Pentecostalism is the fastest-growing segment of Christianity in the world, numbering over 600 million adherents. In America, Pentecostal pastors no longer wear threadbare suits, and our churches are no longer housed in abandoned buildings and temporary tents. We have grown, and in some places we have grown rich.

Unfortunately, growth and prosperity present new temptations that are just as dangerous as those presented by weakness and poverty. We should pay close attention to the dire warning Jesus spoke to the large and prosperous church at Laodicea:

> You say, "I am rich; I have acquired wealth and do not need a thing." But you do not realize that you are wretched, pitiful, poor, blind and naked. I counsel you to buy from me gold refined in the fire, so you can become rich; and white clothes to wear, so you can cover your shameful nakedness; and salve to put on your eyes, so you can see. Those whom I love I rebuke and discipline. So be earnest and repent (Rev. 3:17-19 NIV).

There was a day when we struggled from lack of training, but today we have ministers with the highest levels of education. We have built our buildings, we have acquired technology, we have achieved professional training, and we have honed our skills and talents. Although we should be thankful for these wonderful advances, we should realize our strength presents us with new temptations and challenges. If we focus on outward attainments, we will lose our power with God.

In our lesson this week, we will study the life of Samson—a strong man who was very weak in many ways. Samson's strength set him apart from everyone else, and his enemies searched for a way to rob him of that strength. Similarly, Satan seeks to take away the source of our spiritual strength. In this lesson, we will discover what Samson finally learned—the secret of our strength is dependence on God.

I. SAMSON'S MIRACULOUS BIRTH (Judg. 13:1-14, 24-25)

A. Israel Needs a Deliverer (v. 1)

¹And the children of Israel did evil again in the sight of the Lord; and the Lord delivered them into the hand of the Philistines forty years.

For the seventh time in the Book of Judges, we read that the Israelites did what was evil in the eyes of the Lord. They forsook the Lord in order to worship the idols of Canaan. The Lord had saved Israel from the bondage of Egypt. He had also saved them from the oppression of the Amalekites, Amorites, Moabites, Zidonians, Ammonites, and Maonites (10:11-12). God had been faithful to Israel. Nevertheless, Israel continued to forsake the Lord, breaking their covenant with Him to serve the gods of Canaan instead.

The Lord repeatedly subjected the Israelites to enemy attack in order to discipline them. Over and over, the Israelites sinned; the Lord handed them over to the enemy; the Israelites cried out for God's help; and the Lord raised up a judge who saved them.

This time, the Lord gave them into the power of the Philistines for forty years. The Philistines had oppressed Israel twice before. We read in chapter 3 that Shamgar killed six hundred Philistines with an ox goad (v. 31). Although Shamgar rebuffed the Philistines, they returned and attacked Israel at a later date (10:7). In chapter 13, the Philistines seem to exercise complete domination over the Israelites.

The exact origins of the Philistines are unknown, but it is certain they were not native inhabitants of Canaan. Apparently, they migrated from Greece and settled in southwestern Palestine on the shores of the Mediterranean Sea, an area that is now called the Gaza Strip. Their most prominent cities were Gaza, Ashkelon, Ashdod, Ekron, and Gath. The power of the Philistines consisted in their ability to forge iron weapons during a time when Israel had only weaker bronze weapons. The Philistines continued to be a threat throughout Israel's history. The Bible records battles against the Philistines in the times of Samuel (1 Sam. 7:3-14), Saul (13:17; 14:31), and Hezekiah (2 Kings 18:5-8).

- Describe a contemporary situation that Israel's circumstance brings to mind.

> "Man's mind is like a store of idolatry and superstition; so much so that if a man believes his own mind, it is certain that he will forsake God and forge some idol in his own brain."—John Calvin

---

B. The Lord Sends a Promise (vv. 2-3)

2 And there was a certain man of Zorah, of the family of the Danites, whose name was Manoah; and his wife was barren, and bare not. 3 And the angel of the Lord appeared unto the woman, and said unto her, Behold now, thou art barren, and bearest not: but thou shalt conceive, and bear a son.

Throughout the Book of Judges, we have observed the repeated cycles of rebellion. In each cycle the Lord responds to Israel's cries for help by raising up judges who save Israel from her enemies. In this final cycle, however, the Israelites do not cry out for help. Apparently, they have fallen so far away from God that they no longer look to Him as their source of help. They have become indifferent and apathetic. Nevertheless, the Lord sees their suffering and determines to raise up another judge who will save them from the power of the Philistines.

For the first time, the Lord chooses to raise up a leader from birth; therefore, He sends His angel to announce His plan to a barren woman from the tribe of Dan. She is not named, but her husband's name is *Manoah*. The angel of the Lord appears to Manoah's wife and surprises her with a promise from God. She who has been barren will conceive and give birth to a son.

The city of Zorah was located within the original borders of Dan, which was adjacent to Philistine territory in southwestern Israel. The Danites were eventually forced out of their land in the south and migrated to the northernmost part of Israel (see Judg. 18:1-29).

- Describe another Biblical account that this passage brings to mind.

> "If the Lord be with us, we have no cause of fear. His eye is upon us, His arm over us, His ear open to our prayer—His grace sufficient, His promise unchangeable."—John Newton

---

C. The Child Will Be Set Apart (vv. 4-5)

4 Now therefore beware, I pray thee, and drink not wine nor strong drink, and eat not any unclean thing: 5 For, lo, thou shalt conceive, and bear a son; and no razor shall come on his head: for the child shall be a Nazarite unto God from the womb: and he shall begin to deliver Israel out of the hand of the Philistines.

The woman receives instructions from the angel, telling her to "drink no wine or other fermented drink" and "not eat anything unclean" (v. 4 NIV). These restrictions are important because her son will be a Nazirite unto God from the time of his birth until his death. A *Nazirite* was a person who had made a special vow of consecration to the Lord. The guidelines for the Nazirite vow are found in Numbers 6:1-21. Nazirites were required to abstain from all fruit of the grapevine, including grapes, raisins, grape juice, and wine. They could not drink any kind of strong drink. They were not allowed to cut their hair at all, and they must not touch any dead thing. Even if a family member died, they were not allowed to touch the body.

The Nazirite vow was normally entered into for a temporary period of time by an adult who was willing to fulfill these requirements. With Samson, however, his time of Nazirite service is lifelong and not of his own choosing.

The angel tells Manoah's wife that her son will "begin the deliverance of Israel from the hands of the Philistines" (Judg. 13:5 NIV). The angel does not promise Samson will bring complete deliverance; he will only "begin" that deliverance.

• What did God require of Manoah's wife and son, and why?

> "It is scarce conceivable how straight the way is wherein God leads them that follow Him; and how dependent on Him we must be."—John Wesley

------

D. The Angel Confirms His Promise (vv. 6-14)

(Judges 13:6-14 is not included in the printed text.)

When the angel departs from the woman, she relates the entire episode to her husband. Manoah is not satisfied to be left out of the divine encounter, so he prays that he might see the angel for himself. The angel returns and visits the woman while she is in the field. She hurries and gets her husband, and he comes to where the angel is. The angel repeats to Manoah the same instructions he had given to the woman earlier.

Samson's story stands out from the other judges in numerous ways. Samson is the only judge whom the Lord prepares from before birth to fill the role of judge. The angel of the Lord predicts his birth and he is dedicated as a Nazirite to God (vv. 3-5).The story of Samson's birth signifies he is a person of destiny and creates a sense of eager anticipation. The calling of Samson to be a Nazirite adds to the importance of his purpose and devotion. Except for the puzzling declaration that Samson will only "begin" to save Israel, everything in chapter 13 indicates Samson is poised to be the greatest judge of them all.

------

1. How did the woman describe her angelic encounter (vv. 6-7)?
2. How did God honor Manoah (vv. 8-11)?
3. What did Manoah want to know firsthand (v. 12)?

E. Samson Moved by the Spirit (vv. 24-25)

(Judges 13:24-25 is not included in the printed text.)

Samson's early life is described concisely: "The woman gave birth to a boy and named him Samson. He grew and the Lord blessed him, and the Spirit of the Lord began to stir him while he was in Mahaneh Dan, between Zorah and Eshtaol" (vv. 24-25 NIV).

The Spirit rests upon Samson and we expect him, like earlier judges, to assemble the army of Israel and engage the enemy, but no such action ensues. Our hopeful expectations regarding Samson go entirely unfulfilled, while Samson pursues his own agenda. Time after time, the Spirit comes upon Samson, but still he does not gather the Israelites for battle, and he does not eliminate the Philistine threat. The Spirit enables Samson to tear apart an attacking lion (14:6), to kill thirty Philistines in Ashkelon and take their clothing (v. 19), and to break free of his bonds and kill one thousand Philistines with the jawbone of a donkey (15:14-15).

Each time the Spirit comes upon Samson, the Scripture uses the words, "The Spirit of the Lord came upon him in power" (14:6, 19; 15:14 NIV). The Hebrew term used in these verses suggests a forcefulness that exceeds any of the other terms used in Judges to describe the coming of the Spirit. Samson is overwhelmed every time the Spirit comes upon him, but he remains in control of his actions. Even though he is anointed with the Spirit, many of Samson's actions are unwise and some are even unrighteous.

---

1. Compare verse 24 with the descriptions of two other boys (1 Sam. 2:21; Luke 2:40).
2. How does the Holy Spirit "stir" (v. 25 NIV) people today?

II. SAMSON'S WEAKNESS (Judg. 16:4-20)

A. Samson's Fatal Attraction to Women (vv. 4-5)

⁴And it came to pass afterward, that he loved a woman in the valley of Sorek, whose name was Delilah. ⁵And the lords of the Philistines came up unto her, and said unto her, Entice him, and see wherein his great strength lieth, and by what means we may prevail against him, that we may bind him to afflict him; and we will give thee every one of us eleven hundred pieces of silver.

Samson's willfulness and self-centeredness are evident throughout the stories of chapters 14-16, beginning with his insistence on marrying a Philistine woman, despite the objections of his parents (14:1-3). His unruly behavior persists as he breaks his Nazirite vows by touching the corpse of a dead lion

---

(vv. 8-9), and as he visits a prostitute in Gaza (16:1). Now he falls in love with a Philistine woman named Delilah, but there is no indication that he marries her.

The unholy conduct of Samson makes us wonder how he can be anointed by the Spirit. In response to Samson's sinful behavior, consider the following observations:

1. God is free to give His power to whomsoever He will and, at times, He even uses unbelievers (e.g., Balaam in Num. 24:2).

2. The charismatic endowment of the Spirit in Judges is not always a sign of spiritual maturity or holy character.

3. Nowhere in Judges is sin excused or disobedience treated lightly.

4. The perspective on sin in Judges is focused more on the whole people of God than on the individual. The sanctifying work of the Spirit in the life of the individual is not a dominant concern of Judges; rather, the sanctification of the community in covenant takes precedence over the sanctification of the individual. This communal aspect of holiness deserves more attention, especially in this electronic age when humans, in spite of being better connected than ever before, bear little communal responsibility or accountability.

5. The work of the Spirit in Judges is aimed at the salvation of the people of God. After all, the judges are called "saviors," and their actions are called "salvation." The Israelites are saved from both the physical/political bondage to Canaanite oppressors and from the spiritual bondage to Baal and Asherah, the gods of Canaan.

Samson's love for Delilah is the perfect opportunity for the Philistines to entrap him. Delilah lives in the valley of Sorek, located on the border between Israelite and Philistine territories. Her location appears to be symbolic, because Samson is prone to "live on the edge" and test the boundaries of proper behavior. The Philistine rulers come to Delilah and offer her a large sum of money from each of the rulers (we do not know how many rulers are involved in the deal) in exchange for information regarding the true source of his strength. They hope to be able to capture and imprison him.

• Contrast Samson's love with Delilah's love.

> "Temptation usually comes in through a door that has deliberately been left open."—Arnold Glasow

---

B. Delilah's Scheme (vv. 6-15)

(Judges 16:7-15 is not included in the printed text.)

⁶And Delilah said to Samson, Tell me, I pray thee, wherein thy great strength lieth, and wherewith thou mightest be bound to afflict thee.

Immediately, Delilah began to question Samson about the source of his great strength. At first, Samson was unwilling to reveal the truth. He told Delilah that he would lose his strength if he were tied up with "seven fresh bowstrings" (v. 7 NIV). Delilah did so, and the Philistines tried to capture

Samson, but he broke free easily. Then he said he could be restrained with "new ropes" (v. 11), but they proved to be no match for Samson's great strength. His next ruse was more complicated. He said to Delilah, "If you weave the seven braids of my head into the fabric on the loom and tighten it with the pin, I'll become as weak as any other man" (v. 13 NIV). Delilah did just as he said, but it had no effect on Samson.

- How did Delilah respond to each of Samson's three lies?

> "We are not going to jump out of Delilah's lap into Abraham's bosom."—William Tiptaft

---

C. Samson's Surrender (vv. 16-20)

(Judges 16:18-19 is not included in the printed text.)

¹⁶And it came to pass, when she pressed him daily with her words, and urged him, so that his soul was vexed unto death; ¹⁷That he told her all his heart, and said unto her, There hath not come a razor upon mine head; for I have been a Nazarite unto God from my mother's womb: if I be shaven, then my strength will go from me, and I shall become weak, and be like any other man.

²⁰And she said, The Philistines be upon thee, Samson. And he awoke out of his sleep, and said, I will go out as at other times before, and shake myself. And he wist not that the Lord was departed from him.

Delilah continued to put pressure on Samson daily. She argued that if he really loved her, he should tell her the truth. Finally, she wore him down. He explained he was a Nazirite and, as such, he was not allowed to cut his hair at all. This appears to be the final violation of Samson's three Nazirite vows. By reaching into the dead lion, he had violated the command not to touch a dead corpse, and during his wedding party he had apparently drank wine.

Delilah immediately called for the Philistines, and they brought her the reward they had promised. She enticed Samson to fall asleep on her knees. While he slept, she had a man to cut Samson's hair. Delilah then woke him with the cry, "Samson, the Philistines are upon you!" (v. 20 NIV). Samson fully expected to defeat his attackers just as he had always done in the past, but his strength was gone. Sadly, he did not know the Lord had departed from him. There was no magic or strength in Samson's hair, but his final act of disobedience caused the Lord to depart. The departure of the Lord meant the departure of Samson's strength.

---

1. Why did Samson eventually tell Delilah the truth? What lesson can Christians learn from this?
2. Describe Samson's deadly assumption (v. 20). How do Christians today sometimes make a similar error?

III. SAMSON'S FINAL ACT (Judg. 16:21-31)

A. Samson's Bondage (vv. 21-22)

(Judges 16:21-22 is not included in the printed text.)

Sin always leads to bondage (John 8:34), and Samson's experience was no exception to the rule. His disobedience brought him to a place of servitude. The Philistines put out his eyes, imprisoned him, and sentenced him to hard labor. We read, however, that Samson's hair "began to grow again" (Judg. 16:22), a fact that alludes to the laws of the Nazirite. According to Numbers 6:12, Nazirites who had broken their vows could rededicate themselves to the Lord and begin their consecration anew. The possibility of rededication was open to Samson.

• Describe Samson's condition with four adjectives.

Healed on the Inside

A diving accident in 1967 left Joni Eareckson, then 17, a quadriplegic in a wheelchair, without the use of her hands. Joni learned to recognize that her strength comes from God. She writes, "My wheelchair was the key . . . especially since God's power always shows up best in weakness. So here I sit . . . glad that I have not been healed on the outside, but glad that I have been healed on the inside. Healed from my own self-centered wants and wishes."

B. Samson's Degradation (vv. 23-27)

(Judges 16:24, 26-27 is not included in the printed text.)

23 Then the lords of the Philistines gathered them together for to offer a great sacrifice unto Dagon their god, and to rejoice: for they said, Our god hath delivered Samson our enemy into our hand.

25 And it came to pass, when their hearts were merry, that they said, Call for Samson, that he may make us sport. And they called for Samson out of the prison house; and he made them sport: and they set him between the pillars.

The capture of Samson was reason for great celebration among the Philistines, so they assembled themselves at the temple of their god Dagon with the purpose of giving thanks and offering sacrifices. They praised Dagon for delivering Samson, their greatest enemy, into their hands.

It was not enough that they had captured and blinded Samson; they wanted to mock and abuse him further. Therefore, they placed him between two great pillars near the center of the building, in full view of the crowds.

When Samson was made aware of his location, he thought of a plan. By faith, Samson spoke to the young man who held his hand, "Put me where I can feel the pillars that support the temple, so that I may lean against them" (v. 26 NIV). Samson knew even though he had lost his strength, God's strength remained. Perhaps Samson remembered the time when he was utterly exhausted and cried out to God, and the Lord answered with a miracle, bringing water out of a rock (15:18-19).

---

1. How did the Philistines view Samson (v. 24)?
2. Describe the crowd at Dagon's temple (v. 27).

> "When sin exerts itself and we know its power and by its power we are held in bondage, surely our dire need is for God to deal with the cause, a sinful heart."—Duncan Campbell

---

C. Samson's Victory (vv. 28-31)

(Judges 16:29, 31 is not included in the printed text.)

28 And Samson called unto the Lord, and said, O Lord God, remember me, I pray thee, and strengthen me, I pray thee, only this once, O God, that I may be at once avenged of the Philistines for my two eyes.

30 And Samson said, Let me die with the Philistines. And he bowed himself with all his might; and the house fell upon the lords, and upon all the people that were therein. So the dead which he slew at his death were more than they which he slew in his life.

We are reminded that even though the Israelites were living in subjection to the Philistines, they had not prayed to the Lord for His help. Samson, however, called out to the Lord and asked that his strength might return just once more. He took hold of the two pillars and uttered his final prayer: "Let me die with the Philistines" (v. 30). Then, with all of his God-given strength, he pulled down the pillars, and the temple collapsed on top of the three thousand Philistines who had gathered to worship their god. Samson's last sacrificial act did not defeat the entire Philistine nation but, by destroying their central pagan temple, he won a great victory which signified far more than any of his previous victories.

---

1. How did Samson show His dependence on God (vv. 28, 30)?
2. What did Samson's family do, and why (v. 31)?

> "A necessary pre-cursor of any great spiritual awakening is a spirit of deep humiliation growing out of a consciousness of sin, and fresh revelation of the holiness and power and glory of God."
> —John R. Mott

CONCLUSION

We should be thankful for the abilities, talents, training, and resources God has given to us. However, we must remain humble and obedient, remembering that our effectiveness depends not on our strength but on God's strength. Samson learned this lesson the hard way; let us learn from his example.

GOLDEN TEXT CHALLENGE

"HE AWOKE OUT OF HIS SLEEP, AND SAID, I WILL GO OUT AS AT OTHER TIMES BEFORE, AND SHAKE MYSELF. AND HE WIST NOT THAT THE LORD WAS DEPARTED FROM HIM" (Judg. 16:20).

When the Lord departed from Samson, along with the Lord went His strength. With God, the weakest are indeed strong; without God, the strongest are indeed weak.

Samson took too much for granted. This is always fatal. Never must Christians cease to be spiritually alert. Never must we expose ourselves needlessly to temptation. The Lord's presence can depart from us without our even realizing it.

Daily Devotions:

M. The Wickedly Proud • Psalm 10:1-11
T. Prophecy Against Pride • Isaiah 2:12-18
W. Lesson Learned • Daniel 4:29-37
T. Every Knee Will Bow • Romans 14:7-13
F. Embrace Humility • 1 Peter 5:5-11
S. A Fading World • 1 John 2:15-17

Consequences of Immorality

Judges 19:1—21:3

Unit Theme:

The Era of the Judges

Central Truth:

Sin compounds, taking a person ever farther from God.

Focus:

Seriously reflect on the downward spiral of sinfulness and determine to live righteously.

Context:

Anarchy and violence as the era of the Judges closes

Golden Text:

"Even as they did not like to retain God in their knowledge, God gave them over to a reprobate mind, to do those things which are not convenient" (Rom. 1:28).

Study Outline:

I. **An Inhospitable Place** (Judg. 19:9-21)

II. **Horrible Acts Committed** (Judg. 19:22-30)

III. **Civil War Incurred** (Judg. 20:12-14, 20-21, 25-28, 48; 21:1-3)

INTRODUCTION

Our lives have become extremely complicated and busy. In fact, we can be so occupied with the urgent complexities of life that we fail to give the necessary attention to our spiritual lives. When we ignore our spiritual health, we soon grow weak and frail in our faith. Before we even realize we are drifting away from God, we can find ourselves far away from Him.

The church at Sardis must have been astonished by Jesus' accusation that its spirituality had declined to a critical and dangerous level. He said to the church, "I know your deeds; you have a reputation of being alive, but you are dead" (Rev. 3:1 NIV). How did they reach such a state? Their decline did not happen overnight. Disobedience in small things, inconsistency in prayer, failure to read God's Word, removing God from the center of life—all of these things contribute to a downward spiral that leads to spiritual stagnation and eventual destruction.

The Israelites in the Book of Judges experienced a similar downward spiral. They began to forget the Lord who had brought them up from the bondage of Egypt. They disobeyed the Lord's command to drive out all of the Canaanites. Then, they compromised with the pagan society around them, eventually intermarrying with the Canaanites and worshiping with them. They served the Lord off and on while the judges ruled; but after each judge died, the next generation of Israelites would sin even worse than the previous generation (2:19).

Finally, they found themselves in a state of complete anarchy and rampant immorality, which is detailed in the concluding section of Judges (chs. 17-21).

In this lesson, we will study chapters 19-21 and observe the moral and spiritual decline that occurs when God's people fail to maintain their relationship with Him. The final verse of Judges summarizes the depths to which Israel had fallen: "In those days there was no king in Israel: every man did that which was right in his own eyes" (21:25). Hopefully, we will search our own hearts and take seriously the warning that is implicit in this last section of Judges. Our relationship with God is not something to be played with or taken lightly. Sin and disobedience carry tragic consequences that will grow worse and worse if we continue to disregard God's call to repentance and faithfulness.

I. AN INHOSPITABLE PLACE (Judg. 19:9-21)

To a large degree, the Book of Judges is concerned with the issue of responsibility and accountability. In 1:1, we learn Joshua has died and Israel is without a leader. However, after Joshua's death, the Lord does not name a successor who would lead at the national level. Instead, God institutes a new system of accountability based on the twelve tribes of Israel. Each tribe is to take responsibility for a certain territory within the nation. Whenever needs would arise, God would raise up judges who would lead the people. The judges, however, were not able to keep the people accountable to God. The Israelites repeatedly rebelled against God and worshiped idols. At one point, the people were willing to appoint Gideon as their king, but Gideon declined the offer. He insisted that the Lord was Israel's only King.

Now, near the end of the Book of Judges, the issue of accountability comes to the forefront again in the statement "There was no king in Israel" (Judg. 19:1). This is equivalent to saying there was no system of accountability. Everyone was free to do as they pleased.

In this context of lawlessness, we find the story of a certain Levite, who was living in the remote parts of the hill country in the territory of Ephraim. The descendants of the tribe of Levi were charged with the spiritual leadership of the nation and were required to care for the Tabernacle and perform all of its ceremonies. This Levite had taken for himself a secondary wife (concubine) from Bethlehem in Judah. We are not told anything about the rest of his family.

The Levite's secondary wife was unfaithful to him. Then she left him and returned to her father's house in Bethlehem. Apparently, the unfaithfulness of the secondary wife is a representation of Israel's unfaithfulness to the Lord. After she had been away for four months, the Levite went to Bethlehem in an attempt to convince her to come home with him. He spoke kindly to her, trying to reconcile with her. He even brought a donkey for her to ride, which was very generous of him, considering the wife would normally be required to walk.

The girl's father welcomed the Levite joyfully, and invited him to stay for three days. On the fourth day, the Levite prepared to depart, but the father insisted he stay another night. The extravagant hospitality of the father stands in sharp contrast to the next scene in the story when the Levite can find no hospitality at all.

A. A City Without Hospitality (vv. 9-15)

(Judges 19:9-11, 13-14 is not included in the printed text.)

¹²And his master said unto him, We will not turn aside hither into the city of a stranger, that is not of the children of Israel; we will pass over to Gibeah.

¹⁵And they turned aside thither, to go in and to lodge in Gibeah: and when he went in, he sat him down in a street of the city: for there was no man that took them into his house to lodging.

On the fifth day the Levite again prepared to depart, but the father urged him to stay on. Later in the afternoon, the Levite determined that he must be on his way. Resisting the pleas of his father-in-law, he, his servant, and his secondary wife started toward home (vv. 8-10).

As the evening drew near, the weary travelers were passing by the Canaanite city of Jebus (Jerusalem), and the Levite's servant encouraged him to turn into the city and find lodging for the night. The Levite, however, was not willing to enter the Jebusite city, because they would not be assured of a hospitable welcome. He chose instead to press onward to the Israelite city of Gibeah, which was inhabited by people from the tribe of Benjamin.

The sun had set by the time they reached Gibeah, and they entered the city expecting someone to take them in for the night. In ancient times, when there were very few inns, hospitality was a necessary and respected custom. Travelers were entitled to free food and lodging, and the person who displayed great hospitality was highly esteemed by everyone (see Gen. 18:1-8).

Unexpectedly, when the small company entered Gibeah, they were not approached by anyone. This was a city without hospitality, which meant it was a city with low morals and no conscience.

---

1. How does the phrase "there was no king in Israel" (v. 1) set the stage for this chapter?
2. Describe the surprising situation in Gibeah (v. 15).

> "If God were to eradicate all evil from this planet, He would have to eradicate all evil men."—Billy Graham

---

B. A Hospitable Man (vv. 16-21)

(Judges 19:17-19, 21 is not included in the printed text.)

¹⁶And, behold, there came an old man from his work out of the field at even, which was also of mount Ephraim; and he sojourned in Gibeah: but the men of the place were Benjamites.

²⁰And the old man said, Peace be with thee; howsoever let all thy wants lie upon me; only lodge not in the street.

After sitting alone for some time in the public square, the travelers are approached by an old man who is coming in from working in the fields. He is not a native of Gibeah (not a Benjamite). Rather, he is an Ephraimite who is only sojourning in Gibeah. The old man inquires as to their identity, destination, and origin. The Levite replies they are returning from Bethlehem to his home in Ephraim, and they were expecting to receive hospitality. However, no one has taken them in.

Not wishing to put too much pressure on the old man, the Levite explains he has food and provisions for the three of them and for the donkeys. He adds, "We don't need anything" (v. 19 NIV). All his party wants is a place to sleep for the night. The old man assures them of his goodwill by saying, "Peace be with you!" (v. 20 NKJV), and he insists on serving them and providing all of their needs. In addition, he urges the Levite not to remain in the town square. The old man must be already aware of the perverted morals of the town.

---

1. How did the Levite explain his plight (v. 18)?
2. Describe the old man's hospitality (vv. 20-21).

> "The church is not a select circle of the immaculate, but a home where the outcast may come in."—James H. Aughey

---

II. HORRIBLE ACTS COMMITTED (Judg. 19:22-30)

A. Unspeakable Evil Thrives Unrestrained (vv. 22-24)

(Judges 19:24 is not included in the printed text.)

22 Now as they were making their hearts merry, behold, the men of the city, certain sons of Belial, beset the house round about, and beat at the door, and spake to the master of the house, the old man, saying, Bring forth the man that came into thine house, that we may know him. 23 And the man, the master of the house, went out unto them, and said unto them, Nay, my brethren, nay, I pray you, do not so wickedly; seeing that this man is come into mine house, do not this folly.

The old man welcomes his tired guests into his home, provides water for their feet, and feeds the donkeys. Then they sit down to an evening meal. Everything is done according to the accepted customs of hospitality, and they are having a merry time, until they hear someone beating on the door. In an episode reminiscent of the story of Sodom in Genesis 19:4-8, certain men of the city surround the house and demand that the old man turn over the Levite to them.

These men are "sons of Belial" (Judg. 19:22), which means "worthless" or "good for nothing." They are wicked men who disregard the most basic rules of civilized society, and they represent the depths to which Israel has fallen. These men want to "know" the Levite, which means they want to have sexual relations with him (see Gen. 4:1). The old man, however, is not willing to acquiesce to their wicked plans. He appeals to their sense of decency and reminds them of the customs of hospitality.

Because the old man has taken in the Levite's party, he is responsible for their safety until they leave his house. He begs the wicked men not to do "this folly" (Judg. 19:23). The translation "folly" is too tame in this context; the original Hebrew wording is better translated as "outrage" (NKJV), "infamy" (NJB), or "vile thing" (ESV). It may be defined as "something repulsive," a "willful sin," a "sacrilege."

In order to protect his guest, the old man commits what he considers to be the lesser of two evils: he offers to hand over his own daughter along with the Levite's concubine. "Do whatever you want to them," he says, "but do not mistreat my guest" (see v. 24). Thus, the old man offers to give them two helpless women.

---

1. What motivated "certain men of the city" (v. 22 NKJV)?
2. Describe the old man's shocking response (vv. 23-24). How could this be?

> "Lust makes men brutish."—Thomas Watson

B. Horrific Abuse of the Weak (vv. 25-28)

(Judges 19:26-28 is not included in the printed text.)

25 But the men would not hearken to him: so the man took his concubine, and brought her forth unto them; and they knew her, and abused her all the night until the morning: and when the day began to spring, they let her go.

The men of Gibeah were not in a mood to compromise; they "would not listen" (NIV) to the old man. Their unwillingness to listen to reason echoes the Lord's earlier accusation against Israel: "You have not obeyed My voice" (2:2 NKJV). The wickedness of Judges 19 has its roots in Israel's refusal to hear God in Judges 2. Seeing the determination of the evil men, the Levite grabbed his concubine and shoved her out of the house, shutting the door behind her. His act was a disgraceful attempt at self-preservation. Earlier in the story, the Levite showed evidence of his love and care for his secondary wife, but now he demonstrated no sign of either.

The men of Gibeah took the defenseless woman and had sexual relations with her. Without any hesitation or remorse, they "abused her all the night" (19:25). At dawn, when they had tired of molesting her, they turned her loose.

The battered woman returned to the house where her husband was sleeping, and she fell down on the ground in front of the door, with her hands stretched out on the threshold. The Levite awoke and prepared to depart from Gibeah, apparently willing to leave his concubine behind. When he opened the door, he discovered her lying on the ground. Without a word of apology, a caring comment, or a helping hand, he told her, "Get up; let's go" (19:28 NIV). But there was no answer. She was either unconscious or dead. So the Levite picked her up and put her on a donkey and resumed his homeward journey.

- How could the Levite be so stunningly callous?

> "A person's life is his most precious possession. Consequently, to rob him of it is the greatest sin we can commit against him." —John Stott

C. Gruesome Act (vv. 29-30)

(Judges 19:29 is not included in the printed text.)

³⁰And it was so, that all that saw it said, There was no such deed done nor seen from the day that the children of Israel came up out of the land of Egypt unto this day: consider of it, take advice, and speak your minds.

When the Levite finally reaches his home, he takes a knife and dismembers his concubine. He divides her into twelve pieces and sends the pieces throughout the territory of Israel. The purpose of his gruesome message is to shock the other tribes into action. Speaking of the rape and murder of the concubine, the people agree that no crime of this magnitude had been committed in all the days since the Israelites "came up from the land of Egypt" (v. 30 NKJV).

The reference to the exodus from Egypt points back to Israel's founding moment—a moment marked by God's grace that delivered His people from oppression and bondage. The God of the Exodus is the God who stands on the side of the weak, the slave, the abused. The Exodus brings to mind hopeful expectations of a future free of abuse and fear, expectations that remain unfulfilled given the crimes against this helpless and unprotected woman. Thrown to the mob to be raped and murdered, she was then victimized by her husband when he dismembered her dead body and sent it throughout the land. Israel's exodus, the high point in its history, stands in stark contrast to this low point in Judges, when freedom turned into anarchy and the oppressed became the oppressors.

> "He who allows oppression shares the crime."—Desiderius Erasmus

III. CIVIL WAR INCURRED (Judg. 20:12-14, 20-21, 25-28, 48; 21:1-3)

A. Confronting the Offenders (20:12-13)

¹²And the tribes of Israel sent men through all the tribe of Benjamin, saying, What wickedness is this that is done among you? ¹³Now therefore deliver us the men, the children of Belial, which are in Gibeah, that we may put them to death, and put away evil from Israel. But the children of Benjamin would not hearken to the voice of their brethren the children of Israel.

In a scene that reminds us of Judges 1, all of Israel gathers at Mizpeh to hear the complaint of the Levite against the men of Gibeah. In contrast to chapter 1 when the Israelites assembled in order to decide how to deal with the enemy Canaanites, chapter 20 has them assembled so they might decide how to deal with disruption within their own tribes. In chapter 1, the twelve tribes were united against the enemy, but here they face division and civil war. Disunity and infighting are clear signs of spiritual decline.

The Levite tells his story, and the Israelites are in full agreement that the men of Gibeah must be punished. "So all the men of Israel were gathered against the city, united together as one man" (20:11 NKJV). Messengers go throughout the tribe of Benjamin and demand that the criminals be turned over to authorities (vv. 12-13). However, without any system of accountability (no king), the Benjamites are not inclined to hand over their people for punishment, no matter how evil their acts had been. Once again, we read about a refusal to hear, inasmuch as the Benjamites "would not listen" to the other Israelites (NIV).

---

1. What did the Israelites demand, and was this reasonable?
2. Why was the tribe of Benjamin's response so foolish?

> "Justice is a certain rectitude of mind whereby a man does what he ought to do in the circumstances confronting him."—Thomas Aquinas

---

B. Fighting Against Each Other (vv. 14, 20-21, 25-28)
(Judges 20:20, 26-28 is not included in the printed text.)

14But the children of Benjamin gathered themselves together out of the cities unto Gibeah, to go out to battle against the children of Israel.

21And the children of Benjamin came forth out of Gibeah, and destroyed down to the ground of the Israelites that day twenty and two thousand men.

25And Benjamin went forth against them out of Gibeah the second day, and destroyed down to the ground of the children of Israel again eighteen thousand men; all these drew the sword.

Instead of handing over the guilty parties, the Benjamites decide to fight. They assemble an army from all over the territory of Benjamin and come together at the city of Gibeah. They bring 26,000 men who are added to the 700 men of Gibeah (vv. 15-16). The Israelites who gather against Gibeah, however, number 400,000 soldiers (v. 17).

When the Israelites first attack the city of Gibeah, they are defeated, losing 22,000 men (v. 21). At the end of the day, they weep before the Lord asking, "Shall we go up again to fight the Benjamites?" and the Lord replies in the affirmative (v. 23 NIV). They fight for a second day, and again they are defeated, losing 18,000 more men (v. 25). They weep, fast, offer sacrifices, and inquire again (v. 26). This time, Yahweh not only instructs them to continue the battle, but ensures them of victory (v. 28). The Israelites who once fought together against the Canaanites are now warring against one of their own tribes. On the third day, the Israelites come up with a shrewd battle plan that devastates the Benjamites.

• What can we learn from the Israelites' actions in verses 26-28?

> "When principles that run against your deepest convictions begin to win the day, then battle is your calling, and peace has become sin; you must, at the price of dearest peace, lay your convictions bare before friend and enemy, with all the fire of your faith."
> —Abraham Kuyper

C. Division and Brokenness (20:48; 21:1-3)
 (Judges 21:1-3 is not included in the printed text.)
 20:48 And the men of Israel turned again upon the children of Benjamin, and smote them with the edge of the sword, as well the men of every city, as the beast, and all that came to hand: also they set on fire all the cities that they came to.

The Israelites continued to go throughout the territory of Benjamin, burning their cities and killing the inhabitants who had not been present on the battlefield. The Benjamites are decimated, and the other tribes mourn the aftermath of the civil war (21:2-3). Because of the wickedness of the men of Benjamin, the other Israelites swear not to give any of their daughters in marriage to the Benjamites (v. 1). In the final episode of Judges, in order to prevent the complete extermination of an Israelite tribe, the remaining Benjamite men are encouraged to abduct young girls who are then forced to become their wives.

---

1. Explain the foolish vow made by the men of Israel (21:1).
2. Explain the grief that gripped Israel (vv. 2-3).

> "Who has ever told the evils and the curses and the crimes of war? Who can describe the horrors of the carnage of battle? Who can portray the fiendish passions which reign there! If there is anything in which earth, more than any other, resembles hell, it is its wars."—Albert Barnes

---

CONCLUSION

The Book of Judges ends on a note of tragedy––the Israelites are fighting among themselves, and one of the twelve tribes is almost extinguished. How did Israel fall to such depths of immorality and depravity? How did Israel come to be divided and broken? Israel's decline happened through a downward spiral of unfaithfulness that began as far back as Judges 1. Israel's small acts of disobedience grew into larger and more pervasive patterns of rebellion. Each generation grew worse in breaking God's commandments and departing from their covenant obligations.

God has committed Himself lovingly to His people, and expects them to love Him in return. *Commitment*—that is what God wants from us. We must serve the Lord and love Him with all of our heart, soul, mind, and strength. Whenever we take lightly our relationship to God, we begin the downward spiral that leads to death.

If we find ourselves headed in the wrong direction spiritually, there is only one remedy. Jesus gives us the answer in His words to the church at Sardis: "Wake up! Strengthen what remains and is about to die, for I have found your deeds unfinished in the sight of my God. Remember, therefore, what you have received and heard; hold it fast, and repent" (Rev. 3:2-3 NIV).

GOLDEN TEXT CHALLENGE

"EVEN AS THEY DID NOT LIKE TO RETAIN GOD IN THEIR KNOWLEDGE, GOD GAVE THEM OVER TO A REPROBATE MIND, TO DO THOSE THINGS WHICH ARE NOT CONVENIENT" (Rom. 1:28).

Stubborn refusal to follow God's way and persistence in sin are dangerous matters, because God will eventually abandon habitually resistant people to their wicked ways. God's Spirit will not always strive with humankind (Gen. 6:3), and present judgment is a foretaste of the Final Judgment.—French L. Arrington

Daily Devotions:

M. Rebellion Judged • 1 Samuel 15:22-29
T. The Immoral Woman • Proverbs 5:1-6, 20-23
W. Sin Upon Sin • Isaiah 30:1-5
T. Immorality in the Church • 1 Corinthians 5:9-13
F. Walk in Love • Ephesians 5:1-6
S. Be Sanctified • 1 Thessalonians 4:1-8

The Risen Christ (Easter)

Matthew 27:57—28:20

Unit Theme:
Resurrection of Jesus Christ

Central Truth:
Jesus Christ rose from the dead and lives forever.

Focus:
Appreciate the significance of Christ's resurrection and exalt Him as our risen Lord.

Context:
Jesus Christ was buried and rose from the dead in AD 30.

Golden Text:
"He is not here: for he is risen, as he said. Come, see the place where the Lord lay" (Matt. 28:6).

Study Outline:
  I. **Christ's Burial** (Matt. 27:57-66)
 II. **Christ's Resurrection** (Matt. 28:1-10)
III. **Christ's Mandate** (Matt. 28:16-20)

INTRODUCTION

At the moment Jesus died on the cross, several things happened. First, the curtain of the Temple was torn in two (Matt. 27:51); second, there was an earthquake (v. 51); third, many graves of Old Testament saints were opened (v. 52), although they did not appear in the city until after His resurrection); fourth, the Roman centurion confessed that Jesus was the Son of God (v. 54).

After chronicling those events, Matthew recorded the presence of faithful believers around the Cross. We must remember that except for John, all the eleven disciples fled at Jesus' death and were not gathered together again till later. In verses 55 and 56 the first group of faithful believers is described. They were the women from Galilee who ministered to Jesus. In verse 57 another faithful believer comes into the story.

I. CHRIST'S BURIAL (Matt. 27:57-66)

A. Faithful Believers (vv. 57-61)

(Matthew 27:61 is not included in the printed text.)

⁵⁷When the even was come, there came a rich man of Arimathaea, named Joseph, who also himself was Jesus' disciple: ⁵⁸He went to Pilate, and begged the body of Jesus. Then Pilate commanded the body to be delivered. ⁵⁹And when Joseph had taken the body, he wrapped it in a clean linen cloth, ⁶⁰And laid it in his own new tomb, which he had

hewn out in the rock: and he rolled a great stone to the door of the sepulchre, and departed.

The Gospels present Joseph as a pious, faithful disciple of Jesus who was looking for the kingdom of God. Other references to him include Mark 15:43-46; Luke 23:50-53; and John 19:38-41. From these accounts we learn Joseph was a member of the Jewish Sanhedrin. He was from a tiny village in the hill country of Judea named Ramathaim (the Greek name for that village is *Arimathea*). Matthew's comment that he was "rich" is based on the fact that he had an extra grave. This was a sign of wealth and influence for a man from outside Jerusalem to own property in a garden area for a grave.

His motive for burying Jesus seems to be based on several things. First, he was a loyal, though discreet, disciple of Jesus. It would have been politically impossible to have been too vocal in supporting Jesus in the Sanhedrin. Second, he is described as a righteous, pious Jew who took the Law seriously. The Mosaic Law (Deut. 21:23) required the body of a slain criminal to be buried by nightfall to prevent defilement of the land. A greater urgency would have been given on the occasion of the death of Jesus since both Sabbath and Passover were about to begin.

We do know that Joseph did not approve of the sentence of death imposed by the Sanhedrin (Luke 23:51). How vocal he was is undetermined; it is clear he did not consent to the decision. According to John 19:39, Nicodemus, another member of the Sanhedrin who apparently followed Jesus, assisted Joseph in the burial.

Nothing credible is known of Joseph following these accounts. All we can say about Joseph is he was a man who believed in Jesus and accepted the Lord's teaching about the kingdom of heaven. He was a man of honor and willing to place His reputation on the line for the sake of Christ.

Matthew 27:58 implies Joseph "begged" for the body of Jesus from Pilate. The Greek does not imply our modern sense of "begging." Rather, Joseph simply asked, or requested, permission to have the body of Christ (the Greek word sometimes has the sense of "demand" which would place an interesting twist on the situation).

The remainder of the account of Joseph affirms he did the proper thing in giving Jesus a decent burial. Joseph left and that ends the account.

Verse 61 briefly mentions some of the women who were referred to in verses 55 and 56. The setting of the passage is that these two women, Mary Magdalene and the other Mary, remained seated near the sepulchre of Jesus. The women were there as mourners, but also were faithful followers of Christ.

---

1. Compare Jesus' burial with the prophecy made about it in Isaiah 53:9.
2. What do you learn about Joseph from these verses?
3. Why do you suppose Joseph buried Jesus in his own tomb?
4. What role did Mary and Mary Magdalene play in this scene?

> Tomb, thou shalt not hold Him longer;
> Death is strong, but Life is stronger;
> Stronger than the dark, the light;
> Stronger than the wrong, the right;
> Faith and Hope triumphant say,
> Christ will rise on Easter Day.
>
> —Phillip Brooks

B. Fearful Unbelievers (vv. 62-66)

(Matthew 27:62-66 is not included in the printed text.)

By giving us this record, Matthew shows that the resurrection of Jesus was not simply a hoax. Both the Jews and the Romans went to pains to ensure that the body of Christ could not be stolen and then the claim made He was raised from the dead. This claim was made against the Christians by many Jews in the centuries following. That claim has spread to the unbelieving world of secular humanism, which refuses to admit the presence of God.

The Jews went before Pilate on the Sabbath to ask that the tomb be guarded (v. 62). On what should have been a most holy day, the Jews were more concerned with covering up their sin rather than actually hearing the voice of God.

Pilate met their request for a guard and the Jews set up a guard around the tomb. The "ye have a watch" of verse 65 can mean either the Jews had their own watchmen who could do the job, or could mean Pilate's giving them some Roman soldiers to use as guards. It was likely a Roman guard, since Jesus was actually killed as a revolutionary against the Roman government.

---

1. Why did the chief priests and Pharisees go to Pilate?
2. What two *errors* ("deceptions") were the religious leaders concerned about?
3. How secure did they make Jesus' tomb?

II. CHRIST'S RESURRECTION (Matt. 28:1-10)

A. God's Mighty Power (vv. 1-4)

¹In the end of the sabbath, as it began to dawn toward the first day of the week, came Mary Magdalene and the other Mary to see the sepulchre. ²And, behold, there was a great earthquake: for the angel of the Lord descended from heaven, and came and rolled back the stone from the door, and sat upon it. ³His countenance was like lightning, and his raiment white as snow: ⁴And for fear of him the keepers did shake, and became as dead men.

Jesus had lain in the tomb for three days (from late evening on Friday, all day Saturday, and through the early morning hours on Sunday). The Jews had been anxious to bury Him before nightfall Friday, when their Sabbath began, for their law required that no body be left unburied overnight.

The words "in the end of the sabbath" are better translated "after the sabbath." The two Marys came to mourn and to finish embalming the body, bringing spices with them.

Just as the earth quaked at the death of Jesus, so also it quaked at His glorious resurrection. The focus of this story is completely on God's mighty action. Matthew records that the men became as dead men in the presence of God's mighty act of life in the Resurrection.

This account stands in sharp contrast to the fear of the unbelieving Jews expressed in 27:64. There the Jews were afraid that the last fraud would be as bad as the first fraud. The first supposed fraud had been Jesus' claim that He was the Son of God. In John's Gospel this claim is developed in the following passages: 3:16-18, 34-36; 5:19-24; 6:35-40 (and others). The Jews considered this a blasphemous claim and used it to support their desire to have Him killed (5:18; 8:39-59; 10:22-39). The last fraud, as far as the unbelieving Jews were concerned, dealt with His prophecy that He would rise from the dead. The Jews were convinced the disciples would steal His body and claim a resurrection. To them that would be an even greater fraud.

But Matthew 28:2-4 shows the power of God in the face of people's unbelief. In the resurrection of Jesus the entire plan of redemption is revealed in power and life and is authenticated for all who will believe. God's own faithfulness to bring life out of death was at stake. The legitimacy of Jesus as the Son of God was at stake. The resurrection of Jesus proved God's Word for life to be true. The apostle Paul affirmed that Jesus was raised from the dead by the Spirit of holiness (Rom. 1:4), thus proving the life-giving power of the Holy Spirit. Jesus' defeat of sin was made a reality in His being raised from the dead.

------

1. Why do you think God used such drama in revealing the tomb's emptiness?
2. Why were the Roman soldiers so fearful?

B. Good News (vv. 5-8)

⁵And the angel answered and said unto the women, Fear not ye: for I know that ye seek Jesus, which was crucified. ⁶He is not here: for he is risen, as he said. Come, see the place where the Lord lay. ⁷And go quickly, and tell his disciples that he is risen from the dead; and, behold, he goeth before you into Galilee; there shall ye see him: lo, I have told you. ⁸And they departed quickly from the sepulchre with fear and great joy; and did run to bring his disciples word.

The angel, who was described in verse 3, here proclaims the Resurrection and declares, "Stop being afraid." It is important why the angel could command that fear leave: he knew the women were seekers of Jesus! This is comforting news to all who face fearful times and circumstances. As we seek the presence of Christ, the forces of fear are brought under control and we are comforted by the eternal love of God.

The New Testament does not tell us when, or how, the actual act of resurrection took place. It seems the resurrection of Jesus and His deliverance from the grave took place prior to the rolling away of the stone door. The action involved in the rolling away of the stone simply served to announce His accomplished deliverance. It announced that God's Word was true and announced the victory of Christ over sin and death.

To prove the grave was empty, the angel invited the women to see where the body had been laid. There is an interesting parallel between the angelic announcement of His birth and the angelic announcement of His resurrection. In both instances, the announcement was made to groups of people who were not in the mainstream of Jewish life: the shepherds and the women. In both instances, the groups were invited to come and see. For the shepherds, it meant seeing the infant lying in a manger. For the women, it meant seeing an empty tomb. In both cases, the joy of salvation was apparent.

Verse 6 also notes His resurrection was in accordance with what He had already announced in His ministry. There are several key places in Matthew where Jesus announced He would rise from the dead: 16:21; 17:9, 23; 20:19.

In 28:7 the women were told to go and tell the good news of His resurrection and the validity of God's Word. They were to announce that (1) Christ was alive and (2) He would appear to His followers in Galilee. The first part of this announcement is always our announcement today. All Christian preaching and witnessing affirms that Jesus is alive. It also affirms that He seeks to be present with His followers in the everyday course of life.

The women did not hesitate in obeying the angel's command. Even though their great joy was mixed with some fear, they *ran*—they didn't walk—to find Christ's disciples.

---

1. Why did the two Marys come to the tomb?
2. Why did the angel invite them into the tomb?
3. Why didn't the disciples come to the tomb?
4. What promise had Christ kept, and what promise did the angel make?

"The Gospels do not explain the Resurrection; the Resurrection explains the Gospels."—John S. Whale

---

C. Overwhelmed Worshipers (vv. 9-10)

⁹And as they went to tell his disciples, behold, Jesus met them, saying, All hail. And they came and held him by the feet, and worshipped

him. ¹⁰**Then said Jesus unto them, Be not afraid: go tell my brethren that they go into Galilee, and there shall they see me.**

Bursting with the emotional impact of the sight of the empty tomb and the news from the angel, the women hurried to tell His disciples. Suddenly, Jesus appeared in the path before them! Overcome with joy, they threw themselves at His feet in grateful praise.

Jesus is always willing to meet us on the path of life. Sometimes people do not recognize Him, and they trample Him underfoot in pursuit of other goals.

Jesus' first words, "Be not afraid" (v. 10), must have sounded indescribably sweet to the ears of His loved ones. How often He had used these words in encouraging His followers! But there seemed to be an urgency in His voice as He gave them further instructions, repeating the message of the angel at the tomb: "Go tell my brethren." Over and over, these words were to be repeated: *Go tell, go tell!* It still is an urgent message, and there still are millions of persons who have not heard the news of the crucifixion and resurrection of Christ.

Galilee was eighty miles from Jerusalem. It was there that Jesus had called his first disciples. He was going back, and the call would be given again. Those who had abandoned Him during His trial and crucifixion would be given another opportunity to come after Him and to learn to be fishers of men. By arranging the meeting in Galilee, Jesus removed His disciples from the danger of violence and arrest in Jerusalem. Once again, they would walk the graveled shore of Galilee together and sit on the hillsides overlooking the fields of grain to hear Him speak the words of life.

---

1. Describe and explain the women's response to the resurrected Christ.
2. Why did the women still need to hear the words "Be not afraid"?

III. CHRIST'S MANDATE (Matt. 28:16-20)

A. Christ's Authority (vv. 16-18)

(Matthew 28:16-17 is not included in the printed text.)

¹⁸**And Jesus came and spake unto them, saying, All power is given unto me in heaven and in earth.**

Upon hearing the message of the women, the eleven remaining disciples (Judas having been lost) went to Galilee to the place appointed by Jesus. The mountain is not identified for us. Wherever it was, the disciples obeyed the Lord and He appeared. It seems that obedience is more important in understanding God's will than anything else. Even some doubted when He first appeared; yet, because they obeyed, they were in the place where He could truly manifest Himself. Those who worshiped Him fell at His feet in adoration and praise (the meaning of the word *worship* in verse 17).

It should be noted that Jesus gave His command to both those who worshiped and those who doubted. Observe that even those who doubted had obeyed.

Verse 18 records the first part of the Great Commission. It begins with the authority that belongs to Jesus himself. The Greek for *power* is better translated "authority." Both words, *power* and *authority*, come from the sphere of politics. *Power* means the capacity to actually accomplish things whether legal or not. *Authority* means that the capacity to enforce is done legally. That Christ has asserted His authority over the world is fundamental to all Christian witnessing. It liberates us from the uncertainty of Satan's attacks against us.

That Christ has authority over heaven and earth means His call upon us will be met by His power to accomplish what He desires. The person who knows God has called him or her can also know Christ will make available the power to accomplish that call.

The reference to heaven and earth indicates the total lordship Jesus has over the created order. It means His authority in heaven is in agreement with the eternal will of the Father. It also means God has not deserted the earth but, in Christ, is bringing it to full redemption.

---

1. Why is it significant that all eleven of the remaining disciples obeyed Christ's message to gather in Galilee for His appearance?
2. Why did some doubt Christ even when they saw Him?
3. Why could Jesus now say, "All power is given unto me"?

> "In the Greek Orthodox tradition, the day after Easter was devoted to telling jokes. . . . They felt they were imitating the cosmic joke that God pulled on Satan in the Resurrection. Satan thought he had won, and was smug in his victory, smiling to himself, having the last word. So he thought. Then God raised Jesus from the dead, and life and salvation became the last words."—William J. Bausch (*Storytelling: Imagination and Faith*)

B. Christ's Challenge (v. 19)

¹⁹Go ye therefore, and teach all nations, baptizing them in the name of the Father, and of the Son, and of the Holy Ghost.

The phrase "teach all nations" is better translated "disciple all nations." The words *go* and *baptize* are participles and are telling what is involved in discipling the world. The Great Commission is primarily centered on discipling the world for Jesus. Many Christians have been sidetracked by "go" and "baptize." We have been afraid of where "go" might lead! We have, therefore, been hesitant to fully do the will of the Father. Others have gotten sidetracked over the mode of baptism. In actuality, these are submitted to the primary goal of making disciples.

To make disciples involves seeing the whole world as our mission. It involves seeing nations and governments as legitimate places for the Gospel to be preached. It does not mean establishing the kingdom of God with any particular government system or ideology. But it does mean the principles of Biblical justice and righteousness are proclaimed to the nations.

When Christ returns, the nations of the world will come to Zion and acknowledge His lordship. Our task before the nations today is to bear witness that He is the King and Lord of all nations. It is to proclaim repentance where national policies of any nation are on the side of evil, injustice, and oppression. It is for the Church to be on the side of the kingdom of God, and boldly declare the good news to both rich and powerful, poor and dispossessed.

---

1. Explain the importance of the word *all* in this verse.
2. What emphasis did Jesus place on water baptism?
3. Why is it significant to baptize people in the names of all three members of the Trinity?

"Christ rose from the grave and exploded in our hearts."—Selected

---

C. Christ's Presence (v. 20)

20 Teaching them to observe all things whatsoever I have commanded you: and, lo, I am with you always, even unto the end of the world. Amen.

What we are to teach the world is already revealed in the Bible. If Christians would know the Word and live in its power, our very life would be a continual testimony before the world of the presence of Christ. How can we obey the Great Commission when in our own life we do not observe what the Lord has commanded?

The lesson closes with great hope. Not only does Jesus have full authority in heaven and earth, but He is also with us always. The "end of the world" is better understood as "the end of the age." This task of bearing witness to Christ in such a way that it radically shapes our life in obedience is given hope by the reality of the presence of Christ. We are not alone in the world as we make disciples; He is present with us, "going before" us as we obey.

---

1. How prominent of a role should teaching play in the church, and what must be taught? What need not be taught?
2. Since Christ was about to ascend to heaven, why did He say, "Surely I am with you always" (NIV)?
3. Explain the phrase "even to the end of the world."

CONCLUSION

Genuine believers in Christ's burial and resurrection will help carry out His mandate to spread the Gospel. He lived, died, and was resurrected, and now we must live in resurrection power and tell the good news.

GOLDEN TEXT CHALLENGE

"HE IS NOT HERE: FOR HE IS RISEN, AS HE SAID. COME, SEE THE PLACE WHERE THE LORD LAY" (Matt. 28:6).

Where is the miracle of Easter? Dare we look for one miracle among so many? Angels' appearing? The rolled-back stone? Earthquake mighty and fearful? All of these had occurred before Easter, and they have happened since.

Not even the restoring of life to a dead body is a first. No, the uniqueness of Christ's resurrection lies in its accomplishments.

The miracle of Easter is the conquering of sin. Jesus took all our sins on Himself, but He emerged the Victor, freeing us from sin's power and penalty. The miracle of Easter is the conquering of hell. Satan's forces had thought to win, but the empty tomb testifies to their utter defeat. Hell has now no claim on us. The miracle of Easter is the conquering of death. Christ came forth triumphant—for Himself and for us who trust Him.

See Him now! The key to death's vault dangles from His belt; the chain of sin's dominion hangs broken in His hand; the gate of hell is borne under His arm. He is risen!

Daily Devotions:

M. Resurrection Song • Psalm 16:1-11
T. Resurrection Promise • Daniel 12:1-3
W. Resurrection Message • Romans 1:1-6
T. Resurrection Life • Romans 6:1-11
F. Resurrection Power • Romans 8:11-16
S. Resurrection Hope • 1 Corinthians 15:1-11

Sent by the Holy Spirit

Acts 11:19-30; 13:1-12

Unit Theme:

Paul's Journeys (Acts, Part 2)

Central Truth:

By His Spirit, God calls and sends people into ministry.

Focus:

Acknowledge and submit to the guidance of the Holy Spirit for ministry.

Context:

Luke, the writer of the Acts of the Apostles, was Paul's coworker and a physician.

Golden Text:

"As they ministered to the Lord, and fasted, the Holy Ghost said, Separate me Barnabas and Saul for the work whereunto I have called them" (Acts 13:2).

Study Outline:

  I. **The Antioch Church Founded** (Acts 11:19-26)
 II. **A Ministry-Minded Church** (Acts 11:27-30; 13:1-3)
III. **Missionaries Evangelizing Cyprus** (Acts 13:4-12)

INTRODUCTION

Antioch was the capital of Syria, situated on the Onontes River, 15 miles from the Mediterranean Sea. The church in Antioch consisted of a group of notable men, most of whom were from Cyprus and Cyrene. Barnabas, it seems, was a leader of the group (Acts 11:20-22).

As the work of the Lord prospered, Barnabas went to Tarsus in Cilicia and brought Saul with him to Antioch (v. 25). Barnabas had first befriended Saul at a time when the other Christian leaders were afraid of him (9:26-30).

In today's lesson we read that the Holy Spirit used Barnabas once again to engage Saul in the Lord's work. Saul assisted in the Antiochene church for about a year. During this time, he and Barnabas went into Jerusalem to take contributions to the Judean churches (vv. 26-30).

Another fact of interest during this period is that the disciples first began to be called "Christians" in Antioch (v. 26). Until this time, they had been called simply "disciples." The word *Christian* means "a follower of Christ." Their worship of Christ was the single fact that called all the disciples together.

In Antioch, there was an illustrious group of prophets and teachers brought together by the Holy Spirit. Verse 27 says "prophets from Jerusalem [came] unto Antioch." In this way, Antioch became a central point of spiritual activity for the young church. Barnabas came from the isle of Cyprus and Saul from

Tarsus in Cilicia. "Simeon that was called Niger" possibly came from North Africa (13:1). The word *Niger* indicates "of dark complexion," Niger being an African country. A man named Lucius also came from Cyrene in North Africa. Last of the Antiochene prophets mentioned in this verse is Manaen, who was a close friend of Herod Antipas, son of Herod the Great.

I. THE ANTIOCH CHURCH FOUNDED (Acts 11:19-26)

A. A Missionary Movement (vv. 19-21)

¹⁹Now they which were scattered abroad upon the persecution that arose about Stephen travelled as far as Phenice, and Cyprus, and Antioch, preaching the word to none but unto the Jews only. ²⁰And some of them were men of Cyprus and Cyrene, which, when they were come to Antioch, spake unto the Grecians, preaching the Lord Jesus. ²¹And the hand of the Lord was with them: and a great number believed, and turned unto the Lord.

The death of Stephen was the beginning of intense persecution of the Christians. Led by the raging Saul, the Sanhedrin increased the bitter attacks on the followers of Jesus. There was a determination to root out this new religion because it threatened the power of religious leadership among the Jews.

The word *persecution,* or "tribulation," appropriately describes this period of time. This was to a reference of the threshing instrument or roller with which the Roman farmer separated the grain from the husks.

The phrase "scattered abroad" (v. 19) is translated from a Greek verb which means "to sow thoroughly." This is what persecution did. The Christians were driven out of Jerusalem to distant lands, and they sowed the Gospel seed as they could have done in no other way.

These scattered Christians went as far as Antioch in Syria preaching the Gospel to none but Jews. Meanwhile, verse 20 refers to Jews who had lived abroad among the Gentiles. They were less bound by Jewish prejudices and were more eager to share their Christian experience with other people.

History indicates the Greek language was spoken all over Syria and throughout western Asia; but where "Grecians" are spoken of as opposed to "Jews," the general term "Gentiles" is meant.

The message preached was "the Lord Jesus," which is another way of saying "preaching the Gospel." This always included that Jesus was from Nazareth, He was the Lord of heaven and earth, He was the Messiah and the Son of God, who was crucified and resurrected.

Verse 21 shows the preaching of the Gospel is not just a matter of presenting information. It is the presenting of a call—a call to believe. When the Gentiles believed, they not only accepted the information, they also obeyed a call.

• Describe the positive product of persecution.

> "The Gospel is not speculation but fact. It is truth, because it is the record of a Person who is the Truth."—Alexander MacLaren

B. A Terrific Report (vv. 22-24)

(Acts 11:23-24 is not included in the printed text.)

²²Then tidings of these things came unto the ears of the church which was in Jerusalem: and they sent forth Barnabas, that he should go as far as Antioch.

It is commendable that the Jerusalem church was interested in other people who had accepted the Gospel. When Philip went down to Samaria and the church in Jerusalem learned that many Samaritans had accepted Christ, they sent Peter and John to encourage the new converts (8:14-16). Now the church was sending Barnabas to Antioch on a similar mission (11:22). The Church should always be interested in this important matter—that a person, having accepted Christ, should receive instruction concerning how to live for Him.

When people turn from the world to the Lord Jesus Christ, their lives are changed. This is the result of the action of the grace of God in their hearts. Barnabas saw the people had accepted the Lord, and this caused him to rejoice.

New converts need to be encouraged, strengthened, and stimulated to live for God. So Barnabas exhorted them to have "purpose of heart" and to "cleave unto the Lord" (v. 23). "Purpose of heart" means they would deliberately live for the Lord. "Cleave unto the Lord" means they would stay with Him as a wife does her husband. Barnabas wanted to cheer them up and cheer them on to take Christ as their own and to walk daily with Him.

"For he was a good man, and full of the Holy Ghost and of faith: and much people was added unto the Lord" (v. 24). What more can be said about a Christian than Luke says about Barnabas in this verse? It is a great tribute to a man of God.

---

1. Explain Barnabas' mission.
2. Why was Barnabas chosen for this task?

> "The idea of preaching the Gospel to all nations alike, regardless of nationality, of internal divisions as to rank and color, complexion and religion, constituted the beginning of a new era in history."
> —Albert Barnes

C. A Remarkable Church (vv. 25-26)

²⁵Then departed Barnabas to Tarsus, for to seek Saul: ²⁶And when he had found him, he brought him unto Antioch. And it came to pass, that a whole year they assembled themselves with the church, and taught much people. And the disciples were called Christians first in Antioch.

Barnabas seems to have based his ministry on the idea that you can do something for God if you do not care who gets the credit for it. He was a big man in spirit and in attitude. The job in Antioch was too big for one man. He wanted these people to be taught well. There was one man ideally suited for the task—Saul of Tarsus. Even though Barnabas would be overshadowed by this former rabbi and member of the Sanhedrin, he found him and brought him to Antioch to assist in the work.

Barnabas and Saul labored for Christ in Antioch for over a year and were very successful in winning and nurturing converts. During this time, Antioch made a significant contribution to Christianity—its name. The name *Christian* was probably first given in jest or ridicule, but it stuck and came to mean more than they could have ever dreamed. The first six letters of the name *Christian* spell *Christ*. This is a significant way of saying what a Christian is. We are nothing, apart from Christ. What better name could believers have than "Christ's people"?

• Summarize Saul's service in Antioch.

> "Being a Christian is more than just an instantaneous conversion—it is a daily process whereby you grow to be more and more like Christ."—Billy Graham

---

II. A MINISTRY-MINDED CHURCH (Acts 11:27-30; 13:1-3)

A. A Compassionate Church (11:27-30)

(Acts 11:27-28 is not included in the printed text.)

[29]Then the disciples, every man according to his ability, determined to send relief unto the brethren which dwelt in Judaea: [30]Which also they did, and sent it to the elders by the hands of Barnabas and Saul.

During the time when the new church in Antioch was growing spiritually and numerically under the ministry of Barnabas and Saul, "prophets from Jerusalem" came to offer their kind of ministry (v. 27). This gift of prophecy in the apostolic church, like the gift of tongues, was exercised under the immediate inspiration of the Holy Spirit, but differed from tongues in that it was expressed in the speaker's ordinary language.

The epistles of Paul give recognition to this spiritual gift in the church (1 Cor. 12:28; Eph. 4:11), and in the text before us we have an illustration of how it was exercised. It appears these prophets were sometimes occupied in preaching and interpreting the Word of God, other times in uttering some new revelation from God, and then at times in foretelling events.

Agabus was a New Testament prophet who, at this time, evidently was inspired to predict the future (v. 28). The famine he predicted was intended to arouse the new Christians in Antioch to get prepared not only for their own preservation, but also for helping other Christians in need. The reign of Claudius Caesar was remarkable because a number of severe famines occurred in the first, second, fourth, ninth, and eleventh years of his rule, in one district or another. The date of this particular famine was probably about AD 45, and is mentioned by the historian Josephus.

Sent by the Holy Spirit

The phrase "throughout all the world" suggests that though only one region might be having crop failure, all the rest of the Roman Empire would suffer to some degree at the same time, especially when famines were of frequent recurrence.

The Christians of Antioch took the prediction of Agabus seriously and began to make preparations for the eventuality of a serious famine. Since in time of famine Judea and Jerusalem were liable to suffer severely, the disciples in Antioch, a faraway Syrian city, spontaneously took up a collection for the believing brethren in Judea.

G. Campbell Morgan observed: "This is a glorious and gracious revelation of the consciousness of oneness in the Spirit; obedience to prophecy, expressing itself in love; and love taking the practical form of definite help sent to those in Judea who would suffer most as the result of the coming famine."

When the collection had been taken and all was ready to be sent to Jerusalem, the church in Antioch appointed Barnabas and Saul to act as representatives and take it to the new church (v. 30). So important did the church conceive this work of relief to be, that they set apart their two teachers and spiritual leaders for the carrying of their gifts to the elders of the mother church. Evidently, the character and labors of these God-ordained ministers had distinguished them as the most fit to be entrusted with this gift. Christian leaders must demonstrate integrity and reliability in every area of activity that the church and the community may have full confidence in them.

---

1. How did God use Agabus?
2. What principle of giving is found in verse 29?

"Christian life consists in faith and charity."—Martin Luther

---

B. A Sending Church (13:1-3)

¹Now there were in the church that was at Antioch certain prophets and teachers; as Barnabas, and Simeon that was called Niger, and Lucius of Cyrene, and Manaen, which had been brought up with Herod the tetrarch, and Saul. ²As they ministered to the Lord, and fasted, the Holy Ghost said, Separate me Barnabas and Saul for the work whereunto I have called them. ³And when they had fasted and prayed, and laid their hands on them, they sent them away.

This marks a new beginning in the missionary movement of the early church. Up to this time, the center of the church had been in Jerusalem. From this point on, however, Antioch in Syria became the center, until it shifted to Rome sometime after the Bible was completed.

It is interesting that there were apparently no apostles in Antioch. The forward thrust of the Church was furnished through the direct operation of the Holy Spirit.

In Ephesians 4:11, Paul lists the ministerial offices that Christ left to the Church. Two of them are mentioned as being present in the church at Antioch: "certain prophets and teachers" (Acts 13:1).

In verse 2, we see the Holy Spirit communicating directly to the church. There are a number of views offered as to how the Lord spoke to the church. The most logical explanation is that the mind and will of the Spirit was revealed by the prophets who were present in the church.

Observe the spiritual state of the church at the time the Lord made known His will. They were engaged in a special season of worship and fasting. *Fasting*, a form of self-denial, is often used by Christians when they desire to seek God earnestly in order to know His will.

Men and women are not to enter Christian service lightly. These positions are for those whom the Lord shall call. Preaching and teaching the Word of God, either at home or abroad, are never to be looked upon as just a job, but rather as a high calling.

The ordination of Saul and Barnabas seems to have occurred on a later day; this is inferred by the statement that they "fasted" (v. 3) again. There may have been several days between the time the Lord made known His will to the church and the time they "laid their hands on them."

The greatest need in the Church today is for men and women whom God has called to be "sent away" to carry the Gospel to those who have not yet heard the good news.

---

1. What type of leaders were in the Antioch church?
2. Why did the leaders fast twice?

"Whenever God has a great task, God raises up a man of equal greatness for that task."—Jerry Falwell

---

III. MISSIONARIES EVANGELIZING CYPRUS (Acts 13:4-12)

A. Sent by the Spirit (v. 4)

⁴So they, being sent forth by the Holy Ghost, departed unto Seleucia; and from thence they sailed to Cyprus.

Though the church sent them away, if the Spirit had not called, by speaking to the hearts of Barnabas and Paul, these two men would never have gone. Adam Clarke said the Spirit sent them forth "by His influence, authority, and under his continual direction. Without the first, they were not qualified to go; without the second, they had no authority to go; and, without the third, they could not know where to go." The missionaries first went to Cyprus—an island 148 miles long and some 40 miles wide.

• How can someone know he is being "sent out by the Holy Spirit" (NKJV)?

B. The Word Preached (v. 5)

⁵And when they were at Salamis, they preached the word of God in the synagogues of the Jews: and they had also John to their minister.

Being Jews, they were permitted to speak freely "in the synagogues." It is simply stated that they "preached the word of God"; however, we may safely infer from the total context that they gave special emphasis to the message of the saving grace of Jesus Christ. This would have included the story of His death, burial, and resurrection.

They initially preached in Salamis—the main city on the east coast. Evidently, this was done without incident, as we are not told whether the Jews' response was favorable or not. It may have been that their message was received gladly.

C. The Word Withstood (vv. 6-11)

(Acts 13:9-11 is not included in the printed text).

⁶And when they had gone through the isle unto Paphos, they found a certain sorcerer, a false prophet, a Jew, whose name was Barjesus: ⁷Which was with the deputy of the country, Sergius Paulus, a prudent man; who called for Barnabas and Saul, and desired to hear the word of God. ⁸But Elymas the sorcerer (for so is his name by interpretation) withstood them, seeking to turn away the deputy from the faith.

There are two forces at work in this world: one of them is the Spirit of God, called "the Spirit of truth"; the other is the power of Satan, or "the spirit of error." These two forces are in opposition to each other. Satan sends false prophets to weaken the effect of the truth upon people's minds. If he cannot destroy the truth, he tries to confuse people by the utterances of his "false apostles" (see 2 Cor. 11:13-15). When Paul and Barnabas came to Paphos, the capital of Cyprus, they met the false prophet Bar-jesus, also known as Elymas.

In verse 7, the word translated *prudent* means more than "wise." It carries the idea of "knowledge, above-average intelligence and understanding." These qualities, no doubt, account for the high position held by Sergius Paulus, the Roman proconsul. The most admirable quality in this man was his desire to "hear the word of God."

Ever since the Garden of Eden, where Satan contradicted the word of God, there have been those who delight in resisting the truth and asserting the word of the Lord is untrue. Hence, Jannes and Jambres withstood Moses; the prophets of Baal withstood Elijah; and Elymas withstood Paul and Barnabas. The truth will be resisted, but it will always be vindicated.

Beginning with verse 9, Luke always calls Saul by his Gentile name, *Paul*. Many Jews of that day had both a Hebrew and a Gentile name. As the apostle to the Gentiles, Saul chose to use the name *Paul*.

What follows was made possible because Paul was "filled with the Holy Ghost." Therefore, if we are to successfully withstand the enemy and boldly contend for the truth, we must be filled with the Holy Ghost (see Acts 1:8; Eph. 5:18).

Paul uses strong words, condemnatory and inditing, but they are the words of a Paul in the grip of the Spirit. The apostle sees Elymas as deceitful, guilty of fraud and wickedness, one who is trying different forms of magic and sorcery so he will not lose his influence with the proconsul.

Paul declared, "The hand of the Lord is upon thee, and thou shalt be blind, not seeing the sun for a season" (Acts 13:11). The judgment put upon Elymas was remedial in nature; therefore, his blindness was only "for a season." Paul hoped this judgment would lead the sorcerer to repentance.

This incident reminds one of the temporary blindness Paul himself had experienced on the road to Damascus. We are not, however, told what effect this season of blindness had on Elymas.

---

1. Describe Sergius Paulus and his request (v. 7).
2. Who was Elymas, what did he try to do, and why (vv. 6, 8)?
3. Compare Elymas' crisis (vv. 9-11) with Saul's crisis (9:1-9).

> "As the sun can be seen only by its own light, so Christ can be known only by His own Spirit."—Robert Leighton

---

D. The Word Believed (v. 12)

¹²Then the deputy, when he saw what was done, believed, being astonished at the doctrine of the Lord.

The judgment miracle of blindness had a profound effect on Sergius Paulus. God has, from time to time, used signs to confirm the word to the heart of those who had an honest doubt. The writer of Hebrews said "God [bore] them witness, both with signs and wonders, and with divers miracles, and gifts of the Holy Ghost, according to his own will" (2:4).

• Describe the conversion of Paulus.

> "For God is, indeed, a wonderful Father who longs to pour out His mercy upon us, and whose majesty is so great that He can transform us from deep within."—Teresa of Avila

---

Sent by the Holy Spirit

CONCLUSION

Holy Spirit, use me,
I surrender now,
I want to serve Thee,
Please show me how;
I will wait in patience
Till I hear from Thee,
O Holy Spirit,
Grant this, my plea.

—Leon H. Ellis

GOLDEN TEXT CHALLENGE

"AS THEY MINISTERED TO THE LORD, AND FASTED, THE HOLY GHOST SAID, SEPARATE ME BARNABAS AND SAUL FOR THE WORK WHEREUNTO I HAVE CALLED THEM" (Acts 13:2).

All people who worship God in Spirit and in truth minister to the Lord. In our worship services, we sing not to each other but to the Lord. Mary ministered to Jesus in her personal life. Paul and Silas ministered to the Lord in prayer and singing, even while they were in jail. When we minister to the hungry, naked, thirsty, and those who are sick and in prison, Jesus himself said, "you are ministering unto Me" (see Matt. 25:40).

All Christians are called to be ministers unto the Lord, and for the Lord, whether we are clergy or laity. The Great Commission is a call to all churches and all Christians to minister to all the world the Gospel of the Lord. Jesus said that when He returned to heaven from His earthly ministry, His followers would fast. We are admonished to fast and call solemn assemblies in order to be renewed, refreshed, and revived. Some things come about only by prayer and fasting.

When people minister unto the Lord with prayer and fasting, the Holy Spirit moves. One way He moves is by separating and empowering believers. He responds and things happen. Have we not learned that it is "not by might, nor by power, but by my spirit, saith the Lord" (Zech. 4:6)? The Holy Spirit said, "Separate me Barnabas and Saul for the work whereunto I have called them" (Acts 13:2) for His service. In the Scriptures, *sanctification*, and the enduement of power for service is the baptism in the Spirit. When God calls and empowers us for His kingdom work, it is our privilege and responsibility to obey His call.

Daily Devotions:

M. God Asks, "Who Will Go?" • Isaiah 6:1-8
T. God Says, "I Send You." • Jeremiah 1:1-10
W. God Commands, "Go." • Ezekiel 3:4-14
T. You Will Be My Witnesses • Acts 1:1-8
F. Speaking the Word Boldly • Acts 4:18-31
S. Sent by the Holy Spirit • Acts 10:19-28

Evangelizing in Asia

Acts 13:14—14:28

Unit Theme:
Paul's Journeys (Acts, Part 2)

Central Truth:
The gospel of Jesus Christ is for all nations.

Focus:
Realize the Gospel will prevail in spite of opposition, and persevere in proclaiming and teaching the Word.

Context:
Luke, the writer of the Acts of the Apostles, was Paul's coworker and a physician.

Golden Text:
"When they were come, and had gathered the church together, they rehearsed all that God had done with them, and how he had opened the door of faith unto the Gentiles" (Acts 14:27).

Study Outline:
I. **The Gospel Proclaimed in Asia** (Acts 13:14-17, 24-30, 38-39, 43)
II. **Preaching, Though Opposed** (Acts 13:44—14:7)
III. **Believers in Christ Encouraged** (Acts 14:19-28)

INTRODUCTION

There has never been a period in the world's history when there were so many churches and preachers. Thousands of sermons are preached throughout the world every Lord's Day, and yet there is such a lack of the unadulterated Word of God. In many churches, people are being fed "pastry" instead of "bread." For God's church to recover the flush of health known in the early church, the Word of God must be faithfully proclaimed.

Preachers who determine that by the grace of God they will proclaim the pure word of God will enlarge, not narrow, the scope and power of their ministry. The preacher who obeys this call is a preacher unshackled. All of God's power is behind such a preacher.

There is a great need for orthodoxy in our pulpits, but we need orthodoxy plus spiritual power. We need orthodoxy on fire, not on ice. We need hothouses, not icehouses. The letter kills, but the Spirit gives life. We need the truth proclaimed, energized by the irresistible power of the Holy Spirit.

It would be wonderful if all our preachers could say to their people, as Paul said to the Corinthians, "My speech and my preaching was not with enticing words of man's wisdom, but in demonstration of the Spirit and of power" (1 Cor. 2:4). The "demonstration" Paul referred to was not the sensationalism that turns some preachers into entertainers. Preaching that gets the job done is the kind Paul did in Pisidian Antioch. When he had finished, his hearers "besought that these [same] words might be preached to them the next sabbath" (Acts 13:42).

I. THE GOSPEL PROCLAIMED IN ASIA (Acts 13:14-17, 24-30, 38-39, 43)

A. The Synagogue Meeting (vv. 14-15)

¹⁴But when they departed from Perga, they came to Antioch in Pisidia, and went into the synagogue on the sabbath day, and sat down. ¹⁵And after the reading of the law and the prophets the rulers of the synagogue sent unto them, saying, Ye men and brethren, if ye have any word of exhortation for the people, say on.

Pisidian Antioch was a large and important Roman city, situated on the great highway running east and west across Asia Minor. This highway extended from Ephesus to Antioch, the capital of Syria. Many Jews lived there because Antiochus the Great transplanted about two thousand Jewish families in order to bind together Phrygia and Syria.

The synagogue which Paul and Barnabas attended was probably arranged like all other synagogues with an "ark" at one end containing the rolls of the Law, with a veil and lamps before it. At the same end sat the rulers of the synagogue who were responsible for arranging the services. First, the Shema was recited: "Hear, O Israel: The Lord our God is one Lord" (Deut. 6:4). Then came a prayer service. This was followed by the reading of the day's portion from the Law (the first five books of Moses, which were divided up in a three-year course) and also from the Prophets. Finally, someone selected by the synagogue rulers gave a talk on the Scripture passage, which might be followed by a discussion. The synagogue had no regular minister or preacher.

After the reading of the Scriptures, the rulers of the synagogue sent a message to the two strangers who had come to their city and synagogue, inviting them to speak a word of exhortation to the gathering.

• Describe the opportunity given to Paul.

"Good words are worth much, and cost little."—George Herbert

B. The Basis of Christian Preaching (vv. 16-17, 24-30)

(Acts 13:24-30 is not included in the printed text.)

¹⁶Then Paul stood up, and beckoning with his hand said, Men of Israel, and ye that fear God, give audience. ¹⁷The God of this people of Israel chose our fathers, and exalted the people when they dwelt as strangers in the land of Egypt, and with an high arm brought he them out of it.

Paul accepted the invitation to address the group promptly. Using appropriate gestures, he invited their attention and began his sermon. According to verse 16, the audience consisted of "men of Israel" (Jews by birth or by proselytization) and Gentile God-fearers ("ye that fear God").

Paul's exhortation took the form of a historical retrospect, as Stephen's defense did. He outlined the course of God's dealings with His people Israel, beginning with His choice of their fathers and deliverance of the people in the Exodus.

F. F. Bruce writes: "In the earliest days of the settlement in Canaan the Israelite worshipers acknowledged that God had chosen patriarchs, that He redeemed their descendants, the children of Israel, for Himself in the events of the Exodus, and that He had given them the land of Canaan as their inheritance. To these acts of God, Israelites of latter days added His choice of David to be their king" (*The Book of Acts*).

In verses 24 and 25, Paul declared John's baptism of repentance paved the way for the appearance of Jesus. As John himself made clear, he was the Messiah's forerunner. So far did John think himself beneath the Messiah, whose way he was preparing, that he declared himself unfit to untie the laces of His sandals.

Having established the fact that the Jewish people accepted John the Baptist as a prophet, in verses 26-28 Paul made his next point. He said the rulers of the Jews, because they did not know Jesus, "nor yet the voices of the prophets which are read every sabbath" (v. 27), fulfilled those very prophecies by condemning Christ to death, though "they found no cause of death in him" (v. 28).

The children of Israel condemned the Messiah even though God had given them the land of Canaan, then the judges to rule over them, then their first king, Saul. Afterward He gave them another king, David; and then in keeping with His promise, He had given them the Son of David, but they crucified Him. By describing the cross as "the tree" (v. 29), Paul made a connection with Deuteronomy 21:23.

When all was over, and the prophecies of Christ's passion had been fulfilled, His body was taken down and buried. "But God raised him from the dead" (Acts 13:30).

Unless we see the death of Jesus Christ through the Resurrection, we will only know defeat. If we simply observe Him dying, there is nothing for us. But He did not stay dead; He arose from the grave. His resurrection assures us that death has been conquered.

Whatever the doubters and skeptics may say, the apostles and the early church taught and believed Christ arose from the dead. Without the Resurrection, one cannot explain the existence of the Church at all. The Church would not have lasted one week if the truth of the Resurrection had not revitalized the disciples.

---

1. How did Paul begin his message (vv. 16-17)?
2. What critical role had John the Baptist played (vv. 24-25)?
3. Explain the phrase "word of this salvation" (v. 26).
4. Describe the irony in verses 27-29.
5. How important are the seven words of verse 30?

> "Immanuel: God with us now in our nature, our sorrow, our life-work, our punishment, and our grave; and with us, or rather we with Him, in resurrection, ascension, triumph, and Second Advent splendor."—Charles Spurgeon

---

C. The Hope of Salvation (vv. 38-39, 43)

(Acts 13:39, 43 is not included in the printed text.)

38 Be it known unto you therefore, men and brethren, that through this man is preached unto you the forgiveness of sins.

As Paul neared the end of his sermon, he declared that "through this man" they might have remission of sins and justification from all things by believing on Him (vv. 38-39).

Forgiveness of sins was a keynote in the preaching of the apostles. Here is the first time we find the verb *justify* in relation to salvation. It is the only time it occurs in the Book of Acts, but it appears many times in Paul's epistles to the Romans and Galatians. To be *justified* before God is to stand before Him in perfect righteousness without condemnation. Only one has ever been righteous, the Lord Jesus Christ. His righteousness is imputed to believers, or given to us, when we believe on Him. We are justified before God only by faith in Christ.

As the apostles were leaving the synagogue after Paul's sermon, the congregation of Jews and proselytes crowded around Paul and Barnabas, asking that the same message be preached the next Sabbath. Many of them followed Paul and Barnabas, and the apostles urged them to continue in the faith (vv. 42-43).

---

1. Describe God's incredible offer to all people (vv. 38-39).
2. How did the people respond to Paul's message (v. 43)?

> "I have taken much pains to know everything that is esteemed worth knowing among men; but with all my reading, nothing now remains to comfort me at the close of this life but this passage of Saint Paul: 'Jesus Christ came into the world to save sinners.'"
> —John Selden

II. PREACHING, THOUGH OPPOSED (Acts 13:44—14:7)

A. Blasphemy and Envy (vv. 44-45)

44 And the next sabbath day came almost the whole city together to hear the word of God. 45 But when the Jews saw the multitudes, they were filled with envy, and spake against those things which were spoken by Paul, contradicting and blaspheming.

The message of Paul was the talk of the town. And the next Sabbath most of the city turned out to hear Paul preach again (v. 44). P. J. Gloag notes: "Not only the Jews, the proselytes, and the devout Gentiles, but the heathen inhabitants of Pisidian Antioch flocked into the synagogue" (*Acts, Volume II*).

When the Jews saw the multitude, they were filled with "envy" (v. 45). This word (translated "jealousy," NIV) is from the Greek verb meaning "to boil," transliterated in our word *zeal*. "The Jews were hot with jealousy because of their fear that the Gospel would set aside the distinction between Jew and Gentile and draw away the God-fearers from the synagogue" (French Arrington, *The Acts of the Apostles*). They did not argue against the apostles because they couldn't. Instead, they angrily and haughtily asserted that Paul and Barnabas were lying. They also blasphemed the name of Christ.

• Describe the opposition to Paul's message and the reason behind it.

> "The proud man has no God; the envious man has no neighbor; the angry man has not himself. What good, then, in being a man, if one has neither himself nor a neighbor nor God."—Joseph Hall

---

B. Turning to the Gentiles (vv. 46-49)

(Acts 13:46-48 is not included in the printed text.)

⁴⁹And the word of the Lord was published throughout all the region.

Paul and Barnabas gave a plain answer to the railing of the Jews. It was right and proper that the Jews should have the first opportunity of hearing and believing the good news. But if they would not receive the light themselves, there were others who would appreciate it: it would be offered to the Gentiles.

This was a bold and revolutionary step that would make Christianity what its Founder intended it to be—*the* world religion. This was necessary because it was what Christ commanded.

Paul based his decision for spreading the Word of God, quoting Isaiah 49:6. Isaiah had prophesied the Messiah would bring salvation to all people.

The Gentiles were overjoyed that the Gospel was going to be preached to them. As many as responded in faith were reconciled to God and received eternal life.

By using the term "as many as were ordained to eternal life believed" (Acts 13:48), Luke declared the inclusiveness of the Gospel. All who believe in Christ—Gentile and Jew alike—have been predestined for everlasting life.

The Jewish antagonists could fight against the missionaries, but they could not stop the Gospel from "being spread throughout all the region" (v. 49 NKJV).

---

1. Rephrase Barnabas and Paul's "bold" statement (v. 46).
2. How did Paul characterize his mission (v. 47)?

3. What two statements are made concerning "the word of the Lord" (vv. 48-49)?

> "The Gospel is open to all; the most respectable sinner has no more claim on it than the worst."—Martyn Lloyd-Jones

---

C. Persecution and Departure (vv. 50-52)

⁵⁰But the Jews stirred up the devout and honourable women, and the chief men of the city, and raised persecution against Paul and Barnabas, and expelled them out of their coasts. ⁵¹But they shook off the dust of their feet against them, and came unto Iconium. ⁵²And the disciples were filled with joy, and with the Holy Ghost.

Many Gentile women in the region were converts to Judaism. Among them were devout women who were probably wives of the leading Gentile citizens. The Jews stirred up these women to take action against the missionaries. Paul and his coworkers were expelled from Antioch as troublemakers (v. 50). Before departing from the inhospitable city, they shook the dust from their feet as a symbol that they were free of any responsibility for those who would not hear (v. 51; cf. Mark 6:11).

In spite of persecution, the church flourished in Antioch. After Paul and Barnabas left, apparently the disciples underwent extreme persecution. But during this period of spiritual duress, the Holy Spirit was ministering to their spiritual need. They were being "filled with joy and with the Holy Spirit" (v. 52 NKJV). These disciples had a rich spiritual experience that shaped their lives and laid claim on their whole existence. The Spirit was continually filling and empowering them day by day.

---

1. Explain the missionaries' actions in verse 51 (see Mark 6:11).
2. Explain the double filling seen (v. 52).

> "The apostles went away rejoicing that they were counted worthy to suffer shame for the name of Christ—that they were graced so far as to be disgraced for the name of Christ!"—Thomas Watson

---

D. Persistence Amid Persecution (14:1-7)

(Acts 14:1, 3-4 is not included in the printed text.)

²But the unbelieving Jews stirred up the Gentiles, and made their minds evil affected against the brethren.

⁵And when there was an assault made both of the Gentiles, and also of the Jews with their rulers, to use them despitefully, and to stone them, ⁶They were ware of it, and fled unto Lystra and Derbe, cities of Lycaonia, and unto the region that lieth round about: ⁷And there they preached the gospel.

Filled with the Holy Spirit, Paul and Barnabas preached powerfully in Iconium, and a "great multitude . . . believed" (v. 1). Their preaching was a positive declaration of the Gospel. They "boldly" spoke (v. 3), even in the face of personal physical danger.

The effectiveness of their preaching can be seen in its creating a division of the entire city. The split resulted from the unbelieving Jews, spreading slander about the preachers. The Gospel always divides people into two categories—believers and unbelievers; there is no middle ground.

Paul and Barnabas fled Iconium, but not because they were afraid. They left while they were still free to move about and preach elsewhere.

---

1. How was the city divided (vv. 1-2, 4)?
2. How did the Lord show the missionaries' "message [about His grace] was true" (v. 3 NLT)?

> "If a Christian is not having tribulation in the world, there's something wrong!"—Leonard Ravenhill

---

III. BELIEVERS IN CHRIST ENCOURAGED (Acts 14:19-28)

Not all of the healings performed by the apostles are recorded, but one in Acts 14:8-10 is given because of the great effect it had on the people of Lystra. The power of preaching is illustrated by the fact that Paul was able to stimulate faith in the heart of a man who had never walked, preaching the story of the risen Christ.

The man jumped up with a single bound and began to walk around. "When the people saw what Paul had done, they lifted up their voices, saying in the speech of Lycaonia, The gods are come down to us in the likeness of men" (v. 11). The people tried to worship Paul and Barnabas, but they were horrified at the thought. Instead, they were anxious for the people of Lystra to know the God they served was not an idol. They served the "living God," who has revealed Himself in His creation (v. 15).

A. Miraculous Recovery (vv. 19-20)

19 And there came thither certain Jews from Antioch and Iconium, who persuaded the people, and, having stoned Paul, drew him out of the city, supposing he had been dead. 20 Howbeit, as the disciples stood round about him, he rose up, and came into the city: and the next day he departed with Barnabas to Derbe.

Those who would try to impede the progress of God's cause will go to almost any length to effect it. "Certain Jews" had undertaken a journey of 130 miles to express their enmity.

Observe how fickle the masses are: first, they would worship Paul as a god; now, under the evil influence, they stone him. It is not stated why only Paul was stoned. It could have been that Barnabas was in another part of the city at the time, or perhaps the mob was mainly interested in closing Paul's mouth since he, as the chief speaker, was provoking their hostility; but God was not through with Paul, so he recovered to continue his work.

• How did Paul leave the city (v. 19), and how did he return (v. 20)?

> "Paul never developed a negative attitude. He picked his bloody body up out of the dirt and went back into the city where he had almost been stoned to death, and he said, 'Hey, about that sermon I didn't finish preaching—here it is!'"—John Hagee

---

B. Reassuring Converts (vv. 21-23)

²¹And when they had preached the gospel to that city, and had taught many, they returned again to Lystra, and to Iconium, and Antioch, ²²Confirming the souls of the disciples, and exhorting them to continue in the faith, and that we must through much tribulation enter into the kingdom of God. ²³And when they had ordained them elders in every church, and had prayed with fasting, they commended them to the Lord, on whom they believed.

Paul and Barnabas returned to the places where they had established churches to review the work and to see how the converts were doing. They reinforced (reassured) them in their hope in Christ.

As they ministered to the churches, they found it necessary to point out the need for perseverance; they must "continue" if they are to "enter into the kingdom of God" (v. 22). Final salvation, though it is by the grace of God, is nevertheless conditional. They are to expect persecution, but heaven is worth "many tribulations" (v. 22 NKJV).

It was impossible for the apostles to stay with each church, so in verse 23 we see they "ordained elders" to guide them. They knew if the churches were to continue, they must have leaders; and the most effective leaders for each church were to be found among their own number, not sent in from outside.

• How did Paul and Barnabas minister in "every church" (v. 23)?

> "Lord, make me a crisis man. Bring those I contact to decision. Let me not be a milepost on a single road; make me a fork, that men must turn one way or another on facing Christ in me."—Jim Elliot

---

C. Reporting to Antioch (vv. 24-28)

(Acts 14:24-28 is not included in the printed text.)

Since the church had sent them forth, missionaries felt the need to report to the church concerning the progress they had made. The people would

---

appreciate hearing of their success and could share in that success by contributing funds and carrying a burden in prayer. Both are essential to the effectiveness of any missionary.

---

1. Upon his return to Antioch, what was Paul's report about their first missionary journey?
2. Why do you suppose the missionaries "stayed there a long time" (v. 28 NIV)?

CONCLUSION

This lesson is one of real encouragement, in that it teaches that one can prosper in the work of God even in the face of great opposition. Success is not determined by outward circumstances but by our carefully following the leadership of the Holy Spirit.

GOLDEN TEXT CHALLENGE

"WHEN THEY WERE COME, AND HAD GATHERED THE CHURCH TOGETHER, THEY REHEARSED ALL THAT GOD HAD DONE WITH THEM, AND HOW HE HAD OPENED THE DOOR OF FAITH UNTO THE GENTILES" (Acts 14:27).

The apostles gave a grateful rehearsal of the progress of the Gospel among the Gentiles. Their report did not dwell on the hardships and violence they had encountered, neither did they boast of their dedication or of their persistence in the face of persecution. They did emphasize two things: (1) what "God had done with them;" the glory belonged to God because He worked "with them." They had been His fellow workers doing the work to which the Holy Spirit had called them. (2) God had opened the door of faith to the Gentiles, and thus no one was to shut the door on which was written "salvation by faith alone."— French L. Arrington

Daily Devotions:
M. Proclaim God's Mighty Acts • Isaiah 12:1-6
T. Preaching Brings Persecution • Jeremiah 26:8-15
W. Preaching Brings Repentance • Jonah 3:1-10
T. Jesus Sends the Twelve • Luke 9:1-6
F. Jesus Sends the Seventy • Luke 10:1-12
S. Jesus Commissions the Church • Luke 24:44-53

Gentile Believers Accepted

Acts 15:1—16:5

Unit Theme:
Paul's Journeys (Acts, Part 2)

Central Truth:
Salvation for all is by grace, through faith in Christ.

Focus:
Be grateful to God that the Gospel is for all people, and endeavor to make it known to all.

Context:
Luke, the writer of the Acts of the Apostles, was Paul's coworker and a physician.

Golden Text:
"The scripture, foreseeing that God would justify the heathen [Gentiles] through faith, preached before the gospel unto Abraham, saying, In thee shall all nations be blessed" (Gal. 3:8).

Study Outline:
  I. **Controversy Over Gentile Believers** (Acts 15:1-12)
 II. **Decided by the Word and Spirit** (Acts 15:13-29)
III. **Gentile Believers Rejoice** (Acts 15:30-35, 40-41; 16:4-5)

INTRODUCTION

The Council of Jerusalem, as recorded in Acts 15, was occasioned by the progress of the Gospel among the Gentiles. This success and the Christian freedom they emphasized aroused the religious prejudice of the Pharisees in Jerusalem. To admit Gentiles into the Christian church without observing the Mosaic rite of circumcision was a serious infraction of the ceremonial law, according to this Jewish segment of the church. When this question became a problem of contention in the Antioch church, Jerusalem was consulted and the great council on Christian freedom was called.

Philip Schaff wrote, "It was the first and in some respects the most important council or synod held in the history of Christendom, though differing widely from the councils of later times. It is placed in the middle of the Book of Acts as the connecting link between two sections of the apostolic church and the two epochs of its history."

Paul recognized how crucial this issue was. His letters are full of references to the fact that the act of salvation in Jesus Christ is dependent upon faithful obedience to the lordship of Jesus, and not the demands of Moses' law. Romans 2:25-29 contains Paul's classic defense for the priority of faith and obedience over circumcision.

It is easy for even good things to take the place of a vibrant, personal faith in the lordship of Jesus Christ. But salvation can be obtained only through power of the blood of Jesus.

I. CONTROVERSY OVER GENTILE BELIEVERS (Acts 15:1-12)
A. The Problem (v. 1)

¹And certain men which came down from Judaea taught the brethren, and said, Except ye be circumcised after the manner of Moses, ye cannot be saved.

Our text moves immediately into the crisis faced by the early community: "Some men came down from Judea to Antioch" (NIV). (Note the Jewish custom of always referring to movement away from Jerusalem as "coming down." Regardless of geographical location, the Israelite always "went up" to Jerusalem. Thus Luke retained a Jewish outlook on the world.)

We are not given the identities of these men. They were Judeans who preached that salvation could not be obtained apart from the circumcision of Moses. It is likely these men represented a conservative Jewish-Christian group. They might have been some of the priests and Pharisees who had joined the church (6:7; 15:5). Their theology showed an understanding of the mission of Jesus and His call to salvation, which includes the acceptance of Moses' law as authoritative upon all who believe.

The issue posed by the teachers from Judea was crucial to the Gentile mission of Paul and Barnabas. Gentiles had received the message of salvation throughout Asia Minor; yet, these men were claiming that the reception of the Gospel in faith was not enough to bring salvation.

• What were "certain men" teaching?

> "When a prejudiced man thinks, he just rearranges his thoughts."
> —*Speaker's Sourcebook*

B. The Delegation (vv. 2-5)

²When therefore Paul and Barnabas had no small dissension and disputation with them, they determined that Paul and Barnabas, and certain other of them, should go up to Jerusalem unto the apostles and elders about this question. ³And being brought on their way by the church, they passed through Phenice and Samaria, declaring the conversion of the Gentiles: and they caused great joy unto all the brethren. ⁴And when they were come to Jerusalem, they were received of the church, and of the apostles and elders, and they declared all things that God had done with them. ⁵But there rose up certain of the sect of the Pharisees which believed, saying, That it was needful to circumcise them, and to command them to keep the law of Moses.

A serious debate took place in the Antioch church regarding the salvation issue. Paul and Barnabas did not sit idly while this breach of faith was preached. Recognizing just how much the circumcision controversy endangered the Gentile mission, the church at Antioch determined to send Paul, Barnabas, and certain others to Jerusalem to consult with the apostolic leaders there.

Jerusalem was considered to be the center of the church. Those who had been with Jesus during His ministry were still located there, and their authority was still taken seriously. It was not until the destruction of Jerusalem (AD 70) that the focus of the church shifted from the east (Jerusalem) to the west (Rome).

The group led by Paul and Barnabas went by land through Phoenicia and Samaria. There were churches in these areas, and the group from Antioch took time to tell them of the mighty acts of God in the Gentile world. The Greek word for "declaring" (v. 3) means "to tell in detail." Thus, events of the first missionary journey were related to these churches to ground them in the doctrine of salvation through faith.

This message of salvation caused great joy for the churches in this area. These believers were probably also being forced under the yoke of the Law. Thus their great joy came from the freedom found in Christ Jesus.

The Antioch delegation was received by the Council at Jerusalem, where the church had apostles and elders. The elders were probably laypeople who served in spiritual leadership. In Acts 6, deacons in the Jerusalem church are mentioned. They took care of the administrative needs of the community. The apostles were spiritual leaders who provided care for all the churches.

When Paul and Barnabas came before this group, the missionaries "declared" to them the works which God had accomplished among them (15:4). Here the word *declare* means "to give a report."

No sooner had Paul and Barnabas declared God's saving work among the Gentiles through these two missionaries than certain of the Pharisaic party in Jerusalem stood forth from the church body and lodged their protest against the methods of the Gospel missionaries. To preach Christ to the Gentiles was apparently not criticized, for these were Pharisees who had accepted Jesus as the Messiah, but they insisted that circumcision be an additional "must" for every believer.

---

1. Why were Paul and Barnabas sent to Jerusalem (v. 2)?
2. What caused "great joy" (v. 3)?
3. Why did some Jewish Christians believe circumcision was necessary?

> "The spread of the Gospel must not be limited by the prejudices and traditions of people."—*Evangelical Commentary*

C. The Debate (vv. 6-12)
   (Acts 15:8-9 is not included in the printed text.)

⁶**And the apostles and elders came together for to consider of this matter. ⁷And when there had been much disputing, Peter rose up, and said unto them, Men and brethren, ye know how that a good while ago God made choice among us, that the Gentiles by my mouth should hear the word of the gospel, and believe.**

¹⁰**Now therefore why tempt ye God, to put a yoke upon the neck of the disciples, which neither our fathers nor we were able to bear? ¹¹But we believe that through the grace of the Lord Jesus Christ we shall be saved, even as they. ¹²Then all the multitude kept silence, and gave audience to Barnabas and Paul, declaring what miracles and wonders God had wrought among the Gentiles by them.**

Verse 6 indicates a formal gathering of the church with the apostles and presbyters to discuss the difficult question now before them. If Paul's visit described in Galatians 2:1-10 is identical with his presence at the Jerusalem Council, then there seems to have been a space between the first gathering of the church leaders and the assembly now described. Paul says he had explained his position "privately to them which were of reputation" (v. 2). These private conferences were a necessary preparation for the more public debate which alone is noted by the historian.

As in the days of our Lord upon the earth, so now in the early church, the apostle Peter takes the floor as the foremost of the apostles to defend the cause of Christian freedom. There had been lengthy discussion, but Peter now rose to remind the gathering that the fundamental principle which they were discussing had already been decided, when nearly ten years earlier he had been led by the Lord to the house of Cornelius to bring the Gospel of grace to the Gentiles. Not only were they to hear the Gospel, but believe and be saved.

God alone really knows "the hearts" (Acts 15:8)—the inner thoughts, motives, and intentions of people—whether sincere or not. With His acknowledgment of the believers' sincerity of heart, one can be sure there had been a genuine experience of salvation. God had put the uncircumcised on the same level with the circumcised in giving them the Holy Spirit. God had made no distinction. What was given to the new Gentile converts was the same which had been given at the first outpouring of the Holy Spirit on the Day of Pentecost. Faith in Jesus Christ had purified the hearts of Cornelius and his friends apart from circumcision, and even before evident and oral confession, the Holy Spirit had come upon them. Why, then, should further conditions be imposed upon them which God himself plainly did not require?

Peter's illustration from his preaching mission in the house of Cornelius is undeniable historical fact. A logical deduction and application must follow. They must not "tempt God" (v. 10). People are said to "tempt" God when they distrust His guidance and, in consequence, disobey His revealed will (Ps. 95:8-11; Heb. 3:9; 1 Cor. 10:9).

Peter concluded that to enforce the Law of Moses on the Gentiles would be to "test" God (Acts 15:10 NIV). It is a test in the sense that one says by his actions of legalism that he cannot trust God to save by faith. Thus, the test focuses on the validity of God's Word.

The Greek conjunction translated *but* (v. 11) implies an exhortation for which the remainder of the verse states the reason. That is, do not continue to demand circumcision for salvation in view of the above facts, for salvation is by grace through faith alone for Jews as well as Gentiles. Due to the free kindness of the Lord Jesus, salvation is for us all.

"Said Peter, here is the fact: God has already given the Gentiles all grace without ceremony, ritual, rite, and observance. Here is the deduction: Do not be afraid to follow God, even though He seems to be breaking through things dear to our heart; do not tempt God by refusing His guidance" (G. C. Morgan).

Peter's speech brought the crowd to silence. His sermon had touched the hearts of even the Pharisees. Then Paul and Barnabas were given an opportunity to relate more of what God had done among the Gentiles. The Greek word translated *declaring* in verse 12 means "narrating" or "interpreting events."

The "miracles and wonders" were probably the acts of God during the first missionary journey. *Miracles* is from the Greek word for "signs," which is also the word used in the Gospel of John to describe the miracles of Jesus.

These miracles were meant to point beyond themselves. The multitude was to understand that God had approved the Gentile mission by allowing these signs to take place.

---

1. What convinced Peter there was "no difference between us and them" (v. 9)?
2. Compare the "yoke" (v. 10) with "grace" (v. 11).
3. What did Paul and Barnabas testify about (v. 12)?

Crisis Repeated

The crisis at Antioch is often repeated in the church. Sometimes the crisis is that the church has few who are willing to go into the world and carry out the evangelism call. At other times the crisis occurs as a result of that evangelism.

The church must be willing to live with the fruit of the seed of evangelism. It may not produce what we have always expected, but is certainly fruit which God desires and calls us to reap.
—A. D. Beacham Jr.

II. DECIDED BY THE WORD AND SPIRIT (Acts 15:13-29)

A. Prophecy Fulfilled (vv. 13-18)

(Acts 15:15-18 is not included in the printed text.)

¹³And after they had held their peace, James answered, saying, Men and brethren, hearken unto me: ¹⁴Simeon hath declared how God at the first did visit the Gentiles, to take out of them a people for his name.

We now move to the third major speaker in the drama: James, the brother of Jesus. James was the leader of the Palestinian church. He spoke with authority, commanding the council to listen to him. He began by affirming the message of "Simeon" (Peter) regarding the conversion and acceptance of Cornelius. He tied this event to Amos 9:11-12 to affirm for the community that the Gospel includes all.

The first part of the Amos passage, as interpreted by James, refers to the death and resurrection of Jesus. Verse 16 of the text relates Christ's death to the phrases "the tabernacle of David, which is fallen down" and "the ruins thereof." The resurrection of Christ is depicted in the phrases "I will build again" and "I will set it up."

The death and resurrection of Jesus was the turning point in the history of humanity; Christ was lifted up to draw all people unto Himself (John 3:14; 12:32). James spoke of the "residue of men" (Acts 15:17), meaning all people could seek after the Lord. This includes the Gentiles, specifically mentioned in the last part of verse 17. The phrase "upon whom my name is called" is better translated "who are called by My name" (NKJV).

Verse 18 says God planned to include the Gentiles in His blessings since the beginning of the world. In whatever manner the Jews might have responded to the presence of Christ, the Gentiles were included in the plan of blessing for the world. If the Jews had accepted Jesus as the Messiah, then the Gentiles would have received the blessings as promised to Abraham and would have been blessed through Israel. But since the Jews rejected the message and person of the Messiah, the Gentiles were included through the preaching of the Word.

The Word functions to bring the message of life and liberty to those who are confused and uncertain. We need more men and women who will hear God's Word and act upon it.

---

1. What did God do "at the first" (v. 14)?
2. In verses 16 and 17, why did James quote from Amos 9:11-12?

"The inclusive Gospel cannot be shared by an exclusive people."
—George Sweeting

B. Agreement Reached (vv. 19-21)

¹⁹Wherefore my sentence is, that we trouble not them, which from among the Gentiles are turned to God: ²⁰But that we write unto them, that they abstain from pollutions of idols, and from fornication, and from things strangled, and from blood. ²¹For Moses of old time hath in every city them that preach him, being read in the synagogues every sabbath day.

In view of the foregoing evidence from events and prophecy, James authoritatively announces his decision. All attempts to impose circumcision and its attendant legal obligations on Gentile converts must be refused. They had turned to God in faith, and God had received them, as evidenced by baptism in the Spirit. Such evidence permits no interference.

A further recommendation from James is to send a formal memorandum from the church in Jerusalem to the Gentile Christians exhorting them on practical matters of Christian conduct. Without compromising the Gentiles' Christian liberty, they were to be asked to respect the scruples of their Jewish brethren by following four guidelines. Each of these commandments is rooted in the Old Testament and serves an important function.

1. *Abstain from pollutions of idols.* This is based on Numbers 25:1-2: The children of Israel worshiped the pagan gods as they ate of the meat sacrificed to those gods. For many Gentile Christians, to continue eating of the meat offered to idols could constitute a form of belief that those idols still had power.

2. *Abstain from fornication.* Most commentators take this to mean abstaining from marriages that are unclean for believers, such as marrying a person who is not a believer. Certainly this should also include sexual activity outside of God-ordained marriage. In 1 Corinthians 6:13-20, Paul relates that fornication was practiced by the Gentiles who went to the pagan temples and engaged with the male and female prostitutes in those temples.

3. *Abstain from things strangled.* There were meats considered a delicacy in the pagan world which were strangled. Therefore blood would be mixed with the food. Thus, the prohibition on food strangled is related to the fourth prohibition.

4. *Abstain from blood.* This is a major theme of the Old Testament. In Genesis 9:4 this demand was put upon all people through Noah, and not just upon the Jews (see Lev. 3:17; 17:10-14). The Jews considered blood to be the lifeforce; it was therefore illegal to eat or drink.

Acts 15:21 reflects James' knowledge that the Law of Moses was known in every city, and that the Gentiles should be willing to make these concessions to their brothers in Christ. This would help to foster true Christian unity and fellowship between the Jewish and Gentile believers.

---

1. Explain the phrase "trouble not them" (v. 19).
2. What guidelines did James suggest (v. 20)?

"Grace is not the enemy, but a friend for which I am grateful."
—Jay Kesler

C. A Letter of Reconciliation (vv. 22-29)
(Acts 15:22-27 is not included in the printed text.)

²⁸For it seemed good to the Holy Ghost, and to us, to lay upon you no greater burden than these necessary things; ²⁹That ye abstain from meats offered to idols, and from blood, and from things strangled, and from fornication: from which if ye keep yourselves, ye shall do well. Fare ye well.

After hearing the speeches of Paul, Peter, and James, the council decided to send a delegation to the Antioch church. The Greek for the phrase "then pleased it" (v. 22) was a word used regularly to describe the decision-making process of an assembly. (It is the same word translated "it seemed good" in verses 25 and 28.) They voted to send the delegation, which was tantamount to accepting James' decision.

The men chosen to return to Antioch with Paul and Barnabas were Judas Barsabas and Silas, who was a Roman citizen. Silas becomes more prominent in the chapters ahead.

A letter was sent to the churches at Antioch, Syria (probably Damascus), and Cilicia. The city of Antioch was part of the province of Syria-Cilicia. Thus, we get the impression there were several churches in the area of Antioch, where Gentiles formed the major part of the congregation. The letter was written by the apostles and elders in the Jerusalem church and carried by Silas and Judas.

The contents of the letter are seen in verses 24-29. The letter describes the beginning of the crisis, and clearly indicates the Judaizers were not acting on orders from the Jerusalem church. The debate of the issue was omitted from the letter. But the most important things were mentioned: The sending of the letter by Silas and Judas, who would verify the letter verbally (v. 27); the courageous testimony of Paul and Barnabas (vv. 25-26) was emphasized to make it clear to the Antioch church that it was not considered a second-class church; the fact that the Holy Spirit had been present in the workings of the council (v. 28); and the list of prohibitions (v. 29).

This was a letter of reconciliation. James and the members of the Jerusalem church recognized the validity of the Gentile mission and showed an appreciation for the struggle encountered at Antioch.

---

1. What "pleased . . . the apostles and elders" (v. 22)?
2. How had the teaching on circumcision affected the Gentiles (v. 24)?
3. Explain the phrase "good to the Holy Spirit and to us" (v. 28 NIV).

Teachers Needed

New issues and challenges are facing the Church. The world is constantly changing, and there are new human ideas and religious teachings that are contrary to the clear teaching of Scripture. The situation calls for godly teachers who accept the Spirit-inspired Word of God as the standard for faith and practice and are gifted by the Holy Spirit to teach and guide the Church.

III. GENTILE BELIEVERS REJOICE (Acts 15:30-35, 40-41; 16:4-5)

A. The Joy of Unity (15:30-32)

30 So when they were dismissed, they came to Antioch: and when they had gathered the multitude together, they delivered the epistle: 31 Which when they had read, they rejoiced for the consolation. 32 And Judas and Silas, being prophets also themselves, exhorted the brethren with many words, and confirmed them.

The entire church community of Antioch, and probably those churches in the outlying regions, gathered together to hear the letter read. The scene was one of great rejoicing and ministry. The church understood this as a vindication of its efforts to evangelize the pagan world. Thus, by the efforts of God-fearing men, the call given the Antioch church in Acts 13 was authenticated.

Silas and Judas, as prophets, preached to the people and confirmed through the Word the validity of their effort. Note the low-key role Silas played in the story. There was no hint of conflict between Paul and Barnabas that included Silas as an accomplice. Luke diligently shows that Silas was well qualified to take over the work started by Barnabas, for Silas was a faithful worker for the Lord.

1. How did the Antioch church respond to the decision (v. 31)?
2. Describe the ministry of Judas and Silas (v. 32).

B. Two Missionary Teams (vv. 33-35, 40-41)

(Acts 15:33-35, 40-41 is not included in the printed text.)

Judas and Silas had completed their work in Antioch and were allowed to return to Jerusalem (v. 33), but only Judas returned, as Silas would soon join with the missionary efforts of Paul (v. 34). For a time, Paul and Barnabas carried on the work of teaching and preaching in Antioch (v. 35).

Because of a disagreement between Barnabas and Paul over Barnabas' nephew, Mark (vv. 36-39), two teams of Gospel preachers took to the field instead of one as originally planned. Although the incident was painful to both Barnabas and Paul, each became the leader of his team. Mark traveled with Barnabas (v. 39), while "Paul chose Silas" (v. 40).

For a while, Paul the pioneer missionary, who was so successful in opening new regions to the Gospel, became the traveling pastor (v. 41). Let ministers and other Christian workers know they are as well employed in confirming, strengthening, and teaching those who believe as in converting those who do not. In fact, one is as necessary as the other. Who should be better fitted to nurture babes in Christ than those who introduced them to Him in the beginning?

• How did "many others" minister with Paul and Barnabas (v. 35)?

C. The Church Expands (16:4-5)

⁴And as they went through the cities, they delivered them the decrees for to keep, that were ordained of the apostles and elders which were at Jerusalem. ⁵And so were the churches established in the faith, and increased in number daily.

It is reassuring to note that in spite of Paul's unhappy experience at Lystra (14:19), a Christian community took root there. Among its members was young Timothy (16:1), who had a good reputation among the Christians at Lystra and Iconium (v. 2). Paul decided to take Timothy along as assistant to himself and Silas. This was a rare opportunity for him to grow in grace, knowledge, and experience in the preaching of the Gospel.

The missionaries carried with them the recent decrees of the council at Jerusalem (v. 4)—that circumcision and the observance of ceremonial law should not be imposed upon Gentile Christians. This was the first of many decisions made by the early church which tended to clarify the Gospel and make it what it was intended to be: the power of God for Jew and Gentile alike.

In verse 5, Luke observes that the results were good—the churches were strengthened in their faith, and daily they received new members.

"The Gospel is neither a discussion or a debate. It is an announcement."—Paul Rees

---

CONCLUSION

It is said that all of us have prejudices; some conscious, many unconscious. Our lifestyle is expressed in our speech, which is sometimes marred by careless remarks toward other racial or ethnic groups. Charles Lamb, in offering a frank statement of his own prejudices, stated, "For myself, earthbound and fettered to the scene of my activities, I'm a bundle of prejudices made up of likings and dislikings."

A prejudice is a judgment formed before due examination, or an attitude which is the result of a narrow or closed mind.

Prejudices develop out of a lack of strong and Biblically sound moral principles. An elimination or hindrance from Christian fellowship and involvement, regardless of the circumstances or reason, is fundamentally not a social but a moral issue. The only cure for prejudice is love—love which takes seriously the words and actions of Christ. Prejudices keep us from our brothers and sisters. Love breaks down man-made barriers and teaches us that all God's children are worthy of His and our fellowship.

GOLDEN TEXT CHALLENGE

"THE SCRIPTURE, FORESEEING THAT GOD WOULD JUSTIFY THE HEATHEN [GENTILES] THROUGH FAITH, PREACHED BEFORE THE

GOSPEL UNTO ABRAHAM, SAYING, IN THEE SHALL ALL NATIONS BE BLESSED" (Gal. 3:8).

Paul used the Old Testament to demonstrate that right standing before God comes through faith. Particularly, he pointed to Abraham, whose life illustrated what faith is.

God entered into covenant with faithful Abraham, promising, "All the nations will be blessed in you" (Gal. 3:8 NASB). Today, that means people from every cultural and racial group, living in every country on every continent, can receive the blessings of God by putting their faith in Him, as Abraham did.

Daily Devotions:

M. All Families to Be Blessed • Genesis 12:1-3
T. Christ for All Nations • Psalm 72:11-17
W. Conversion of Gentiles Foretold • Isaiah 60:1-5
T. Light to the Gentiles • Luke 2:25-32
F. Gentiles Receive the Spirit • Acts 10:44—11:1
S. Gentiles Justified by Faith • Galatians 3:6-14

Evangelizing in Europe

Acts 16:6—17:15

Unit Theme:
Paul's Journeys (Acts, Part 2)

Central Truth:
To succeed in evangelism, we must have the power of the Holy Spirit working in and through us.

Focus:
Realize we need God for successful ministry, and determine to know and do His will.

Context:
Paul's second missionary journey

Golden Text:
"Our gospel came not unto you in word only, but also in power, and in the Holy Ghost, and in much assurance; as ye know what manner of men we were among you for your sake" (1 Thess. 1:5).

Study Outline:
I. **Directed to Europe by the Spirit** (Acts 16:6-15)
II. **Dynamic Ministry in Philippi** (Acts 16:16-40)
III. **Teaching in Thessalonica and Berea** (Acts 17:1-15)

INTRODUCTION

Paul's "second missionary journey" begins at Acts 16:1. This journey retraced some of the steps taken in the first journey; however, the most important event was Paul's entering into Europe and evangelizing in Greece.

In the contemporary world, Europe again needs evangelists. In 1900, 68 percent of the world's Christians lived in Europe. By 2005, that number had dropped to 26 percent. If current trends continue, only 20 percent of the world's Christians will be living in Europe by 2025, reported the Pew Forum.

In 1900, eight of the world's ten nations with the largest Christian population were in Europe. By 2005, only one of those nations, Russia, was in the top ten.

The Church must pray for the nations of Europe, asking God to raise up Spirit-filled evangelists like the apostle Paul to bring revival.

I. DIRECTED TO EUROPE BY THE SPIRIT (Acts 16:6-15)

A. Two Stop Signs (vv. 6-8)

(Acts 16:6-8 is not included in the printed text.)

In these verses we see Paul and his companions were twice turned away from a particular field of service by the hand of the Lord. We are not told exactly how the two prohibitions came to Paul. The primary point Luke wishes to make is that the Holy Spirit, not the directions of men, directed the mission.

Apparently Paul planned to go to the major cities of Asia, located in the west, then probably on to Ephesus. However, this was not the will of God. They were told not to preach in that part of Asia.

Therefore, they went in a northwesterly direction and came to the region of Mysia. They meant to go into the region of Bithynia, which was north of Mysia. Again, the Spirit directed them not to go.

Unable to go in any particular direction, Paul and his companions passed by the region of Mysia and settled in Troas. This city was a normal port of call between the mainland of Asia and the mainland of northern Greece (Macedonia). We are not given any idea of the time lapse during this journey. The narrative moves quickly as Luke was primarily concerned to show the mighty purposes of God and less concerned with details of time and places.

- Describe the relationship between the Holy Spirit and the missionaries.

> "We need men so possessed by the Spirit of God that God can think His thoughts through our minds, that He can plan His will through our actions, that He can direct His strategy of world evangelization through His church."—Alan Redpath

---

B. Call to Europe (vv. 9-10)

⁹And a vision appeared to Paul in the night; There stood a man of Macedonia, and prayed him, saying, Come over into Macedonia, and help us. ¹⁰And after he had seen the vision, immediately we endeavoured to go into Macedonia, assuredly gathering that the Lord had called us for to preach the gospel unto them.

The Lord's will was revealed through a vision to Paul. Since the vision happened at night, it has been suggested that Paul was asleep. One truth is for certain: the vision was precise and there was no misunderstanding its meaning.

A Macedonian stood before Paul in the vision. The man "prayed" for Paul to come—he was "pleading" or "beseeching." He pleaded for Paul to "come over." The Greek word translated "come over" was used primarily to describe a person crossing a body of water to get to the other side. Thus, the vision was precise about the geographical situation of Paul in regard to Macedonia.

The man also cried for Paul to "help us," for the Greeks needed salvation. Thus, the Holy Spirit operated in this vision to clearly mark the way of Paul as he headed west with the Gospel.

Verse 10 begins the first of the "we" sections of Acts. These passages are selections from Luke's diary. However, Luke does not indicate how he met Paul or any connection he had with this traveling missionary band.

We know Luke was a physician (Col. 4:14). Also, according to Galatians 4:12-15, Paul apparently suffered from an eye ailment. Possibly he and Luke became acquainted in Troas as Paul needed medical attention. It has even been conjectured that Luke was originally from Philippi.

While we cannot be certain regarding how Paul and Luke met, we know the group affirmed the vision of Paul and immediately determined to go to Macedonia with the expressed intention of preaching the Gospel.

• Describe Paul's Macedonian call.

"Spend time in prayer today asking for God to share His vision for your life and the work He wants you to do for Him. Pray that He molds your heart into that of a willing servant."—Michael Youssef

---

C. Personal Evangelism (vv. 11-15)

(Acts 16:11-12 is not included in the printed text.)

¹³And on the sabbath we went out of the city by a river side, where prayer was wont to be made; and we sat down, and spake unto the women which resorted thither. ¹⁴And a certain woman named Lydia, a seller of purple, of the city of Thyatira, which worshipped God, heard us: whose heart the Lord opened, that she attended unto the things which were spoken of Paul. ¹⁵And when she was baptized, and her household, she besought us, saying, If ye have judged me to be faithful to the Lord, come into my house, and abide there. And she constrained us.

Macedonia was the portion of Greece lying north of Achaia. It was the home of Alexander the Great, but, more important to our lesson, it was the country nearest Troas where Paul was during the time of his vision.

Upon seeing the vision, Paul decided to leave at once for Macedonia. There was no debating, no evasion, no tarrying. As soon as they heard the orders, these followers of Christ made haste to depart. They probably could not leave at once, for ships to Macedonia did not sail every day. In the meantime they made inquiries, then took the first available ship.

Macedonia knew nothing about Paul and was even unconscious of its need of Christ, but its dire need of the Gospel appealed to Paul and brought him to offer help.

That there was no synagogue in Philippi indicates the scarcity of Jews living in the city. In such places the Jewish people gathered for prayer in a *proseuche*, which means, literally, "a place of prayer." Because of Jewish ceremonial washings, these places of prayer were not enclosed but located near a river on the seashore. The river mentioned here was probably the Gangites, about one mile west of the city.

When the missionaries reached the river, they found many worshipers, and they were all women. This was Paul's first congregation in Philippi—all women and no men, no building to meet in, no prestige or influence in the city to count on. Nevertheless, it grew into one of the most generous of all the churches that Paul founded (*Interpreter's Bible*).

Among the women gathered at the river was one named Lydia, who, though from Thyatira, was living in Philippi at the time. She was evidently a successful businesswoman and probably had been sent to Philippi to represent a firm that sold fabric colored with rich purple dyes. This purple dye was made in Thyatira from shellfish. Lydia was obviously financially independent, but greater than her financial and business acumen was her godliness.

Lydia listened readily to Paul's exhortations and accepted Christ. She desired to be baptized, after which she influenced her household (possibly her servants) also to be baptized in water. Following the baptismal service, she invited the missionaries to enjoy the hospitality of her home.

---

1. What happened for "some days" (v. 12), and what took place on a certain "Sabbath day" (v. 13 NKJV)?
2. Describe Lydia's openness to the Lord (v. 14) and to the missionaries (v. 15).

> "He [John Wesley] has generally blown the Gospel trumpet and rode twenty miles [on horseback] before most of the professors who despise his labors have left their downy pillows."—John Fletcher

---

II. DYNAMIC MINISTRY IN PHILIPPI (Acts 16:16-40)

A. Deliverance and Imprisonment (vv. 16-24)

(Acts 16:19-24 is not included in the printed text.)

16 And it came to pass, as we went to prayer, a certain damsel possessed with a spirit of divination met us, which brought her masters much gain by soothsaying: 17 The same followed Paul and us, and cried, saying, These men are the servants of the most high God, which shew unto us the way of salvation. 18 And this did she many days. But Paul, being grieved, turned and said to the spirit, I command thee in the name of Jesus Christ to come out of her. And he came out the same hour.

The literal meaning of *divination* here is that the young girl had a "spirit of python." Greeks used the name *python* to denote a prophetic demon. The pagan inhabitants of Philippi regarded the girl as inspired by the Greek god Python.

The poor girl was a slave, controlled by her masters, to whom she had proved so popular and profitable that more than one person had charge of her. The demented girl followed Paul and his companions, shouting out to them. In spite of her demon possession, she could not but speak the truth. *Weymouth* translates her cry thus: "These men are the servants of the Most High God, and are proclaiming to you the way of salvation." She had heard the apostles preach and had retained in her confused mind some of their often-repeated statements. Thus the evil spirits in her, even as the evil spirits in the days of Christ, were led to testify of Christ (Mark 1:24; Luke 4:41).

Paul was greatly annoyed and troubled by the girl's cries. He, like Christ, would not receive the testimony of a demon. Therefore, he turned upon the raving girl and, in the name of Jesus Christ, solemnly ordered the evil spirit to come out of her. At once her frenzy left her; her shoutings were silenced, and she was once again in her right mind.

The slave girl was now no longer of any use to her greedy masters, so they arrayed themselves against Paul and his companions. Enraged at their loss, they seized Paul and Silas and dragged them through the streets to their rulers. There were two of these rulers who exercised the authority of Rome. The owners of the slave girl announced that their captives were Jews, well knowing that the Jews were generally unpopular. Then they claimed they were seditious, inciting riots and teaching unlawful customs.

So violent were their charges that the excitable crowd which followed was worked into a frenzy. The magistrates, not willing to give Paul and Silas a hearing, ordered them to be scourged with rods. This was a terribly cruel punishment, cutting through the skin to the bone and often resulting in death. After being beaten with "many stripes" (v. 23), Paul and Silas were dragged off and handed over to the city jailer with instructions to regard them as dangerous.

The jailer thrust the missionaries into the innermost of two stone rooms, a prison as dark as midnight. It swarmed with vermin and reeked of foul odor. The missionaries' feet were stretched apart in stocks, which were heavy bars of wood with holes just large enough for their legs. They were held in a most painful position, while chains held their arms fast to the wall.

---

1. Describe two ways this girl was enslaved (v. 16).
2. How did the gift of discernment operate in this situation (vv. 17-18)?
3. What charges were made against Paul and Silas (vv. 19-20)?

> "For if God be on our side, what matter maketh it who be against us, be they bishops, cardinals, popes, or whatsoever names they will?"—William Tyndale

---

B. Earthquake and Near Suicide (vv. 25-28)

25 And at midnight Paul and Silas prayed, and sang praises unto God: and the prisoners heard them. 26 And suddenly there was a great earthquake, so that the foundations of the prison were shaken: and immediately all the doors were opened, and every one's bands were loosed. 27 And the keeper of the prison awaking out of his sleep, and seeing the prison doors open, he drew out his sword, and would have killed himself, supposing that the prisoners had been fled. 28 But Paul cried with a loud voice, saying, Do thyself no harm: for we are all here.

With heroic cheerfulness, Paul and Silas passed the night of darkness with prayer and hymns. To every Jew, as well as to every Christian, the Psalms furnish an inexhaustible storehouse of sacred songs. Perhaps this is what Job meant when he spoke of "songs in the night" (Job 35:10).

Whoever the other prisoners were, they probably listened with surprise, envy, and admiration to those who were praising God in such circumstances. One of the blessed realities of living for God is the experience of being able, in nights of despair, to have a song in our hearts to Him.

Acts 16:26 underscores God does not always manifest Himself in a still, small voice. On this occasion, He manifested Himself through an earthquake. This was God's reaffirmation for His servants—His answer to their prayer and song. The earthquake trembled through the prison, opening doors and loosening bonds.

Startled from sleep, and catching sight of the prison doors standing open, the jailer instantly drew his sword and was on the verge of killing himself. He thought the prisoners had escaped, and he knew he would have to pay with his life for their escape. Suicide was a common refuge of the day against disaster and might have been regarded at Philippi as an act not only natural but heroic.

Evidently, no prisoner used the occasion to escape. But a new fear, more awful than the former, seized the jailer's soul.

---

1. Would you call this earthquake a natural disaster? Why or why not?
2. What was Paul's first concern following the quake?

"So long as we are occupied with any other object than God himself, there will be neither rest for the heart nor peace for the mind."
—A. W. Pink

C. Conviction and Salvation (vv. 29-34)

(Acts 16:29-30, 34 is not included in the printed text.)

31 And they said, Believe on the Lord Jesus Christ, and thou shalt be saved, and thy house. 32 And they spake unto him the word of the Lord, and to all that were in his house. 33 And he took them the same hour of the night, and washed their stripes; and was baptized, he and all his, straightway.

The jailer became convicted of his wickedness and realized his dire need of salvation. He could not have asked a more important question than "What must I do to be saved?" (v. 30).

What does it mean to *believe*? The word *believe* in the Bible means "to have confidence, trust, and faith." That is what the apostles were talking about in verse 31. They were telling the jailer to put his confidence, his trust, and his faith in Jesus Christ.

"The word of the Lord" (v. 32) refers to the Gospel, the good news that God so loved the world that He gave His Son to die for sinners. The apostles did not try to persuade the man with their opinions. They went directly to the Word. The message was designed for the entire family, or household.

There was an immediate response on the part of the jailer to the invitation given by the apostles. He displayed sincere evidence of the change that had occurred in his heart. His first concern was the physical welfare of the prisoners, so he "washed their stripes" (v. 33). The apostles responded to the jailer's action by baptizing him and his entire household. There was no delay.

The jailer was well aware that the apostles had not eaten since their exhausting experiences of the afternoon before; and even though it was still night, he offered them the courtesy of his hospitality. This was another proof of the change that had taken place in his heart. As they ate together, there was rejoicing because Christ had become real to the jailer and his family (v. 34).

---

1. Describe the jailer's mind-set (vv. 29-30).
2. What does it mean to "believe on the Lord Jesus Christ" (v. 31)?
3. How did Paul minister to the jailer, and how did the jailer serve Paul (vv. 32-33)?

> "While God had work for Paul, He found him friends both in court and prison."—William Gurnall

---

D. Rights and Release (vv. 35-40)

(Acts 16:35-40 is not included in the printed text.)

Rather than being released from prison quietly and getting out of town, Paul chose to remain and let the authorities worry about the legal implications of having beaten, without a trial, two Roman citizens (v. 37). Paul forced them to come and apologize for the injustice they had committed. Probably he did this to make it easier for the small church to live in Philippi without harassment from the city government. Since the founder was a Roman citizen, the government would be less likely to trouble the church.

Here we see a pragmatic man of God. One truth we need to remember is that our Lord taught us to be as innocent as doves, but also "wise as serpents" (Matt. 10:16).

Paul was not ashamed to affirm his rights as a Roman citizen. One can only wonder why those rights were not affirmed earlier, before the beating. Apparently, the Holy Spirit desired that they suffer and be present to win this jailer's family to the Lord. Perhaps the scene in Acts 16:22-24 was so chaotic they could not say anything. Regardless, Paul knew his rights and opportunities as a citizen and used them to their full purpose.

---

1. Why does Paul refuse to simply "go in peace" (v. 36)?

Evangelizing in Europe

2. How does Lydia come back into the narrative (v. 40)?

> "If God gives you rights, no man and no government can take them away from you."—Judge Roy Moore

---

III. TEACHING IN THESSALONICA AND BEREA (Acts 17:1-15)

A. The Gospel Proclaimed (vv. 1-4)

(Acts 17:2-3 is not included in the printed text.)

¹Now when they had passed through Amphipolis and Apollonia, they came to Thessalonica, where was a synagogue of the Jews.

⁴And some of them believed, and consorted with Paul and Silas; and of the devout Greeks a great multitude, and of the chief women not a few.

After the great persecution perpetrated against them, Paul and Silas left Philippi and went to Thessalonica, a city about seventy-three miles from Philippi. It was a great center of commerce.

Since there "was a synagogue of the Jews" at Thessalonica (v. 1), it is reasonable to assume that there was not a synagogue in Amphipolis and Apollonia. The former was a pure Greek town, and the latter was too small a place for Jews to settle. Paul probably bypassed these towns because there were not enough Jews. Some authorities think Thessalonica was the only city in all of Macedonia that had a Jewish synagogue.

Paul had a plan that he followed in spreading the Gospel story. First, he would locate the place of religious worship, a synagogue if possible. This would give him an opportunity to bring up the subject of religion. Those who had gathered at the synagogue had done so because they were religious-minded. They already believed in God, a fact which gave Paul a point of agreement with them. It is always good to begin a Christian witness at a place of common ground.

Second, these Jews already believed the Scriptures were the Word of God, and were, therefore, the final authority in matters of religion.

Paul based all of his claims on the Scriptures, making every effort to convince the Jews that the Old Testament prophecies had Jesus in mind. His method was one of reasoning, which points to a conversational give-and-take between Paul and his fellow countrymen. And he "reasoned with them out of the scriptures" (v. 2), meaning he either drew his proof from them, or started his argument with them.

Though the Gospel is always the same, it must be presented with the particular audience in mind. The congregations to whom Paul spoke on these occasions were Jews; therefore, he had to present the Gospel in a way that would be convincing to a Jewish mind. While they accepted the Old Testament, the "stumblingblock" for the Jews was "Christ crucified" (1 Cor. 1:23). They found it difficult to believe Jesus was their Messiah and that His death was necessary for their salvation.

The Jews believed the Christ was to come, but they did not understand He was to suffer. They looked on Him as one that was to be a great deliverer. It was, therefore, necessary for Paul to show Christ was to give His life for an atonement.

After showing the true nature of the Christ's work, Paul then explained Jesus had fulfilled all of the requirements of the Old Testament and, therefore, He was the Christ for whom they looked.

Paul's appeal was accepted by more non-Jews than Jews—a "great multitude of the devout Greeks" and several wives of prominent officials, as contrasted with "some" of the Jews (Acts 17:4 NKJV).

• Describe Paul's three Sabbath days in Thessalonica.

> "Seek each day to do or say something to further Christianity among the heathen."—Jonathan Goforth

---

B. The Gospel Opposed (vv. 5-9)

(Acts 17:6-9 is not included in the printed text.)

⁵But the Jews which believed not, moved with envy, took unto them certain lewd fellows of the baser sort, and gathered a company, and set all the city on an uproar, and assaulted the house of Jason, and sought to bring them out to the people.

The Jews had become uncontrollably jealous, both over the teaching concerning the Messiah and the success it was enjoying; so, with the help of the ignorant, rude, and shiftless, who had an easy propensity to evil, they sent the whole city into an uproar. They then directed the mob to Jason's house, hoping to find the missionaries and inflict vengeance upon them, then and there.

It appears Paul and Silas were staying in the home of Jason. This might be the same Jason of whom Paul writes in Romans 16:21. If that is the case, then he was Paul's "kinsman" and, therefore, a Jew. If this assumption is true, then Jason, either at this time or later, joined Paul and was with him in Corinth when the letter to the Romans was written.

Since they could not find Paul and Silas—probably because they were not, at that time, at the house—they arrested Jason and some of the Thessalonian brethren who were visiting Jason. The Greek word for "drew" (Acts 17:6) is literally "dragged." This shows the utter disregard the mob had for Christians. They violently forced them to the offices of "the rulers of the city."

So powerful was the ministry of the apostles that they had a reputation that preceded them wherever they went. They always caused a commotion and disturbed the status quo. Their preaching was revolutionary. This is what is meant by the statement that they "turned the world upside down."

Since the mob was momentarily unable to lay hands on Paul and Silas, they had to implicate Jason. The phrase "these all" (v. 7), though, has a wider application than Jason and the accused; it probably means "all Christians, wherever found." The charge made was treason, the same one brought against our Lord (Luke 23:2), and would suggest a Jewish source on this occasion.

Since the rulers did not consider the evidence to be very weighty, they took "security" from them and released them (Acts 17:9). This security certainly involved a promise of good behavior from Jason and the others, that nothing unlawful should be done by them.

---

1. What motivated Paul's Jewish opponents (v. 5)?
2. How are the missionaries described in verse 6? Was this accurate?
3. Who was Jason, and how did he suffer for the Gospel?

> "Nothing which is good and true can be destroyed by persecution, but that the effect ultimately is to establish more firmly, and to spread more widely, that which it was designed to overthrow."
> —Albert Barnes

C. The Gospel Believed (vv. 10-15)

(Acts 17:12-15 is not included in the printed text.)

¹⁰And the brethren immediately sent away Paul and Silas by night unto Berea: who coming thither went into the synagogue of the Jews. ¹¹These were more noble than those in Thessalonica, in that they received the word with all readiness of mind, and searched the scriptures daily, whether those things were so.

The apostles immediately left Thessalonica as a result of a direct charge by the rulers, or in fear of a recurrence of the disorder. Such a departure pained Paul; and, although he recognized the necessity of the move, he regretted it (1 Thess. 2:17-20). Yet, his spirit seemed undaunted by the persecution he had experienced; so, we see him again following his custom of going first to the "synagogue of the Jews" in Berea (Acts 17:10).

These Jews were of "more noble [character] than those in Thessalonica" (v. 11)—more reasonable and understanding and, therefore, more receptive to the claims of the Gospel. They were willing to "search the scriptures daily" to verify if the things they were hearing were reliable.

"Many of them" were thoroughly convinced the Scriptures were fulfilled in Jesus Christ (v. 12). A faith based on such study will be more likely to stand in the hour of temptation. It is not enough for us to know what we believe; we should be able to "give an answer to every man that asketh [us] a reason of the hope that is in [us]" (1 Peter 3:15).

The bitter and enduring malice of the Jews caused them to follow Paul from one place to another. His enemies came to Berea and "stirred up the people" (Acts 17:13). The Word of God always condemns those who are not willing to submit to its authority. Some people, in order to vindicate their own position, make every effort to stamp out the Word of God. Some use words while others

---

resort to physical violence. Those Jews who came from Thessalonica were of the latter sort.

Had Paul remained in Berea, there would likely have been a recurrence of the events that transpired in Thessalonica. So, to ensure his personal safety, Paul was ushered away (v. 15). Nevertheless, Paul left behind him a good number of believers. The seed had been planted and a new church had been organized.

• How should we be like the Bereans?

"Belief is a wise wager. Granted that faith cannot be proved, what harm will come to you if you gamble on its truth and it proves false? If you gain, you gain all; if you lose, you lose nothing. Wager, then, without hesitation, that He exists."—Blaise Pascal

---

CONCLUSION

This lesson underscores the truth that whenever the Gospel is preached, it will be met with different reactions from those who hear it. These reactions were foretold by the Lord in the parables of the sower and the tares, as recorded in Matthew 13. Let us learn that God's Word will not return unto Him empty, but will accomplish that which He pleases, and the purpose for which He sends it (see Isa. 55:11).

GOLDEN TEXT CHALLENGE

"OUR GOSPEL CAME NOT UNTO YOU IN WORD ONLY, BUT ALSO IN POWER, AND IN THE HOLY GHOST, AND IN MUCH ASSURANCE; AS YE KNOW WHAT MANNER OF MEN WE WERE AMONG YOU FOR YOUR SAKE" (1 Thess. 1:5).

How many people have received Jesus Christ because they saw someone leading a genuine Christian life? How many other people have rejected Christianity because of the unholy life of a professing Christian? Is your life a reflection of God's power that brings conviction to your unsaved neighbors, or is it a life of empty words that turns people away from the Gospel?

Through the indwelling Spirit of God and the implanted Word of God, we can all be powerful witnesses for Christ.

Daily Devotions:

M. Samuel Preaches to Israel • 1 Samuel 12:16-25
T. A Righteous King Sends Teachers • 2 Chronicles 17:1-9
W. A Godly King Leads Revival • 2 Chronicles 34:27-33
T. Remembering the Philippians • Philippians 1:1-11
F. Remembering the Thessalonians • 1 Thessalonians 1:1-10
S. Instructing the Thessalonians • 2 Thessalonians 3:10-18

Evangelizing Corinth and Ephesus

Acts 18:1—19:20

Unit Theme:

Paul's Journeys (Acts, Part 2)

Central Truth:

Proclaiming God's Word in the power of the Holy Spirit can change lives.

Focus:

Consider and appreciate the fact God's Word is powerful and will prevail over evil.

Context:

After ministering in Corinth for eighteen months, Paul preaches in Ephesus for two years.

Golden Text:

"God wrought special miracles by the hands of Paul. . . . So mightily grew the word of God and prevailed" (Acts 19:11, 20).

Study Outline:

 I. **Eighteen Months at Corinth** (Acts 18:1-11)

 II. **Two Years at Ephesus** (Acts 19:1-10)

 III. **God's Word Spreads and Prevails** (Acts 19:11-20)

INTRODUCTION

After Paul and Silas escaped an attempted assault in Thessalonica, they came to Berea (Acts 17:10-14). There they initially were well-received, and many of the Bereans believed in Christ; but the Jews from Thessalonica came and caused difficulty, forcing Paul to flee.

Separated from Silas and Timothy, Paul was taken in the safe custody of Christians to Athens, Greece (v. 15)—one of the most important cities in classical history. Even in Paul's time (about AD 55), it was noted for its contributions to political/philosophical history. Many of the great Greek philosophers had called it home: Plato, Aristotle, and Zeno.

It did not take Paul long in visiting the ancient historical sites of Athens to realize there was something terribly wrong in the spiritual realm. These sites were not merely historical sites in his time; they remained active sites of worship and idolatry (v. 16). As a Jew who accepted the first commandment (Ex. 20:3), the sight of so many idols was terribly offensive.

After finding an altar dedicated to "an unknown god," Paul declared, "This is what I am going to proclaim to you" (Acts 17:23 NIV), and then told the story of the living God's interaction with humanity, from Creation to Christ's resurrection. In response, "some of the people . . . believed" (v. 34 NIV).

I. EIGHTEEN MONTHS AT CORINTH (Acts 18:1-11)
A. Bi-vocational Ministry (vv. 1-4)
   (Acts 18:2-3 is not included in the printed text.)
   **¹After these things Paul departed from Athens, and came to Corinth;
   ⁴And he reasoned in the synagogue every sabbath, and persuaded
   the Jews and the Greeks.**

Following his ministry efforts in Athens with the philosophers, Paul continued his mission to Corinth. That a church could be founded in this city is a miracle of divine grace, for it was a place of dishonesty, drunkenness, and immorality. There were a thousand prostitutes devoted to the immoral worship of the sensual goddess Astorath. No wonder Paul could write, "Where sin abounded, grace did much more abound" (Rom. 5:20)!

While waiting for Silas and Timothy to join him, Paul found it necessary to follow his trade of tentmaking in order to support himself. Manual work was never beneath Paul. His working, however, was only a means of providing the necessities of life. His main goal was always to declare the message of salvation through Jesus Christ.

In following his trade, Paul quickly made new friends (18:2). There is no evidence that Aquila and Priscilla were believers before they met Paul; in fact, it seems Paul was responsible for their conversion. It was impossible for one to meet Paul and not, at the same time, be introduced to Jesus Christ.

During the week, Paul was engaged in physical work, but on the Sabbath he went to the synagogue to worship and to reason with those he met there (v. 4). He took advantage of every opportunity to witness and spread the gospel of Jesus Christ.

There were many Greeks who attended the synagogue to hear the word of the Lord. It appears that the dispersion of the Jews throughout the empire was used of the Lord as a preparation for the spreading of the Gospel. First came the Jews with their message of a coming Messiah; then followed the apostles with their message that the Messiah had come, and that He was none other than Jesus of Nazareth, who had been crucified but was now risen from the dead.

---

1. How was Paul similar to Aquila and Priscilla?
2. How did Paul minister in Corinth?

"Be active, be diligent. Avoid all laziness, sloth, indolence. From . . . every appearance of it; else you will never be more than half a Christian."
—John Wesley

B. Opposite Responses (vv. 5-8)
   (Acts 18:5, 7 is not included in the printed text.)
   **⁶And when they opposed themselves, and blasphemed, he shook his
   raiment, and said unto them, Your blood be upon your own heads; I am
   clean; from henceforth I will go unto the Gentiles.**

⁸And Crispus, the chief ruler of the synagogue, believed on the Lord with all his house; and many of the Corinthians hearing believed, and were baptized.

After Silas and Timothy arrived, Paul gave up his job and made preaching his full business. Possibly, he had earned enough to take care of them for a while, or it could be that Silas and Timothy could now help with providing a means of support. In any case, Paul was "pressed," or driven, by the Holy Spirit to make every effort to convince "the Jews that Jesus was Christ"—the Messiah (v. 5).

Paul felt he was responsible to tell everyone he could about the Lord; so we hear him saying to the Romans, "I am debtor both to the Greeks, and to the Barbarians; both to the wise, and to the unwise" (1:14). However, after he had preached the Gospel to the Jews in Corinth, he felt the burden of responsibility shift from the preacher to the hearer. Therefore, he symbolically "shook his raiment" (Acts 18:6), indicating both his freedom from responsibility and his contempt because of their refusal to believe. He later wrote to the church in Corinth, "If any man love not the Lord Jesus Christ, let him be Anathema [accursed]" (1 Cor. 16:22).

After abandoning his meetings in the synagogue, the home of a man named Justus became his place of meeting (Acts 18:7). Paul's spirit had been stirred; he would not be defeated, even if his fellow Jews were determined to refuse the truth. He went into a house close to the synagogue so easy access could be gained to his services by all who wished to come, whether Greeks or Jews.

Though most of the Jews rejected the truth, some received it gladly. Among those who accepted Christ was "Crispus, the chief ruler of the synagogue" (v. 8). It was a blow to the Jews that one of their leaders would accept Christ, which explains why they felt so hostile toward Paul. Crispus was one of the few people whom the apostle personally baptized (see 1 Cor. 1:14).

The major part of the "many" who believed in the city were Gentiles (Acts 18:8). The spread of the new faith among them was gradual and continuous; and from this group was formed one of the most gifted churches.

---

1. Describe the content of Paul's message (v. 5).
2. Describe the response to the message and Paul's severe reaction (v. 6).
3. How did God show favor to Paul's preaching (vv. 7-8)?

> "A preacher should have the mind of a scholar, the heart of a child, and the hide of a rhinoceros. His biggest problem is how to toughen his hide without hardening his heart."—Vance Havner

---

C. Encouraging Vision (vv. 9-11)

⁹Then spake the Lord to Paul in the night by a vision, Be not afraid, but speak, and hold not thy peace: ¹⁰For I am with thee, and no man

shall set on thee to hurt thee: for I have much people in this city. [11]And he continued there a year and six months, teaching the word of God among them.

Wilbur G. Williams said:

> By reading the Thessalonian letters, we can discover much about Paul during his stay in Corinth, for they were written within a few months of each other, the first after Timothy had brought news of the church to Corinth. We discover that Paul had become apprehensive about the persecution he was suffering at Corinth, for he was being hindered from ministering even to non-Jews (1 Thess. 2:15-16). However, he did receive comfort from the way the church there was growing (3:7). Yet, he needed more comfort, and God gave it to him [in a vision at night].

Paul is given two reasons why he should not fear. The first and greatest reason is the presence of Christ. This was in fulfillment of the Great Commission, when Christ said, "I am with you alway, even unto the end of the world [age]" (Matt. 28:20).

The second reason is the Lord had "much people in this city" (Acts 18:10). By his foreknowledge, God knew a large number of the people of Corinth would be favorably disposed to the apostle and the Gospel, thus assuring Paul's success in establishing a church.

The vision was enough to quiet the troubled spirit of Paul; he saw that although he wanted to revisit the Macedonian churches (1 Thess. 2:18), the strength of Satan would have to be broken in Corinth first. Evil men attacked the apostle to do him personal injury, but they were without success, as his year-and-six-month stay verifies.

• How did the Lord encourage Paul, and what was the outcome?

> "I will not fear, for You are ever with me, and You will never leave me to face my perils alone."—Thomas Merton

---

II. TWO YEARS AT EPHESUS (Acts 19:1-10)

A. Paul Finds Disciples (vv. 1-2)

[1]And it came to pass, that, while Apollos was at Corinth, Paul having passed through the upper coasts came to Ephesus: and finding certain disciples, [2]He said unto them, Have ye received the Holy Ghost since ye believed? And they said unto him, We have not so much as heard whether there be any Holy Ghost.

It is possible that Paul knew of these disciples before he went to Ephesus. It may be that Apollos had informed him where he could find these men. Perhaps, like Apollos, these men had served the Lord diligently but knew only the baptism of John and needed to be taught "the way of God more perfectly" (18:24-26). This was a period of transition, and some of the true followers of

God were unaware of all that had taken place in other parts of the world. It is possible that these men were believers long before Christ was crucified.

They did not know the Holy Spirit had been given. This does not mean they knew about the Holy Spirit, for John, whose disciples they were, had said, "I indeed baptize you with water unto repentance: but he that cometh after me is mightier than I, whose shoes I am not worthy to bear: he shall baptize you with the Holy Ghost, and with fire" (Matt. 3:11). They were not in Jerusalem when the Holy Spirit was poured out on the Day of Pentecost. They were living up to the knowledge they had.

We should never criticize those who have not had the privileges or light that we have had. Instead, like Aquila and Priscilla, we should do all we can, in a spirit of humility, to help all to reach a place of greater understanding. It could be, too, that someone may have a fuller knowledge than we, in which case we should be willing to learn.

• Describe the status of "certain disciples" in Ephesus.

> "We need the indwelling and leading of the Holy Spirit, but we also need Him in baptismal portion."—Horace S. Ward

---

B. Believers Filled With the Spirit (vv. 3-7)

(Acts 19:3-4 is not included in the printed text.)

5When they heard this, they were baptized in the name of the Lord Jesus. 6And when Paul had laid his hands upon them, the Holy Ghost came on them; and they spake with tongues, and prophesied. 7And all the men were about twelve.

There was essentially no difference between John's requirements and those of the Gospel, except one set was given before the atonement of Christ was accomplished on the cross and the other was given after. In both cases, followers were to believe in Him who was to come, or who had come—Jesus Christ the Messiah. Those who served God before Calvary looked forward to the Deliverer who was to come, while those who serve God on this side of Calvary look back to the One who has already come. To the former, it was hope in what was to be and faith in the promise of God; to the latter, it is a faith in a fact of history.

In Ephesus, there was a group of twelve men who, through the teachings of John, had understood and practiced repentance toward God. They had a real faith in Christ, though perhaps it was a little vague; for they had not heard His disclosures about "another Comforter," and had missed the gift of His baptism. Hungry for truth, they wasted no time making up for the deficiency; they were baptized in the name of Jesus.

Following their water baptism, Paul laid his hands on these men and prayed for them to be filled with the Holy Spirit. The Spirit descended upon them and manifested Himself, partly by their speaking words they had not learned, and partly in prophetic inspiration, uttering truth they had not known.

It is necessary for those who accept the Lord to be filled with the Spirit in order to be the effective witnesses God calls them to be (see Acts 1:8).

---

1. Why were these Ephesian believers baptized in water a second time (vv. 3-5)?
2. How did Paul know these twelve men had been baptized in the Spirit (vv. 6-7)?

> "*Amplius* means broader, fuller, wider. That is God's perpetual word to us in relation to the filling of the Holy Spirit. We can never have enough to satisfy His yearning desire."—F. B. Meyer

---

C. The Word Spreads (vv. 8-10)

⁸And he went into the synagogue, and spake boldly for the space of three months, disputing and persuading the things concerning the kingdom of God. ⁹But when divers were hardened, and believed not, but spake evil of that way before the multitude, he departed from them, and separated the disciples, disputing daily in the school of one Tyrannus. ¹⁰And this continued by the space of two years; so that all they which dwelt in Asia heard the word of the Lord Jesus, both Jews and Greeks.

Following his custom of preaching to the Jews first, Paul enters the synagogue and disputes and persuades. He must have known what sort of opposition he would meet and how their hearts would be hardened to the truth; yet, with courage and determination, he boldly proclaimed the message of salvation.

Paul was bold because he was completely convinced of the truthfulness of the Gospel which he preached. Furthermore, he had a love for people, even when they opposed him. He knew that without the Christ he preached, they would be lost. Perhaps if we believed this with the same conviction Paul had, we would be much more zealous in our efforts to bring lost people to the Lord.

Often the Lord uses opposition as a means to draw attention to the Gospel. By speaking against the Gospel, Paul's opponents caused others to consider the Gospel and to make a choice concerning it. Rather than remaining indifferent, they are made to decide. This dispute caused the disciples to be separated from the synagogue, and Paul preached daily in a lecture hall.

Being so strategically located, and such a center of importance in commerce and religion (people came to see and worship the goddess Diana from all over that part of the world), Ephesus was an ideal place for Paul to spend extra time. Probably the seven churches of Asia were founded during this period. They were all centers of trade and within easy reach of Ephesus.

Paul made it his business to see that everyone had "heard the word of the Lord" (v. 10). No church should allow the people of its city to go about without even knowing of its existence. Wherever Paul was, it was the center of activity. All may not believe, but all would hear.

- Compare Paul's first three months in Ephesus with the ensuing two years.

> "If you have no opposition in the place you serve, you're serving in the wrong place."—G. Campell Morgan

III. GOD'S WORD SPREADS AND PREVAILS (Acts 19:11-20)

A. Miracle Ministry (vv. 11-12)

¹¹And God wrought special miracles by the hands of Paul: ¹²So that from his body were brought unto the sick handkerchiefs or aprons, and the diseases departed from them, and the evil spirits went out of them.

Whenever a New Testament revival or spiritual renewal takes place, miracles are to be expected. It is one of the marks of a Holy Spirit-inspired awakening. At Ephesus, the activeness of the Holy Spirit is seen not only in the twelve receiving the Baptism but also in a number of supernatural miracles and deliverances.

The means is what separates these events from other miracles recorded in the New Testament. Verse 11 specifically states Paul was used of God to bring about these miracles. However, it was an indirect use. Neither of these two verses state or hint at his going to where the miracles occurred. He did not lay hands on or pray directly for the people receiving the miracles.

Apparently, other believers came to Paul's workplace and took pieces of material with which he had been in contact physically. These pieces of material were then placed on those individuals needing healing or deliverance. Miraculously the diseases left the sick, and evil spirits departed from those possessed. It reminds us how unlimited the Holy Spirit is. He can work across great distances and through a variety of contact means.

These pieces of material were of two types. The *handkerchiefs* literally refer to sweat rags which were tied around the head to keep perspiration from running down a person's face. The *aprons* were the common waist aprons worn by craftsmen. In themselves these materials were undesirable, especially in consideration of their use. But they became the means of a contact point with the apostle Paul and the powerful ministry of the Holy Spirit which flowed through him.

- Describe how "God worked unusual miracles" (v. 11 NKJV).

> "The man who is going through with God to be used in healing must be a man of longsuffering."—Smith Wigglesworth

B. Imitation Ministry (vv. 13-16)

(Acts 19:13-14, 16 is not included in the printed text.)

¹⁵And the evil spirit answered and said, Jesus I know, and Paul I know; but who are ye?

Paul's powerful ministry through the Holy Spirit drew attention. Especially interested were those who practiced exorcism and were involved in various magic arts. The city of Ephesus had a historical reputation as a center for the practice of magic.

According to verse 13, some itinerant Jewish exorcists were at Ephesus and knew of Paul's ministry. Paul's presentation of Jesus and the power which flowed from him through this name caused them to decide to also use it. Apparently, it appeared to them as just another power which might become useful to them. And, of course, if successful, there would be monetary benefit.

In verse 14, Luke included a specific account of a family of brothers who attempted to cast out an evil spirit by using the name of Jesus. Their father, Sceva, may have been from one of the families of the high priests. But, more than likely, he had taken the title since, by doing so, it would give him great prestige. A chief priest could pronounce the name of Israel's God correctly and, thus, supposedly invoke great power. He and his sons apparently traveled from location to location setting up business where it seemed profitable.

The demon's response let them know they were in unfamiliar territory (v. 15). This evil spirit knew who Jesus was. He knew Christ's position and power. He also knew Paul and his ministry through the Holy Spirit. But these seven men were unknown in their spiritual world. They had no power and no reputation to be feared.

Energized with demonic strength, the man attacked these interferers (v. 16). Unable to flee quickly due to the confines of the house, all seven of them received a beating. Their clothing was ripped from them, and all received injuries. Their attempt at glory degenerated into a nightmare. They wrongly assumed the power of Jesus would radiate through them by the simple use of His name even though they did not know Him.

---

1. What error did seven brothers make (vv. 13-14)?
2. What do verses 15 and 16 reveal about evil spirits?

"Satan is not an initiator but an imitator."—A. W. Pink

C. Means of Belief (vv. 17-18)

¹⁷And this was known to all the Jews and Greeks also dwelling at Ephesus; and fear fell on them all, and the name of the Lord Jesus was magnified. ¹⁸And many that believed came, and confessed, and shewed their deeds.

News spread fast. The seven brothers' failure in the exorcism plus the physical beating became known throughout the practitioners of the city. Jesus Christ was not a power just anyone could use. There had to be a personal, believing relationship.

The impact of this event was threefold: (1) Fear came upon those who practiced magic. (2) The name of Jesus became magnified. Not only did they come to realize Paul's message about Jesus was true, but they also began to recognize who Jesus was and accept Him. (3) Many believed on Him, confessed their sins, and began a new life.

• Explain the connection between fear, worship, and confession in these verses.

> "Persistent calling upon the name of the Lord breaks through every stronghold of the devil, for nothing is impossible with God. For Christians in these troubled times there is simply no other way." —Jim Cymbala

---

D. Rejection of Sorcery (vv. 19-20)

19Many of them also which used curious arts brought their books together, and burned them before all men: and they counted the price of them, and found it fifty thousand pieces of silver. 20So mightily grew the word of God and prevailed.

Spiritual renewal in the life of the unbeliever begins with belief in Jesus and confession of sins. It also, however, must include a change in lifestyle. Those activities and possessions which cause the previous life of sin to remain need to be discontinued and destroyed. Verse 19 records the actions of some of these new believers as they disassociated themselves from the past and turned to a new future in Christ.

These parchments of magical directions and spells could have been burned in private, but not with the same effect. Public burning served as an open rejection of their content and practice. This was another form of public witness of their new life in Christ. The economic value of the materials burned was considerable. A *drachma*, or silver coin, equaled about one day's wages. Their bonfire destroyed fifty thousand days of wages.

Verse 20 summarizes the total revival event in Ephesus. The word of the Lord spread and prevailed. People were changed. They were led into new depths of spirituality and life in Christ through the move of the Holy Spirit.

---

1. How do you know these sorcerers' repentance was genuine (v. 19)?
2. What does verse 20 declare about the Word of God?

> "The Bible is no dead book of ink on paper, bound in leather and cloth, but it is life to those who in faith receive it."—Charles W. Conn

---

CONCLUSION

Planting churches in pagan lands has always been hazardous; nevertheless, if one is led of the Lord, he or she can be assured of His favor. The

Gospel will never be accepted by all people, but there are those who hunger for God in the most unlikely places. Evangelism knows no bounds.

GOLDEN TEXT CHALLENGE

"GOD WROUGHT SPECIAL MIRACLES BY THE HANDS OF PAUL. . . . SO MIGHTILY GREW THE WORD OF GOD AND PREVAILED" (Acts 19:11, 20).

Equipped for ministry by the Spirit, the apostle Paul not only had success in preaching the Gospel but, also, his ministry was attested by extraordinary miracles, healings, and exorcisms. God wrought signs and wonders through Paul's laying his hands on the sick; handkerchiefs and aprons that had touched his body were used in healings and exorcisms. The apostle, as he himself bears witness, effected extraordinary miracles and ministered to human needs (Rom. 15:18; 2 Cor. 12:12). These mighty deeds glorified Jesus Christ and both advertised and sealed the saving power of "the word of God" in Asia.

Daily Devotions:

M. God's Word Humbles a Sinner • 1 Kings 21:20-29
T. Power of a Testimony • 2 Kings 8:1-6
W. Wise counsel by Letter • Jeremiah 29:1-7
T. The Church at Corinth • 1 Corinthians 1:1-9
F. Exhorting the Corinthians • 2 Corinthians 13:5-14
S. Exhorting the Ephesians • Ephesians 2:11-22

Teaching the Gospel at Rome

Acts 23:11; 25:10-12; 27:13-25; 28:16-31

Unit Theme:

Paul's Journeys (Acts, Part 2)

Central Truth:

God provides us with opportunities for ministry.

Focus:

Give thanks for and use wisely ministry opportunities God sets before us.

Context:

Paul travels from Jerusalem to Caesarea, to Malta, and on to Rome.

Golden Text:

"I would ye should understand, brethren, that the things which happened unto me have fallen out rather unto the furtherance of the gospel" (Phil. 1:12).

Study Outline:

  I. **Sent by God to Rome** (Acts 23:11; 25:10-12; 27:13-15, 20-25)

  II. **Testifying to the Jews** (Acts 28:16-23)

  III. **Proclaiming the Kingdom of God** (Acts 28:24-31)

INTRODUCTION

Saul the Pharisee, who became Paul the apostle, was a Roman citizen who would eventually witness for Christ in Rome, because this was God's will. However, getting there would be quite a process.

In Acts 23, the Roman commander of the guard in Jerusalem, named Claudius Lysias, brought Paul before the Jewish court to find out why the Jews were bringing charges against him. Paul began his defense by speaking of his own life before God. He used the term "good conscience" (v. 1) to describe his relationship with God. Paul used the word *conscience* in Romans 2:15; 1 Corinthians 8:7; and 2 Corinthians 1:12; and it appears he helped to develop the meaning of the word during the Christian era.

Paul barely got these words out of his mouth before he was struck on the mouth (v. 2). He was smitten either because he claimed to have a clear conscience before God, or because he called the members of the council "brethren." Regardless, it must have created quite a stir.

The high priest is identified as Ananias. His order to strike Paul fits in well with what is known of his life. He became high priest about AD 47 and ruled till AD 58. The historian Josephus writes that he took for himself the tithe that should have gone to the common priests. He went on to describe Ananias as "a bold man in his temper, and very insolent; he was also of the sect of the

Sadducees, who are very stern in judging offenders above all the rest of the Jews."

Paul responded with righteous indignation, asserting they had no right to judge him when they had broken the Law themselves by striking him (v. 3).

Paul recognized the precarious state of the proceedings and that the assembly consisted of the two largest Jewish religious groups: the Pharisees and the Sadducees. He took advantage of this opportunity to deflect attention from himself and focus it on his participation as a Pharisee. He said he was on trial regarding "the hope and resurrection of the dead" (v. 6), which the Sadducees disbelieved (v. 8). Upon hearing this, the two rival parties were divided. After a period of raucous debate, the scribes took the floor and argued on partisan grounds for Paul (v. 9).

I. SENT BY GOD TO ROME (Acts 23:11; 25:10-12; 27:13-15, 20-25)

A. Divine Promise (23:11)

¹¹And the night following the Lord stood by him, and said, Be of good cheer, Paul: for as thou hast testified of me in Jerusalem, so must thou bear witness also at Rome.

The partisan position by the Pharisees added to the crisis of the situation. Both sides became violent and Paul was caught in the middle. Paul was rescued by a Roman officer, the "chief captain," and brought back to the barracks for his own safety (v. 10).

This must have been a traumatic experience for the apostle. He had been warned before coming to Jerusalem of the inherent danger (20:22; 21:4, 11-12). He felt strongly that he must obey the voice of the Lord, who was directing him. We can suppose that through the rest of that day he wondered about his mission to Rome and to Spain (Rom. 15:23-24).

In the midst of this uncertainty, the Lord appeared to him and brought marvelous news. The message was that Paul would carry the Gospel to Rome. It may not have been the way the apostle had planned, but it was the way God willed it.

• Of what did the Lord assure Paul, and how?

"There is more stuff and substance of good in the Lord's promises than the sharpest-sighted saint did or can perceive; for when we have followed the promise, to find out all the truth which is in it, we meet with a cloud of unsearchable riches, and are forced to leave it there."—David Dickson

---

B. Appeal to Caesar (25:10-12)

¹⁰Then said Paul, I stand at Caesar's judgment seat, where I ought to be judged: to the Jews have I done no wrong, as thou very well knowest. ¹¹For if I be an offender, or have committed any thing worthy of death, I refuse not to die: but if there be none of these things whereof these

**accuse me, no man may deliver me unto them. I appeal unto Caesar.
¹²Then Festus, when he had conferred with the council, answered, Hast
thou appealed unto Caesar? unto Caesar shalt thou go.**

In the first six verses of Acts 25, the new procurator of Judea became
acquainted with the Jewish case against Paul. Three days after he arrived in
Caesarea, he went to Jerusalem to pay his respects to the religious leaders
and to cultivate their friendship. Immediately the Jewish leaders asked that
Festus grant them a favor. They told him about Paul and asked that he send
the prisoner to Jerusalem. Festus told the Jews to come to Caesarea instead
and present their case there.

The Jews issued the same charges against Paul with the additional charge
of treason against Caesar. This charge seems to have come from Tertullus'
accusation that Paul had agitated the "Jews throughout the world" (24:5).

Paul denied all accusations, but the Jews still charged him with heresy
because he did not require his Gentile converts to observe the Jewish law.

Festus was caught in a difficult position. He wanted to retain favor with the
Jews, but he was obliged to respect Roman justice. As a compromise, he
asked Paul, "Are you willing to go up to Jerusalem and stand trial before me
there on these charges?" (25:9 NIV).

Paul's response was couched in a restatement of his innocence and with
an affirmation that, if he were an offender, he was willing to die. He also
reminded Festus that he had done no wrong to the Jews "as thou very well
knowest" (v. 10). Paul felt he stood a better chance of getting justice from the
Romans than from his own people, so he made his appeal to go to Caesar.

Commenting on the Roman's right of appeal, T. C. Smith writes: "In Paul's
day no citizen could ask for a trial before Caesar's court if he had already been
sentenced by a lower tribunal. Since no judgment had been passed upon the
apostle, he was well within his rights to make the appeal. He took advantage of
his inherited prerogative, not simply for his own safety, but for use as a wedge
to gain legal recognition of the Christians in the Empire" (*The Broadman Bible
Commentary*, Vol. 10).

Festus was apparently fearful of having to refer his first case to the imperial
government. So, he conferred with the council (v. 12) to be advised if Paul was
within his right to make such an appeal. From his response, Festus seemed
to have been assured Paul was within his rights and privileges to appeal to
Caesar, and he consented for Paul to go to Rome.

• Describe Paul's confidence.

"No great principle ever triumphed but through much evil."
—Frederick W. Robertson

C. A Sure Word (27:13-15, 20-25)
    (Acts 27:13-15, 20 is not included in the printed text.)

²¹But after long abstinence Paul stood forth in the midst of them, and said, Sirs, ye should have hearkened unto me, and not have loosed from Crete, and to have gained this harm and loss. ²²And now I exhort you to be of good cheer: for there shall be no loss of any man's life among you, but of the ship. ²³For there stood by me this night the angel of God, whose I am, and whom I serve, ²⁴Saying, Fear not, Paul; thou must be brought before Caesar: and, lo, God hath given thee all them that sail with thee. ²⁵Wherefore, sirs, be of good cheer: for I believe God, that it shall be even as it was told me.

Acts 27 details Paul's harrowing voyage from Caesarea to Malta (an unplanned stop). Thinking that the soft wind meant good sailing (v. 13), the ship sailed along the coast of Crete until it ran into a storm from the northeast. The Scripture records the half-Greek, half-Latin name of this kind of storm, "Euroclydon" (v. 14), meaning "a northeast wind." The storm took control and drove them in the midst of its powerful winds (v. 15).

Verse 18 describes the continued violence of the storm and the need for the craft to be made lighter and more stable by throwing overboard all unnecessary items. The passengers' despair reached its lowest ebb as days passed without relief from the stormy cloud cover (v. 20). Luke makes it clear that everyone, including Paul, was deeply concerned about their hopeless plight.

We do not know how long they had been without food. Probably they had been too sick from the raging seas to eat. In the midst of the storm, the Lord appeared to Paul and promised that he would be delivered to Rome. Paul understood this to mean the Lord would spare the lives of all 276 people on the vessel, although the ship would be lost.

The apostle began his speech in verse 21 with a Biblical "I told you so." This was not done in arrogance, but was meant to affirm his knowledge of the matter. Verse 24 affirms the same message Paul received from the Lord in a vision in 23:11. In both instances, Paul was promised by the Lord that he would arrive in Rome. Paul emphasized that the messenger during the night came from the God to whom he belonged and served.

The message from heaven did not mean Paul would stand trial as a common criminal. Rather, it meant that before the highest-ranking person in the world, the Caesar (emperor) of Rome, Paul would have an opportunity to proclaim the Gospel.

---

1. Describe the voyagers' crisis (vv. 13-15).
2. How did things move from "lost all hope" to "take hope" (vv. 20-22 NLB)?
3. What do you suppose would have happened if Paul had not been aboard the ship, and why?

Cast an Anchor

A Christian may for many days together see neither sun nor star, neither light in God's countenance, nor light in his own heart,

---

though even at that time God darts some beams through those clouds upon the soul; the soul again, by a spirit of faith, sees some light through those thickest clouds, enough to keep it from utter despair, though not to settle it in peace. In this dark condition, if they do as Paul and his company did, cast an anchor even in the dark night of temptation, and pray still for day, God will appear, and all shall clear up, we shall see light without and light within; the day-star will arise in their hearts.—Richard Sibbes

II. TESTIFYING TO THE JEWS (Acts 28:16-23)

As the angel had promised, all 276 people on the dangerous voyage survived the shipwreck, which occurred on the island of Malta. Paul lived and ministered there for three months, and then the trek to Rome resumed.

A. For the Hope of Israel (vv. 16-20)

(Acts 28:18-20 is not included in the printed text.)

16And when we came to Rome, the centurion delivered the prisoners to the captain of the guard: but Paul was suffered to dwell by himself with a soldier that kept him. 17And it came to pass, that after three days Paul called the chief of the Jews together: and when they were come together, he said unto them, Men and brethren, though I have committed nothing against the people, or customs of our fathers, yet was I delivered prisoner from Jerusalem into the hands of the Romans.

The use of the word "suffered" (v. 16) gives a false impression of Paul's living conditions during his stay in Rome. He was "allowed" (NIV) to live in his own rented home (see also v. 30) and basically was under house arrest. Verse 20 shows he was "bound with . . . chain." F. F. Bruce suggests he was "lightly chained by the wrist." While the New Testament does not say, it is likely he was released after this early period of house arrest.

He spent about three days getting settled, and then called the Jews of Rome together for a meeting. There were several synagogues in Rome. Whether Paul was dealing with representatives of all of them, or with leaders of a local synagogue, we do not know. It is clear that he felt under obligation to preach the Gospel to the Jews first in the capital city (Rom. 1:16).

When they came together, Paul began his defense (Acts 28:17). He indicated his innocence of all charges brought against him by the Jews in Jerusalem. The use of the phrase "I was delivered as a prisoner" (NKJV) hints at treachery or betrayal.

In verses 18 and 19, Paul indicated why he had to appeal to Caesar and come to Rome in this fashion. He was not a common criminal nor a rioter; he was a fellow Jew who desired to announce the arrival of the Messiah. In Philippians 1:12-18, Paul wrote that his situation in Rome served the cause of the Gospel. While opponents came and mocked his situation of house arrest, he remained thankful that the Gospel was still preached and people were emboldened in spreading the message.

Acts 28:20 climaxes this initial speech. Here Paul laid the foundation for his teaching of the Gospel, which would take place in the following months in

Rome. He spoke of the "hope of Israel." Normally this was a reference to the resurrection of Jesus and everlasting life.

---

1. Describe the favor God granted Paul (v. 16).
2. How did Paul explain his being a prisoner (vv. 17-20)?

"Without Christ there is no hope."—Charles Spurgeon

B. Persuading Concerning Jesus (vv. 21-23)

(Acts 28:21-22 is not included in the printed text.)

²³ And when they had appointed him a day, there came many to him into his lodging; to whom he expounded and testified the kingdom of God, persuading them concerning Jesus, both out of the law of Moses, and out of the prophets, from morning till evening.

The Jews indicated they knew nothing of Paul's background in Judea (vv. 21-22). They had no letters of warning from the Jews and seemed to be ignorant of his ministry and the cause that brought him to Rome. However, they were aware of the "sect" called *Christianity*, and knew that "everywhere it is spoken against" (v. 22). Thus, the Jews of Rome had a negative view of Christians (as did the majority of the empire), yet they were willing to hear more of what Paul thought.

French Arrington writes:

> After they had heard about his imprisonment, a day was appointed for them to hear him speak at length on the great subject of the gospel of Jesus Christ. More came on the appointed day to the place where Paul was staying than had come in response to his first invitation. He spent a whole day expounding to them the kingdom of God, that is, God's rule established by His mighty acts in the death and the resurrection of Jesus. As always in his effort to convince the Jews, he appealed to the Old Testament. What Moses and the prophets had predicted about the Messiah was fulfilled in Jesus' death and His resurrection. Paul attempted to get the Jews to see in the life and ministry of Jesus the fulfillment of the prophecies regarding the Messiah (*The Acts of the Apostles*).

• Why is the Old Testament critical to our Christian witness?

"We are the Bibles the world is reading; we are the creeds the world is needing; we are the sermons the world is heeding."—Billy Graham

---

III. PROCLAIMING THE KINGDOM OF GOD (Acts 28:24-31)

A. The Promised Messiah (vv. 24-29)

(Acts 28:25-26 is not included in the printed text.)

---

²⁴ **And some believed the things which were spoken, and some believed not.**

²⁷ **For the heart of this people is waxed gross, and their ears are dull of hearing, and their eyes have they closed; lest they should see with their eyes, and hear with their ears, and understand with their heart, and should be converted, and I should heal them.** ²⁸ **Be it known therefore unto you, that the salvation of God is sent unto the Gentiles, and that they will hear it.** ²⁹ **And when he had said these words, the Jews departed, and had great reasoning among themselves.**

Paul's teaching was drawn from the Old Testament as he attempted to show that both the Prophets and the Law pointed to the coming of Jesus Christ. The preaching of the kingdom of God meant God was close to people through Christ. Through Jesus and the activity of the Spirit, God was making His claim for lordship in the lives of all people.

Some gave heed to what Paul was saying, and wanted to hear more about the new way in Christ. However, those who did not believe his message began to dispute with those who were receptive. Before the crowd dispersed, Paul spoke one last word to them. He attributed Isaiah 6:9-10 to the Holy Spirit and quoted it to the Jews. It was a powerful indictment of their stubborn hearts and unwillingness to believe the truth. They could see physically, but they were blind spiritually; they could hear Paul's words, but their ears were sealed shut with unbelief. They refused to hear the Holy Spirit beckon them to new life.

Acts 28:28-29 closes out Paul's ministry among the Jews of Rome. They had been offered the message of grace but refused to hear. The Gentiles, who had walked in great darkness, would hear the Gospel and see the light of the glory of God. The Jews left Paul and discussed among themselves what the apostle had said.

The acceptance of faith in the Lord is not a matter of intellectual debate. It is rare that we can win an argument with an unbeliever and, thereby, cause him or her to accept the Lord. The faithful preaching and teaching of the Gospel will bring its own results. The Holy Spirit must do His convicting work in the life of a person if he or she is to turn and find the way of life.

---

1. Why did most of Paul's Jewish audience hear without believing and see without perceiving (vv. 24-27)?
2. To whom did Paul turn, and why (v. 28)?

> "If all things were made through Him, clearly so must the splendid revelations have been which were made to the fathers and prophets, and became to them the symbols of the sacred mysteries of religion."—Origen

---

B. The Kingdom of God (vv. 30-31)

³⁰ **And Paul dwelt two whole years in his own hired house, and received all that came in unto him,** ³¹ **Preaching the kingdom of God, and teaching**

those things which concern the Lord Jesus Christ, with all confidence, no man forbidding him.

The apostle remained in his location for two years. This time was important to Paul's case. According to Roman law, if the prosecution did not bring the case within two years, the charges were dropped. What happened at the end of the two years is uncertain. Whether Paul argued his case before Caesar is unknown. We do know he wrote to the Philippian Christians that there were believers even in Caesar's household (4:22). Whether or not they became believers after his arrival and a subsequent defense before Caesar is only conjecture.

It is clear from verse 30 of the text that Paul was able to continue an effective ministry in Rome for these two years. People were free to come and meet with him. That must have been a wonderful time of teaching and fellowship in the Roman church!

Verse 31 indicates the major thesis of his preaching was the kingdom of God. This theme would be quite appropriate for a mission in the city which represented the epitome of man's kingdom. For two years, he sharply contrasted this man-made kingdom with the Kingdom not made by hands, but by the Spirit of God. This included overtones of comparison of the two kings of the kingdoms: Jesus was truly the Lord; the Caesar was not.

During this time, Paul was able to preach and teach boldly and without hindrance. Luke closes by making it clear that "the Lord Jesus Christ" was the subject of Paul's ministry.

• What did Paul preach about?

"Thousands of pastors, Sunday school teachers, and Christian workers are powerless because they do not make the Word the source of their preaching or teaching."—Billy Graham

---

CONCLUSION

After reaching Burma, pioneer missionary Adoniram Judson yearned to preach the Gospel before he learned the language of the natives. One day he embraced a Burmese man and beamed Christlike concern into his eyes.

The national said to a friend, "I have seen an angel."

Do people see the love of Christ reflected in our eyes?

GOLDEN TEXT CHALLENGE

"I WOULD YE SHOULD UNDERSTAND, BRETHREN, THAT THE THINGS WHICH HAPPENED UNTO ME HAVE FALLEN OUT RATHER UNTO THE FURTHERANCE OF THE GOSPEL" (Phil. 1:12).

"What sort of progress ("furtherance") might Paul be intending here?" asks Lynn Cohick in *The Story of God Bible Commentary*. "The progress is not with the Gospel itself, but with the telling of the Gospel. . . . Advancement of the Gospel for Paul is both the increased number of people hearing that message and the increased number of believers sharing."

How are you and I involved in spreading the good news to those who desperately need to hear it?

Daily Devotions:

M. Blessed in Spite of Adversity • Genesis 31:24, 36-42

T. Afflicted and Exalted to Save • Genesis 45:1-9

W. Prophet to Gentile Kings • Daniel 5:10-17

T. If God Be for Us • Romans 8:31-39

F. Seeing the Light • 2 Corinthians 4:1-10

S. Serve Faithfully • 1 Peter 5:1-4

Introduction to Summer Quarter

The first unit, "Good Lessons From Bad Examples" (lessons 2-6), focus on the lives of Lot, Jephthah, Manasseh, Nebuchadnezzar, and others.

The studies were written by the Reverend Dr. Jerald Daffe (B.A., M.A., D.Min.), who earned his degrees from Northwest Bible College, Wheaton College Graduate School, and Western Conservative Baptist Seminary. An ordained minister in the Church of God, Dr. Daffe served in pastoral ministry for ten years and has been a faculty member at Northwest Bible College and Lee University for over thirty years. Dr. Daffe received the Excellence in Advising Award at Lee University. His newest book is *Crosses, Coffee, Couches, and Community.*

The Pentecost lesson (1) was compiled by Lance Colkmire (see biographical information on page 16).

Lessons 7-13, "Good Lessons From Good Examples," highlight Caleb, Phinehas, Rahab, Jehoshaphat, Daniel, Andrew, Philip, and Barnabas.

Lessons 7, 9-12 were compiled by Lance Colkmire (see biographical information on page 16).

Lessons 8 and 13 were written by Homer G. Rhea (see biographical information on page 150).

All of the Golden Text Challenges for this quarter were written by the Reverend Dr. J. Ayodeji Adewuya (Ph.D., University of Manchester). Dr. Adewuya is professor of New Testament and Greek at the Pentecostal Theological Seminary in Cleveland, Tennessee.

Why the Holy Spirit Came (Pentecost)

Unit Theme:

Pentecost

Central Truth:

The Holy Spirit enables us to live for Christ and make the Gospel known to the world.

Focus:

Understand God's purpose in sending the Holy Spirit and rely on the Spirit's help for Christian living and witness.

Context:

New Testament teachings about the ministry of the Holy Spirit

Golden Text:

"When the Comforter is come, whom I will send unto you from the Father, even the Spirit of truth, which proceedeth from the Father, he shall testify of me" (John 15:26).

Study Outline:

I. **The Spirit Came at Pentecost** (John 14:15-18; Acts 2:1-4)

II. **The Spirit Helps Believers** (John 14:26; 16:12-14; Rom. 8:26-27)

III. **The Spirit Convinces the World** (John 15:26-27; 16:7-11)

INTRODUCTION

For the writers of Scripture, the Holy Spirit was not a mere influence but God himself. Speaking theologically, we identify the Holy Spirit as the "third" person of the Trinity. However, the Scripture places Him on the same level as the Father and the Son (2 Cor. 13:14; Matt. 28:19; 1 Cor. 12:4-6). As the One who carries to completion the saving work of the Father and Son, the Spirit is called by such names as "the Spirit of God," "the Holy Spirit of God," "the Spirit of adoption," "the Spirit of the Son," and "the Spirit of Christ." The Holy Spirit is a person, just as God the Father and Christ the Son are persons. In the Bible the Holy Spirit is represented as One who thinks (Rom. 8:27), feels (15:30), wills (1 Cor. 12:11), teaches (John 14:26), guides (Acts 8:29), and intercedes (Rom. 8:26-27). The Spirit shows love and affection (15:30) and bears witness that we are children of God (8:16). These are activities of a person, not a mere force or influence.

As well as performing works as a person, the Holy Spirit is affected as a person by the acts of others. Ananias and Sapphira lied to the Spirit (Acts 5:3, 9). He can be blasphemed (Matt. 12:31-32) and grieved (Eph. 4:30). The apostle Peter called the Holy Spirit "God" (Acts 5:3-4). He is God, personally present in believers. Believers are "the temple of God"—"the temple of the Holy Spirit" (1 Cor. 3:17; 6:19). The Holy Spirit also has divine attributes. He is omnipresent (Ps. 139:7-10), omnipotent (Zech. 4:6; Rom. 15:18-19), eternal (Heb. 9:14), and Co-Creator of the world (Gen. 1:2; Ps. 104:30). The Holy Spirit is divine because God is divine, and He is personal because God is personal. He lives in perfect unity with the Father and the Son, but He is also a distinct person, as is each of them.

This world has never been without the Holy Spirit. Jesus promised His disciples the power of the Holy Spirit (Acts 1:8), but the Spirit was a powerful presence in the lives of God's people before New Testament times. As the Old Testament reveals, the Holy Spirit worked in Creation and in the lives of God's people long before the days of the New Testament.—French L. Arrington

I. THE SPIRIT CAME AT PENTECOST (John 14:15-18; Acts 2:1-4)

A. Loving Obedience Required (John 14:15)

¹⁵If ye love me, keep my commandments.

Verse 15 is a direct practical exhortation. It says the way to prove love for Jesus is by doing His will. The commandments referred to by Jesus would include all of His moral teachings while on earth.

Jesus does not expect us to live an obedient life through our own ability. We are to depend on His Spirit, as the following verses reveal.

• How do we show our love for God (v. 15)?

B. The Comforter Promised (vv. 16-18)

¹⁶And I will pray the Father, and he shall give you another Comforter, that he may abide with you for ever; ¹⁷Even the Spirit of truth; whom the world cannot receive, because it seeth him not, neither knoweth him: but ye know him; for he dwelleth with you, and shall be in you. ¹⁸I will not leave you comfortless: I will come to you.

Four times in His farewell discourse Jesus referred to the Holy Spirit as the Comforter. The Greek word for "Comforter" is *parakletos*. It carries with it the idea of an advocate who stands by, not only as an intercessor but as a helper, comforter, and consoler.

From its derivation we rightly conclude that *comforter* suggests the idea of "strengthening, empowering in weakness." Jesus himself declared, "I will not leave you comfortless" (v. 18). We also correctly infer that the thought of comfort in sorrow is also included in the meaning.

However, it is important to consider that the thought of sorrow was not prominent in the mind of Jesus as He used the word *Comforter* in His Upper Room discourse. Three times He identified the Comforter as the Spirit of truth, who was to lead the disciples into all truth (v. 17; 15:26; 16:13). Once His function is said to be that of rememberer of and witness to Christ (14:26). And once the Spirit is seen convicting the human heart of sin, righteousness, and judgment (16:8). As Jesus used the word *Comforter*, it becomes clear that the idea of consolation and comfort is distinctly secondary to that of strength and help.

Why the Holy Spirit Came

The word *Spirit* (14:17) comes from the Latin word *spiritus*, which is synonymous with the Greek word *pneuma*. Both literally signify "breath" or "wind." The Holy Spirit is called the "breath of God" with reference to His mode of subsistence, proceeding from God as the breath from the mouth. Observe the characteristic action of Jesus in John 20:22.

The Holy Spirit is not called *Spirit* merely because of the spirituality of His essence, for this is likewise true of the Father and Son. Neither is He called *Holy* in reference to the exclusive holiness of His nature, for He is no more holy than either of the other persons of the Trinity. But this term has reference to God's official character—He is the author of all holiness.

The Holy Spirit is called the "Spirit of truth." It is His special office to apply the truth to the hearts of Christians. He is to guide them into all truth and to sanctify them by the truth.

The Holy Spirit is said to be One whom the world cannot know and receive. His operations are foolishness to sinners. The inward feelings of conviction, repentance, faith, hope, fear, and love—which He always produces—are aspects of religion which the world cannot understand.

The Holy Spirit is said to dwell in believers. He is known of them. They know the feelings He creates and the fruit He produces. They may not be able to understand them or to perceive how God could be pleased to bless them in such ways, but they can know Him.

It was very appropriate that Jesus referred to the Holy Spirit as the Comforter. He knew the disciples would need this kind of assistance. He himself had been a Paraclete to them. They had leaned on Him in every perplexity and trial. Now He was going away, and these words concerning another Comforter would be welcome. They were not to be deserted, but another Paraclete—the Holy Spirit—was to come to them.

---

1. What did Jesus pray for (v. 16)?
2. What did Jesus reveal about the Holy Spirit (v. 17)?
3. What did Jesus promise in verse 18?

> "There was a promise! The coming of the Holy Spirit was based upon the promise of the Lord Jesus Christ."—Billy Graham

---

C. The Promise Fulfilled (Acts 2:1-4)

¹And when the day of Pentecost was fully come, they were all with one accord in one place. ²And suddenly there came a sound from heaven as of a rushing mighty wind, and it filled all the house where they were sitting. ³And there appeared unto them cloven tongues like as of fire, and it sat upon each of them. ⁴And they were all filled with the Holy Ghost, and began to speak with other tongues, as the Spirit gave them utterance.

The Day of Pentecost came fifty days after the Passover. It was one of three Jewish festivals to which every male Jew living within twenty miles of

Jerusalem was legally bound to come—the Passover, Pentecost, and the Feast of Tabernacles. It commemorated the giving of the Law to Moses on Mount Sinai.

As people gathered in Jerusalem from around the world, about 120 believers were gathered in the Upper Room awaiting the coming of the Holy Spirit. They spent time in prayer and personal preparation so they could receive the Spirit.

These followers of the Lord were assembled in one place for one purpose. They were in one accord, that is, the occasion was marked by unity. The expression indicates they were knit together with a bond stronger than death. This kind of unity is needed in the church today.

After ten days of waiting, the Spirit came suddenly upon the believers. When God acts, He often acts suddenly. This is true of the conversion experience. The very instant one repents and believes, he or she is saved.

Waiting in the Upper Room, the believers heard a sound as of the blowing of a violent wind. Living in that area, they had witnessed many storms at sea and they had heard the blowing of violent wind many times. What they heard was the same sound, but this sound came out of a clear sky. They were sure of one thing—it came from heaven. It was a symbol of the Spirit; it indicated His power—mighty, mysterious, and heavenly, but unseen. The suddenness and strength of the sound struck the believers with awe, and completed their preparation for the heavenly gift.

The followers of the Lord in the Upper Room not only heard a sound as of a rushing mighty wind; they also saw what appeared to be tongues of fire that separated and came to rest on each of them.

In the Word, fire is frequently used as a symbol of the divine presence. It also represents fervor and enthusiasm. Touched by fire from heaven, one cannot remain cold and indifferent. Fire is a beautiful symbol of the Spirit's burning energy that is abundantly available to the Church.

The Pentecostal fire came in the shape of tongues. The tongue is the instrument God uses to proclaim the Gospel. Witnessing for Christ is directly linked with the coming of the Spirit. Jesus said: "Ye shall be witnesses unto me" (Acts 1:8). A witness is one who tells what he knows. A Christian is one who keeps the faith but does not keep it to himself.

The tongues of fire came to rest upon each person present in the Upper Room. They did not come to the apostles alone, but to every believer present. This is encouraging to believers at all levels of life.

These believers received an inward experience: "they were all filled with the Holy Ghost" (2:4). To be filled with the Spirit is to be brought completely under His control. This is essentially what happened to these believers. The power of the Spirit flooded their souls. Thereafter He manifested Himself in their lives on numerous occasions.

These devoted disciples also received an outward manifestation: they spoke "with other tongues." It is clear that the speakers themselves did not understand what they were saying. Their words were completely beyond their conscious control. They spoke in a language of which they had no command in normal circumstances.

These Christians spoke in other tongues as the Spirit enabled them. Luke is careful to point out that the Spirit initiated their utterances.

---

1. Explain the two uses of the word "one" in verse 1.
2. What was the significance of the wind (v. 2) and the fire (v. 3)?
3. What did the Holy Spirit do for the believers (v. 4)?

> "Tongues of fire sat upon them; hearts were aglow and tongues were aflame witnessing the wonderful works of God. Pentecost then became a personal experience."—Ray H. Hughes Sr.

II. THE SPIRIT HELPS BELIEVERS (John 14:26; 16:12-14; Rom. 8:26-27)

A. The Spirit Teaches (John 14:26)

26But the Comforter, which is the Holy Ghost, whom the Father will send in my name, he shall teach you all things, and bring all things to your remembrance, whatsoever I have said unto you.

The disciples did not have the power and wisdom to be proper witnesses without the Holy Spirit. Of course they remembered experiences from the life and ministry of Jesus. As eyewitnesses they could have painted word pictures of His death, His resurrection, and His ascension. They could have done this with conviction and enthusiasm. No one can doubt that the disciples were bound to one another in one fellowship through their love for Christ and His love for them. But Jesus knew that even these virtues would not be sufficient for the task ahead. Therefore, He promised them the power from on high—an infilling of God's wisdom, strength, courage, and vision. Their new Spirit baptism would serve to comfort, teach, and challenge them in their life and witness.

If we allow the Holy Spirit to bring the words of Jesus to our remembrance, we will understand that they are the only infallible text of real orthodoxy, the only unerring touchstone of truth, the only immaculate code of laws, the only faultless system of morals, and the only immutable ground of hope.

• Describe the teaching role of the Holy Spirit.

> "The Holy Spirit is called 'the Spirit of truth' because He is the great revealer of truth. He takes the things of Christ and makes them known to believers."—French Arrington

---

B. The Spirit Guides (16:12-14)

12I have yet many things to say unto you, but ye cannot bear them now. 13Howbeit when he, the Spirit of truth, is come, he will guide you

into all truth: for he shall not speak of himself; but whatsoever he shall hear, that shall he speak: and he will shew you things to come. ¹⁴He shall glorify me: for he shall receive of mine, and shall shew it unto you.

The disciples' need for the Holy Spirit is seen in the fact that they could not understand the many things Jesus had yet to say to them. But Jesus assured them the Holy Spirit would guide them into all truth concerning Himself and the doctrines He taught. The reference here is to spiritual truth.

The ministry of the Holy Spirit is Christ-centered. It is characteristic of Him not to speak of Himself but of Christ.

The statement "He will shew you things to come" undoubtedly refers to the finished New Testament—the establishing of the church to include both Gentiles and Jews and the proclaiming of the full-gospel message.

Verse 14 reminds us that rivalry does not exist within the Godhead. Each person in the Trinity delights in serving the others. Christ's passion was to manifest and to glorify the excellence of the Father (John 8:54; 17:4-5).

The primary concern of the Holy Spirit is to glorify Christ and to see Him enthroned as Lord in the hearts of believers. He does not add anything to the personal glories of the ascended Christ but glorifies Christ in the believer's experience. The Spirit reveals and explains Christ. What light is to the earth, the Holy Spirit is to Christ.

---

1. Why didn't Jesus reveal certain things to the disciples (v. 12)?
2. List ministries of the Holy Spirit (vv. 13-14).

> "The Comforter serves as a truth-guide amid the maze of deceptive religious teachings in our world."—Anthony Lombard

---

C. The Spirit Intercedes (Rom. 8:26-27)

²⁶Likewise the Spirit also helpeth our infirmities: for we know not what we should pray for as we ought: but the Spirit itself maketh intercession for us with groanings which cannot be uttered. ²⁷And he that searcheth the hearts knoweth what is the mind of the Spirit, because he maketh intercession for the saints according to the will of God.

In this chapter, Paul deals with three kinds of groanings. First, he pictures the creation growning and travailing in pain (v. 22). Then, he says that believers groan inwardly, awaiting our full adoption as sons—the redemption of our bodies (v. 23). Now, he writes of the Spirit making intercession for us with groans that words cannot utter.

As God, through the Holy Spirit, will take care of the future needs represented by the groanings of creation and of believers, so He will take care of the present needs of believers. He comes to our aid in our weaknesses and understands our present limitations.

We need the help of the Holy Spirit in prayer because we don't know how we ought to pray. We cannot foresee the future. God knows the past, the present, and the future. Our knowledge of the past and the present is limited, and our knowledge of the future is practically nil. But God knows it all. The help of the Spirit is, then, essential to effective and Christ-honoring prayer.

Also, we need the help of the Spirit in prayer because in any given situation we do not know what is best for us. We may think we do, but in reality only God knows best. So, the only really perfect prayer we can offer is the prayer Jesus prayed: "Not my will, but thine, be done" (Luke 22:42). We cannot go wrong with this prayer.

Then, we can bring to God an inarticulate sigh which the Spirit will translate to God for us. He will plead our case with inexpressible yearnings, with groans that are too deep for words. His assistance is invaluable.

John Phillips observed: "We have an Advocate with the Father in heaven in the Person of the Lord Jesus (1 John 2:1), and we have One within our hearts as well who can lay bare before the eyes of God the deepest needs of our souls."

God knows all about us. He searches our inmost being. The psalmist wrote: "O Lord, thou hast searched me, and known me. . . . Search me, O God, and know my heart . . . and see if there be any wicked way in me, and lead me in the way everlasting" (Ps. 139:1, 23-24). God searches our heart as no one else can. Nothing is hidden from Him. No one knows us so well or understands as completely as He does. His eye is ever upon us.

God, who knows the needs of the human heart, also understands what the Spirit's meaning is even though the expressions have been inarticulate. He knows the unspoken desire of the Spirit, who always puts our prayer in the context of God's constructive purpose for our life. As someone has said, "Here is the secret of victorious Christian living. Without the Spirit's help in all these areas, no human being would be wise or strong enough to succeed. With it there is no reason for failure."

The Spirit pleads our case before God and He always intercedes in a manner that is in harmony with God's will. As believers, we need to avail ourselves of this help from the Spirit of God. By leaning upon Him, we may be guided in the path of righteousness and may be given a clearer and stronger assurance of God's presence. He assists us in our prayers and places within us high and holy aspirations.

• What is the Holy Spirit's role in the Christian's prayer life?

Help in Prayer

The Christian is not alone when he prays. He has Jesus Christ as intercessor and advocate on his behalf at the right hand of God (Heb. 7:25; 1 John 2:1). Then, dwelling in his heart, the Christian has the Holy Spirit who makes intercession for him according to the will of God (Rom. 8:26-27).—Daniel Black

III. THE SPIRIT CONVINCES THE WORLD (John 15:26-27; 16:7-11)

A. The Spirit of Truth (15:26-27)

26But when the Comforter is come, whom I will send unto you from the Father, even the Spirit of truth, which proceedeth from the Father, he shall testify of me: 27And ye also shall bear witness, because ye have been with me from the beginning.

The context of these verses is set in verse 18 at the beginning of this section of teaching. Christ said the world hated Him and would also hate the disciples. In light of this hatred, Christ instructs them so that they will not "stumble" (16:1 NKJV). The grammar of "hate" in 15:18 indicates a permanent attitude of hate. The world hates Christians as a basic attitude. It is not an occasional spurt of emotion. The attitude of the world is permanently set against Christ as well. Christ goes further in verse 19. The reason that the world hates the Christian is Christ's choosing of the Christian for His purposes.

The climax of the description of hatred is found in verse 25 when Christ says the world hated Him "without a cause." Christians feel this attack as well and need a secure foundation to stand on.

Christ introduces this foundation with the word *but* in verse 26, when He says that despite the unjustified and brutal attack of the world there is a foundation. In contrast to the attack of the world, the "Comforter"—the Holy Spirit—will be the Spirit of truth.

"Spirit of truth" describes a vital work of the Holy Spirit in establishing the believer when the world would attack him. When the cause of the Christian to stand for Christ is attacked unjustifiably, the Holy Spirit works to establish the Christian. Despite the false claims of the world against the Christian, still there is stability. The Holy Spirit establishes truth in the life of the Christian.

Christ locates the source and the authority of the work of truth by the Holy Spirit. The source is "the Father." The work of the Spirit in establishing truth in the life of the Christian is to "testify of [Christ]."

---

1. Describe the relationship between Jesus and the Holy Spirit (v. 26).
2. What would the disciples do (v. 27)?

> "In essence, Jesus said, 'I'll not let you down. I'll not leave you without help. I will come to you. So don't give up . . . and don't lose heart. Help is on the way. I will send Him to you.'"
> —Ray H. Hughes Sr.

B. The Convincer (16:7-11)

7Nevertheless I tell you the truth; It is expedient for you that I go away: for if I go not away, the Comforter will not come unto you; but if I depart, I will send him unto you. 8And when he is come, he will reprove the world of sin, and of righteousness, and of judgment: 9Of sin, because they believe not on me; 10Of righteousness, because I go to my Father,

---

and ye see me no more; ¹¹Of judgment, because the prince of this world is judged.

The disciples were "filled with grief" (v. 6 NIV) because Jesus had told them He would soon be leaving them. The departure of Jesus was a disappointment of their greatest hopes. They had placed all their Jewish hopes concerning the Messiah in Jesus. They had expected Jesus to restore the kingdom of Israel. His telling them that instead of sitting on the throne of His father David He was going to die brought to them a paralyzing fear.

Understanding the attitude of the disciples, Jesus reassured them by saying, "Unless I go away, the Counselor will not come to you; but if I go, I will send him to you" (v. 7 NIV). He went on to point out that the coming of the Holy Spirit would be a greater blessing to them than His personal presence had been.

From these words of Jesus it can be seen that under certain conditions absence is better than presence. For the disciples it was worthwhile to lose Jesus' physical presence if they might find for themselves the way into that spiritual world in which they had seen Him moving. Jesus wanted them to learn to walk in the Spirit—to walk by faith and not by sight.

To "reprove" (v. 8) is to convince one of error or sinfulness. This is the work of the Holy Spirit in relation to man's condition before God.

In his book *The Holy Spirit in the Gospels*, J. R. Smith says of the Holy Spirit, "He so presents the truth to men that they ought to believe. . . . The end sought in conviction is conversion. The Truth is made plain, not that men may be condemned, but that they might be saved."

Jesus said the Holy Spirit would "convict the world of sin, of righteousness, and of judgment" (v. 8 NKJV). Sin is the basis of all the world's ills; but apart from the work of the Holy Spirit, the world does not recognize this. The world is aware of the defects that exist in humanity. We say that a person is unjust, cruel, proud, sensuous, or covetous. Yet, these are simply surface manifestations of a greater fundamental evil in the character of humanity. It is this that the world does not understand.

The Holy Spirit, working in people's hearts as the Word of God is presented, convinces individuals of their sin and of their need for a Savior. The Holy Spirit also convinces the world of the righteousness that is found in Christ. Jesus Christ, the Son of God, took upon Himself human flesh and in the flesh condemned sin. His entire life exemplified righteousness. His every thought, word, deed, and action was right in the highest sense. He lived among the ordinary people of His time. He was exposed to the same temptations, corruption, and weaknesses, yet He did not sin. He was God manifest in a human body. He was the world's model of a perfectly holy life. This was what the world needed to see. But the world was not wiling to receive the heaven-sent Light that penetrated its darkness.

Instead of accepting Christ as the Son of God, some of the religious leaders banded together and agreed that Jesus was blaspheming God when He declared that He was life and the pattern of holiness. They condemned Him to death on this pretext. He was crucified, but He arose, ascended to the Father, and sent the Holy Spirit into the world to convince sinners that He was the

Son of God. So it was actually "the prince of this world" (v. 11)—Satan—who was condemned through Christ's suffering. And it is still the Holy Spirit who is convincing all who will listen that Jesus is the Savior.

---

1. What was to the disciples' advantage, and why (v. 7)?
2. What did Jesus say the Holy Spirit would do (vv. 8-11)?

> "No clergyman however brilliant, no evangelist no matter how eloquent or compelling, can bring about the revival we need. Only the Holy Spirit can do this."—Billy Graham

CONCLUSION

In the person of the Holy Spirit, God himself has been empowering, teaching, guiding interceding on behalf of, and comforting Christians for more than two thousand years. His Spirit will continue ministering in all those ways and more until the return of Jesus Christ.

GOLDEN TEXT CHALLENGE

"WHEN THE COMFORTER IS COME, WHOM I WILL SEND UNTO YOU FROM THE FATHER, EVEN THE SPIRIT OF TRUTH, WHICH PROCEEDETH FROM THE FATHER, HE SHALL TESTIFY OF ME" (John 15:26).

The Holy Spirit testifies to His relationship with Christ. In Matthew 1:20 we see that the Holy Spirit was related to Christ in Christ's conception. The Spirit was also related to Christ in the anointing for Christ's ministry (Acts 10:38).

It is recorded in Luke 4:1 that Jesus was filled with the Spirit, who gave Jesus direction. There was nothing in the life of Jesus that was opposed to the Holy Spirit.

Luke also records that Jesus accomplished His ministry in the power of the Holy Spirit (vv. 14, 18-19). And according to the writer of Hebrews, Jesus sacrificially offered Himself in death through the Holy Spirit (9:14). In Romans 8:11, Paul wrote that "the Spirit . . . raised up Jesus from the dead."

The ministry of the Holy Spirit is not to magnify Himself but to give prominence to Christ. So efficient has He been in discharging His trust that His own existence has been questioned. But He is real! Any information we have of Christ comes to us through the Spirit's illumination of the Scriptures He has inspired. As the Spirit of Christ, He delights in unveiling His glories to believing hearts.

Daily Devotions:

M. Anointed by the Spirit • 1 Samuel 16:10-13
T. Led by the Spirit • Ezekiel 3:10-14
W. Born of the Spirit • John 3:1-8
T. Ministry of the Spirit • John 16:5-15
F. Witness of the Spirit • Romans 8:12-17
S. Filled With the Spirit • Ephesians 5:15-21

Why the Holy Spirit Came

The Cost of Worldliness (Lot)

**Genesis 13:1—14:16; 19:1-29; Luke 17:28-33;
James 4:4-6; 2 Peter 2:6-9; 1 John 2:15-17**

Unit Theme:

Good Lessons From Bad Examples

Central Truth:

Christians should guard themselves against the lure of worldliness.

Focus:

Consider how worldliness affected Lot and reject worldliness.

Context:

Lot, whose name means "veil" or "covering," was the son of Haran and the nephew of Abraham.

Golden Text:

"Love not the world, neither the things that are in the world. If any man love the world, the love of the Father is not in him" (1 John 2:15).

Study Outline:

  I. **Danger of Evil Influences** (Gen. 13:10-13; 14:8-16; James 4:4-6)

  II. **God Rescues From Temptation** (Gen. 19:1-3, 12-29; 2 Peter 2:6-9)

  III. **Reject Worldliness** (Luke 17:28-33; 1 John 2:15-17)

INTRODUCTION

Every morning when we awaken, there are a multitude of choices needing to be made. Will I hit the snooze button? What should I wear? Will it be breakfast on the run or not at all? These are just a few of the hundreds of choices most of us make every day. Choices tend to be placed under the heading "Decisions," but they still necessitate our choosing a particular action.

Some choices appear as the result of a sovereign appointment. God interjects the desire for us through the Scriptures or special encounters through the ministry of the Holy Spirit. This is an ongoing process as we live the Christian life.

Other choices come through peer pressure, which does not end when a person graduates from high school or college. It can be ongoing as one attempts to "keep up with the Joneses." This may include where you live, the type of home you live in, vehicles you own, where you vacation, all the latest electronic toys you have, and so on. It can easily lead to a facade which does not provide happiness but does incur a huge amount of indebtedness.

There are also choices that stem from one's family background and personality. An unbelieving family may press children toward materialism, while discouraging them from becoming too religious. The opposite is seen when godly parents demonstrate and encourage moral choices that reflect integrity and commitment to Christ. Then there is the impact of each person's personality as it pushes forward toward either positive or negative choices.

This lesson focuses on a man named Lot. Initially he makes a choice which appears beneficial for his flocks and herds. However, gradually he is drawn into an environment of worldliness which will have disastrous results for both him and his family. He probably had no idea of the depths of immorality which would affect him and his family from the first decision that brought him close to the city of Sodom.

Today's lesson should be a wake-up call showing how worldliness can creep into one's lifestyle without recognizing what is happening. Believers must guard against the lure of worldliness. It is a trap which may not be immediately recognized until it flexes a tight grip on one's attitudes and actions.

I. DANGER OF EVIL INFLUENCES (Gen. 13:10-13; 14:8-16; James 4:4-6)
A. The Influence of Environment (Gen. 13:10-13)

¹⁰And Lot lifted up his eyes, and beheld all the plain of Jordan, that it was well watered every where, before the Lord destroyed Sodom and Gomorrah, even as the garden of the Lord, like the land of Egypt, as thou comest unto Zoar. ¹¹Then Lot chose him all the plain of Jordan; and Lot journeyed east: and they separated themselves the one from the other. ¹²Abram dwelled in the land of Canaan, and Lot dwelled in the cities of the plain, and pitched his tent toward Sodom. ¹³But the men of Sodom were wicked and sinners before the Lord exceedingly.

The narrative of Lot's life begins on a positive note of influence. Instead of remaining in Haran, he continues with his uncle, Abram, into the Promised Land (12:5). This association apparently enables him to accumulate considerable wealth even as Abram is blessed. Prosperity eventually becomes a major problem. There isn't sufficient pasture for the combined flocks and herds. In an attempt to care for their animals, tension arises as both groups of shepherds jockey to provide the necessary grass (13:5-7).

As the patriarchal head of the family, Abram takes responsibility to solve the issue. He recognizes how unhealthy it is for the family and their herdsmen to continually be at odds with one another (v. 8). They must find separate grazing grounds. By virtue of his position, Abram has the right to make a decision which would have been final. This was the normative pattern in the Oriental culture—the oldest male in the clan made the decisions. However, Abraham allows Lot to make this decision (v. 9).

As Lot surveys the land, there are two opposite choices. One area lacks abundance of pasture and a ready source of water. In marked contrast is the plain of Jordan with an abundant supply of water which provides excellent grazing for herds and flocks. Notice the comparison to what had been available in Eden ("the garden of the Lord," v. 10) and could be found in Egypt.

Lot's choice of the better land doesn't automatically label him as a person with suspect values. He had animals which needed provision. However, it does suggest a sense of materialism which negated an acute awareness of how he and his family could be impacted by the worldliness of the twin cities of Sodom and Gomorrah. It is doubtful that Lot could have been unaware of the sinfulness of the population of these cities.

Verse 12 describes Lot's pitching "his tent toward Sodom." This seems to indicate an interest in being part of an extended community. As will be seen later, he becomes quite attached to the business of the city. His choice of land becomes the door to a secular, worldly approach, which is in opposition to the holiness God requires.

• How was Lot's choice both smart and foolish?

> "Sin is the act of the will, and is only possible when the will assents to some unholy influence."—F. B. Meyer

---

B. The Impact of Association (14:8-16)

(Genesis 14:8-10, 13-15 is not included in the printed text.)

¹¹And they took all the goods of Sodom and Gomorrah, and all their victuals, and went their way. ¹²And they took Lot, Abram's brother's son, who dwelt in Sodom, and his goods, and departed.

¹⁶And he brought back all the goods, and also brought again his brother Lot, and his goods, and the women also, and the people.

The timeline is unknown, but it appears Lot moves from simply living in the surrounding area to living within the city of Sodom. It means he and his family will be directly affected by whatever economic, political, and moral issues arise in Sodom. For twelve years Sodom and Gomorrah have been under the domination of Chedorlaomer, king of Elam (v. 4). Upon the cities' rebellion, Chedorlaomer and his allies not only defeat the rebels but also take captives and other spoils of war. Lot, his family, and possessions become part of what is taken captive (vv. 11-12).

Hearing of the situation, Abram takes immediate action by arming his servants and pursuing the invading forces. Abram's having 318 servants who are trained for war further indicates the wealth and strength of Abram (v. 14). The battle tactic utilized by Abram shows his military skill. The enemy is defeated, and all of the captives and goods are recovered.

It is easy to speculate that during this time, Lot may have regretted his earlier choices. Wealth and position can quickly vanish, leading an individual to reevaluate everything.

Lot demonstrated two bad examples of decision making. First, he selected the fertile plains of Jordan near Sodom. Second, he became part of that society by moving into the city and becoming one of the decision makers at the city gate, as seen in Genesis 19:1. Can a person live a holy life while surrounded by worldliness? Yes. However, there is a qualifier. This occurs only if a person makes a conscious, ongoing effort to maintain a close relationship with God. Only by constantly guarding one's heart and mind will there be escape from worldliness.

1. What befell Lot (vv. 8-11)?
2. How did Abraham act as a redeemer (vv. 12-16)?

> "If any occupation or association is found to hinder our communion with God or our enjoyment of spiritual things, then it must be abandoned. . . . Whatever I cannot do for God's glory must be avoided."—A. W. Pink

---

C. The Separation of Choice (James 4:4-6)

(James 4:5-6 is not included in the printed text.)

⁴Ye adulterers and adulteresses, know ye not that the friendship of the world is enmity with God? whosoever therefore will be a friend of the world is the enemy of God.

These three verses explicitly indicate how choice of commitment determines one's relationship with God. Choosing the actions and ideas of the world places a person in direct opposition to God (v. 4). No one can be a friend of the world and assume a right relationship with God. Our God is a jealous God in the sense of not sharing worship or honor with anything or anyone (see v. 5).

Verse 6 includes a quote from Proverbs 3:34. It is a strong statement pointing to the difference of relationship God has with those who are friends of the world and those who humble themselves before Him. The proud are those who choose to be independent and serve their own pleasures.

God's response is directly related to how each individual chooses to live his or her life. Rejection of God eventually results in His opposition. However, humble commitment brings God's grace. Why would anyone choose opposition rather than submission?

---

1. Who is an "adulterer" or "adulteress" (vv. 4-5)?
2. What do we need from God, and how can we receive it (v. 6)?

> "Many of our troubles occur because we base our choices on unreliable authorities: culture ("everyone is doing it"), tradition ("we've always done it"), reason ("it seems logical"), or emotion ("it just felt right")."—Rick Warren

---

II. GOD RESCUES FROM TEMPTATION (Gen. 19:1-3, 12-29; 2 Peter 2:6-9)
A. The Angelic Visit (Gen. 19:1-3, 12-14)

(Genesis 19:1-3, 12 is not included in the printed text.)

¹³For we will destroy this place, because the cry of them is waxen great before the face of the Lord; and the Lord hath sent us to destroy it. ¹⁴And Lot went out, and spake unto his sons in law, which married

his daughters, and said, Up, get you out of this place; for the Lord will destroy this city. But he seemed as one that mocked unto his sons in law.

In chapter 18, we see Abraham praying in an attempt to save the city of Sodom from the destruction which is going to occur. This probably originates from concern for Lot and his family. He is not aware of the grace that will be extended to Lot by the angelic visit.

At evening, the two heavenly visitors in the form of humans arrive at Sodom (19:1). Immediately Lot rises, offers the greeting of a deep bow, and invites them to his home. In the Oriental culture, guests were seen as sent from God and were to be offered all aspects of hospitality possible. When they initially do not accept the invitation, Lot persists. It was common for a first invitation to be rejected so the host would have the opportunity to share his great desire for company through a second invitation.

Only after this encounter with the men of Sodom who try to forcibly take the guests to sexually abuse them (vv. 4-10) do the angels reveal their identity and mission. Because of the people's wanton wickedness, they have become ripe for God's judgment. There is a point when God's mercy ends because of the sin being so grievous to His holiness. Judgment is inevitable. In this case, God sends two of His angels to inflict the destruction, but not before bringing safety to Lot and his family.

Lot attempts to offer to rescue his sons-in-law. Apparently, they are *betrothed* to the daughters without yet having lived as husband and wife. (It was the same as being married but not yet having the right of physical intimacy.) His attempt to warn them of the coming judgment is disregarded. They "thought he was joking" (v. 14 NIV).

---

1. Why were the angels sent to Lot (v. 12)?
2. Why was Sodom doomed (v. 13)?
3. Explain the actions of Lot's sons-in-law (v. 14).

> "Believers, look up—take courage. The angels are nearer than you think."—Billy Graham

---

B. The Family Flight (vv. 15-29)

(Genesis 19:17-25, 27-28 is not included in the printed text.)

¹⁵And when the morning arose, then the angels hastened Lot, saying, Arise, take thy wife, and thy two daughters, which are here; lest thou be consumed in the iniquity of the city. ¹⁶And while he lingered, the men laid hold upon his hand, and upon the hand of his wife, and upon the hand of his two daughters; the Lord being merciful unto him: and they brought him forth, and set him without the city.

²⁶But his wife looked back from behind him, and she became a pillar of salt.

²⁹And it came to pass, when God destroyed the cities of the plain, that God remembered Abraham, and sent Lot out of the midst of the overthrow, when he overthrew the cities in which Lot dwelt.

In the face of immediate judgment, Lot lingers rather than moving quickly to leave the city. One can only speculate why. Maybe he was hopeful his sons-in-law would choose to take the warning seriously. There might have been thought about the material possessions which would be destroyed. Regardless of the reasons, the angels took the hands of Lot, his wife, and daughters and led them from the city (v. 16). They are directed to escape to the nearby mountains in order to save their lives (v. 17).

Lot asked for a change of plans, saying, "I can't flee to the mountains; this disaster will overtake me, and I'll die" (v. 19 NIV). Possibly his physical strength would not allow this strenuous journey, in his opinion. Maybe the ascent would be on a dangerous path. Regardless, it seems presumptuous for his asking for a change, since it is only through God's mercy that he will escape. The four people escaping is well below the last number of ten which Abraham had asked for in his intercession to save the city (18:32). The angels allow them to escape to a small town (19:22).

During their flights from Sodom, strict directions were given to not look back (v. 17). There is symbolism here in their not holding to the sinful conditions of the city, but looking forward to the life God is now providing. However, tragically Lot's wife looks back as judgment is rained on the cities, and she is turned into a pillar of salt (v. 26).

It is hard to imagine the scene in which sulfurous rain created a fierce firestorm destroying everything in its path. Surely the sound of the explosions and the rising smoke would have been heard and seen for miles around.

Verse 29 points out God's mercy to Lot stemmed from his uncle's righteous intercession. Without Abraham's prayer, the entire family would have been decimated.

---

1. Describe the angels' actions, and their motivation (vv. 15-16).
2. How was more favor shown to Lot (vv. 21-22)?
3. Compare Genesis 19:26 with Jesus' statement in Luke 9:62.
4. Explain the statement, "God remembered Abraham" (Gen. 19:29).

> "Everything in your life is a reflection of a choice you once made. If you want different results, make different choices."—Kemmy Nola

---

C. The Righteous Delivered (2 Peter 2:6-9)

    (2 Peter 2:6, 8 is not included in the printed text.)

⁷And delivered just Lot, vexed with the filthy conversation of the wicked.

⁹The Lord knoweth how to deliver the godly out of temptations, and to reserve the unjust unto the day of judgment to be punished.

The apostle Peter's second epistle describes the judgment God has and will bring upon those who are living in rebellion against Him. In verse 6, Peter addresses the account of the destruction of Sodom and Gomorrah. The reference to *ashes* indicates the complete destruction of people and buildings. Then and now, it stands as an example of God's intense judgment on those who persist in ungodly living.

In verses 7-9 we are given a picture of Lot's character. He lived righteously, in contrast to the immorality of the community. Daily, Lot was conflicted with the evil which surrounded him. One cannot help but ask, "Why did he continue to reside there?" For most of his life, Lot had been a wealthy nomad.

Thankfully, God knows our spiritual condition and judges accordingly. In His mercy, God delivered Lot from the temptation surrounding him and the judgment which was soon to come to the city. Today, God still delivers godly people from their trials.

In His justice, in the same manner, God reserves judgment for those who refute His laws and persist in fulfilling their own desires. The humanistic philosophy that "man is the measure of all things" separates people from God. It, in turn, results in His judgment either in this life or in the one to come after death.

---

1. To whom is Sodom an example, and how (v. 6)?
2. To whom is Lot an example, and how (vv. 7-9)?

> "God knows our situation; He will not judge us as if we had no difficulties to overcome. What matters is the sincerity and perseverance of our will to overcome them."—C. S. Lewis

---

III. REJECT WORLDLINESS (Luke 17:28-33; 1 John 2:15-17)

A. The Judgment on Worldliness (Luke 17:28-29)

²⁸Likewise also as it was in the days of Lot; they did eat, they drank, they bought, they sold, they planted, they builded; ²⁹But the same day that Lot went out of Sodom it rained fire and brimstone from heaven, and destroyed them all.

These verses are part of Jesus' response to the Pharisee's questioning Him about when the kingdom of God would come (v. 20). Part of His response is a description of the worldly activities which will be taking place at that time. He begins with Noah and then immediately follows with the example of Lot. The actions of eating, drinking, buying, selling, planting, and building may appear normal (v. 28); however, here it indicates a total commitment to self and fulfilling one's own pleasures while disregarding God.

In both situations, the individuals surrounding these righteous men are seemingly oblivious to God's coming judgment or choose to disregard the truth until it is too late. Once Noah and his family are safe in the ark, it begins to rain. A similar situation takes place at Sodom. Once Lot and his family are out of the city, God's judgment rains down destruction.

Consider two truths. First, worldliness with its disregard for God will result in judgment on His timetable. God's holiness demands justice for sin. Second, the righteous may be all that withholds God's judgment in certain cases. Believers are urged to pray for God's mercy so lost people will have an opportunity to repent.

• How was one "day" (v. 29) different than all other "days" (v. 28), and what does this teach us?

"Worldliness is what makes sin look normal in any age and righteousness seem odd."—David F. Wells

---

B. The Contrast to Worldliness (vv. 30-33)

³⁰Even thus shall it be in the day when the Son of man is revealed. ³¹In that day, he which shall be upon the housetop, and his stuff in the house, let him not come down to take it away: and he that is in the field, let him likewise not return back. ³²Remember Lot's wife. ³³Whosoever shall seek to save his life shall lose it; and whosoever shall lose his life shall preserve it.

Verse 31 describes a situation in which a city was under attack. Anyone on the roof would be in grave danger if he or she attempted to gather valuables from the lower floor before escaping. Delay would probably lead to disaster. Similarly, anyone working in the fields outside the city walls would walk into harm's way by trying to salvage any of their belongings from their home.

Jesus is speaking of the time of His return to earth (v. 30) and emphasizes the need to separate from worldly pleasures in order to be prepared to meet Him. To emphasize the importance of this separation, Jesus simply states, "Remember Lot's wife" (v. 32). Those three words tell the whole story. We need to lose in order to gain.

Worldliness seeks to please self. This provides a marked contrast with a life of holiness which seeks to follow the righteousness God requires. Pleasing self brings immediate satisfaction but will end in eternal destruction. The opposite path may not bring what the world perceives as success, but will result in eternal life.

---

1. What will happen suddenly (vv. 30-31)?
2. Who must we "remember," and why (v. 32)?
3. Explain the meaning of verse 33.

C. The Fleetingness of Worldliness (1 John 2:15-17)

¹⁵Love not the world, neither the things that are in the world. If any man love the world, the love of the Father is not in him. ¹⁶For all that is in the world, the lust of the flesh, and the lust of the eyes, and the pride of life, is not of the Father, but is of the world. ¹⁷And the world passeth away, and the lust thereof: but he that doeth the will of God abideth for ever.

Under the guidance of the Holy Spirit, the apostle John provides a simple statement concerning a person's allegiance. Regardless of an individual's verbal claims of allegiance to the heavenly Father, the truth is revealed in what the person values. When it becomes evident that the activities of worldliness take precedent, this person is not being a faithful servant of the Lord Jesus Christ (v. 15).

Verse 16 labels the three major categories into which all sins fall—lust of the flesh, lust of the eyes, and pride. Consider Eve's temptation in the Garden of Eden. *Pride* causes her to assume she could decide right and wrong. Her *eyes* saw the aesthetic beauty of the forbidden fruit. The *fleshly desire* causes her to take and to eat of the fruit. David's sin with Bathsheba displays a similar pattern. He *looks* at the beautiful woman and *physically desires* her. When a pregnancy occurs, his *pride* causes him to hide the immorality by causing her husband, Uriah, to die in battle.

Verse 17 emphasizes how all the pleasures of worldliness are short-lived and quickly subside, leaving nothing. In marked contrast are the results of serving God. Christians are the only ones who find joy and peace now while looking for the rewards of life forever with our heavenly Father.

1. What does it mean to "love the world," and why is it so easy to do so (vv. 15-16)?
2. Why is it critical for Christians to keep in mind the truth of verse 17?

CONCLUSION

The account of Lot's taking up residence in Sodom and then being divinely rescued provides some life principles for us: (1) One wrong choice may initially seem fairly innocent, but it has the potential to expand into a major catastrophe. (2) The ties to worldliness quickly become bonds which are not easily broken, even in the face of personal disaster. (3) Even the righteous may need divine intervention to rescue them from the tentacles of the world's temptation. (4) It is possible to live separate from worldliness. However, constantly being in its environment may influence us in a far greater degree than realized. (5) We need to guard ourselves against the lure of worldliness.

One more critical concept can be drawn from Lot's experience: Nothing is more valuable than having a righteous family member (or members) who intercede on our behalf.

GOLDEN TEXT CHALLENGE

"LOVE NOT THE WORLD, NEITHER THE THINGS THAT ARE IN THE WORLD. IF ANY MAN LOVE THE WORLD, THE LOVE OF THE FATHER IS NOT IN HIM" (1 John 2:15).

The term *world* in this verse does not refer to the world of people (John 3:16) nor to the created world (17:24), but to the evil world order controlled by Satan. It includes all that goes to make up the organized system of evil on this earth.

This scripture warns us against becoming so involved in the world that we are emotionally tied to it and come to value it as a way of life. Although Christians are of necessity in the world, we are not to be intimately related to the world. Its things, its ways, its attitudes, and its spirit are not to be accepted by us as the people of God.

Daily Devotions:

M. Choose Obedience • Joshua 23:6-16
T. Repent of Worldliness • Ezra 9:5-15
W. The Righteous Reject Worldliness • Proverbs 11:4-11
T. Separate Yourself From Worldliness • 1 Corinthians 5:6-13
F. Stand Firm for God • 1 Corinthians 10:1-13
S. Say "No" to Ungodliness • Titus 2:11-14

Do Not Make Rash Vows (Jephthah)

Deuteronomy 23:21-23; Judges 10:6—11:40; Ecclesiastes 5:1-7

Unit Theme:

Good Lessons From Bad Examples

Central Truth:

God holds people accountable for their vows.

Focus:

Discuss Jephthah's rash vow and honor God by keeping our vows.

Context:

Jephthah was judge of Israel for six years.

Golden Text:

"Be not rash with thy mouth, and let not thine heart be hasty to utter any thing before God: for God is in heaven, and thou upon earth: therefore let thy words be few" (Eccl. 5:2).

Study Outline:

  I. **A Rash Vow** (Judg. 11:1-14, 28-33; Deut. 23:21-23)
 II. **The Vow Fulfilled** (Judg. 11:34-40)
III. **Reverence God by Keeping Vows** (Eccl. 5:1-7)

INTRODUCTION

A foundational Scripture verse for this lesson is Ecclesiastes 5:2: "Be not rash with thy mouth, and let not thine heart be hasty to utter any thing before God: for God is in heaven, and thou upon earth: therefore let thy words be few."

A *vow* can be defined as "a voluntary promise indicating a willingness to do some service in return for an anticipated benefit." Some vows include refraining from particular actions to receive the desired result. There are many Scriptural references to individuals making vows to God. Religious vows were never a spiritual or religious duty. However, once made, they were considered binding for males. This was not the case for females, unless they were widows or divorced (Num. 30:9). Unmarried women's vows were subject to their father's authority and willingness for them to follow through (vv. 3-5). For a married woman, her husband determined whether or not the vow would be fulfilled (vv. 6-15).

It is amazing how quickly individuals will make a vow hoping they can bribe God. Do any of these sound familiar? "God, if You will get me out of this jam, I will serve You!" "God, restore my health, and I will 'pay' my tithes and give generously in the offerings." These vows appear as a desperate attempt to bribe or move the hand of God on future righteous deeds.

Individuals utilizing these vows seem to neglect the Biblical example of bargaining with God. Abraham attempts to save Sodom and Gomorrah on the basis of righteous individuals living. Hezekiah reminds God of his righteous actions as he faces an announced death. In both cases, God willingly listens and considers the possibility. Not even ten righteous people are found in Sodom and Gomorrah, so they encounter judgment. In contrast is Hezekiah's being granted an extra fifteen years of life.

This lesson begins with a focus on Old Testament culture with distinct statements which reflect the need to fulfill God's laws. Anyone who made a vow was to fulfill it as a means of giving honor to God. Though we do not live under the Law, we still have the responsibility not to speak rashly but fulfill our commitment to God.

I. A RASH VOW (Judg. 11:1-14, 28-33; Deut. 23:21-23)

A. A Desperate Situation (Judg. 11:1-14, 28)

(Judges 11:1-6, 9-10, 12-14, 28 is not included in the printed text.)

⁷And Jephthah said unto the elders of Gilead, Did not ye hate me, and expel me out of my father's house? and why are ye come unto me now when ye are in distress? ⁸And the elders of Gilead said unto Jephthah, Therefore we turn again to thee now, that thou mayest go with us, and fight against the children of Ammon, and be our head over all the inhabitants of Gilead.

¹¹Then Jephthah went with the elders of Gilead, and the people made him head and captain over them: and Jephthah uttered all his words before the Lord in Mizpeh.

The various accounts included in the Book of Judges must first be seen as punishment for rebellion against God. He allows Israel's pagan neighbors to overrun them for extended periods of time. After they repent, a deliverer arises to lead them in victorious overthrow of their oppressors.

Jephthah and his efforts for Israel are somewhat different than most of those recorded. His birth comes from the physical relationship of a Jewish man, Gilead, and an unnamed prostitute (v. 1). Jephthah is raised in the home of his birth father, but the legitimate sons of Gilead refuse to allow their illegitimate half-brother to have any part in sharing in their father's future estate (v. 2). They throw him out of the family, and he flees. Jephthah then becomes the captain of a group of "worthless men" (v. 3 NKJV), or renegades. It sounds similar to the case of David and the men who joined him as he lived the life of a fugitive (1 Sam. 22:1-2).

Jephthah's activities earned him the reputation of a warrior. When oppressed by the Ammonites, the elders of the area of Gilead reach out to Jephthah (Judg. 11:6). Their pleading initially is met by Jephthah's reminding them, "Didn't you hate me and drive me from my father's house?" (v. 7 NIV). Without denying the past, they again request his help but include their willingness to make him their ruler (v. 8).

Once established in his new position of authority, Jephthah contacts the Ammonite king concerning their aggressive conquest (v. 12). The response goes back to events of centuries past when Israel had journeyed from Egypt to take up residence in Canaan (v. 13). They claim Israel had taken their land and it should now be returned without any conflict.

Do Not Make Rash Vows

Jephthah refutes this claim with a detailed rehearsal of how Israel came to possess the land (vv. 14-26). He concludes by declaring the Lord will be the Judge and determine who is right (v. 27). "Howbeit the king of the children of Ammon hearkened not unto the words of Jephthah which he sent him" (v. 28).

---

1. How does verse 1 describe Jephthah?
2. Why did Jephthah settle in Tob, and what did he do there (vv. 2-3)?
3. What caused the Gileadites' opinion of Jephthah to change (vv. 4-7)?
4. Did the Gileadites keep their promise to Jephthah (vv. 8-11)?
5. Why were the Ammonites threatening Israel (vv. 12-13)?

> "Circumstances which we have resented, situations which we have found desperately difficult, have all been the means in the hands of God of driving the nails into the self-life which so easily complains."—Alan Redpath

---

B. Foolish Vow (vv. 29-31)

29 Then the Spirit of the Lord came upon Jephthah, and he passed over Gilead, and Manasseh, and passed over Mizpeh of Gilead, and from Mizpeh of Gilead he passed over unto the children of Ammon. 30 And Jephthah vowed a vow unto the Lord, and said, If thou shalt without fail deliver the children of Ammon into mine hands, 31 Then it shall be, that whatsoever cometh forth of the doors of my house to meet me, when I return in peace from the children of Ammon, shall surely be the Lord's, and I will offer it up for a burnt offering.

God's raising up Jephthah to be the deliverer is evident by the Holy Spirit's coming upon him and equipping for the task (v. 29). He makes a circuit through the immediate area. Though the purpose isn't given, it seems only logical for him to be building support and possibly recruiting soldiers.

Prior to going into the conflict, Jephthah makes an unnecessary vow. Having already stated God would be the Judge (v. 27), one wonders whether he thought it possible to influence Him in his favor. The vow seems to be a willingness to offer whatever animal first greets him upon returning from battle. Homes were frequently part of a compound located some distance from the gate. Animals were free to roam within the open area. Curiosity, as well as familiarity with the owner and his family, would cause the animals to come to the gate whenever anyone approached. The problem will arise in the wording of the vow—he states "whatever" (v. 31 NKJV). There is no limitation.

Further, notice his intention is to offer a "burnt offering" to the Lord. If Jephthah was open to a human sacrifice, since the Hebrew text offers the possibility of "whoever," his concept of worship is horribly misunderstood. It reminds us how easy it can be to confuse genuine worship with our perception of worship that has been strongly tainted by other religions and secularism.

Let's be reminded that God does not require vows as part of our relationship with Him. *Obedience?* Yes! *Vows?* No. Vows lean toward bribery as well as a works response instead of love and thanksgiving for God's provision.

1. What "came upon" Jephthah, and why (v. 29)?
2. Why do you suppose Jephthah made this vow to God (vv. 30-31)?

"Make no vows to perform this or that; it shows no great strength, and makes thee ride behind thyself."—Thomas Fuller

C. Complete Victory (vv. 32-33)

³²**So Jephthah passed over unto the children of Ammon to fight against them; and the Lord delivered them into his hands. ³³And he smote them from Aroer, even till thou come to Minnith, even twenty cities, and unto the plain of the vineyards, with a very great slaughter. Thus the children of Ammon were subdued before the children of Israel.**

Empowered by the Holy Spirit, Jephthah initiates an attack on the Ammonites. Notice the absence of any reference to soldiers accompanying him. This does not indicate it was a solo operation like those of Samson. We know Jephthah led a band of renegades. It seems logical they would have accompanied him, along with Israelites of the region. Also, we need to keep in mind the centrality of Jephthah to this narrative. He made the vow and, with victory, will be the one to fulfill it.

The Lord grants victory to Jephthah as they march through the land of the Ammonites. "Twenty cities" fall under the sword (v. 33). The description of "a very great slaughter" indicates a huge loss of Ammonite lives. Any attempt to take away some of Israelite land has been destroyed. God has honored the repentance of His people and preserved their inheritance.

- Describe the outcome of the battle.

"If you are under the power of evil, and you want to get under the power of God, cry to Him to bring you over to His service; cry to Him to take you into His army."—D. L. Moody

D. Vows Not Required (Deut. 23:21-23)

(Deuteronomy 23:21-22 is not included in the printed text.)

²³**That which is gone out of thy lips thou shalt keep and perform; even a freewill offering, according as thou hast vowed unto the Lord thy God, which thou hast promised with thy mouth.**

This passage is from the midst of laws God gave to Israel through Moses. We can learn three important principles from these verses.

First, if we make a vow to the Lord but do not keep it, we have sinned. Second, God does not require us to make vows, so "it is not a sin to refrain from making a vow" (v. 22 NLT). Third, a vow is made to God out of our free will; but once made, we are no longer free, but obligated to keep our vow.

---

1. What is sinful (v. 21)?
2. What is not sinful (v. 22)?
3. How serious does God take our vows (v. 23)? Would this include one's marriage vows?

II. THE VOW FULFILLED (Judges 11:34-40)

A. A Disastrous Homecoming (vv. 34-35)

³⁴And Jephthah came to Mizpeh unto his house, and, behold, his daughter came out to meet him with timbrels and with dances: and she was his only child; beside her he had neither son nor daughter. ³⁵And it came to pass, when he saw her, that he rent his clothes, and said, Alas, my daughter! thou hast brought me very low, and thou art one of them that trouble me: for I have opened my mouth unto the Lord, and I cannot go back.

Jephthah comes home as the triumphant victor, only to perhaps be reduced to wishing he had been defeated. As he comes to his home, the first "whatever" of his vow is none other than his daughter. Dancing and playing the timbrels, she joyously welcomes home her father, the conquering hero. This form of celebration is seen in several other Old Testament accounts. The prophetess Miriam led the women of Israel with timbrels and dancing as they rejoiced over God's destroying the Egyptian army in the Red Sea (Ex. 15:20-21). When David and King Saul returned from soundly defeating the Philistines, they were greeted by the women dancing and playing various musical instruments (1 Sam. 18:6).

The anguish of Jephthah becomes immediately evident by tearing his clothes. In the Oriental culture there were various means of showing sorrow; they included weeping, wailing, and putting dust on one's head. However, the most significant expression of sorrow was to literally tear the outer garment. The depth of Jephthah's mourning is then verbally expressed: "Oh! My daughter! You have made me miserable and wretched" (Judg. 11:35 NIV).

Jephthah's misery and anguish comes from his perspective of a vow. Vows made to God were not to be broken, no matter the actions needed to fulfill them. Notice Jephthah's wording, "I cannot go back" (KJV). Or, "I have made a vow to the Lord that I cannot break (NIV)."

• Contrast the emotions of Jephthah's daughter (v. 34) with his emotions (v. 35).

B. A Daughter's Response (vv. 36-38)

(Judges 11:37-38 is not included in the printed text.)

³⁶And she said unto him, My father, if thou hast opened thy mouth unto the Lord, do to me according to that which hath proceeded out of thy mouth; forasmuch as the Lord hath taken vengeance for thee of thine enemies, even of the children of Ammon.

Here is where we wish there was more information about this unnamed daughter. We do not know her age but, due to her request, we may assume she was approaching a point where she could soon be married. Keep in mind that girls often married in their mid-teens.

The daughter asks her father to delay the fulfillment of the vow for two months (v. 37). She requests the time to grieve with her friends that she will never have the opportunity to marry. Marriage in this culture was the door to self-worth. Marriage and bearing children, especially sons, brought value to women in this patriarchal society.

In verse 36, we see her encouraging the work of the Lord in her father's victory. She says her father must fulfill his vow in light of the Lord's intervention. This commitment provides an outstanding example of response to God's work. Regretfully, it involves actions which He does not require or expect in any vow.

Jephthah grants her request (v. 38). One can only imagine the heaviness of heart this father must have felt during these two months. He must have experienced overwhelming mental and emotional anguish. He must have pondered over other vows he could have made without the possibility of such dire consequences to him and his family.

---

1. What does verse 36 reveal about Jephthah's daughter?
2. Describe the two months of lament (vv. 37-38).

C. A Difficult Conclusion (vv. 39-40)

³⁹And it came to pass at the end of two months, that she returned unto her father, who did with her according to his vow which he had vowed: and she knew no man. And it was a custom in Israel, ⁴⁰That the daughters of Israel went yearly to lament the daughter of Jephthah the Gileadite four days in a year.

Did Jephthah really offer his daughter as a burnt offering? Or, did he commit his daughter to a life of perpetual virginity? Here we come to a crossroads.

Do we accept the Scriptural account as truth or, do we attempt to soften the reality of the Word and the historical culture?

A quote from the *Beacon Bible Commentary*, volume 2, summarizes how we should look at the event and what actually takes place:

> We must never allow pious sentiment to influence our interpretation of God's Word. The rather clean meaning of the text is that Jephthah offered his daughter as a human sacrifice. It is undeniable that Jephthah's conduct falls far short of Biblical standards, which strongly forbade human sacrifices. But, Jephthah was the product of a corse, barbarous, pre-Christian age, and was half-Canaanite as well. This incident illustrates the extent to which the pagan religions of Canaan had influenced Hebrew monotheism at this time.

One of the reasons to believe in the divine inspiration of the Bible is that it consistently includes accounts of all types of people and their actions, good and bad. If only the righteous, obedient accounts were included, we would not have a complete picture of our own humanity.

• Describe the commemoration that took place.

> "How one handles grief is a personal matter. Let the one who has suffered the loss take the lead."—Abigail Van Buren

---

III. REVERENCE GOD BY KEEPING VOWS (Eccl. 5:1-7)

A. Guarding Our Actions (vv. 1-3)

(Ecclesiastes 5:1, 3 is not included in the printed text.)

²Be not rash with thy mouth, and let not thine heart be hasty to utter any thing before God: for God is in heaven, and thou upon earth: therefore let thy words be few.

The Book of Ecclesiastes is attributed to the writings of King Solomon and, along with the books of Psalms and James, is considered a book of wisdom. The opening verses of Ecclesiastes 5 are especially important, as they provide a guideline for our actions and our words in reference to worship. Verse 1 cautions us concerning how we go to the house of worship. Listening and understanding must precede our words if they are to honor God. When there is no true worship, Solomon describes it as "the sacrifice of fools." This will not be acceptable to the heavenly Father.

Verse 2 reminds us of the saying, "Put brain in gear prior to engaging mouth." It emphasizes the need for wise thinking and careful evaluation of our motives before making statements about God or commitments to Him. Emotions are part of how God made us, but they fluctuate, so we must not let them hinder a consistent life in Christ. Thoughtful silence and reverent prayer, not our feelings, provide the foundation for God-honoring speech and worship.

There are many worship styles by which God's people can honor Him. However, worship leaders and the congregation need moments of quiet so genuine words of praise and thanksgiving can pour out. Psalm 19:14 is a prayer we should offer consistently: "Let the words of my mouth, and the meditation of my heart, be acceptable in thy sight, O Lord, my strength, and my redeemer."

Verse 3 of the text compares the many words of a foolish person to what happens to an individual who is consumed with an abundance of business activities. Even while sleeping, dreams flood the mind. Many of them make no sense. Others may cause fear or distress. No wonder the words of the foolish are compared to these dreams.

---

1. How should we approach the house of God (v. 1)?
2. Describe the warning in verse 2.

> "When you've got a word on the tip of your tongue, sometimes it's best to leave it there."—*Quotable Quotations*

B. Fulfilling One's Vows (vv. 4-7)

⁴When thou vowest a vow unto God, defer not to pay it; for he hath no pleasure in fools: pay that which thou hast vowed. ⁵Better is it that thou shouldest not vow, than that thou shouldest vow and not pay. ⁶Suffer not thy mouth to cause thy flesh to sin; neither say thou before the angel, that it was an error: wherefore should God be angry at thy voice, and destroy the work of thine hands? ⁷For in the multitude of dreams and many words there are also divers vanities: but fear thou God.

Unless they are brought to completion, good intentions have little to no value. The only reason for stating they may have a little value is their indicating some positive thinking and a desire to accomplish. It looks good to others. However, unless there is the effort and sometimes endurance to bring those intentions to fruition, they accomplish nothing.

The same holds true when a person chooses to make a vow. Usually we see vows in relationship to some aspect of our spiritual life with the Lord. Other vows may be directed toward bettering a relationship with another person or not falling back into some undesirable behaviors. The former is indicated here, with some possible application to the latter.

In this setting, a vow needs to be seen as a contract with God. Knowing we have committed to God himself, we should not be careless in its completion. To contract and then not fulfill places us in the category of the foolish (v. 4). Strong devotion to God results in pressing on toward fulfilling the vow. Failure to complete a vow eventually may lead to a separation from the Lord God.

Verses 6 and 7 reflect on verses 2 and 3. Great care needs to be taken prior to making a vow. No one has the option of later claiming to have made a mistake in what was said. It can result only in God's bringing judgment on one's plans and hopes for success. When a person simply dreams without substance and speaks without the boundaries of faith and reason, everything then has no meaning. This indicates a complete lack of recognition of God's awesome presence and power.

---

1. Who is a fool (v. 4)?
2. What is "better" (v. 5)?
3. What can we not simply call "an error" (v. 6)?

> "Many good purposes and intentions lie in the churchyard."
> —Matthew Henry

CONCLUSION

The account of Jephthah's foolish vow is one of the saddest stories in Scripture. The Lord chooses him to be the deliverer whom the people desperately desire. This man goes into battle with the Holy Spirit upon him. However, a foolish vow is offered.

Vows can have a positive purpose in believers' lives, provided they are not loose talk based on dreams or visions with no divine guidance. The bottom line is accountability to God himself.

GOLDEN TEXT CHALLENGE

"BE NOT RASH WITH THY MOUTH, AND LET NOT THINE HEART BE HASTY TO UTTER ANY THING BEFORE GOD: FOR GOD IS IN HEAVEN, AND THOU UPON EARTH: THEREFORE LET THY WORDS BE FEW" (Eccl. 5:2).

We must be cautious concerning what we say *about* God and *to* Him. We must "not be hasty in word or impulsive in thought to bring up a matter in the presence of God" (NASB). This was Jephthah's error, and we must not follow his tragic example.

The second part of this verse reveals why we must not be rash or hasty. The vast difference between the creation and the Creator is measured in God being "in heaven, and thou upon earth"—and that demands thoughtful reverence, not extravagant words. God cannot be manipulated into answering prayer. He hears the simple, sincere, brief words of those who truly submit to His majesty and seek His help.

Daily Devotions:

M. Honor Your Promises • 1 Samuel 1:9-11, 19-28
T. God Hears Our Vows • Psalm 61:1-8
W. God Keeps His Word • Jeremiah 34:12-22
T. Keep Your Word • Matthew 5:33-37
F. Accountable for Your Words • Matthew 12:33-37
S. Powerful Use of Words • James 5:12-16

Reject Ungodly Attitudes (Various Individuals)

1 Samuel 2:12-35; 4:17; Acts 5:1-11; 8:9-24

Unit Theme:

Good Lessons From Bad Examples

Central Truth:

Motives of the heart lead to a lifestyle that either pleases God or rejects Him.

Focus:

Identify and avoid attitudes that lead to ungodliness.

Context:

Accounts of individuals whose wrong attitudes brought condemnation

Golden Text:

"Search me, O God, and know my heart: try me, and know my thoughts: And see if there be any wicked way in me, and lead me in the way everlasting" (Ps. 139:23-24).

Study Outline:

  I. **Total Disregard for God** (1 Sam. 2:12-17, 22-25, 34-35; 4:17)
 II. **Motivated by Greed and Acclaim** (Acts 5:1-11)
III. **Lust for Power and Fame** (Acts 8:9-24)

INTRODUCTION

This lesson focuses on a variety of individuals who have one thing in common—their self-serving motives. The central truth of this lesson provides the foundation: "Motives of the heart lead to a lifestyle that either pleases God or rejects Him."

Motives can be best understood as the reason for a particular course of action. Individuals may be conscious of their motives and know exactly what is driving them. However, it is also possible for unconscious motives to impact behavior. Unhealthy motives may stem from one's environment, distinct negative events, or influential people. These negative motives are not easily eradicated. A new healthy setting, positive role models, and forgiveness are part of change. Also, a person must want to adopt a new set of motives.

As believers, we understand the power of spiritual regeneration through the work of the Holy Spirit. One way the Spirit works is through the Scriptures. It is amazing to hear the testimonies of people whose lives have been changed by reading the Bible. Some were reading to disapprove its content but fell under conviction and became believers.

Today's lesson introduces us to people who, by virtue of their position or supposed relationship with God, should never have exhibited the motives which led to unspiritual actions. These, in turn, provided a path to physical and spiritual disaster. Accounts come from both Old Testament and New Testament characters, reminding us that human nature does not change though separated by time and culture. The actions of Eli's sons are separated from the New Testament examples by some 1,100 years, yet, in each case, motives contribute to the very same actions.

In our own lives, we can be so concerned about what we want to do or what others want for us that we overlook the motives behind our actions. We need to ask, "What is driving me?" and "What do I really want out of this?" Yet, we can slide through those questions without giving genuine answers. For that reason, having a trusted friend who knows us and will ask difficult, penetrating questions enables our true motives to surface.

The objective of this lesson is "to identify and avoid attitudes that lead to ungodliness." These attitudes rise from our undergirding motives.

I. TOTAL DISREGARD FOR GOD (1 Sam. 2:12-17, 22-25, 34-35; 4:17)
A. Self-serving Sons (2:12-17)
   (1 Samuel 2:13-16 is not included in the printed text.)
   ¹²Now the sons of Eli were sons of Belial; they knew not the Lord.
   ¹⁷Wherefore the sin of the young men was very great before the Lord: for men abhorred the offering of the Lord.

The introduction of Hophni and Phinehas to the Biblical narrative is completely negative. They are called the *sons of Belial*, meaning "corrupt," "worthless," or "wicked." Notice their names are not included (until v. 34), only a description of their character. The wickedness practiced by these two men stems from their complete disregard for God and His law.

As the sons of Eli, they are members of the priestly tribe, Levi. Their father is the high priest of Israel. By virtue of their heritage, they are priests ministering in the Tabernacle as the people come to offer sacrifice. However, the character of these men is far from what God expected of them. They were to lead holy lives, following the Law in their life and actions of ministry.

Instead, Hophni and Phinehas were motivated by unholy, self-serving greediness. They cared only for what *they* wanted, in complete disregard for God's plans of how worship and provision for them was to be accomplished. Their actions could be attributed to procedural ignorance. Not only would they have known the Law, but also trained to keep it.

Instead of following the regulations as prescribed in Leviticus 7:28-36 for obtaining their share of the meat sacrifices, they preempted it (1 Sam. 2:13-15). They did not wait for the fat to be burned on the altar to take a portion of the boiled meat. Also, they asked for their portion of the meat while it was still raw so it could be roasted. They changed God's law to fit their human desires.

Verse 16 indicates there was resistance by some of the Israelites. They knew the proper manner and pushed for the right sequence of events, but it was to no avail. Their statements were met with the threat, "Give it to me now; and if not, I will take it by force" (NKJV). It is hard to imagine such an environment. People came obediently to worship and were coerced by unscrupulous priests. Regretfully, as one studies the history of the Christian church, there are similar examples of individuals in ministering offices who took advantage of their positions for personal gain.

Verse 17 indicates how grievous their sins were in the eyes of God. This was not an error in judgment or a single falling to temptation. Rather, it speaks of a lifestyle of contempt for God and divine worship.

As contemporary believers, we must not carelessly assume God will accept any words and actions we perceive as worship. Giving the leftovers of our time, energy, and money is not acceptable worship.

---

1. Explain the phrase "they did not know the Lord" (v. 12 NKJV).
2. How does verse 17 summarize the situation?

> "He that boasts of being one of God's elect, while he is willfully and habitually living in sin, is only deceiving himself, and talking wicked blasphemy."—J. C. Ryle

---

B. Nondisciplining Father (vv. 22-25)

(1 Samuel 2:22-23, 25 is not included in the printed text.)

²⁴Nay, my sons; for it is no good report that I hear: ye make the Lord's people to transgress.

Eli, the high priest, was aware of the sins of his sons. Their sins were not limited to changing the means of receiving the priestly portion of the sacrifices. Their wickedness included sexual relations with the women who were a part of the operation of the Tabernacle (see Ex. 38:8). What an abomination! We are not told if this was done under the guise of "sacred prostitution," as took place in some pagan temples, or just unbridled lust. Regardless, their immoral actions were condemned by the law of God.

Eli confronted his sons in a weak manner. Yes, he was an old man nearing the end of his life. However, that did not excuse him from maintaining the holiness of God's laws. Perhaps he would have removed these two from office if they had not been his own flesh and blood. On the other hand, how much more should a father have wanted to bring his sons back into alignment to escape God's judgment?

Eli's question, "Why do you do such things?" (1 Sam. 2:23 NKJV) was unnecessary. No logical reason can be projected for their behavior. His indicating the reports of their behavior not being good (v. 24) consists little more of a light slap on the wrist. He then says they have placed themselves in a position where no one can plead their case before God (v. 25). All of this has little effect on Hophni and Phinehas. They do not change their ways and now will be facing the judgment God intends for their desecration of worship.

---

438   Reject Ungodly Attitudes

Could Eli have done more? Absolutely! He was the high priest with spiritual authority and responsibility for the Tabernacle and the spiritual life of the nation.

---

1. Whom did Eli's sons take advantage of, and how?
2. What was wrong with Eli's reaction to his sons' corrupt deeds?

> "If we never have headaches through rebuking our children, we shall have plenty of heartaches when they grow up."—Charles Spurgeon

---

C. Sin's Judgment (2:34-35; 4:17)

(1 Samuel 2:35 and 4:17 are not included in the printed text.)

³⁴And this shall be a sign unto thee, that shall come upon thy two sons, on Hophni and Phinehas; in one day they shall die both of them.

The ongoing sins of Hophni and Phinehas, along with Eli's failure to properly discipline them, does not go unnoticed by God. An unnamed man of God comes to the high priest with a specific message concerning the situation (v. 27). He begins with a brief historical review of God's selecting the tribe of Levi to be His ministering servants, the priests. Verse 28 refers to the pattern by which the priests would receive a portion of some offerings for their livelihood.

Though Eli did not personally participate in his sons' activities, he became guilty by association. He chose his sons over the responsibility of being God's chosen spiritual leader fulfilling the Law. God rescinded His intention for the continuance of Eli's family in the priesthood (v. 31). Also, Eli's descendants would not live to old age; rather, they would die in the prime of life (v. 32).

As confirmation of God's word and intention, both Hophni and Phinehas would die on the same day (v. 34). This tragedy would be a visible sign of the judgment for sin. The time period from this statement of judgment until its fulfilment is not stated.

In verse 35, the unnamed prophet adds that God would raise up for Himself "a faithful priest who shall do according to what is in My heart and in My mind" (NKJV). This would be fulfilled through the priest Zadok (see 1 Kings 2:27, 33), and ultimately fulfilled in Jesus Christ, the "anointed forever."

In 1 Samuel 4, the predicted judgment on Hophni and Phinehas becomes a reality. Once again, Israel and the Philistines are engaged in war. Experiencing a significant defeat, the Israelites bring the ark of the covenant to the battlefield, thinking they will turn the tide. This brings Eli's two sons into the conflict.

However, God's favor is not with Israel. The Philistines experience a tremendous victory, killing thirty thousand soldiers. Part of their victory includes the death of Eli's two sons (vv. 11, 17). Even more importantly, they capture the ark of the covenant—that is an ultimate catastrophe.

Back in Shiloh, the elderly Eli sits by the side of the road waiting for news and fearing what may have happened to the ark. Hearing the tragic news, this ninety-eight-year-old, overweight man falls off his chair, breaks his neck, and dies (v. 18). Thus, his forty years of service as the high priest comes to a sad end.

---

1. What would happen "in one day" (2:34), and how did it happen (4:11, 17)?
2. How would the next priest of Israel be different (2:35)?

"Sin wouldn't be so attractive if the wages were paid immediately."
—Author unknown

II. MOTIVATED BY GREED AND ACCLAIM (Acts 5:1-11)

A. Plan of Deceit (Acts 5:1-2)

¹But a certain man named Ananias, with Sapphira his wife, sold a possession, ²And he kept back part of the price, his wife also being privy to, and brought a certain part, and laid it at the apostles' feet.

The backdrop for this event can be seen in chapter 4. There was a voluntary communal treasury into which many of the believers contributed. They willingly sold property and gave the proceeds to the Twelve for distribution as needed. Some would have been used for care of the widows (ch. 6). The rest was probably used to support those who had given up their occupations and now were in "full-time ministry."

Ananias and Sapphira wanted to participate financially after having sold one of their possessions (5:1). There was probably some sense of genuine desire to support the community's ministry. Maybe there was an attempt to appear to be as generous as others, but a fear of insecurity caused them to hold back part of the proceeds. When Ananias presented the money to the apostles, he used misleading words as to the amount of the sale and what was being donated.

Verse 2 notes how both husband and wife were part of the deception. It was a precalculated attempt to deceive and receive credit for more than was actually being done.

• How was this couple deceitful?

"In the deceitfulness of our hearts, we sometimes play with temptation by entertaining the thought that we can always confess and later ask forgiveness. Such thinking is exceedingly dangerous."
—Jerry Bridges

Reject Ungodly Attitudes

B. Discernment of Deceit (vv. 3-6)

³But Peter said, Ananias, why hath Satan filled thine heart to lie to the Holy Ghost, and to keep back part of the price of the land? ⁴Whiles it remained, was it not thine own? and after it was sold, was it not in thine own power? why hast thou conceived this thing in thine heart? thou hast not lied unto men, but unto God. ⁵And Ananias hearing these words fell down, and gave up the ghost: and great fear came on all them that heard these things. ⁶And the young men arose, wound him up, and carried him out, and buried him.

Peter's response to Ananias' bringing the money to the community treasure indicates the Holy Spirit's revealing the truth of the situation. Ananias apparently presented the money as if it were the entire proceeds from the sale, but the Holy Spirit revealed the deception to Peter. This was the spiritual gift of knowledge in operation.

Peter attributed Ananias' actions to yielding to Satan's temptation. Peter pointed out the property and subsequent proceeds belonged to Ananias and Sapphira. They could do whatever they chose—give none, give all, or give some. The choice of the couple points to greed and the desire for affirmation. The greatest failure here was not lying to their brothers and sisters, but lying to God, causing separation from Him.

God's judgment was immediate. Why was there such drastic punishment when others seem to be given more grace prior to God's taking action? David presents a prime example. The prophet Nathan did not confront him until nine months after his sin of adultery with Bathsheba and arranging for the death of her husband, Uriah (see 2 Sam. 11—12). We know God's ways are just. His judgment doesn't need to fit our timetable; His timing always fits His purpose.

Ananias' death had a tremendous effect on the infant church. "Great fear" developed upon hearing of what had taken place (Acts 5:5). This was a milestone emphasizing the importance of personal integrity before God.

Verse 6 records the immediate burial of Ananias. The Jewish pattern was for burial to take place within twenty-four hours, since there was no form of embalming. However, here the body was immediately wound in cloth and buried. Even his wife was not notified of his death! The usual pattern of mourning and then having a simple meal after the burial did not take place.

---

1. If you were Ananias' defense attorney, how might you answer Peter's four questions in verses 3 and 4?
2. Describe the speed and severity of God's judgment (vv. 5-6).

> "Lying insults not only those whom you manage to fool, but also God, whom you can never fool."—J. I. Packer

---

C. Continuance of Deceit (vv. 7-11)
(Acts 5:7, 10-11 is not included in the printed text.)

8And Peter answered unto her, Tell me whether ye sold the land for so much? And she said, Yea, for so much. 9Then Peter said unto her, How is it that ye have agreed together to tempt the Spirit of the Lord? behold, the feet of them which have buried thy husband are at the door, and shall carry thee out.

No reason stands out as to why Ananias and Sapphira did not come together when presenting their money to the apostles. She arrives just three hours after his burial and stands totally ignorant of the preceding events. Peter immediately presses the issue to test her integrity. He asks directly concerning the amount of money received for the property. He states the price Ananias had indicated, and she agrees.

Her response causes Peter to first ask how she could ever agree to test the Holy Spirit's ability to know truth. He then states her fate to be that of her husband, immediately falling to the ground and dying. The same young men who took Ananias and buried him do likewise for Sapphira (v. 10).

Verse 11 indicates "great fear" gripping the whole church as they hear of these two events. This fear reaches deep into their being and brings an awesome awareness of God's holiness and need to live a holy, faithful life in Christ.

---

1. Ultimately, what had Ananias and Sapphira "agreed together" to do (v. 9)?
2. How did this event affect the church and community?

Shiny but Worthless

An old method for catching raccoons is to place a piece of foil inside a small barred box that is staked to the ground. When a raccoon comes by, he reaches his paw into the box to get the foil. But, once he has grasped the foil, his paw changes shape and will not fit back through the bars on the box. Many times a raccoon would rather give up his freedom, and perhaps his life, just for the sake of a shiny but useless piece of foil.—Michael Green, ed., *Illustrations for Biblical Preaching*

III. LUST FOR POWER AND FAME (Acts 8:9-24)

A. Conversion of a Sorcerer (vv. 9-13)

(Acts 8:10-13 is not included in the printed text.)

9But there was a certain man, called Simon, which beforetime in the same city used sorcery, and bewitched the people of Samaria, giving out that himself was some great one.

This account of one man's inordinate desire for power and fame is couched in the middle of a dramatic expansion of the church in Samaria. Here is a fulfillment of Jesus' words of how believers would witness in Jerusalem, Judea, and then Samaria. We see the geographical and ethnic expansion of the Gospel. Philip, initially seen as one of the seven selected to oversee the benevolence work of the church (ch. 6), begins to preach Christ in the city of Samaria. Dramatic healings and release from demon possession accompany his ministry. Many believe, including a most unlikely convert, Simon the sorcerer. Not only had this man boasted of his powerful magic, but he had drawn a following.

Through magic potions and ties to demonic forces, this type of individual performed miracles and showed revelation knowledge (8:9). Simon's practice of the occult arts had convinced people that he was "the great power of God" (v. 10). Verse 11 says, "He had astonished them with his sorceries for a long time" (NKJV).

In marked contrast, we see how Philip's preaching the kingdom of God and invoking the name of Jesus brought salvation to many people (v. 12), including Simon, who was baptized in water (v. 13). Simon "continued with Philip, amazed by the miracles which were part of this evangelistic outreach.

---

1. What did Simon claim about himself, and how did people respond (vv. 9-11)?
2. How was Samaria turned upside down (vv. 12-13)?

> "The charm of fame is so great that we like every object to which it is attached, even death."—Blaise Pascal

---

B. Empowerment of the Holy Spirit (vv. 14-17)
   (Acts 8:14-17 is not included in the printed text.)
   The Samaritans' acceptance of the gospel of Jesus Christ is a major event. No longer does the Church consist of only Jewish believers. Now Jesus' words of their being witnesses in Samaria has been fulfilled. No wonder the apostles send two of their own to personally see what has taken place. Upon arriving in Samaria, Peter and John immediately begin to pray that these believers experience the baptism in the Holy Spirit. They follow the pattern of laying hands on the new believers, and they receive this empowerment of the Holy Spirit.

• Who came to the Samaritan revival, and what resulted (vv. 14-17)?

C. Rebuke of a Sinful Request (vv. 18-24)
   (Acts 8:21-24 is not included in the printed text.)
   18And when Simon saw that through laying on of the apostles' hands the Holy Ghost was given, he offered them money, 19Saying, Give me also this power, that on whomsoever I lay hands, he may receive the

Holy Ghost. ²⁰But Peter said unto him, Thy money perish with thee, because thou hast thought that the gift of God may be purchased with money.

Old habits and attitudes can be hard to break. Unless there is a concentrated effort to eradicate them, they can creep back into our words and actions. Simply suppressing them can only delay their reappearance. Simon's request to buy the power of the Holy Spirit provides a classic example. As seen earlier in verse 13, he continued to have a special fascination and interest in the miraculous. This was a part of his old life as a sorcerer. Now, as a believer, he had a temptation for power for personal fame.

Simon's desire did not remain hidden. He offered money to Peter and John so he too could lay hands on people, and they would receive the Holy Spirit.

What caused this desire to rise up in Simon? What did he see or hear? It seems only logical, from the other accounts of people receiving the Holy Spirit, that the Samaritans spoke languages they had not learned when baptized in the Spirit. They obviously had received a powerful spiritual experience.

Peter strongly rebuked Simon for thinking he could receive a gift from God with money (v. 20). In verse 21, Peter says this is a heart matter; sin has invaded. Simon cannot have any part in this marvelous ministry while thinking of personal power and influence, such as was true prior to salvation.

Immediately, Peter directed Simon to the need for repentance (v. 22). Without it, there could be no reconciliation with God. By using the word *perhaps* regarding forgiveness, Peter reveals the issue here does not lie with God—He forgives anyone who comes to Him with a contrite heart. The problem rests with Simon. Will he honestly come before God with a repentant heart, recognizing his sin, and desiring to be forgiven?

Verse 23 sheds further light on the inner attitude of Simon. Peter discerns bitterness having filled Simon's heart. Here we can only speculate. However, it is possible that his no longer being a great man of influence had gnawed at him. Philip, Peter, and John are the leading individuals in the Samaritan revival, which includes miracles. Simon's desire for position among the people becomes a dominant desire over his living in relationship with Christ.

Having incurred such a stern rebuke by spiritually powerful people, Simon recognizes his perilous position. He immediately asks for Peter's intercession to the Lord so he may avoid the declared punishment (v. 24). No further account of Simon is included in Scripture, so we do not know the rest of the story. However, we can see the need for discipleship of new believers so they can move beyond their past.

---

1. What did Simon's request reveal about his heart (vv. 18-21)?
2. How do some people today try to buy (or sell) the power of God?
3. What did Peter tell Simon to do, and how did he respond (vv. 22-24)?

"Riches are the pettiest and least worthy gifts which God can give a man. . . . Yet men toil for them day and night, and take no rest.

CONCLUSION

The three examples of ungodly attributes have something in common. Each comes from within a spiritual environment which should have produced a totally different response: (1) As the high priest, Eli had the responsibility to maintain the integrity of the ministering priests, but he did not (2). Having experienced the power of the Holy Spirit and the growth of the Church, one would have hoped Ananias and Sapphira would have resisted temptation, but they did not. (3) Simon witnessed the miraculous power of the Holy Spirit, yet wanted to exploit it for selfish gain.

All three of these incidents remind us of the need to guard our hearts from temptation and strive to lead a holy life acceptable to our heavenly Father.

GOLDEN TEXT CHALLENGE

"SEARCH ME, O GOD, AND KNOW MY HEART: TRY ME, AND KNOW MY THOUGHTS: AND SEE IF THERE BE ANY WICKED WAY IN ME, AND LEAD ME IN THE WAY EVERLASTING" (Ps. 139:23-24).

The psalmist turns the spotlight on the secret things of his own heart. It is easy for us to condemn what we perceive as a wrong mind-set in others, sometimes using only one outward action by which to judge them, but we tend to be much more cavalier about a search of our own mind and motives. Not only did David invite the Lord to search his heart, but also to test him to see if his actions under fire matched the good intentions of his thoughts and plans.

Once we have started with God, it is the direction of our lives—our continuing in the grace of God—that determines where we will spend eternity. David called it "the way everlasting" (v. 24). Paul referred to it as "your conversation," or way of life (Phil. 1:27).

Daily Devotions:

M. Respect Holy Things • Leviticus 22:1-9
T. Danger of Greed • 2 Kings 5:16-27
W. Give Your Best to God • Malachi 1:6-14
T. Jesus Condemns Irreverence • Matthew 21:10-13
F. Be Characterized by Humility • Matthew 23:1-12
S. Pursue Eternal Priorities • Luke 12:13-21

Trust God's Infinite Grace (Manasseh)

2 Kings 21:16; 2 Chronicles 33:1-20; Ezekiel 18:21-23; Romans 2:4-11

Unit Theme:

Good Lessons From Bad Examples

Central Truth:

No one who repents is beyond God's willingness to forgive.

Focus:

Recognize God can forgive any sin and trust Him to forgive.

Context:

Manasseh was king in Judah from 697 until 642 BC.

Golden Text:

"If the wicked will turn from all his sins that he hath committed, and keep all my statutes, and do that which is lawful and right, he shall surely live, he shall not die" (Ezek. 18:21).

Study Outline:

  I. **The Worst of the Worst** (2 Chron. 33:1-10; 2 Kings 21:16)

 II. **Judgment, Repentance, Restoration** (2 Chron. 33:11-20)

III. **God Will Forgive Anyone** (Ezek. 18:21-23; Rom. 2:4-11)

INTRODUCTION

In this lesson, the central truth and evangelism emphasis are the same: "No one who repents is beyond God's willingness to forgive." It sounds right because we know anyone who repents of sin and accepts Jesus Christ as Savior comes into a right relationship with the heavenly Father. But, when it comes to the reality of applying the concept to a particular cruel, Godless person, do we believe it still applies?

This lesson reminds us of two important doctrinal truths inherent in the plan of salvation. First is God's grace. His holiness and humanity's sinfulness provide a huge chasm which cannot be crossed by our efforts to be good. Because of God's love for us, He offers a bridge that enables us to be reconciled to Himself; we are not worthy in ourselves. His grace—His unmerited favor to sinners—offers the wonderful opportunity of salvation.

The second part of salvation depends on us. As the Holy Spirit convicts us of our sinful state, will we repent and believe in Jesus as our Savior? No human deeds can take the place of this action and commitment. Those who believe in the inherent goodness of humankind may attempt to come into relationship with God, but they are only deceiving themselves and ignoring the Word of God.

Today's lesson focuses on a king of Judah who is often overlooked when considering bad examples. Typically, we think of King Ahab and his wicked wife, Jezebel—an evil duo who lead Israel into idolatry. God sends His most powerful prophet, Elijah, to confront them. They never repent and thus experience God's judgment. In marked contrast is Manasseh. He too falls into the category of the most sinful kings to rule God's people, but instead of continuing in his ways, he repents and God forgives.

I. THE WORST OF THE WORST (2 Chron. 33:1-10; 2 Kings 21:16)
A. Idolatry Promoted (2 Chron. 33:1-10)
(2 Chronicles 33:2-5, 7-8 is not included in the printed text.)

¹Manasseh was twelve years old when he began to reign, and he reigned fifty and five years in Jerusalem:

⁶And he caused his children to pass through the fire in the valley of the son of Hinnom: also he observed times, and used enchantments, and used witchcraft, and dealt with a familiar spirit, and with wizards: he wrought much evil in the sight of the Lord, to provoke him to anger.

⁹So Manasseh made Judah and the inhabitants of Jerusalem to err, and to do worse than the heathen, whom the Lord had destroyed before the children of Israel. ¹⁰And the Lord spake to Manasseh, and to his people: but they would not hearken.

Manasseh is the fourteenth king to rule over the southern kingdom known as Judah. He holds two distinctive records. First, he reigns longest of the nineteen kings of Judah. Second, Manasseh's heritage of a godly father makes it ironic that he stands as the worst of the worst. Hezekiah, Manasseh's father, followed righteousness, which was the basis for his bargaining with God when informed he was going to die (2 Kings 20:1-6; Isa. 38:1-5). During the additional fifteen years granted to Hezekiah, his son is born.

The opening verse of 2 Chronicles 33 states the basics—age when Manasseh begins to reign and length of his kingship. He might have been a co-regent with his father for nine years. Verse 2 begins the description of evil which Manasseh imposed on the people. It provides an overview with a general description of his participating in and promoting the detestable spiritual practices of the heathen nations. In the previous centuries, God directed the leadership to destroy the pagan peoples who perpetuated such wickedness. Here we see a leader, the king of Judah, personally engaged in those same practices! One can only wonder of the influences which caused Manasseh to fall into such depths of depraved sinfulness. Also, where were the spiritual leaders who should have been a positive influence in his life?

Verses 3-7 provide a description of the various ways Manasseh introduced heathen worship into the kingdom. It began with rebuilding the high places his father destroyed (31:1). The *high places* refer to mountain tops, higher knolls, or elevated places which had been constructed as pagan worship sites, featuring altars. The altars could be of various shapes, but they always had a sacred column or pillar. There, the Baals were worshiped (33:3).

Manasseh's idolatrous worship included worshiping the heavenly bodies (v. 3). There was the pagan belief that they determined events on earth. What a terrible contrast to the sun, moon, and stars being God's light to the earth and providing a means to mark day, night, and years (Gen. 1:14-15).

Second Chronicles 33:6 points to Manasseh's heavy involvement in all the various forms of the occult. It would have included various forms of witchcraft and types of divination, as well as consulting mediums and spiritualists. Was this a means of his attempting to cast spells on his enemies? Possibly, but we cannot know for sure. Horribly, the king even caused his own "sons to pass through the fire" (NKJV) as an act of worship to the gods Molech and Chemosh.

Manasseh did not stop with participating in pagan rituals of worship and offering allegiance to false gods at high places. He brought this worship into the sacred Temple dedicated to the Lord God. The king apparently wanted to worship God and have these other gods alongside. Setting up a carved image further broke the Ten Commandments. God alone was to receive worship and there were to be no images erected as part of that worship (see Ex. 20:3-7). God had promised Canaan would be His people's home, but He required their obedience (2 Chron. 33:8). When Solomon gave his dedicatory prayer at the Temple, he noted how the people's sins eventually would cause them to be taken as captives from their homeland (6:38; 1 Kings 8:46).

Manasseh's actions led the people into a path from which they refused to return (2 Chron. 33:9). It sealed their doom. God attempted to bring them back to Himself, but to no avail (v. 10). In Josephus' historical work *Antiquities*, he records how Manasseh slaughtered many prophets. Apparently, these unnamed men came with a word from the Lord but were murdered for urging Manasseh to repent of his wicked ways and turn back to God.

---

1. Whose pattern did Manasseh follow (v. 2)? Why do you suppose he did this?
2. How did Manasseh undermine his father's legacy (v. 3)?
3. How did Manasseh act like Ahaz, his grandfather (v. 6; see 28:3)?
4. How did Manasseh profane God's house (vv. 4-5, 7)?
5. How did the king influence the entire nation (vv. 8-10)?

> "What each one honors before all else, what before all things he admires and loves, this for him is God."—Origen

---

B. Innocent Bloodshed (2 Kings 21:16)

¹⁶Moreover Manasseh shed innocent blood very much, till he had filled Jerusalem from one end to another; beside his sin wherewith he made Judah to sin, in doing that which was evil in the sight of the Lord.

Not only did Manasseh lead Judah into the depths of idolatry; he murdered innocent people. *Filling Jerusalem with innocent blood* was not just a simple uprising or isolated incident; it speaks of constant brutality. This can be expected when the ruler himself participates in child sacrifices as part of supposed worship.

Let's consider some possible reasons Manasseh followed such a path of idolatry and immorality. One suggestion is he followed some of the patterns of his grandfather, Ahaz. Another suggestion is wanting to be seen favorably by the Assyrians and their rising influence. The bottom line is, Manasseh chose to reject God and indulge in his own passion for sin. *Did he really expect God to overlook his sins?* Very likely, the answer is "yes." Lawbreakers do not expect to be caught and have to pay the consequences.

• What "innocent blood" is being shed in our nation today?

"Men never do evil so completely and cheerfully as when they do it from religious conviction."—Blaise Pascal

---

II. JUDGMENT, REPENTANCE, RESTORATION (2 Chron. 33:11-20)
A. God's Judgment (v. 11)

¹¹Wherefore the Lord brought upon them the captains of the host of the king of Assyria, which took Manasseh among the thorns, and bound him with fetters, and carried him to Babylon.

God destroyed the Canaanites who previously occupied Canaan due to their pagan religions. Now His own chosen people, under the leadership of Manasseh, are participating in horrible sins. The depth of their sinful idolatry has deafened their ears and blinded their eyes to any return to God.

Harsh, deserved judgment comes on Manasseh. The Assyrians were known for their brutal treatment of their captives. They would put hooks in their noses and lead them as livestock. Also, they were known to put hooks into a person's buttocks and lead them with ropes. Every movement would cause intense pain. Not only is a nose hook placed on Manasseh, but his hands are shackled. In this manner, he is taken to Babylon. What a marked change from the monarch who freely moved about his kingdom worshiping a plethora of pagan gods!

---

1. How did Manasseh suffer for his sins?
2. Describe ways many people are "bound" today.

"The agony of man's affliction is often necessary to put him into the right mood to face the fundamental things of life."—Oswald Chambers

---

B. Manasseh's Repentance (vv. 12-13)

¹²And when he was in affliction, he besought the Lord his God, and humbled himself greatly before the God of his fathers, ¹³And prayed unto him: and he was intreated of him, and heard his supplication, and brought him again to Jerusalem into his kingdom. Then Manasseh knew that the Lord he was God.

Up to this point, nothing good could be said concerning the wicked King Manasseh. However, now in the distress of Assyrian captivity, he turns to the Lord and seeks His favor. Notice the description of "humbled himself greatly" (v. 12). It speaks of laying aside every sense of arrogance and personal pride.

Manasseh returns to "the God of his fathers." There now exists an understanding of who can deliver and who needs to be served. In previous years, all of his worship and commitment had been given to pagan gods who had done nothing of any lasting effect for him but bring judgment. Now, in the middle of disaster, Manasseh prays to God.

Although there is no record of the specific words spoken, verse 13 provides a sense of what might have been said. His humble supplications included an acknowledgment of his sins and recognition of the only true God. Mercifully, "the Lord . . . listened to his plea" (NIV). Manasseh could not ask for God's intervention on the basis of past righteousness as did his father, Hezekiah (see 2 Kings 20:2-3). All he could hope for was God's grace and forgiveness to be extended to a repentant heart, and it happened.

We need to know our humble repentance in the middle of disastrous circumstances does not obligate God to reverse them. He forgives and restores our relationship with Himself, but it is only in His mercy that we are lifted out of the depths brought on by our selfish pursuit of sin.

The circumstances of Manasseh's release and return to his position was a miraculous restoration. The last line of verse 13 speaks of a new confession of faith and commitment: "Then Manasseh knew that the Lord is God" (NIV).

• Describe the king's transformation.

A Criminal's Turnaround

About fifteen years ago at the Church of God national convention in Peru, a humble pastor, surrounded by his family, received his ordination certificate from the national overseer. At one time this man had been greatly feared in the city for his ruthless behavior, which even included murder. One day an evangelism team was witnessing on "his street." Seeing him, all went to the other side, except for one saintly lady who boldly shared the Gospel with him. He made a commitment to Christ that day and, shortly thereafter, became a minister of the Gospel.

C. True Worship Restored (vv. 14-20)

(2 Chronicles 33:14, 17-20 is not included in the printed text.)

¹⁵And he took away the strange gods, and the idol out of the house of the Lord, and all the altars that he had built in the mount of the house of the Lord, and in Jerusalem, and cast them out of the city. ¹⁶And he repaired the altar of the Lord, and sacrificed thereon peace offerings

and thank offerings, and commanded Judah to serve the Lord God of Israel.

What are the signs of true repentance? That person demonstrates a significant transformation of heart, mind, and emotion. For some it occurs in stages, while others have an on-the-spot miraculous change which is immediately noticed.

In the life of King Manasseh, the distinction lies in the direction of his worship. He destroys the foreign gods with their images and altars (v. 15). Everything used to desecrate God's holy temple, along with the rubble of the other gods, are thrown outside of the city. He does not allow them to even remain in sight. Following this, Manasseh sanctifies the temple of God and offers appropriate sacrifices (v. 16). In spite of all this good, one failure does remain. The high places outside of Jerusalem are not destroyed (v. 17). Though the people use them to worship God, it still allows the temptation for the Israelites to return to their previous sinful idolatrous practices.

Here we are reminded of how one's sinful actions can have long-term effects, even after changing to live for Christ. For years, Manasseh had served a great number of gods. He now tells the people of Judah to serve God, and they do. But, the temptation remains.

Verse 14 points to a king who now takes care of state business. Specifically, he cares for the safety of the capital city and the kingdom as a whole, strengthening the walls of Jerusalem, and placing military leaders in key cities of Judah.

This results from an imprisoned king who pled for God to intervene, despite the sins he had committed and promoted for many years. God graciously intervened, and a new man led the nation of Judah until he was "buried . . . in his own house" (v. 20).

---

1. Describe the physical changes Manasseh brought about (vv. 14-15).
2. Describe the new example the king set for the nation (v. 16).

> "The amazing thing about Jesus is that He doesn't just patch up our lives; He gives us . . . a clean slate to start over, all new."
> —Gloria Gaither

III. GOD WILL FORGIVE ANYONE (Ezek. 18:21-23; Rom. 2:4-11)

A. Forgiveness Available (Ezek. 18:21-23)

21 But if the wicked will turn from all his sins that he hath committed, and keep all my statutes, and do that which is lawful and right, he shall surely live, he shall not die. 22 All his transgressions that he hath committed, they shall not be mentioned unto him: in his righteousness that he hath done he shall live. 23 Have I any pleasure at all that the wicked should die? saith the Lord God: and not that he should return from his ways, and live?

Now we turn our attention to the Lord's word on forgiveness as given to the prophet Ezekiel. Ezekiel's ministry occurs during the dark days of Judah's being taken into Babylonian captivity. The ongoing sins of the kings and the people leaves God no other choice but to bring judgment on them. Ezekiel will share in their suffering in a foreign land and be God's voice to His people.

In verse 21, the Lord says if a wicked man leaves his sinful acts and dedicates himself to following the decrees of God, he will not die because of the previous sins—he will live. Verse 22 emphasizes how repentance and the subsequent forgiveness erase the past record of sin. Life now replaces death.

Frequently, we hear individuals speak of God as being unjust or harsh in His judgment on sinners (v. 26). However, nothing is further from the truth. Verse 23 states God takes no delight in bringing death to the sinner. However, God delights in those who leave their life of sin and turn to righteousness. They find forgiveness and a loving heavenly Father. "Therefore turn and live!" says the Lord (v. 32 NKJV).

---

1. What does God choose to forget (vv. 21-22)?
2. What displeases God (v. 23)?

"Forgiveness is the giving, and so the receiving, of life."—George MacDonald

---

B. Impartial Judgment (Rom. 2:4-11)

(Romans 2:5-10 is not included in the printed text.)

⁴Or despisest thou the riches of his goodness and forbearance and longsuffering; not knowing that the goodness of God leadeth thee to repentance?

¹¹For there is no respect of persons with God.

This last portion of our lesson presents a strong case for realizing God's goodness to individuals, even when faced with their sins. His forbearance and long-suffering causes there to be a delay in executing judgment for sin. Our sins deserve His wrath. Without His restraint, there would be no opportunity for repentance and salvation.

God's forbearance and long-suffering does not erase His wrath and judgment on sinners, for "God will give to each person according to what he has done" (v. 6 NIV). For the self-seeking and truth-rejecting there is wrath (v. 5). In contrast, those who continue to do good will experience God's glory, honor, and peace (v. 7). This must not be understood as good deeds providing salvation. Rather, once we have accepted Christ as Savior and Lord, leading a life of righteousness brings divine rewards.

Verse 11 provides a strong statement of God's equal concern for each person, regardless of ethnicity, gender, or age. He shows no favoritism in offering forgiveness. No person's sins are so many or so hideous that God's mercy will not be offered when they seek His forgiveness.

Great care needs to be taken to avoid a misapplication of this wonderful offering of God. His forbearance must never be interpreted as *cheap grace*. This term is used to describe the concept of choosing to sin and then repenting afterward. A continued practice indicates a person's state of heart. They are not concerned with regularly following the Lord in holiness. They want to serve God and pursue self. That is impossible.

---

1. How do verses 4 and 11 describe God?
2. When and how will God's "righteous judgment" (vv. 5-6) be revealed?
3. How will perseverance and righteousness be rewarded (vv. 7, 10)?
4. What awaits those who are "self-seeking" (vv. 8-9 NKJV)?

"God's delays are not God's denials."—Robert H. Schuller

CONCLUSION

This lesson on Manasseh provides a dramatic contrast. On one side stands the son of a righteous king who sells himself to the most hideous of pagan gods. On the other side, we see a holy God who despises sin and calls His people to follow the path of holiness.

Manasseh's dramatic turn to God and a lifestyle of righteousness demonstrates the mercy of God, who accepts all repentant sinners—even the worst of the worst. No one who repents is beyond God's willingness to forgive.

GOLDEN TEXT CHALLENGE

"IF THE WICKED WILL TURN FROM ALL HIS SINS THAT HE HATH COMMITTED, AND KEEP ALL MY STATUTES, AND DO THAT WHICH IS LAWFUL AND RIGHT, HE SHALL SURELY LIVE, HE SHALL NOT DIE" (Ezek. 18:21).

The axiom that says, "To err is human, to forgive is divine" is true. Paul said, "For all have sinned, and come short of the glory of God" (Rom. 3:23).

God's words through Ezekiel provide the answer to all of our erring. The simple answer is, *Repent and live right.*

This supports the second half of the axiom, "to forgive is divine." John said, "If we confess our sins, he is faithful and just to forgive us our sins, and to cleanse us from all unrighteousness" (1 John 1:9). There is no other attribute of God that so reveals His love than His ability and willingness to forgive.

Daily Devotions:

M. Recognize Your Need for Forgiveness • Psalm 51:1-12
T. Repentance Brings Forgiveness • Jonah 3:1-10
W. Return to the Lord • Zechariah 1:1-6
T. Forgiveness Offered and Accepted • Luke 23:32-43
F. Cleansed by Jesus • 1 Corinthians 6:9-11
S. God Forgives the Worst • 1 Timothy 1:12-16

The Danger of Pride (Nebuchadnezzar)

Psalm 10:4; Proverbs 16:5, 18-19; Daniel 4:1-37; 1 Peter 5:5-7

Unit Theme:
Good Lessons From Bad Examples

Central Truth:
Christians are called to live humbly before God.

Focus:
Be warned of the danger of pride and humble ourselves before God.

Context:
Nebuchadnezzar, the most powerful of the Babylonian kings, reigned for forty-three years.

Golden Text:
"Be subject one to another, and be clothed with humility: for God resisteth the proud, and giveth grace to the humble" (1 Peter 5:5).

Study Outline:
I. **Warned Against Being Prideful** (Dan. 4:19-27; Ps. 10:4; Prov. 16:5)
II. **Pride Leads to a Fall** (Dan. 4:28-33; Prov. 16:18-19)
III. **Humble Yourself Before God** (Dan. 4:34-37; 1 Peter 5:5-7)

INTRODUCTION

Pride has two dimensions or opposites. There is a *proper pride*. This occurs when a person feels pleasure or a sense of accomplishment in a performance, one's family, or particular development. It covers satisfaction and positive behavior toward others. The opposite dimension of pride can be defined as an "inordinate and unreasonable self-esteem, attended with insolence and rude treatment of others." These two types of pride cannot reside side-by-side within the same individual or group of people.

Though we usually think of pride on an individual or personal level, we must also consider *corporate pride*. Throughout the Old Testament there are references to various nations expressing pride, usually of the type which brings God's judgment.

Our lesson emphasizes the dangerous side of pride; it leads to destruction and death. This comes as a result of pride deceiving one's heart and hardening the mind to the reality of his or her condition. The Lord told the arrogant Edomites, "The pride of your heart [has] deceived you" (Jer. 49:16 NIV). In today's lesson, while recounting the narrative of King Nebuchadnezzar of the Babylonian Empire, we will be warned of the danger of pride and the need to humble ourselves before God.

Too frequently, individuals associate *humility* with *weakness*. Nothing can be further from the truth. To be humble demands greater strength and commitment than being prideful. When people refuse to humble themselves before God and become obsessed with personal pride, it sets the stage for God bringing them face-to-face with reality. Then they quickly understand who they are in comparison to Almighty God.

I. WARNED AGAINST BEING PRIDEFUL (Dan. 4:19-27; Ps. 10:4; Prov. 16:5)

To set the stage for God's judgment on Nebuchadnezzar for his pride, we need to take a brief look at his background. His rise to power is a sovereign act of God, so he could be the means of God's judgment on Judah for their extended commitment to pagan gods. On three separate occasions, his armies invade Judah. On the third invasion, the Temple (Solomon's temple) is destroyed.

Nebuchadnezzar was the genius of this empire. It did not last very long after his death. The successors seem to have lacked the will and ability to continue the greatness of the kingdom. Historians celebrate this king's military brilliance, as well as the splendor of his many building projects. All of this seems to have taken its toll on his personal perspective. In Daniel 4:1, he presents himself as though he were the monarch of the universe. That speaks of a strong sense of personal pride. It was God who had allowed his ascendance to this powerful position, and now God will bring him to a position of humility.

A. A Prophetic Dream (Dan. 4:19-27)

(Daniel 4:19-23 is not included in the printed text.)

24 This is the interpretation, O king, and this is the decree of the most High, which is come upon my lord the king: 25 That they shall drive thee from men, and thy dwelling shall be with the beasts of the field, and they shall make thee to eat grass as oxen, and they shall wet thee with the dew of heaven, and seven times shall pass over thee, till thou know that the most High ruleth in the kingdom of men, and giveth it to whomsoever he will. 26 And whereas they commanded to leave the stump of the tree roots; thy kingdom shall be sure unto thee, after that thou shalt have known that the heavens do rule. 27 Wherefore, O king, let my counsel be acceptable unto thee, and break off thy sins by righteousness, and thine iniquities by shewing mercy to the poor; if it may be a lengthening of thy tranquillity.

It is interesting how God chooses the medium of dreams to speak to some powerful monarchs. In Genesis, Pharaoh has two dreams that set the stage for Joseph's rise to power and the move of Jacob's entire family to Egypt. Here we see the second time Nebuchadnezzar experiences dreams and will need an interpretation (also see Dan. 2). Each time, Daniel becomes the man who steps in and reveals their meaning.

This second dream greatly disturbs the king (4:5). He calls for various individuals who he assumes should have the skills or connections to give him the interpretation. However, just like the previous time, they are of no help. Eventually, Daniel answers. He is referred to as "Belteshazzar," since that was the Babylonian name given to him when he was chosen to serve in the royal court (1:7). Nebuchadnezzar expresses great confidence in Daniel's ability to interpret, since he recognizes God's Spirit dwells in him (4:9, 18).

The dream begins with the picture of a stately, beautiful tree which Daniel realizes represents the king. A messenger from heaven states it is to be cut down, but the roots will remain (vv. 10-15).

Daniel finds himself in a difficult position, and is both terrified of the implications and perplexed (v. 19). How do you tell the most powerful monarch of that era he is about to be reduced to the position of an animal foraging in the fields? There is no easy way to break the news. Recognizing Daniel must have a dilemma, Nebuchadnezzar encourages him not to be alarmed at what he knows.

Prior to stating the interpretations, Daniel states his wish that the dream would apply to the enemies of the king rather than to Nebuchadnezzar. He then launches into the dream's meaning. The large, strong tree represents the king and the greatness of his kingdom. The second part of the dream is judgment on Nebuchadnezzar. Rather than death, God chooses to humble this man. He needs to recognize the greatness of his kingdom does not rest on his abilities alone. God is "sovereign over the kingdoms of men and gives them to anyone he wishes" (v. 25 NIV).

This judgment of his having the mind of an animal and living in the fields as one of them will last for seven years. At the end of this time, the kingdom will be restored. Daniel finishes with practical advice. If Nebuchadnezzar will repent of his sins, live right, and stop oppressing individuals in his kingdom, possibly God will relent from His judgment and allow him to rule without interruption (v. 27). Daniel's practical advice still holds true today, and it can be applied to individuals and groups.

Nebuchadnezzar has been warned, but how will he respond?

---

1. Why does God sometimes speak through dreams?
2. How did the king try to calm Daniel's concerns (v. 19)?
3. How was the tree an apt symbol (vv. 20-22)?
4. How was the dream prophetic (vv. 24-26)?
5. What was Daniel's advice (v. 27)?

"The chief occupational hazard of leadership is pride."—John Stott

---

B. Pride Separates (Ps. 10:4; Prov. 16:5)

Psalm 10:4 The wicked, through the pride of his countenance, will not seek after God: God is not in all his thoughts.

Proverbs 16:5 Every one that is proud in heart is an abomination to the Lord: though hand join in hand, he shall not be unpunished.

These two scriptures show how pride not only separates the wicked from God, but also sets the stage for His judgment to be unleashed on them. These verses also provide the platform for our discussion of the next stage in Nebuchadnezzar's life.

The first part of Psalm 10 gives a detailed description of the wicked person who yields to arrogance and pride. Verse 4 specifically points to the prideful person's separating himself from God. Pride allows room only for self-pleasures and personal pursuits. This person does not think about God. All attention is given to personal plans and enjoying the prosperity of gain obtained through devious means.

Proverbs 16:5 shows the Lord's attitude toward the pride of the wicked. He isn't just disturbed by it or slightly frustrated. He detests their pride and its ongoing impact. As a result, the prideful will assuredly experience God's judgment.

These two verses leave no doubt as to the impact of pride. Unless prideful people repent, they will be punished by God.

---

1. Describe the likely tone of voice Nebuchadnezzar used in verse 30.
2. Describe the likely tone of voice that sounded from heaven (vv. 31-32).
3. Describe Nebuchadnezzar's drastic change (v. 33).

> "It was pride that changed angels into devils; it is humility that makes men as angels."—Augustine

---

II. PRIDE LEADS TO A FALL (Dan. 4:28-33; Prov. 16:18-19)
A. The Dream Fulfilled (Dan. 4:28-33)

(Daniel 4:28-29, 32-33 is not included in the printed text.)

³⁰The king spake, and said, Is not this great Babylon, that I have built for the house of the kingdom by the might of my power, and for the honour of my majesty? ³¹While the word was in the king's mouth, there fell a voice from heaven, saying, O king Nebuchadnezzar, to thee it is spoken; The kingdom is departed from thee.

Verse 28 sets the stage for the narrative of events which follows. Everything which had been predicted in the dream interpreted by Daniel takes place. Twelve months go by from the warning to repent until God's judgment falls on Nebuchadnezzar.

This provides us an opportunity to consider God's mercy in allowing the sinner time to repent. Remember how God did not confront King David concerning his adulterous act with Bathsheba and arranging the death of her husband, Uriah, until the child was born. In this case, God provides a seemingly generous amount of time for Nebuchadnezzar to consider the predicted future. It is almost unbelievable that Nebuchadnezzar would continue as though nothing is wrong. However, we can attribute this to the destructive nature of pride. Pride fights a gallant battle against humility, unless there is a distinct event which provides a motivating factor.

It is amazing how God personally encounters this prideful living. He doesn't send a messenger but speaks directly with a voice from heaven. One can only imagine the surprise and shock Nebuchadnezzar must have experienced. He has just been viewing the greatness of his capital city and boasting of its being his accomplishment. He saw this city with its magnified temple and hanging gardens as symbols of his personal glory.

No sooner has he uttered those words than God verbally issues judgment. This event has similarity to the parable of the rich fool (Luke 12:13-21). In that narrative, the man takes pride in his material possessions and immediately God speaks of his foolishness and immediate death.

God speaks specifically concerning Nebuchadnezzar's fate (Dan. 4:31-32): (1) His authority as king is going to be removed. (2) He will live in the fields away from people as a wild animal. (3) His diet will be the same as the cattle. (4) This scenario will last for seven years. (5) After this period he will need to acknowledge God as the sovereign monarch of the world.

Verse 33 not only points to the fulfillment of God's judgment, but also provides a graphic picture of Nebuchadnezzar. The once mighty king of the dominant kingdom, the man who used to bring judgment on Judah, now lives and looks like an animal. One can only speculate as to what the people may have said when getting a glimpse of their humbled king.

The remaining verses in the chapter, which will be further discussed in section three, reveal the impact of God's judgment on Nebuchadnezzar. At the end of the appointed time and having his sanity return, this king understands who truly has dominion over the earth. His humility causes God to restore him to the previous position of honor. Once again, he is surrounded with the advisers and nobles who had previously been present in his court. Verse 37 provides a distinct summary of how Nebuchadnezzar now views God: "Everything he does is right and all his ways are just. And those who walk in pride he is able to humble" (NIV). What a dramatic change in perspective!

---

1. Describe the wicked person's mind-set (Ps. 10:4).
2. Restate Proverbs 16:5 in language a child could understand.

> "Pride thrust Nebuchadnezzar out of men's society, Saul out of his kingdom, Adam out of Paradise, Haman out of court, and Lucifer out of heaven."—Thomas Adams

---

B. The Better Attitude (Prov. 16:18-19)

(Proverbs 16:18 is not included in the printed text.)

[19]Better it is to be of an humble spirit with the lowly, than to divide the spoil with the proud.

Frequently, we hear people share a shortened paraphrase of verse 18. They say "pride goeth before the fall." This mini statement shares truth; however, the whole verse provides a much better picture by the repetition of the concept with two separate statements. This pattern of repetition is one of the styles of Hebrew poetry.

Destruction, as a result of *pride*, can be seen in a variety of areas. First, it evades the time sense of reality. It causes an assumption of what may not be true. Second, it places a barrier between people. Thinking of oneself as better or above others negates receiving the benefits of relationships which bring personal growth. Third, it easily sets the stage for a fall from position due to others choosing to oppose and to replace. Pride contains within itself the opportunity to "crash and burn" from the lofty perception.

For those reasons and many more, verse 19 shows a better attitude; maintain a humble spirit and be among those who are oppressed by the proud. This position and attitude completely removes the destructive position pride provides. Proverbs 8:13 reminds us that wisdom never promotes pride, but rather hates it.

---

1. Describe a contemporary situation in which the truth of verse 18 was manifest.
2. What is "better," and why (v. 19)?

Not Quite Unsinkable

When the *Titanic* was to launch, a news magazine stated the ship was almost unsinkable. Overlooked was the word *almost*. On its maiden voyage, the ship received several warnings of ice in the area. Yet, the ship maintained full speed ahead. It was thought the larger ships were immune to danger from floating ice. Edward Smith, the captain, declared he could not "imagine any condition which would cause a ship to founder. Modern ship-building has gone far beyond that" (April 1912).

III. HUMBLE YOURSELF BEFORE GOD (Dan. 4:34-37; 1 Peter 5:5-7)
A. The Words of Humility (Dan. 4:34-37)

(Daniel 4:35 is not included in the printed text.)

34And at the end of the days I Nebuchadnezzar lifted up mine eyes unto heaven, and mine understanding returned unto me, and I blessed the most High, and I praised and honoured him that liveth for ever, whose dominion is an everlasting dominion, and his kingdom is from generation to generation.

36At the same time my reason returned unto me; and for the glory of my kingdom, mine honour and brightness returned unto me; and my counsellors and my lords sought unto me; and I was established in my kingdom, and excellent majesty was added unto me. 37Now I Nebuchadnezzar praise and extol and honour the King of heaven, all whose works are truth, and his ways judgment: and those that walk in pride he is able to abase.

At the completion of the stated time, God graciously restores Nebuchadnezzar's mind. We can only assume he returns to a sound mind but that his animal appearance remains. He will need to cut his hair and nails and begin eating normal food. His appearance would have been a definite confirmation of God's judgment having been brought against him.

Verse 34 demonstrates a complete change—a stance of humility. Now he speaks of God's honor and glory. He understands God exists eternally. His kingdom doesn't end with a generation or particular dynasty. Nebuchadnezzar follows these statements with a presentation of God's omnipotence. He exists as the Almighty Sovereign doing what He chooses, and no one can resist Him.

Another gracious action toward a humble Nebuchadnezzar can be seen in the various restorations which take place. The leading men of the kingdom seek out their former king and restore him to the throne. He then proceeds to lead the Babylonian kingdom to even greater heights.

Notice how this chapter concludes. The king now worships the God of heaven and recognizes His ways are just. He also now understands God can humble anyone who demonstrates pride.

---

1. Compare Nebuchadnezzar's transformation (v. 34) with the one seen in Mark 5:5, 15.
2. How did the king describe God's authority (Dan. 4:35)?
3. How did God bless the king, and why (v. 36)?
4. How did the king describe God's character (v. 37)?

> "A man must be big enough to admit his mistakes, smart enough to profit from them, and strong enough to correct them."—John C. Maxwell

---

B. The Choice of Humility (1 Peter 5:5-7)
  (1 Peter 5:6-7 is not included in the printed text.)
  ⁵Likewise, ye younger, submit yourselves unto the elder. Yea, all of you be subject one to another, and be clothed with humility: for God resisteth the proud, and giveth grace to the humble.

There are three "S" words which constantly appear in our desire to live for Christ. The first is *sin*. It separates us from God. We must strive to overcome its attempts to invade our hearts and minds regardless of the temptation. The second is *sacrifice*. Life in Christ does not occur without our putting forth the necessary effort to fulfill His will, regardless of the circumstances in which we may find ourselves. The third is *submission*. This brings the attitude of humility into our lives. Regardless of one's ability and intelligence, the attitude is an absolute necessity.

The apostle Peter writes to Jewish believers who are struggling because of persecution. These verses are taken from a position of chapter 5 in which he provides some guidelines for the elders as they serve as shepherds, or overseers serve the church. In verse 5 he addresses their relationship with the younger members. *Younger* here does not seem to refer to chronological age. Instead, it refers to those who are in the category of "laity" and are not in a ruling position. This provides the possibility of their being chronologically older and having been believers longer than their leadership.

These believers are directed to submit themselves to the authority of their leadership. However, this submission is not just to be one way. Genuinely being clothed with humility understands that being in leadership does not exempt from submission as well. Peter does not list specific areas. Instead, he states the principle which needs to be applied. Failure to practice humility places a person in opposition to God, for He is in opposition to pride. Pride is sin and open to God's judgment.

Verse 6 describes an opposite scenario from pride. Whereas pride brings God's anger and judgment, humility sets the stage for God's exaltation. "Due time" does not indicate the immediate future of this lifetime. It will probably take place at the Day of Judgment. However, let's not overlook the possibility of its being fulfilled partially while here on earth. We must not forget Nebuchadnezzar's humility, which results in his restoration as the king of Babylon.

The last verse in this section (v. 7) seems to be saying "relax." There are many things that probably cause anxiety in their lives with the issue of persecution. Only those who are cultivating humility in their lives can rest in God's care. This verse should be compared with Psalm 55:22: "Cast your burden on the Lord, and He shall sustain you; He shall never permit the righteous to be moved" (NKJV).

---

1. What blessing comes from submitting oneself to fellow Christians (v. 5)?
2. Who will be exalted, when, and how (v. 6)?

> "When our Lord says, we must be converted and become as little children, I suppose He means also that we must be sensible of our weakness, comparatively speaking, as a little child."—George Whitefield

---

CONCLUSION

The objective of this lesson is to be warned of the danger of pride and humble ourselves before God. Nebuchadnezzar provides an excellent example of how easy it can be to disregard God's role in setting us up and then, full of pride, assume what we have and do rests solely on our own ability. As individuals, we likely will never rise to the position of a world leader such as Nebuchadnezzar. However, that does not eliminate us from having the same struggle with pride.

Maybe you heard of someone who is "so humble they are proud of it." That describes a *pseudo-pride*. Genuine humility pushes back against the temptation of pride when it appears; it is a choice. We practice it in our lives through commitment to Scripture and by the empowerment of the Holy Spirit.

GOLDEN TEXT CHALLENGE

"BE SUBJECT ONE TO ANOTHER, AND BE CLOTHED WITH HUMILITY: FOR GOD RESISTETH THE PROUD, AND GIVETH GRACE TO THE HUMBLE" (1 Peter 5:5).

Parents tell me how their children need to change. Children say their parents need to change. Married people emphatically list each spouse's shortcomings. As a family therapist, I tell them, "Thank you. Now tell me some of the changes you might need to make in yourself." This usually elicits either a blank or a somewhat hostile stare from the client.

Therapists call it "resistance"; the Bible calls it "pride." The Golden Text speaks directly to this problem through the subject of *submission*.

The word *submit*, as it appears in the New Testament, literally means we are to fashion and order our lives under the authority of another. The concept is markedly out of step with society's present stampede toward personal independence, but I maintain it represents the pivotal solution to the crisis in the American family.

Submission cannot be forced or cajoled or argued into existence; neither can it be artificially produced through discipline or therapy. Submission flows from a humble and quiet spirit. May God grant each of us the wisdom to seek that silence for ourselves.—John Abuso

Daily Devotions:

M. Do Not Forget the Lord • Deuteronomy 8:10-20
T. Repent of All Pride • 2 Chronicles 32:24-29
W. The Humble Receive God's Favor • Proverbs 3:31-35
T. Pride Separates Us From God • Romans 1:28-32
F. Marks of This Fallen World • 2 Timothy 3:1-7
S. Submit to God • James 4:4-10

Follow the Lord Wholeheartedly (Caleb)

Numbers 13:1—14:30; Joshua 14:6-14

Unit Theme:

Good Lessons From Good Examples

Central Truth:

Wholehearted devotion to God pleases Him.

Focus:

Examine and emulate Caleb's wholehearted devotion to God.

Context:

In the 15th century BC, witnessing Caleb's devotion to God over the decades

Golden Text:

"Ye shall seek me, and find me, when ye shall search for me with all your heart" (Jer. 29:13).

Study Outline:

I. **Trust God Against All Odds** (Num. 13:1-2, 25—14:9)

II. **Have a Different Spirit** (Num. 14:20-30)

III. **Wholehearted Devotion** Rewarded (Josh. 14:6-14)

INTRODUCTION

The time of this lesson is about one and one-half to two years after Israel's departure from Egypt. The Israelites had spent about a year at Mount Sinai as the Lord completed His revelation of the Law and perfected their organization as a nation. Then they moved northward to the southern extremities of Canaan, at or near the oasis town of Kadesh-barnea. Here was a natural launching point for their occupation of Canaan—the climax to all the great things the Lord had been doing for them.

But at this point, all of the progress of the past two years will come to a grinding halt. Unbelief rears its ugly head, and the people sink into a morass of fear and confusion. Because of their doubts, Israel's move into Canaan is delayed for nearly forty years.

However, we meet a man, Caleb, who follows God wholeheartedly before, during, and after Israel's wilderness experience.

I. TRUST GOD AGAINST ALL ODDS (Num. 13:1-2, 25—14:9)

A. Selecting the Spies (13:1-2)

¹**And the Lord spake unto Moses, saying,** ²**Send thou men, that they may search the land of Canaan, which I give unto the children of Israel: of every tribe of their fathers shall ye send a man, every one a ruler among them.**

Following the instructions given him by the Lord, Moses selected men to go into Canaan and search out the land. He chose one from each tribe of Israel, with each being a leader from his group.

This action was closely associated with the movement of the people toward the Promised Land. The hour had come in which they were to go forward; according to verses 1-3, the spies were sent in obedience to the divine command. However, a comparison with Deuteronomy 1:22-24 shows the command followed the people's determination to do this very thing. This in itself was an act of suspicion and doubt. However, as the people had decided, so they were commanded to do.

In Numbers 13:6, we read that one of the men chosen was "Caleb the son of Jephunneh." His name means "capable" and "bold," and he lived up to it.

• What did the Lord declare about Canaan?

"He that takes truth for his guide . . . may safely trust God's providence to lead him aright."—Blaise Pascal

---

B. Reporting on the Land (vv. 25-33)

(Numbers 13:26, 29, 32-33 is not included in the printed text.)

25And they returned from searching of the land after forty days.

27And they told him, and said, We came unto the land whither thou sentest us, and surely it floweth with milk and honey; and this is the fruit of it. 28Nevertheless the people be strong that dwell in the land, and the cities are walled, and very great: and moreover we saw the children of Anak there.

30And Caleb stilled the people before Moses, and said, Let us go up at once, and possess it; for we are well able to overcome it. 31But the men that went up with him said, We be not able to go up against the people; for they are stronger than we.

After forty days, the spies returned to the camp of Israel to report on their findings. They brought with them a magnificent cluster of grapes (vv. 23-24). The mode of carrying the cluster cut down by the spies was evidently adopted to preserve it entire, as a specimen of the produce of the Promised Land. The impression made by the sight of it would be all the greater since the Israelites were only familiar with the scanty vines and small grapes of Egypt.

The general report the spies brought with them contained two elements: (1) the excellence of the land (which must have appeared beautiful indeed after more than a year of life in the desert) and (2) the great strength of its inhabitants.

The spies could not deny the land of Canaan was fruitful land. God had promised them "a land flowing with milk and honey" (Ex. 3:8), and the twelve spies acknowledged it was such a place.

Follow the Lord Wholeheartedly

Although Canaan was a land of milk and honey and grapes, the spies were awed by the presence of "the children of Anak" (Num. 13:28). Accustomed to the Egyptians—who, as may be inferred from their mummies, were slight and short of stature—the tall, muscular appearance of the mountaineers of Hebron must have formed a striking contrast. No wonder they inspired terror; for, combined with an extraordinary stature, they were a fierce, wild, wicked race, engaged in continual warfare. The spies were also awed by Canaan's walled cities.

Besides the children of Anak, the spies also saw the Amalekites, the Hittites, the Jebusites, the Amorites, and the Canaanites (v. 29). The Amalekites were descendants of Esau. They formed wild roving bands, which infested rather than inhabited the whole country between Judea and Egypt, including the Negev. They were not numbered among the inhabitants of Canaan proper.

As the difficulties of the conquest are given, one can almost feel the people's terror mounting. Then one of the spies interrupted the report of the others, in an attempt to slow down this reaction. "Caleb stilled the people," asserting they were able to conquer the land (v. 30).

Caleb opposed the majority with the confidence of victory: "We are well able to overcome it." Relying on God's promise, he believed they would be successful, and thus boldly foretold it. The others did not take into consideration that, with the banner of the Lord before them, they would come into the promised inheritance.

The Israelites had seen the strength of God manifested on their behalf. Were not the Egyptians as much stronger than they as the Canaanites were? And yet, without a sword drawn by Israel or a stroke struck, the chariots and horsemen of Egypt were routed and ruined.

Besides, God promised His people victory and success. He gave Abraham all possible assurances that He would put His seed in possession of that land (see Gen. 15:18; 17:8). God had expressly promised the Israelites by Moses that He would "drive out the Canaanites [from before them]" (Ex. 33:2), and He would do it "by little and little" (23:30). After all this, for them to say, "We [are] not able to go up against [them]" (Num. 13:31) was in effect to say, "God is not able to make His word good; He has undertaken more than He can perform."

In spite of the promises of God, the spies spread an "evil report of the land" among the Israelites (v. 32). They exaggerated the difficulties of the conquest in their unbelieving despair, and described Canaan as "a land that eateth up the inhabitants thereof."

The ten spies had confessed the land was rich; they now declared it consumed or devoured its inhabitants—which was entirely the reverse. They stressed the difficulties and dangers connected with the conquest and maintenance of the land, on account of the tribes inhabiting it and surrounding it. They said, "There we saw the giants, the sons of Anak . . . and we were like grasshoppers in our own sight, and so we were in theirs" (see v. 33).

---

1. Who heard the spies' account (v. 26)?
2. How did Canaan live up to its promise (v. 27)?

3. What did ten spies say about the desert, the hills, and the sea (v. 29)?
4. Contrast Caleb's report (v. 30) with the majority report (vv. 31-33).

> "God's commands are designed to guide you into life's very best. You will not obey Him if you do not believe Him and trust Him. You cannot believe Him if you do not love Him. You cannot love Him unless you know Him."—Henry Blackaby

---

C. Rejecting the Lord (14:1-4)

(Numbers 14:1-4 is not included in the printed text.)

Given the choice between faith in the judgment of the spies, who stood before them, and faith in the invisible God, the mass of the people put their faith in the word of the spies. All the memories of the great words God had said through Moses were as nothing against the words of these men. Filled with despair, the people thought of selecting a new leader and going back to Egypt.

How strong is your faith in God? Is it strong enough to withstand discouragement, disappointment, and disillusionment? Is it strong enough to stand firm when all the odds seem to be against you? The faith of Israel failed them at the time they needed it most. Don't let yours!

---

1. How did the negative report affect the nation (vv. 1-2)?
2. What fears did the Israelite men express (v. 3)?
3. Describe the people's "plan B" (vv. 3-4).

> "Keep your fears to yourself; share your courage with others." —Robert L. Stevenson

---

D. Pleading With the People (vv. 5-9)

⁵Then Moses and Aaron fell on their faces before all the assembly of the congregation of the children of Israel. ⁶And Joshua the son of Nun, and Caleb the son of Jephunneh, which were of them that searched the land, rent their clothes: ⁷And they spake unto all the company of the children of Israel, saying, The land, which we passed through to search it, is an exceeding good land. ⁸If the Lord delight in us, then he will bring us into this land, and give it us; a land which floweth with milk and honey. ⁹Only rebel not ye against the Lord, neither fear ye the people of the land; for they are bread for us: their defence is departed from them, and the Lord is with us: fear them not.

Moses, Aaron, Joshua, and Caleb pleaded with the congregation to look at the positive factors which supported their contention that a victorious occupation of Canaan was possible. To lend weight to their judgment, and as an expression of their deep concern, Caleb and Joshua tore their clothes, declaring, "The land . . . is an exceeding good land" (v. 7). They contended there was no reason why Israel could not enter. "If the Lord is pleased with us, he will lead us into that land" (v. 8 NIV). Only rebellion and fear could defeat God's people; obedience, courage, and faith were the secrets of victory.

However, the people cried out that Caleb and Joshua should be stoned. Such is the world's reward of many who have sought to be true messengers of God across the centuries (see Acts 6:8—7:60). The stoning was averted on this occasion, however, by God's intervention. He appeared in His glory before the Tent of Meeting, visible to all the congregation (Num. 14:10).

1. How did Moses, Aaron, Joshua, and Caleb express the seriousness of the situation (vv. 5-7)?
2. Describe the leaders' confidence in God (v. 8).
3. List three reasons why the Israelites need not fear Canaan's inhabitants (v. 9).

"Just as we must learn to obey God one choice at a time, we must also learn to trust God one circumstance at a time."—Jerry Bridges

II. HAVE A DIFFERENT SPIRIT (Num. 14:20-30)

A. Judgment Against a Nation (vv. 20-23)

20And the Lord said, I have pardoned according to thy word: 21But as truly as I live, all the earth shall be filled with the glory of the Lord. 22Because all those men which have seen my glory, and my miracles, which I did in Egypt and in the wilderness, and have tempted me now these ten times, and have not hearkened to my voice; 23Surely they shall not see the land which I sware unto their fathers, neither shall any of them that provoked me see it.

The act of pardon from God was in relation to His initial statement to completely destroy the people and build a new people from Moses (v. 12). Instead, God pardoned in response to Moses' request (v. 20).

Moses' intercession points to the power of the Christian in prayer before God. It is clearly expressed in the New Testament in Matthew 16:19 (with the power of the keys) and in John 20:22-23 (with the power of the Holy Spirit). In both passages there is the affirmation of the tremendous power of the Christian to intercede in behalf of the sinner. God does listen to our prayers.

Numbers 14:21-23 reveals that behind God's wrath and judgment stand His glory. Israel was meant to be the people who would show God's glory on the basis of their obedience. God is so committed to the integrity of His Word and will that He even used Israel's disobedience to manifest His glory to the earth. This generation would not inherit the Promised Land.

1. Why didn't God destroy the Israelites (v. 20)?
2. How was "ten times" too much (v. 22)?

3. What did God declare about the Israelites (v. 23)?

_____

B. Blessings on a Servant (vv. 24-30)
(Numbers 14:25-29 is not included in the printed text.)

²⁴But my servant Caleb, because he had another spirit with him, and hath followed me fully, him will I bring into the land whereinto he went; and his seed shall possess it.

³⁰Doubtless ye shall not come into the land, concerning which I sware to make you dwell therein, save Caleb the son of Jephunneh, and Joshua the son of Nun.

The preceding verses concluded with the sentence of death upon all who rebelled against God in siding with the "doubting ten." Verse 24 shows God does reward the obedient. Caleb had a "different spirit" (NIV)—he was willing to obey God. Caleb "followed [God] fully."

The joy Caleb experienced was in ultimately receiving the land he had seen. According to Hebrews 12:2, Jesus "endured the cross, despising the shame," because of "the joy that was set before him." Christian joy is not based on the instant gratification of our society but, instead, looks forward to the future God has ordained.

Along with God's blessing on Caleb and Joshua (Num. 14:30), all those twenty years of age or younger were to be pardoned (v. 29). From them would come a new people whom God would lead and protect and bring at last into the Promised Land. As for the rest, they would remain in the wilderness and die for their rebellion. For their steadfast faith in God, Joshua and Caleb were rewarded; for their utter lapse of faith, the children of Israel were punished.

_____

1. How did the Lord describe Caleb (v. 24)?
2. What directions did God give Moses, and why (v. 25)?
3. How would the people's words become their fate (vv. 28-29)?
4. Caleb and Joshua were distinguished as two among two million (v. 30). How should this encourage you?

"Trust God or die."—Winkie Pratney

_____

III. WHOLEHEARTED DEVOTION REWARDED (Josh. 14:6-14)
This passage's setting follows seven years of war. Israel now controlled the Promised Land as a whole, and Joshua had dismissed the army. He had divided the territories up among the various tribes as God directed, but part of the land had not been conquered. Chapter 13 lists the various peoples, cities, and areas left to be subjugated. God's plan was that the various tribes prove their trust in Him by finishing the work.

Caleb was one man who recognized the difference between *inheritance* and *possession*. We will see how he claimed all that had been promised to him forty-five years earlier. As an old man, he was willing to accept the challenge of taking possession of what was his.

A. Caleb's Wholehearted Faithfulness (vv. 6-8)

(Joshua 14:6 is not included in the printed text.)

⁷Forty years old was I when Moses the servant of the Lord sent me from Kadesh-barnea to espy out the land; and I brought him word again as it was in mine heart. ⁸Nevertheless my brethren that went up with me made the heart of the people melt: but I wholly followed the Lord my God.

Caleb remained true and faithful all his life. He was forty years old when Moses sent him into Canaan as one of the twelve spies. Thus, Caleb was no stranger to standing alone on God's promises.

The eighty-five-year-old man could point to the confidence he had in the Lord. He and Joshua were the oldest citizens of Israel. Everyone else in the generation had died in the wilderness.

What made Caleb so special? Surely he could see Israel's enemies were superior in terms of military strength. Caleb didn't look at the enemy, however. Instead, he focused on the supreme strength of God and the prize to be won by trusting Him.

---

1. Of what did Caleb remind Joshua (v. 6)?
2. How did Caleb contrast his heart with the heart of the Israelite nation (vv. 7-8)?

> "The reward of being 'faithful over a few things' is the same as being 'faithful over many things'; for the emphasis falls upon the same word; it is the 'faithful' who will enter into 'the joy of the Lord'" (see Matt. 25:20-23).—Charles S. Robinson

---

B. Caleb's Inheritance (v. 9)

⁹And Moses sware on that day, saying, Surely the land whereon thy feet have trodden shall be thine inheritance, and thy children's for ever, because thou hast wholly followed the Lord my God.

Can you imagine claiming something that was verbally promised to you forty-five years earlier? Caleb was an old man who appeared to have very few years left in this life. At age eighty-five, most men would not think of clearing land and building a new home (not to mention that he would have to drive out a whole tribe of people claiming squatter's rights).

Caleb knew he could trust God's promise. Although it took many years to see His promise fulfilled, Caleb never doubted the Lord's integrity.

• Describe Caleb's reward.

C. Caleb's Strength (vv. 10-11)

¹⁰And now, behold, the Lord hath kept me alive, as he said, these forty and five years, even since the Lord spake this word unto Moses, while the children of Israel wandered in the wilderness: and now, lo, I am this day fourscore and five years old. ¹¹As yet I am as strong this day as I was in the day that Moses sent me: as my strength was then, even so is my strength now, for war, both to go out, and to come in.

Caleb was still healthy, vital, and strong for his years. He was as much an able warrior in the army of Israel as the day Moses had sent him on the spy mission. He attributed his health to the Lord, whom He knew would allow him to claim his inheritance. He had accepted the Lord's promises and lived positively to see them fulfilled. "God seemed to prolong Caleb's life as a reminder to a younger generation that He fulfills His word" (*The Word in Life Study Bible*).

• Over 45 years, how had Caleb not changed, and why?

> "Oftentimes God demonstrates His faithfulness in adversity by providing for us what we need to survive. He does not change our painful circumstances. He sustains us through them."—Charles Stanley

---

D. Caleb's Mountain (vv. 12-14)

¹²Now therefore give me this mountain, whereof the Lord spake in that day; for thou heardest in that day how the Anakims were there, and that the cities were great and fenced: if so be the Lord will be with me, then I shall be able to drive them out, as the Lord said. ¹³And Joshua blessed him, and gave unto Caleb the son of Jephunneh Hebron for an inheritance. ¹⁴Hebron therefore became the inheritance of Caleb the son of Jephunneh the Kenezite unto this day, because that he wholly followed the Lord God of Israel.

Hebron, the area given to Caleb, had been attacked at least once by Joshua and the army of Israel during the years of conquest. Joshua 10:36-37 informs us the city and all its inhabitants were destroyed. Still, there were apparently many warriors in the vicinity—the Anakim—whom Caleb must drive out.

Hebron had a long history in the Biblical account, even before it was given to Caleb. Here was the cave of Machpelah, where Abraham buried Sarah hundreds of years earlier. Hebron was one of the oldest cities of the ancient world, occupied since at least 3,000 BC.

Caleb's battle cry, "Give me this mountain," was a bold request for an old man. Still, he was able to drive out the Anakim. This was a direct fulfillment of the faith proclamation he had made forty-five years earlier when he tried to convince the Israelites to take Canaan: "We should go up and take possession of the land, for we can certainly do it" (Num. 13:30 NIV). Hebron was one of the specific sections of Canaan explored by the twelve spies (v. 22). Caleb may have even then set his sights on the area to claim as his inheritance.

---

1. Explain Caleb's confidence (v. 12).
2. Can it be said about you, "He [or she] wholly follows the Lord God" (see v. 14)? If not, how can this become true?

"He that overcomes shall inherit all things."—Dwight L. Moody

CONCLUSION

Today the things that test our faith may be altogether different from those of Caleb's day and the days of the early Christians, yet they can be just as real, hard, and discouraging. And we must have our priorities well defined and our value system firmly in place so we can "stand against the wiles of the devil" (Eph. 6:11).

We have a great and effective promise the Old Testament believers did not have in their day: Paul declared, "There hath no temptation taken you but such as is common to man: but God is faithful, who will not suffer you to be tempted above that ye are able; but will with the temptation also make a way to escape, that ye may be able to bear it" (1 Cor. 10:13). Take heart: "If God be for us, who can be against us?" (Rom. 8:31).

GOLDEN TEXT CHALLENGE

"YE SHALL SEEK ME, AND FIND ME, WHEN YE SHALL SEARCH FOR ME WITH ALL YOUR HEART" (Jer. 29:13).

God's people were in captivity in Babylon. Some among them had aroused false hopes of returning soon to Jerusalem. Jeremiah urged them to patience and prayer. Through prayer, God could be found by the waters of Babylon. "I will listen to you . . . when you seek Me with all your heart" (see vv. 12-13). Prayer here is more than words; it is the whole heart reaching out to God.

Prayer has been defined as "talking to God," but not all petitions and supplications directed to heaven qualify as prayer. They may seem to be ardent enough and framed in the proper words, but rise no higher than the ceiling. Unless commitment is present, words addressed to God are not real prayer.

Genuine prayer assumes commitment to Christ and the Gospel. When full commitment undergirds prayer, our hearts reach out to God and our souls are poured out before Him.

Daily Devotions:

M. Abraham Followed God's Call • Genesis 12:1-9
T. Commitment to Follow the Lord • Joshua 24:22-31
W. Faithfulness Rewarded • Psalm 15:1-5
T. Follow Christ Wholeheartedly • Matthew 10:32-39
F. Called to Follow Christ • Mark 1:14-20
S. Christ's Followers Receive Eternal Life • John 10:23-30

Zealous for God (Phinehas)

Numbers 25:1-13; Joshua 22:10-34; John 2:13-17;
Romans 12:11; Hebrews 3:12-15

Unit Theme:

Good Lessons From Good Examples

Central Truth:

Zeal for God motivates Christians to effective service.

Focus:

Study examples of being zealous for God and serve Him with zeal.

Context:

Phinehas the priest demonstrates his zeal for God as does Jesus, the Great High Priest.

Golden Text:

"[Be] not slothful in business; fervent in spirit; serving the Lord" (Rom. 12:11).

Study Outline:

I. **Zealous for God's Honor** (Num. 25:1-13)

II. **Zealous for Faithfulness to God** (Josh. 22:10-34; Heb. 3:12-15)

III. **Be Zealous for God** (John 2:13-17; Rom. 12:11)

INTRODUCTION

Today's lesson begins with an account about a little-known, seldom-discussed Biblical character named Phinehas. His passion for the Lord and for righteousness is first expressed in intense anger at Zimri for his immoral conduct. His zeal led him to kill Zimri and the Midianite woman he had an illicit relationship with. Clearly, there are times when the cause of God calls for extraordinary zeal. When evil raises its head shamelessly, it is time for the righteous to act boldly and daringly. That is exactly what Phinehas did.

Yet, there is another side to Phinehas. He was also a trusted priest who interceded between God and people. He was known for his fairness and compassion. When a dispute arose between two factions of God's people, Phinehas was called on to negotiate the situation. Through his calm demeanor and wise counsel, he was able to stop an encounter between the two sides that could have ended in a bloody confrontation. So, we see Phinehas played a major role at one point in the history of God's people.

This lesson also calls on believers to be zealous for God and to encourage one another. What a blessing we can be by being an encourager! At some point in life, everyone needs to hear an uplifting word. We never know what burden our fellow believers are carrying, and how showing care and compassion can make a difference in their lives.

In John 2:13-17, we see a display of righteous indignation displayed when Jesus saw the sacred Temple being defiled and used for unacceptable purposes. Turning "the house of prayer" into "a den of thieves" (Matt. 21:13) was enough to cause the Lord to show, in the strongest terms, His indignation. He was consumed by zeal for God's house.

Jesus is looking for a people who will serve Him wholeheartedly. He has no patience with a half-hearted commitment. Be hot or cold, but not lukewarm.

I. ZEALOUS FOR GOD'S HONOR (Num. 25:1-13)

A. Illicit Relationships (vv. 1-3)

(Numbers 25:1-2 is not included in the printed text.)

³And Israel joined himself unto Baalpeor: and the anger of the Lord was kindled against Israel.

In the preceding chapters, a strange character by the name of Balaam comes on the scene. He was an eloquent but apostate prophet who was also known as a sorcerer. He had a fear of God, but he also loved money. He gave forth four blessings in response to the request of Balak, a Moabite king, to curse the people of God. Of Israel, he said, "I see a people who live by themselves, set apart from other nations" (23:9 NLT). He affirmed God's favor on Israel when he said, "The Lord his God is with him, and the shout of a king is among them" (v. 21). He said of Israel, "Blessed is he who blesses you, and cursed is he who curses you" (24:9 NKJV). Balaam also foretold the coming of a Person like no other: "I shall see him, but not now: I shall behold him, but not nigh: there shall come a Star out of Jacob, and a Sceptre shall rise out of Israel" (v. 17). After this fourth glorious word, Balaam and Balak returned to their respective homes.

While Balak was unsuccessful in getting Israel cursed, he succeeded in seducing them to engage in unbecoming behavior. This the apostle John addressed to the church at Pergamos, saying Balak had "cast a stumblingblock before the children of Israel, to eat things sacrificed unto idols, and to commit fornication" (Rev. 2:14). Just how devastating this was to the children of Israel is shown in Numbers 25.

While camping in Shittim on the border of the Promised Land, the Israelites engaged in illicit relationships with the daughters of Moab (v. 1). Perceiving their lustful inclinations, the daughters of Moab invited the men of Israel to participate in their feasts, which included sacrifices to their god, Baal-Peor (vv. 2-3). Such activity was forbidden to the Israelites and incurred the wrath of God. Their actions directly opposed God's nature, honor, and glory.

- Why was God angry with His people?

> "Loving the world destroys our relationship with God, it denies our faith in God, and it discounts our future with God."—David Jeremiah

---

B. Sin's Wages (vv. 4-9)

(Numbers 25:4-6, 9 is not included in the printed text.)

⁷And when Phinehas, the son of Eleazar, the son of Aaron the priest, saw it, he rose up from among the congregation, and took a javelin in his hand; ⁸And he went after the man of Israel into the tent, and thrust both of them through, the man of Israel, and the woman through her belly. So the plague was stayed from the children of Israel.

It is hard to imagine how low the Israelites sank in their depraved activity. Not only did they participate in sexual relations with the Moabite women, they also joined in their festivities and worshiped their god, Baal-Peor. Their behavior angered the Lord and resulted in the unleashing of His wrath upon them.

Because of this flagrant departure from the Lord and His standards, He called for severe punishment on the leaders of Israel (v. 4). Since the whole nation was involved in the profligate activity, the representatives of the people were held accountable. After all, those in leadership did not restrain their followers. The chiefs of the people were to be executed and then hanged and put on public display as a warning to the people of just how angry the Lord was at their conduct. Since their sin was public and scandalous, their punishment was meted out in broad daylight.

To illustrate how brazen some of the people were, we are told of Zimri (see v. 14), son of one of the leaders, who took a Midianite woman into the midst of the camp in the presence of Moses and the congregation of Israel (v. 6). Prior to this, the immoral liaisons with foreign women took place outside the camp. Such contempt for God and His covenant resulted in the people weeping at the entrance to the Tabernacle.

Phinehas was so incensed by Zimri's brazen action that he followed the couple into the tent and thrust his javelin all the way through Zimri's body and into the woman's stomach. The indication is that Phinehas slew them in the very act of intercourse.

To our minds this might seem to be a crude act of justice, but we must remember how critical this situation was. When Phinehas slew this couple, he acted in keeping with the command the Lord gave to Moses. That his action met with divine approval is shown by the fact the plague was now lifted from the Israelites. Nevertheless, their sin and degradation led to the death of twenty-four thousand Israelites. Surely, "the wages of sin is death" (Rom. 6:23).

---

1. What harsh remedy did God prescribe (vv. 4-5)?
2. What stopped a deadly plague (vv. 6-9)?
3. How should Christians today respond to the "plague" of immorality?

"If sin is estrangement from God, this very estrangement is death."—Henry Drummond

C. Strong Action (vv. 10-13)

(Numbers 25:10, 12-13 is not included in the printed text.)

¹¹Phinehas, the son of Eleazar, the son of Aaron the priest, hath turned my wrath away from the children of Israel, while he was zealous for my sake among them, that I consumed not the children of Israel in my jealousy.

Phinehas had a significant role in the history of his people. He was the son of Eleazar and the grandson of Aaron. He is credited here with the slaying of a rebellious Israelite and a pagan Midianite woman who were engaged in an illicit relationship, thereby stopping a plague. He also had a prominent part in a subsequent war against Midian, leading twelve thousand soldiers to win a great victory (see 31:6-12). During the period of the judges, Phinehas was an officiating priest (see Judg. 20:28).

There are times when the cause of God calls for extraordinary zeal, which comes from a heart set on fire for God. Jeremiah became weary in his service for the Lord and declared, "I will not make mention of Him, nor speak anymore in His name" (Jer. 20:9a, NKJV), but something inside him would not let him quit. So he continued, "But His word was in my heart like a burning fire shut up in my bones; I was weary of holding it back, and I could not" (v. 9b NKJV). Have you ever been in that place where truth was burning so intensely in your soul that you could not hold back any longer? You felt compelled to speak forth for the Lord.

The Lord commended and rewarded Phinehas for his zealous priestly service. He mediated between God and the nation, obtaining and preserving his own and Israel's peace and relationship with God. The *Ryrie Study Bible* says, "Because of his hatred of sin, Phinehas' family was promised the high priesthood in Israel, thus bypassing the other grandsons of Aaron." This would be a "perpetual priesthood" (Num. 25:13 NASB).

• Describe God's covenant with Phinehas.

The Lightning Bolt

John Knox is one of my favorites—thirty-two years younger than Martin Luther, but every bit as zealous. A history book said, "He was a stern man for a stern age in the midst of a violent people." Luther is described by some as the thunderclap of the Reformation. If so, then John Knox was the lightning bolt. Queen Mary once said, "I fear his pulpit more than the armies of England put together." John Knox hit the floor running, three-fourths gristle and the rest bone. The man was an unbelievable giant. He took the message to Scotland and they accepted it freely, quickly.—Herbert Lockyer (*All the Prayers of the Bible*)

II. ZEALOUS FOR FAITHFULNESS TO GOD (Josh. 22:10-34; Heb. 3:12-15)
A. The Misunderstanding (Josh. 22:10-20)

(Joshua 22:11-12, 15, 17-20 is not included in the printed text.)

¹⁰And when they came unto the borders of Jordan, that are in the land of Canaan, the children of Reuben and the children of Gad and the half tribe of Manasseh built there an altar by Jordan, a great altar to see to.

¹³And the children of Israel sent unto the children of Reuben, and to the children of Gad, and to the half tribe of Manasseh, into the land of Gilead, Phinehas the son of Eleazar the priest, ¹⁴And with him ten princes, of each chief house a prince throughout all the tribes of Israel; and each one was an head of the house of their fathers among the thousands of Israel.

¹⁶Thus saith the whole congregation of the Lord, What trespass is this that ye have committed against the God of Israel, to turn away this day from following the Lord, in that ye have builded you an altar, that ye might rebel this day against the Lord?

This chapter begins at the time the Israelites had defeated the Canaanites and divided the conquered territory. Two and one-half tribes—the Reubenites, the Gadites, and half the tribe of Manasseh—had been promised land east of the Jordan River. Now that the fighting was over, Joshua released them to return to their homes and families. He commended them for their faithfulness to the directions of Moses and himself. He challenged them to be faithful to God in the days ahead, and then blessed them and sent them on their way. The western tribes also made their way to their own territories.

When the eastern tribes reached the Jordan River, they stopped and built a massive altar (v. 10). When the western tribes heard about this, they were infuriated (v. 11). They assumed the altar had been built as a rival to the altar at Shiloh. If so, the eastern tribes were guilty of apostasy. The whole assembly of Israel gathered at Shiloh to make war with the eastern tribes (v. 12). What a turn of events! The two groups had recently separated after fighting side-by-side against their mutual enemy, the Canaanites. Now they were ready to go to war against each other.

Before they engaged in any combat with the eastern tribes, the children of Israel sent a delegation of ten men, a leader from each tribe, led by Phinehas, to determine what was going on and to negotiate with them (vv. 13-14). This delegation was candid with these eastern tribes, calling what they were doing *treachery* if they had built an altar in opposition to the altar of God in Shiloh (v. 16). The ten men suggested that, if the land the other tribes had been given was defiled, they could come over and live with them; they would give them some of their land (v. 19). Wouldn't it be wonderful if when differences arise in the church on any level that cooler heads would prevail and a path to peace be found?

---

1. Describe the building project in verse 10.
2. What accusation was made by ten tribal leaders (v. 16)?
3. What had they learned from the plague at Peor (vv. 17-18)?

4. What did Israel recall from the judgment against Achan (v. 20; Josh. 7:1-26)?

> "It does grieve me to think there are people misunderstanding my heart on an issue."—Kirk Cameron

---

B. The Peacemaker (vv. 21-34)
   (Joshua 22:21-22, 25-28, 30, 32-34 is not included in the printed text.)

²³That we have built us an altar to turn from following the Lord, or if to offer thereon burnt offering or meat offering, or if to offer peace offerings thereon, let the Lord himself require it; ²⁴And if we have not rather done it for fear of this thing, saying, In time to come your children might speak unto our children, saying, What have ye to do with the Lord God of Israel?

²⁹God forbid that we should rebel against the Lord, and turn this day from following the Lord, to build an altar for burnt offerings, for meat offerings, or for sacrifices, beside the altar of the Lord our God that is before his tabernacle.

³¹And Phinehas the son of Eleazar the priest said unto the children of Reuben, and to the children of Gad, and to the children of Manasseh, This day we perceive that the Lord is among us, because ye have not committed this trespass against the Lord: now ye have delivered the children of Israel out of the hand of the Lord.

The delegation from the western tribes learned they had misunderstood the intention of the eastern tribes (v. 30). They thought the eastern tribes had erected this altar to worship another god and to deny the Lord God Almighty. Actually, the eastern tribes had built the altar as a memorial that would remind them of the history they shared with the western tribes (vv. 24-25). It was not to be used to offer sacrifices to replace the altar at Shiloh, where they continued to worship and serve the Lord (v. 26). It was not intended to bring a division between the eastern and western tribes, but to remind all that the twelve tribes were united in their worship of Jehovah (vv. 27-28).

What started out with the potential to become a disaster ended well. In the final analysis, all parties stood in support of the truth and acted in love. In *Joshua and the Flow of Biblical History*, Francis A. Schaeffer wrote:

> If there had only been a stand for truth, there would never have been a happy ending. There would have only been war because the ten tribes would have torn across the river and killed the other Israelites without talking to anybody. There would have been sadness in the midst of misunderstanding. But because of the love of God, the tribes talked to each other openly, and the love and holiness of God were able to come together. Psalm 85 speaks of the righteousness of God and the love of God kissing each other (v. 10). This is what happened.

What does this incident say to the church and to individual Christians today? Is it enough just to be zealous for the truth? What part does love play when we are defending the truth? Clearly, when we share the truth in love, we have a better chance of convincing others that God has the answer for the needs in their life. An open and compassionate conversation can show we genuinely care about the individual, thereby touching their heart and leading to a surrender to the Lord. Zeal grounded in love and compassion is a powerful combination.

---

1. How did the two and a half tribes explain their actions (vv. 21-25)?
2. Describe these tribes' concern for future generations (vv. 25-28).
3. Describe the leadership displayed by Phinehas (vv. 30-33).
4. What was the altar at Jordan named, and why (v. 34)?

"Speak, move, act in peace, as if you were in prayer. In truth, this is prayer."—Francois Fenelon

---

C. Be an Encourager (Heb. 3:12-15)
(Hebrews 3:14-15 is not included in the printed text.)
¹²Take heed, brethren, lest there be in any of you an evil heart of unbelief, in departing from the living God. ¹³But exhort one another daily, while it is called To day; lest any of you be hardened through the deceitfulness of sin.

The writer of Hebrews issues a warning that calls for soul-searching. Believers are called upon to be very cautious that no evil or evil thoughts take hold of their hearts and lead them away from God. Such thoughts and deeds will lead to unbelief, and unbelief will lead to turning away from God, which is no small matter. When the Israelites rebelled against Moses, it resulted in their failure to enter the Promised Land, but to turn away from Christ is to surrender the privilege of everlasting life. The greater mistake anyone could make is to reject "the living God" (v. 12). This matter is addressed later in this book in these words: "It is a fearful thing to fall into the hands of the living God" (10:31).

To avoid stumbling and falling, believers are admonished to encourage one another daily (3:13). The present time is the time to be an encouragement to fellow Christians. This day will not last forever, and neither will the day of grace. *Now* is the opportune time to lift up one another, showing the love of Christ. Such loving care can steer a believer away from the deceitfulness of sin, which aims to harden the heart toward God. God can use a word of encouragement to stop the soul from drifting in the wrong direction.

The writer of Hebrews urges his readers to finish as strong as they started (v. 14). Do you remember your zeal at the beginning of your Christian journey? Are you still as excited and determined as then? Are you even more committed to run this race successfully and finish strong? Is your trust in Christ as strong as when you first believed? The result of such trust is to become co-heirs with Christ and partakers in all of His benefits.

---

1. What can Christian encouragement help to prevent (vv. 12-13)?
2. Who are genuine "partakers of Christ" (v. 14)?
3. What must we do "today" (v. 15)?

Zealous for God

III. BE ZEALOUS FOR GOD (John 2:13-17; Rom. 12:11)

A. Jesus' Zeal (John 2:13-16)

(John 2:13-14 is not included in the printed text.)

15And when he had made a scourge of small cords, he drove them all out of the temple, and the sheep, and the oxen; and poured out the changers' money, and overthrew the tables; 16And said unto them that sold doves, Take these things hence; make not my Father's house an house of merchandise.

John's Gospel is always careful to identify the Passover as being a Jewish festival. He knew many of his readers would be Gentiles who were not familiar with the customs of the Jews. Every year Jesus' parents went to Jerusalem to observe this festival (Luke 2:41). It was a gathering of this nature that Jesus attended when He was twelve years old (v. 42). While there, He astounded the teachers and leaders with His wisdom and understanding (vv. 46-47).

What Jesus was taught in His youth He continued to practice in adulthood. So, in John 2:13, we find Him making His way to Jerusalem to participate in the annual Passover celebration.

At first glance, we are somewhat astonished at Jesus' reaction to the activities going on during the Passover festival. However, He was not there to put a stop to Temple worship; He was there to put it back on track. What Jesus found upon His arrival were animals acceptable to sacrifice: oxen, sheep, and doves. He also saw money changers who exchanged foreign money into the local currency (v. 14). This was intended to be a convenience for those who had traveled long distances, making bringing an animal sacrifice with them difficult.

After observing the situation, Jesus made a whip by tying cords together and drove the animals out. He then turned over the tables of the money changers, pouring their money to the floor, and He ordered those selling doves to set them free (v. 15). He explained His actions by saying, "How dare you turn my Father's house into a market!" (v. 16 NIV). When He cleansed the Temple on another occasion, Jesus said, "Is it not written, My house shall be called of all nations the house of prayer? but ye have made it a den of thieves" (Mark 11:17).

- By His actions and words, what does Jesus reveal about Himself in this event?

B. Consumed by Love (v. 17)

¹⁷And his disciples remembered that it was written, The zeal of thine house hath eaten me up.

Observing Jesus' actions, the disciples remembered Psalm 69:9: "Zeal for Your house has consumed me" (NASB). They saw the words of the psalmist fulfilled in what Jesus did. So much of what we see in Jesus' life and ministry, we observe to be the fulfillment of Old Testament passages revealing Jesus to be the Messiah.

It was astonishing for a single person to make a whip and, with authority, drive the buyers and sellers out of the Temple with no opposition. Oh, they questioned His authority, but did nothing more (v. 18). These men who were driven out had been selected and approved by the priests and rulers. They saw Someone so consumed by His love for God's house and proper worship until He was unstoppable.

While the enemies of Christ did not raise their hand to stop Him, this was one more event that increased their determination to find a way to kill Him. In *The Gospel of John: An Expositional Commentary*, James Montgomery Boice raised this question: "How do you stop Jesus? How do you stop a Man who has no guns, no tanks, no ammunition, but still is shaking the whole Roman Empire? How do you stop a Man, who, without firing a shot, is getting revolutionary results? They [the enemies of Christ] figured there's only one answer—get rid of Him."

Christ was willing to pay the supreme price to see the honor of God and sacred things preserved. How great is your passion? How far are you willing to go to see holiness defended? The call of the Lord is to follow His example.

• How zealous are you for God and His house?

> "The Lord intends us to be powerful people—mighty in optimism and hopeful of spirit, powerful in evangelistic zeal, potent in influence, sturdy in moral fiber and purity."—David Jeremiah

---

C. Fervent in Service (Rom. 12:11)

¹¹Not slothful in business; fervent in spirit; serving the Lord.

The apostle Paul here is concerned about spiritual matters, not secular ones. The apostle challenges believers to exercise the abilities God has given them in a manner that advances His kingdom. He wants believers to be fervent in their service for the Master. The term *fervent* carries the thought of "water brought to a boiling point." The Lord despises lukewarmness (Rev. 3:16). Where is the passion in being aflame for Christ? Is it missing in today's church?

The words of Solomon echo the thoughts of the apostle: "Whatsoever thy hand findeth to do, do it with thy might; for there is no work, nor device, nor knowledge, nor wisdom, in the grave, whither thou goest" (Eccl. 9:10).

Contrast that with the lazy servant who earned the rebuke of his master: "You wicked and lazy servant, you knew that I reap where I have not sown, and gather where I have not scattered seed. So you ought to have deposited my money with the bankers, and at my coming I would have received back my own with interest. So take the talent from him, and give it to him who has ten talents" (Matt. 25:26-28 NKJV).

Our challenge is to do whatever we do with all our might, diligently and fervently performing all that is required of us to God's honor and glory. Our allegiance is to God, not to man.

• What should characterize our service to God?

> "The highest form of worship is the worship of unselfish Christian service."—Billy Graham

---

CONCLUSION

Where do you rate on the "passion for Christ" scale? Are you hot, cold, or lukewarm? In what ways do you show your zeal? Is purity of worship important to you? Does it bother you when the house of God is not respected as sacred? What do you do on a daily basis to keep the flame of passion burning in your soul? In what ways do you encourage fellow believers to stay close to Christ and to serve Him fervently?

GOLDEN TEXT CHALLENGE

"[BE] NOT SLOTHFUL IN BUSINESS; FERVENT IN SPIRIT; SERVING THE LORD" (Rom. 12:11).

Christians are never to be lazy but, instead, must be zealous in carrying out our responsibilities in the workplace, the home, and the church . . . all to the glory of God. Henry Ward Beecher wrote:

When God wanted sponges and oysters, He made them; and He put one on a rock and the other in the mud. When He made man, He did not make him to be a sponge or an oyster; He made him with feet and hands, and head, and heart, and vital blood, and a place to use them, and said to him, "Go, work!"

Daily Devotions:

M. Zeal to Obey God • 2 Kings 10:9-17
T. Zealous Despite Opposition • Psalm 119:137-144
W. Be Zealous, Not Jealous • Proverbs 23:15-18
T. Zealous for God • Romans 12:11-21
F. Zeal Refocused • Philippians 3:1-11
S. Zealous of Good Works • Titus 2:7-14

Put Faith Into Action (Rahab)

Joshua 2:1-24; 6:22-25; Matthew 1:5-6; Hebrews 11:31; James 2:14-26

Unit Theme:
Good Lessons From Good Examples

Central Truth:
Faith in God should compel us to obey Him.

Focus:
Examine Rahab's faith-inspired actions and express our faith through actions.

Context:
Old and New Testament passages concerning the faith of Rahab

Golden Text:
"Even so faith, if it hath not works, is dead, being alone" (James 2:17).

Study Outline:
 I. **Faith and Fear Expressed** (Josh. 2:1-14)
 II. **Faith in Action** (Josh. 2:15-24; James 2:14-17, 25-26)
 III. **Faith Rewarded** (Josh. 6:22-25; Heb. 11:31; Matt. 1:5-6)

INTRODUCTION

Isn't it amazing to see whom God chooses for service in His kingdom? Humans tend to select those individuals whose appearance—looks, height, build—meets their standards. Ability and intelligence also play a part in the selection process. The best and the brightest are assumed to be the right individuals for the important tasks. In some case, one's family name may be the factor in whether or not an individual receives a particular opportunity.

Sometimes overlooked are those who do not make a great first impression or have not received honors and recognition. People with lower-level jobs, limited education, and a minimal range of skills are often bypassed. It is amazing the bias, prejudice, and discrimination which often comes into play.

Isn't it wonderful how God does not use the same criteria? He sees the heart and what each person can become. He knows the potential when given the opportunity. Such is the situation when Rahab, an unlikely woman to be in the lineage of Christ, had her faith rewarded.

Rahab lived in the city of Jericho on the eastern edge of Canaan near the Jordan River. The population was probably about 3,000, with the area of the city being somewhere between 7 and 13 acres. People mainly worked outside the city and returned at night for housing and safety. Jericho was a double-walled city. The outer wall was 6 feet thick and the inner was 12 feet. The walls stood 15 feet apart and rose 30 feet above ground.

From a human perspective, Jericho stood as a mighty fortress providing safety for its population. It is significant that God led Israel to this city as the first military target in Canaan. From a military perspective, this was brilliant strategy. By taking possession of the middle ground, the Israelites were cutting off the routes from north to south. Also, the destruction of this major fortress would send a message to the Canaanites. They would constantly have in mind the power of Israel and her God, Jehovah. However, that would not stop them from fighting against these perceived invaders.

That Rahab played a pivotal role in this story is amazing. Her occupation raises eyebrows. Her faith appears so strong while lacking so much knowledge of God. Her reward emphasizes God's grace and abundant blessings.

I. FAITH AND FEAR EXPRESSED (Josh. 2:1-14)

A. The Risk (vv. 1-7)

(Joshua 2:5-7 is not included in the printed text.)

¹And Joshua the son of Nun sent out of Shittim two men to spy secretly, saying, Go view the land, even Jericho. And they went, and came into an harlot's house, named Rahab, and lodged there. ²And it was told the king of Jericho, saying, Behold, there came men in hither to night of the children of Israel to search out the country. ³And the king of Jericho sent unto Rahab, saying, Bring forth the men that are come to thee, which are entered into thine house: for they be come to search out all the country. ⁴And the woman took the two men, and hid them, and said thus, There came men unto me, but I wist not whence they were.

Everything was ready for Israel to conquer and take possession of the Promised Land. At this point, it appears God had not given Joshua any specific directions or battle plan. Being a military man, he understood the need for inside information prior to attacking. So Joshua sent two men to secretly gather information about the land and the city of Jericho. Upon arriving in Jericho, they stayed at the home of Rahab.

Why would these men go to the house of a prostitute? Initially, it appears questionable. Further knowledge points to the same Hebrew word being used for "female innkeeper" and "harlot." It is likely that Rahab had rooms to rent and her services could be purchased for those who so desired. Some have suggested their staying at her home would give them less visibility. Visits of strange men would not raise suspicion as would their staying in another location.

Any attempt of being incognito failed. Keep in mind the relatively small size of the city. It would be difficult not to be seen. Also, the report to the king specifically pointed to their being Israelites. Verse 3 says the king was told these men's purpose in coming—they were spies.

Immediately, messengers were sent to Rahab with the directive to bring these men to the king. Would she obey the king of her city or take the risk of hiding the men who represented Israel? She decided to protect the Israelites, but what would she say in response to the king's men?

Without hesitancy, Rahab glibly lied. Her story contained three separate falsehoods (vv. 4-5): (1) She claimed not to know where the men were from. (2) She stated they left just before the time of the evening gate closing. (3) She indicated a lack of knowledge as to their direction but assured that swift pursuit would result in their being caught.

All along, the two spies were hidden on the flat roof under bundles of flax (v. 6). Since the roofs were used for storage of drying grain, the flax became a convenient hiding location. There would be no reason to search the roof, having heard Rahab's story. Also, it would be logical for spies to operate under the cover of darkness and leave at that hour. All the pieces of the puzzle seemed to fall into place.

---

1. What did Joshua want the two spies to find out?
2. Why do you suppose the spies' names are not given?
3. Explain whether Rahab's actions were right or wrong.

> "Courage is a special kind of knowledge: the knowledge of how to fear what ought to be feared and how not to fear what ought not to be feared."—Ben Gurion

---

B. The Request (vv. 8-14)

(Joshua 2:8, 10 is not included in the printed text.)

⁹And she said unto the men, I know that the Lord hath given you the land, and that your terror is fallen upon us, and that all the inhabitants of the land faint because of you.

¹¹And as soon as we had heard these things, our hearts did melt, neither did there remain any more courage in any man, because of you: for the Lord your God, he is God in heaven above, and in earth beneath. ¹²Now therefore, I pray you, swear unto me by the Lord, since I have shewed you kindness, that ye will also shew kindness unto my father's house, and give me a true token: ¹³And that ye will save alive my father, and my mother, and my brethren, and my sisters, and all that they have, and deliver our lives from death. ¹⁴And the men answered her, Our life for yours, if ye utter not this our business. And it shall be, when the Lord hath given us the land, that we will deal kindly and truly with thee.

After the king's messengers left, Rahab spoke to the men on the rooftop. In verse 9, she acknowledged God's having given Jericho to Israel and that His terror had fallen on the people. She said, "All who live in this country are melting in fear" (NIV). They somehow knew of the distant past when God miraculously opened the Red Sea for Israel (v. 10). Also known to them was the immediate past as God enabled Israel to destroy the army of the Amorites (Num. 21:21-35).

These two events on either side of a forty-year span point to God's enabling of His people. Nothing could stand in His way. As a result, the people

Put Faith Into Action

of Jericho's courage had melted. Where there once was strength, only weakness now resided. Apparently, the people sensed the hopelessness of the future.

In verse 11 of the text, Rahab made a major confession regarding the God of Israel: He is the God of the heavens and earth. This can be seen as a statement in which she abandoned the gods of Canaan for the sovereign Almighty God.

Having made a confession concerning the true God, Rahab then requested kindness for herself and her father's household. She asked that the favor shown to the spies would be returned in like kind. She provided security and safety, despite the king's request. Would they return a similar act of kindness when Israel's army invaded? Rahab also requested a token, or "sure sign" (v. 12 NIV), of this agreement. The spies responded by agreeing to spare her life and those of her family in exchange for her actions. There was one requirement: Rahab must remain silent about their actions and intent (v. 14). This points to the need for Rahab to continue on the path of commitment to God and His plans for Israel.

---

1. How did the people of Jericho know about the Israelites' triumphs, and how did it affect them (vv. 9-10)?
2. What was Rahab's belief about the God of Israel (v. 11)?
3. What positive characteristic does verse 13 reveal about Rahab?
4. What did the spies promise Rahab in verse 14?

"Promises may get friends, but it is performance that keeps them." —Owen Feltham

---

II. FAITH IN ACTION (Josh. 2:15-24; James 2:14-17, 25-26)
A. The Escape (Josh. 2:15-24)

(Joshua 2:16-21, 24 is not included in the printed text.)

¹⁵Then she let them down by a cord through the window: for her house was upon the town wall, and she dwelt upon the wall.

²²And they went, and came unto the mountain, and abode there three days, until the pursuers were returned: and the pursuers sought them throughout all the way, but found them not. ²³So the two men returned, and descended from the mountain, and passed over, and came to Joshua the son of Nun, and told him all things that befell them.

Rahab's assistance to the spies went far beyond that of the initial hiding. Next, they must leave the city unnoticed. Through the use of a rope, the men were lowered to the ground outside the city walls. It is not likely this rope remained tied to the window; otherwise it would reveal Rahab's duplicity and aiding of the spies. She was, however, to place a scarlet marker of some type in the window. Symbolically, it seems similar to the blood on the doorposts when the death angel passed over Egypt. The scarlet cord became the sign of security.

Rahab's thoughtfulness can be seen in her directing the spies to go to the mountains for three days. By that time, those watching the fording places would have given up and gone home. The spies followed her directions and returned safely to report to Joshua.

Before leaving, the spies reminded Rahab of the requirements of safety (vv. 18-20). The scarlet marker needed to be in place. Family members were to stay in her house and not wander into the streets. She was to maintain complete silence about their activities.

These verses remind us of the need to follow God's plans and directives. Our salvation is not a do-it-yourself job in which we determine the parameters of belief and action. God sets the stage and writes the script.

---

1. What did the spies' response (v. 22) to Rahab's instructions (v. 16) reveal about their confidence in her?
2. What contingency did the spies add to their agreement with Rahab, and why (v. 20)?
3. Describe the spies' report to Joshua (v. 24).

B. Faith in Action (James 2:14-17, 25-26)

(James 2:15-16, 26 is not included in the printed text.)

14What doth it profit, my brethren, though a man say he hath faith, and have not works? can faith save him?

17Even so faith, if it hath not works, is dead, being alone.

25Likewise also was not Rahab the harlot justified by works, when she had received the messengers, and had sent them out another way?

According to James, faith is more than right doctrine; faith must include right action as well. Faith without right action is not merely passive; it is dead. Just as medical personnel check the vital signs of patients in the hospital, so Christians look for the vital signs of true faith. Right actions are those vital signs.

Having a proper creed is not enough. One who believes in the one true God yet has no works is no better off than the demons who also believe in one God, and tremble in fear of Him (v. 19).

James illustrated his point by envisioning a scene that could occur in any church (vv. 15-16). A poor brother or sister comes in with a desperate need. His eyes brimming with tears, the leader says, "Let's pray for this dear brother (or sister) that God may meet the need." The prayer is exhilarating. At the "amen," the leader addressing the needy person says, "Praise God! Go in peace, be warmed and fed. Just keep using your faith!" Quietly, desperately, this poor soul often goes home just as he or she came in: hungry, penniless, and depressed.

This story, which is an imaginative elaboration of James' statement, is not intended to put down faith or prayer. It is an effort to point out what is often missing from faith—namely, works.

In verse 25, James points to the uselessness of Rahab's having faith but not following through. Without her positive actions toward the spies, she would not have obtained righteousness. She would never have been in the lineage of Christ. Instead, Rahab and her relatives would have died with the rest of the city.

Verse 26 summarizes the whole concept. James says, "The body without the spirit is dead." He is using the analogy of the human body and the life-giving spirit to demonstrate the relationship between faith and works. *Faith*, then, is basic to the Christian life—belief in who God is and what He can do. *Righteous works* reflect the vitality and reality of our faith.

---

1. Answer the questions in verse 14.
2. What specific works should Christians practice (vv. 15-16)?
3. Explain the phrase "justified by works" (v. 25).
4. Based on verses 17 and 26, is your faith dead or alive?

"Firm and steadfast in good works make me, and in Thy service make me to persevere."—Claire of Assisi

---

III. FAITH REWARDED (Josh. 6:22-25; Heb. 11:31; Matt. 1:5-6)

A. Rahab and Household Spared (Josh. 6:22-25)

(Joshua 6:22-23 is not included in the printed text.)

24And they burnt the city with fire, and all that was therein: only the silver, and the gold, and the vessels of brass and of iron, they put into the treasury of the house of the Lord. 25And Joshua saved Rahab the harlot alive, and her father's household, and all that she had; and she dwelleth in Israel even unto this day; because she hid the messengers, which Joshua sent to spy out Jericho.

Besides saving her and her family from destruction, Rahab's reward increased. She was allowed to continue to live in the land and was incorporated into God's people. This is not the picture of an outcast being tolerated. No, Rahab was a woman who, by faith and action, bravely made a commitment to God and His people. She had heard of Israel's God and His mighty works, and when the opportunity arose, she began her walk of faith by the risky business of hiding the spies and aiding in their escape.

Something similar occurs when we accept Jesus as our Savior and Lord. With this commitment we become part of another people, God's family. We may live in the same region, but now there is a new citizenship.

• Who was spared from destruction, and why?

B. Rahab's Faith (Heb. 11:31)

[31]By faith the harlot Rahab perished not with them that believed not, when she had received the spies with peace.

Hebrews 11 is frequently referred to as the Hall of Faith. Inclusion in this lineup does not make any one of them better than believers who have lived since then. It does provide a wide variety of examples of people demonstrating faith in God, regardless of the circumstances or the amount of their knowledge of God. This chapter follows a chronological order. In verse 30, the faith of Israel in God's plan of attack on Jericho is shown. Immediately following, we read of Rahab's faith, which was the reason her life was spared. The writer then points to the action which resulted from her faith. She believed what she heard God had done in the past, she believed God and His people would triumph over her city and its surrounding land, and she acted on her faith.

Recognizing who the men were when they came to her home, Rahab had a choice: Would they be received in peace or revealed as spies? Receiving them in peace demanded taking a risk. There was no assurance of her personal fate when choosing to hide the two men. Only later would she enter into an agreement with the spies providing for the safety of herself and her family.

• What did the people of Jericho "not believe" (NKJV)?

> "Faith, as Paul saw it, was a living, flaming thing leading to surrender and obedience to the commands of Christ."—A. W. Tozer

C. Christ's Lineage (Matt. 1:5-6)

(Matthew 1:6 is not included in the printed text.)

[5]And Salmon begat Booz of Rachab; and Booz begat Obed of Ruth; and Obed begat Jesse.

Believers tend to skip over the genealogies recorded in the Old and New Testaments. The names are often difficult to pronounce. Yet they serve a vital part in validating other portions of Scripture and providing key information. In the New Testament, both the Gospel of Matthew and the Gospel of Luke include a genealogy of Jesus. Matthew traces Jesus' lineage through Joseph, His legal father. Luke records Jesus' lineage through Mary, His mother. Each reflects the fulfillment of the Davidic covenant (2 Sam. 7), which promised a descendant would be on His throne forever.

In Matthew's genealogy we find Rahab's inclusion. Normally women are not included in these lineage lists. Matthew includes two—Ruth and Rahab (in one verse)—and both have "a past." Ruth was not an immoral woman, but she was a Moabitess, one of the forbidden people for intermarriage. Rahab was known for her sexual immorality. We are thereby reminded that Christ does not hold the past against any person, but opens the door for restoration for those who will believe and live a new life.

Rahab's inclusion in Christ's lineage reflects a person who had "two strikes" against her. First, she was part of the Canaanites, who were to be completely destroyed for their sins. Second, she participated in immoral sexual behavior. But when she turned to God in faith, He responded in love, acceptance, and protection.

"Faith rests upon character. Faith must rest in confidence upon the One who made the promise."—A. W. Tozer

---

CONCLUSION

The life of Rahab shows the tremendous contrast between one's past and future potential. The key is *faith*. Only when she chose to place her lot with the people of God and hold to faith in Him was she able to escape judgment. Death became life as she combined her faith and works.

GOLDEN TEXT CHALLENGE

"EVEN SO FAITH, IF IT HATH NOT WORKS, IS DEAD, BEING ALONE" (James 2:17).

Our faith and our relationship with God . . . are dynamic and living. Our faith grows and affects our actions, or it dies. "Faith by itself" (NKJV), static faith, does not save. We must nurture our faith in God and love for Him through our works.—*Orthodox Study Bible*

Daily Devotions:

M. Faith Brings Salvation • Genesis 6:9-22
T. Faith Brings Provision • 2 Kings 4:1-7
W. Hezekiah Prays in Faith • 2 Kings 19:14-20, 35-37
T. Persistent Faith • Matthew 15:21-28
F. Mountain-Moving Faith • Matthew 21:18-22
S. The Prayer of Faith • James 5:13-18

The Battle Is the Lord's (Jehoshaphat)

2 Chronicles 20:1-30

Unit Theme:
Good Lessons From Good Examples

Central Truth:
God's promise of victory encourages Christians through life's challenges.

Focus:
Affirm that God is with us in difficulties and trust Him for victory.

Context:
Jerusalem, around 853 BC.

Golden Text:
"Thus saith the Lord unto you, Be not afraid nor dismayed by reason of this great multitude; for the battle is not yours, but God's" (2 Chron. 20:15).

Study Outline:
  I. **Look to God When in Distress** (2 Chron. 20:1-12)
 II. **Trust God for His Help** (2 Chron. 20:13-21)
III. **Praise God for the Victory** (2 Chron. 20:22-30)

INTRODUCTION

To understand King Jehoshaphat, we need to have some comprehension of his father, Asa—the third king of Judah after Israel split into the southern and northern kingdoms. Asa set himself to rid Judah of the idolatry his father and grandfather had allowed, and to bring the people back to seeking God. Second Chronicles 14 gives a glowing picture of the young monarch as he removed high places, incense altars, and Asherah poles. He shored up the defenses of Judah and equipped a large army.

When the horde of Ethiopians under Zerah came against Asa, Judah was far outnumbered, and victory seemed impossible. Yet, Asa had done everything he could to prepare his country and his army. He prayed, "Help us, O Lord our God, for we rely on you, and in your name we have come against this vast army. O Lord, you are our God; do not let man prevail against you" (v. 11 NIV). The Lord honored Asa's prayer and gave him a massive victory.

Upon returning from the battle, the Lord sent the prophet Azariah with this message for Asa: "The Lord is with you when you are with him. If you seek him, he will be found by you, but if you forsake him, he will forsake you" (15:2 NIV). This fueled the king's desire to further serve the Lord and bring reforms. He reigned for a total of forty-one years, doing great things for most of those years. Jehoshaphat was born in his father's sixth year as king.

Though Asa had been a good king, in the thirty-sixth year of his reign, he made a treaty with the king of Syria; therefore, God sent the prophet Hanani to rebuke Asa. Instead of humbling himself and admitting his mistake, Asa imprisoned the prophet. He also began to oppress some of his own people. Eventually he came down with a terrible disease in his feet, but he did not seek the Lord for help. He stubbornly held on to his pride and died from the disease (16:1-13).

This brings us to the subject of our lesson—Jehoshaphat. He had been raised and mentored during the great years of his father's reign. He was an adult when his father hardened his heart. Jehoshaphat had the benefit of clearly seeing his father's strengths and weaknesses.

Jehoshaphat learned much from his father's life, but he made several decisions that reflected the negative aspects of his father's example. Clearly, at every difficult time, Jehoshaphat turned to the Lord for help and guidance, but he proved lax in the more mundane times. He allowed his son to marry Athaliah, the daughter of King Ahab and Jezebel. Athaliah proved to be just as wicked as her parents. Jehoshaphat also entered a terrible alliance with Ahab, which nearly cost him his life. Later, he unwisely got involved in a shipbuilding scheme with Ahab's son, which the Lord himself wreaked havoc upon.

Both Jehoshaphat and his father stand out in Biblical history as strong lights against paganism. They had their weaknesses, but their faith in the Lord brought good to the nation and to them.

Our lesson deals with one of the critical episodes of Jehoshaphat's life—a time when he had no doubt that God must intervene.

I. LOOK TO GOD WHEN IN DISTRESS (2 Chron. 20:1-12)

A. Grave Crisis (vv. 1-2)

(2 Chronicles 20:2 is not included in the printed text.)

¹It came to pass after this also, that the children of Moab, and the children of Ammon, and with them other beside the Ammonites, came against Jehoshaphat to battle.

Everything Jehoshaphat had learned from his father (both good and bad), as well as what he had learned from his own mistakes (such as the foolish alliance with Ahab), was now about to be tested. He knew from these past experiences he could not rely on himself. The circumstances coming against him were nearly impossible to overcome. The Moabites, Ammonites, and some Edomites all combined their forces against Judah.

The attack force was coming by means of a little-used route, up from the southern point of the Dead Sea. Because their movement was not detected by the Israelite villages west of the Judean mountains, they had marched treacherously close before word came to the king. By this time, they were only about fifteen hours from Jerusalem.

Jehoshaphat's first reaction was probably to recognize this as the Lord's discipline for his recent foolish alliance with Ahab and attack against Ramoth-gilead. The prophet Jehu, son of Hanani, had told him, "The wrath of the Lord is upon you" (19:2 NIV). However, God had tempered His discipline with grace. Jehu had continued by saying, "There is, however, some good in you, for you have rid the land of the Asherah poles and have set your heart on seeking God" (v. 3 NIV). This last statement had to bring comfort to the king now as he faced the most crucial test of his reign.

- Describe the crisis facing the people of Judah.

> "Often we become apathetic in our lives until we face a severe storm. Whether loss of a job, health crisis, loss of a loved one, or financial struggle; God often brings storms into our lives to change our perspective, to shift the focus from ourselves and our lives to Him."—Paul Chappell

B. A National Fast (vv. 3-4)

³And Jehoshaphat feared, and set himself to seek the Lord, and proclaimed a fast throughout all Judah. ⁴And Judah gathered themselves together, to ask help of the Lord: even out of all the cities of Judah they came to seek the Lord.

There had been general fasts in Israel before, but this was the first time a monarch proclaimed a national fast to deal with a crisis. Though he knew he was under the discipline of the Lord for his recent foolish actions, Jehoshaphat realized his only hope was to cry out to God. He recognized his own inability to stop the invaders. Certainly he felt the guilt for the situation, realizing news of Ahab's death and his own brush with death was probably spread abroad. His enemies would suspect him to be in a weakened position and vulnerable for attack.

The people of Judah responded to the king's call by coming together in mass. They saw his humility and humbled themselves with him. Fasting "stressed the sincerity of the prayers of God's people when they were facing special needs" (*Zondervan NIV Bible Commentary*).

We are not told whether the king prepared his military, but most likely he did. However, his greatest care was to invoke the Lord's assistance. He knew he could not presume on God's help (even though he was the Davidic ruler of God's people). We should not expect God's help if we do not ask and seek His face. Scripture says, "You do not have, because you do not ask God" (James 4:2 NIV).

1. What was Jehoshaphat's initial reaction to the crisis, and what did he "set himself" to do (v. 3)?
2. What did the king ask the people of Judah to do, and how did they respond?

Fasting in China

"In Shansi I found Chinese Christians who were accustomed to spend time in fasting and prayer. They recognized that this fasting,

C. Jehoshaphat's Prayer (vv. 5-12)

(2 Chronicles 20:7-11 is not included in the printed text.)

⁵And Jehoshaphat stood in the congregation of Judah and Jerusalem, in the house of the Lord, before the new court, ⁶and said, O Lord God of our fathers, art not thou God in heaven? and rulest not thou over all the kingdoms of the heathen? and in thine hand is there not power and might, so that none is able to withstand thee?

¹²O our God, wilt thou not judge them? for we have no might against this great company that cometh against us; neither know we what to do: but our eyes are upon thee.

Further sign of Jehoshaphat's humility is seen in his standing in the middle of the assembly and taking on the role of priest for them all. His prayer was spontaneous and totally from the heart. This took place in the outer Temple court.

He reminded the Lord this was a land He had given to their forefathers, this was His Temple, and they were His people. Thus, he entreated the Lord to protect His own possessions. He referred back to Deuteronomy 2:5, where the Israelites had not been allowed to invade the lands of Seir (from which these present enemies were coming) when they came out of Egypt. This being the case, these descendants had no right to make an unprovoked invasion into Hebrew lands.

Jehoshaphat's prayer was humble; he cried out, "We do not know what to do, but our eyes are upon you" (v. 12 NIV).

1. In his prayer, what did Jehoshaphat declare about God's ability (v. 6)?
2. Why did he make a reference to the past (v. 7)?
3. What did he say about the people's confidence in God (vv. 8-9)?
4. Describe the king's request (v. 12).

"It is not the body's posture, but the heart's attitude that counts when we pray."—Billy Graham

II. TRUST GOD FOR HIS HELP (2 Chron. 20:13-21)

A. Standing in Unity (vv. 13-14)

(2 Chronicles 20:13-14 is not included in the printed text.)

The entire body of people who had gathered were in one accord. The fast had extended to all Judah—meaning every man, woman, and child. When a people become so united in their heart toward the Lord, mighty things will happen. The sad aspect of humanity, however, is that it generally takes crises to bring people into unity.

"Then the Spirit of the Lord came upon Jahaziel" (v. 14 NKJV). The supposition is that Jahaziel was a prophet (based on the reverence with which the people listened to his words), although he is not mentioned anywhere else in Scripture. He was a Levite of the lineage of Asaph. Asaph had been one of the three families given responsibility for music and singing in the Temple by David (see 1 Chron. 25:1-9). Psalm 83 may have been written by Jahaziel to commemorate the victory.

- Who stood before the Lord as the king prayed? Why is this important?

"There is unusual power in united prayer. God has planned for His people to join together in prayer, not only for Christian fellowship, spiritual nurture, and growth, but also for accomplishing His divine purposes and reaching His chosen goals."—Wesley L. Duewel

---

B. Divine Direction (vv. 15-17)

¹⁵And he said, Hearken ye, all Judah, and ye inhabitants of Jerusalem, and thou king Jehoshaphat, Thus saith the Lord unto you, Be not afraid nor dismayed by reason of this great multitude; for the battle is not yours, but God's. ¹⁶To morrow go ye down against them: behold, they come up by the cliff of Ziz; and ye shall find them at the end of the brook, before the wilderness of Jeruel. ¹⁷Ye shall not need to fight in this battle: set yourselves, stand ye still, and see the salvation of the Lord with you, O Judah and Jerusalem: fear not, nor be dismayed; to morrow go out against them: for the Lord will be with you.

The word that came was one of assurance. Repeating what David had said just before going against Goliath (1 Sam. 17:47), Jahaziel exhorted the people not to fear. God was on their side, and it was His battle to fight. In order to give the people confidence, God was reminding them of His faithful intervention in the past. It took great fear to bring the people humbly before God, but now they were to release that fear.

The fear that drives us to the Lord is the same fear that will redeem us. The psalmist said, "The fear of the Lord is the beginning of wisdom" (111:10); Proverbs 19:23 says, "The fear of the Lord leads to life: Then one rests content, untouched by trouble" (NIV).

God instructed Jehoshaphat to lead his army out the next day. They would find the enemy at a specific valley location. There they were to stand still and see what the Lord would do. This is the same type of instruction God gave Moses when the people came to the Red Sea (Ex. 14:13). Simple as this may sound, completely releasing a situation into God's hand can be difficult to do. Human nature always demands some type of human effort, but God insists we leave certain battles to Him.

---

1. Why should the Jews not be afraid (v. 15)?
2. Describe the battle plan (vv. 16-17).

> "Cultivate prompt, exact, unquestioning, joyous obedience to every command that it is evident from its context applies to you. . . . God's commands are but signboards that mark the road to present success and blessedness and to eternal glory."—R. A. Torrey

---

C. Response of Worship (vv. 18-19)
(2 Chronicles 20:19 is not included in the printed text.)

¹⁸And Jehoshaphat bowed his head with his face to the ground: and all Judah and the inhabitants of Jerusalem fell before the Lord, worshipping the Lord.

Everyone present knew the Lord had spoken. Jehoshaphat bowed to the ground and worshiped, and all the people followed his example. When God truly speaks, there will be a peaceful recognition of His presence. If we hear someone give a "word" and we are left with anxiety, there is room to question the validity of the prophecy. God's true word comes with a sense of assurance, not trepidation.

Verse 19 says certain "Levites . . . stood up to praise the Lord—doubtless by the king's command; and their anthem was sung with such a joyful acclaim as showed that they universally regarded the victory as already obtained" (*studylight.org*).

• Describe the response to the prophetic word.

> "Do you feel more loved when God makes much of you, or do you feel more loved when God, at the cost of His Son, allows you to make much of Him?"—John Piper

---

D. Confident Instructions (vv. 20-21)

²⁰And they rose early in the morning, and went forth into the wilderness of Tekoa: and as they went forth, Jehoshaphat stood and said, Hear me, O Judah, and ye inhabitants of Jerusalem; Believe in the Lord your God, so shall ye be established; believe his prophets, so shall ye prosper. ²¹And when he had consulted with the people, he appointed singers unto the Lord, and that should praise the beauty of holiness, as they went out before the army, and to say, Praise the Lord; for his mercy endureth for ever.

The sting of the discipline Jehoshaphat had been feeling was now past. His faith was fully empowered. He could lead the people with total assurance that God would deliver them.

People who have heard from God will inspire others to follow them, not because of their own personal strengths, but because they have full trust in the Almighty. Jehoshaphat encouraged the people to not only trust the word they had received the day before, but to trust every word God's prophets had given in the past (v. 20).

Ahead of the army, Jehoshaphat organized Levitic singers to sing out praise unto the Lord. There was precedent for this; Joshua had sent the priests ahead blowing trumpets as they marched around Jericho (Josh. 6). The song the people used was Psalm 136.

---

1. What did Jehoshaphat declare about faith in God?
2. Describe the army's "weapons."

> "How happy it is to believe, with a steadfast assurance, that our petitions are heard even while we are making them; and how delightful to meet with a proof of it in the effectual and actual grant of them."—William Cowper

---

III. PRAISE GOD FOR THE VICTORY (2 Chron. 20:22-30)

A. Ambush Set by the Lord (vv. 22-23)

²²And when they began to sing and to praise, the Lord set ambushments against the children of Ammon, Moab, and mount Seir, which were come against Judah; and they were smitten. ²³For the children of Ammon and Moab stood up against the inhabitants of mount Seir, utterly to slay and destroy them: and when they had made an end of the inhabitants of Seir, every one helped to destroy another.

As the singers began to sing, going out ahead of the army, the Lord set some type of ambush for the enemy. The ambush may have come from Edomites planted among the invaders, or from other individuals the Lord had planted who suddenly came out of hiding, or from a supernatural source. Whoever they were, they were not men of Judah, for God had told Jehoshaphat not to have his people fight. The result of the confusion was that the various groups in the coalition began to fight each other. This is the same thing that had happened with Gideon (Judg. 7:22).

• How did confusion serve God's purpose?

> "Thank God for the battle verses in the Bible. We go into the unknown every day of our lives, and especially every Monday morning, for the week is sure to be a battlefield, outwardly and inwardly

B. The Spoils Reaped (vv. 24-25)

(2 Chronicles 20:24 is not included in the printed text.)

²⁵And when Jehoshaphat and his people came to take away the spoil of them, they found among them in abundance both riches with the dead bodies, and precious jewels, which they stripped off for themselves, more than they could carry away: and they were three days in gathering of the spoil, it was so much.

The march of the people of Judah from Jerusalem would have taken several hours. By the time they arrived at the hill (or watchtower) overlooking the scene, the mayhem was over and dead bodies lay everywhere. They did not have anyone to fight, for the Lord had totally handled the situation. All that was left to do was collect the huge amount of supplies and treasures that lay there. The amount was so immense that it took three days to gather it all.

• What "spoils" can be won through spiritual battles?

"The greater the battle—the greater the spoils."—T. D. Jakes

C. Worship and Thanksgiving Given (vv. 26-30)

(2 Chronicles 20:27-30 is not included in the printed text.)

²⁶And on the fourth day they assembled themselves in the valley of Berachah; for there they blessed the Lord: therefore the name of the same place was called, The valley of Berachah, unto this day.

After all the goods from the defeated enemy were collected, Jehoshaphat called everyone together to praise the Lord for this amazing victory. They named this place *Berachah*, which means "blessing."

Some six centuries earlier, when Israel passed over the Red Sea after leaving Egyptian bondage, there was great singing on the other side. However, there had been no singing praises to the Lord before the sea parted. Anyone can sing to the Lord after the fact.

Jehoshaphat and the people of Judah were able to sing on both sides of their "Red Sea" experience. Because of the Lord's intervention, Judah was at peace, her enemies at bay out of recognition that God was with them.

1. Describe the people's feelings as they returned to Jerusalem.
2. How did other nations respond when they heard how God had fought for Judah?

3. How did God bless Jehoshaphat's reign?

"The unthankful heart discovers no mercies; but let the thankful heart sweep through the day and, as the magnet finds the iron, so it will find, in every hour, some heavenly blessings!"—Henry Ward Beecher

---

CONCLUSION

Will the Lord fight for us in our time of desperation? Jehoshaphat, even though he was nursing the reprimand given him by the Lord for his involvement with King Ahab, still had the privilege to pray for divine help.

We must not think God has forsaken us during times when He is disciplining us. Job 5:17-18 says, "Blessed is the man whom God corrects; so do not despise the discipline of the Almighty. For he wounds, but he also binds up; he injures, but his hands also heal" (NIV).

The actions of Jehoshaphat and the people of Judah show us a pattern for approaching God for help: (1) Recognize that God will fight for His children because He absolutely loves us. (2) Recognize our human limitations, but also the unlimited power and resources of the Lord. (3) Seek God's will, not our own selfish interests, for He knows what is right and best for all. (4) Trust Him completely, and leave it in His hands. (5) Do what He tells us to do.

GOLDEN TEXT CHALLENGE

"THUS SAITH THE LORD UNTO YOU, BE NOT AFRAID NOR DISMAYED BY REASON OF THIS GREAT MULTITUDE; FOR THE BATTLE IS NOT YOURS, BUT GOD'S" (2 Chron. 20:15).

When Jehoshaphat was warned of the coming invasion by three armies, he did not put his trust in chariots and horses but, instead, called on the name of the Lord (cf. Ps. 20:7). In response, God assured the king that He would take care of the enemy.

It is a wonderful relief to know there are some situations for which the Lord takes complete responsibility when we turn to Him. In those situations, He will make us "more than conquerors through him that loved us" (Rom. 8:37).

Daily Devotions:
M. God Equips Us for Battle • 2 Samuel 22:29-37
T. God Is Our Refuge • Psalm 46:1-11
W. God Strengthens Against Opposition • Isaiah 41:8-16
T. More Than Conquerors Through Christ • Romans 8:31-39
F. Victory Over Death • 1 Corinthians 15:50-58
S. Do Not Fear Others • Hebrews 13:1-8

Stand Resolutely for the Lord (Daniel)

Daniel 1:1-20; 6:1-28

Unit Theme:

Good Lessons From Good Examples

Central Truth:

The Lord empowers Christians to stand firm in the face of opposition.

Focus:

Examine how Daniel remained true to God and stand fast in our faith.

Context:

As a young man and a mature adult, Daniel courageously served God while living in Babylon.

Golden Text:

"That the trial of your faith, being much more precious than of gold that perisheth, though it be tried with fire, might be found unto praise and honor and glory at the appearing of Jesus Christ" (1 Peter 1:7).

Study Outline:

 I. **Always Honor God** (Dan. 1:1-15)

 II. **Always Do What Is Right** (Dan. 6:1-11)

 III. **Trust God to Keep You** (Dan. 6:12-28)

INTRODUCTION

Some of the greatest exploits of faith found in the Scriptures are recorded in the Book of Daniel. What stories are more filled with the fervor of faith than the three Hebrew children in the fiery furnace, Daniel before Belshazzar at the banquet feast, and Daniel in the lion's den?

Today's lesson focuses on two events from the life of Daniel. His nobility of character is an example for believers to emulate.

I. ALWAYS HONOR GOD (Dan. 1:1-15)

A. Choice Exiles (vv. 1-4)

(Daniel 1:1-4 is not included in the printed text.)

When Nebuchadnezzar, king of Babylon, conquered Judah, he took some vessels from the house of God in Jerusalem. These vessels were placed in the treasure-house of his god. He was not satisfied, however, with the best of Judah's material treasures alone. He also desired to draw from the nation's mental resources. His standards for these captives whom he would bring into his own court was high. They had to be "children of Israel, and of the king's seed, and of the princes" (v. 3). Only the choicest young men of Israel could meet his standards.

Some have suggested these young people were about twelve to fourteen years old. No doubt, the king expected to shape the thinking of these captives that they might serve him. They were to be taught "the learning and the tongue of the Chaldeans" (v. 4). He hoped to break them away from their own heritage and tradition. His failure should be a lesson to us on the effectiveness of the early training of a child.

---

1. Why was Daniel living in Babylon (vv. 1-2)?
2. Describe King Nebuchadnezzar's plan for select captives (vv. 3-4).

"He has seen but little of life who does not discern everywhere the effect of early education on men's opinions and habits of thinking. Children bring out of the nursery that which displays itself throughout their lives."—Richard Cecil

---

B. The King's Table (vv. 5-8)

(Daniel 1:6-7 is not included in the printed text.)

⁵And the king appointed them a daily provision of the king's meat, and of the wine which he drank: so nourishing them three years, that at the end thereof they might stand before the king.

⁸But Daniel purposed in his heart that he would not defile himself with the portion of the king's meat, nor with the wine which he drank: therefore he requested of the prince of the eunuchs that he might not defile himself.

Four of the children of Judah who were selected by the king are named. Daniel is one of them. They were set apart for training and preparation for their official duties. This training lasted three years. They had special physical attention, and their food and drink were supplied from the king's table.

To eat from the king's table would have been looked upon as an honor by most people. No doubt, the king intended it as an honor for the Hebrew children. However, the meat from the king's table came from unclean animals and had been offered as a sacrifice to the gods of the Babylonians. For these young Hebrews to eat this meat would have been the same as worshiping these pagan gods. Therefore, "Daniel was determined not to defile himself by eating the food and wine given to them by the king" (v. 8 NLT).

There is great power in purpose. A minister titled his sermon about Ahab's desire for Naboth's vineyard, "Beware of What You Want—You Will Get It." Much truth is contained in that statement. In Daniel's case, what he wanted was good. He resolved that he would be true to God and keep his body undefiled. His making that decision in a strange land showed strength of character.

• Why is the phrase "purposed in his heart" so significant (v. 8)?

Stand Resolutely for the Lord

C. Favor and Good Will (vv. 9-13)

(Daniel 1:10-11, 13 is not included in the printed text.)

⁹Now God had brought Daniel into favour and tender love with the prince of the eunuchs.

¹²Prove thy servants, I beseech thee, ten days; and let them give us pulse to eat, and water to drink.

When Daniel decided he would not defile himself with the king's food, he made his request to the prince of the eunuchs ("chief of staff," NLT). God, who looks after His own, moved upon the official's heart, giving him "respect and affection for Daniel" (v. 9 NLT).

The chief of staff was answerable to the king. If he neglected the responsibilities entrusted to him, he would be held accountable. Therefore, Daniel's request posed some problems for him. He reminded Daniel that the king had ordered the menu he was to follow. If he did not eat the food the king ordered, he might become sick. When he appeared before the king pale and weak, the king would want to know why he was ill. If the others looked better than Daniel, the king would know something was wrong. If this happened, the official's life would be endangered (v. 10).

Since the chief of staff felt the wish was too great for him to grant, Daniel turned to one of the underofficers and repeated his request (v. 11). His faith was not shaken by the failure of his first attempt to realize his purpose.

When the opportunity came, Daniel proposed a plan to Melzar (a title meaning "steward"), whom the chief of staff had "set over" Daniel and his three companions (v. 11 NKJV). Daniel asked that his plan be tested for ten days. In the place of the king's meat and wine, he and his companions would eat vegetables and drink water (v. 12). The implication was that if they appeared pale and sickly after ten days, they would go on the king's diet.

After ten days of eating a restricted diet, Daniel was willing for the countenance of himself and his friends to be compared with the countenance of those who had eaten the king's meat. He would leave their fate in the steward's hands. "As you see fit, so deal with your servants" (v. 13 NKJV).

---

1. How did the Lord intervene (v. 9)?
2. Explain Daniel's proposal (vv. 12-13).

D. The Test (vv. 14-15)

¹⁴So he consented to them in this matter, and proved them ten days. ¹⁵And at the end of ten days their countenances appeared fairer and fatter in flesh than all the children which did eat the portion of the king's meat.

The result of Daniel's faith is recorded. After eating vegetables and drinking water for ten days, the countenances of Daniel and his friends "appeared fairer and fatter" than all those who had eaten the king's meat. We are not to conclude that in such a short time the vegetable diet in itself produced this contrast. Rather, the God of Israel heard the prayers of His people and answered in this way.

Many times God has miraculously intervened to meet the needs of His own. When Israel needed bread or water, God miraculously provided for them: bitter water made sweet; water out of a rock; manna from heaven; quails for meat. How else would Israel have won many of the wars they waged except that God fought for them? The history of God's dealings with His people is a record of miracles. He still works in a miraculous manner to meet the needs of those who trust in Him.

"When we do the best that we can, we never know what miracle is wrought in our life, or in the life of another."—Helen Keller

---

II. ALWAYS DO WHAT IS RIGHT (Dan. 6:1-11)

A. Daniel's Advancement (vv. 1-3)

(Daniel 6:1-2 is not included in the printed text.)

³Then this Daniel was preferred above the presidents and princes, because an excellent spirit was in him; and the king thought to set him over the whole realm.

More than forty years after Daniel refused to eat the food from Nebuchadnezzar's table, Darius the Mede became the ruler of Babylon. Darius set 120 princes over the whole kingdom, each being responsible for a given area; then he set three presidents over these princes. The princes were accountable to the presidents who, in turn, would report to the king. Of these presidents, Daniel was first. The king even considered setting him over the entire kingdom. Daniel was elevated because "an excellent spirit was in him" (v. 3). The Spirit of the living God worked through him. It was this divine influence that impressed the king.

- Describe Daniel's appointment.

"It is not the situation which makes the man, but the man who makes the situation. The slave may be a freeman. The monarch

may be a slave. Situations are noble or ignoble, as we make them."
—Frederick W. Robertson

B. Daniel's Adversaries (vv. 4-9)
(Daniel 6:6-7 is not included in the printed text.)
⁴Then the presidents and princes sought to find occasion against Daniel concerning the kingdom; but they could find none occasion nor fault; forasmuch as he was faithful, neither was there any error or fault found in him. ⁵Then said these men, We shall not find any occasion against this Daniel, except we find it against him concerning the law of his God.

⁸Now, O king, establish the decree, and sign the writing, that it be not changed, according to the law of the Medes and Persians, which altereth not. ⁹Wherefore king Darius signed the writing and the decree.

Daniel impressed the king by his life, and the king honored him above the others. This naturally stirred up jealousy among the presidents and princes. So they cunningly planned Daniel's downfall.

They observed him in his duties, imagining they could find something to report to the king. However, they found no fault in his work. In everything he was faithful. They concluded the only way they could find anything against him would be in his relationship to God. So they devised a plan.

They presented a plan to the king whereby "for the next thirty days any person who prays to anyone, divine or human—except to you, Your Majesty—will be thrown into the den of lions" (v. 7 NLT). They said all the presidents and other rulers had agreed to this. However, this was not true. Daniel had not been a party to it.

Nevertheless, their flattery induced the king to sign the decree, which was designed to discredit Daniel with him. How sad are the words, "Therefore King Darius signed the written decree" (v. 9 NKJV)!

---

1. Compare Daniel with the other officials (v. 4).
2. How did Daniel frustrate the other leaders (vv. 5-6)?

"Some persons are always ready to level those above them down to themselves, while they are never willing to level those below them up to their own position."—Jonathan Edwards

---

C. Daniel's Faithfulness (vv. 10-11)
¹⁰Now when Daniel knew that the writing was signed, he went into his house; and his windows being open in his chamber toward Jerusalem, he kneeled upon his knees three times a day, and prayed, and gave thanks before his God, as he did aforetime. ¹¹Then these men assembled, and found Daniel praying and making supplication before his God.

How did Daniel react to the news that the king had signed the decree? Did he change his prayer habits? Did he elevate the law of man above the law of God?

To know Daniel is to know the answer to these questions. His loyalty to God never swerved. He continued to pray as had been his custom.

Those who had been responsible for having the king sign the decree watched for an occasion to accuse Daniel. They found him "praying and asking for God's help" (v. 11 NLT). This was the chance they were looking for.

---

1. What did Darius agree to do, and why (v. 9)?
2. Describe Daniel's boldness (vv. 10-11).

> "The reason why many fail in battle is because they wait until the hour of battle. The reason why others succeed is because they have gained their victory on their knees long before the battle came."
> —R. A. Torrey

III. TRUST GOD TO KEEP YOU (Dan. 6:12-28)
A. The King's Regret (vv. 12-15)
   (Daniel 6:12-15 is not included in the printed text.)

Daniel's enemies approached Darius, reminding him he had signed a decree that no petitions could be made to anyone but himself. They also reminded him of the penalty the decree imposed. Then they told the king they had caught Daniel in prayer.

The king realized he had been trapped into doing something he did not want to do. He labored diligently to discover a way whereby he could deliver Daniel, but the rulers kept reminding him "no decree nor statute which the king establisheth may be changed" (v. 15).

Though he was king, Darius could not rescue Daniel from the judgment that had been rendered. He had much power at his disposal, but not enough power to help his top official.

---

1. How did Daniel's fellow leaders expose their hidden agenda?
2. How were the king's hands tied?

> "Live thoughtfully today and you won't have to live regretfully tomorrow."—Woodrow Kroll

---

B. The King's Anxiety (vv. 16-20)
   (Daniel 6:17-19 is not included in the printed text.)

¹⁶Then the king commanded, and they brought Daniel, and cast him into the den of lions. Now the king spake and said unto Daniel, Thy God whom thou servest continually, he will deliver thee.

²⁰And when he came to the den, he cried with a lamentable voice unto Daniel: and the king spake and said to Daniel, O Daniel, servant of the living God, is thy God, whom thou servest continually, able to deliver thee from the lions?

As Daniel was being cast into the den, Darius spoke encouraging words to him. The king reminded Daniel of his faithfulness to his God and that God would deliver him. The king's later actions indicate he did not really believe this himself. It seems he was expressing what he hoped, rather than what he believed.

Daniel was different—he believed in the power of God. He remembered what God had done for him when he refused to eat the king's meat and drink his wine. He recalled the visions and dreams God had revealed to him. His confidence was placed in God.

Once Daniel was lowered into the lions' den, a stone was placed over the opening, and the king "sealed it with his own signet ring and with the signets of his lords" (v. 17 NKJV). The king was too worried to eat or sleep that night. When the sun rose, Darius hurried to the lions' den and cried out to Daniel, "Has your God . . . been able to deliver you from the lions?" (v. 20 NKJV). Was the Creator more powerful than the creature?

———————————

1. How did Darius describe Daniel (v. 16)?
2. Explain the king's actions in verse 18.
3. Describe the miracle (vv. 20-22).
4. How can you be spared from a "roaring lion" (1 Peter 5:8-9)?

"Where does your security lie? Is God your refuge, your hiding place, your stronghold? . . . If He is, you don't need to search any further for security."—Elisabeth Elliot

———————————

C. Daniel's Deliverance (vv. 21-24)

²¹Then said Daniel unto the king, O king, live for ever. ²²My God hath sent his angel, and hath shut the lions' mouths, that they have not hurt me: forasmuch as before him innocency was found in me; and also before thee, O king, have I done no hurt. ²³Then was the king exceedingly glad for him, and commanded that they should take Daniel up out of the den. So Daniel was taken up out of the den, and no manner of hurt was found upon him, because he believed in his God. ²⁴And the king commanded, and they brought those men which had accused Daniel, and they cast them into the den of lions, them, their children, and their wives; and the lions had the mastery of them, and brake all their bones in pieces or ever they came at the bottom of the den.

The sound of Daniel's voice must have been music to the ears of the king. All his fears could now vanish. God had protected His faithful servant.

Daniel's reply was an expression of esteem for the king. He did not blame the king for the fate that had befallen him. Rather, he expressed the wish that the king would have a long and sustained reign.

Daniel explained to Darius what had taken place. While the king was spending a sleepless night in the palace, the prophet was resting in the presence of the Lord's angel. This heavenly visitor had protected Daniel from the lions. The mouths of the lions had been shut so they could do him no harm.

Daniel said his protection came because he was "found innocent in [God's] sight" (v. 22 NLT). Though people may misjudge us, God judges us fairly. The king's men looked upon Daniel as a threat to them. This resulted in their cunningly devised plot to get rid of him. On the other hand, God looked at the same life and found no fault in it.

Daniel reminded Darius, "Also, O king, I have done no wrong before you" (v. 22 NKJV). He was innocent before God and man. His faithfulness was apparent to the king.

When Daniel was taken up out of the den, there was not a scratch on him. God's protective care had been complete. The same shield that surrounded the Hebrew children in the fiery furnace (ch. 3) surrounded Daniel in the den of lions.

Daniel was protected "because he believed in his God" (6:23). Faith is a powerful factor in the life of the believer. The writer of Hebrews said, "Without faith it is impossible to please him: for he that cometh to God must believe that he is, and that he is a rewarder of them that diligently seek him" (11:6).

Once Daniel's health was verified, the king issued another command, directed toward those who accused Daniel. They were cast into the den of lions, along with their wives and children. The lions devoured all of them immediately. No angel came down to restrain the lions.

These adversaries of Daniel had sown to the flesh, and they were reaping the rewards of their sowing. They had defied the living God and had persecuted His servant, and God took vengeance on them. It was not necessary for Daniel to take matters into his own hands, for God fought his battles for him. And God still fights the battles of His people.

---

1. Why did God deliver Daniel (vv. 23-24)?
2. Why doesn't God save all of His faithful followers from their enemies?

D. The King's Command (vv. 25-28)
   (Daniel 6:25, 27-28 is not included in the printed text.)
   26 I make a decree, That in every dominion of my kingdom men tremble and fear before the God of Daniel: for he is the living God, and stedfast for ever, and his kingdom that which shall not be destroyed, and his dominion shall be even unto the end.

Darius took immediate steps to further correct the situation in his kingdom. He directed a communique to "all people, nations, and languages, that dwell in all the earth" (v. 25).

Darius called upon people in every dominion of his kingdom to "tremble and fear before the God of Daniel" (v. 26). His language was much stronger than that used by Nebuchadnezzar in his decree. Nebuchadnezar had pronounced judgment upon any who were to "speak any thing amiss against the God of Shadrach, Meshach, and Abednego" (3:29); but Darius called upon his subjects to "tremble and fear" before the God of Daniel.

The king then gave his reasons for this decree: the God of Daniel was "the living God" (6:26). There were many other gods worshiped in the land, but there was only one living God. Gods of gold, silver, stone, or wood were helpless to meet the needs of their followers. On the other hand, the God of Daniel had proven His ability to meet the need of His servant.

Darius also recognized the durability of God's kingdom; it will never be destroyed. Those who are a part of His kingdom are assured of ultimate triumph.

The king described God as the One who "worketh signs and wonders in heaven and in earth" (v. 27). He delivered Daniel from the power of the lions, and He is still the God who works wonders. His power has not changed. His care for us is as great as was His care for Daniel. He stands ready to meet our every need.

The chapter concludes with this statement: "So this Daniel prospered in the reign of Darius, and in the reign of Cyrus the Persian" (v. 28).

• Describe Darius' decree regarding the Lord God (vv. 27-28).

> "Knowing God is more than knowing about Him; it is a matter of dealing with Him as He opens up to you, and being dealt with by Him as He takes knowledge of you. Knowing about Him is a necessary precondition of trusting in Him, but the width of our knowledge about Him is no gauge of our knowledge of Him."—J. I. Packer

---

CONCLUSION

This lesson highlights Daniel's *resolve*, which can be defined as "firm determination." One might even say Daniel practiced a "holy stubbornness"—he refused to do anything that would offend God.

Like Daniel, we need to purpose in our heart to fully obey God no matter the consequences.

GOLDEN TEXT CHALLENGE

"THAT THE TRIAL OF YOUR FAITH, BEING MUCH MORE PRE-CIOUS THAN OF GOLD THAT PERISHETH, THOUGH IT BE TRIED

WITH FIRE, MIGHT BE FOUND UNTO PRAISE AND HONOUR AND GLORY AT THE APPEARING OF JESUS CHRIST" (1 Peter 1:7).

Just as gold can be purified by applying great heat, which burns off the impurities, our faith can be purified and made of greater value and permanence if it is subjected to trials.

Gold is valuable, but faith is of greater value. Gold is durable, but faith is even more durable. Real faith can endure trials better than gold can endure heat.

When Christ comes again, will He "find faith on the earth" (Luke 18:8)? The answer is yes. Christians in all ages have shown themselves able to remain loyal to Christ during the most terrible persecutions.

Daily Devotions:

M. Follow God's Commands • Deuteronomy 8:1-6

T. Obedience in Trials • Job 23:8-12

W. Trust God in Troubled Times • Psalm 86:1-7

T. Stand Firm in the Lord • Ephesians 6:10-17

F. Unwavering Faith • James 1:2-8

S. Resist Opposition Steadfastly • 1 Peter 5:8-11

Bring Others to Jesus
(Andrew and Philip)

John 1:35-51; Acts 8:26-39

Unit Theme:
Good Lessons From Good Examples

Central Truth:
Christians are called to bring others to Christ.

Focus:
Review how Andrew and Philip brought others to Jesus and witness to others.

Context:
An apostle and a deacon bring people to Jesus.

Golden Text:
"He [Andrew] first findeth his own brother Simon, and saith unto him, We have found the Messia, which is, being interpreted, the Christ. And he brought him to Jesus" (John 1:41-42).

Study Outline:
I. **Andrew Brings His Brother** (John 1:35-42)
II. **Philip Brings a Friend** (John 1:43-51)
III. **Philip Witnesses to a Stranger** (Acts 8:26-39)

INTRODUCTION

In John 1:29, John the Baptist points his hearers to Jesus by calling Him "the Lamb of God who takes away the sin of the world" (NKJV). The next day, two of John's disciples leave him to follow Jesus. His role in the Kingdom diminishes as the ministry of Jesus is established (3:30).

God uses many people to accomplish His will. It requires cooperation with others to fulfill our ministries effectively. Always, the focus must be on Jesus.

Methods of evangelism are revealed in both of today's lesson texts—John 1:35-51 and Acts 8:26-39. First, we will see the power of personal experience in witnessing. We must tell others who Jesus is and what He has done for us. Second, we will see the importance of obeying the Holy Spirit.

I. ANDREW BRINGS HIS BROTHER (John 1:35-42)
A. John the Baptist (vv. 35-37)
(John 1:35-37 is not included in the printed text.)
John the Baptist preached to a crowd and testified about Jesus Christ, the Son of God (vv. 29-34). The next day, he stood with "two of his disciples" (v. 35). The Baptist knew how to minister to the multitudes, but also was available to provide personal attention to those who needed it.

Later on in the narrative, we find that one of these two was Andrew (v. 40). The other is never named, yet even this might be a clue. The writer of the Gospel, the apostle John, according to tradition, only referred to himself as "the disciple whom Jesus loved" (19:26; 21:20). Like John the Baptist, he wanted to step out of the spotlight so the ministry of Jesus would be the focus. Therefore, it seems logical that the apostle John is the unnamed disciple. In the lists of the twelve disciples, his name occurs as one of the first four, and the order is consistent with the order of calling by Jesus (Matt. 10:2-4; Luke 6:14-16).

As they stood there, the Baptist was "looking upon Jesus" (John 1:36). This was a poignant moment for John. The previous day Jesus was walking toward him. John's ministry was at its peak. This day, Jesus was walking away from him (see v. 38), not in abandonment but as a shift in the strategy of God. John had accomplished his role as the forerunner to the Messiah.

At that moment, John proclaimed, "Behold the Lamb of God!" (v. 36). It was the same testimony as the day before, but for a different audience and purpose. He was preparing the hearts of two of his disciples.

In response, Andrew and Peter "followed Jesus" (v. 37). *Follow* is often used in the Gospels to signify acceptance of discipleship and commitment of faith (see Matt. 9:9; Mark 8:34; John 8:12; 10:4).

- What does John the Baptist call Jesus, and why?

"The men who followed Him were unique in their generation. They turned the world upside down because their hearts had been turned right side up. The world has never been the same."—Billy Graham

----

B. Jesus' Call (vv. 38-39)

38 Then Jesus turned, and saw them following, and saith unto them, What seek ye? They said unto him, Rabbi, (which is to say, being interpreted, Master,) where dwellest thou? 39 He saith unto them, Come and see. They came and saw where he dwelt, and abode with him that day: for it was about the tenth hour.

Jesus turned around and "saw" Andrew and John following Him. Given what is revealed about Jesus in this passage, it is evident He knew they were behind Him (see v. 48). The two were "following" Jesus, choosing to become disciples.

In the first century, a disciple entered into a relationship with a teacher. The disciple became identified with the teacher and was considered to be a reliable source of the teacher's wisdom and doctrine. The disciple's destiny was also tied to that of the teacher.

The first words spoken by Jesus in the Gospel of John are directed to these two disciples. He asked them, "What do you seek?" (v. 38 NASB). He did not ask, "Whom do you seek," but "what?" It has been said this is the first question to be answered by everyone coming to Jesus.

The two followers addressed Him as *Rabbi*, which John interpreted for his readers. It is an Aramaic term of polite address, meaning "teacher" or "master," or literally, "my great one."

The two disciples responded to Jesus with a puzzling, "Where are You staying?" (v. 38 NASB). Perhaps they were unsure how to respond, or were asking if He had a school with which they could become associated, as teachers often did.

Jesus' response was not one of rebuke or annoyance. He simply replied, "Come and see" (v. 39). It was an invitation to those who wanted uninterrupted time with Jesus. The invitation still stands. They saw where He was staying and their following led to "abiding" ("remaining," NKJV) with Jesus. It would be a permanent relationship.

• What is Jesus called here, and why?

"If we are followers of Christ, we are His disciples and should have the primary devotion in our lives to see as He does, think as He thinks, and understand with His heart."—Rick Joyner

---

C. The Messiah (vv. 40-41)

40One of the two which heard John speak, and followed him, was Andrew, Simon Peter's brother. 41He first findeth his own brother Simon, and saith unto him, We have found the Messias, which is, being interpreted, the Christ.

In verse 40, John identifies one of the two as *Andrew*, a Greek name meaning "manly." He is further identified as "Simon Peter's brother." Andrew "first" found Simon (v. 41). Before doing anything else, he wanted his brother to share in the discovery he made.

Andrew informed Simon that he and John had found the *Messiah*, a Hebrew word meaning "Anointed One." In the Old Testament, several offices were set apart through anointing. The king of Israel was known as "the Lord's anointed" (1 Sam. 16:6; 2 Sam. 1:14). The high priest (Ex. 29:7; Lev. 4:3) and prophets (1 Kings 19:16) were anointed. Jesus, as the Messiah, the Anointed One, fulfilled the offices of prophet, priest, and king. The anticipation and searching for the Messiah, the declaration of John the Baptist, and the daylong visit convinced them Jesus was "the Christ" (Greek equivalent of *Messiah*).

• What is Jesus called here, and why?

"When Andrew went to find his brother, he little imagined how eminent Simon would become. You may be very deficient in talent yourself, and yet you may be the means of drawing to Christ one who shall become eminent in grace and service."—Charles Spurgeon

---

D. Simon Peter (v. 42)

42And he brought him to Jesus. And when Jesus beheld him, he said, Thou art Simon the son of Jona: thou shalt be called Cephas, which is by interpretation, A stone.

Andrew "brought" Simon "to Jesus." This is the natural order of evangelism: we lead people to the same place we received help. The place to start is with our family and friends.

"Jesus beheld" Simon. The phrase denotes intentionality—Jesus looked him over. He looked deep within. Jesus' statement is a prophecy of what Simon would become, not a declaration of what he then was. Before Simon ever spoke a word, Jesus accepted him as a disciple and gave him a new name, a new character, and the new work to fulfill in the unfolding of God's redemptive plan. He would be a "stone," or "rock."

• What does Jesus call Simon, and why?

"God is the author of who we are and where we are to go."—Ley Anne

---

II. PHILIP BRINGS A FRIEND (John 1:43-51)
A. The Finding of Philip (1:43-45)

43The day following Jesus would go forth into Galilee, and findeth Philip, and saith unto him, Follow me. 44Now Philip was of Bethsaida, the city of Andrew and Peter. 45Philip findeth Nathanael, and saith unto him, We have found him, of whom Moses in the law, and the prophets, did write, Jesus of Nazareth, the son of Joseph.

Jesus is still at Bethany before the Jordan; He desires to go to Galilee, which would require crossing over the Jordan and traveling west. Perhaps while making preparations, He "finds," or seeks out, Philip and says, "Follow Me." This is a different person than Philip the deacon and evangelist of Acts 6 and 8.

John also tells the readers that Philip, like Andrew and Simon Peter, was originally from Bethsaida, a fishing village in a predominantly Greek area. In the account of the feeding of the five thousand, Jesus asked him about feeding the multitude. Philip focused on the cost, while Andrew found the lad (John 6:5-9). On another occasion, Philip was slow to understand that one purpose of Jesus' mission was to reveal the Father (14:8-9). Apparently, he tended to examine things from a natural perspective.

Part of the discipleship process is to move the eyes of the disciple from the human perspective to God's perspective. This is an ongoing process. If the disciple is confident he or she has reached that goal, the change in perspective is not complete.

Philip immediately found Nathanael (1:45), who was from Cana in Galilee (21:2). Philip's declaration displayed great enthusiasm. The reference to "the law, and the prophets" (1:45) usually means the entire Old Testament.

That Philip referred to Jesus as "the son of Joseph" was not a denial of the Virgin Birth. According to the custom of his day, Philip identified Jesus by His native home and His legal father, who was Joseph (see Matt. 1:16). Just as Jesus found Philip, Philip found Nathanael.

- How does Philip describe Jesus?

"We don't follow Him in order to be loved; we are loved so we follow Him."—Neil T. Anderson

---

B. Skepticism Answered (vv. 46-49)

⁴⁶And Nathanael said unto him, Can there any good thing come out of Nazareth? Philip saith unto him, Come and see. ⁴⁷Jesus saw Nathanael coming to him, and saith of him, Behold an Israelite indeed, in whom is no guile! ⁴⁸Nathanael saith unto him, Whence knowest thou me? Jesus answered and said unto him, Before that Philip called thee, when thou wast under the fig tree, I saw thee. ⁴⁹Nathanael answered and saith unto him, Rabbi, thou art the Son of God; thou art the King of Israel.

Nathanael was skeptical about Philip's assertion that the Messiah was from Nazareth. Perhaps he objected to the Messiah having such a lowly origin, as did the Jewish leaders (6:42; 7:52). The idea that the Messiah could come from Nazareth was as offensive as His being born in a stable, dying for people's sins, or taking on the flesh of humanity to suffer what we suffer and feel what we feel. Or, perhaps Nathanael's objection was based on the understanding that neither the anticipated prophet nor the Messiah would come out of Galilee (7:40-42). This, then, would depict Nathanael as a student of the Scriptures, though he misunderstood them.

Nathanael agreed to go with Philip to see Jesus, who saw him approaching and declared he was a true "Israelite" (1:47)—a member of God's chosen community. Jesus further declared Nathanael had "no deceit" (NKJV)—his integrity was visible. However, even people of integrity and high morals need a Savior (Rom. 3:23).

Jesus' description hit its mark and surprised Nathanael, who responded, "How do You know me?" (John 1:48 NKJV). He may have thought Philip told Jesus more about him than he desired. Jesus quickly cleared up that misconception, telling him that "before Philip" ever approached him, He saw him "under the fig tree." Since Jesus saw Nathanael under the fig tree, He could have heard him disparage His hometown, yet He still accepted him.

Nathanael was convinced of Jesus' ability and status. With deep emotion he cried, "Rabbi, You are the Son of God! You are the King of Israel!" (1:49 NKJV). It is a confession of faith and a statement of revelation (see Matt. 16:16-17). While he may not have understood the full implication of his statement, he did see Jesus as the restorer of the kingship of God to Israel (see Ps. 2).

---

1. Why did Nathanael question Jesus' messiahship (v. 46)?

2. What does Nathanael call Jesus, and why (vv. 47-49)?

C. The Promise of Things Greater (vv. 50-51)

(John 1:50-51 is not included in the printed text.)

Jesus responded with a rhetorical question to Nathanael's declaration by making a personal promise to Nathanael of "greater things" to come (v. 50). While it was directed toward Nathanael, others would share in this promise also.

"Greater" can be taken in a qualitative or quantitative sense. Jesus could be saying to Nathanael, "You will see things of a greater nature than My ability to see you under a fig tree." Or He could be saying, "You will see a greater number of works like this in the future." It seems to be inclusive of both.

In verse 51, Jesus told Nathanael, "Ye [plural] shall see heaven open." When the heavens open, there is mediation between God and humanity and a special union is established. Through Jesus, the gateway to heaven is now open.

The next element of the promise speaks of angels "ascending and descending upon the Son of man" (v. 51). This title establishes a connection with humanity. He is the Son of Man who suffers humiliation and pain so He might reconcile people to God. He is also the Son of Man who receives dominion and glory, whose kingdom is eternal (Dan. 7:13-14).

The disciples could not grasp all that at this point, but they would before their journey on earth with Jesus was complete (see John 6:66-71; 13:7). It was after the Resurrection that they began to understand the full significance of their time with Jesus (2:22; 12:16). This example reveals to us that our understanding of God need not be fully developed to accept who He is and what He has to offer us. He is just looking for disciples who will answer His call to know, be, and do greater things.

• Describe Jesus' promise to Nathanael.

III. PHILIP WITNESSES TO A STRANGER (Acts 8:26-39)

Acts 8:1-12 chronicles a powerful move of God that took place in Samaria through Philip the evangelist. Many people were saved, delivered, healed, and baptized, "and there was great joy in that city" (v. 8). Then God moved Philip from ministry to a multitude to a one-on-one encounter.

Bring Others to Jesus

A. "Arise, and Go" (vv. 26-28)

26And the angel of the Lord spake unto Philip, saying, Arise, and go toward the south unto the way that goeth down from Jerusalem unto Gaza, which is desert. 27And he arose and went: and, behold, a man of Ethiopia, an eunuch of great authority under Candace queen of the Ethiopians, who had the charge of all her treasure, and had come to Jerusalem for to worship, 28Was returning, and sitting in his chariot read Esaias the prophet.

These verses describe Philip as a man prepared to do the Lord's bidding anywhere and at any time. When the angel said "go," Philip went.

On the lonely road to Gaza to which Philip was directed, he found a covered wagon moving in a southerly direction. In it was seated the treasurer of the Ethiopian court. He was likely a native African who had become a proselyte to Judaism. This dignitary was returning from a pilgrimage to Jerusalem and was occupied in reading aloud the prophecy of Isaiah. The fact he had traveled about twelve hundred miles from his native country to worship in the capital of Judaism indicates his inner longing for a satisfaction that his position and money could not buy. And his reading of the inspired Hebrew Scriptures had created a greater hunger still.

---

1. How did Philip respond to the angel's command?
2. List everything revealed about the man in the chariot.

> "The will of God for your life is simply that you submit yourself to Him each day and say, 'Father, Your will for today is mine. Your pleasure for today is mine. Your work for today is mine. I trust You to be God. You lead me today and I will follow.'"—Kay Arthur

---

B. "Go Near" (vv. 29-35)

(Acts 8:32-34 is not included in the printed text.)

29Then the Spirit said unto Philip, Go near, and join thyself to this chariot. 30And Philip ran thither to him, and heard him read the prophet Esaias, and said, Understandest thou what thou readest? 31And he said, How can I, except some man should guide me? And he desired Philip that he would come up and sit with him.

35Then Philip opened his mouth, and began at the same scripture, and preached unto him Jesus.

Philip was prepared for his mission to this man by his knowledge of Scripture, his love for souls, and his responsiveness to the voice of the Holy Spirit. The Spirit commanded him to approach the eunuch's wagon as a witness of the Lord. The words "join thyself" express strong determination to accomplish a purpose, and Philip promptly obeyed.

Philip's tactful approach indicates the method of a Spirit-led personal evangelist. His question "Do you understand what you are reading?" (v. 30

NKJV) was intended to arrest the man's attention to the interpretation and application Philip was prepared to give. The eunuch's responsive question, as well as his invitation to Philip to take his place at his side in the chariot, indicated an earnest desire for more enlightenment.

The text being read was Isaiah 53:7-8. An intelligent reader could see the prophet was speaking of an Individual who suffered in silence like a lamb before its shearer. Moreover, in His humiliation and suffering, justice was denied Him.

The theme for Philip's witnessing to this man was simply "Jesus." Whether or not the Ethiopian had ever heard of Jesus is not known, but he now heard an exposition of Jesus, the Suffering Servant, that enlightened his understanding and moved his heart. This is in accord with Jesus' own words: "Search the scriptures; for in them ye think ye have eternal life: and they are they which testify of me" (John 5:39).

---

1. Explain the eunuch's dilemma.
2. Do you think most people in your community would correctly interpret verses 32 and 33? Why or why not?

"Your job today is to be a witness."—Warren Wiersbe

C. "Here Is Water" (vv. 36-39)

36And as they went on their way, they came unto a certain water: and the eunuch said, See, here is water; what doth hinder me to be baptized? 37And Philip said, If thou believest with all thine heart, thou mayest. And he answered and said, I believe that Jesus Christ is the Son of God. 38And he commanded the chariot to stand still: and they went down both into the water, both Philip and the eunuch; and he baptized him. 39And when they were come up out of the water, the Spirit of the Lord caught away Philip, that the eunuch saw him no more: and he went on his way rejoicing.

Philip's witnessing evidently included instruction relative to Christian baptism, since this was the common symbol of confession of faith in Jesus Christ as Savior. It is evident, too, that Philip's testimony of Christ's redeeming death and resurrection in fulfillment of the Servant prophecy had produced conviction and kindled saving faith in the heart of the Ethiopian. Hence, upon arrival at a stream of water, the man requested baptism as a visible confession of his faith.

Philip was satisfied with the sincerity of the Ethiopian's testimony and thus water baptism was in order. The chariot driver was ordered to stop, and Philip and the eunuch "went down both into the water" (v. 38). This seems to be in harmony with the universality of immersion in the practice of the early church.

Following the baptism, Philip the evangelist was suddenly and supernaturally snatched away, while the new convert, assured of the salvation experience, "went on his way rejoicing" (v. 39). While human feeling may have moved

Philip to accompany his new convert with further instruction, the Lord had other plans for His witness and other places for him to work.

---

1. What "hinders" (v. 36 NKJV) some people from being baptized?
2. Who should be baptized, and why (v. 37)?
3. Describe the story's happy conclusion (vv. 38-39).

> "Baptism in New Testament theology is a loyalty oath, a public avowal of who is on the Lord's side in the cosmic war between good and evil."—Michael Heiser

---

CONCLUSION

L. C. Hester was a Texan known as "the witnessing plumber." A minister said of him, "That witnessing plumber has won hundreds to Christ since he became a Christian. Many will listen to a workingman who will not listen to a preacher, you know."

GOLDEN TEXT CHALLENGE

"HE [ANDREW] FIRST FINDETH HIS OWN BROTHER SIMON, AND SAITH UNTO HIM, WE HAVE FOUND THE MESSIAS, WHICH IS, BEING INTERPRETED, THE CHRIST. AND HE BROUGHT HIM TO JESUS" (John 1:41-42).

This is a testimony of a new convert who wishes to share his glorious discovery with others—especially with another member of his family. Andrew was the first of John's disciples to heed John's message to follow "the Lamb of God." He then went immediately to tell his brother Simon.

Andrew's testimony was positive. He did not say, "I think I've found a good thing," or "I hope this is it." He said, rather, "I have found the Christ." How heartwarming it is to see new converts cry out, "I have found Him!"

Andrew's enthusiasm did not stop with this brief witness, but it continued to make a tremendous difference in the rest of his life. He forsook all and followed Jesus.

Have you found Him? Are you following Him? Are you telling others?

Daily Devotions:

M. Leading Families to God • Deuteronomy 6:4-15
T. A Gentile Believes • 2 Kings 5:8-19
W. God's Goodness Draws People • Psalm 67:1-7
T. A Woman's Testimony • John 4:4-7, 39-42
F. Preaching Despite Opposition • Acts 4:1-4
S. Share the Good News • Romans 10:13-17

Be an Encourager (Barnabas)

Acts 4:32-37; 9:26-28; 11:19-30; 13:1-5; 14:1-28; 15:36-40; 1 Timothy 6:17-19

Unit Theme:

Good Lessons From Good Examples

Central Truth:

Christians should build up one another in Christ.

Focus:

Investigate and imitate how Barnabas encouraged others.

Context:

Accounts of Barnabas, "the son of encouragement"

Golden Text:

"Let us therefore follow after the things which make for peace, and things wherewith one may edify another" (Rom. 14:19).

Study Outline:

I. **A Generous Man** (Acts 4:32-37; 1 Tim. 6:17-19)

II. **A Compassionate Mentor** (Acts 9:26-27; 11:19-30; 15:36-40)

III. **An Effective Missionary** (Acts 13:1-5; 14:1-7, 21-28)

INTRODUCTION

In his book *The Other Twelve*, Leslie Flynn says his wife has followed six daily rules for years. He wrote: "She resolved every day to do something for herself, to do something she doesn't want to do but which needs doing, to do a physical exercise, to do a mental exercise, and to offer an original prayer that includes thanks for blessings. The sixth item (though first on her list) is to do something for someone else . . . she does this without telling anyone."

Although Barnabas probably did not have a daily list of good things to do, his deeds speak volumes about his character. He was a generous man. When believers decided to pool their resources to help the less fortunate in their community, Barnabas said, in effect, "You can count me in." He sold the land he owned and brought the proceeds to the apostles to be distributed among those in need.

Barnabas was a man who could be trusted. His trustworthiness surfaced in two different ways. When the saints at Antioch learned a great famine was going to strike Judea, they pitched in as much as they could to bring relief to their brothers and sisters there. Then they trusted Barnabas and Saul to deliver the goods to the fellow believers. The second way was when the Christians at Jerusalem were reluctant to accept Paul as one of their own. Barnabas testified that Saul's conversion was genuine and, on his word, the church received Saul in open fellowship.

When Paul refused to let Mark travel with him because he had deserted them on an earlier trip, Barnabas was loyal to his cousin. He defended him as worthy of a second chance. This difference of opinion resulted with Mark traveling with Barnabas, and Silas accompanying Paul. Later in life, Paul acknowledged Mark had something to offer his ministry. Also, he and Barnabas were reconciled over time and worked together again.

The church needs more encouragers like Barnabas—people who leave a trail of grateful people wherever they go.

I. A GENEROUS MAN (Acts 4:32-37; 1 Tim. 6:17-19)

A. A Model of Unity (Acts 4:32)

32And the multitude of them that believed were of one heart and of one soul: neither said any of them that ought of the things which he possessed was his own; but they had all things common.

Unity often rises out of persecution, as we see in Acts 3 and 4. A lame man was healed and disciples landed in jail. Moreover, they were threatened and severely warned against preaching anymore in the name of Jesus. The believers stood their ground and expressed their determination to speak the truth, regardless of the consequences. Facing these circumstances, they went to the Lord in prayer, seeking boldness to remain faithful in ministering the Word and asking the Lord to confirm their work with signs and wonders. "When they had prayed, the place was shaken where they were assembled together; and they were all filled with the Holy Ghost, and they spake the word of God with boldness" (4:31).

The combination of persecution and the powerful display of the Lord's presence resulted in complete unity in the church. They were united in their attitude toward each other, and in their doctrine; they were one in heart and soul. At this point, they reflected the unity Jesus prayed about and longed for among His people (John 17:20-23). Verse 21 says, "That they all may be one; as thou, Father, art in me, and I in thee, that they also may be one in us: that the world may believe that thou hast sent me."

This unity extended to their possessions; they shared everything they had. Remembering God loved them so much that He gave His only begotten Son so they might be saved, they shared what they had. Can you picture a people with such deep affection for one another that they were as willing for other believers in need to enjoy their possessions as much as they themselves did?

• What happens when believers are "of one heart and one soul"?

"Nothing unites people as sharing the same affliction."—Jack Hyles

---

B. The Son of Encouragement (vv. 33-37)
(Acts 4:33-35 is not included in the printed text.)

36And Joses, who by the apostles was surnamed Barnabas, (which is, being interpreted, The son of consolation,) a Levite, and of the country

of Cyprus, ³⁷Having land, sold it, and brought the money, and laid it at the apostles' feet.

It appears the distribution of goods was delegated to others while the apostles continued to preach the Word. The Holy Spirit confirmed the preaching of the Gospel with mighty miracles that showed the resurrection of Jesus to be valid (v. 33). These mighty manifestations of the Spirit were proof to all that Jesus was alive.

The result of a unified church is the bestowing of "great grace" upon the believers (v. 33). The apostle John tells us Jesus was "full of grace and truth" (John 1:14). Jesus blessed these believers in Jerusalem with the grace to grasp the message of salvation, to proclaim the good news, and to lead a life of holiness. God's grace was manifested in their words and deeds.

Again, Acts 4:34 spotlights the charitable attitude of the early Christians. Their desire to share their possessions came from genuine Christian love motivated by the Holy Spirit. What they did, they did voluntarily. Their action was prompted by mutual love. They viewed fellow believers as brothers and sisters in the body of Christ. When they discovered some among them were in need, they rallied to their cause and shared what they had.

At this point, we are introduced to Barnabas (v. 36). His name is interpreted in a variety of ways. He is called "the son of consolation," "the son of encouragement," and "the son of comfort." When we study his life carefully, we discover he earned those titles. He was a Jew, a Levite from Cyprus, who had relatives living in Jerusalem, and who owned a piece of land. We are not told whether his land was a farm or not. Whatever the case may be, he sold his property and gave the proceeds to be used by the community of believers.

In Acts 5, the generosity of Barnabas and his fellow believers is placed in contrast to the greed of Ananias and Sapphira.

---

1. How are "great power" and "great grace" connected (v. 33)?
2. How were the needs of the poor met (vv. 34-35)?
3. What do verses 36 and 37 reveal about Barnabas?

"You Are My Center Fielder"

After Willie Mays joined the Giants, there was a period when he made only one hit in twenty-six times at bat. He could have been benched or sent back to the minors. Neither happened. One day, the twenty-year-old player came to his manager, Leo Durocher, weeping, and begged to be benched. Durocher draped a fatherly arm about the strong young man's shoulders: "Don't you worry, Son, you are my center fielder, even if you don't get another hit all season." Willie left Leo's office and promptly began hitting the ball. He became one of baseball's immortals. What a difference a word of encouragement can make!—*Putting Faith to Work*, Robert McCracken

---

Be an Encourager

C. The Wise Use of Wealth (1 Tim. 6:17-19)

17Charge them that are rich in this world, that they be not highminded, nor trust in uncertain riches, but in the living God, who giveth us richly all things to enjoy; 18That they do good, that they be rich in good works, ready to distribute, willing to communicate; 19Laying up in store for themselves a good foundation against the time to come, that they may lay hold on eternal life.

In this chapter, Paul has a lot to say about money. In verses 6-10, his message is to Christians who are poor and warns of the temptations into which one might become ensnared in the pursuit of riches. In verses 17-19, his message is to Christians who are rich. He offers them instructions both negative and positive. He does not tell those who are wealthy that they need to get rid of their money. He does warn them of the temptations they may face because of their money and the danger of putting their trust in their wealth; but he also gives them guidance as to how they can wisely use their wealth.

Paul admonishes Timothy to tell the wealthy to put their trust in God and to use their riches to benefit others. James addressed this when he defined true religion: "Pure religion and undefiled before God and the Father is this, To visit the fatherless and widows in their affliction, and to keep himself unspotted from the world" (James 1:27).

---

1. List two errors a wealthy person must avoid (v. 17).
2. Describe the proper use of wealth, and its results (v. 19).

"Since much wealth too often proves a snare and an encumbrance in the Christian's race, let him lighten the weight by 'dispersing abroad and giving to the poor'; whereby he will both soften the pilgrimage of his fellow travelers, and speed his own way the faster."—Augustus Toplady

---

II. A COMPASSIONATE MENTOR (Acts 9:26-27; 11:19-30; 15:36-40)
A. Barnabas Embraces Saul (9:26-27)

26And when Saul was come to Jerusalem, he assayed to join himself to the disciples: but they were all afraid of him, and believed not that he was a disciple. 27But Barnabas took him, and brought him to the apostles, and declared unto them how he had seen the Lord in the way, and that he had spoken to him, and how he had preached boldly at Damascus in the name of Jesus.

Saul, who came to Damascus to work havoc against the followers of Christ, found himself the object of the hatred of the Jews. After his conversion to Christ, he went about preaching the Gospel. The Jewish resistance to him was so great that his life was now in danger. So he left Damascus and sought the solitude of Arabia, where he became better acquainted with Christ and His teachings. Now, he was ready to return and share his experience with the disciples of Christ. He especially wanted to meet with Peter and James. He recorded his thoughts about this visit when he wrote his letter to the church in Galatia:

> When it pleased God, who separated me from my mother's womb, and called me by his grace, to reveal his Son in me, that I might preach him among the heathen; immediately I conferred not with flesh and blood: Neither went I up to Jerusalem to them which were apostles before me; but I went into Arabia, and returned again unto Damascus. Then after three years I went up to Jerusalem to see Peter, and abode with him fifteen days. But other of the apostles saw I none, save James the Lord's brother (1:15-19).

No welcoming committee awaited Saul when he arrived in Jerusalem. The believers were all afraid of him. Since Jerusalem was a considerable distance from Damascus, many of them had probably not heard of his conversion. Many of those who remembered him still trembled at the thought of the persecutions he perpetrated upon Christians. Even some who had heard of his commitment to Christ were suspicious that he was faking and, thereby, setting a trap in which to ensnare them.

Then, Barnabas came on the scene. Somehow he saw through the distrust so many felt, believed the account Saul gave of his relationship with Christ, and embraced him as a true believer. Having already earned the respect of the disciples, Barnabas was able to convince them that Saul's testimony was true. They admitted Saul into their fellowship and treated him as a brother in Christ. During his brief stay with them, Saul boldly preached Christ.

• Describe the breakthrough Barnabas brought about.

"The most vital question to ask about all who claim to be Christian is this: Have they a soul thirst for God? . . . Is their life centered on Him?"—Martyn Lloyd-Jones

---

B. Barnabas in Antioch (11:19-30)

(Acts 11:19-21, 26-30 is not included in the printed text.)

²²Then tidings of these things came unto the ears of the church which was in Jerusalem: and they sent forth Barnabas, that he should go as far as Antioch. ²³Who, when he came, and had seen the grace of God, was glad, and exhorted them all, that with purpose of heart they would cleave unto the Lord. ²⁴For he was a good man, and full of the Holy Ghost and of faith: and much people was added unto the Lord. ²⁵Then departed Barnabas to Tarsus, for to seek Saul.

After witnessing the persecution Stephen faced, many believers left Jerusalem and traveled to several other places, including Antioch of Syria (v. 19). Antioch was the capital of Syria and was situated on the Orontes River. It was founded by one of the generals of Alexander the Great, but received its name from Antiochus, a king of Syria. Verse 26 says believers

Be an Encourager

were first called Christians in Antioch. This city became a hub for Christian missions.

As the persecuted believers entered various cities, their audience was primarily made up of Jews. However, "some of them" began to reach out to the Gentiles in Antioch, sharing the message of Christ with them (v. 20). The Holy Spirit anointed their message and a large number of Gentiles responded in faith, accepting Jesus Christ as their Savior (v. 21).

When the church at Jerusalem heard what was happening, they sent Barnabas to check out the situation (v. 22). What he found brought joy to his heart. He immediately observed that their experience was genuine and he, as was his nature, encouraged them to remain faithful to the Lord (v. 23). Perceiving the type of spiritual work that was needed in Antioch, Barnabas knew just the person for the job. He left for Tarsus to find Saul and bring him to Antioch (v. 25). He knew Saul had the spiritual aptitude needed to establish these believers in Christ. He and Saul stayed in Antioch for a year, working together and teaching the people the truths of God's Word (v. 26).

When a prophet named Agabus was impressed by the Holy Spirit that a great famine was going to hit the entire Roman Empire, some of the believers contributed what they could of their goods to help the believers in Judea. They entrusted Barnabas and Saul to deliver their gifts to the elders of that area (vv. 27-30).

Barnabas' character is described by three terms in verse 24: (1) "He was a good man." His evil disposition was gone, and he had the mind of Christ, "who went about doing good" (10:38). (2) Barnabas was "full of the Holy Spirit" (NKJV). He was entirely under the influence of the Holy Spirit and displayed the fruit of the Spirit in his life. (3) He was "full . . . of faith." His faith never failed because it was anchored in God, who never changes. He knew God's Word would never fail.

---

1. Describe the positive results of persecution (vv. 19-21).
2. Why was Barnabas sent to Antioch, and what was the result (vv. 22-24)?
3. Describe Barnabas' and Saul's teamwork (vv. 25-26).
4. Explain the trust given to Barnabas (vv. 27-30).

> "Christians are like the several flowers in a garden that have each of them the dew of heaven, which, being shaken with the wind, they let fall at each other's roots, whereby they are jointly nourished, and become nourishers of each other."—John Bunyan

---

C. A Compassionate Act (15:36-40)

(Acts 15:36, 38-40 is not included in the printed text.)

37And Barnabas determined to take with them John, whose surname was Mark.

Out of concern for the well-being of those whom they had won to Christ and sought to establish in the faith, Paul suggested to Barnabas that they visit each of the churches where they had ministered to see how these new believers were doing. He knew there were unbelievers who would like nothing better than to disrupt their Christian journey. Also, there were Jews who would try to convince them that they needed to carry out the rituals of Judaism. Paul wanted to make sure they were staying on the right track.

Barnabas liked the idea, and he wanted to take John Mark along. Mark was a cousin of Barnabas (Col. 4:10) who had traveled with them before. For whatever reason, Mark had deserted them in Pamphylia, failing to complete the journey they had started (Acts 13:13). Paul had a problem with that and objected to Mark's accompanying them this time. He felt very strongly about this, and their disagreement led to them going their separate ways. Barnabas took Mark with him, and Paul chose Silas as his companion.

Paul's attitude toward Mark changed through the years, implying that Barnabas' compassion and mentoring of his cousin was fruitful. When Paul was in prison and Timothy was coming to visit him, Paul wrote to him, "Only Luke is with me. Take Mark, and bring him with thee: for he is profitable to me for the ministry" (2 Tim. 4:11).

Also, Paul and Barnabas would work together again. Paul wrote to the Galatians, "Fourteen years after I went up again to Jerusalem with Barnabas, and took Titus with me also. . . . When James, Cephas, and John, who seemed to be pillars, perceived the grace that was given unto me, they gave to me and Barnabas the right hands of fellowship; that we should go unto the heathen, and they unto the circumcision" (2:1, 9).

• How did a difficult circumstance have a positive outcome?

"The purpose of human life is to serve, and to show compassion and the will to help others."—Albert Schweitzer

---

III. AN EFFECTIVE MISSIONARY (Acts 13:1-5; 14:1-7, 21-28)
A. The Spirit in Charge (13:1-5)
   (Acts 13:1, 3-5 is not included in the printed text.)
   2As they ministered to the Lord, and fasted, the Holy Ghost said, Separate me Barnabas and Saul for the work whereunto I have called them.

There was no shortage of prophets and teachers in the church at Antioch. Five are named in this passage. These two offices might work through the same person, or one gift might operate through one person and another in someone else. *Barnabas* is listed, and we are quite familiar with him and the work God called him to do. *Simeon* was also called *Niger*, meaning "black." He was so called either because of his complexion or his hair. Nothing more is known about him. *Lucius* is a native of Cyrene, an African city where a large population of Jews resided. *Manaen* is identified as the foster brother of Herod Antipas (i.e., Herod the Tetrarch). Josephus says this Herod was educated at Rome, and it is likely this prophet or teacher spent his early childhood with him. The other person listed is *Saul*, who became known as Paul the apostle.

As the church worshiped the Lord, the Holy Spirit intervened with a message for them. We are not told how the Spirit communicated this message. It could have been an operation of the gift of prophecy, or the gift of tongues and interpretation. Or, it could have been the voice of the Spirit through an unmistakable inward urge. However the Spirit spoke, the church understood clearly what the Spirit was asking of them. They were to send Saul and Barnabas forth to do the work the Lord had called them to do. In obedience to the Spirit, they laid hands on them and sent them on their way (vv. 3-4). Notice that all of this was accompanied by prayer and fasting (vv. 2-3). Also, observe that John Mark went with them as their assistant (v. 5).

---

1. What resulted from prayer and fasting (vv. 1-2)?
2. Why did they pray and fast a second time (v. 3)?
3. What does it mean to be "sent out by the Holy Spirit" (v. 4 NASB)?

"[Christ's] authority on earth allows us to dare to go to all the nations. His authority in heaven gives us our only hope of success. And His presence with us leaves us no other choice."—John Stott

---

B. Ministry in Iconium (14:1-7)

(Acts 14:2, 4-7 is not included in the printed text.)

¹And it came to pass in Iconium, that they went both together into the synagogue of the Jews, and so spake, that a great multitude both of the Jews and also of the Greeks believed.

³Long time therefore abode they speaking boldly in the Lord, which gave testimony unto the word of his grace, and granted signs and wonders to be done by their hands.

Paul and Barnabas are now in Iconium, the capital city of Lycaonia, about 120 miles from the Mediterranean Sea. The population was made up of a variety of citizens, including Greeks whose main interest was the theater and the marketplace; an older population mainly living in the country; a few Roman officials; and an established colony of Jews who exercised their trade during the week and met in the synagogue on the Sabbath.

As Paul and Barnabas had already learned, not everyone welcomed them with open arms. Everywhere they went, some people accepted them and their message, while others would try anything to stop them. Iconium is no exception. As was their custom, Paul and Barnabas enter the synagogue together. Paul is the primary spokesperson, while Barnabas is by his side supporting him. The Holy Spirit anoints their message, and a large number of Jews and Gentiles receive Christ as their Savior. This infuriates the unbelieving Jews.

Despite the persecution leveled against them, these messengers from the Lord stay in Iconium a "long time," boldly declaring the word of the Lord (v. 3). God honors His word by manifesting miraculous signs and wonders. Eventually, the persecution becomes so intense that Paul and Barnabas are forced to leave Iconium and preach the Gospel elsewhere (vv. 5-7).

1. Who caused trouble for Paul and Barnabas, and why (vv. 1-2)?
2. How did the Lord confirm their ministry (v. 3)?
3. Describe the missionaries' persistence (vv. 5-7).

"The mission of the Church is to seek and to save them that are lost."—James H. Aughey

C. Healing in Lystra (vv. 21-28)
(Acts 14:23-28 is not included in the printed text.)
21And when they had preached the gospel to that city, and had taught many, they returned again to Lystra, and to Iconium, and Antioch, 22Confirming the souls of the disciples, and exhorting them to continue in the faith, and that we must through much tribulation enter into the kingdom of God.

In Lystra, Paul and Barnabas encountered a crippled man, perceived he had faith to be healed, and instructed him to stand up. The man responded by leaping and walking about (vv. 8-10). The local populace mistook this as the action of gods in human form and tried to worship Paul and Barnabas (v. 11), but the missionaries declared they were mere men and this was the work of "the living God" (v. 15).

The next day, Paul and Barnabas departed for Derbe. After preaching the Gospel there, the pair continued their journey by retracing their steps, encouraging believers to continue in the faith, even in the face of persecution. They appointed elders in each church (in Lystra, Iconium, and Antioch), strengthening the organization of the church.

This was a spiritual endeavor; they committed all the elders to the Lord with prayer and fasting. Returning to Antioch in Syria, they reported how the blessing of God had come to the entire region. They especially rejoiced that the Lord had opened the door of faith to the Gentiles.

• How did the missionaries strengthen the churches they had planted?

"To win men to acceptance of Jesus Christ as Savior and Lord is the only reason Christians are left in this world."—R. A. Torrey

Be an Encourager

CONCLUSION

Who are the influential mentors in your life? In what ways is your life better because of their input? What characteristics did you see in Barnabas' life that you would like to imitate? To whom are you a mentor? Do you seek to encourage others? How have you gone out of your way, or even sacrificed, so someone else's dreams could be fulfilled?

GOLDEN TEXT CHALLENGE

"LET US THEREFORE FOLLOW AFTER THE THINGS WHICH MAKE FOR PEACE, AND THINGS WHEREWITH ONE MAY EDIFY ANOTHER" (Rom. 14:19).

Making peace and building up others, even in the face of turmoil, creates a sense of stability and dependability.

The ocean is a good analogy. There are times when the sea is calm and seemingly undisturbed, such as at sunset on a calm summer's evening. There are other times when the sea rages, driven by high winds, with huge waves. Even when the sea is raging on the surface, research findings indicate there is no noticeable effect a few hundred feet down.

Christians must have the deep, abiding, inner peace and stability the Holy Spirit gives in His abiding presence. Those who have this kind of inner peace will be able to edify others as they interact with them.

Daily Devotions:

M. Generosity Toward the Poor • Deuteronomy 15:7-11
T. Mentoring Youth • 1 Samuel 3:1-10
W. Warn Others • Ezekiel 3:17-21
T. Give Generously • 2 Corinthians 9:6-15
F. Have Concern for Others • Philippians 2:1-4
S. Paul's Words of Encouragement • Colossians 4:7-15